The Leadership Experience

Fourth Edition

Richard L. Daft

Owen Graduate School of Management
Vanderbilt University

With the assistance of
Patricia G. Lane

THOMSON

SOUTH-WESTERN

Australia • Brazil • Canada • Mexico • Singapore • Spain • United Kingdom • United States

THOMSON

SOUTH-WESTERN

The Leadership Experience, Fourth Edition
Richard L. Daft

with the assistance of Patricia G. Lane

VP/Editorial Director:
Jack W. Calhoun

Editor-in-Chief:
Melissa Acuña

Sr. Acquisitions Editor:
Joe Sabatino

Sr. Developmental Editor:
Emma Newsom

Editorial Assistant:
Ruth Belanger

Sr. Content Project Manager:
Cliff Kallemeyn

Sr. Marketing Manager:
Kimberly Kanakes

Marketing Coordinator:
Sarah Rose

Sr. Marketing Communications Manager:
Jim Overly

Technology Project Manager:
Kristen Meere

Sr. Art Director:
Tippy McIntosh

Sr. First Print Buyer:
Doug Wilke

Internal and Cover Design:
Craig Ramsdell, Ramsdell Design

Cover Image:
The Image Bank/Getty Images

Printer:
Edwards Brothers

Library of Congress Control Number:
2007928702

For more information about our
products, contact us at:

**Thomson Learning Academic
Resource Center**

1-800-423-0563

Thomson Higher Education
5191 Natorp Boulevard
Mason, OH 45040
USA

To the spiritual leaders who shaped my growth and development as a leader and as a human being.

brief contents

contents

Part 3: The Personal Side of Leadership   95

Part 4: The Leader as a Relationship Builder 223

Part 5: The Leader as Social Architect — 385

Richard L. Daft, Ph.D., is the Brownlee O. Currey, Jr., Professor of Management in the Owen Graduate School of Management at Vanderbilt University. Professor Daft specializes in the study of leadership and organization theory. Dr. Daft is a Fellow of the Academy of Management and has served on the editorial boards of *Academy of Management Journal, Administrative Science Quarterly,* and *Journal of Management Education*. He was the Associate Editor-in-Chief of *Organization Science* and served for three years as associate editor of *Administrative Science Quarterly*.

Professor Daft has authored or co-authored 12 books, including *Organization Theory and Design* (South-Western, 2007), *The Leadership Experience* (South-Western, 2008) and *What to Study: Generating and Developing Research Questions* (Sage, 1982). He co-authored, with Robert Lengel, *Fusion Leadership: Unlocking the Subtle Forces That Change People and Organizations* (Berrett-Koehler, 2000). He has also authored dozens of scholarly articles, papers, and chapters. His work has been published in *Administrative Science Quarterly, Academy of Management Journal, Academy of Management Review, Strategic Management Journal, Journal of Management, Accounting Organizations and Society, Management Science, MIS Quarterly, California Management Review,* and *Organizational Behavior Teaching Review*. Professor Daft has been awarded several government research grants to pursue studies of organization design, organizational innovation and change, strategy implementation, and organizational information processing.

Dr. Daft also is an active teacher and consultant. He has taught management, leadership, organizational change, organizational theory, and organizational behavior. He has served as associate dean, produced for-profit theatrical productions, and helped manage a start-up enterprise. He has been involved in management development and consulting for many companies and government organizations including the American Banking Association, AutoZone, Bell Canada, Nortel, TVA, Pratt & Whitney, Alsstate Insurance, State Farm Insurance, the United States Air Force, the U.S. Army, J. C. Bradford & Co., Central Parking System,, Bristol-Myers Squibb, First American National Bank, and the Vanderbilt University Medical Center.

My vision for the fourth edition is to give students an exciting, applied, and comprehensive view of what leadership is like in today's world. *The Leadership Experience* integrates recent ideas and applications with established scholarly research in a way that makes the topic of leadership come alive. The world of leadership and organizations is undergoing major changes, and this textbook addresses the qualities and skills leaders need in this rapidly evolving world.

Recent ethical scandals, global crises, the growing need for creativity and innovation in organizations, the emergence of e-business, learning organizations, virtual teams, globalization, knowledge work, and other ongoing transformations place new demands on leaders far beyond the topics traditionally taught in courses on management or organizational behavior. My experiences teaching leadership to students and managers, and working with leaders to change their organizations, have affirmed for me the value of traditional leadership concepts, while highlighting the importance of including new ideas and applications.

The Leadership Experience thoroughly covers the history of leadership studies and the traditional theories, but goes beyond that to incorporate valuable ideas such as leadership vision, shaping culture and values, and the importance of moral leadership. The book expands the treatment of leadership to capture the excitement of the subject in a way that motivates students and challenges them to develop their leadership potential.

New to the Fourth Edition

A primary focus for revising *The Leadership Experience,* fourth edition, has been to offer students greater potential for self-assessment and leadership development. An important aspect of learning to be a leader involves looking inward for greater self-understanding, and the fourth edition provides more opportunities for this reflection. Each chapter includes multiple questionnaires or exercises that enable students to learn about their own leadership beliefs, values, competencies, and skills. These exercises help students gauge their current standing and connect the chapter concepts and examples to ideas for expanding their own leadership abilities. A few of the new self-assessment topics are: innovation, networking, personality traits, leading diverse people, developing a personal vision, spiritual leadership, leader feedback, and leading with love versus leading with fear. Self-assessments related to basic leadership abilities such as listening skills, emotional intelligence, motivating others, and using power and influence are also included.

In addition, each chapter of *The Leadership Experience* has been thoroughly revised and updated, and one chapter has been cut to focus more attention on current issues that leaders face. Topics that have been added or expanded in the fourth edition include: creativity and innovation, ethical leadership, leading diverse people, asking questions, social perception and attribution theory, gender-driven leadership styles, framing a noble purpose, changing mental models, leadership courage, spiritual leadership, shaping a high-performance culture, integrative and distributive negotiation, and matching leaders with leadership roles.

A special opportunity for student leadership growth in conjunction with this text is the computer-based simulation called Virtual Leader. John Dunning, Troy University, used Virtual Leader in conjunction with *The Leadership Experience* and wrote an instructor's guide to show others how to use the simulation with the text. If you want to explore cost and possible use of Virtual Leader with *The Leadership Experience,* please go the website: http://www.simulearn.net. The title of the guide is "Integrating Leadership Theory and Practice Through Computer-based Simulation: A guide to Integrating vLeader 2007 with The Leadership Experience, 4th ed," by John E. Dunning.

Organization

The organization of the book is based on first understanding basic ways in which leaders differ from managers, and the ways leaders set direction, seek alignment between organizations and followers, build relationships, and create change. Thus the organization of this book is in five parts:

1. Introduction to Leadership
2. Research Perspectives on Leadership
3. The Personal Side of Leadership
4. The Leader as Relationship Builder
5. The Leader as Social Architect

The book integrates materials from both micro and macro approaches to leadership, from both academia and the real world, and from traditional ideas and recent thinking.

Distinguishing Features

This book has a number of special features that are designed to make the material accessible and valuable to students.

In the Lead *The Leadership Experience* is loaded with new examples of leaders in both traditional and contemporary organizations. Each chapter opens with a real-life example that relates to the chapter content, and several additional examples are highlighted within each chapter. These spotlight examples are drawn from a wide variety of organizations including education, the military, government agencies, businesses, and nonprofit organizations.

Consider This! Each chapter contains a Consider This! box that is personal, compelling, and inspiring. This box may be a saying from a famous leader, or wisdom from the ages. These Consider This! boxes provide novel and interesting material to expand the reader's thinking about the leadership experience.

Leader's Bookshelf Each chapter also includes a review of a recent book relevant to the chapter's content. The Leader's Bookshelf connects students to issues and topics being read and discussed in the worlds of academia, business, military, education, and nonprofit organizations.

Action Memo This margin feature helps students apply the chapter concepts in their own lives and leadership activities, as well as directs students to self-assessments related to various chapter topics.

Leader's Self-Insight boxes provide self-assessments for learners and an opportunity to experience leadership issues in a personal way. These exercises take the form of questionnaires, scenarios, and activities.

Student Development Each chapter ends with Discussion Questions and then two activities for student development. The first, **Leadership at Work**, is a practical, skill-building activity that engages the student in applying chapter concepts to real-life leadership. These exercises are designed so students can complete them on their own outside of class or in class as part of a group activity. Instructor tips are given for maximizing in-class learning with the Leadership at Work exercises. **Leadership Development—Case for Analysis**, the second end-of-chapter activity, provides two short, problem-oriented cases for analysis. These cases test the student's ability to apply concepts when dealing with real-life leadership issues. The cases challenge the student's cognitive understanding of leadership ideas while the Leadership at Work exercises and the feedback questionnaires assess the student's progress as a leader.

Ancillaries

This edition offers a wider range than previous editions of instructor ancillaries to fully enable instructors to bring the leadership experience into the classroom. These ancillaries include:

Instructors Manual with Test Bank (ISBN: 0-324-568479)

A comprehensive Instructor's Manual and Test Bank is available to assist in lecture preparation. Included in the Instructor's Manual are the chapter outlines, suggested answers to end chapter materials and suggestions for further study. The Test Bank includes approximately 100 questions per chapter to assist in writing examinations. Types of questions include true/false, multiple choice, essay, and matching questions.

Instructor's Resource CD-ROM (ISBN: 0-324-56827-4)

Key instructor ancillaries (Instructor's Manual, Test Bank, ExamView, and Power-Point slides) are provided on CD-ROM, giving instructors the ultimate tool for customizing lectures and presentations.

ExamView

Available on the Instructor's Resource CD, ExamView contains all of the questions in the printed test bank. This program is an easy-to-use test creation software compatible with Windows or Macintosh. Instructors can add or edit questions, instructions, and answers, and select questions (randomly or numerically) by previewing them on the screen.

PowerPoint Lecture Presentation

An asset to any instructor, the lectures provide outlines for every chapter, graphics of the illustrations from the text, and additional examples providing instructors with a number of learning opportunities for students.

Videos (ISBN: 0-324-56829-0)

Videos compiled specifically to accompany *The Leadership Experience,* fourth edition utilize real-world companies to illustrate international business concepts as outlined in the text. Focusing on both small and large businesses, the video gives students an inside perspective on the situations and issues that global corporations face.

Companion Web site

The Leadership Experience's Web site at **http://daft.swlearning.com/** provides a multitude of resources for both Instructors and Students.

Acknowledgments

Textbook writing is a team enterprise. This book has integrated ideas and support from many people whom I want to acknowledge. I especially thank Bob Lengel, at the University of Texas at San Antonio. Bob's enthusiasm for leadership many years ago stimulated me to begin reading, teaching, and training in the area of leadership development. His enthusiasm also led to our collaboration on the book, *Fusion Leadership: Unlocking the Subtle Forces that Change People and Organizations.* I thank Bob for keeping our shared leadership dream alive, which in time enabled me to pursue my dream of writing this leadership textbook.

Here at Vanderbilt I want to thank my assistant, Barbara Haselton, for the tremendous volume and quality of work she accomplished on my behalf that gave me time to write. Jim Bradford, the Dean at Owen, and Joe Blackburn, the Senior Associate Dean, have maintained a positive scholarly atmosphere and supported me with the time and resources to complete the revision of this book. I also appreciate the intellectual stimulation and support from friends and colleagues at the Owen School—Bruce Barry, Ray Friedman, Neta Moye, Rich Oliver, David Owens, Bart Victor, and Tim Vogus.

I want to acknowledge the reviewers who provided feedback and a very short turnaround. Their ideas helped me improve the book in many areas:

Thomas H. Arcy
University of Houston—Central Campus

Janey Ayres
Purdue University

Kristin Backhaus
SUNY New Paltz

Bill Bommer
Georgia State University

Ron Franzen
Saint Luke's Hospital

Delia J. Haak
John Brown University

Nell Hartley
Robert Morris College

Ellen Jordan
Mount Olive College

Gregory Manora
Auburn University-Montgomery

Richard T. Martin
Washburn University

Mark Nagel
Normandale Community College

Ranjna Patel
Bethune Cookman College

Chad Peterson
Baylor University

Gordon Riggles
University of Colorado

Bill Service
Samford University

Dan Sherman
University of Alabama at Huntsville

Bret Simmons
North Dakota State University

Shane Spiller
University of Montevallo

Ahmad Tootonchi
Frostburg State University

Mary L. Tucker
Ohio University

Xavier Whitaker
Baylor University

Jean Wilson
The College of William and Mary

I want to extend special thanks to my editorial associate, Pat Lane. I could not have undertaken this revision without Pat's help. She skillfully drafted materials for the chapters, found original sources, and did an outstanding job with last-minute changes, the copyedited manuscript, art, and galley proofs. Pat's talent and personal enthusiasm for this text added greatly to its excellence.

The editors at South-Western also deserve special mention. Joe Sabatino, Senior Acquisitions Editor, supported the concept for this book and obtained the resources necessary for its completion. Emma Newsom, Senior Developmental Editor, provided terrific support for the book's writing, reviews, copyediting, and production. Mike Guendelsberger, Developmental Editor, also assisted during the development of the text. Cliff Kallemeyn, Senior Content Project Manager, smoothly took the book through the production process. Tippy McIntosh, Art Director, created the design for the fourth edition.

Finally, I want to acknowledge my loving family. I received much love and support from my wife, Dorothy Marcic, and daughters Elizabeth at George Washington University, Solange in Ecuador, Roxanne in Israel, and Amy and Danielle in Texas. I appreciate the good feelings and connections with my daughters and grandchildren. On occasion, we have been able to travel, ski, watch a play, or just be together—all of which reconnect me to the things that really count.

PART 1
Introduction to Leadership

Chapter 1
What Does It Mean to Be a Leader?

Chapter 1

Your Leadership Challenge

After reading this chapter, you should be able to:

- Understand the full meaning of leadership and see the leadership potential in yourself and others.

- Recognize and facilitate the six fundamental transformations in today's organizations and leaders.

- Identify the primary reasons for leadership derailment and the new paradigm skills that can help you avoid it.

- Recognize the traditional functions of management and the fundamental differences between leadership and management.

- Appreciate the crucial importance of providing direction, alignment, relationships, personal qualities, and outcomes.

- Explain how leadership has evolved and how historical approaches apply to the practice of leadership today.

What Does It Mean to Be a Leader?

At 694 feet long, 105 feet wide, 13 stories tall, and 25,000 tons, the *USS San Antonio* is breathtaking—and a bit intimidating. But not to Commander Brad Lee, the 40-year-old Navy officer who recently took command of the ship. As commander of one of the most technologically advanced amphibious assault vessels ever built, Lee is responsible for up to 400 sailors, twice that many Marines, numerous aircraft, fighting vehicles, smaller vessels, and tactical support for a Marine AirGround Task Force. Lee admits that it's not exactly *comfortable* being in charge of a ship the size of the *USS San Antonio,* simply due to the enormity of having so many people's lives in your hands. Yet he is confident in himself—and, more significantly, in his crew. "Every sailor is important," Lee tells his crew members, stressing that success is never a one-man mission. "Each [person] brings a certain perspective to the table. So, it's not about me. It's about the ship and the success of our mission."

Lee joined the Navy as a way to make a difference in the world after seeing an article in *Ebony* magazine that featured Admiral Anthony Watson, an African-American Naval officer who grew up in a rough Chicago housing development. Although Lee originally didn't think of the Navy as a lifetime career, his first four-year stint showed him that he had "a real opportunity, and more importantly, the ability, to make a difference in the lives of sailors." It was the desire to help other sailors, rather than personal ambition, which spurred Lee to seek increasing levels of leadership responsibility.

By the time he took command of the *USS San Antonio,* Lee had served 18 years in the Navy and earned numerous awards and medals. More important to him, though, is earning the respect and commitment of his crew. As Anthony Ray Cade, Senior Chief of Information Technology serving on the ship, said, "The best part of what I do every day is working for a guy like that."[1]

What does it mean to be a leader? For Commander Brad Lee, it means striving to make a difference in the lives of others and the world. It means believing in yourself and those you work with, loving what you do and infusing others with energy and enthusiasm. You probably have never heard of Commander Brad Lee. His face isn't splashed on the covers of magazines. His adventures and accomplishments aren't featured on the national news. Yet leaders like Brad Lee are making a difference every day, not just in the military, but in businesses and nonprofit organizations, educational systems and governmental agencies, sports teams and volunteer groups, huge cities and small rural communities.

When most people think of leaders, they recall great historical figures such as Abraham Lincoln, Napoleon, and Alexander the Great, or think of "big names" in the news, such as former General Electric CEO Jack Welch, who still commands a spotlight nearly five years after his retirement. Yet there are leaders working in every organization, large and small. In fact, leadership is all around us every day, in all facets of our lives—our families, schools, communities, churches, social clubs, and volunteer organizations, as well as in the world of business, sports, and the military. The qualities that make Commander Brad Lee a good leader can be effective whether one is leading a military unit, a basketball team, a business, or a family.

The Nature of Leadership

Before we can examine what makes an effective leader, we need to know what leadership means. Leadership has been a topic of interest to historians and philosophers since ancient times, but scientific studies began only in the twentieth century. Scholars and other writers have offered hundreds of definitions of the term *leadership,* and one authority on the subject has concluded that leadership "is one of the most observed and least understood phenomena on earth."[2] Defining leadership has been a complex and elusive problem largely because the nature of leadership itself is complex. Some have even suggested that leadership is nothing more than a romantic myth, perhaps based on the false hope that someone will come along and solve our problems by sheer force of will.[3]

There is some evidence that people do pin their hopes on leaders in ways that are not always realistic. Think about how some struggling companies recruit well-known, charismatic CEOs and invest tremendous hopes in them, only to find that their problems actually get worse.[4] For example, Carly Fiorina rocketed to the top of Hewlett-Packard's (HP) CEO search list because of her bold ideas and charismatic personality. Her appointment quickly became front-page news, with the focus as much on Fiorina's star power as on HP's business issues. Unfortunately, implementing Fiorina's plans turned out to cause even more problems for the struggling company, leading to unexpected losses, layoffs, the departure of key executives, and a declining stock performance. Whether Fiorina, who was ousted by HP's board in early 2005, has gotten more or less blame than she deserves for the problems is debatable, but the example serves to illustrate the unrealistic expectations people often have of "larger-than-life" leaders. Particularly when times are tough, people may look to a grand, heroic type of leader to alleviate fear and uncertainty. In recent years, the romantic or heroic view of leadership has been challenged.[5] Much progress has been made in understanding the essential nature of leadership as a real and powerful influence in organizations and societies.

Definition of Leadership

Leadership studies are an emerging discipline and the concept of leadership will continue to evolve. For the purpose of this book, we will focus on a single definition that delineates the essential elements of the leadership process: **Leadership** is an influence relationship among leaders and followers who intend real changes and outcomes that reflect their shared purposes.[6]

Exhibit 1.1 summarizes the key elements in this definition. Leadership involves influence, it occurs among people, those people intentionally desire significant changes, and the changes reflect purposes shared by leaders and followers. *Influence* means that the relationship among people is not passive; however, also inherent in this definition is the concept that influence is multidirectional and noncoercive. The basic cultural values in North America make it easiest to think of leadership as something a leader does to a follower.[7] However, leadership is reciprocal. In most organizations, superiors influence subordinates, but subordinates also influence superiors. The people involved in the relationship want substantive *changes*—leadership involves creating change, not maintaining the status quo. In addition, the changes sought are not dictated by leaders, but reflect *purposes* that leaders and followers share. Moreover, change is toward an

Leadership
an influence relationship among leaders and followers who intend real changes and outcomes that reflect their shared purposes

Exhibit 1.1 What Leadership Involves

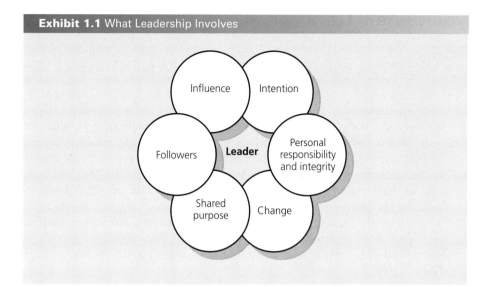

outcome that leader and followers both want, a desired future or shared purpose that motivates them toward this more preferable outcome. An important aspect of leadership is influencing others to come together around a common vision. Thus, leadership involves the influence of people to bring about change toward a desirable future.

Also, leadership is a *people* activity and is distinct from administrative paperwork or planning activities. Leadership occurs *among* people; it is not something done *to* people. Since leadership involves people, there must be *followers*. An individual performer who achieves excellence as a scientist, musician, athlete, or woodcarver may be a leader in her field of expertise but is not a leader as it is defined in this book unless followers are involved. Followers are an important part of the leadership process, and all leaders are sometimes followers as well. Good leaders know how to follow, and they set an example for others. The issue of *intention* or will means that people—leader and followers—are actively involved in the pursuit of change. Each person takes personal responsibility to achieve the desired future.

One stereotype is that leaders are somehow different, that they are above others; however, in reality, the qualities needed for effective leadership are the same as those needed to be an effective follower.[8] Effective followers think for themselves and carry out assignments with energy and enthusiasm. They are committed to something outside their own self-interest, and they have the courage to stand up for what they believe. Good followers are not "yes people" who blindly follow a leader. Effective leaders and effective followers may sometimes be the same people, playing different roles at different times. At its best, leadership is shared among leaders and followers, with everyone fully engaged and accepting higher levels of responsibility.

Leadership and the Business of Living

Think for a moment about someone you personally have known that you would consider a leader—a grandparent, a supervisor, a coach, or even a fellow student. Perhaps you consider yourself a leader, or know that you want to be one. If we stop equating leadership with greatness and public visibility, it becomes easier to see our own opportunities for leadership and recognize the leadership of people we interact with every day. Leaders come in all shapes and sizes, and many true leaders are working behind the scenes. Leadership that has big outcomes often starts small.

- Greg Mortenson had a vision that the best way to fight terrorism was by building secular schools and promoting education, especially for girls, in northern Pakistan and neighboring Afghanistan. He wrote nearly 600 letters and submitted 16 grant applications, but received only one favorable reply—a $100 check from Tom Brokaw. Undeterred, Mortenson sold all his possessions and began appealing to everyday people. School-children donated hundreds of dollars in pennies, inspiring adults to donate as well. With the $12,000 he eventually raised, Mortenson built his first school in Korphe in 1996. Today, he runs the Central Asia Institute (CAI), which has built 55 schools with 520 teachers serving 22,000 students, as well as 24 potable water projects, 14 women's vocational centers, and several rural health camps. CAI has continued its "Pennies for Peace" project (http://www.penniesforpeace.org) to educate American children about the larger world and show them they can have a positive impact.[9]

- While attending a diabetes fundraiser, 17-year-old Kimberly Ross overheard some parents talking about not being able to go out because they couldn't find a baby-sitter who understood the special needs of a diabetic child. Having struggled with diabetes for half her life, Ross understood, and she knew that other teens with diabetes would as well. Ross talked with a school nurses' association and then started Safe Sitting, a baby-sitting network of teens with diabetes who care for children with the disease. The service was such a hit that Ross set up a Web site and is now helping diabetic teens establish similar networks in other cities.[10]

- Several years ago, hundreds of unarmed residents of an Argentinean farming village stormed the local police station after officials had refused to search for a missing child who was later found by villagers, raped and strangled. The siege ended only when the provincial government agreed to replace the entire police department, with the villagers allowed to name the new chief.[11] The villagers could not have pulled off the siege without leadership, and yet no one stepped forward to claim the title of "leader," and no one was able to specifically state who had provided the leadership for this initiative.

- During his five years working as a car salesman, Robert Chambers was disgusted by how some dealers and finance institutions preyed on low-income customers. After he retired from a varied career, the 62-year-old electrical engineer decided to do something about it. He founded Bonnie CLAC (for Car Loans and Counseling), which steers low-income people toward buying new, base-model cars at low prices and on good loan terms. With branches in New Hampshire, Vermont, and Maine, Bonnie CLAC has negotiated price and extended warranty deals with a dozen or so auto dealers and worked with banks to provide low interest rates. Bonnie CLAC guarantees the loan, and then works with clients to help them manage their finances.[12]

There are opportunities for leadership all around us that involve influence and change toward a desired goal or outcome. Without leadership, our families and communities, as well as our organizations, would fall apart. The leaders of tomorrow's organizations will come from anywhere and everywhere, just as they always have. You can start now, wherever you are, to practice leadership in your own life. Leadership is an everyday way of acting and thinking that has little to do with a title or formal position in an organization. As we will discuss in the following section, business leaders need to understand this tenet more than ever in the world of the twenty-first century.

Action Memo
As a leader, you can recognize opportunities for leadership and act to influence others and bring about changes for a better future.

The New Reality for Today's Organizations

Globalization. Shifting geopolitical forces. Outsourcing. Advancing technologies. Virtual teams. E-business. People in organizations around the world are feeling the impact of these and other trends, and are forced to adapt to new ways of working. Add to this the recent economic uncertainty, widespread ethical scandals, and the insecurity associated with war and terrorism, and leaders are facing a really tough job to keep people grounded, focused, and motivated toward accomplishing positive goals. It takes particularly strong leaders to guide people through the uncertainty and confusion that accompanies periods of rapid change.

Some historians and other scholars believe our world is undergoing a transformation more profound and far-reaching than any experienced since the dawn of the modern age and the Industrial Revolution some 500 years ago. Rapid environmental changes are causing fundamental shifts that have a dramatic impact on organizations and present new challenges for leaders.[13] These shifts represent a transition from a traditional to a new paradigm, as outlined in Exhibit 1.2. A **paradigm** is a shared mindset that represents a fundamental way of thinking about, perceiving, and understanding the world.

Although many leaders are still operating from an old-paradigm mindset, as outlined in the first column of Exhibit 1.2, they are increasingly ineffective. Successful leaders in the twenty-first century will respond to the new reality outlined in the second column of the exhibit.

Paradigm
a shared mindset that represents a fundamental way of thinking about, perceiving, and understanding the world

From Stability to Change and Crisis Management

In the past, many leaders assumed that if they could just keep things running on a steady, even keel, the organization would be successful. Yet today's world is

Exhibit 1.2 The New Reality for Leadership

OLD Paradigm	NEW Paradigm
Stability	Change and crisis management
Control	Empowerment
Competition	Collaboration
Uniformity	Diversity
Self-centered	Higher ethical purpose
Hero	Humble

in constant motion, and nothing seems certain anymore. If leaders still had an illusion of stability at the dawn of the twenty-first century, it is surely shattered by now. Consider the following string of events that occurred in the first five years of the new century:

1. Terrorists commandeered United and American Airlines jets and crashed them into the Pentagon and the twin towers of the World Trade Center in New York City, killing thousands and temporarily halting economic activity around the world. Soon afterward, the United States became involved in a costly and controversial war in Iraq.

2. Hurricane Katrina slammed into the Gulf Coast, virtually wiping out New Orleans, killing more than 1,500 people, and destroying homes, businesses, schools, and towns in several states. The social and economic impact of the largest natural disaster in U.S. history was felt nationwide, and the region still has not recovered.

3. General Motors, one of the world's largest companies and central to the U.S. economy, slid toward bankruptcy, faced with declining sales, slipping market share, and mounting health care costs for 1.1 million employees, retirees, and dependents.

4. China and India emerged from dismal poverty to become the "dragon and the tiger" of global commerce, experiencing growth rates unmatched by any other large country.[14] The effects are reverberating around the world and reshaping the global economy.

Most leaders, whether in the military, business, politics, education, social services, the arts, or the world of sports, recognize that maintaining stability in a world of such rapid and far-reaching change is a losing battle. In addition, many organizations face small crises on an almost daily basis—anything from a factory fire, to a flu epidemic, to charges of racial discrimination.

The new paradigm of leadership acknowledges that, as suggested by the science of chaos theory, we live in a world characterized by randomness and uncertainty, and small events often have massive and widespread consequences. For example, the ethical cloud that enveloped many giant companies, and the passage of the 2002 Sarbanes-Oxley Act, which dramatically increased government regulation of U.S. businesses, began with some relatively simple, unsuspecting questions about Enron Corporation's stock valuation and business model.

Today's best leaders accept the inevitability of change and crisis and recognize them as potential sources of energy and self-renewal. Rather than being laid low, they develop effective *crisis management* skills that help their organizations weather the storm and move toward something better. This chapter's Leader's Bookshelf describes some qualities needed for effective leadership during times of crisis or uncertainty. Real leaders know that the benefits associated with stability are a myth; that when things do not change, they die.

From Control to Empowerment

Leaders in powerful positions once thought workers should be told what to do and how to do it. They believed strict control was needed for the organization to function efficiently and effectively. Rigid organizational hierarchies, structured jobs and work processes, and detailed, inviolate procedures let everyone know that those at the top had power and those at the bottom had none.

Leader's Bookshelf

Leadership

Getty Images

by Rudolph Giuliani, with Ken Kurson

Some people probably looked to Rudy Giuliani, former mayor of New York, for inspiration even before September 11, 2001, when terrorists crashed jetliners into the twin towers of the World Trade Center. But after that horrendous event, practically the whole country recognized New York City's mayor as the epitome of what a leader should be: calm and steady in the face of crisis, strong but compassionate, honest but diplomatic. Giuliani's book, titled simply *Leadership,* shows that he has given a lot of thought, both before and after September 11, to what makes a great leader.

The Hallmarks of Great Leadership

In a clear, interesting style, Giuliani lays out his prescription for success as a leader in a complex and turbulent world. Some of his principles include:

- *Develop and communicate strong beliefs.* Great leaders lead by ideas, so they have to know what they stand for and be able to communicate it in a compelling way. A leader "cannot simply impose his will. . . ." Giuliani writes. "He must bring people aboard, excite them about his vision, and earn their support."

- *Accept responsibility.* Leaders set an example for others by performing their jobs honestly and effectively and by accepting responsibility for what happens during their watches. Good leaders welcome being held accountable, and they hold others accountable for living up to high standards as well.

- *Surround yourself with great people.* The most effective leaders are those who hire the best people they can possibly find, motivate them, provide them with challenges and opportunities to grow, and direct their energies toward positive outcomes. Giuliani recalls the September 11 aftermath: "Faced with the worst disaster New York had ever seen, it might have been understandable for some people in my administration to go through the motions. . . . Instead, without exception, my staff distinguished themselves."

- *Study, Read, Learn Independently.* Leaders should never leave important decisions to the experts. "No matter how talented your advisors and deputies, you have to attack challenges with as much of your own knowledge as possible." Giuliani believes the best leaders are lifelong learners who "put time aside for deep study." Leaders also prepare relentlessly so they can identify potential problems before they happen.

The Making of a Leader

Giuliani makes the key point that leadership does not just happen. It can be learned and developed through practice as well as by studying the leadership ideas and behavior of great leaders. *Leadership* incorporates not only Giuliani's ideas but the thinking of numerous people—from his mother, to President Ronald Reagan, to Winston Churchill—who have shaped him as a leader. Through insights and anecdotes, Giuliani offers us a chance to learn from their wisdom as well.

Leadership, by Rudolph Giuliani with Ken Kurson, is published by Hyperion.

Today, the old assumptions about the distribution of power are no longer valid. An emphasis on control and rigidity serves to squelch motivation, innovation, and morale rather than produce desired results. Today's leaders share power rather than hoard it and find ways to increase an organization's brain power by getting everyone in the organization involved and committed.

One reason for this is that the financial basis of today's economy is rapidly becoming *information* rather than the tangible assets of land, buildings, and machines. Fifty years ago, tangible assets represented 73 percent of the assets of non-financial corporations in the United States. By 2002, the proportion was down to around 53 percent and still declining.[15] This means that the primary factor of production is human knowledge, which increases the power of employees. The educational and skill level of employees in the United States and other developed countries has also steadily increased over the past several decades, and many people are no longer satisfied working in an organization that doesn't give them opportunities to participate and learn.

When all the organization needed was workers to run machines eight hours a day, traditional command-and-control systems generally worked quite well, but the organization received no benefit from employees' minds. Today, success depends on the intellectual capacity of all employees, and leaders have to face a hard fact: Buildings and machines can be owned; people cannot. One of the leader's most challenging jobs is to guide workers by using their power effectively to creat and develop a climate of respect and development for employees.[16]

From Competition to Collaboration

The move to empowerment also ties directly into new ways of working that emphasize collaboration over competition and conflict. Although some companies still encourage internal competition and aggressiveness, most of today's organizations stress teamwork and cooperation. Self-directed teams and other forms of horizontal collaboration are breaking down boundaries between departments and helping to spread knowledge and information throughout the organization. Compromise and sharing are recognized as signs of strength, not weakness.

Some competition can be healthy for an organization, but many leaders are resisting the idea of competition as a struggle to win while someone else loses. Instead, they direct everyone's competitive energy toward being the best that they can be. There is a growing trend toward increasing collaboration with other organizations so that companies think of themselves as teams that create value jointly rather than as autonomous entities in competition with all others.[17] A new form of global business is made up of networks of independent companies that share financial risks and leadership talents and provide access to one another's technologies and markets.[18]

The move to collaboration presents greater challenges to leaders than did the old concept of competition. It is often more difficult to create an environment of teamwork and community that fosters collaboration and mutual support. The call for empowerment, combined with an understanding of organizations as part of a fluid, dynamic, interactive system, makes the use of intimidation and manipulation obsolete as a means of driving the competitive spirit.

> **Action Memo**
>
> Go to Leader's Self-Insight 1.1 to learn about your own "intelligence" for dealing with collaboration and with the other new realities facing organizations.

From Uniformity to Diversity

Many of today's organizations were built on assumptions of uniformity, separation, and specialization. People who think alike, act alike, and have similar job skills are grouped into a department, such as accounting or manufacturing, separate from other departments. Homogenous groups find it easy to get along, communicate, and understand one another. The uniform thinking that arises, however, can be a disaster in a world becoming more multinational and diverse.

Two business school graduates in their twenties discovered the importance of diversity when they started a specialized advertising firm. They worked hard, and as the firm grew, they hired more people just like themselves—bright, young, intense college graduates who were committed and hard working. The firm grew to about 20 employees over two and a half years, but the expected profits never materialized. The two entrepreneurs could never get a handle on what was wrong, and the firm slid into bankruptcy. Convinced the idea was still valid, they started over, but with a new philosophy. They sought employees with different

Multiple Intelligence theory suggests that there are several different ways of learning about things, hence there are multiple "intelligences," of which five are interpersonal (learn via interactions with others), intrapersonal (own inner states), logical/mathematical (rationality and logic), verbal/linguistic (words and language), and musical (sounds, tonal patterns, and rhythms). Most people prefer one or two of the intelligences as a way of learning, yet each person has the potential to develop skills in each of the intelligences.

The items below will help you identify the forms of intelligence that you tend to use or enjoy most, as well as the forms which you utilize less. Please check each item below as Mostly False or Mostly True for you.

	Mostly False	Mostly True
1. I like to work with and solve complex problems.	_____	_____
2. I recently wrote something that I am especially proud of.	_____	_____
3. I have three or more close friends.	_____	_____
4. I like to learn about myself through personality tests.	_____	_____
5. I frequently listen to music on the radio or iPod-type player.	_____	_____
6. Math and science were among my favorite subjects.	_____	_____
7. Language and social studies were among my favorite subjects.	_____	_____
8. I am frequently involved in social activities.	_____	_____
9. I have or would like to attend personal growth seminars.	_____	_____
10. I notice if a melody is out of tune or off-key.	_____	_____
11. I am good at problem solving that requires logical thinking.	_____	_____
12. My conversations frequently include things I've read or heard about.	_____	_____
13. When among strangers I easily find someone to talk to.	_____	_____
14. I spend time alone meditating, reflecting, or thinking.	_____	_____
15. After hearing a tune once or twice I am able to sing it back with some accuracy.	_____	_____

Scoring and Interpretation

Count the number of items checked Mostly True that represent each of the four intelligences as indicated below.

Questions 1, 6, 11, Logical-mathematical intelligence
Mostly True = _____.
Questions 2, 7, 12, Verbal-linguistic intelligence.
Mostly True = _____.
Questions 3, 8, 13, Interpersonal intelligence.
Mostly True = _____.
Questions 4, 9, 14, Intrapersonal intelligence.
Mostly True = _____.
Questions 5, 10, 15, Musical intelligence.
Mostly True = _____.

Educational institutions tend to stress the logical-mathematical and verbal-linguistic forms of learning. How do your intelligences align with the changes taking place in the world? Would you rather rely on using one intelligence in-depth or develop multiple intelligences? Any intelligence above for which you received a score of three is a major source of learning for you, and a score of zero means you may not use it at all. How do your intelligences fit your career plans and your aspirations for the type of leader you want to be?

Source: Based on Kirsi Tirri, Petri Nokelainen, and Martin Ubani, "Conceptual Definition and Empirical Validation of the Spiritual Sensitivity Scale," *Journal of Empirical Theology* 19 (2006), pp. 37–62; and David Lazear, Seven Ways of Knowing: Teaching for Multiple Intelligences (Palentine, IL: IRI/Skylight Publishing, 1991).

ages, ethnic backgrounds, and work experience. People had different styles, yet the organization seemed to work better. People played different roles, and the diverse experiences of the group enabled the firm to respond to unique situations and handle a variety of organizational and personal needs. The advertising firm is growing again, and this time it is also making a profit.

The world is rapidly moving toward diversity at both national and international levels, and bringing diversity into the organization is the way to attract the best human talent and develop an organizational mindset broad enough to thrive in a multinational world. Organizations suffer when leaders don't respond to the reality of today's diverse environment.

From Self-Centered to Higher Ethical Purpose

The ethical turmoil of the early twenty-first century has prompted a determined and conscious shift in leader mindset from a self-centered focus to emphasis on a higher ethical purpose. Public confidence in business leaders in particular is at an all-time low, but politics, sports, and non-profit organizations have also been affected.

Over years of business growth and success, many leaders slipped into a pattern of expecting—and getting—more. Pay for CEOs of large organizations in the United States quadrupled between the years of 1993 and 2005. By then, the average CEO pay was 369 times as much as the average employee's.[19] Unfortunately, the old-paradigm emphasis on individual ability, success, and prosperity has sometimes pushed people to cross the line, culminating in organizational corruption on a broad scale and ugly headlines exposing leaders from companies such as Enron, WorldCom, Tyco, and Adelphia Communications as unethical and self-serving rogues. At Enron, top executives rewarded highly competitive managers who were willing to do whatever it took—whether it was hiding their mistakes, fudging their reports, or backstabbing colleagues—to make the numbers and keep the stock price high. The overriding emphasis on individual ambition created an environment of vanity and greed whereby executives profited at the expense of employees, shareholders, and the community.[20] And Enron managers didn't hold a monopoly on greed. Top executives at companies including Qwest Communications, AOL Time Warner, Global Crossing, and Broadcom sold billions of dollars worth of stock at vastly inflated prices, making themselves rich even as their companies deteriorated and average investors lost as much as 90 percent of their holdings.[21]

In the new paradigm, leaders emphasize accountability, integrity, and responsibility to something larger than individual self-interest, including employees, customers, the organization, and all stakeholders.[22] This chapter's *Consider This* box presents ten commandments based on 1950s western film star Gene Autry's Cowboy Code that can be regarded as applicable to new paradigm leaders.

New-paradigm leaders reinforce the importance of doing the right thing, even if it hurts. One example is Aramark Worldwide Corp., the giant outsourcing company that provides food services for many universities and corporations. After a huge investment of time and money, CEO Joseph Neubauer walked away from a once-promising overseas merger when he discovered that the company's business practices didn't live up to Aramark's ethical standards. "It takes a lifetime to build a reputation, and only a short time to lose it all," Neubauer says.[23]

From Hero to Humble

A related shift is the move from the celebrity "leader-as-hero" to the hardworking behind-the-scenes leader who quietly builds a strong enduring company by supporting and developing others rather than touting his own abilities and successes.[24]

During the last two decades of the twentieth century, good leadership became equated with larger-than-life personalities, strong egos, and personal

Consider This!

Should Leaders Live by the Cowboy Code?

1. A cowboy never takes unfair advantage—even of an enemy.
2. A cowboy never goes back on his word or betrays a trust.
3. A cowboy always tells the truth.
4. A cowboy is kind and gentle with children, the elderly, and animals.
5. A cowboy is free from racial or religious prejudice.
6. A cowboy is always helpful and lends a hand when anyone's in trouble.
7. A cowboy is a good worker.
8. A cowboy stays clean in thought, speech, action, and personal habits.
9. A cowboy respects womanhood, parents, and the laws of his nation.
10. A cowboy is a patriot to his country.

Source: Gene Autry's Cowboy Commandments are reported, with some variations in wording, in multiple sources.

ambition. The media attention helped cultivate the image.[25] In the early 1980s, Lee Iacocca was portrayed almost as a white knight riding in to save Chrysler. Over the next 20 years, corporate CEOs became superstars, featured on the covers of business and news magazines and celebrated for their charismatic or outrageous personalities as much as for their abilities. A remark made by Albert J. Dunlap, nicknamed "Chainsaw Al" for his slash-and-run tactics at companies such as Scott Paper and Sunbeam Corp. in the mid-1990s, captures the mindset of the leader-as-hero: "Most CEOs are ridiculously overpaid, but I deserved the $100 million," Dunlap wrote in his self-congratulatory autobiography. "I'm a superstar in my field, much like Michael Jordan in basketball."[26] As we now know, Dunlap's "turnarounds" were smoke and mirrors, based mostly on short-term accounting gimickry. His efforts netted him millions, but left the companies, their employees, and shareholders much worse off than they were before.

Although the majority of high-profile leaders are not so self-serving, the recent ethical maelstrom in the business world has contributed to a shift in mindset away from the individual leader as hero. When a business magazine recently asked a number of successful leaders about the best advice they ever got, several, including Meg Whitman of eBay and Howard Schultz of Starbucks, included "letting others take the credit" in their answers. Brian Roberts, CEO of Comcast, got this advice from his father. "You're in a lucky position and you know it," Ralph Roberts told his son. "You don't need all the glory. If you let others take the credit, it makes them feel like they're part of something special."[27]

The new-paradigm leader is characterized by an almost complete lack of ego, coupled with a fierce resolve to do what is best for the organization. Jim Collins, author of *Good to Great: Why Some Companies Make the Leap . . . and Others*

Action Memo

As a leader, you can respond to the reality of change and crisis, the need for empowerment, collaboration, and diversity, and the importance of a higher, ethical purpose. You can channel your ambition toward achieving larger organizational goals rather than feeding your own ego.

Don't, calls this new breed Level 5 leaders.[28] In contrast to the view of great leaders as larger-than-life personalities with strong egos and big ambitions, Level 5 leaders often seem shy and unpretentious. A classic example is Darwin E. Smith, who led Kimberly-Clark from 1971 to 1991.

Darwin E. Smith, Kimberly-Clark

During his 20 years as CEO, Darwin Smith turned Kimberly-Clark into the world's leading consumer paper products company, yet few people have ever heard of him. And that's just the way he wanted it.

Smith was somewhat shy and awkward in social situations, and he would never make anybody's best-dressed list. He wasn't the feature of articles in *Business Week, Fortune,* or *The Wall Street Journal.* Yet, far from being meek, Smith demonstrated an aggressive determination to revive Kimberly-Clark, which at the time was a stodgy old paper company that had seen years of falling stock prices. Anyone who interpreted his appearance and demeanor as a sign of ineptness soon learned differently, as Smith made difficult decisions that set Kimberly-Clark on the path to greatness. When Smith took over, the company's core business was in coated paper. Convinced that this approach doomed the company to mediocrity, Smith took the controversial step of selling the company's paper mills and investing all its resources in consumer products like Kleenex and Huggies diapers.

It proved to be a stroke of genius. Over the 20 years Smith led Kimberly-Clark, the company generated cumulative stock returns that were 4.1 times greater than those of the general market. When asked after his retirement about his exceptional performance, Smith said simply, "I never stopped trying to become qualified for the job."[29]

As the example of Darwin Smith illustrates, despite their personal humility, Level 5 leaders are highly ambitious for their organizations, with a fierce determination to produce great and lasting results. They develop a solid corps of leaders throughout the organization and create a culture focused on high performance and integrity. Although Level 5 leaders accept full responsibility for mistakes, poor results, or failures, they typically give credit for successes to other people. Reuben Mark, current CEO of Colgate-Palmolive, shuns personal publicity and turns down requests for media profiles because he believes being personally profiled takes credit for the efforts of his employees. At annual meetings, Mark pays tribute to employees around the world who make even seemingly minor contributions to innovation, market increases, or business operations.[30]

Egocentric leaders often build an organization as a hero with a thousand helpers. New-paradigm leaders, though, build their organizations with many strong leaders who can step forward and continue the company's success long into the future. Although most research regarding the new type of leader has been on corporate CEOs such as Reuben Mark and Darwin Smith, it's important to remember that new-paradigm or Level 5 leaders are in all positions in all types of organizations.

Comparing Management and Leadership

Management
the attainment of organizational goals in an effective and efficient manner through planning, organizing, staffing, directing, and controlling organizational resources

Management can be defined as the attainment of organizational goals in an effective and efficient manner through planning, organizing, staffing, directing, and controlling organizational resources. So, what is it that distinguishes the process of leadership from that of management? Hundreds of books and articles have been written in recent years about the difference between the two. Unfortunately, with the current emphasis on the need for leadership, managers have gotten a bad name.[31] Yet

Exhibit 1.3 Comparing Management and Leadership

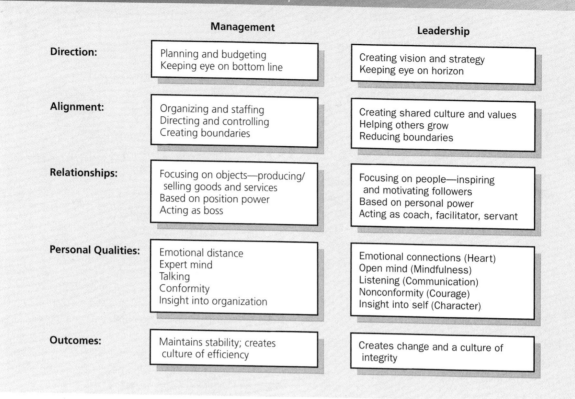

	Management	Leadership
Direction:	Planning and budgeting Keeping eye on bottom line	Creating vision and strategy Keeping eye on horizon
Alignment:	Organizing and staffing Directing and controlling Creating boundaries	Creating shared culture and values Helping others grow Reducing boundaries
Relationships:	Focusing on objects—producing/ selling goods and services Based on position power Acting as boss	Focusing on people—inspiring and motivating followers Based on personal power Acting as coach, facilitator, servant
Personal Qualities:	Emotional distance Expert mind Talking Conformity Insight into organization	Emotional connections (Heart) Open mind (Mindfulness) Listening (Communication) Nonconformity (Courage) Insight into self (Character)
Outcomes:	Maintains stability; creates culture of efficiency	Creates change and a culture of integrity

managers and leaders are not inherently different types of people, and many managers already possess the abilities and qualities needed to be good leaders. Both management and leadership are essential in organizations and must be integrated effectively to lead to high performance.[32] That is, leadership cannot replace management; it should be in addition to management.

At Aetna, CEO Ronald A. Williams has used an integrated management and leadership approach to rescue the nation's largest health insurance provider from a steep decline. Williams clearly practices good management, such as controlling costs, implementing operational changes and new technologies, establishing goals and plans, and monitoring performance. However, he is also a consummate leader who creates a culture that allows others to flourish, builds an environment that fosters integrity and accountability, and provides vision and inspiration for employees. "People will walk through walls for him," said one health care industry observer.[33] There are managers at all hierarchical levels in today's organizations who are also good leaders, and most people can develop the qualities needed for effective leadership.

Exhibit 1.3 compares management to leadership in five areas crucial to organizational performance—providing direction, aligning followers, building relationships, developing personal qualities, and creating leader outcomes.[34]

Action Memo
You can evaluate your own leadership potential by completing the quiz in Leader's Self-Insight 1.2 on page 16.

Providing Direction

Both leaders and managers are concerned with providing direction for the organization, but there are differences. Management focuses on establishing detailed plans and

Getty Images

Questions 1–6 below are about you right now. Questions 7–22 are about how you would like to be if you were the head of a major department at a corporation. Answer Mostly False or Mostly True to indicate whether the item describes you accurately, or whether you would strive to perform each activity as a department head.

NOW

	Mostly False	Mostly True
1. When I have a number of tasks or homework assignments to do, I set priorities and organize the work to meet the deadlines.	_____	_____
2. When I am involved in a serious disagreement, I hang in there and talk it out until it is completely resolved.	_____	_____
3. I would rather sit in front of my computer than spend a lot of time with people.	_____	_____
4. I reach out to include other people in activities or when there are discussions.	_____	_____
5. I know my long-term vision for career, family, and other activities.	_____	_____
6. When solving problems, I prefer analyzing things myself to working through them with a group of people.	_____	_____

HEAD OF MAJOR DEPARTMENT

7. I would help subordinates clarify goals and how to reach them.	_____	_____
8. I would give people a sense of long-term mission and higher purpose.	_____	_____
9. I would make sure jobs get out on time.	_____	_____
10. I would scout for new product or service opportunities.	_____	_____
11. I would give credit to people who do their jobs well.	_____	_____
12. I would promote unconventional beliefs and values.	_____	_____
13. I would establish procedures to help the department operate smoothly.	_____	_____
14. I would verbalize the higher values that I and the organization stand for.	_____	_____

Scoring and Interpretation

Count the number of Mostly True answers to even-numbered questions: _____. Count the number of Mostly True answers to odd-numbered questions: _____. Compare the two scores.

The even-numbered items represent behaviors and activities typical of leadership. Leaders are personally involved in shaping ideas, values, vision, and change. They often use an intuitive approach to develop fresh ideas and seek new directions for the department or organization. The odd-numbered items are considered more traditional management activities. Managers respond to organizational problems in an impersonal way, make rational decisions, and work for stability and efficiency.

If you answered yes to more even-numbered than odd-numbered items, you may have potential leadership qualities. If you answered yes to more odd-numbered items, you may have management qualities. Management qualities are an important foundation for new leaders because the organization first has to operate efficiently. Then leadership qualities can enhance performance. Both sets of qualities can be developed or improved with awareness and experience.

Sources: John P. Kotter, *Leading Change* (Boston, MA: Harvard Business School Press, 1996), p. 26; Joseph C. Rost, *Leadership for the Twenty-first Century* (Westport, CT; Praeger, 1993), p. 149; and Brian Dumaine, "The New Non-Manager Managers," *Fortune* (February 22, 1993), pp. 80–84.

schedules for achieving specific results, then allocating resources to accomplish the plan. Leadership calls for creating a compelling vision of the future and developing farsighted strategies for producing the changes needed to achieve that vision. Whereas management calls for keeping an eye on the bottom line and short-term results, leadership means keeping an eye on the horizon and the long-term future.

A **vision** is a picture of an ambitious, desirable future for the organization or team.[35] It can be as lofty as Motorola's aim to "become the premier company in the world" or as down-to-earth as the Swedish company IKEA's simple vision "to provide affordable furniture for people with limited budgets."

To be compelling for followers, the vision has to be one they can relate to and share. Consider that in *Fortune* magazine's study of the "100 Best Companies to Work for in America," two of the recurring traits of great companies are a powerful, visionary leader and a sense of purpose beyond increasing shareholder value.[36] At Google, people are energized by the psychic rewards they get from working on intellectually stimulating and challenging technical problems, as well as by the potentially beneficial global impact of their work. Leaders stress a vision of unifying data and information around the world, one day totally obliterating language barriers via the Internet.[37] Similarly, employees at mutual fund company Vanguard are motivated by a vision of helping people pay for a happy retirement.[38]

Vision
a picture of an ambitious, desirable future for the organization or team

Aligning Followers

Management entails organizing a structure to accomplish the plan; staffing the structure with employees; and developing policies, procedures, and systems to direct employees and monitor implementation of the plan. Managers are thinkers and workers are doers. Leadership is concerned instead with communicating the vision and developing a shared culture and set of core values that can lead to the desired future state. This involves others as thinkers, doers, and leaders themselves, fostering a sense of ownership in everyone.[39] Whereas the vision describes the destination, the culture and values help define the journey toward it. Leadership focuses on getting everyone lined up in the same direction. Gertrude Boyle, a housewife and mother who took charge of Columbia Sportswear after her husband's early death, created a comfortable, down-to-earth corporate culture that propelled the outdoor clothing manufacturer from sales of $800,000 to just under $300 million. She came into the company with no business experience, but says, "Running a company is like raising kids. You all have to be in the same line of thinking."[40]

Management often means organizing by separating people into specialties and functions, with boundaries separating them by department and hierarchical level. Leaders break down boundaries so people know what others are doing, can coordinate easily, and feel a sense of teamwork and equalness for achieving outcomes.

Rather than simply directing and controlling employees to achieve specific results, leaders "align [people] with broader ideas of what the company should be and why."[41] Leaders encourage people to expand their minds and abilities and to assume responsibility for their own actions. Think about classes you have taken at your college or university. In some college classes, the professor tells students exactly what to do and how to do it, and many students expect this kind of direction and control. Have you ever had a class where the instructor instead inspired and encouraged you and your classmates to find innovative ways to meet goals? The difference reflects a rational management versus a leadership approach. Whereas the management communication process generally involves providing answers and solving problems, leadership entails asking questions, listening, and involving others.[42]

Building Relationships

In terms of relationships, management focuses on objects such as machines and reports, on taking the steps needed to produce the organization's goods and services. Leadership, on the other hand, focuses on motivating and inspiring people.

Whereas the management relationship is based on position and formal authority, leadership is a relationship based on personal influence. Formal **position power** means that there is a written, spoken, or implied contract wherein people accept either a superior or subordinate role and see the use of coercive as well as noncoercive behavior as an acceptable way to achieve desired results.[43] For example, in an authority relationship, both people accept that a manager can tell a subordinate to be at work at 7:30 A.M. or her pay will be docked. Leadership, on the other hand, relies on influence, which is less likely to use coercion. Followers are empowered to make many decisions on their own. Leadership strives to make work stimulating and challenging and involves pulling rather than pushing people toward goals. The role of leadership is to attract and energize people, motivating them through identification rather than rewards or punishments.[44] The formal position of authority in the organization is the source of management power, but leadership power comes from the personal character of the leader. Leadership does not require that one hold a formal position of authority, and many people holding positions of authority do not provide leadership. The differing source of power is one of the key distinctions between management and leadership. Take away a manager's formal position and will people choose to follow her? That is the mark of a leader. Leadership truly depends on who you are rather than on your position or title.

> **Position power**
> a written, spoken, or implied contract wherein people accept either a superior or subordinate role and see the use of coercive as well as noncoercive behavior as an acceptable way of achieving desirable results

Developing Personal Leadership Qualities

Leadership is more than a set of skills; it relies on a number of subtle personal qualities that are hard to see, but are very powerful. These include things like enthusiasm, integrity, courage, and humility. First of all, good leadership springs from a genuine passion for the work and a genuine concern for other people. Great leaders are people who love what they do and want to share that love with others. The process of management generally encourages emotional distance, but leadership means being emotionally connected to others. Where there is leadership, people become part of a community and feel that they are contributing to something worthwhile.[45]

Whereas management means providing answers and solving problems, leadership requires the courage to admit mistakes and doubts, to take risks, to listen, and to trust and learn from others. Emotional connections can be uncomfortable for some managers, but they are necessary for true leadership to happen. George Sparks, a graduate of the Air Force Academy and general manager of Hewlett-Packard's measuring-equipment business, says he learned this from a Girl Scout leader.

> **Action Memo**
> As a leader, you can awaken your leadership qualities of enthusiasm, integrity, courage, and moral commitment. You can make emotional connections with followers to increase your leadership effectiveness.

Frances Hesselbein and the Girl Scout Way

"The best two days of my career" is how George Sparks describes the time he spent following Frances Hesselbein around. Hesselbein is currently chairman of the board of governors of the Leader to Leader Institute and an acclaimed author and editor of more than 20 books, the most recent of which is titled *Hesselbein on Leadership*. But she began her career more than 40 years ago as a volunteer Scout leader. She eventually rose to CEO of the Girl Scouts, inheriting a troubled organization of 680,000 people, only 1 percent of whom were paid employees.

By the time she retired in 1990, Hesselbein had turned around declining membership, dramatically increased participation by minorities, and replaced a brittle hierarchy with one of the most vibrant organizations in the non-profit or business world.

Hesselbein describes how she works with others as a circle in which everyone is included. As Sparks observed her in action, the most compelling quality he noted was her ability to sense people's needs on an emotional level. He explains, "Time and again, I have seen people face two possible solutions. One is 20 percent better, but the other meets their personal needs—and that is the one they inevitably choose." He noticed that Hesselbein would listen carefully and then link people in such a way that their personal needs were met at the same time they were serving the needs of the organization. Hesselbein recognizes that the only way to achieve high performance is through the work of others, and she consistently treats people with care and respect. In her talks and writings for leaders, one of her primary lessons is that taking people for granted is contrary to the definition of what makes a leader.

Her definition of leadership, she says, was "very hard to arrive at, very painful. . . . [It] is not a basket of tricks or skills. It is the quality and character and courage of the person who is the leader. It's a matter of ethics and moral compass, the willingness to remain highly vulnerable."[46]

As Frances Hesselbein noted, developing leadership qualities can sometimes be painful. Abraham Zaleznik has referred to leaders as "twice-born personalities," who struggle to develop their sense of self through psychological and social change.[47] For leadership to happen, leaders have to undergo a journey of self-discovery and personal understanding.[48] Leadership experts agree that a top characteristic of effective leaders is that they know who they are and what they stand for. In addition, leaders have the courage to act on their beliefs.[49] By knowing what they believe in, leaders remain constant, so that followers know what to expect. One study revealed that people would much rather follow individuals they can count on, even when they disagree with their viewpoint, than people they agree with but who frequently shift their viewpoints or positions.[50] One employee described the kind of person she would follow as this: ". . . it's like they have a stick down through the center of them that's rooted in the ground. I can tell when someone has that. When they're not defensive, not egotistical. They're open-minded, able to joke and laugh at themselves. They can take a volatile situation and stay focused. They bring out the best in me by making me want to handle myself in the same way. I want to be part of their world."[51]

True leaders draw on a number of subtle but powerful forces within themselves. For example, leaders tend to have open minds that welcome new ideas rather than closed minds that criticize new ideas. Leaders tend to care about others and build personal connections rather than maintain emotional distance. Leaders listen and discern what people want and need more than they talk to give advice and orders. Leaders are willing to be nonconformists, to disagree and say no when it serves the larger good, and to accept nonconformity from others rather than try to squeeze everyone into the same mindset. They and others step outside the traditional boundary and comfort zone, take risks, and make mistakes to learn and grow. Moreover, leaders are honest with themselves and others to the point of inspiring trust. They set high moral standards by doing the right thing, rather than just going along with standards set by others. Leadership causes wear and tear on the individual, because leaders are vulnerable, take risks, and initiate change, which typically encounters resistance.

Creating Outcomes

The differences between management and leadership create two differing outcomes, as illustrated at the bottom of Exhibit 1.3. Management maintains a degree of stability, predictability, and order through a *culture of efficiency.* Good management helps the organization consistently achieve short-term results and meet the expectations of various stakeholders. Leadership, on the other hand, creates change, often radical change, within a *culture of integrity* that helps the organization thrive over the long haul by promoting openness and honesty, positive relationships, and a long-term focus. Leadership facilitates the courage needed to make difficult and unconventional decisions that may sometimes hurt short-term results.

Leadership means questioning and challenging the status quo so that outdated, unproductive, or socially irresponsible norms can be replaced to meet new challenges. Good leadership can lead to extremely valuable change, such as new products or services that gain new customers or expand markets. Thus, although good management is needed to help organizations meet current commitments, good leadership is needed to move the organization into the future. Remember that the two must be combined for the organization to succeed.

Evolving Theories of Leadership

To understand leadership as it is viewed and practiced today, it is important to recognize that the concept of leadership has changed over time. Leadership typically reflects the larger society, and theories have evolved as norms, attitudes, and understandings in the larger world have changed.

Historical Overview of Major Approaches

The various leadership theories can be categorized into six basic approaches, each of which is briefly described below. Many of these ideas are still applicable to leadership studies today and are discussed in various chapters of this text.

Great Man Theories This is the granddaddy of leadership concepts. The earliest studies of leadership adopted the belief that leaders (who were always thought of as male) were born with certain heroic leadership traits and natural abilities of power and influence. In organizations, social movements, religions, governments, and the military, leadership was conceptualized as a single "Great Man" who put everything together and influenced others to follow along based on the strength of inherited traits, qualities, and abilities.

Trait Theories Studies of these larger-than-life leaders spurred research into the various traits that defined a leader. Beginning in the 1920s, researchers looked to see if leaders had particular traits or characteristics, such as intelligence or energy, that distinguished them from non-leaders and contributed to success. It was thought that if traits could be identified, leaders could be predicted, or perhaps even trained. Although research failed to produce a list of traits that would always guarantee leadership success, the interest in leadership characteristics has continued to the present day.

Behavior Theories The failure to identify a universal set of leadership traits led researchers in the early 1950s to begin looking at what a leader does, rather than who he or she is.[52] One line of research focused on what leaders actually do on the job, such as various management activities, roles, and responsibilities. These studies were soon expanded to try to determine how effective leaders differ in their behavior from ineffective ones. Researchers looked at how a leader behaved toward followers and how this correlated with leadership effectiveness or ineffectiveness. Chapter 2 discusses trait and behavior theories.

Contingency Theories Researchers next began to consider the contextual and situational variables that influence what leadership behaviors will be effective. The idea behind contingency theories is that leaders can analyze their situation and tailor their behavior to improve leadership effectiveness. Major situational variables are the characteristics of followers, characteristics of the work environment and follower tasks, and the external environment. Contingency theories, sometimes called situational theories, emphasize that leadership cannot be understood in a vacuum separate from various elements of the group or organizational situation. Chapter 3 covers contingency theories.

Influence Theories These theories examine influence processes between leaders and followers. One primary topic of study is *charismatic leadership* (Chapter 12), which refers to leadership influence based not on position or formal authority but, rather, on the qualities and charismatic personality of the leader. Related areas of study are *leadership vision* (Chapter 13) and *organizational culture* (Chapter 14). Leaders influence people to change by providing an inspiring vision of the future and shaping the culture and values needed to attain it. Several chapters of this text relate to the topic of influence because it is essential to understanding leadership.

Relational Theories Since the late 1970s, many ideas of leadership have focused on the relational aspect, that is, how leaders and followers interact and influence one another. Rather than being seen as something a leader does to a follower, leadership is viewed as a relational process that meaningfully engages all participants and enables each person to contribute to achieving the vision. Interpersonal relationships are seen as the most important facet of leadership effectiveness.[53] Two significant relational theories are *transformational leadership* (Chapter 12) and *servant leadership* (Chapter 6).

Other important relational topics covered in various chapters of the text include the personal qualities that leaders need to build effective relationships, such as emotional intelligence, a leader's mind, integrity and high moral standards, and personal courage. In addition, leaders build relationships through motivation and empowerment, leadership communication, team leadership, and embracing diversity.

A Model of Leadership Evolution

Exhibit 1.4 provides a framework for examining the evolution of leadership from the early Great Man theories to today's relational theories. Each cell in the model summarizes an era of leadership thinking that was dominant in its time but may be less appropriate for today's world.

Leadership Era 1 This era may be conceptualized as pre-industrial and pre-bureaucratic. Most organizations were small and were run by a single individual who many times hired workers because they were friends or relatives, not necessarily because of their skills or qualifications. The size and simplicity of organizations and the stable nature of the environment made it easy for a single person to understand the big picture, coordinate and control all activities, and keep things on track. This is the era of Great Man leadership and the emphasis on personal traits of leaders. A leader was conceptualized as a single hero who saw the big picture and how everything fit into a whole.

Exhibit 1.4 Leadership Evolution

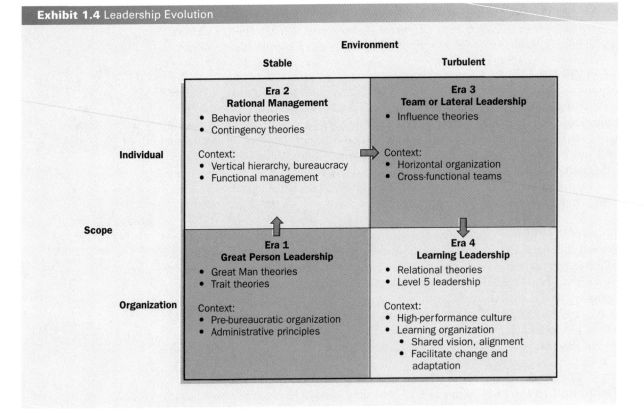

Leadership Era 2 In Era 2, we see the emergence of hierarchy and bureaucracy. Although the world remains stable, organizations have begun to grow so large that they require rules and standard procedures to ensure that activities are performed efficiently and effectively. Hierarchy of authority provides a sensible mechanism for supervision and control of workers, and decisions once based on rules of thumb or tradition are replaced with precise procedures. This era sees the rise of the "rational manager" who directs and controls others using an impersonal approach. Employees aren't expected to think for themselves; they are expected to do as they're told, follow rules and procedures, and accomplish specific tasks. The focus is on details rather than the big picture.

The rational manager was well-suited to a stable environment. The behavior and contingency theories worked here because leaders could analyze their situation, develop careful plans, and control what happened. But rational management is no longer sufficient for leadership in today's world.

Leadership Era 3 This era represented a tremendous shock to managers in North America and Europe. Suddenly, the world was no longer stable, and the prized techniques of rational management were no longer successful. Beginning with the OPEC oil embargo of 1972 to 1973 and continuing with the severe global competition of the 1980s and early 1990s, many managers saw that environmental conditions had become chaotic. The Japanese began to dominate world commerce with their ideas of team leadership and superb quality. This became an era of great confusion for leaders. They tried team-based approaches, downsizing, re-engineering, quality programs, and empowerment as ways to improve performance and get more motivation and commitment from employees.

This is the era of the team leader and the change leader. Influence was important because of the need to change organizational structures and cultures. This era sees the emergence of knowledge work, an emphasis on horizontal collaboration, and a shift to influence theories. Rather than conceiving of leadership as one person always being firmly "in charge," leadership is often shared among team leaders and members, shifting to the person with the most knowledge or expertise in the matter at hand.[54] Many leaders have become comfortable with ideas of team leadership, empowerment, diversity, and open communication. However, some are still trapped in old ways of thinking, trying to use rational management for a stable world when their organizations and the environment have already moved on.

Leadership Era 4 Enter the digital information age. It seems that everything is changing, and changing fast. Era 4 represents the **learning leader** who has made the leap to giving up control in the traditional sense. Leaders emphasize relationships and networks, and they influence others through vision and values rather than power and control. They are constantly experimenting, learning, and changing, both in their personal and professional lives, and they encourage the development and growth of others. Era 4 requires the full scope of leadership that goes far beyond rational management or even team leadership.

Learning leader
a leader who is open to learning and change and encourages the growth and development of others

Implications The flow from Great Man leadership to rational management to team and change leadership to learning leadership illustrates trends in the larger world. The implication is that leadership reflects the era or context of the organization and society. Most of today's organizations and leaders are still struggling with the transition from a stable to a chaotic environment and the new skills and qualities needed in this circumstance. Thus, issues of diversity, team leadership, empowerment, and horizontal relationships are increasingly relevant. In addition, many leaders are rapidly shifting into Era 3 and 4 leadership by focusing on change management and facilitating a vision and values to transform their companies into learning organizations. Era 3 and Era 4 leadership is what much of this book is about.

Leadership Is Not Automatic

Many leaders are caught in the transition between the practices and principles that defined the industrial era and the new reality of the twenty-first century. Attempts to achieve collaboration, empowerment, and diversity in organizations may fail because the beliefs and thought processes of leaders as well as employees are stuck in an old paradigm that values control, stability, and homogeneity. The difficult transition between the old and the new partly explains the current crisis in organizational leadership. It is difficult for many leaders to let go of methods and practices that have made them and their organizations successful in the past.

One of the most important aspects of the new paradigm of leadership is the ability to use human skills to build a culture of performance, trust, and collaboration. A few clues about the importance of acquiring new leadership skills were brought to light by the Center for Creative Leadership in Greensboro, North Carolina.[55] The study compared 21 derailed executives with 20 executives who successfully arrived at the top of a company. The derailed managers were successful people who were expected to go far, but they reached a plateau, were fired, or were forced to retire early. They were all bright, worked hard, and excelled in a technical area such as accounting or engineering.

Action Memo
As a leader, you can use the leadership skills that fit the correct era for your organization. You can use influence and relational aspects as appropriate for your organization.

Action Memo
As a leader, you can cultivate your people skills to avoid executive derailment. You can treat others with kindness, interest, and respect, and avoid over-managing by selecting good followers and delegating effectively.

Exhibit 1.5 Top Seven Reasons for Executive Derailment

1. Acting with an insensitive, abrasive, intimidating, bullying style
2. Being cold, aloof, arrogant
3. Betraying personal trust
4. Being overly ambitious, self-centered, thinking of next job, playing politics
5. Having specific performance problems with the business
6. Overmanaging, being unable to delegate or build a team
7. Being unable to select good subordinates

The striking difference between the two groups was the ability to use human skills. Only 25 percent of the derailed group were described as being good with people, whereas 75 percent of those who arrived at the top had people skills. Exhibit 1.5 lists the top seven reasons for failure. Unsuccessful managers were insensitive to others, abrasive, cold, arrogant, untrustworthy, overly ambitious and selfish, unable to delegate or build teams, and unable to acquire appropriate staff to work for them.

Interestingly, even people who do make it to the top of organizations sometimes fail in the role of CEO because of poor human skills. For example, Philip Purcell was forced out as CEO of Morgan Stanley largely because he was a remote, tyrannical leader who treated many employees with contempt and failed to build positive relationships with other managers or clients. His lack of human skills left Purcell with little goodwill to back him up when things started going against him.[56]

The inability to surround oneself with good people and help them learn and contribute can doom a top leader. The best leaders, at all levels, are those who are genuinely interested in other people and find ways to bring out the best in them.[57] In addition, today's successful leaders value change over stability, empowerment over control, collaboration over competition, diversity over uniformity, and integrity over self-interest, as discussed earlier. The new industry of *executive coaching* has emerged partly to help people through the transition to a new paradigm of leadership. Whereas management consultants typically help executives look outward, at company operations and strategic issues, executive coaches help them look inward. Executive coaches encourage leaders to confront their own flaws and hang-ups that inhibit effective leadership, then help them develop stronger emotional and interpersonal skills.

This brings up an interesting question: How do people become good leaders? As Kembrel Jones, associate dean of full-time MBA programs at Emory University's Goizueta Business School said, "If the elements of leadership were easy . . . we wouldn't be seeing the problems we see today."[58] But can leadership be taught? Many people don't think so, because so much of leadership depends on self-discovery. But it can be learned.

Action Memo

Leader's Self-Insight 1.3 gives you a chance to test your people skills and see if there are areas you need to work on.

Learning the Art and Science of Leadership

As we have discussed in this chapter, the concept of leadership has evolved through many perspectives and continues to change. Today's reality is that the old ways no longer work, but the new ways are just emerging. Everywhere, we hear the cry for leadership as the world around us is rocked by massive and often painful events.

How can a book or a course on leadership help you to be a better leader? It is important to remember that leadership is both an art and a science. It is an art

Leader's Self-Insight 1.3

Are You on a Fast Track to Nowhere?

Many fast-trackers find themselves suddenly derailed and don't know why. Many times, a lack of people skills is to blame. To help you determine whether you need to work on your people skills, take the following quiz answering each item as Mostly False or Mostly True. Think about a job or volunteer position you have now or have held in the past as you answer the following items.

PEOPLE SKILLS

	Mostly False	Mostly True
1. Other people describe me as a real "people person."	_____	_____
2. I spend a part of each day making small talk with coworkers (or teammates or classmates).	_____	_____
3. I see some of my coworkers (or teammates or classmates) outside of work, and I know many of them socially.	_____	_____
4. Because I have good work relationships, I often succeed where others fail.	_____	_____

WORKING WITH AUTHORITY

5. When I have a good reason for doing so, I will express a view that differs from that of leaders in the organization.	_____	_____
6. If I see a leader making a decision that seems harmful to the organization, I speak up.	_____	_____
7. People see me as someone who can independently assess an executive decision and, when appropriate, offer an alternative perspective.	_____	_____
8. When senior people ask for my opinion, they know that I'll respond with candor.	_____	_____

NETWORKING

9. I spend at least part of each week networking with colleagues.	_____	_____
10. I belong to organizations where I can make professional contacts.	_____	_____
11. A few times each month, I am invited to join key members of my team or organization for lunch.	_____	_____
12. I regularly interact with peers at other organizations.	_____	_____

Scoring and Interpretation

Tally the number of "Mostly Trues" checked for each set of questions.

People Skills:_____; Working with Authority: _____; Networking: _____

If you scored 4 in an area, you're right on track. Continue to act in the same way.

If your score is 2–3, you can fine tune your skills in that area. Review the questions where you said Mostly False and work to add those abilities to your leadership skill set.

A score of 0–1 indicates that you're dangerously close to derailment. You should take the time to do an in-depth self-assessment and find ways to expand your interpersonal skills.

Source: Adapted from "Are You Knocking Out Your Own Career?" *Fast Company* (May 1999), p. 230, based on Lois P. Frankel's *Jump-Start Your Career* (New York: Three Rivers Press).

because many leadership skills and qualities cannot be learned from a textbook. Leadership takes practice and hands-on experience, as well as intense personal exploration and development. However, leadership is also a science because a growing body of knowledge and objective facts describes the leadership process and how to use leadership skills to attain organizational goals.

Knowing about leadership research helps people analyze situations from a variety of perspectives and learn how to be more effective as leaders. By exploring leadership in both business and society, students gain an understanding of the importance of leadership to an organization's success, as well as the difficulties and challenges involved in being a leader. Studying leadership can also lead to the discovery of abilities you never knew you had. When students in a leadership seminar at Wharton were asked to pick one leader to represent the class, one woman was surprised when she outpolled all other students. Her leadership was drawn out not in the practice of leadership in student government, volunteer activities, or athletics, but in a classroom setting.[59]

Studying leadership gives you skills you can apply in the practice of leadership in your everyday life. Many people have never tried to be a leader because they have no understanding of what leaders actually do. The chapters in this book are designed to help you gain a firm knowledge of what leadership means and some of the skills and qualities that make a good leader. You can build competence in both the art and the science of leadership by completing the Self-Insight exercises throughout the book, by working on the activities and cases at the end of each chapter, and by applying the concepts you learn in class, in your relationships with others, in student groups, at work, and in voluntary organizations. Although this book and your instructors can guide you in your development, only you can apply the concepts and principles of leadership in your daily life. Learning to be a leader starts now, with you. Are you up to the challenge?

Organization of the Rest of the Book

The plan for this book reflects the shift to a new paradigm summarized in Exhibit 1.2 and the discussion of management versus leadership summarized in Exhibit 1.3. The framework in Exhibit 1.6 illustrates the organization of the book. Part 1 introduces leadership, its importance, and the transition to a new leadership paradigm.

Exhibit 1.6 Framework for the Book

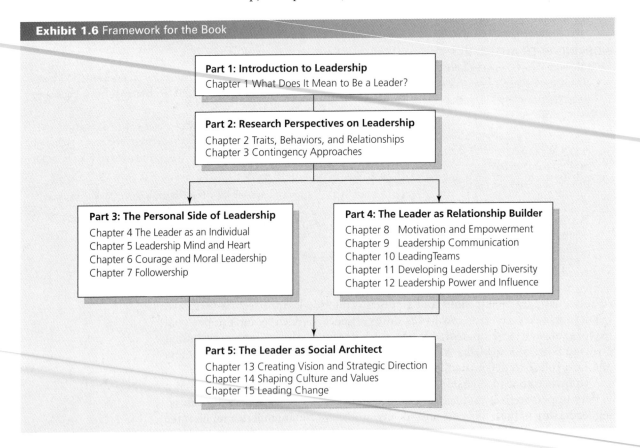

Part 1: Introduction to Leadership
Chapter 1 What Does It Mean to Be a Leader?

Part 2: Research Perspectives on Leadership
Chapter 2 Traits, Behaviors, and Relationships
Chapter 3 Contingency Approaches

Part 3: The Personal Side of Leadership
Chapter 4 The Leader as an Individual
Chapter 5 Leadership Mind and Heart
Chapter 6 Courage and Moral Leadership
Chapter 7 Followership

Part 4: The Leader as Relationship Builder
Chapter 8 Motivation and Empowerment
Chapter 9 Leadership Communication
Chapter 10 Leading Teams
Chapter 11 Developing Leadership Diversity
Chapter 12 Leadership Power and Influence

Part 5: The Leader as Social Architect
Chapter 13 Creating Vision and Strategic Direction
Chapter 14 Shaping Culture and Values
Chapter 15 Leading Change

Part 2 explores basic research perspectives that evolved during a more stable time when rational management approaches were effective. These basic perspectives, including the Great Man and trait theories, behavior theories, and contingency theories, are relevant to dealing with specific tasks and individuals and are based on a premise that leaders can predict and control various aspects of the environment to keep the organization running smoothly.

Parts 3, 4, and 5 switch to leadership perspectives that reflect the paradigm shift to the chaotic, unpredictable nature of the environment and the need for fresh leader approaches. Part 3 focuses on the personal side of leadership and looks at some of the qualities and forces that are required to be effective in the new reality. These chapters emphasize the importance of self-awareness and self-understanding, the development of one's own leadership mind and heart, moral leadership and courage, and appreciating the role of followership. Part 4 is about building effective relationships, including motivating and empowering others, communicating as a leader, leading teams, embracing the diversity of today's world, and using power and influence.

Part 5 brings together all of these ideas to examine the leader as builder of a social architecture that can help an organization create a brighter future. These chapters deal with creating vision and strategic direction, aligning culture and values to achieve the vision, and leading change.

Taken together, the sections and chapters paint a complete portrait of the leadership experience as it has evolved to the present day and emphasize the new paradigm skills and qualities that are relevant from today and into the future. This book blends systematic research evidence with real-world experiences and impact.

Summary and Interpretation

This chapter introduced the concept of leadership and explained how individuals can grow as leaders. Leadership is defined as an influence relationship among leaders and followers who intend real changes and outcomes that reflect their shared purposes. Thus leadership involves people in a relationship, influence, change, a shared purpose, and taking personal responsibility to make things happen. Most of us are aware of famous leaders, but most leadership that changes the world starts small and may begin with personal frustrations about events that prompt people to initiate change and inspire others to follow them. Your leadership may be expressed in the classroom, your neighborhood, community, or volunteer organizations.

Concepts of leadership have evolved over time. Major research approaches include Great Man theories, trait theories, behavior theories, contingency theories, influence theories, and relational theories. Elements of all these approaches are still applicable to the study of leadership.

The biggest challenge facing leaders today is the changing world that wants a new paradigm of leadership. The new reality involves the shift from stability to change and crisis management, from control to empowerment, from competition to collaboration, from uniformity to diversity, and from a self-centered focus to a higher ethical purpose. In addition, the concept of leader as hero is giving way to that of the humble leader who develops others and shares credit for accomplishments. These dramatic changes suggest that a philosophy based on control and personal ambition will probably fail in the new era. The challenge for leaders is to evolve to a new mindset that relies on human skills, integrity, and teamwork.

The "soft" skills of leadership complement the "hard" skills of management, and both are needed to effectively guide organizations. Although leadership is often equated with good management, leadership and management are different processes. Management strives to maintain stability and improve efficiency. Leadership, on the other hand, is about creating a vision for the future, designing social architecture that shapes culture and values, inspiring and motivating followers, developing personal qualities, and creating change within a culture of integrity. Leadership can be integrated with management to achieve the greatest possible outcomes. Organizations need to be both managed and led, particularly in today's turbulent environment. Many managers already have the qualities needed to be effective leaders, but they may not have gone through the process needed to bring these qualities to life. It is important to remember that most people are not born with natural leadership skills and qualities, but leadership can be learned and developed.

Discussion Questions

1. What do you consider your own strengths and weaknesses for leadership? Discuss your answer with another student.
2. How do you feel about changing yourself first in order to become a leader who can change an organization?
3. Of the elements in the leadership definition as illustrated in Exhibit 1.1, which is the easiest for you? Which is hardest? Explain.
4. What does the paradigm shift from control to empowerment mean for you? Discuss.
5. Describe the best leader you have known. How did this leader acquire his or her capability?
6. Why do you think there are so few people who succeed at both management and leadership? Is it reasonable to believe someone can be good at both? Discuss.
7. Discuss some recent events and societal changes that might have contributed to a shift "from hero to humble." Do you agree or disagree that humility is important for good leadership?
8. "Leadership is more concerned with people than is management." Do you agree? Discuss.
9. What personal capacities should a person develop to be a good leader versus those developed to be a good manager?
10. Why is leadership considered both an art and a science?

Leadership at Work

Leadership Right–Wrong

Leader Wrong. Think of a specific situation in which you were working with someone who was in a leadership position over you, and that person was doing something that was wrong for you. This person might have been a coach, teacher, team leader, employer, immediate boss, family member, or anyone who had a leadership position over you. "Wrong for you" means that person's behavior reduced your effectiveness, made you and/or your coworkers less productive, and was de-motivating to you and/or your colleagues. *Write a few words below that describe what the leader was doing that was wrong for you.*

_____

_____

_____

Think of a second situation in which someone in a leadership position did something wrong for you. *Write a few words below that describe what the leader was doing that was wrong for you.*

_____

_____

_____

Leader Right. Think of a specific situation in which you were working with someone who was in a leadership position over you, and that person was doing something that was *right* for you. This person might have been a coach, teacher, team leader, employer, immediate boss, family member, or anyone who had a leadership position over you. "Right for you" means that person's behavior made you and/or your coworkers more productive, highly motivated you and/or others, and removed barriers to make you more successful. *Write a few words below that describe what the leader was doing that was right for you.*

_____

_____

_____

Think of a second situation in which someone in a leadership position did something right for you. *Write a few words below that describe what the leader was doing that was right for you.*

_____

_____

_____

The previous answers are data points that can help you understand the impact of leader behaviors. Analyze your four incidents—what are the underlying qualities of leadership that enable you to be an effective performer? Discuss your answers with another student. What leadership themes are present in the eight combined incidents? What do these responses tell you about the qualities you both want and don't want in your leaders?

In Class: An interesting way to use this exercise in class is to have students write (five words maximum) their leader "rights" on one board and their leader "wrongs" on another board. The instructor can ask small groups to identify underlying themes in the collective set of leader data points on the boards to specify what makes an effective leader. After students establish four or five key themes, they can be challenged to identify the one key theme that distinguishes leaders who are effective with subordinates from those who are not.

Source: Based on Melvin R. McKnight, "Organizational Behavior as a Phenomenological, Free-Will Centered Science," Working Paper, College of Business Administration, Northern Arizona University, 1997.

Leadership Development: Cases for Analysis

Sales Engineering Division

When DGL International, a manufacturer of refinery equipment, brought in John Terrill to manage its Sales Engineering division, company executives informed him of the urgent situation. Sales Engineering, with 20 engineers, was the highest-paid, best-educated, and least-productive division in the company. The instructions to Terrill: Turn it around. Terrill called a meeting of the engineers. He showed great concern for their personal welfare and asked point blank: "What's the problem? Why can't we produce? Why does this division have such turnover?"

Without hesitation, employees launched a hail of complaints. "I was hired as an engineer, not a pencil pusher." "We spend over half of our time writing asinine reports in triplicate for top management, and no one reads the reports." "We have to account for every penny, which doesn't give us time to work with customers or new developments."

After a two-hour discussion, Terrill began to envision a future in which engineers were free to work with customers and join self-directed teams for product improvement. Terrill concluded he had to get top management off the engineers' backs. He promised the engineers, "My job is to stay out of your way so you can do your work, and I'll try to keep top management off your backs too." He called for the day's reports and issued an order effective immediately that the originals be turned in daily to his office rather than mailed to headquarters. For three weeks, technical reports piled up on his desk. By month's end, the stack was nearly three feet high. During that time no one called for the reports. When other managers entered his office and saw the stack, they usually asked, "What's all this?" Terrill answered, "Technical reports." No one asked to read them.

Finally, at month's end, a secretary from finance called and asked for the monthly travel and expense report. Terrill responded, "Meet me in the president's office tomorrow morning."

The next morning the engineers cheered as Terrill walked through the department pushing a cart loaded with the enormous stack of reports. They knew the showdown had come.

Terrill entered the president's office and placed the stack of reports on his desk. The president and the other senior executives looked bewildered.

"This," Terrill announced, "is the reason for the lack of productivity in the Sales Engineering division. These are the reports your people require every month. The fact that they sat on my desk all month shows that no one reads this material. I suggest that the engineers' time could be used in a more productive manner, and that one brief monthly report from my office will satisfy the needs of the other departments."

QUESTIONS

1. Does John Terrill's leadership style fit the definition of leadership in Exhibit 1.1? Explain.

2. With respect to Exhibit 1.4, in what leadership era is Terrill? In what era is headquarters?

3. What approach would you have taken in this situation?

Airstar, Inc.

Airstar, Inc. manufactures, repairs, and overhauls pistons and jet engines for smaller, often privately owned aircraft. The company had a solid niche, and most managers had been with the founder for more than 20 years. With the founder's death five years ago, Roy Morgan took over as president at Airstar. Mr. Morgan has called you in as a consultant.

Your research indicates that this industry is changing rapidly. Airstar is feeling encroachment of huge conglomerates like General Electric and Pratt & Whitney, and its backlog of orders is the lowest in several years. The company has always been known for its superior quality, safety, and customer service. However, it has never been under threat before, and senior managers are not sure which direction to take. They have considered potential acquisitions, imports and exports, more research, and additional repair lines. The organization is becoming more chaotic, which is frustrating Morgan and his vice presidents.

Before a meeting with his team, he confides to you, "Organizing is supposed to be easy. For maximum efficiency, work should be divided into simple, logical, routine tasks. These business tasks can be grouped by similar kinds of work characteristics and arranged within an organization under a particularly suited executive. So why are we having so many problems with our executives?"

Morgan met with several of his trusted corporate officers in the executive dining room to discuss what was happening to corporate leadership at Airstar. Morgan went on to explain that he was really becoming concerned with the situation. There have been outright conflicts between the vice president of marketing and the controller over merger and acquisition opportunities. There have been many instances of duplication of work, with corporate officers trying to outmaneuver each other.

"Communications are atrocious," Morgan said to the others. "Why, I didn't even get a copy of the export finance report until my secretary made an effort to find one for me. My basis for evaluation and appraisal of corporate executive performance is fast becoming obsolete. Everyone has been working up their own job descriptions, and they all include overlapping responsibilities. Changes and decisions are being made on the basis of expediency and are perpetuating too many mistakes. We must take a good look at these organizational realities and correct the situation immediately."

Jim Robinson, vice president of manufacturing, pointed out to Morgan that Airstar is not really following the "principles of good organization." "For instance," explained Robinson, "let's review what we should be practicing as administrators." Robinson believed they should be following six principles:

1. Determine the objectives, policies, programs, and plans that will best achieve the desired results for our company.
2. Determine the various business tasks to be done.
3. Divide the business tasks into a logical and understandable organizational structure.
4. Determine the suitable personnel to occupy positions within the organizational structure.
5. Define the responsibility and authority of each supervisor clearly in writing.
6. Keep the number of kinds and levels of authority at a minimum.

Robinson proposed that the group study the corporate organizational chart, as well as the various corporate business tasks. After reviewing the corporate organizational chart, Robinson, Morgan, and the others agreed that the number and kinds of formal corporate authority were logical and not much different from other corporations. The group then listed the various corporate business tasks that went on within Airstar.

Robinson continued, "How did we ever decide who should handle mergers or acquisitions?" Morgan answered, "I guess it just occurred over time that the vice president of marketing should have the responsibility." "But," Robinson queried, "where is it written down? How would the controller know it?" "Aha!" Morgan exclaimed. "It looks like I'm part of the problem. There isn't anything in writing. Tasks were assigned superficially, as they became problems. This has all been rather informal. I'll establish a group to decide who should have responsibility for what so things can return to our previous level of efficiency."

Source: Adapted from Bernard A. Deitzer and Karl A. Shilliff, Contemporary Management Incidents (Columbus, OH: Grid, Inc., 1977), pp, 43–46. Copyright ©1997 by John Wiley & Sons, Inc. This material is used by permission of John Wiley & Sons, Inc.

QUESTIONS

1. What is your reaction to this conversation? What would you say to Morgan to help him lead the organization?
2. To what extent do you rate both Morgan and Robinson as a good manager versus a good leader according to the dimensions in Exhibit 1.3?
3. If you were to take over as president of Airstar, what would you do first? Second? Third?

References

1　Nikitta A. Foston, "Commander Brad Lee Takes Charge," *Ebony* (September 2006), p. 52ff.

2　Warren Bennis and Burt Nanus, *Leaders: The Strategies for Taking Charge* (New York: Harper & Row, 1985), 4; James MacGregor Burns, *Leadership* (New York: Harper & Row, 1978), p. 2.

3　J. Meindl, S. Ehrlich, and J. Dukerich, "The Romance of Leadership," *Administrative Science Quarterly* 30 (1985), pp. 78–102.

4　Rakesh Khurana, "The Curse of the Superstar CEO," *Harvard Business Review* (September 2002), pp. 60–66.

5　Khurana, "The Curse of the Superstar CEO"; Joseph A. Raelin, "The

Myth of Charismatic Leaders," *Training and Development* (March 2003), p. 46; and Betsy Morris, "The New Rules," *Fortune* (July 24, 2006), pp. 70–87.

6   Joseph C. Rost, *Leadership for the Twenty-First Century* (Westport, CT: Praeger, 1993), p. 102; and Joseph C. Rost and Richard A. Barker, "Leadership Education in Colleges: Toward a 21st Century Paradigm," *The Journal of Leadership Studies* 7, no. 1 (2000), pp. 3–12.

7   Peter B. Smith and Mark F. Peterson, *Leadership, Organizations, and Culture: An Event Management Model* (London: Sage Publications, 1988), p. 14.

8   Robert E. Kelley, "In Praise of Followers," *Harvard Business Review*, (November–December 1988), pp. 142–148.

9   Kevin Fedarki. "He Fights Terror with Books," *Parade Magazine* (April 6, 2003), pp. 4–6; Richard Halicks, "Schools for Pakistan and Afghanistan: Moving Mountains," *The Atlanta Journal-Constitution* (April 16, 2006), p. F1; and http://www.ikat.org/projects.html; Mortenson's amazing story is told in Greg Mortenson and David Oliver Relin, *Three Cups of Tea; One Man's Mission to Fight Terrorism and Build Nations . . . One School at a Time* (New York: Penguin, 2006).

10 Tara Parker Pope, "Chronic Conditions Inspire Two Teens to Help Others with Similar Problems," *The Wall Street Journal* (August 22, 2006), p. D1.

11 Robin Wright and Doyle McManus, *Flashpoints: Promise and Peril in a New World* (New York: Alfred A. Knopf, 1991), pp. 107–110.

12 Scott R. Schmedel, "Making a Difference," *The Wall Street Journal* (August 21, 2006), pp. R5, R12.

13 The discussion of these transformations is based in part on Daniel C. Kielson, "Leadership: Creating a New Reality," *The Journal of Leadership Studies* 3, No. 4 (1996), pp. 104–116; and Mark A. Abramson, "Leadership for the Future: New Behaviors, New Roles, and New Attitudes," *The Public Manager* (Spring 1997). See also Frances Hesselbein, Marshall Goldsmith, and Richard Beckhard, eds. *The Leader of the Future: New Visions, Strategies, and Practices for the Next Era* (San Francisco: Jossey-Bass, 1996).

14 Marvin J. Cetron and Owen Davies, "The Dragon vs. the Tiger," *The Futurist* (July–August 2006), p. 38ff.

15 Greg Ip, "Mind Over Matter—Disappearing Acts: The Rapid Rise and Fall of the Intangible Asset," *The Wall Street Journal* (April 4, 2002), pp. A1, A6.

16 Charles Handy, *The Age of Paradox* (Boston: Harvard Business School Press, 1994), pp. 146–147.

17 Richard L. Daft, *Organization Theory and Design,* 6th ed. (Cincinnati, OH: South-Western College Publishing, 1998), p. 523.

18 Cyrus F. Friedheim Jr., *The Trillion-Dollar Enterprise: How the Alliance Revolution Will Transform Global Business* (Reading, MA: Perseus Books, 1999).

19 Jerry Useem, "Tyrants, Statesmen, and Destroyers (A Brief History of the CEO)," *Fortune,* (November 18, 2002), pp. 82–90; Joann S. Lublin and Scott Thurm, "Money Rules; Behind Soaring Executive Pay, Decades of Failed Restraints," *The Wall Street Journal* (October 12, 2006), p. A1.

20 Bethany McLean, "Why Enron Went Bust," *Fortune* (December 24, 2001), pp. 58–68; and John A. Byrne with Mike France and Wendy Zellner, "The Environment Was Ripe for Abuse," *BusinessWeek* (February 25, 2002), pp. 118–120.

21 Mark Gimein, "You Bought, They Sold," *Fortune* (September 2, 2002), pp. 64–74.

22 Patricia Sellers, "The New Breed," *Fortune* (November 18, 2002), pp. 66–76.

23 Nanette Byrnes with John A. Byrne, Cliff Edwards, Louise Lee, Stanley Holmes, and Joann Muller, "The Good CEO," *BusinessWeek* (September 23, 2002), pp. 80–88.

24 See James Collins, *Good to Great: Why Some Companies Make the Leap . . . And Other Don't* (New York: HarperCollins, 2001); Charles A. O'Reilly III and Jeffrey Pfeffer, *Hidden Value: How Great Companies Achieve Extraordinary Results with Ordinary People* (Boston, MA: Harvard Business School Press, 2000); Rakesh Khurana, *Searching for a Corporate Savior: The Irrational Quest*

for Charismatic CEOs (Princeton University Press, 2002); Joseph Badaracco, *Leading Quietly* (Boston, MA: Harvard Business School Press, 2002); Jason Jennings, *Think Big, Act Small: How America's Best Performing Companies Keep the Startup Spirit Alive* (New York: Portfolio/Penguin, 2005); Ryan Underwood, "The CEO Next Door," *Fast Company* (September 2005), pp. 64–66; and Linda Tischler, "The CEO's New Clothes," *Fast Company* (September 2005), pp. 27–28,

25 Useem, "Tyrants, Statesmen, and Destroyers" and Rakesh Khurana, "The Curse of the Superstar CEO," *Harvard Business Review* (September 2002), pp. 60–66.

26 Ibid.

27 "The Best Advice I Ever Got," *Fortune* (March 21, 2005), p. 90ff.

28 Jim Collins, "Level 5 Leadership: The Triumph of Humility and Fierce Resolve," *Harvard Business Review* (January 2001), pp. 67–76; Collins, "Good to Great," *Fast Company* (October 2001), pp. 90–104; Edward Prewitt, "The Utility of Humility," *CIO* (December 1, 2002), pp. 104–110; A. J. Vogl, "Onward and Upward" (an interview with Jim Collins), *Across the Board* (September–October 2001), pp. 29–34; and Jerry Useem, "Conquering Vertical Limits," *Fortune* (February 19, 2001), pp. 84–96.

29 Collins, "Level 5 Leadership."

30 James Lardner, "In Praise of the Anonymous CEO," *Business 2.0* (September 2002), pp. 104–108; and Byrnes, et al., "The Good CEO."

31 Martha H. Peak, "Anti-Manager Named Manager of the Year," *Management Review* (October 1991), p. 7.

32 Gary Yukl and Richard Lepsinger, "Why Integrating the Leading and Managing Roles Is Essential for Organizational Effectiveness," *Organizational Dynamics* 34, no. 4 (2005), pp. 361–375.

33 Sonia Alleyne, "The Turnaround King," *Black Enterprise* (September 2006), p. 96ff.

34 This section is based largely on John P. Kotter, *A Force for Change: How Leadership Differs from Management* (New York: The Free Press, 1990), pp. 3–18.

35 *Leadership, A Forum Issues Special Report* (Boston, MA: The Forum Corporation, 1990), p. 13.

36 See Geoff Colvin, "The 100 Best Companies to Work For, 2006," *Fortune* (January 23, 2006), pp. 71–74; "2004 Special Report: The 100 Best Companies to Work For," *Fortune* (January 12, 2004), pp. 56–80; and Kevin E. Joyce, "Lessons for Employers from Fortune's 100 Best," *Business Horizons* (March–April 2003), pp. 77–84.

37 Alan Deutschman, "Can Google Stay Google?" *Fast Company* (August 2005), pp. 62–68.

38 Colvin, "The 100 Best Companies to Work For, 2006."

39 *Leadership: A Forum Issues Special Report* (Boston, MA: The Forum Corporation, 1990), p. 15.

40 James Kaplan, "Amateur's Hour," *Working Woman* (October 1997), pp. 28–33.

41 John P. Kotter, quoted in Thomas A. Stewart, "Why Leadership Matters," *Fortune* (March 2, 1998), pp. 71–82.

42 John P. Kotter, *Leading Change* (Boston, MA: Harvard Business School Press, 1996), p. 26.

43 Joseph C. Rost, *Leadership for the Twenty-First Century* (Westport, CT: Praeger, 1993), pp. 145–146.

44 Warren Bennis, *Why Leaders Can't Lead* (San Francisco: Jossey-Bass, 1989).

45 Bennis, *Why Leaders Can't Lead;* and Stewart, "Why Leadership Matters."

46 Stratford Sherman, "How Tomorrow's Best Leaders Are Learning Their Stuff," *Fortune* (November 27, 1995), pp. 90–102; Frances Hesselbein, "The Search for Common Ground," *Leader to Leader* no. 25 (2002), accessed at *http://www.pfdf.org;* and Frances Hesselbein, *Hesselbein on Leadership* (San Francisco: Jossey–Bass, 2002).

47 Abraham Zaleznik, "Managers and Leaders: Are They Different?" *Harvard Business Review* (March–April 1992): pp. 126–135.

48 David Rooke and William R. Torbert, "7 Transformations of Leadership," *Harvard Business Review* (April 2005), pp. 67–76;

and Rooke and Torbert, *Action Inquiry: The Secret of Timely and Transforming Leadership* (San Francisco: Berrett-Koehler, 2004).

49 Tricia Bisoux, "What Makes Leaders Great," *BizEd* (September–October 2005), pp. 40–45.

50 Bennis, *Why Leaders Can't Lead.*

51 Sherman, "How Tomorrow's Best Leaders Are Learning Their Stuff."

52 Susan R. Komives, Nance Lucas, Timothy R. McMahon, *Exploring Leadership: For College Students Who Want to Make a Difference* (San Francisco: Jossey-Bass Publishers, 1998), p. 38.

53 Based on Komives, et al., *Exploring Leadership;* and Shann R. Ferch and Matthew M. Mitchell, "Intentional Forgiveness in Relational Leadership: A Technique for Enhancing Effective Leadership," *The Journal of Leadership Studies* 7, no. 4 (2001), pp. 70–83.

54 Craig L. Pearce, "The Future of Leadership: Combining Vertical and Shared Leadership to Transform Knowledge Work," *Academy of Management Executive* 18, no. 1 (2004), pp. 47–57.

55 Morgan W. McCall, Jr., and Michael M. Lombardo, "Off the Track: Why and How Successful Executives Get Derailed" (Technical Report No. 21, Greensboro, NC: Center for Creative Leadership, January 1983); Carol Hymowitz, "Five Main Reasons Why Managers Fail," *The Wall Street Journal* (May 2, 1988).

56 Tischler, "The CEO's New Clothes"; Joseph Nocera, "In Business, Tough Guys Finish Last," *The New York Times* (June 18, 2005), p. C1; Carol Hymowitz, "Rewarding Competitors Over Collaborators No Longer Makes Sense" (In the Lead column), *The Wall Street Journal* (February 13, 2006), p. B1.

57 Ram Charan and Geoffrey Colvin, "Why CEOs Fail," *Fortune* (June 21, 1999), pp. 68–78.

58 Bisoux, "What Makes Leaders Great."

59 Russell Palmer, "Can Leadership Be Learned?" *Business Today* (Fall, 1989), pp. 100–102.

PART 2
Research Perspectives on Leadership

Chapter 2

Your Leadership Challenge

After reading this chapter, you should be able to:

- Identify personal traits and characteristics that are associated with effective leaders.

- Recognize autocratic versus democratic leadership behavior and the impact of each.

- Know the distinction between people-oriented and task-oriented leadership behavior and when each should be used.

- Understand how the theory of individualized leadership has broadened the understanding of relationships between leaders and followers.

- Recognize how to build partnerships for greater effectiveness.

Chapter Outline

Traits, Behaviors, and Relationships

Imagine slogging through near-freezing water up to your waist, or walking for miles and then discovering you're only 100 yards closer to your destination. That's what happened when Robert Swan led a team to the North Pole and the ice cap melted beneath their feet. Swan's carefully planned expedition, made up of eight people from seven countries, became a nightmare when the ice cap began to melt in April—four months earlier than usual.

The group survived—barely—because of teamwork and Swan's extraordinary leadership. Swan's honesty, as well as his ability to maintain his poise, self-confidence, and sense of purpose amid life-threatening and constantly changing conditions, helped to nourish the spirit and motivation of the team. With the completion of the journey, Swan became the first person ever to walk to both the North and the South Poles. Today, he recounts his adventures to groups around the world, including businesspeople hungry to learn what it means to be a leader in a dangerous and hostile environment.

Swan had dreamed of walking to the South Pole, tracing the route taken by Robert Falcon Scott in 1912, since he was a child. As a young adult, he spent seven years working as a taxi driver, a tree cutter, a gardener, and a hotel dishwasher to earn money, all the while selling the dream to others to help raise funds. His first expedition to Antarctica in 1986 changed his life completely. Motivated by firsthand observation of the destruction of the ozone layer and the waste and pollution he encountered, Swan became deeply committed to environmental issues. He took on the difficult challenge of raising money for his second expedition, to the North Pole, inspired primarily by a vision of helping to save the polar regions from human destruction.

From an organizational viewpoint, Swan's stories of courage, adventure, determination, and risk taking are good metaphors for what many leaders feel in today's complex and challenging world.[1]

Robert Swan is a world-renowned explorer who is influencing young people, world leaders, businesspeople, and organizations around the globe. He works tirelessly for what he believes in and has inspired others to become more actively involved. Those who participate in his expeditions take what they learn back to their organizations, further extending Swan's influence. Several personal attributes contribute to Swan's leadership. He had the courage, self-confidence, and determination to try something that everyone told him couldn't be done. He had the drive and the commitment to work for years in menial jobs to make his dream a reality, and he continues to raise money for the causes he believes in. His poise and ability to maintain a positive attitude have helped team members survive harrowing conditions.

In considering Swan's influence, it seems evident that characteristics such as courage, self-confidence, drive, determination, and a willingness to take risks are part of the personality that make him a good leader. Indeed, personal traits are what captured the imagination of the earliest leadership researchers. Many leaders possess traits that researchers believe affect their leadership impact. For example, four-star Army General John Abizaid, who leads U.S. forces in the Middle East, is known for his intelligence, honesty, and ease in coping with uncertainty and chaos.[2] An example from the business world is Julia Stewart, whose first job was serving food at an International House of Pancakes (IHOP) in San Diego.

Traits such as ambition, persistence, responsibility, and enthusiasm have helped Stewart through a series of jobs since then, eventually landing her in the CEO's chair at IHOP.[3]

Leaders display traits through patterns in their behavior. Consequently, many researchers have examined the behavior of leaders to determine what behavioral features comprise leadership style and how particular behaviors relate to effective leadership. Later research specified behavior between a leader and each distinct follower, differentiating one-on-one behavior from leader-to-group behavior.

This chapter provides an overview of the initial leadership research in the twentieth century. We examine the evolution of the trait approach and the behavior approach, and introduce the theory of individualized leadership. The path illuminated by the research into leader traits and behaviors is a foundation for the field of leadership studies and still enjoys remarkable dynamism for explaining leader success or failure.

The Trait Approach

Traits
the distinguishing personal characteristics of a leader, such as intelligence, honesty, self-confidence, and appearance

Great Man approach
a leadership perspective that sought to identify the inherited traits leaders possessed that distinguished them from people who were not leaders

Early efforts to understand leadership success focused on the leader's personal traits. **Traits** are the distinguishing personal characteristics of a leader, such as intelligence, honesty, self-confidence, and appearance. Research early in the twentieth century examined leaders who had achieved a level of greatness, and hence became known as the Great Man approach. Fundamental to this theory was the idea that some people are born with traits that make them natural leaders. The **Great Man approach** sought to identify the traits leaders possessed that distinguished them from people who were not leaders. Generally, research found only a weak relationship between personal traits and leader success.[4] Indeed, the diversity of traits that effective leaders possess indicates that leadership ability is not necessarily a genetic endowment.

Nevertheless, with the advancement of the field of psychology during the 1940s and 1950s, trait approach researchers expanded their examination of personal attributes by using aptitude and psychological tests. These early studies looked at personality traits such as creativity and self-confidence, physical traits such as age and energy level, abilities such as knowledge and fluency of speech, social characteristics such as popularity and sociability, and work-related characteristics such as the desire to excel and persistence against obstacles. Effective leaders were often identified by exceptional follower performance, or by a high status position within an organization and a salary that exceeded that of peers.[5]

In a 1948 literature review,[6] Stogdill examined more than 100 studies based on the trait approach. He uncovered several traits that appeared consistent with effective leadership, including general intelligence, initiative, interpersonal skills, self-confidence, drive for responsibility, and personal integrity. Stogdill's findings also indicated, however, that the importance of a particular trait was often relative to the situation. Initiative, for example, may contribute to the success of a leader in one situation, but it may be irrelevant to a leader in another situation. Thus, possessing certain personal characteristics is no guarantee of success.

Many researchers desisted their efforts to identify leadership traits in light of Stogdill's 1948 findings and turned their attention to examining leader behavior and leadership situations. However, others continued with expanded trait lists and research projects. Stogdill's subsequent review of 163 trait studies conducted between 1948 and 1970 concluded that some personal traits do indeed seem to contribute to effective leadership.[7] The study identified many of the same traits found in the 1948 survey, along with several additional characteristics, including aggressiveness, independence, and tolerance for stress. However, Stogdill again cautioned that the value of a particular trait or set of traits varies with the organizational situation.

In recent years, there has been a resurgence of interest in examining leadership traits. A review by Kirkpatrick and Locke identified a number of personal traits that distinguish leaders from non-leaders, including some pinpointed by Stogdill.[8] Other studies have focused on followers' perceptions and indicate that certain traits are associated with individuals' perceptions of who is a leader. For example, one study found that the traits of intelligence, masculinity, and dominance were strongly related to how individuals perceived leaders.[9] In summary, trait research has been an important part of leadership studies throughout the twentieth century and continues into the twenty-first. Many researchers still contend that some traits are essential to effective leadership, but only in combination with other factors.[10] Influential business consultant Ram Charan says successful leaders are those who apply their personal traits to develop *leadership know-how,* as discussed in the Leader's Bookshelf.

Exhibit 2.1 presents some of the traits and their respective categories that have been identified through trait research over the years. Some of the traits considered important are optimism and self-confidence, honesty and integrity, and drive.

Optimism and Self-Confidence

Emerging research points to a positive outlook as key to effective leadership.[11] **Optimism** refers to a tendency to see the positive side of things and expect that things will turn out well. Numerous surveys indicate that the one characteristic most common to top executives, for example, is an optimistic attitude. People rise to the top because they have the ability to see opportunities where others see problems and can instill in others a sense of hope for the future. Leaders at all levels need a degree of optimism to see possibilities even through the thickest fog and rally people around a vision for a better tomorrow. One leadership researcher has gone so far as to say that "The opposite of a leader isn't a follower. The opposite of a leader is a pessimist."[12]

A related characteristic is having a positive attitude about oneself, which doesn't mean being arrogant and prideful. Leaders who know themselves develop **self-confidence**, which is assurance in one's own judgments, decision making, ideas, and capabilities. A leader with a positive self-image who displays certainty about his or her own ability fosters confidence among followers, gains respect and admiration, and meets challenges. The confidence a leader displays and develops creates motivation and commitment among followers for the mission at hand.

Active leaders need self-confidence and optimism. How many of us willingly follow someone who is jaded and pessimistic, or someone who obviously doesn't believe in him or herself? Leaders initiate changes and they often must make decisions without adequate information. Problems are solved continuously. Without the confidence to move forward and believe things will be okay, even if an occasional decision is wrong, leaders could be paralyzed into inaction. Setbacks have to be overcome. Risks have to be taken. Competing points of view have to be

Optimism
a tendency to see the positive side of things and expect that things will turn out well

Self-confidence
assurance in one's own judgments, decision making, ideas, and capabilities

Getty Images

by Ram Charan

What does it take to be a great leader? Executive consultant Ram Charan admits that it can help to possess traits such as intelligence, self-confidence, energy, and enthusiasm, but in his book *Know-How: The 8 Skills That Separate People Who Perform From Those Who Don't*, he emphasizes that traits alone are not enough. "A person may possess the entire panoply of personal traits that everyone admires, but without the know-hows of running a business," Charan contends, "that person can be a recipe for disaster." Charan has applied the understanding he's gained from three decades of hands-on experience with leaders in diverse industries to identify key skills that are the bedrock of leadership success.

DEVELOP THE KNOW-HOW TO BE A GREAT LEADER

Leaders are made, not born, Charan says, and they're made by hard work and commitment to personal development. He describes eight essential skills that all great leaders share, and he emphasizes that anyone can develop these *leadership know-hows*, no matter what their personality traits. Here are a few of the essential leadership skills:

1. **Learn how to judge people accurately.** Great leaders are people experts, which enables them to put the right people in the right jobs. Leaders carefully observe patterns of behavior, actions, and decisions, and they learn how to ask the right questions to judge people's capabilities, needs, and interests.
2. **Mold a team of leaders.** Judging people accurately enables leaders to put together a team of people who submerge their own agendas for the sake of common goals. An effective team in which everyone acts like a

leader, Charan says, "is a huge multiplier of your capability for making better decisions and getting things done."

3. **Manage the social system.** For any organization to succeed, people have to work together smoothly. Great leaders invest time and energy in shaping and reinforcing collaborative working relationships. They identify areas where interaction is needed and make sure there are mechanisms in place to bring the right people together for the sharing of ideas and information.
4. **Set the right goals.** Poorly chosen goals is a common problem in struggling organizations. Too often, leaders simply take last year's goal and add some incremental improvement to it, rather than taking a fresh look at current conditions. Charan uses the example of General Motors, where leaders are struggling under a misguided goal of winning back U.S. market share rather than looking at the reality of a critical need to improve profitability.

Don't Let Traits Get in the Way

Charan says anyone can become a better leader by "consciously working to improve these skills and becoming aware of how your own personality affects them." He cautions that some personality traits can get in the way. Optimism can be a positive characteristic for a leader, for example, but if a leader is overly optimistic, his or her assessments of people will be distorted, and goals may be unrealistic. The key, Charan says, is to be self-aware and consider personality traits that might be holding you back from fully developing leadership know-how.

Know-How: The 8 Skills That Separate People Who Perform From Those Who Don't, by Ram Charan, is published by Crown Business.

Action Memo

Do you believe you have the self-confidence to be a strong and effective leader? Complete the questionnaire in Leader's Self-Insight 2.1 on page 42 to assess your level of self-confidence.

managed, with some people left unsatisfied. Optimism and self-confidence enables a leader to face all these challenges.[13]

Honesty and Integrity Positive attitudes have to be tempered by strong ethics or leaders can get into trouble. Consider Jeffrey Skilling, former CEO of Enron, who was convicted and sent to jail on 19 criminal charges related to the largest corporate fraud case in history. As a leader, Skilling displayed strong self-confidence and optimism. The problem was that he didn't have strong ethics to match. Ethics refers to a code of moral principles and values that governs a person's behavior with respect to what is right or wrong. In today's world, effective leaders are ethical leaders.

Exhibit 2.1 Personal Characteristics of Leaders

Personal Characteristics	Social Characteristics
Energy	Sociability, interpersonal skills
Physical stamina	Cooperativeness
Intelligence and Ability	Ability to enlist cooperation
Intelligence, cognitive ability	Tact, diplomacy
Knowledge	**Work-Related Characteristics**
Judgment, decisiveness	Drive, desire to excel
Personality	Responsibility in pursuit of goals
Optimism	Persistence against obstacles, tenacity
Self-confidence	**Social Background**
Honesty and integrity	Education
Enthusiasm	Mobility
Desire to lead	
Independence	

Sources: *Bass and Stogdill's Handbook of Leadership: Theory, Research, and Management Applications*, 3rd ed. (New York: The Free Press, 1990), pp. 80–81; and S. A. Kirkpatrick and E. A. Locke, "Leadership: Do Traits Matter?" *Academy of Management Executive* 5, no. 2 (1991), pp. 48–60.

One aspect of being an ethical leader is being honest with followers, customers, shareholders, and the public, and maintaining one's integrity. **Honesty** refers to truthfulness and non-deception. It implies an openness that followers welcome. **Integrity** means that a leader's character is whole, integrated, and grounded in solid moral principles, and he or she acts in keeping with those principles. When leaders model their convictions through their daily actions, they command admiration, respect, and loyalty. These virtues are the foundation of trust between leaders and followers.

In the wake of widespread corporate scandals, trust is sorely lacking in many organizations. Leaders need the traits of ethics, honesty, and integrity to rebuild trusting and productive relationships. People today are wary of authority and the deceptive use of power, and they are hungry for leaders who hold high standards and reinforce them through everyday actions. Successful leaders have also been found to be highly consistent, doing exactly what they say they will do when they say they will do it. Successful leaders are easy to trust. They have basic principles and consistently apply them. One survey of 1,500 managers asked the values most desired in leaders. Integrity was the most important characteristic. The authors concluded:

> *Honesty is absolutely essential to leadership. After all, if we are willing to follow someone, whether it be into battle or into the boardroom, we first want to assure ourselves that the person is worthy of our trust. We want to know that he or she is being truthful, ethical, and principled. We want to be fully confident in the integrity of our leaders.*[14]

Drive Another characteristic considered essential for effective leadership is drive. Leaders often are responsible for initiating new projects as well as guiding projects to successful completion. **Drive** refers to high motivation that creates a high effort level by a leader. Leaders with drive seek achievement, have energy and

Honesty
truthfulness and nondeception

Integrity
the quality of being whole, integrated, and acting in accordance with solid moral principles

Action Memo
As a leader, you can develop the personal traits of self-confidence, integrity, and drive, which are important for successful leadership in every organization and situation. You can work to keep an optimistic attitude and be ethical in your decisions and actions.

Drive
high motivation that creates a high effort level by a leader

This questionnaire is designed to assess your level of self-confidence as reflected in a belief in your ability to accomplish a desired outcome. There are no right or wrong answers. Please indicate your personal feelings about whether each statement is Mostly False or Mostly True by checking the answer that best describes your attitude or feeling.

	Mostly False	Mostly True
1. When I make plans, I am certain I can make them work.	_____	_____
2. One of my problems is that I often cannot get down to work when I should.	_____	_____
3. When I set important goals for myself, I rarely achieve them.	_____	_____
4. I often give up on things before completing them.	_____	_____
5. I typically put off facing difficult situations.	_____	_____
6. If something looks too complicated, I may not even bother to try it.	_____	_____
7. When I decide to do something, I go right to work on it.	_____	_____
8. When an unexpected problem occurs, I often don't respond well.	_____	_____
9. Failure just makes me try harder.	_____	_____
10. I consider myself a self-reliant person.	_____	_____

Scoring and Interpretation

Give yourself one point for checking Mostly True for items 1,7,9, and 10. Also give yourself one point for checking Mostly False for items 2,3,4,5,6, and 8. Enter your score here: _____. If your score is 8 or higher, it may mean that you are high on self confidence. If your score is 3 or less, your self confidence may be low. If your score is low, what can you do to increase your self-confidence?

Source: This is part of the general self-efficacy subscale of the self-efficacy scale published in M. Sherer, J. E. Maddux, B. Mercadante, S. Prentice-Dunn, B. Jacobs, and R. W. Rogers, "The Self-Efficacy Scale: Construction and Validation," *Psychological Reports* 51 (1982), pp. 663–671. Used with permission.

tenacity, and are frequently seen to have ambition and initiative to achieve their goals. If people don't strive to achieve something, they rarely do. Leaders actively pursue goals. Ambition enables them to set challenging goals and take initiative to reach them.[15]

A strong drive is associated with high energy. Leaders work long hours over many years. They have stamina and are vigorous and full of life in order to handle the pace, the demands, and the challenges of leadership. Jeff Immelt, CEO of General Electric, provides an excellent example of strong drive, as well as several other traits listed in Exhibit 2.1 that are associated with successful leaders.

Jeff Immelt, General Electric

IN THE LEAD

"There are 24 hours in a day, and you can use them all," says Jeff Immelt. Immelt claims he's been working 100 hours a week for nearly a quarter of a century, long before he took over the top job at General Electric. "You have to have real stamina," he says.

Immelt has shown a drive for achievement since his days at Harvard Business School, which he says he approached like a job. That's where he began budgeting his time with steely discipline and pursuing goals with gritty determination.

IN THE LEAD

As CEO of GE, Immelt is known as a demanding boss who isn't afraid to push aside his own hand-picked managers if they don't meet performance standards. However, Immelt is also praised by employees (which he calls teammates) for his pleasant, approachable manner. His optimism about GE's future is infectious; despite a slowdown in the company's sales and a slide in the stock price, Immelt helps people see a world of promising opportunities that can make GE as central to this new century as it was to the previous one.

For such a hard-charging leader, Immelt can seem surprisingly relaxed, almost serene, partly due to his confidence in his abilities and his belief in GE's superior capabilities and quality people. Yet, as *Fortune* magazine put it, "his apparent serenity masks rigor, toughness, and a white-hot desire to win."[16]

Working 100-hour weeks certainly isn't necessary for effective leadership, but all leaders have to display drive and energy to be successful. Clearly, various traits such as drive, self-confidence, optimisim, and honesty have great value for leaders. One study of 600 executives by Hay Group, a global organizational and human resources consulting firm, found that 75 percent of the successful executives studied possessed the characteristics of self-confidence and drive.[17] This chapter's *Consider This* box presents the notion that personal characteristics of the leader are ultimately responsible for leadership outcomes. In Chapter 4, we will further consider individual characteristics and qualities that play a role in leadership effectiveness. However, as indicated earlier, traits alone cannot define effective leadership. The inability of researchers to define effective leadership based solely on personal traits led to an interest in looking at the behavior of leaders and how it might contribute to leadership success or failure.

Behavior Approaches

Rather than looking at an individual's personal traits, the behavior approach says that anyone who adopts the appropriate behavior can be a good leader. Diverse research programs on leadership behavior have sought to uncover the behaviors that leaders engage in rather than what traits a leader possesses. Behaviors can be learned more readily than traits, enabling leadership to be accessible to all.

Autocratic Versus Democratic Leadership

One study that served as a precursor to the behavior approach recognized autocratic and democratic leadership styles. An **autocratic** leader is one who tends to centralize authority and derive power from position, control of rewards, and coercion. A **democratic** leader delegates authority to others, encourages participation, relies on subordinates' knowledge for completion of tasks, and depends on subordinate respect for influence.

The first studies on these leadership behaviors were conducted at the University of Iowa by Kurt Lewin and his associates.[18] The research included groups of children, each with its own designated adult leader who was instructed to act in either an autocratic or democratic style. These experiments produced some interesting findings. The groups with autocratic leaders performed highly so long as the leader was present to supervise them. However, group members were displeased with the close, autocratic style of leadership, and feelings of hostility frequently arose. The performance of groups who were assigned democratic leaders was almost as good, and these groups were characterized by positive feelings rather than hostility. In addition, under the democratic style of leadership, group members performed well even when the leader was absent. The participative techniques and majority-rule decision making used by the democratic leader trained and involved the group members so that they performed well with or without the leader present. These characteristics of democratic leadership may partly explain why the empowerment of employees is a popular trend in companies today.

This early work implied that leaders were either autocratic or democratic in their approach. However, further work by Tannenbaum and Schmidt indicated that leadership behavior could exist on a continuum reflecting different amounts of employee participation.[19] Thus, one leader might be autocratic (boss-centered), another democratic (subordinate-centered), and a third a mix of the two styles. Exhibit 2.2 illustrates the leadership continuum.

Tannenbaum and Schmidt also suggested that the extent to which leaders should be boss-centered or subordinate-centered depended on organizational circumstances, and that leaders might adjust their behaviors to fit the circumstances. For example, if there is time pressure on a leader or if it takes too long for subordinates to learn how to make decisions, the leader will tend to use an autocratic style. When subordinates are able to learn decision-making skills readily, a participative style can be used. Also, the greater the skill difference, the more autocratic the leader approach, because it is difficult to bring subordinates up to the leader's expertise level.[20]

Jack Hartnett, president of D. L. Rogers Corp. and franchise owner of 54 Sonic drive-in restaurants, provides an example of the autocratic leadership style.[21] The style works well in the fast-food restaurant business where turnover is typically high and many employees are young and low-skilled. In contrast, the CEO of Applegate Farms, a purveyor of organic and natural meats, is an extreme example of a democratic leader.

Autocratic
a leader who tends to centralize authority and derive power from position, control of rewards, and coercion

Democratic
a leader who delegates authority to others, encourages participation, relies on subordinates' knowledge for completion of tasks, and depends on subordinate respect for influence

Action Memo
As a leader, you can use a democratic leadership style to help followers develop decision-making skills and perform well without close supervision. An autocratic style might be appropriate when there is time pressure or followers have low skill levels.

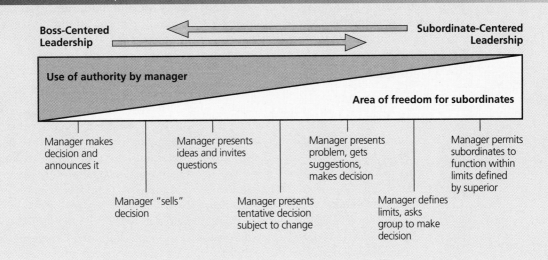

Exhibit 2.2 Leadership Continuum

Boss-Centered Leadership ← → Subordinate-Centered Leadership

Use of authority by manager

Area of freedom for subordinates

Manager makes decision and announces it

Manager "sells" decision

Manager presents ideas and invites questions

Manager presents tentative decision subject to change

Manager presents problem, gets suggestions, makes decision

Manager defines limits, asks group to make decision

Manager permits subordinates to function within limits defined by superior

Source: *Harvard Business Review*. An exhibit from Robert Tannenbaum and Warren Schmidt, "How to Choose a Leadership Pattern" (May–June 1973). Copyright 1973 by the president and Fellows of Harvard College.

Stephen McDonnell, Applegate Farms

For most of Applegate Farms' history, its CEO hasn't even been in the office. When Stephen McDonnell bought a struggling meat products company (then called Jugtown Mountain Smokehouse) nearly 20 years ago, he spent the first six months working full-time on-site, but since then he's been working mostly from home.

From his experience at other companies, McDonnell had observed that most organizational problems were more easily diagnosed, and more effectively solved, within specific teams or work groups rather than by top managers. He decided that the best way to get a company running smoothly was to give everyone constant access to relevant information, empower them with the freedom and responsibility to act on it, and then stay out of the way.

What's most interesting about the whole story is that McDonnell is a self-confessed control-freak boss, full of anxiety and obsessed with meeting goals and moving on quickly. He realized that working mostly from home was the best way to protect the company from his tendency to micromanage. McDonnell goes into the office only on Wednesdays, when he does everything from taste-test new products, observe twice-a-day team "huddles" (10-minute stand-up meetings to discuss key problems or issues), meet with senior staff members to discuss strategic issues, and deal with any staff problems that might threaten the company's smooth functioning.

Applegate is thriving under this system of extreme democratic leadership. The company has grown to sales of more than $35 million. Profits and productivity go up every year. To McDonnell, a hands-off leadership style "doesn't mean they don't need you—it means they need you looking ahead."[22]

The findings about autocratic and democratic leadership in the original University of Iowa studies indicated that leadership behavior had a definite effect on outcomes such as follower performance and satisfaction. Equally important was the recognition that effective leadership was reflected in behavior, not simply by what personality traits a leader possessed. The Stephen McDonnell example above indicates that leaders can adopt behaviors that are almost in direct opposition to their natural traits when its necessary. Jay Vogt, a consultant to Applegate, says of McDonnell: "If he's at the company on some days he might do more harm than good, and he knows that. How many CEOs have that self-awareness?"[23]

Ohio State Studies

The idea that leadership is reflected in behavior and not just personal traits provided a focus for subsequent research. One early series of studies on leadership behavior was conducted at the Ohio State University. Researchers conducted surveys to identify specific dimensions of leader behavior. Narrowing a list of nearly 2,000 leader behavirs into a questionnaire containing 150 examples of definitive leader behaviors, they developed the Leader Behavior Description Questionnaire (LBDQ) and administered it to employees.[24] Hundreds of employees responded to behavior examples according to the degree to which their leaders engaged in the various behaviors. The analysis of ratings resulted in two wide-ranging categories of leader behavior types, later called consideration and initiating structure.

Consideration
the extent to which a leader is sensitive to subordinates, respects their ideas and feelings, and establishes mutual trust

Initiating Structure
the extent to which a leader is task oriented and directs subordinates' work activities toward goal achievement

　　　Consideration describes the extent to which a leader cares about subordinates, respects their ideas and feelings, and establishes mutual trust. Showing appreciation, listening carefully to problems, and seeking input from subordinates regarding important decisions are all examples of consideration behaviors.

　　　Initiating structure describes the extent to which a leader is task oriented and directs subordinates' work activities toward goal achievement. This type of leader behavior includes directing tasks, getting people to work hard, planning, providing explicit schedules for work activities, and ruling with an iron hand.

　　　Although many leaders fall along a continuum that includes both consideration and initiating structure behaviors, these behavior categories are independent of one another. In other words, a leader can display a high degree of both behavior types, or a low degree of both behavior types. Additionally, a leader might demonstrate high consideration and low initiating structure, or low consideration and high initiating structure behavior. Research indicates that all four of these leader style combinations can be effective.[25] The following examples describe two U.S. Marine leaders who display different types of leadership behavior that correlate to the *consideration* and *initiating structure* styles. Sometimes these styles clash.

IN THE LEAD

Col. Joe D. Dowdy and Maj. Gen. James Mattis, U.S. Marine Corps

Only a few weeks into the war in Iraq, Marine Col. Joe D. Dowdy had both accomplished a grueling military mission and been removed from his command by Maj. Gen. James Mattis. The complicated and conflicting tales of why Col. Dowdy was dismissed are beyond the scope of this text, but one issue that came under examination was the differing styles of Col. Dowdy and Gen. Mattis, as well as the difficult, age-old wartime tension of "men versus mission."

　　　Gen. Mattis has been referred to as a "warrior monk," consumed with the study of battle tactics and whose own battle plans in Iraq were considered brilliant. Gen. Mattis saw speed as integral to success in the early days of the Iraqi war, pushing for regiments to move quickly to accomplish a mission despite significant risks. For Col. Dowdy, some risks seemed too high, and he made decisions that delayed his mission, but better protected his Marines. Col. Dowdy was beloved by his followers because he was deeply concerned about their welfare, paid attention to them as inviduals, and treated them as equals, going so far as to decline certain privileges that were available only to officers.

What's Your Leadership Orientation?

The questions below ask about your personal leadership orientation. Each item describes a specific kind of behavior but does not ask you to judge whether the behavior is desirable or undesirable.

Read each item carefully. Think about how frequently you engage in the behavior described by the item in a work or school group. Please indicate whether each statement is Mostly False or Mostly True by checking the answer that best describes your behavior.

	Mostly False	Mostly True
1. I put into operation suggestions agreed to by the group.	_____	_____
2. I treat everyone in the group with respect as my equal.	_____	_____
3. I back up what other people in the group do.	_____	_____
4. I help others with their personal problems.	_____	_____
5. I bring up how much work should be accomplished.	_____	_____
6. I help assign people to specific tasks.	_____	_____
7. I frequently suggest ways to fix problems.	_____	_____
8. I emphasize deadlines and how to meet them.	_____	_____

Scoring and Interpretation

Consideration behavior score—count the number of checks for Mostly True for items 1–4. Enter your consideration score here _____.

A higher score (3 or 4) suggests a relatively strong orientation toward consideration-oriented behavior by you as a leader. A low score (2 or less) suggests a relatively weak consideration orientation.

Initiating structure behavior score—count the number of checks for Mostly True for items 5–8. Enter your initiating structure score here _____.

A higher score (3 or 4) suggests a relatively strong orientation toward initiating structure-oriented behavior by you as a leader. A low score (2 or less) suggests a relatively weak orientation toward initiating structure behavior.

Source: Sample items adapted from: Edwin A Fleishman's *Leadership Opinion Questionnaire.* (Copyright 1960, Science Research Associates, Inc., Chicago, IL.) This version is based on Jon L. Pierce and John W. Newstrom, *Leaders and the Leadership Process: Readings, Self-Assessments & Applications,* 2nd edition (Boston: Irwin McGraw-Hill, 2000).

IN THE LEAD

Despite their different styles, both leaders were highly respected by followers. When asked about Gen. Mattis, Gunnery Sgt. Robert Kane, who has served under both leaders, says he would certainly "follow him again." However, when he learned that Col. Dowdy had been dismissed, Sgt. Kane says he "wanted to go with him. If [he] had said 'Get your gear, you're coming with me,' I would've gone, even if it meant the end of my career.[26]

Gen. Mattis might be considred highly task-oriented, reflecting an initiating structure approach, while Col. Dowdy seems more people-oriented, reflecting a consideration behavioral style. Whereas Gen. Mattis typically put the mission first, combined with a concern for the Marines under his command, Col. Dowdy typically put Marines first, even though he also gave his all to accomplish the mission.

Additional studies that correlated the two leader behavior types and impact on subordinates initially demonstrated that "considerate" supervisors had a more positive impact on subordinate satisfaction than did "structuring" supervisors.[27] For example, when leader effectiveness was defined by voluntary turnover or amount of grievances filed by subordinates, considerate leaders generated less turnover and grievances. But research that utilized performance criteria, such as group output and productivity, showed initiating structure behavior was rated more effective. Other studies involving aircraft commanders

Action Memo
Discover your leadership orientation related to consideration and initiating structure by completing the self-assessment exercise in Leader's Self-Insight 2.2.

and university department heads revealed that leaders rated effective by subordinates exhibited a high level of both consideration and initiating structure behaviors, whereas leaders rated less effective displayed low levels of both behavior styles.[28]

University of Michigan Studies

Studies at the University of Michigan took a different approach by directly comparing the behavior of effective and ineffective supervisors.[29] The effectiveness of leaders was determined by productivity of the subordinate group. Initial field studies and interviews at various job sites gave way to a questionnaire not unlike the LBDQ, called the Survey of Organizations.[30]

Over time, the Michigan researchers established two types of leadership behavior, each type consisting of two dimensions.[31] First, **employee-centered** leaders display a focus on the human needs of their subordinates. Leader support and interaction facilitation are the two underlying dimensions of employee-centered behavior. This means that in addition to demonstrating support for their subordinates, employee-centered leaders facilitate positive interaction among followers and seek to minimize conflict. The employee-centered style of leadership roughly corresponds to the Ohio State concept of consideration. Because relationships are so important in today's work environment, many organizations are looking for leaders who can facilitate positive interaction among others. Damark International, a general merchandise catalogue company, even has a position designed to help people get along better. Although his official title is director of leadership and team development, Mark Johansson calls himself a "relationship manager." Johansson works with managers throughout the organization to help them improve their relationship and interpersonal skills and become more employee-centered.[32]

In contrast to the employee-centered leader, the **job-centered** leader directs activities toward scheduling, accomplishing tasks, and achieving efficiency. Goal emphasis and work facilitation are dimensions of this leadership behavior. By focusing on reaching task goals and facilitating the structure of tasks, job-centered behavior approximates that of initiating structure.

However, unlike the consideration and initiating structure styles defined by the Ohio State studies, Michigan researchers considered employee-centered leadership and job-centered leadership to be distinct styles in opposition to one another. A leader is identifiable by behavior characteristic of one or the other style, but not both. Another hallmark of later Michigan studies is the acknowledgment that often the behaviors of goal emphasis, work facilitation, support, and interaction facilitation can be meaningfully performed by a subordinate's peers, rather than only by the designated leader. Other people in the group could supply these behaviors, which enhanced performance.[33]

In addition, while leadership behavior was demonstrated to affect the performance and satisfaction of subordinates, performance was also influenced by other factors related to the situation within which leaders and subordinates worked. The situation will be explored in the next chapter.

The Leadership Grid

Blake and Mouton of the University of Texas proposed a two-dimensional leadership theory called **The Leadership Grid** that builds on the work of the Ohio State and Michigan studies.[34] Based on a week-long seminar, researchers rated leaders on a scale of one to nine according to two criteria: the concern for people and the concern for production. The scores for these criteria are plotted on a grid with an axis corresponding to each concern. Exhibit 2.3 depicts the two-dimensional model and five of the seven major leadership styles.

Employee-centered
a leadership behavior that displays a focus on the human needs of subordinates

Job-centered
leadership behavior in which leaders direct activities toward efficiency, cost-cutting, and scheduling, with an emphasis on goals and work facilitation

The Leadership Grid
a two-dimensional leadership model that describes major leadership styles based on measuring both concern for people and concern for production

Exhibit 2.3 The Leadership Grid® Figure

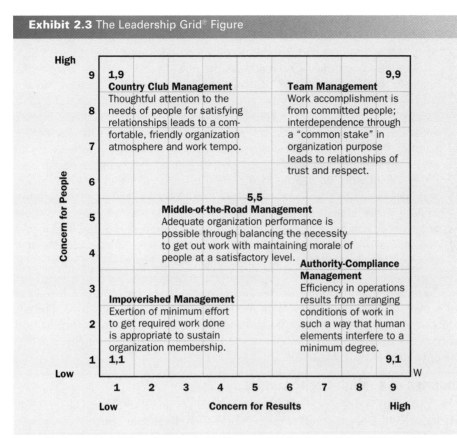

Source: The Leadership Grid figure from *Leadership Dilemma—Grid Solutions* by Robert R. Blake and Anne Adams McCanse (formerly the Managerial Grid by Robert R. Blake and Jane S. Mouton). Houston: Gulf Publishing Company, p. 29. Copyright 1991 by Scientific Methods, Inc. Reproduced by permission of the owners.

Team management (9,9) often is considered the most effective style and is recommended because organization members work together to accomplish tasks. *Country club management* (1,9) occurs when primary emphasis is given to people rather than to work outputs. *Authority-compliance management* (9,1) occurs when efficiency in operations is the dominant orientation. *Middle-of-the-road management* (5,5) reflects a moderate amount of concern for both people and production. *Impoverished management* (1,1) means the absence of a leadership philosophy; leaders exert little effort toward interpersonal relationships or work accomplishment. Consider these examples:

TruServ and North Jackson Elementary School

When Pamela Forbes Lieberman learned that her subordinates called her *the dragon lady,* she embraced the moniker and hung a watercolor of a dragon in her office. Lieberman makes no apologies for her hard-driving management style. Her emphasis on tough goals and bottom-line results is helping to restore the health of hardware cooperative TruServ, which supplies inventory to True Value hardware stores. As soon as Lieberman became CEO, she began slashing costs and setting tough performance targets. "If [people] succeed, they will be rewarded, but if they don't, then we're going to have to look for new people sitting in their chairs," Lieberman says. Despite her hard-nosed approach, Lieberman also believes in the importance of keeping morale high. She's been known to join in karaoke nights, and she uses

IN THE LEAD

humor and stories to lighten up intense meetings. At the end of every meeting to outline new tasks or performance targets, she plays the song, "Nothing's Gonna Stop Us Now" to keep people motivated and focused on goals.

Compare Lieberman's approach as a new CEO at TruServ to Joyce Pully's approach as the new principal of North Jackson Elementary School in Jackson, Mississippi. Pully had a vision of transforming North Jackson into a model of creative learning. However, she didn't make any changes at all during the first year, working instead to build trust with teachers, staff, and students. She listened carefully to teachers' concerns and began involving them closely in decision making. When she presented ideas for new ways of teaching and learning, Pully assured people she'd provide them with the training they needed to succeed. When teachers realized that Pully respected them and truly valued their input, they became more involved in planning the future of the school. Today, rote teaching and rote learning are gone at North Jackson, replaced by a vibrant educational process that relies on innovation and discovery. Pully believes the change was possible only because the staff, teachers, and students played an active role in making it happen.[35]

The leadership of Pamela Forbes Lieberman is characterized by high concern for tasks and production and low-to-moderate concern for people. Joyce Pully, in contrast, is high on concern for people and moderate on concern for production. In each case, both concerns shown in the Leadership Grid are present, but they are integrated at different levels.

Theories of a "High-High" Leader

The leadership styles described by the researchers at Ohio State, University of Michigan, and University of Texas pertain to variables that roughly correspond to one another: consideration and initiating structure; employee-centered and job-centered; concern for people and concern for production, as illustrated in Exhibit 2.4. The research into the behavior approach culminated in two predominate types of leadership behaviors—people-oriented and task-oriented.

The findings about two underlying dimensions and the possibility of leaders rated high on both dimensions raise four questions to think about. The first is whether these two dimensions are the most important behaviors of leadership. Certainly, these two behaviors are important. They capture fundamental, underlying aspects of human behavior that must be considered for organizations to succeed. One reason why these two dimensions are compelling is that the findings are based on empirical research, which means that researchers went into the field to study real leaders across a variety of settings. When independent streams of field research reach similar conclusions, they probably represent a fundamental theme in leadership behavior. One recent review of 50 years of leadership research, for example, identified task-oriented behavior and people-oriented behavior as primary categories related to effective

Action Memo

As a leader, you can succeed in a variety of situations by showing concern for both tasks and people. People-oriented behavior is related to higher follower satisfaction, and task-oriented behavior is typically associated with higher productivity.

Exhibit 2.4 Themes of Leader Behavior Research

	People-Oriented	Task-Oriented
Ohio State University	Consideration	Initiating Structure
University of Michigan	Employee-Centered	Job-Centered
University of Texas	Concern for People	Concern for Production

leadership in numerous studies.[36] Concern for tasks and concern for people must be shown toward followers at some reasonable level, either by the leader or by other people in the system. Although these are not the only important behaviors, as we will see throughout this book, they certainly require attention.

The second question is whether people orientation and task orientation exist together in the same leader, and how. The Grid theory argues that yes, both are present when people work with or through others to accomplish an activity. Although leaders may be high on either style, there is considerable belief that the best leaders are high on both behaviors. John Fryer, superintendent of Florida's Duvall County Schools, provides an example of a leader who succeeds on both dimensions. A former U.S. Air Force officer, Fryer developed a strategic plan for the school system, set high performance standards for both teachers and students, and directed everyone toward the accomplishment of specific tasks and goals. At first skeptical of the new superintendent, teachers were won over by his genuine concern for their ideas and their anxieties. He gained commitment by involving teachers in the planning process and learning what they needed to succeed. "We finally got a superintendent who will listen," said Terrie Brady, president of the teachers' union.[37]

How does a leader achieve both behaviors? Some researchers argue that "high-high" leaders alternate the type of behavior from one to the other, showing concern one time and task initiation another time.[38] Another approach says that effective "high-high" leaders encompass both behaviors simultaneously in a fundamentally different way than people who behave in one way or the other. For example, Fryer sets challenging goals for student performance and also works closely with teachers to provide the tools and training they feel they need to achieve those goals. A task-oriented leader might set difficult goals and simply pressure subordinates to improve quality. On the other hand, a person-oriented leader might ignore student achievement scores and goal attainment and simply seek to improve schools by consulting with teachers and building positive relationships with them. The "high-high" leaders seem to have a knack for displaying concern for both people and production in the majority of their behaviors.[39]

The third question is whether a "high-high" leadership style is universal or situational. Universal means that the behavior will tend to be effective in every situation, whereas situational means the behavior succeeds only in certain settings. Research has indicated some degree of universality with respect to people-oriented and task-oriented behavior. In other words, the leader behavior of concern for people tended to be related to higher employee satisfaction and fewer personnel problems across a wide variety of situations. Likewise, task-oriented behavior was associated with higher productivity across a large number of situations.

The fourth question concerns whether people can actually change themselves into leaders high on people and/or task-orientation. In the 1950s and 1960s, when the Ohio State and Michigan studies were underway, the assumption of researchers was that the behaviors of effective leaders could be emulated by anyone wishing to become an effective leader. In general it seems that people can indeed learn new leader behaviors. There is a belief that "high-high" leadership is a desirable quality, because the leader will meet both needs simultaneously. Although "high-high" leadership is not the only effective style, researchers have looked to this kind of leader as a candidate for success in a wide variety of situations. However, as we will see in the next chapter, the next generation of leadership studies refined the understanding of situations to pinpoint more precisely when each type of leadership behavior is most effective.

Individualized Leadership

Individualized leadership
a theory based on the notion
that a leader develops a
unique relationship with each
subordinate or group member,
which determines how the
leader behaves toward the
member and how the member
responds to the leader

Traditional trait and behavior theories assume that a leader adopts a general leadership style that is used with all group members. A more recent approach to leadership behavior research, *individualized leadership,* looks instead at the specific relationship between a leader and each individual member.[40] **Individualized leadership** is based on the notion that a leader develops a unique relationship with each subordinate or group member, which determines how the leader behaves toward the member and how the member responds to the leader. In this view, leadership is a series of *dyads,* or a series of two-person interactions.

Sometimes called *dyadic theory,* individualized leadership examines why leaders have more influence over and greater impact on some members than on others. To understand leadership, then, a closer look at the specific relationship in each leader-member dyad is necessary.[41] The dyadic view focuses on the concept of *exchange,* what each party gives to and receives from the other. Leaders can meet followers' emotional needs and offer a sense of support for the follower's self-worth, whereas followers provide leaders with commitment and high performance. Some dyads might be "rich," meaning there is a high level of both giving and receiving by both partners in the exchange, whereas others are "poor," reflecting little giving and receiving by dyadic partners.[42]

The first individualized leadership theory was introduced more than 25 years ago and has been steadily revised ever since. Exhibit 2.5 illustrates the development of this viewpoint. The first stage was the awareness of a relationship between a leader and each individual, rather than between a leader and a group of subordinates. The second stage examined specific attributes of the exchange relationship. The third stage explored whether leaders could intentionally develop

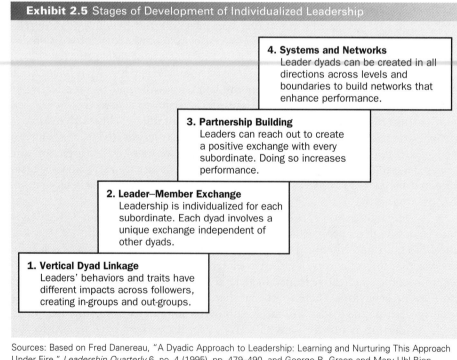

Exhibit 2.5 Stages of Development of Individualized Leadership

4. Systems and Networks
Leader dyads can be created in all directions across levels and boundaries to build networks that enhance performance.

3. Partnership Building
Leaders can reach out to create a positive exchange with every subordinate. Doing so increases performance.

2. Leader–Member Exchange
Leadership is individualized for each subordinate. Each dyad involves a unique exchange independent of other dyads.

1. Vertical Dyad Linkage
Leaders' behaviors and traits have different impacts across followers, creating in-groups and out-groups.

Sources: Based on Fred Danereau, "A Dyadic Approach to Leadership: Learning and Nurturing This Approach Under Fire," *Leadership Quarterly* 6, no. 4 (1995), pp. 479–490, and George B. Graen and Mary Uhl-Bien, "Relationship-Based Approach to Leadership: Development of Leader-Member Exchange (LMX) Theory of Leadership Over 25 Years: Applying a Multi-level, Multi-domain Approach," *Leadership Quarterly* 6, no. 2 (1995), pp. 219–247.

partnerships with each group member, and the fourth stage expanded the view of dyads to include larger systems and networks.

Vertical Dyad Linkage Model

The **Vertical Dyad Linkage (VDL) model** argues for the importance of the dyad formed by a leader with each member of the group. Initial findings indicated that subordinates provided very different descriptions of the same leader. For example, some subordinates reported a leader, and their relationship with the leader, as having a high degree of mutual trust, respect, and obligation. These high-quality relationships might be characterized as high on both people and task orientation. Other subordinates reported a low-quality relationship with the same leader, such as having a low degree of trust, respect, and obligation. These subordinates perceived the leader as being low on important leadership behaviors.

Based on these two extreme exchange patterns, subordinates were found to exist in either an in-group or an out-group in relation to the leader. Exhibit 2.6 delineates the differences in leader behavior toward in-group versus out-group members. Most of us who have had experience with any kind of group, whether it be a college class, an athletic team, or a work group, recognize that some leaders may spend a disproportionate amount of time with certain people, and that these "insiders" are often highly trusted and may obtain special privileges. In the terminology of the VDL model, these people would be considered to participate in an *in-group exchange* relationship with the leader, whereas other members of the group who did not experience a sense of trust and extra consideration would participate in an *out-group exchange*.

In-group members, those who rated the leader highly, had developed close relationships with the leader and often became assistants who played key roles in the functioning of the work unit. Out-group members were not key players in the work unit. Because of these differences, individuals often fell into subgroups, which might be considered supporters and opponents of the leader. Some subordinates were getting their needs met, whereas others were not. These differences were based on the dyad between the leader and each subordinate. The in-group had high access

Vertical Dyad Linkage (VDL) Model
a model of individualized leadership that argues for the importance of the dyad formed by a leader with each member of the group

---

Exhibit 2.6 Leader Behavior toward In-Group Versus Out-Group Members

In-Group	Out-Group
• Discusses objectives; gives employee freedom to use his or her own approach in solving problems and reaching goals	• Gives employee specific directives for how to accomplish tasks and attain goals
• Listens to employee's suggestions and ideas about how work is done	• Shows little interest in employee's comments and suggestions
• Treats mistakes as learning opportunities	• Criticizes or punishes mistakes
• Gives employee interesting assignments; may allow employee to choose assignment	• Assigns primarily routine jobs and monitors employee closely
• Sometimes defers to subordinate's opinion	• Usually imposes own views
• Praises accomplishments	• Focuses on areas of poor performance

Source: Based on Jean-François Manzoni and Jean-Louis Barsoux, "The Set-Up-to-Fail Syndrome," *Harvard Business Review* (March–April, 1988), pp. 101–113.

to the leader, whereas the out-group members tended to be passive and did not have positions of influence or access to the leader. In-group members expressed greater mutual influence and collaborative effort with the leader, and they had opportunities to receive greater rewards and perform additional duties. Out-group members tended not to experience positive leader relationships and influence, and the leader was more likely to use formal authority and coercive behavior with these subordinates. In-group members typically received more attention, more approval, and probably more status, but they were also expected to be loyal, committed, and productive.

Thus, by focusing on the relationship between a leader and each individual, the Vertical Dyad Linkage research found great variance of leader style and impact within a group of subordinates.

Leader–Member Exchange

Leader–Member Exchange (LMX)
individualized leadership model that explores how leader-member relationships develop over time and how the quality of exchange relationships impacts outcomes

Stage two in the development of the individual leadership theory explored the **leader–member exchange (LMX)** in more detail, discovering that the impact on outcomes depends on how the leader–member exchange process develops over time. Studies evaluating characteristics of the LMX relationship explored such things as communication frequency, value agreement, characteristics of followers, job satisfaction, performance, job climate, and commitment. Leaders typically tend to establish in-group exchange relationships with individuals who have characteristics similar to those of the leader, such as similarity in background, interests, and values, and with those who demonstrate a high level of competence and interest in the job. Overall, studies have found that the quality of the leader–member exchange relationship is substantially higher for in-group members. LMX theory proposes that this higher-quality relationship will lead to higher performance and greater job satisfaction for in-group members, and research in general supports this idea.[43] High-quality LMX relationships have been found to lead to very positive outcomes for leaders, followers, work units, and the organization. For followers, a high-quality exchange relationship may mean more interesting assignments, greater responsibility and authority, and tangible rewards such as pay increases and promotions. Leaders and organizations clearly benefit from the increased effort and initiative of in-group participants to carry out assignments and tasks successfully.

LMX theorists identified three stages dyad members go through in their working relationship. In the initial stage, the leader and follower, as strangers, test each other to identify what kinds of behaviors are comfortable. The relationship is negotiated informally between each follower and the leader. The definition of each group member's role defines what the member and leader expect the member to do. Next, as the leader and member become acquainted, they engage in shaping and refining the roles they will play together. Finally, in the third stage, as the roles reach maturity, the relationship attains a steady pattern of behavior. Leader-member exchanges are difficult to change at this point. The exchange tends to determine in-group and out-group status.

Action Memo
Answer the questions in Leader's Self-Insight 2.3 to understand how LMX theory applies to your own work experience.

Partnership Building

In this third phase of research, the focus was on whether leaders could develop positive relationships with a large number of subordinates. Critics of early LMX theory pointed out the dangers of leaders establishing sharply differentiated in-group and out-group members, in that this may lead to feelings of resentment or even hostility among out-group participants.[44] If leaders are perceived to be granting excessive benefits and advantages to in-group members, members of the out-group may rebel, which can damage the entire organization. Moreover, some

Your "LMX" Relationship

What was the quality of your leader's relationship with you? Think back to a job you held and recall your feelings toward your leader, or if currently employed use your supervisor. Please answer whether each item below was Mostly False or Mostly True for you.

	Mostly False	Mostly True
1. I very much liked my supervisor as a person.	_____	_____
2. My supervisor defended my work to people above him if I made a mistake.	_____	_____
3. The work I did for my supervisor went well beyond what was required.	_____	_____
4. I admired my supervisor's professional knowledge and ability.	_____	_____
5. My supervisor was enjoyable to work with.	_____	_____
6. I applied extra effort to further the interests of my work group.	_____	_____
7. My supervisor championed my case to others in the organization.	_____	_____
8. I respected my supervisor's management competence.	_____	_____

Scoring and Interpretation

LMX theory is about the quality of a leader's relationship with subordinates. If you scored 6 or more Mostly True, your supervisor clearly had an excellent relationship with you, which is stage two in Exhibit 2.5. You had a successful dyad. If your supervisor had an equally good relationship with every subordinate, that is a stage three level of development (partnership building). If you scored 3 or fewer Mostly True, then your supervisor was probably at level one, perhaps with different relationships with subordinates, some or all of which were unsucessful. What do you think accounted for the quality of your and other subordinates' relationships (positive or negative) with your supervisor? Discuss with other students to learn why some supervisors have good LMX relationships.

Source: Based on Robert C. Liden and John M. Maslyn, Multidimensionality of Leader-Member Exchange: An Empirical Assessment through Scale Development, *Journal of Management* 24 (1998), pp. 43–72.

studies have found that leaders tend to categorize employees into in-groups and out-groups as early as five days into their relationship.[45]

Thus, the third phase of research in this area focused on whether leaders could develop positive relationships with all subordinates, not just a few "favorites." The emphasis was not on how or why discrimination among subordinates occurred, but rather on how a leader might work with each subordinate on a one-on-one basis to develop a partnership. The idea was that leaders could develop a unique, beneficial relationship with each individual and provide all employees with access to high-quality leader-member exchanges, thereby providing a more equitable environment and greater benefits to leaders, followers, and the organization.

In this approach, the leader views each person independently, and may treat each individual in a different but positive way. Leaders strive to actively develop a positive relationship with each subordinate, although the positive relationship will have a different form for each person. For example, one person might be treated with "consideration," another with "initiating structure," depending on what followers need to feel involved and to succeed. Heather Coin, director of operations for Calabasas, California-based Cheesecake Factory, emphasizes that developing a personal, positive relationship with each employee is one of a restaurant manager's most critical jobs because it enables each person to contribute his or her best to the organization. As a former general manager for several of the company's restaurants, Coin practiced what she now preaches in leading a team of 11 managers and dozens of staff, helping keep turnover low and morale and performance high.[46]

In the LMX research study, leaders were trained to offer the opportunity for a high-quality relationship to all group members, and the followers who responded to the offer dramtically improved their performance. As these relationships matured, the entire work group became more productive, and the payoffs were tremendous. Leaders could count on followers to provide the assistance needed for high performance, and followers participated in and influenced decisions. Leaders provided support, encouragement, and training, and followers responded with high performance. In some sense, leaders were meeting both the personal and work-related needs of each subordinate, one at a time. The implications of this finding are that true performance and productivity gains can be achieved by having the leader develop positive relationships one-on-one with each subordinate.

Action Memo
As a leader, you can build a positive, individualized relationship with each follower to create an equitable work environment and provide greater benefits to yourself, followers, and the organization.

Systems and Networks

The final stage of this work suggests that leader dyads can be expanded to larger systems. Rather than focusing on leaders and subordinates, a systems-level perspective examines how dyadic relationships can be created across traditional boundaries to embrace a larger system. This larger network for the leader may cut across work unit, functional, divisional, and even organizational boundaries. In this view, leader relationships are not limited to subordinates, but include peers, teammates, and other stakeholders relevant to the work unit. To this point, there has been little systematic research on a broader systemic view of dyadic relationships. But the theory suggests the need for leaders to build networks of one-on-one relationships and to use their traits and behaviors selectively to create positive relationships with as many people as possible. A large number of people thereby can be influenced by the leader, and these stakeholders will contribute to the success of the work unit.

One organization that is promoting the idea of creating partnerships across a larger system is University Public Schools in Stockton, California.

IN THE LEAD

University Public Schools

Education has always been a service business, with each child highly individualized and needing a specific approach. However, many schools operate on an old-fashioned factory model that treats students like pieces of equipment. University Public Schools (UPS) of Stockton, California, takes a different approach.

UPS's San Joaquin campus is a model of partnership. Leaders have established network linkages across traditional boundaries. Teachers at San Joaquin are expected to develop partnerships with students, each other, parents, and other community members. They are given an unprecedented amount of freedom to set their own goals and develop their own curriculum. If parents want something taught that isn't being covered, they can request that it be included. "Parents can have a say about what's important to them," says Christina Cross, whose son attends UPS. "It's nice to be involved in the education that goes on here."

Teachers' pay raises are based on merit and tied to meeting both individual and team goals. Teachers sign one-year contracts and there is no notion of tenure. Despite the lack of job security, people are so willing to work at the Stockton school that some make a daily commute of nearly four hours. One reason is that teachers feel they are involved in a genuine partnership with the school system, one another, and the community. UPS is trying to build a system that empowers everyone to shape a new vision of learning and make a real difference in the lives of students and the larger world.[47]

Summary and Interpretation

The point of this chapter is to understand the importance of traits and behaviors in the development of leadership theory and research. Traits include self-confidence, honesty, and drive. A large number of personal traits and abilities distinguish successful leaders from nonleaders, but traits themselves are not sufficient to guarantee effective leadership. The behavior approach explored autocratic versus democratic leadership, consideration versus initiating structure, employee-centered versus job-centered leadership, and concern for people versus concern for production. The theme of people versus tasks runs through this research, suggesting these are fundamental behaviors through which leaders meet followers' needs. There has been some disagreement in the research about whether a specific leader is either people- or task-oriented or whether one can be both. Today, the consensus is that leaders can achieve a "high-high" leadership style.

Another approach is the dyad between a leader and each follower. Followers have different relationships with the leader, and the ability of the leader to develop a positive relationship with each subordinate contributes to team performance. The leader-member exchange theory says that high-quality relationships have a positive outcome for leaders, followers, work units, and the organization. Leaders can attempt to build individualized relationships with each subordinate as a way to meet needs for both consideration and structure.

The historical development of leadership theory presented in this chapter introduces some important ideas about leadership. Although certain personal traits and abilities indicate a greater likelihood for success in a leadership role, they are not in themselves sufficient to guarantee effective leadership. Rather, behaviors are equally significant, as outlined by the research at several universities. Therefore, the style of leadership demonstrated by an individual greatly determines the outcome of the leadership endeavor. Often, a combination of styles is most effective. To understand the effects of leadership upon outcomes, the specific relationship behavior between a leader and each follower is also an important consideration.

Discussion Questions

1. Is the "Great Man" perspective on leadership still alive today? Think about some recent popular movies that stress a lone individual as hero or savior. How about some business stories? Discuss.

2. Suggest some personal traits of leaders you have known. What traits do you believe are most valuable? Why?

3. What is the difference between trait theories and behavioral theories of leadership?

4. Would you prefer working for a leader who has a "consideration" or an "initiating-structure" leadership style? Discuss the reasons for your answer.

5. The Vertical Dyad Linkage model suggests that followers respond individually to the leader. If this is so, what advice would you give leaders about displaying people-oriented versus task-oriented behavior?

6. Does it make sense to you that a leader should develop an individualized relationship with each follower? Explain advantages and disadvantages to this approach.

7. Why would subordinates under a democratic leader perform better in the leader's absence than would subordinates under an autocratic leader?

8. What type of leader—task-oriented or people-oriented—do you think would have an easier time becoming a "high-high" leader? Why?

Leadership at Work

Your Ideal Leader Traits

Spend some time thinking about someone you believe is an ideal leader. For the first part of the exercise, select an ideal leader you have heard about whom you don't personally know. It could be someone like Mother Teresa, Rudolph Giuliani, Martin Luther King, Abraham Lincoln, or any national or international figure that you admire. Write the person's name here: _____ . Now, in the space below, write down three things you admire about the person, such as what he or she did or the qualities that person possesses.

_____

_____

_____

For the second part of the exercise, select an ideal leader whom you know personally. This can be anyone from your life experiences. Write the person's name here: _____ _____. *Now, in the space below, write down three things you admire about the person, such as what he or she did or the qualities that person possesses.*

_____

_____

_____

The first leader you chose represents something of a projective test based on what you've heard or read. You imagine the leader has the qualities you listed. The deeds and qualities you listed say more about what you admire than about the actual traits of the leader you chose. This is something like an inkblot test, and it is important because the traits you assign to the leader are traits you are aware of, have the potential to develop, and indeed can develop as a leader. The qualities or achievements you listed are an indicator of the traits you likely will express as you develop into the leader you want to become.

The second leader you chose is someone you know, so it is less of a projective test and represents traits you have had direct experience with. You know these traits work for you and likely will become the traits you develop and express as a leader.

What is similar about the traits you listed for the two leaders? Different? Interview another student in class about traits he or she admires. What do the traits tell you about the person you are interviewing? What are the common themes in your list and the other student's list of traits? To what extent do you display the same traits as the ones on your list? Will you develop those traits even more in the future?

_____

_____

_____

Leadership Development: Cases for Analysis

Consolidated Products

Consolidated Products is a medium-sized manufacturer of consumer products with nonunionized production workers. Ben Samuels was a plant manager for Consolidated Products for 10 years, and he was very well liked by the employees there. They were grateful for the fitness center he built for employees, and they enjoyed the social activities sponsored by the plant several times a year, including company picnics and holiday parties. He knew most of the workers by name, and he spent part of each day walking around the plant to visit with them and ask about their families or hobbies.

Ben believed that it was important to treat employees properly so they would have a sense of loyalty to the company. He tried to avoid any layoffs when production demand was slack, figuring that the company could not afford to lose skilled workers that are so difficult to replace. The workers knew that if they had a special problem, Ben would try to help them. For example, when someone was injured but wanted to continue working, Ben found another job in the plant that the person could do despite having a disability. Ben believed that if you treat people right, they will do a good job for you without close supervision or prodding. Ben applied the same principle to his supervisors, and he mostly left them alone to run their departments as they saw fit. He did not set objectives and standards for the plant, and he never asked the supervisors to develop plans for improving productivity and product quality.

Under Ben, the plant had the lowest turnover among the company's five plants, but the second worst record for costs and production levels. When the company was acquired by another firm, Ben was asked to take early retirement, and Phil Jones was brought in to replace him.

Phil had a growing reputation as a manager who could get things done, and he quickly began making changes. Costs were cut by trimming a number of activities such as the fitness center at the plant, company picnics and parties, and the human relations training programs for supervisors. Phil believed that human relations training was a waste of time; if employees don't want to do the work, get rid of them and find somebody else who does.

Supervisors were instructed to establish high performance standards for their departments and insist that people achieve them. A computer monitoring system was introduced so that the output of each worker could be checked closely against the standards. Phil told his supervisors to give any worker who had substandard performance one warning, and then if performance did not improve within two weeks, to fire the person. Phil believed that workers don't respect a supervisor who is weak and passive. When Phil observed a worker wasting time or making a mistake, he would reprimand the person right on the spot to set an example. Phil also checked closely on the performance of his supervisors. Demanding objectives were set for each department, and weekly meetings were held with each supervisor to review department performance. Finally, Phil insisted that supervisors check with him first before taking any significant actions that deviated from established plans and policies.

As another cost-cutting move, Phil reduced the frequency of equipment maintenance, which required machines to be idled when they could be productive. Since the machines had a good record of reliable operation, Phil believed that the current maintenance schedule was excessive and was cutting into production. Finally, when business was slow for one of the product lines, Phil laid off workers rather than finding something else for them to do.

By the end of Phil's first year as plant manager, production costs were reduced by 20 percent and production output was up by 10 percent. However, three of his seven supervisors left to take other jobs, and turnover was also high among the machine operators. Some of the turnover was due to workers who were fired, but competent machine operators were also quitting, and it was becoming increasingly difficult to find any replacements for them. Finally, there was increasing talk of unionizing among the workers.

Source: Reprinted with permission from Gary Yukl, *Leadership in Organizations*, 4th ed. (Englewood Cliffs, NJ: Prentice Hall, 1998), pp. 66–67.

QUESTIONS

1. Compare the leadership traits and behaviors of Ben Samuels and Phil Jones.
2. Which leader do you think is more effective? Why? Which leader would you prefer to work for?
3. If you were Phil Jones' boss, what would you do now?

D. L. Woodside, Sunshine Snacks

D. L. Woodside has recently accepted the position of research and development director for Sunshine Snacks, a large snack food company. Woodside has been assistant director of research at Skid's, a competing company, for several years, but it became clear to him that his chances of moving higher were slim. So, when Sunshine was looking for a new director, Woodside jumped at the chance.

At Skid's, Woodside had worked his way up from the mail room, going to school at night to obtain first a bachelor's degree and eventually a Ph.D. Management admired his drive and determination, as well as his ability to get along with just about anyone he came in contact with, and they gave him opportunities to work in various positions around the company over the years. That's when he discovered he had a love for developing new products. He had been almost single-handedly responsible for introducing four new successful product lines at Skid's. Woodside's technical knowledge and understanding of the needs of the research and development department were excellent. In addition, he was a tireless worker—when he started a project he rarely rested until it was finished, and finished well.

Despite his ambition and his hard-charging approach to work, Woodside was considered an easy-going fellow. He liked to talk and joke around, and whenever anyone had a problem they'd come to Woodside rather than go to the director. Woodside was always willing to listen to a research assistant's personal problems. Besides that, he would often stay late or come in on weekends to finish an assistant's work if the employee was having problems at home or difficulty with a particular project. Woodside knew the director was a hard taskmaster, and he didn't want anyone getting into trouble over things they couldn't help. In fact, he'd been covering the mistakes of George, an employee who had a drinking problem, ever since he'd been appointed assistant director. Well, George was on his own now. Woodside had his own career to think about, and the position at Sunshine was his chance to finally lead a department rather than play second fiddle.

At Sunshine, Woodside is replacing Henry Meade, who has been the director for almost 30 years. However, it seems clear that Meade has been slowing down over the past few years, turning more and more of his work over to his assistant, Harmon Davis. When Woodside was first introduced to the people in the research department at Sunshine, he sensed not only a loyalty to Davis, who'd been passed over for the top job because of his lack of technical knowledge, but also an undercurrent of resistance to his own selection as the new director.

Woodside knows he needs to build good relationships with the team, and especially with Davis, quickly. The company has made it clear that it wants the department to initiate several new projects as soon as possible. One reason they selected Woodside for the job was his successful track record with new product development at Skid's.

Source: Based in part on *"The Take Over,"* Incident 52 in Bernard A. Deitzer and Karl A. Shilliff, *Contemporary Management Incidents* (Columbus, OH: Grid, Inc., 1977), pp. 161–162; and *"Choosing a New Director of Research,"* Case 2.1 in Peter G. Northouse, Leadership Theory and Practice, 2nd ed. *(Thousand Oaks, CA: Sage Publications, 2001), pp. 25–26.*

QUESTIONS

1. What traits does Woodside possess that might be helpful to him as he assumes his new position? What traits might be detrimental?

2. Would you consider Woodside a people-oriented or a task-oriented leader? Discuss which you think would be best for the new research director at Sunshine.

3. How might an understanding of individualized leadership theory be useful to Woodside in this situation? Discuss.

References

1   Curtis Sittenfeld, "Leader on the Edge," Fast Company (October 1999), pp. 212–226.

2   Greg Jaffe, "A General's New Plan to Battle Radical Islam," *The Wall Street Journal* (September 2–3, 2006), pp. A1, A4.

3   "IHOP's CEO Has a Lot on Her Plate," *Fortune* (March 31, 2003), p. 143.

4   G. A. Yukl, *Leadership in Organizations* (Englewood Cliffs, NJ: Prentice Hall, 1981); and S. C. Kohs and K. W. Irle, "Prophesying Army Promotion," *Journal of Applied Psychology* 4 (1920), pp. 73–87.

5   Yukl, *Leadership in Organizations*, p. 254.

6   R. M. Stogdill, "Personal Factors Associated with Leadership: A Survey of the Literature," *Journal of Psychology* 25 (1948), pp. 35–71.

7   R. M. Stogdill, *Handbook of Leadership: A Survey of the Literature* (New York: Free Press, 1974); and Bernard M. Bass, *Bass & Stogdill's Handbook of Leadership: Theory, Research, and Managerial Applications,* 3rd ed. (New York: Free Press, 1990).

8   S. A. Kirkpatrick and E. A. Locke, "Leadership: Do Traits Matter?" *The Academy of Management Executive* 5, No. 2 (1991), pp. 48–60.

9   R. G. Lord, C. L. DeVader, and G. M. Alliger, "A Meta-Analysis of the Relation Between Personality Traits and Leadership Perceptions: An Application of Validity Generalization Procedures," *Journal of Applied Psychology* 71 (1986), pp. 402–410.

10 Edwin Locke and Associates, *The Essence of Leadership* (New York: Lexington Books, 1991).

11 A summary of various studies and surveys is reported in Del Jones, "Optimism Puts Rose-Colored Tint in Glasses of Top Execs," *USA Today* (December 15, 2005).

12 Marcus Buckingham, quoted in Jones, "Optimism Puts Rose-Colored Tint in Glasses of Top Execs."

13 Shelley A. Kirkpatrick and Edwin A. Locke, "Leadership: Do Traits Matter?" *Academy of Management Executive* 5, No. 2 (1991), pp. 48–60.

14 James M. Kouzes and Barry Z. Posner, *Credibility: How Leaders Gain and Lose It, Why People Demand It* (San Francisco: Jossey-Bass Publishers, 1993), p. 14.

15 This discussion is based on Kirkpatrick and Locke, "Leadership: Do Traits Matter?"

16 Geoffrey Colvin, "The Bionic Manager," *Fortune* (September 19, 2005), pp. 88–100.

17 "Towards a More Perfect Match: Building Successful Leaders By Effectively Aligning People and Roles," Hay Group Working Paper, 2004.

18 K. Lewin, "Field Theory and Experiment in Social Psychology: Concepts and Methods," *American Journal of Sociology* 44 (1939), pp. 868–896; K. Lewin and R. Lippet, "An Experimental Approach to the Study of Autocracy and Democracy: A Preliminary Note," *Sociometry* 1 (1938), pp. 292–300; and K. Lewin, R. Lippett, and R. K. White, "Patterns of Aggressive Behavior in Experimentally Created Social Climates," *Journal of Social Psychology* 10 (1939), pp. 271–301.

19 R. Tannenbaum and W. H. Schmidt, "How to Choose a Leadership Pattern," *Harvard Business Review* 36 (1958), pp. 95–101.

20 F. A. Heller and G. A. Yukl, "Participation, Managerial Decision-Making and Situational Variables," *Organizational Behavior and Human Performance* 4 (1969), pp. 227–241.

21 "Jack's Recipe (Management Principles Used by Jack Hartnett, President of D. L. Rogers Corp.)," sidebar in Marc Ballon, "Equal Parts Old-Fashioned Dictator and New Age Father Figure, Jack Hartnett Breaks Nearly Every Rule of the Enlightened Manager's Code," *Inc.* (July 1998), p. 60.

22 Donna Fenn, "The Remote Control CEO," *Inc. Magazine* (October 2005), pp. 96–101, 144–146.

23 Ibid.

24 J. K. Hemphill and A. E. Coons, "Development of the Leader Behavior Description Questionnaire," in *Leader Behavior: Its Description and Measurement,* Eds. R. M. Stogdill and A. E. Coons (Columbus, OH: Ohio State University, Bureau of Business Research, 1957).

25 P. C. Nystrom, "Managers and the High-High Leader Myth," *Academy of Management Journal* 21 (1978) pp. 325–331; and L. L. Larson, J. G. Hunt and Richard N. Osborn, "The Great High-High Leader Behavior Myth: A Lesson from Occam's Razor," *Academy of Management Journal* 19 (1976), pp. 628–641.

26 Christopher Cooper, "Speed Trap; How a Marine Lost His Command in Race to Baghdad," *The Wall Street Journal* (April 5, 2004), pp. A1, A15.

27 E. W. Skinner, "Relationships Between Leadership Behavior Patterns and Organizational-Situational Variables," *Personnel Psychology* 22 (1969), pp. 489–494; and E. A. Fleishman and E. F. Harris, "Patterns of Leadership Behavior Related to Employee Grievances and Turnover," *Personnel Psychology* 15 (1962), pp. 43–56.

28 A. W. Halpin and B. J. Winer, "A Factorial Study of the Leader Behavior Descriptions," in *Leader Behavior: Its Descriptions and Measurement,* Eds. R. M. Stogdill and A. E. Coons, (Columbus, OH: Ohio State University, Bureau of Business Research, 1957); and J. K. Hemphill, "Leadership Behavior Associated with the Administrative Reputations of College Departments," *Journal of Educational Psychology* 46 (1955), pp. 385–401.

29 R. Likert, "From Production- and Employee-Centeredness to Systems 1–4," *Journal of Management* 5 (1979), pp. 147–156.

30 J. Taylor and D. Bowers, *The Survey of Organizations: A Machine Scored Standardized Questionnaire Instrument* (Ann Arbor, MI: Institute for Social Research, University of Michigan, 1972).

31 D. G. Bowers and S. E. Seashore, "Predicting Organizational Effectiveness with a Four-Factor Theory of Leadership," *Administrative Science Quarterly* 11 (1966), pp. 238–263.

32 Carol Hymowitz, "Damark's Unique Post: A Manager Who Helps Work on Relationships," (In the Lead column), *The Wall Street Journal* (September 7, 1999), p. B1.

33 Bowers and Seashore, "Predicting Organizational Effectiveness with a Four-Factor Theory of Leadership."

34 Robert Blake and Jane S. Mouton, *The Managerial Grid III* (Houston: Gulf, 1985).

35 Jo Napolitano, "No, She Doesn't Breathe Fire," *The New York Times* (September 1, 2002), Section 3, p. 2; "The Transformed School," segment in Sara Terry, "Schools That Think," *Fast Company* (April 2000), pp. 304–320.

36 Gary Yukl, Angela Gordon, and Tom Taber, "A Hierarchical Taxonomy of Leadership Behavior: Integrating a Half Century of Behavior Research," *Journal of Leadership and Organizational Studies* 9, no. 1 (2002), pp. 15–32.

37 Stephanie Desmon, "Schools Chief an Executive, Not an Educator," *The Palm Beach Post* (December 26, 1999), pp. 1A, 22A.

38 J. Misumi, *The Behavioral Science of Leadership: An Interdisciplinary Japanese Research Program* (Ann Arbor, MI: University of Michigan Press, 1985).

39 Fleishman and Harris, "Patterns of Leadership Behavior Related to Employee Grievances and Turnover"; and Misumi, *The Behavioral Science of Leadership: An Interdisciplinary Japanese Research Program.*

40 Francis J. Yammarino and Fred Dansereau, "Individualized Leadership," *Journal of Leadership and Organizational Studies* 9, no. 1 (2002), pp. 90–99.

41 This discussion is based on Fred Dansereau, "A Dyadic Approach to Leadership: Creating and Nurturing This Approach Under Fire," *Leadership Quarterly* 6, No. 4 (1995), pp. 479–490; and George B. Graen and Mary Uhl-Bien, "Relationship-Based Approach to Leadership: Development of Leader Member Exchange (LMX) Theory of Leadership Over 25 Years: Applying a Multi-Level Multi-Domain Approach," *Leadership Quarterly* 6, No. 2 (1995), pp. 219–247.

42 Yammarino and Dansereau, "Individualized Leadership."

43 See A. J. Kinicki and R. P. Vecchio, "Influences on the Quality of Supervisor-Subordinate Relations: The Role of Time Pressure, Organizational Commitment, and Locus of Control," *Journal of Organizational Behavior,* (January 1994), pp. 75–82; R. C. Liden, S. J. Wayne, and D. Stilwell, "A Longitudinal Study on the Early Development of Leader-Member Exchanges," *Journal of Applied Psychology* (August 1993), pp. 662–674; Yammarino and Dansereau, "Individualized Leadership"; and Jean-François Manzoni and Jean-Louis Baraoux, "The Set-Up-to-Fail Syndrome," *Harvard Business Review* (March-April 1998), pp. 101–113.

44 W. E. McClane, "Implications of Member Role Differentiation: Analysis of a Key Concept in the LMX Model of Leadership," *Group and Organization Studies* 16 (1991), pp. 102–113; and Gary Yukl, *Leadership in Organizations,* 2nd ed. (New York: Prentice-Hall, 1989).

45 Manzoni and Barsoux, "The Set-Up-to-Fail Syndrome."

46 Bret Thorn, "Best GMs Must Have Heart, Be Smart to Succeed in Business," *Nation's Restaurant News* (November 1, 2004), p. 42; and Susan Spielberg, "The Cheesecake Factory: Heather Coin," *Nation's Restaurant News* (January 26, 2004), p. 38.

47 "The Service School," segment in Sara Terry, "Schools That Think," *Fast Company* (April 2000), pp. 304–320.

Chapter 3

Your Leadership Challenge

After reading this chapter, you should be able to:

- Understand how leadership is often contingent on people and situations.

- Apply Fiedler's contingency model to key relationships among leader style, situational favorability, and group task performance.

- Apply Hersey and Blanchard's situational theory of leader style to the level of follower readiness.

- Explain the path–goal theory of leadership.

- Use the Vroom–Jago model to identify the correct amount of follower participation in specific decision situations.

- Know how to use the power of situational variables to substitute for or neutralize the need for leadership.

Contingency Approaches

For Pat McGovern, founder and chairman of International Data Group, a technology publishing and research firm that owns magazines such as *CIO, PC World,* and *Computerworld,* having personal contact with employees and letting them know they're appreciated is a primary responsibility of leaders. McGovern treats people to lunch at the Ritz on their 10th anniversary with IDG to tell them how important they are to the success of the company. He personally thanks almost every person in every business unit once a year, which takes about a month of his time. Managers provide him with a list of accomplishments for all their direct reports, which McGovern memorizes the night before his visit so he can congratulate people on specific accomplishments. Rather than establishing strict goals and standards for task accomplishment, McGovern decentralizes decision making so that people have the autonomy to make their own decisions about how best to do their jobs.

Wolfgang Bernhard, a member of Volkswagen AG's board of management responsible for the core VW brand, displays a very different style of leadership. When he came to the struggling company, Bernhard moved quickly to cut jobs, scale back investments in underperforming units, and get people focused on quality and productivity issues. He ordered more than 200 employees to report to an auditorium a few miles from headquarters, formed them into teams and told them to figure out ways to meet specific cost reduction goals, and instructed them not to return to their workplaces until they'd done so. Often working until midnight, the teams took four weeks to meet the targets. Bernhard has also tied managers' bonuses to demonstrated improvements in quality and productivity. His hard-charging style has rankled some long-time employees and managers, but Bernhard doesn't mind. "I am quick and focused, and I like to cut the formalites," he says.[1]

IDG's Pat McGovern is strongly people-oriented—that is, characterized by high concern for people and low concern for production. Wolfgang Bernhard, in contrast, is a strong, task-oriented leader, high on concern for production and relatively low on concern for people. Two leaders, both successful, with two very different approaches to leading. This difference points to what researchers of leader traits and behaviors eventually discovered: Many different leadership styles can be effective. What, then, determines the success of a leadership style?

In the above example, Bernhard and McGovern are performing leadership in very different situations. Volkswagen AG recruited Bernhard to assist in a massive restructuring and help the company reverse a steep drop in profits. Many people, including CEO Bernd Pischetsrieder, believe Bernhard's blunt honesty and task-oriented approach is just what is needed to get the automaker back on track. McGovern, on the other hand, is operating in a much more favorable business situation. As a smaller, privately-held company, IDG isn't under the same kind of public pressures from investors and analysts as Volkswagen. IDG is a leader in its industry, publishes more than 300 magazines and newspapers, and consistently earns industry awards. Morale and motivation among employees is high.[2]

This chapter explores the relationship between leadership effectiveness and the situation in which leadership activities occur. Over the years, researchers have observed that leaders frequently behave situationally—that is, they adjust their leadership style depending on a variety of factors in the situations they face. In this chapter, we discuss the elements of leader, follower, and the situation, and the impact each has upon the others. We examine several theories that define how leadership styles, follower attributes, and organizational characteristics fit together to enable successful leadership. The important point of this chapter is that the most effective leadership approach depends on many factors. Understanding the contingency approaches can help a leader adapt his or her approach, although it is important to recognize that leaders also develop their ability to adapt through experience and practice.

The Contingency Approach

The failure to find universal leader traits or behaviors that would always determine effective leadership led researchers in a new direction. Although leader behavior was still examined, the central focus of the new research was the situation in which leadership occurred. The basic tenet of this focus was that behavior effective in some circumstances might be ineffective under different conditions. Thus, the effectiveness of leader behavior is *contingent* upon organizational situations. Aptly called *contingency approaches*, these theories explain the relationship between leadership styles and effectiveness in specific situations.

The universalistic approach as described in Chapter 2 is compared to the contingency approach used in this chapter in Exhibit 3.1. In the previous chapter, researchers were investigating traits or behaviors that could improve performance and satisfaction in any or all situations. They sought universal leadership traits and behaviors. **Contingency** means that one thing depends on other things, and for a leader to be effective there must be an appropriate fit between the leader's behavior and style and the conditions in the situation. A leadership style that works in one situation might not work in another situation. There is no one best way of leadership. Contingency means "it depends." This chapter's Leader's Bookshelf talks about a new approach to leadership for a new kind of contingency facing today's organizations.

Contingency
a theory meaning one thing depends on other things

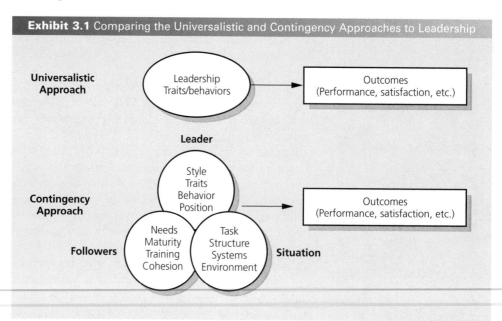

Exhibit 3.1 Comparing the Universalistic and Contingency Approaches to Leadership

Leader's Bookshelf

Leadership and the New Science

Getty Images

by Margaret J. Wheatley

In searching for a better understanding of organizations and leadership, Margaret Wheatley looked to science for answers. In the world of Newtonian physics, every atom moves in a unique predictable trajectory determined by the forces exerted on it. Prediction and control are accomplished by reducing wholes into discrete parts and carefully regulating the forces that act on those parts. Applied to organizations, this view of the world led to rigid vertical hierarchies, division of labor, task description, and strict operating procedures designed to obtain predictable, controlled results.

Just as Newton's law broke down as physics explored ever-smaller elements of matter and ever-wider expanses of the universe, rigid, control-oriented leadership doesn't work well in a world of instant information, constant change, and global competition. The physical sciences responded to the failure of Newtonian physics with a new paradigm called quantum mechanics. In *Leadership and the New Science,* Wheatley explores how leaders are redesigning organizations to survive in a quantum world.

CHAOS, RELATIONSHIPS, AND FIELDS

From quantum mechanics and chaos theory emerge new understandings of order, disorder, and change. Individual actions, whether by atoms or people, cannot be easily predicted and controlled. Here's why:

- Nothing exists except in relationship to everything else. It is not things, but the relationships among them that are the key determinants of a well-ordered system we perceive. Order emerges through a web of relationships that make up the whole, not as a result of controls on individual parts.
- The empty space between things is filled with fields, invisible material that connects elements together.

In organizations, the fields that bind people include vision, shared values, culture, and information.

- Organizations, like all open systems, grow and change in reaction to disequilibrium, and disorder can be a source of new order.

IMPLICATIONS FOR LEADERSHIP

These new understandings provide a new way to see, understand, and lead today's organizations. The new sciences can influence leaders to:

- Nurture relationships and the fields between people with a clear vision, statements of values, expressions of caring, the sharing of information, and freedom from strict rules and controls.
- Focus on the whole, not on the parts in isolation.
- Reduce boundaries between departments and organizations to allow new patterns of relationships.
- Become comfortable with uncertainty and recognize that any solutions are only temporary, specific to the immediate context, and developed through the relationship of people and circumstances.
- Recognize that healthy growth of people and organizations is found in disequilibrium, not in stability.

Wheatley believes leaders can learn from the new sciences how to lead in today's fast-paced, chaotic world, suggesting that "we can forgo the despair created by such common organization events as change, chaos, information overload, and cyclical behaviors if we recognize that organizations are conscious entities, possessing many of the properties of living systems."

Leadership and the New Science, by Margaret J. Wheatley, is published by Berrett-Koehler Publishers.

The contingencies most important to leadership as shown in Exhibit 3.1 are the situation and followers. Research implies that situational variables such as task, structure, context, and environment are important to leadership style, just as we saw in the opening examples. The nature of followers has also been identified as a key contingency. Thus, the needs, maturity, and cohesiveness of followers make a significant difference to the best style of leadership.

Several models of situational leadership have been developed. The contingency model developed by Fiedler and his associates, the situational theory of Hersey and Blanchard, path-goal theory, the Vroom–Jago model of decision participation, and the substitutes for leadership concept will all be described

Contingency approaches
approaches that seek to
delineate the characteristics
of situations and followers and
examine the leadership styles
that can be used effectively

in this chapter. The **contingency approaches** seek to delineate the characteristics of situations and followers and examine the leadership styles that can be used effectively. Assuming that a leader can properly diagnose a situation and muster the flexibility to behave according to the appropriate style, successful outcomes are highly likely.

Two basic leadership behaviors that can be adjusted to address various contingencies are *task behavior* and *relationship behavior*, introduced in the previous chapter. Research has identified these two *meta-categories*, or broadly defined behavior categories, as applicable to leadership in a variety of situations and time periods.[3] A leader can adapt his or her style to be high or low on both task and relationship behavior. Exhibit 3.2 illustrates the four possible behavior approaches—high task–low relationship, high task–high relationship, high relationship–low task, and low task–low relationship. The exhibit describes typical task and relationship behaviors. High task behaviors include planning short-term activities, clarifying tasks, objectives, and role expectations, and monitoring operations and performance. High relationship behaviors include providing support and recognition, developing followers' skills and confidence, and consulting and empowering followers when making decisions and solving problems.

> **Action Memo**
> Complete the questionnaire in Leader's Self-Insight 3.1 to assess your relative emphasis on two important categories of leadership behavior.

Both Fiedler's contingency model and Hersey and Blanchard's situational theory, discussed in the following sections, use these meta-categories of leadership behavior but apply them based on different sets of contingencies.

Fiedler's Contingency Model

Fiedler's contingency model
a model designed to diagnose
whether a leader is task-oriented
or relationship-oriented and match
leader style to the situation

An early extensive effort to link leadership style with organizational situation was made by Fiedler and his associates.[4] The basic idea is simple: Match the leader's style with the situation most favorable for his or her success. **Fiedler's contingency model** was designed to enable leaders to diagnose both leadership style and organizational situation.

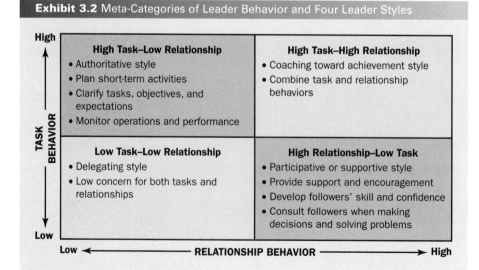

Exhibit 3.2 Meta-Categories of Leader Behavior and Four Leader Styles

High Task–Low Relationship	**High Task–High Relationship**
• Authoritative style	• Coaching toward achievement style
• Plan short-term activities	• Combine task and relationship behaviors
• Clarify tasks, objectives, and expectations	
• Monitor operations and performance	
Low Task–Low Relationship	**High Relationship–Low Task**
• Delegating style	• Participative or supportive style
• Low concern for both tasks and relationships	• Provide support and encouragement
	• Develop followers' skill and confidence
	• Consult followers when making decisions and solving problems

(TASK BEHAVIOR: High ↕ Low; RELATIONSHIP BEHAVIOR: Low ← → High)

Source: Based on Gary Yukl, Angela Gordon, and Tom Taber, "A Hierarchical Taxonomy of Leadership Behavior: Integrating a Half Century of Behavior Research," *Journal of Leadership and Organizational Studies* 9, no. 1 (2002), pp. 15–32.

T–P Leadership Questionnaire: An Assessment of Style

The following items describe aspects of leadership behavior. *Assume you are under great pressure for performance improvements as the leader of a manufacturing work group of six machine operators. Respond to each item according to the way you would most likely act in this pressure situation.* Indicate whether each item below is Mostly False or Mostly True for you as a work group leader.

	Mostly False	Mostly True
1. I would take charge of what should be done and when to do it.	_____	_____
2. I would stress getting ahead of competing groups.	_____	_____
3. I would ask the members to work harder.	_____	_____
4. I would speak for the group if there were visitors present.	_____	_____
5. I would keep the work moving at a rapid pace.	_____	_____
6. I would permit members to use their own judgment in solving problems.	_____	_____
7. I would ask for group feedback on my ideas.	_____	_____
8. I would let members do their work the way they think best.	_____	_____
9. I would turn the members loose on a job and let them go for it.	_____	_____
10. I would permit the group to set its own pace.	_____	_____
T _____ P _____	_____	_____

Scoring and Interpretation

The T–P Leadership Questionnaire is scored as follows: Your "T" score is the number of Mostly True answers for questions 1–5. Your "P" score is the number of Mostly True answers for questons 6–10. A score of 4 or 5 would be considered high for either T or P.

Some leaders deal with people needs, leaving task details to followers. Other leaders focus on specific details with the expectation that followers will carry out orders. Depending on the situation, both approaches may be effective. The important issue is the ability to identify relevant dimensions of the situation and behave accordingly. Through this questionnaire, you can identify your relative emphasis on two dimensions of leadership: task orientation (T) and people orientation (P). These are not opposite approaches, and an individual can rate high or low on either or both.

What is your leadership orientation? Compare your results from this assignment to your result from the quiz in Leader's Self-Insight 2.2 in the previous chapter. What would you consider an ideal leader situation for your style?

Source: Based on the T-P Leadership Questionnaire as published in "Toward a Particularistic Approach to Leadership Style: Some Findings," by T. J. Sergiovanni, R. Metzcus, and L. Burden, *American Educational Research Journal* 6, no. 1 (1969), pp. 62–79.

Leadership Style

The cornerstone of Fiedler's theory is the extent to which the leader's style is relationship-oriented or task-oriented. A *relationship-oriented leader* is concerned with people. As with the consideration style described in Chapter 2, a relationship-oriented leader establishes mutual trust and respect, and listens to employees' needs. A *task-oriented leader* is primarily motivated by task accomplishment. Similar to the initiating structure style described earlier, a task-oriented leader provides clear directions and sets performance standards.

Leadership style was measured with a questionnaire known as the least preferred coworker (LPC) scale. The LPC scale has a set of 16 bipolar adjectives along an eight-point scale. Examples of the bipolar adjectives used by Fiedler on the LPC scale follow:

open	guarded
quarrelsome	harmonious
efficient	inefficient
self-assured	hesitant
gloomy	cheerful

If the leader describes the least preferred coworker using positive concepts, he or she is considered relationship-oriented; that is, a leader who cares about and is sensitive to other people's feelings. Conversely, if a leader uses negative concepts to describe the least preferred coworker, he or she is considered task-oriented; that is, a leader who sees other people in negative terms and places greater value on task activities than on people.

Situation

Fiedler's model presents the leadership situation in terms of three key elements that can be either favorable or unfavorable to a leader: the quality of leader–member relations, task structure, and position power.

Leader–member relations refers to group atmosphere and members' attitudes toward and acceptance of the leader. When subordinates trust, respect, and have confidence in the leader, leader–member relations are considered good. When subordinates distrust, do not respect, and have little confidence in the leader, leader–member relations are poor.

Task structure refers to the extent to which tasks performed by the group are defined, involve specific procedures, and have clear, explicit goals. Routine, well-defined tasks, such as those of assembly-line workers, have a high degree of structure. Creative, ill-defined tasks, such as research and development or strategic planning, have a low degree of task structure. When task structure is high, the situation is considered favorable to the leader; when low, the situation is less favorable.

Position power is the extent to which the leader has formal authority over subordinates. Position power is high when the leader has the power to plan and direct the work of subordinates, evaluate it, and reward or punish them. Position power is low when the leader has little authority over subordinates and cannot evaluate their work or reward them. When position power is high, the situation is considered favorable for the leader; when low, the situation is unfavorable.

Combining the three situational characteristics yields a list of eight leadership situations, which are illustrated in Exhibit 3.3. Situation I is most favorable to the leader because leader–member relations are good, task structure is high, and leader position power is strong. Situation VIII is most unfavorable to the leader because leader–member relations are poor, task structure is low, and leader position power is weak. Other octants represent intermediate degrees of favorableness for the leader.

Contingency Theory

When Fiedler examined the relationships among leadership style, situational favorability, and group task performance, he found the pattern shown at the top of Exhibit 3.3. Task-oriented leaders are more effective when the situation is either highly favorable or highly unfavorable. Relationship-oriented leaders are more effective in situations of moderate favorability.

Exhibit 3.3 Fiedler's Classification: How Leader Style Fits the Situation

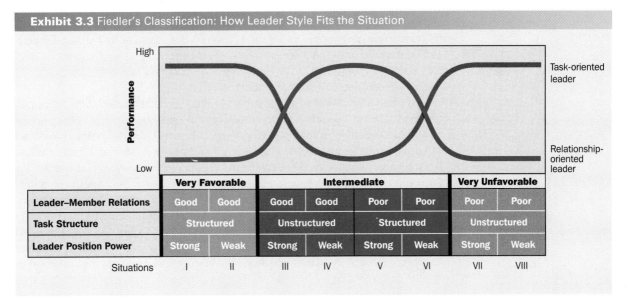

	Very Favorable		Intermediate				Very Unfavorable	
Leader–Member Relations	Good	Good	Good	Good	Poor	Poor	Poor	Poor
Task Structure	Structured		Unstructured		Structured		Unstructured	
Leader Position Power	Strong	Weak	Strong	Weak	Strong	Weak	Strong	Weak
Situations	I	II	III	IV	V	VI	VII	VIII

Source: Based on Fred E. Fiedler, "The Effects of Leadership Training and Experience: A Contingency Model Interpretation," *Administrative Science Quarterly* 17 (1972), p. 455.

The task-oriented leader excels in the favorable situation because everyone gets along, the task is clear, and the leader has power; all that is needed is for someone to take charge and provide direction. Similarly, if the situation is highly unfavorable to the leader, a great deal of structure and task direction is needed. A strong leader defines task structure and can establish authority over subordinates. Because leader–member relations are poor anyway, a strong task orientation will make no difference to the leader's popularity.

The relationship-oriented leader performs better in situations of intermediate favorability because human relations skills are important in achieving high group performance. In these situations, the leader may be moderately well liked, have some power, and supervise jobs that contain some ambiguity. A leader with good interpersonal skills can create a positive group atmosphere that will improve relationships, clarify task structure, and establish position power.

A leader, then, needs to know two things in order to use Fiedler's contingency theory. First, the leader should know whether he or she has a relationship- or task-oriented style. Second, the leader should diagnose the situation and determine whether leader–member relations, task structure, and position power are favorable or unfavorable. Consider the following example of Tom Freston, former CEO of MTV Networks and Viacom, Inc.

Tom Freston, Viacom, Inc.

A few years ago, Tom Freston was regarded as one of the best leaders in the entertainment industry. In the fall of 2006, the 26-year company veteran, credited with building MTV into a global powerhouse, was fired. What went wrong?

One way to look at Freston's rise and fall is to examine his leadership in terms of Fiedler's theory. As CEO of MTV Networks and later its parent company Viacom, Freston fostered a relaxed atmosphere and gave people freedom to explore, imagine, and make many of their own decisions. In interviews, he often credited employees for the company's success rather than taking all the applause for himself. Employees liked Freston's laid-back approach and appreciated his trust and respect for their judgment. For many years, MTV Networks and Viacom maintained a steady level of success under Freston's style of leadership.

But things in the media industry have changed dramatically with the emergence of Internet startups such as MySpace and YouTube. As the power of these new media outlets mushroomed, MTV began to lose its hip status. Viacom launched its own broadband channels, but they have fared poorly. At the same time, the traditional cable network audience is shrinking, along with advertising dollars. MTV's 2006 annual Video Music Awards provided the ultimate example of how much things have changed. Despite the show's serious star power, ratings fell nearly 30 percent from the previous year and nearly 50 percent from two years earlier.

Viacom's stock price has reflected the company's flagging fortunes. Chairman Sumner Redstone believed something had to be done, and fast. Despite his earlier support of Freston, Redstone convened the Viacom board and got their approval to fire the unsuspecting CEO. Redstone is now putting his hopes for Viacom's future on Philippe Dauman, a numbers-oriented former lawyer who says he's committed to putting the company "on the fast track."[5]

Action Memo

As a leader, you can effectively use a task-oriented style when the organizational situation is either highly favorable or highly unfavorable to your leadership. Use a relationship-oriented style in situations of intermediate favorability because human relations skills can create a positive atmosphere.

Tom Freston might be characterized as using a relationship-oriented style in an unfavorable situation. The environment has grown more challenging, the nature of tasks in the media industry is unstructured, and Freson's personal power with employees has begun to erode somewhat as the company has grown larger and faced bigger problems. Viacom Chairman Sumner Redstone grew impatient with the lack of results and the slow response to increased competition, and he felt that Freston's leadership approach was no longer working. Redstone believed a leader using a more task-oriented style might be able to impose the structure and discipline needed for the organization to succeed in its current situation. In discussing his appointment as the new CEO, Philippe Dauman said Redstone "told me I was the right guy at the right time."[6] Read the *Consider This* box for an interesting perspective on the disadvantages of persisting in a behavior style despite the processes of change.

An important contribution of Fiedler's research is that it goes beyond the notion of leadership styles to try to show how styles fit the situation. Many studies have been conducted to test Fiedler's model, and the research in general provides some support for the model.[7] However, Fiedler's model has also been criticized.[8] Using the LPC score as a measure of relationship- or task-oriented behavior seems simplistic to some researchers, and the weights used to determine situation favorability seem to have been determined in an arbitrary manner. In addition, some observers argue that the empirical support for the model is weak because it is based on correlational results that fail to achieve statistical significance in the majority of cases. The model also isn't clear about how the model works over time. For instance, if a task-oriented leader is matched with an unfavorable situation and is successful the organizational situation is likely to improve and become a situation more appropriate for a relationship-oriented leader.

Finally, Fiedler's model and much of the subsequent research fails to consider *medium* LPC leaders, who some studies indicate are more effective than either high or low LPC leaders in a majority of situations.[9] Leaders who score in the mid-range on the LPC scale presumably balance the concern for relationships

Consider This!

The phrase "too much of a good thing" is relevant in leadership. Behavior that becomes overbearing can be a disadvantage by ultimately resulting in the opposite of what the individual is hoping to achieve.

POLARITIES

All behavior consists of opposites or polarities. If I do anything more and more, over and over, its polarity will appear. For example, striving to be beautiful makes a person ugly, and trying too hard to be kind is a form of selfishness.

Any over-determined behavior produces its opposite:

- An obsession with living suggests worry about dying.
- True simplicity is not easy.
- Is it a long time or a short time since we last met?
- The braggart probably feels small and insecure.
- Who would be first ends up last.

Knowing how polarities work, the wise leader does not push to make things happen, but allows process to unfold on its own.

Source: John Heider, *The Tao of Leadership: Leadership Strategies for a New Age* (New York: Bantam Books, 1986), p. 3. Copyright 1985 Humanic Ltd., Atlanta, GA. Used with permission.

with a concern for task achievement more effectively than high or low LPC leaders, making them more adaptable to a variety of situations.

New research has continued to improve Fiedler's model,[10] and it is still considered an important contribution to leadership studies. However, its major impact may have been to stir other researchers to consider situational factors more seriously. A number of other situational theories have been developed in the years since Fiedler's original research.

Hersey and Blanchard's Situational Theory

The **situational theory** developed by Hersey and Blanchard is an interesting extension of the leadership grid outlined in Chapter 2. This approach focuses on the characteristics of followers as the important element of the situation, and consequently of determining effective leader behavior. The point of Hersey and Blanchard's theory is that subordinates vary in readiness level. People low in task readiness, because of little ability or training, or insecurity, need a different leadership style than those who are high in readiness and have good ability, skills, confidence, and willingness to work.[11]

According to the situational theory, a leader can adopt one of four leadership styles, based on a combination of relationship (concern for people) and task (concern for production) behavior. The appropriate style depends on the readiness level of followers. Exhibit 3.4 summarizes the relationship between leader style and follower readiness. The upper part of the exhibit indicates the four leader styles: telling, selling, participating, and delegating. The *telling style* reflects a high concern for tasks and a low concern for people and relationships. This is a very

Situational theory
Hersey and Blanchard's extension of the Leadership Grid focusing on the characteristics of followers as the important element of the situation, and consequently, of determining effective leader behavior

directive style. The leader gives explicit directions about how tasks should be accomplished. The *selling style* is based on a high concern for both relationships and tasks. With this approach, the leader explains decisions and gives followers a chance to ask questions and gain clarity about work tasks. The *participating style* is characterized by high relationship and low task behavior. The leader shares ideas with followers, encourages participation, and facilitates decision making. The fourth style, the *delegating style,* reflects a low concern for both tasks and re-lationships. This leader provides little direction or support because responsibility for decisions and their implementation is turned over to followers.

The bell-shaped curve in Exhibit 3.4 is called a prescriptive curve because it indicates when each leader style should be used. The readiness level of followers is indicated in the lower part of the exhibit. R1 is low readiness and R4 represents very high readiness. The essence of Hersey and Blanchard's situational theory is for the leader to diagnose a follower's readiness and select a style that is appropriate

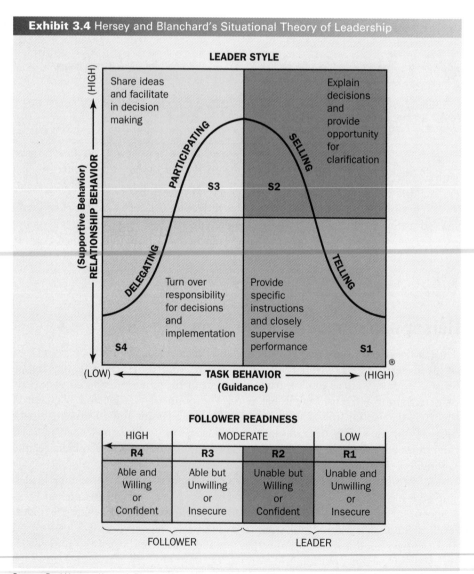

Exhibit 3.4 Hersey and Blanchard's Situational Theory of Leadership

Source: Paul Hersey, Kenneth Blanchard, and Dewey Johnson, *Management of Organizational Behavior: Utilizing Human Resources,* 7th ed. (Englewood Cliffs, NJ: Prentice Hall, 1996), p. 200. Used with permission.

for the readiness level, such as their degree of education and skills, experience, self-confidence, and work attitudes.

Low Readiness Level When one or more followers exhibit very low levels of readiness, the leader has to be very specific, "telling" followers exactly what to do, how to do it, and when. For example, Phil Hagans owns two McDonald's franchises in northeast Houston and gives many young workers their first job. He uses a telling style regarding everything from how to dress to the correct way to clean the grill, giving young workers the strong direction they need to develop to higher levels of skill and self-confidence.[12]

Moderate Readiness Level A selling leadership style works well when followers lack some education and experience for the job but demonstrate confidence, ability, interest, and willingness to learn. With a selling style, the leader gives some direction but also seeks input from and clarifies tasks for followers rather than merely instructing how tasks be performed. Kierstin Higgins, founder of Accommodations by Apple, a small company that handles corporate relocations, finds the selling style appropriate for her young employees, who are very energetic and enthusiastic about their jobs but have not yet gained a lot of experience. By seeking their input and clarifying tasks, Higgins believes she helps her workers learn from the challenges they face rather than being frustrated by them.[13]

High Readiness Level A participating style can be effective when followers have the necessary education, skills, and experience, but they might be insecure in their abilities and need some guidance from the leader. The leader can guide followers' development and act as a resource for advice and assistance. An example of the participating style is Eric Brevig, a visual-effects supervisor with Industrial Light and Magic, who maximizes the creativity of artists and animators by encouraging participation. Rather than telling people how to do their jobs, Brevig presents them with a challenge and works with them to figure out the best way to meet it.[14]

Very High Readiness Level The delegating style of leadership can be effectively used when followers have very high levels of education, experience, and readiness to accept responsibility for their own task behavior. The leader provides a general goal and sufficient authority to do the tasks as followers see fit. Highly educated professionals such as lawyers, college professors, and social workers would typically fall into this category. There are followers in almost every organization who demonstrate high readiness. For example, many fast-food outlets have had great success hiring retirees for part-time jobs. These older employees often have high levels of readiness because of their vast experience and positive attitudes, and leaders can effectively use a delegating style.

In summary, the telling style works best for followers who demonstrate very low levels of readiness to take responsibility for their own task behavior, the selling and participating styles are effective for followers with moderate-to-high readiness, and the delegating style is appropriate for employees with very high readiness.

This contingency model is easier to understand than Fiedler's model because it focuses only on the characteristics of followers, not those of the larger

Action Memo
As a leader, you can tell followers how to perform their tasks if they have few skills, little experience, or low self-confidence. If followers have a moderate degree of skill and show enthusiasm and willingness to learn, provide direction but seek followers' input and explain your decisions.

Action Memo
As a leader, you can act as a resource to provide advice and assistance when followers have a high level of skill, experience, and responsibility. Delegate responsibility for decisions and their implementation to followers who have very high levels of skill and positive attitudes.

A leader's style can be contingent upon the readiness level of followers. Think of yourself working in your current or former job. Answer the questions below based on how you are on that job. Please answer whether each item below is Mostly False or Mostly True for you in that job.

	Mostly False	Mostly True
1. I typically do the exact work required of me, nothing more or less.	_____	_____
2. I am often bored and uninterested in the tasks I have to perform.	_____	_____
3. I take extended breaks whenever I can.	_____	_____
4. I have great interest and enthusiasm for the job.	_____	_____
5. I am recognized as an expert by colleagues and coworkers	_____	_____
6. I have a need to perform to the best of my ability.	_____	_____
7. I have a great deal of relevant education and experience for this type of work.	_____	_____
8. I am involved in "extra-work" activities such as committees.	_____	_____
9. I prioritize my work and manage my time well.	_____	_____

Scoring and Interpretation

In the Situational Theory of Leadership, the higher the follower's readiness, the more participative and delegating the leader can be. Give yourself one point for each Mostly False answer to items 1–3 and one point for each Mostly True answer to items 4–9. A score of 8–9 points would suggest a "very high" readiness level. A score of 7–8 points would indicate a "high" readiness level. A score of 4–6 points would suggest "moderate" readiness, and 0–3 points would indicate "low" readiness. What is the appropriate leadership style for your readiness level? What leadership style did your supervisor use with you? What do you think accounted for your supervisor's style? Discuss your results with other students to explore which leadership styles are actually used with subordinates who are at different readiness levels.

Action Memo

Answer the questions in Leader's Self-Insight 3.2 to determine your own readiness level and the style of leadership that would be most appropriate for you as a follower.

situation. The leader should evaluate subordinates and adopt whichever style is needed. The leader's style can be tailored to individual subordinates similar to the leader–member exchange theory described in Chapter 2. If one follower is at a low level of readiness, the leader must be very specific, telling exactly what to do, how to do it, and when. For a follower high in readiness, the leader provides a general goal and sufficient authority to do the task as the follower sees fit. Leaders can carefully diagnose the readiness level of followers and then tell, sell, participate, or delegate.

Classroom teachers face one of the toughest leadership challenges around because they usually deal with students who are at widely different levels of readiness. Consider how Carole McGraw of the Detroit, Michigan, school system met the challenge.

Carole McGraw, Detroit Public Schools

IN THE LEAD

Carole McGraw describes what she sees when she walks into a classroom for the first time: "A ubiquitous sea of easily recognizable faces. There's Jamie, whose eyes glow with enthusiasm for learning. And Terrell, who just came from the crib after having no breakfast, no supervision of his inadequate homework, and a chip on his shoulder because he needed to flip hamburgers 'til 10 o'clock at night. . . . And Matt, who slumps over his desk, fast asleep from the Ritalin he took for a learning disorder that was probably misdiagnosed to correct a behavior problem. . . ." And on and on.

McGraw diagnosed what teenagers have in common to find the best way to help students of such varying degrees of readiness learn. She realized that teenagers are exposed to countless hours of social networking Web sites, television programs, CDs, and disc jockeys. They spend a lot of time playing sports, eating junk food, talking on the phone, playing computer games, going to the movies, reading pop magazines, hanging out with peers, and avoiding adults. After considering this, McGraw developed her teaching method focused on three concepts: painless, interesting, and enjoyable. Students in McGraw's biology class now do almost all of their work in labs or teamwork sessions. During the labs, a captain is selected to act as team leader. In teams, students select a viable problem to investigate and then split up the work and conduct research in books, on the Internet, and in laboratory experiments. Teams also spend a lot of time engaged in dialogue and brainstorming. McGraw will throw out an idea and let the students take off with it.

McGraw's teaching method combines telling and participating. Students are provided with direction about certain concepts, vocabulary words, and so forth that they must master, along with guidelines for doing so. This provides the structure and discipline some of her low-readiness level students need to succeed. However, most of her leadership focuses on supporting students as they learn and grow on their own. Does McGraw's innovative approach work? Sixty percent of the students get a grade of A and all score fairly well on objective tests McGraw gives after the teamwork is complete. Students from her classes score great on standardized tests like the SAT because they not only accumulate a lot of knowledge but also gain self-confidence and learn how to think on their feet. "All the stress my kids lived with for years disappears," McGraw says. "My classroom buzzes with new ideas and individual approaches."[15]

Path–Goal Theory

Another contingency approach to leadership is called the path–goal theory.[16] According to the **path–goal theory**, the leader's responsibility is to increase subordinates' motivation to attain personal and organizational goals. As illustrated in Exhibit 3.5, the leader increases follower motivation by either (1) clarifying the follower's path to the rewards that are available or (2) increasing the rewards that the follower values and desires. Path clarification means that the leader works with subordinates to help them identify and learn the behaviors that will lead to successful task accomplishment and organizational rewards. Increasing rewards means that the leader talks with subordinates to learn which rewards are important to them—that is, whether they desire intrinsic rewards from the work itself or extrinsic rewards such as raises or promotions. The leader's job is to increase personal payoffs to subordinates for goal attainment and to make the paths to these payoffs clear and easy to travel.[17]

This model is called a contingency theory because it consists of three sets of contingencies—leader style, followers and situation, and the rewards to meet followers' needs.[18] Whereas the Fiedler theory made the assumption that new leaders could take over as situations change, in the path–goal theory, leaders change their behaviors to match the situation.

Leader Behavior

The path–goal theory suggests a fourfold classification of leader behaviors.[19] These classifications are the types of behavior the leader can

Path–goal theory
a contingency approach to leadership in which the leader's responsibility is to increase subordinates' motivation by clarifying the behaviors necessary for task accomplishment and rewards

Action Memo
As a leader, you can increase follower motivation, satisfaction and performance by adopting a leadership behavior that will clarify the follower's path to receiving available rewards or increase the availability of rewards the follower desires.

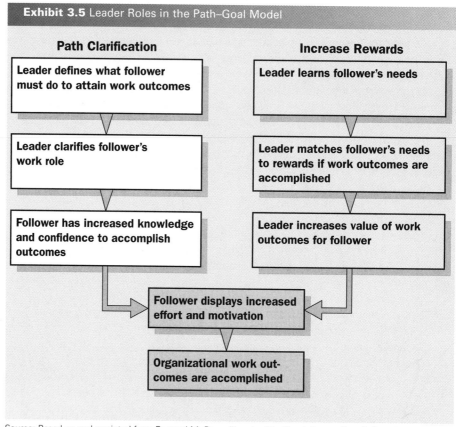

Exhibit 3.5 Leader Roles in the Path–Goal Model

Path Clarification

Leader defines what follower must do to attain work outcomes

Leader clarifies follower's work role

Follower has increased knowledge and confidence to accomplish outcomes

Increase Rewards

Leader learns follower's needs

Leader matches follower's needs to rewards if work outcomes are accomplished

Leader increases value of work outcomes for follower

Follower displays increased effort and motivation

Organizational work outcomes are accomplished

Source: Based on and reprinted from Bernard M. Bass, "Leadership: Good, Better, Best," *Organizational Dynamics* 13 (Winter 1985), pp. 26–40. Copyright 1985, with permission from Elsevier.

adopt and include supportive, directive, achievement-oriented, and participative styles.

Supportive leadership shows concern for subordinates' well-being and personal needs. Leadership behavior is open, friendly, and approachable, and the leader creates a team climate and treats subordinates as equals. Supportive leadership is similar to the consideration or people-oriented leadership described earlier.

Directive leadership tells subordinates exactly what they are supposed to do. Leader behavior includes planning, making schedules, setting performance goals and behavior standards, and stressing adherence to rules and regulations. Directive leadership behavior is similar to the initiating structure or task-oriented leadership style described earlier.

Participative leadership consults with subordinates about decisions. Leader behavior includes asking for opinions and suggestions, encouraging participation in decision making, and meeting with subordinates in their workplaces. The participative leader encourages group discussion and written suggestions, similar to the selling or participating style in the Hersey and Blanchard model.

Achievement-oriented leadership sets clear and challenging goals for subordinates. Leader behavior stresses high-quality performance and improvement over current performance. Achievement-oriented leaders also show confidence in subordinates and assist them in learning how to achieve high goals.

To illustrate achievement-oriented leadership, consider the training of army officers in the Reserve Officers' Training Corps (ROTC). This training goes far beyond how to command a platoon. It involves the concepts of motivation, responsibility, and the creation of a team in which decision making is expected of everyone. Fundamentally, this training will enable officers to respond to any situation, not just those outlined in the manual. Thus achievement-oriented leadership is demonstrated: The set goals are challenging, require improvement, and demonstrate confidence in the abilities of subordinates.[20]

The four types of leader behavior are not considered ingrained personality traits as in the earlier trait theories; rather, they reflect types of behavior that every leader is able to adopt, depending on the situation.

Situational Contingencies

The two important situational contingencies in the path–goal theory are (1) the personal characteristics of group members and (2) the work environment. Personal characteristics of followers are similar to Hersey and Blanchard's readiness level and include such factors as ability, skills, needs, and motivations. For example, if an employee has a low level of ability or skill, the leader may need to provide additional training or coaching in order for the worker to improve performance. If a subordinate is self-centered, the leader may use monetary rewards to motivate him or her. Subordinates who want or need clear direction and authority require a directive leader to tell them exactly what to do. Craft workers and professionals, however, may want more freedom and autonomy and work best under a participative leadership style.

The work environment contingencies include the degree of task structure, the nature of the formal authority system, and the work group itself. The task structure is similar to the same concept described in Fiedler's contingency theory; it includes the extent to which tasks are defined and have explicit job descriptions and work procedures. The formal authority system includes the amount of legitimate power used by leaders and the extent to which policies and rules constrain employees' behavior. Work-group characteristics consist of the educational level of subordinates and the quality of relationships among them.

Use of Rewards

Recall that the leader's responsibility is to clarify *the path to rewards* for followers or to increase *the amount of rewards* to enhance satisfaction and job performance. In some situations, the leader works with subordinates to help them acquire the skills and confidence needed to perform tasks and achieve rewards already available. In others, the leader may develop new rewards to meet the specific needs of subordinates.

Exhibit 3.6 illustrates four examples of how leadership behavior is tailored to the situation. In the first situation, the subordinate lacks confidence; thus, the supportive leadership style provides the social support with which to encourage the subordinate to undertake the behavior needed to do the work and receive the rewards. In the second situation, the job is ambiguous, and the employee is not performing effectively. Directive leadership behavior is used to give instructions and clarify the task so that the follower will know how to accomplish it and receive rewards. In the third situation, the subordinate is unchallenged by the task; thus, an achievement-oriented behavior is used to set higher goals. This clarifies the path to rewards for the employee. In the fourth situation, an incorrect reward is given to a subordinate, and the participative leadership style is used to

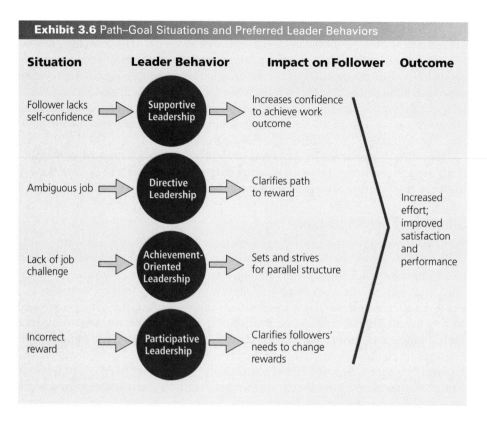

Exhibit 3.6 Path–Goal Situations and Preferred Leader Behaviors

change this. By discussing the subordinate's needs, the leader is able to identify the correct reward for task accomplishment. In all four cases, the outcome of fitting the leadership behavior to the situation produces greater employee effort by either clarifying how subordinates can receive rewards or changing the rewards to fit their needs.

At The Home Depot, former CEO Bob Nardelli reinvigorated employee morale—and retail sales—with his achievement-oriented leadership, which cascades down from headquarters to the store level.

Bob Nardelli, The Home Depot

When Bob Nardelli took over as CEO of The Home Depot, one of his first moves was to impose high goals for everyone from headquarters down to the store level. By doing so, he turned a retail chain where employees were becoming complacent and bored into a company full of enterprising people who thrive on challenge, responsibility, and recognition.

Many low-performing store managers, who were accustomed to a more relaxed approach, left the company. Nardelli slowly began building a cadre of talented people, from top to bottom, and instituting a "no-bull performance culture" that gave people challenging goals and generous rewards for achieving them. Rigorous talent assessments, new approaches to hiring, new performance measurement systems, and programs such as the Store Leadership Program and Accelerated Leadership Program enhanced employee skills and reduced turnover. Nardelli monitored stores in real time via computer, and he spent 1 week a quarter as a "mystery shopper," popping in unannounced to as many as 10 stores a day.

Nardelli's achievement-oriented leadership worked. Within five years, sales grew from $45.7 billion to around $80 billion, earnings per share increased by 20 percent annually, and the retailer gained an edge in lucrative new segments, such as the $410 billion professional construction market. "His real ability," says Jack Welch, who was Nardelli's boss at General Electric, "is to motivate lots of people around a mission, excite them about it, and make it happen."[21]

Bob Nardelli's achievement-oriented leadership encouraged every manager in the organization to focus on keeping people challenged and motivated to reach goals. Despite Nardelli's success increasing sales and profits at the retail chain, however, Home Depot's stock price did not increase. Unhappy shareholders, concerns over Nardelli's huge pay package, his refusal to tie his stock awards to shareholder gains, and growing resentment over Nardelli's often brusque approach led Nardelli and the board to mutually agree that he would resign in early 2007.[22] Nardelli's rise and abrubt fall at The Home Depot provides a good example of how an achievement-oriented leader can drive positive internal performance but still face external dissatisfaction in today's corporate environment.

Path–goal theorizing can be complex, but much of the research on it has been encouraging.[23] Using the model to specify precise relationships and make exact predictions about employee outcomes may be difficult, but the four types of leader behavior and the ideas for fitting them to situational contingencies provide a useful way for leaders to think about motivating subordinates.

The Vroom–Jago Contingency Model

The **Vroom–Jago contingency model** shares some basic principles with the previous models, yet it differs in significant ways as well. This model focuses specifically on varying degrees of participative leadership, and how each level of participation influences quality and accountability of decisions. A number of situational factors shape the likelihood that either a participative or autocratic approach will produce the best outcome.

This model starts with the idea that a leader faces a problem that requires a solution. Decisions to solve the problem might be made by a leader alone, or through inclusion of a number of followers.

The Vroom–Jago model is very applied, which means that it tells the leader precisely the correct amount of participation by subordinates to use in making a particular decision.[24] The model has three major components: leader participation styles, a set of diagnostic questions with which to analyze a decision situation, and a series of decision rules.

Leader Participation Styles

The model employs five levels of subordinate participation in decision making, ranging from highly autocratic (leader decides alone) to highly democratic (leader delegates to group), as illustrated in Exhibit 3.7.[25] The exhibit shows five decision styles, starting with the leader making the decision alone (Decide), presenting the problem to subordinates individually for their suggestions, and then making the decision (Consult Individually), presenting the problem to subordinates as a group, collectively obtaining their ideas and suggestions, then making the decision (Consult Group), sharing the problem with subordinates as a group and acting as a facilitator to help the group arrive at a decision (Facilitate), or delegating the problem and permitting the group to make the decision within prescribed limits

Vroom–Jago contingency model
a contingency model that focuses on varying degrees of participative leadership, and how each level of participation influences quality and accountability of decisions.

Exhibit 3.7 Five Leader Decision Styles

Area of Influence by Leader				Area of Freedom for Group
Decide	**Consult Individually**	**Consult Group**	**Facilitate**	**Delegate**
You make the decision alone and either announce or "sell" it to the group. You may use your expertise in collecting information that you deem relevant to the problem from the group or others.	You present the problem to the group members individually, get their suggestions, and make the decision.	You present the problem to the group members in a meeting, get their suggestions, and then make the decision.	You present the problem to the group in a meeting. You act as facilitator, defining the problem to be solved and the boundaries within which the decision must be made. Your objective is to get concurrence on a decision. Above all, you take care to show that your ideas are not given any greater weight that those of others simply because of your position.	You permit the group to make the decision within prescribed limits. The group undertakes the identification and diagnosis of the problem, developing alternative procedures for solving it, and deciding on one or more alternative solutions. While you play no direct role in the group's deliberations unless explicitly asked, your role is an improtant one behind the scenes, providing needed resources and encouragement.

Source: Victor H. Vroom, "Leadership and the Decision Making Process," *Organizational Dynamics* 28, no. 4 (Spring 2000), pp. 82–94. This is Vroom's adaptation of Tannenbaum and Schmidt's Taxonomy.

(Delegate). The five styles fall along a continuum, and the leader should select one depending on the situation.

Diagnostic Questions

How does a leader decide which of the five decision styles to use? The appropriate degree of decision participation depends on a number of situational factors, such as the required level of decision quality, the level of leader or subordinate expertise, and the importance of having subordinates commit to the decision. Leaders can analyze the appropriate degree of participation by answering seven diagnostic questions.

1. **Decision significance:** *How significant is this decision for the project or organization?* If the decision is highly important and a high-quality decision is needed for the success of the project or organization, the leader has to be actively involved.

2. **Importance of commitment:** *How important is subordinate commitment to carrying out the decision?* If implementation requires a high level of commitment to the decision, leaders should involve subordinates in the decision process.

3. **Leader expertise:** *What is the level of the leader's expertise in relation to the problem?* If the leader does not have a high amount of information, knowledge, or expertise, the leader should involve subordinates to obtain it.

4. **Likelihood of commitment:** *If the leader were to make the decision alone, would subordinates have high or low commitment to the decision?* If subordinates typically go along with whatever the leader decides, their involvement in the decision-making process will be less important.

5. **Group support for goals:** *What is the degree of subordinate support for the team's or organization's objectives at stake in this decision?* If subordinates have low support for the goals of the organization, the leader should not allow the group to make the decision alone.

6. **Goal expertise:** *What is the level of group members' knowledge and expertise in relation to the problem?* If subordinates have a high level of expertise in relation to the problem, more responsibility for the decision can be delegated to them.

7. **Team competence:** *How skilled and committed are group members to working together as a team to solve problems?* When subordinates have high skills and high desire to work together cooperatively to solve problems, more responsibility for the decision making can be delegated to them.

These questions seem detailed, but considering these seven situational factors can quickly narrow the options and point to the appropriate level of group participation in decision making.

Selecting a Decision Style

Further development of the Vroom–Jago model added concern for time constraints and concern for follower development as explicit criteria for determining the level of participation. That is, a leader considers the relative importance of time versus follower development in selecting a decision style. This led to the development of two decision matrixes, *a time-based model,* to be used if time is critical, for example, if the organization is facing a crisis and a decision must be made immediately, and a *development-based model,* to be used if time and efficiency are less important criteria than the opportunity to develop the thinking and decision-making skills of followers.

Consider the example of a small auto parts manufacturer, which owns only one machine for performing welds on mufflers. If the machine has broken down and production has come to a standstill, a decision concerning the purchase of a new machine is critical and has to be made immediately to get the production line moving again. In this case, a leader would follow the time-based model for selecting the decision style. However, if the machine is scheduled for routine replacement in three months, time is not a critical factor. The leader is then free to consider the importance of involving production workers in the decision making to develop their skills. Thus, the leader may follow the development-based model because time is not a critical concern.

Exhibits 3.8 and 3.9 illustrate the two decision matrixes—a time-based model and a development-based model—that enables leaders to adopt a participation style by answering the diagnostic questions in sequence. Returning to the example of the welding machine, if the machine has broken down and must be replaced immediately, the leader would follow the time-based model in Exhibit 3.8. The leader enters the matrix at the left side, at Problem Statement, and considers the seven situational questions in sequence from left to right, answering high (H) or low (L) to each one and avoiding crossing any horizontal lines.

Action Memo
As a leader, you can use the Vroom–Jago model to determine the appropriate amount of follower participation to use in making a decision. You can follow the time-based guidelines when time is of the essence, but use development-based guidelines when cultivating followers' decision-making skills is also important.

Exhibit 3.8 Time-Driven Model for Determining an Appropriate Decision-Making Style—Group Problems

Instructions: The matrix operates like a funnel. You start at the left with a specific decision problem in mind. The column headings denote situational factors which may or may not be present in that problem. You progress by selecting High or Low (H or L) for each relevant situational factor. Proceed down from the funnel, judging only those situational factors for which a judgment is called for, until you reach the recommended process.

The table below represents the PROBLEM STATEMENT funnel.

Decision Significance?	Importance of Commitment?	Leader Expertise?	Likelihood of Commitment?	Group Support?	Group Expertise?	Team Competence?	Process
H	H	H	H	—	—	—	Decide
H	H	H	L	H	H	H	Delegate
H	H	H	L	H	H	L	Consult (Group)
H	H	H	L	H	L	—	Consult (Group)
H	H	H	L	L	—	—	Consult (Group)
H	H	L	H	H	H	H	Facilitate
H	H	L	H	H	H	L	Consult (Individually)
H	H	L	H	H	L	—	Consult (Individually)
H	H	L	H	L	—	—	Consult (Individually)
H	H	L	L	H	H	H	Facilitate
H	H	L	L	H	H	L	Consult (Group)
H	H	L	L	H	L	—	Consult (Group)
H	H	L	L	L	—	—	Consult (Group)
H	L	H	—	—	—	—	Decide
H	L	L	—	H	H	H	Facilitate
H	L	L	—	H	H	L	Consult (Individually)
H	L	L	—	H	L	—	Consult (Individually)
H	L	L	—	L	—	—	Consult (Individually)
L	H	—	H	—	—	—	Decide
L	H	—	L	—	—	H	Delegate
L	H	—	L	—	—	L	Facilitate
L	L	—	—	—	—	—	Decide

Source: Victor H. Vroom, "Leadership and the Decision Making Process," *Organizational Dynamics* 28, no. 4 (Spring 2000), pp. 82–94.

Exhibit 3.9 Development-Driven Model for Determining an Appropriate Decision-Making Style—Group Problems

Decision Significance?	Importance of Commitment?	Leader Expertise?	Likelihood of Commitment?	Group Support?	Group Expertise?	Team Competence?	
H	H	-	H	H	H	H	Delegate
						L	Facilitate
					L	-	Consult (Group)
				L	-	-	Consult (Group)
			L	H	H	H	Delegate
						L	Facilitate
					L	-	Facilitate
				L	-	-	Consult (Group)
	L	-	-	H	H	H	Delegate
						L	Facilitate
					L	-	Consult (Group)
				L	-	-	Consult (Group)
L	H	-	H	-	-	-	Decide
			L	-	-	-	Delegate
	L	-	-	-	-	-	Decide

Source: Victor H. Vroom, "Leadership and the Decision Making Process," *Organizational Dynamics* 28, no. 4 (Spring 2000), pp. 82–94.

The first question would be: *How significant is this decision for the project or organization?* If the answer is High, the leader proceeds to importance of commitment: *How important is subordinate commitment to carrying out the decision?* If the answer is High, the next question pertains to leader expertise: *What is the level of the leader's expertise in relation to the problem?* If the leader's knowledge and expertise is High, the leader next considers likelihood of commitment: *If the leader were to make the decision alone, how likely is it that subordinates would be committed to the decision?* If there is a high likelihood that subordinates would be committed, the decision matrix leads directly to the Decide style of decision making, in which the leader makes the decision alone and presents it to the group.

As noted earlier, this matrix assumes that time and efficiency are the most important criteria. However, consider how the selection of a decision style would differ if the leader had several months to replace the welding machine and considered follower development of high importance and time of little concern. In this case, the leader would follow the development-driven decision matrix in

Exhibit 3.9. Beginning again at the left side of the matrix: *How significant is this decision for the project or organization?* If the answer is High, proceed to importance of commitment: *How important is subordinate commitment?* If high, the next question concerns likelihood of commitment (leader expertise is not considered because the development model is focused on involving subordinates, even if the leader has knowledge and expertise): *If the leader were to make the decision alone, how likely is it that subordinates would be committed to the decision?* If there is a high likelihood, the leader next considers group support: *What is the degree of subordinate support for the team's or organization's objectives at stake in this decision?* If the degree of support for goals is low, the leader would proceed directly to the Group Consult decision style. However, if the degree of support for goals is high, the leader would then ask: *What is the level of group members' knowledge and expertise in relation to the problem?* An answer of High would take the leader to the question: *How skilled and committed are group members to working together as a team to solve problems?* An answer of High would lead to the delegate style, in which the leader allows the group to make the decision within certain limits.

Note that the time-driven model takes the leader to the first decision style that preserves decision quality and follower acceptance, whereas the development-driven model takes other considerations into account. It takes less time to make an autocratic decision (Decide) than to involve subordinates by using a Facilitate or Delegate style. However, in many cases, time and efficiency are less important than the opportunity to further subordinate development. In many of today's organizations, where knowledge sharing and widespread participation are considered critical to organizational success, leaders are placing greater emphasis on follower development when time is not a critical issue.

Leaders can quickly learn to use the model to adapt their styles to fit the situation. However, researchers have also developed a computer-based program that allows for greater complexity and precision in the Vroom–Jago model and incorporates the value of time and value of follower development as situational factors rather than portraying them in separate decision matrixes.

The Vroom–Jago model has been criticized as being less than perfect,[26] but it is useful to decision makers, and the body of supportive research is growing.[27] Leaders can learn to use the model to make timely, high-quality decisions. Let's try applying the model to the following problem.

Dave Robbins, Whitlock Manufacturing

IN THE LEAD

When Whitlock Manufacturing won a contract from a large auto manufacturer to produce an engine to power its flagship sports car, Dave Robbins was thrilled to be selected as a project manager. The engine, of Japanese design and extremely complex, has gotten rave reviews in the automotive press. This project has dramatically enhanced the reputation of Whitlock Manufacturing, which was previously known primarily as a producer of outboard engines for marine use.

Robbins and his team of engineers have taken great pride in their work on the project, but their excitement was dashed by a recent report of serious engine problems in cars delivered to customers. Fourteen owners of cars produced during the first month have experienced engine seizures. Taking quick action, the auto manufacturer suspended sales of the sports car, halted current production, and notified owners of the current model not to drive the car. Everyone involved knows this is a disaster. Unless the engine problem is solved quickly, Whitlock Manufacturing could be exposed to extended litigation. In addition, Whitlock's valued relationship with one of the world's largest auto manufacturers would probably be lost forever.

As the person most knowledgeable about the engine, Robbins has spent two weeks in the field inspecting the seized engines and the auto plant where they were installed. In addition, he has carefully examined the operations and practices in Whitlock's plant where the engine is manufactured. Based on this extensive research, Robbins is convinced that he knows what the problem is and the best way to solve it. However, his natural inclination is to involve other team members as much as possible in making decisions and solving problems. He not only values their input, but thinks that by encouraging greater participation he strengthens the thinking skills of team members, helping them grow and contribute more to the team and the organization. Therefore, Robbins chooses to consult with his team before making his final decision. The group meets for several hours that afternoon, discussing the problem in detail and sharing their varied perspectives, including the information Robbins has gathered during his research. Following the group session, Robbins makes his decision. He will present the decision at the team meeting the following morning, after which testing and correction of the engine problem will begin.[28]

In the Whitlock Manufacturing case, either a time-driven or a development-driven decision tree can be used to select a decision style. Although time is of importance, a leader's desire to involve subordinates can be considered equally important. Do you think Robbins used the correct leader decision style? Let's examine the problem using the development-based decision tree, since Robbins is concerned about involving other team members. Moving from left to right in Exhibit 3.9, the questions and answers are as follows: *How significant is this decision for the organization?* Definitely high. Quality of the decision is of critical importance. The company's future may be at stake. *How important is subordinate commitment to carrying out the decision?* Also high. The team members must support and implement Robbins's solution. *If Robbins makes the decision on his own, will team members have high or low commitment to it?* The answer to this question is probably also high. Team members respect Robbins, and they are likely to accept his analysis of the problem. This leads to the question, *What is the degree of subordinate support for the team's or organization's objectives at stake in this decision?* Definitely high. This leads to the question, *What is the level of group members' knowledge and expertise in relation to the problem?* The answer to this question is probably Low, which leads to the Consult Group decision style. Thus, Robbins used the style that would be recommended by the Vroom–Jago model.

Now, assume that Robbins chose to place more emphasis on time than on participant involvement and development. Using the time-based decision matrix in Exhibit 3.8, trace the questions and answers based on the information just provided and rate Robbins's level of expertise as high. Remember to avoid crossing any horizontal lines. What decision style is recommended? Is it the same or different from that recommended by the development-based tree?

Substitutes for Leadership

The contingency leadership approaches considered so far have focused on the leader's style, the follower's nature, and the situation's characteristics. The final contingency approach suggests that situational variables can be so powerful that they actually substitute for or neutralize the need for leadership.[29] This approach outlines those organizational settings in which task-oriented and people-oriented leadership styles are unimportant or unnecessary.

Exhibit 3.10 Substitutes and Neutralizers for Leadership

Variable		Task-Oriented Leadership	People-Oriented Leadership
Organizational variables:	Group cohesiveness	Substitutes for	Substitutes for
	Formalization	Substitutes for	No effect on
	Inflexibility	Neutralizes	No effect on
	Low positional power	Neutralizes	Neutralizes
	Physical separation	Neutralizes	Neutralizes
Task characteristics:	Highly structured task	Substitutes for	No effect on
	Automatic feedback	Substitutes for	No effect on
	Intrinsic satisfaction	No effect on	Substitutes for
Follower characteristics:	Professionalism	Substitutes for	Substitutes for
	Training/experience	Substitutes for	No effect on
	Low value of rewards	Neutralizes	Neutralizes

Substitute
a situational variable that makes leadership unnecessary or redundant

Neutralizer
a situational characteristic that counteracts the leadership style and prevents the leader from displaying certain behaviors

Exhibit 3.10 shows the situational variables that tend to substitute for or neutralize leadership characteristics. A **substitute** for leadership makes the leadership style unnecessary or redundant. For example, highly educated, professional subordinates who know how to do their tasks do not need a leader who initiates structure for them and tells them what to do. In addition, long-term education often develops autonomous, self-motivated individuals. Thus, task-oriented and people-oriented leadership is substituted by professional education and socialization.[30]

A **neutralizer** counteracts the leadership style and prevents the leader from displaying certain behaviors. For example, if a leader is physically removed from subordinates, the leader's ability to give directions to subordinates is greatly reduced. Kinko's, a nationwide copy center, includes numerous locations widely scattered across regions. Regional managers enjoy very limited personal interaction due to the distances between stores. Thus, their ability to both support and direct is neutralized.

Situational variables in Exhibit 3.10 include characteristics of the followers, the task, and the organization itself. For example, when subordinates are highly professional, such as research scientists in companies like Merck or Monsanto, both leadership styles are less important. The employees do not need either direction or support. With respect to task characteristics, highly structured tasks substitute for a task-oriented style, and a satisfying task substitutes for a people-oriented style. When a task is highly structured and routine, like auditing cash, the leader should provide personal consideration and support that is not provided by the task. Satisfied people don't need as much consideration. Likewise, with respect to the organization itself, group cohesiveness substitutes for both leader styles. For example, the relationship that develops among air traffic controllers and jet fighter pilots is characterized by high-stress interactions and continuous peer training. This cohesiveness provides support and direction that substitutes for formal leadership.[31] Formalized rules and procedures substitute for leader task orientation because the rules tell people what to do. Physical separation of leader and subordinate neutralizes both leadership styles.

The value of the situations described in Exhibit 3.10 is that they help leaders avoid leadership overkill. Leaders should adopt a style

Action Memo
As a leader, you can avoid leadership overkill. Adopt a style that is complementary to the organizational situation to ensure that both task needs and people needs are met.

Action Memo
Measure how the task characteristics of your job or a job you've held in the past might act as substitutes for leadership by answering the questions in Leader's Self-Insight 3.3.

Measuring Substitutes for Leadership

Think about your current job, or a job you have held in the past. Please answer whether each item below is Mostly False or Mostly True for you in that job.

TASK STRUCTURE

	Mostly False	Mostly True
1. Because of the nature of the tasks I perform, there is little doubt about the best way to do them.		
2. My job duties are so simple that almost anyone could perform them well after a little instruction.		
3. It is difficult to figure out the best way to do many of my tasks and activities.		
4. There is really only one correct way to perform most of the tasks I do.		

TASK FEEDBACK

5. After I've completed a task, I can tell right away from the results I get whether I have performed it correctly.		
6. My job is the kind where you can finish a task and not know if you've made a mistake or error.		
7. Because of the nature of the tasks I do, it is easy for me to see when I have done something exceptionally well.		

INTRINSIC SATISFACTION

8. I get lots of satisfaction from the work I do.		
9. It is hard to imagine that anyone could enjoy performing the tasks I have performed on my job.		
10. My job satisfaction depends primarily on the nature of the tasks and activities I perform.		

Scoring and Interpretation

For your task structure score, give yourself one point for Mostly True answers to items 1, 2, and 4, and for a Mostly False answer to item 3. This is your score for Task Structure: _____

For your task feedback score, give yourself one point for Mostly True answers to items 5 and 7, and for a Mostly False answer to item 6. This is your score for Task Feedback: _____

For your intrinsic satisfaction score, score one point for Mostly True answers to items 8 and 10, and for a Mostly False answer to item 9. This is your score for Intrinsic Satisfaction: _____

A high score (3 or 4) for Task Structure or Task Feedback indicates a high potential for those elements to act as a substitute for *task-oriented leadership*. A high score (3) for Intrinsic Satisfaction indicates the potential to be a substitute for *people-oriented leadership*. Does your leader adopt a style that is complementary to the task situation, or is the leader guilty of *leadership overkill*? How can you apply this understanding to your own actions as a leader?

Source: Based on "Questionnaire Items for the Measurement of Substitutes for Leadership," Table 2 in Steven Kerr and John M. Jermier, "Substitutes for Leadership: Their Meaning and Measurement," *Organizational Behavior and Human Performance* 22 (1978), pp. 375–403.

with which to complement the organizational situation. For example, the work situation for bank tellers provides a high level of formalization, little flexibility, and a highly structured task. The head teller should not adopt a task-oriented style because the organization already provides structure and direction. The head teller should concentrate on a people-oriented style. In other organizations, if group cohesiveness or previous training meets employee social needs, the leader is free to concentrate on task-oriented behaviors. The leader can adopt a style complementary to the organizational situation to ensure that both task needs and people needs of followers are met. Leadership overkill can help to explain the problems Lawrence Summers encountered as president of Harvard University.

Lawrence H. Summers, Harvard University

Leading a major university has many challenges, and one of the biggest is choosing the right approach with deans, faculty members, and other professionals who are highly educated, independent, and often perform their jobs as much for the intrinsic satisfaction of the work as for the pay and other extrinsic benefits.

As president of Harvard University, former U.S. Treasury Secretary Lawrence Summers tried to use a heavy, primarily task-oriented style of leadership, which led to serious conflicts with some faculty members and eventual demands for his ouster. The assertive top-down style rankled followers who have been accustomed to thinking of themselves not as employees but as partners in an academic enterprise. Faculty members at Harvard, as at many universities, have long been used to decentralized, democratic decision making, such as having a say in matters such as department mergers or new programs of study. Summers made many decisions on his own that followers thought should be put to a faculty vote and then used a directive style to get things done.

Although students in general supported Summers, the conflicts and a vote of no-confidence from some faculty convinced Summers to resign with many of his goals and plans for the university unrealized. There are a variety of reasons for Summers' troubles and eventual departure, but his heavy-handed task-oriented approach likely played a role.[32]

> **Action Memo**
> As a leader, you can use a people-oriented style when tasks are highly structured and followers are bound by formal rules and procedures. You can adopt a task-oriented style if group cohesiveness and followers' intrinsic job satisfaction meet their social and emotional needs.

> **Action Memo**
> As a leader, you can provide minimal task direction and personal support to highly-trained employees; followers' professionalism and intrinsic satisfaction substitute for both task- and people-oriented leadership.

Lawrence Summers infuriated some Harvard faculty members by failing to appreciate the substitutes for leadership concept. In this situation, professionalism, education, and intrinsic satisfaction make both task- and people-oriented leadership behavior less important. Summers likely would have been more successful using a light-handed, primarily people-oriented style.

Recent studies have examined how substitutes (the situation) can be designed to have more impact than leader behaviors on outcomes such as subordinate satisfaction.[33] The impetus behind this research is the idea that substitutes for leadership can be designed into organizations in ways to complement existing leadership, act in the absence of leadership, and otherwise provide more comprehensive leadership alternatives. For example, Paul Reeves, a foreman at Harmon Auto Parts, shared half-days with his subordinates during which they helped him perform his leader tasks. After Reeves' promotion to middle management, his group no longer required a foreman. Followers were trained to act on their own.[34] Thus, a situation in which follower ability and training were highly developed created a substitute for leadership.

The ability to utilize substitutes to fill leadership "gaps" is often advantageous to organizations. Indeed, the fundamental assumption of substitutes-for-leadership researchers is that effective leadership is the ability to recognize and provide the support and direction not already provided by task, group, and organization.

Summary and Interpretation

The most important point in this chapter is that situational variables affect leadership outcomes. The contingency approaches were developed to systematically address the relationship between a leader and the organization. The contingency approaches focus on how the components of leadership style, subordinate characteristics, and situational elements impact one another. Fiedler's contingency model, Hersey and Blanchard's situational theory, the path–goal theory, the Vroom–Jago model, and the substitutes-for-leadership concept each examine how different situations call for different styles of leadership behavior.

According to Fiedler, leaders can determine whether the situation is favorable to their leadership style. Task-oriented leaders tend to do better in very easy or very difficult situations, whereas relationship-oriented leaders do best in situations of intermediate favorability. Hersey and Blanchard contend that leaders can adjust their task or relationship style to accommodate the readiness level of their subordinates. The path–goal theory states that leaders can use a style that appropriately clarifies the path to desired rewards. The Vroom–Jago model indicates that leaders can choose a participative decision style based on contingencies such as quality requirement, commitment requirement, or the leader's information. In addition, concern for time (the need for a fast decision) versus concern for follower development are taken into account. Leaders can analyze each situation and answer a series of questions that help determine the appropriate level of follower participation. Finally, the substitutes-for-leadership concept recommends that leaders adjust their style to provide resources not otherwise provided in the organizational situation.

By discerning the characteristics of tasks, subordinates, and organizations, leaders can determine the style that increases the likelihood of successful leadership outcomes. Therefore, effective leadership is about developing diagnostic skills and being flexible in your leadership behavior.

Discussion Questions

1. Consider Fiedler's theory as illustrated in Exhibit 3.3. How often do you think very favorable, intermediate, or very unfavorable situations occur to leaders in real life? Discuss.

2. Do you think leadership style is fixed and unchangeable or flexible and adaptable? Why?

3. Consider the leadership position of the managing partner in a law firm. What task, subordinate, and organizational factors might serve as substitutes for leadership in this situation?

4. Compare Fiedler's contingency model with the path–goal theory. What are the similarities and differences? Which do you prefer?

5. If you were a first-level supervisor of a team of telemarketers, how would you go about asessing the readiness level of your subordinates? Do you think most leaders are able to easily shift their leadership style to suit the readiness level of followers?

6. Think back to teachers you have had, and identify one each who fits a supportive style, directive style, participative style, and achievement-oriented style according to the path–goal theory. Which style did you find most effective? Why?

7. Do you think leaders should decide on a participative style based on the most efficient way to reach the decision? Should leaders sometimes let people participate for other reasons?

8. Consider the situational characteristics of group cohesiveness, organizational formalization, and physical separation. How might each of these substitute for or neutralize task-oriented or people-oriented leadership? Explain.

Leadership at Work

Task Versus Relationship Role Play

You are the new distribution manager for French Grains Bakery. Five drivers report to you that deliver French Grains baked goods to grocery stores in the metropolitan area. The drivers are expected to complete the Delivery Report to keep track of actual deliveries and any changes that occur. The Delivery Report is a key element in inventory control and provides the data for French Grains invoicing of grocery stores. Errors become excessive when drivers fail to complete the report each day, especially when store managers request different inventory when the driver arrives. As a result, French Grains may not be paid for several loaves of bread a day for each mistake in the Delivery Report. The result is lost revenue and poor inventory control.

One of the drivers accounts for about 60 percent of the errors in the Delivery Reports. This driver is a nice person and generally reliable, but sometimes is late for work. His major problem is that he falls behind in his paperwork. A second driver accounts for about 30 percent of the errors, and a third driver for about 10 percent of the errors. The other two drivers turn in virtually error-free Delivery Reports.

You are a high task-oriented (and low relationship-oriented) leader, and have decided to talk to the drivers about doing a more complete and accurate job with the Delivery Report. Write below exactly how you will go about correcting this problem as a task-oriented leader. Will you meet with drivers individually or in a group? When and where will you meet with them? Exactly what will you say and how will you get them to listen?

Now adopt the role of a high relationship-oriented (and low task-oriented) leader. Write below exactly what you will do and say as a relationship-oriented distribution manager. Will you meet with the drivers individually or in a group? What will you say and how will you get them to listen?

In Class: The instructor can ask students to volunteer to play the role of the Distribution Manager and the drivers. A few students can take turns role playing the Distribution Manager in front of the class to show how they would handle the drivers as task- and relationship-oriented leaders. The instructor can ask other students for feedback on the leader's effectiveness and on which approach seems more effective for this situation, and why.

Source: Based on K. J. Keleman, J. E. Garcia, and K. J. Lovelace, *Management Incidents: Role Plays for Management Development* (Kendall Hunt Publishing Company, 1990), pp. 69–72.

Leadership Development: Cases for Analysis

Alvis Corporation

Kevin McCarthy is the manager of a production department in Alvis Corporation, a firm that manufactures office equipment. After reading an article that stressed the benefits of participative management, Kevin believes that these benefits could be realized in his department if the workers are allowed to participate in making some decisions that affect them. The workers are not unionized. Kevin selected two decisions for his experiment in participative management.

The first decision involved vacation schedules. Each summer the workers were given two weeks vacation, but no more than two workers can go on vacation at the same time. In prior years, Kevin made this decision himself. He would first ask the workers to indicate their preferred dates, and he considered how the work would be affected if different people were out at the same time. It was important to plan a vacation schedule that would ensure adequate staffing for all of the essential operations performed by the department. When more than two workers wanted the same time period, and they had similar skills, he usually gave preference to the workers with the highest productivity.

The second decision involved production standards. Sales had been increasing steadily over the past few years, and the company recently installed some new equipment to increase productivity. The new equipment would allow Kevin's department to produce more with the same number of workers. The company had a pay incentive system in which workers received a piece rate for each unit produced above a standard amount. Separate standards existed for each type of product, based on an industrial engineering study conducted a few years earlier. Top management wanted to readjust the production standards to reflect the fact that the new equipment made it possible for the workers to earn more without working any harder. The savings from higher productivity were needed to help pay for the new equipment.

Kevin called a meeting of his 15 workers an hour before the end of the workday. He explained that he wanted them to discuss the two issues and make recommendations. Kevin figured that the workers might be inhibited about participating in the discussion if he were present, so he left them alone to discuss the issues. Besides, Kevin had an appointment to meet with the quality control manager. Quality problems had increased after the new equipment was installed, and the industrial engineers were studying the problem in an attempt to determine why quality had gotten worse rather than better.

When Kevin returned to his department just at quitting time, he was surprised to learn that the workers recommended keeping the standards the same. He had assumed they knew the pay incentives were no longer fair and would set a higher standard. The spokesman for the group explained that their base pay had not kept up with inflation and the higher incentive pay restored their real income to its prior level.

On the vacation issue, the group was deadlocked. Several of the workers wanted to take their vacations during the same two-week period and could not agree on who should go. Some workers argued that they should have priority because they had more seniority, whereas others argued that priority should be based on productivity, as in the past. Since it was quitting time, the group concluded that Kevin would have to resolve the dispute himself. After all, wasn't that what he was being paid for?

Source: Reprinted with permission from Gary Yukl, *Leadership in Organizations,* Fourth Edition (Englewood Cliffs, NJ: Prentice Hall, 1998), pp. 147–148.

QUESTIONS

1. Analyze this situation using the Hersey–Blanchard model and the Vroom–Jago model. What do these models suggest as the appropriate leadership or decision style? Explain.

2. Evaluate Kevin McCarthy's leadership style before and during his experiment in participative management.

3. If you were Kevin McCarthy, what would you do now? Why?

Finance Department

Ken Osborne stared out the window, wondering what he could do to get things back on track. When he became head of the finance department of a state government agency, Osborne inherited a group of highly trained professionals who pursued their jobs with energy and enthusiasm. Everyone seemed to genuinely love coming to work every day. The tasks were sometimes mundane, but most employees liked the structured, routine nature of the work. In addition, the lively camaraderie of the group provided an element of fun and excitement that the work itself sometimes lacked.

Ken knew he'd had an easy time of things over the last couple of years—he had been able to focus his energies on maintaining relationships with other departments and agencies and completing the complex reports he had to turn in each month. The department practically ran itself. Until now. The problem was Larry Gibson, one of the department's best employees. Well-liked by everyone in the department, Gibson had been a key contributor to developing a new online accounting system, and Ken was counting on him to help with the implementation. But everything had changed after Gibson attended a professional development seminar at a prestigious university. Ken had expected him to come back even more fired up about work, but lately Larry was spending more time on his outside professional activities than he was on his job. "If only I'd paid more attention when all this began," Ken thought, as he recalled the day Larry asked him to sign his revised individual development plan. As he'd done in the past, Ken had simply chatted with Larry for a few minutes, glanced at the changes, and initialed the modification. Larry's revised plan included taking a more active role in the state accountants' society, which he argued would enhance his value to the agency as well as improve his own skills and professional contacts.

Within a month, Ken noticed that most of Gibson's energy and enthusiasm seemed to be focused on the society rather than the finance department. On "first Thursday," the society's luncheon meeting day, Larry spent most of the morning on the phone notifying people about the monthly meeting and finalizing details with the speaker. He left around 11 A.M. to make sure things were set up for the meeting and usually didn't return until close to quitting time. Ken could live with the loss of Gibson for one day a month, but the preoccupation with society business seemed to be turning his former star employee into a part-time worker. Larry shows up late for meetings, usually doesn't participate very much, and seems to have little interest in what is going on in the department. The new accounting system is floundering because Larry isn't spending the time to train people in its effective use, so Ken is starting to get complaints from other departments. Moreover, his previously harmonious group of employees is starting to whine and bicker over minor issues and decisions. Ken has also noticed that people who used to be hard at work when he arrived in the mornings seem to be coming in later and later every day.

"Everything's gone haywire since Larry attended that seminar," Ken brooded. "I thought I was one of the best department heads in the agency. Now, I realize I haven't had to provide much leadership until now. Maybe I've had things too easy."

Source: Based on David Hornestay, "Double Vision," *Government Executive* (April 2000), pp. 41–44.

QUESTIONS

1. Why had Ken Osborne's department been so successful even though he has provided little leadership over the past two years?

2. How would you describe Osborne's current leadership style? Based on the path–goal theory, which style do you think he might most effectively use to turn things around with Larry Gibson?

3. If you were in Osborne's position, describe how you would evaluate the situation and handle the problem.

References

1 Leigh Buchanan, "Pat McGovern . . . For Knowing the Power of Respect," segment in "25 Entrepreneurs We Love," *Inc Magazine* 25th Anniversary Issue (April 2004), pp. 110–147; Stephen Power, "Aggressive Driver: Top Volkswagen Executive Tries U.S.-Style Turnaround Tactics; Blunt-Talking Mr. Bernhard Rankles Charman, Union," *The Wall Street Journal* (July 18, 2006), p. A1.

2 "International Data Group Named 'One of the Best Places to Work'; IDG Honored for Second Straight Year," Boston Business Journal award, *Business Wire* (June 23, 2006), p. 1; and "IDG Executives Honored for Their Influence and Innovation in Publishing; IDG Publications Receive Nearly Two Dozen Awards in 2004," *Business Wire* (June 7, 2004), p. 1.

3 Gary Yukl, Angela Gordon, and Tom Taber, "A Hierarchical Taxonomy of Leadership Behavior: Integrating a Half Century of Behavior Research," *Journal of Leadership and Organization Studies* 9, no. 1 (2002), pp. 15–32.

4 Fred E. Fiedler, "Assumed Similarity Measures as Predictors of Team Effectiveness," *Journal of Abnormal and Social Psychology* 49 (1954), pp. 381–388; F. E. Fiedler, *Leader Attitudes and Group Effectiveness* (Urbana, IL: University of Illinois Press, 1958); and F. E. Fiedler, *A Theory of Leadership Effectiveness* (New York: McGraw-Hill, 1967).

5 Matthew Karnitschnig, "Ouster of Viacom Chief Reflects Redstone's Impatience for Results," *The Wall Street Journal*

(September 6, 2006), pp. A1, A16; "Matthew Karnitschnig and Brooks Barnes, "Does MTV Still Rock? Freston Firing Sparks Soul-Searching at Network," *The Wall Street Journal* (September 7, 2006), pp. B1, B3; and Bill Carter, "He's Cool, He Keeps MTV Sizzling, and, Oh Yes, He's 56," *The New York Times* (June 16, 2002), Section 3, p. 1.

6   Karnitschnig, "Ouster of Viacom Chief Reflects Redstone's Impatience."

7   M. J. Strube and J. E. Garcia, "A Meta-Analytic Investigation of Fiedler's Contingency Model of Leadership Effectiveness," *Psychological Bulletin* 90 (1981), pp. 307–321; and L. H. Peters, D. D. Hartke, and J. T. Pohlmann, "Fiedler's Contingency Theory of Leadership: An Application of the Meta-Analysis Procedures of Schmidt and Hunter," *Psychological Bulletin* 97 (1985), pp. 274–285.

8   R. Singh, "Leadership Style and Reward Allocation: Does Least Preferred Coworker Scale Measure Tasks and Relation Orientation?" *Organizational Behavior and Human Performance* 27 (1983), pp. 178–197; D. Hosking, "A Critical Evaluation of Fiedler's Contingency Hypotheses," *Progress in Applied Psychology* 1 (1981), pp. 103–154; Gary Yukl, "Leader LPC Scores: Attitude Dimensions and Behavioral Correlates," *Journal of Social Psychology* 80 (1970), pp. 207–212; G. Graen, K. M. Alvares, J. B. Orris, and J. A. Martella, "Contingency Model of Leadership Effectiveness: Antecedent and Evidential Results," *Psychological Bulletin* 74 (1970), pp. 285–296; R. P. Vecchio, "Assessing the Validity of Fiedler's Contingency Model of Leadership Effectiveness: A Closer Look at Strube and Garcia," *Psychological Bulletin* 93 (1983), pp. 404–408.

9   J. K. Kennedy, Jr., "Middle LPC Leaders and the Contingency Model of Leadership Effectiveness," *Organizational Behavior and Human Performance* 30 (1982), pp. 1–14; and S. C. Shiflett, "The Contingency Model of Leadership Effectiveness: Some Implications of Its Statistical and Methodological Properties," *Behavioral Science* 18, no. 6 (1973), pp. 429–440.

10 Roya Ayman, M. M. Chemers, and F. Fiedler, "The Contingency Model of Leadership Effectiveness: Its Levels of Analysis," *Leadership Quarterly* 6, no. 2 (1995), pp. 147–167.

11 Paul Hersey and Kenneth H. Blanchard, *Management of Organizational Behavior: Utilizing Human Resources*, 4th ed. (Englewood Cliffs, NJ: Prentice-Hall, 1982).

12 Jonathan Kaufman, "A McDonald's Owner Becomes a Role Model for Black Teenagers," *The Wall Street Journal* (August 23, 1995), pp. A1, A6.

13 Michael Barrier, "Leadership Skills Employees Respect," *Nation's Business* (January 1999).

14 Cheryl Dahle, "Xtreme Teams," *Fast Company* (November 1999), pp. 310–326.

15 Carole McGraw, "Teaching Teenagers? Think, Do, Learn," *Education Digest* (February 1998), pp. 44–47.

16 M. G. Evans, "The Effects of Supervisory Behavior on the Path–Goal Relationship," *Organizational Behavior and Human Performance* 5 (1970), pp. 277–298; M. G. Evans, "Leadership and Motivation: A Core Concept," *Academy of Management Journal* 13 (1970), pp. 91–102; and B. S. Georgopoulos, G. M. Mahoney, and N. W. Jones, "A Path–Goal Approach to Productivity," *Journal of Applied Psychology* 41 (1957), pp. 345–353.

17 Robert J. House, "A Path–Goal Theory of Leadership Effectiveness," *Administrative Science Quarterly* 16 (1971), pp. 321–338.

18 M. G. Evans, "Leadership," in *Organizational Behavior*, ed. S. Kerr (Columbus, OH: Grid, 1974), pp. 230–233.

19 Robert J. House and Terrence R. Mitchell, "Path–Goal Theory of Leadership," *Journal of Contemporary Business* (Autumn 1974), pp. 81–97.

20 Dyan Machan, "We're Not Authoritarian Goons," *Forbes* (October 24, 1994), pp. 264–268.

21 Jennifer Reingold, "Bob Nardelli Is Watching," *Fast Company* (December 2005), pp. 76–83.

22 Brian Grow, with Dean Foust, Emily Thornton, Roben Farzad, Jena McGregor, and Susan, "Out at Home Depot," *Business Week* (January 15, 2007), p. 56ff.

23 Charles Greene, "Questions of Causation in the Path-Goal Theory of Leadership," *Academy of Management Journal* 22 (March 1979), pp. 22–41; and C. A. Schriesheim and Mary Ann von Glinow, "The Path-Goal Theory of Leadership: A Theoretical and Empirical Analysis," *Academy of Management Journal* 20 (1977), pp. 398–405.

24 V. H. Vroom and Arthur G. Jago, *The New Leadership: Managing Participation in Organizations* (Englewood Cliffs, NJ: Prentice-Hall, 1988).

25 The following discussion is based heavily on Victor H. Vroom, "Leadership and the Decision-Making Process," *Organizational Dynamics* 28, no. 4 (Spring 2000), pp. 82–94.

26 R. H. G. Field, "A Test of the Vroom–Yetton Normative Model of Leadership," *Journal of Applied Psychology* (October 1982), pp. 523–532; and R. H. G. Field, "A Critique of the Vroom–Yetton Contingency Model of Leadership Behavior," *Academy of Management Review* 4 (1979), pp. 249–251.

27 Vroom, "Leadership and the Decision-Making Process"; Jennifer T. Ettling and Arthur G. Jago, "Participation Under Conditions of Conflict: More on the Validity of the Vroom–Yetton Model," *Journal of Management Studies* 25 (1988), pp. 73–83; Madeline E. Heilman, Harvey A. Hornstein, Jack H. Cage, and Judith K. Herschlag, "Reactions to Prescribed Leader Behavior as a Function of Role Perspective: The Case of the Vroom–Yetton Model," *Journal of Applied Psychology* (February 1984), pp. 50–60; and Arthur G. Jago and Victor H. Vroom, "Some Differences in the Incidence and Evaluation of Participative Leader Behavior," *Journal of Applied Psychology* (December 1982), pp. 776–783.

28 Based on a decision problem presented in Victor H. Vroom, "Leadership and the Decision-Making Process," *Organizational Dynamics* 28, no. 4 (Spring, 2000), pp. 82–94.

29 S. Kerr and J. M. Jermier, "Substitutes for Leadership: Their Meaning and Measurement," *Organizational Behavior and Human Performance* 22 (1978), pp. 375–403; and Jon P. Howell and Peter W. Dorfman, "Leadership and Substitutes for Leadership Among Professional and Nonprofessional Workers," *Journal of Applied Behavioral Science* 22 (1986), pp. 29–46.

30 J. P. Howell, D. E. Bowen, P. W. Doreman, S. Kerr, and P. M. Podsakoff, "Substitutes for Leadership: Effective Alternatives to Ineffective Leadership," *Organizational Dynamics* (Summer 1990), pp. 21–38.

31 Howell, et al., "Substitutes for Leadership: Effective Alternatives to Ineffective Leadership."

32 Robert Tomsho and John Hechinger, "Crimson Blues; Harvard Clash Pits Brusque Leader Against Faculty," *The Wall Street Journal* (February 18, 2005), pp. A1, A8; and Ruth R. Wisse, "Cross Country; Coup d'Ecole," *The Wall Street Journal* (February 23, 2006), p. A17.

33 P. M. Podsakoff, S. B. MacKenzie, and W. H. Bommer, "Transformational Leader Behaviors and Substitutes for Leadership as Determinants of Employee Satisfaction, Commitment, Trust, and Organizational Behaviors," *Journal of Management* 22, no. 2 (1996), pp. 259–298.

34 Howell, et al., "Substitutes for Leadership."

PART 3
The Personal Side of Leadership

Getty Images

Chapter 4

Your Leadership Challenge

After reading this chapter, you should be able to:

- Identify major personality dimensions and understand how personality influences leadership and relationships within organizations.

- Clarify your instrumental and end values, and recognize how values guide thoughts and behavior.

- Define *attitudes* and explain their relationship to leader behavior.

- Explain attribution theory and recognize how perception affects the leader-follower relationship.

- Recognize individual differences in cognitive style and broaden your own thinking style to expand leadership potential.

- Understand different types of leadership roles and the cognitive skills, personalities, and behaviors that might contribute to your success and happiness in each type of role.

The Leader as an Individual

Thom Keeton, an offshore oil rig manager for Transocean Sedco Forex, keeps a color chart under the glass covering his desk. When a crew member comes in, Keeton checks the color of the dot on his hard hat to help him know how to relate to the worker. The colored dots are a shorthand way to help people understand one another's personality styles. *Reds* tend to be strong-willed and decisive, whereas *Greens* are cautious and serious. *Blues* are sensitive and dislike change, and sunny *Yellows* are emotional and talkative. If Keeton, a red–green leader, sees that a worker is a blue–yellow, he knows to tone down his blunt, to-the-point style to enhance communication and understanding.

The color-coding system, which grew out of a training program that profiled employees' personalities, started as a way to help people communicate better and work together more smoothly. Color charts are posted not only in offices, but on the bulkheads of Transocean's rigs. Cramped living conditions, aggressive bosses, and frayed nerves can lead to volatile and dangerous conditions on an oil rig, and Transocean leaders believe the training has relieved tensions and helped people get along better. One worker, who's a laid-back blue-yellow, says he can now cope with "those high-strung red-greens" because he understands where they're coming from.

Employees aren't required to show their colors, and some don't. One employee who doesn't reveal his colors publicly is CEO J. Michael Talbert, who says he needs to be a bit of a chameleon because he has to change his own personality to suit the people he's dealing with at the time. Transocean's training instructor reveals that Talbert's really a green–blue. However, he can act like a competitive red when he needs to, the instructor says, referring to a recent merger. "Once the merger stuff settles down, he'll go back to green and blue."[1]

We all know that people differ in many ways. Some are quiet and shy while others are gregarious; some are thoughtful and serious while others are impulsive and fun-loving. All these individual differences affect the leader–follower interaction. Differences in personality, attitudes, values, and so forth influence how people interpret an assignment, whether they like to be told what to do, how they handle challenges, and how they interact with others. Leaders' personalities and attitudes, as well as their ability to understand individual differences among employees, can profoundly affect leadership effectiveness. Many of today's organizations are using personality and other psychometric tests as a way to help people better understand and relate to one another.

In Chapter 2, we examined studies of some personality traits, individual qualities, and behaviors that are thought to be consistent with effective leadership. Chapter 3 examined contingency theories of leadership, which consider the relationship between leader activities and the situation in which they occur, including followers and the environment. Clearly, organizational leadership is both an individual and an organizational phenomenon. This chapter explores the individual in more depth, looking at some individual differences that can influence leadership abilities and success. We begin by looking at personality and some leader-related personality dimensions. Then, the chapter considers how values affect leadership and the ways in which a leader's attitudes toward self and others influence behavior. We also explore the role of perception, discuss attribution theory, and look at cognitive differences, including a discussion of thinking and decision-making styles and the concept of brain dominance. Finally, the chapter considers the idea that different personalities and thinking styles are better suited to different types of leadership roles.

Personality and Leadership

Some people are consistently pleasant in a variety of situations, whereas others are moody or aggressive. To explain this behavior, we may say, "He has a pleasant personality," or "She has an aggressive personality." This is the most common usage of the term *personality,* and it refers to an individual's behavior patterns as well as how the person is viewed by others. However, there is also a deeper meaning to the term. **Personality** is the set of unseen characteristics and processes that underlie a relatively stable pattern of behavior in response to ideas, objects, or people in the environment. Leaders who have an understanding of how individuals' personalities differ can use this understanding to improve their leadership effectiveness.

A Model of Personality

Most people think of personality in terms of traits. As we discussed in Chapter 2, researchers have investigated whether any traits stand up to scientific scrutiny, and we looked at some traits associated with effective leadership. Although investigators have examined thousands of traits over the years, their findings have been distilled into five general dimensions that describe personality. These often are called the **Big Five personality dimensions**, which describe an individual's extraversion, agreeableness, conscientiousness, emotional stability, and openness to experience.[2] Each dimension contains a wide range of specific traits—for example, all of the personality traits that you would use to describe a teacher, friend, or boss could be categorized into one of the Big Five dimensions. These factors represent a continuum, in that a person may have a low, moderate, or high degree of each of the dimensions.

Extraversion is made up of traits and characteristics that influence behavior in group settings. Extraversion refers to the degree to which a person is outgoing, sociable, talkative, and comfortable meeting and talking to new people. Someone low on extraversion may come across as quiet, withdrawn, and socially unassertive. This dimension also includes the characteristic of *dominance*. A person with a high degree of dominance likes to be in control and have influence over others. These people often are quite self-confident, seek out positions of authority, and are competitive and assertive. They like to be in charge of others or have responsibility for others. It is obvious that both dominance and extraversion could be valuable for a leader. However, not all effective leaders necessarily have a high degree of these characteristics.

For example, many successful top leaders, including Bill Gates, Charles Schwab, and Steven Spielberg, are introverts, people who become drained by social encounters and need time alone to reflect and recharge their batteries. One study found that 4 in 10 top executives test out to be introverts.[3] Thus, the quality of extraversion is not as significant as is often presumed. In addition, a high degree of dominance could even be detrimental to effective leadership if not tempered by other qualities, such as agreeableness or emotional stability.

Personality

the set of unseen characteristics and processes that underlie a relatively stable pattern of behavior in response to ideas, objects, and people in the environment

Big Five personality dimensions

five general dimensions that describe personality: extraversion, agreeableness, conscientiousness, emotional stability, and openness to experience

Extraversion

the degree to which a person is outgoing, sociable, talkative, and comfortable meeting and talking to new people

Action Memo

See where you fall on the Big Five scale for extraversion, agreebleness, conscientiousness, emotional stability, and openness to experience by answering the questions in Leader's Self-Insight 4.1.

The Big Five Personality Dimensions

Getty Images

Each individual's collection of personality traits is different; it is what makes us unique. But, although each *collection* of traits varies, we all share many common traits. The following phrases describe various traits and behaviors. Rate how accurately each statement describes you, based on a scale of 1 to 5, with 1 being very inaccurate and 5 very accurate. Describe yourself as you are now, not as you wish to be. There are no right or wrong answers.

	1	2	3	4	5
Very Inaccurate				Very Accurate	

Extraversion

I am usually the life of the party.	1	2	3	4	5
I feel comfortable around people.	1	2	3	4	5
I am talkative.	1	2	3	4	5

Neuroticism (Low Emotional Stability)

I often feel critical of myself.	1	2	3	4	5
I often envy others.	1	2	3	4	5
I am temperamental.	1	2	3	4	5

Agreeableness

I am kind and sympathetic.	1	2	3	4	5
I have a good word for everyone.	1	2	3	4	5
I never insult people.	1	2	3	4	5

Openness to New Experiences

I am imaginative.	1	2	3	4	5
I prefer to vote for liberal political candidates.	1	2	3	4	5
I really like art.	1	2	3	4	5

Conscientiousness

I am systematic and efficient.	1	2	3	4	5
I pay attention to details.	1	2	3	4	5
I am always prepared for class.	1	2	3	4	5

Which are your most prominent traits? For fun and discussion, compare your responses with those of classmates.

Source: These questions were adapted from a variety of sources.

Agreeableness refers to the degree to which a person is able to get along with others by being good-natured, cooperative, forgiving, compassionate, understanding, and trusting. A leader who scores high on agreeableness seems warm and approachable, whereas one who is low on this dimension may seem cold, distant, and insensitive. People high on agreeableness tend to make friends easily and often have a large number of friends, whereas those low on agreeableness generally establish fewer close relationships.

Traits of agreeableness seem to be particularly important for leaders in today's collaborative organizations. The days are over when a hard-driving manager can run roughshod over others to earn a promotion. Today's successful leaders are not the tough guys of the past but those men and women who know how to get people to like and trust them.[4] One recent book even argues that the secret to success in work and in life is *likability*. We all know we're more willing to do something for someone we like than for someone we don't, whether it be a teammate, a neighbor, a professor, or a supervisor. Leaders can increase their likability by developing characteristics of agreeableness, including being friendly and cooperative, understanding other people in a genuine way, and striving to

Agreeableness
the degree to which a person is able to get along with others by being good-natured, cooperative, forgiving, compassionate, understanding, and trusting

make people feel positive about themselves.[5] Bob and Stan Lee, brothers who run a family-owned manufacturing plant that makes parts for machines that produce cardboard boxes, are striving to incorporate this advice to improve their leadership effectiveness.

Bob and Stan Lee, *Corrugated Replacements Inc.*

Corrugated Replacements Inc. (CRI) has been successful since the day Bob and Stan Lee founded it in their family's barn more than 25 years ago. But the industry is changing, with consolidation in the paper industry and the outsourcing of manufacturing to lower-wage countries. To meet the new challenges, the company requested the advice of experts about what internal changes they needed to make.

Although the two top leaders were concerned mainly about strategic issues, the team of consultants pointed out that one of the company's biggest problems was poor morale and alienation among employees. In a small, family-owned company, one might expect to find a warm, family feeling, but that wasn't the case at CRI. One staff member joked that it seemed the leaders feared that sales might actually increase if they listened to their staff. Comments from the shop floor were even more biting. "In the time I've worked here, the owner has said maybe two words [to me and given me] no handshake when I've come through the door," one production worker said. Another added, "A pat on the back would go a long way with me."

The hazards of failing to make people feel appreciated became painfully clear when the Lees moved CRI from the original plant in Atlanta to a new facility in northern Georgia. More than 80 percent of employees, including a top-notch plant foreman, chose not to make the move, forcing the Lees to hire a new and largely untrained workforce.

Based on suggestions from the team of consultants, the Lees started holding monthly management meetings to foster better communication, placed a suggestion box on the plant floor, and boosted benefits. The biggest challenge, though, is for the leaders to learn to be friendlier with their employees, such as by building time into each workday to connect with shop floor workers.[6]

At Corrugated Replacements Inc., Bob and Stan Lee have begun their change initiative with the more easily-implemented ideas, such as a suggestion box. However, unless they can adopt behaviors that make them more agreeable and likable, employees aren't likely to respond positively to any of the other iniatives aimed at improving morale.

Conscientiousness
the degree to which a person is responsible, dependable, persistent, and achievement-oriented

The next personality dimension, **conscientiousness**, refers to the degree to which a person is responsible, dependable, persistent, and achievement-oriented. A conscientious person is focused on a few goals, which he or she pursues in a purposeful way, whereas a less conscientious person tends to be easily distracted and impulsive. This dimension of personality relates to the work itself rather than to relationships with other people. Many entrepreneurs show a high level of conscientiousness. For example, Mary Clare Murphy and Christie Miller started FSBOMadison to help people sell their homes without going through a traditional real estate agent. As one of the country's largest for-sale-by-owner Web sites, FSBOMadison now lists almost 15 percent of all houses for sale in and around Madison, Wisconsin. The two women stayed focused on their goal despite resistance from the local real estate industry, and they work around the clock to manage the thriving business. One woman called at midnight to ask whether she should paint a closet to make her house more marketable. "Calls come at all hours, even on Christmas," Miller says.[7]

The dimension of **emotional stability** refers to the degree to which a person is well-adjusted, calm, and secure. A leader who is emotionally stable handles stress well, is able to handle criticism, and generally doesn't take mistakes and failures personally. In contrast, leaders who have a low degree of emotional stability are likely to become tense, anxious, or depressed. They generally have lower self-confidence and may explode in emotional outbursts when stressed or criticized. The related topic of *emotional intelligence* will be discussed in detail in the next chapter.

Emotional stability
the degree to which a person is well-adjusted, calm, and secure

The final Big Five dimension, **openness to experience**, is the degree to which a person has a broad range of interests and is imaginative, creative, and willing to consider new ideas. These people are intellectually curious and often seek out new experiences through travel, the arts, movies, reading widely, or other activities. Steve Odland, CEO of Office Depot, for example, has spent his vacation for the past 11 years at the Chautauqua Institution in upstate New York, which offers arts performances, participation in sports, classes for adults and children, and daily lectures on a wide range of topics, from religion to governance. "When I'm at a Chautauqua lecture with 1,000 people who are intellectually curious," Odland says, "that opens my mind to a breadth of issues and points of view."[8]

Openness to experience
the degree to which a person has a broad range of interests and is imaginative, creative, and willing to consider new ideas

People lower in this dimension tend to have narrower interests and stick to the tried-and-true ways of doing things. Open-mindedness is important to leaders because, as we learned in Chapter 1, leadership is about change rather than stability. In an interesting study of three nineteenth-century leaders—John Quincy Adams, Frederick Douglass, and Jane Addams—one researcher found that early travel experiences and exposure to different ideas and cultures were critical elements in developing open-minded qualities in these leaders.[9] Travel during the formative years helped these leaders develop a greater degree of openness to experience because it put them in situations that required adaptability.

Despite the logic of the Big Five personality dimensions, they can be difficult to measure precisely. In addition, since each dimension is made up of numerous traits, a person can be high on some of the specific traits but low on others. For example, concerning the dimension of conscientiousness, it might be possible for a person to be highly responsible and dependable and yet also have a low degree of achievement-orientation. Furthermore, research has been mostly limited to subjects in the United States, so the theory is difficult to apply cross-culturally.

Action Memo
As a leader, you can learn about your own basic personality dimensions and how to emphasize the positive aspects of your personality in dealing with followers.

Few studies have carefully examined the connection between the Big Five and leadership success. One recent summary of more than 70 years of personality and leadership research did find evidence that four of the five dimensions were consistently related to successful leadership.[10] The researchers found considerable evidence that people who score high on the dimensions of extraversion, agreeableness, conscientiousness, and emotional stability are more successful leaders. Results for openness to experience were less consistent; that is, in some cases, higher scores on this dimension related to better performance, but they did not seem to make a difference in other cases. Yet, in a recent study by a team of psychologists of the personality traits of the greatest U.S. presidents (as determined by historians), openness to experience produced the highest correlation with historians' ratings of greatness. The study noted that presidents such as Abraham Lincoln and Thomas Jefferson were high on this personality dimension. Other personality dimensions the team found to be associated with great presidents were extraversion and conscientiousness, including traits such as aggressiveness, setting ambitious goals, and striving for achievement. Although agreeableness did not correlate with greatness, the ability to empathize with others and being concerned for others, which could be considered elements of emotional stability, did.[11]

It is important to note that few leaders have consistently high scores across all of the Big Five dimensions, yet there are many successful leaders. Higher scores on the Big Five dimensions are not necessarily predictive of leadership effectiveness, and persons who score toward the lower end of the scale can also be good leaders. The value of the Big Five for leaders is primarily to help them understand their own basic personality dimensions, and then learn to emphasize the positive and mitigate the negative aspects of their own natural style.

Exhibit 4.1 gives some tips for both introverts and extraverts to help them be better leaders. Many factors contribute to effective leadership. As we learned in the previous two chapters, situational factors play a role in determining which traits may be most important. In addition, a leader's intelligence, knowledge of the business, values and attitudes, and problem-solving styles, which are not measured by the Big Five, also play a role in leadership effectiveness. Later in this chapter, we will discuss values and attitudes, as well as examine some cognitive differences that affect leadership. First, let's look more closely at two personality attributes that have significant implications for leaders.

Exhibit 4.1 Maximizing Leadership Effectiveness

Tips for Extraverts	Tips for Introverts
• *Don't bask in the glow of your own personality.* Learn to hold back and listen to others when the situation calls for it.	• *Get out and about.* Resist the urge to hibernate.
• *Try to underwhelm.* Your natural exuberance can be intimidating and miss important facts and ideas.	• *Practice being friendly and outgoing in settings outside of work.* Take your new skills to the office.
• *Talk less, listen more.* Develop the discipline to let others speak first on an issue to avoid the appearance of arrogance.	• *Give yourself a script.* Come up with a few talking points you can rely on to cover silences in conversations.
• *Don't be Mr. or Ms. Personality.* Extraverts tend to agree too quickly just to be liked. These casual agreements can come back to haunt you.	• *Smile.* A frown or a soberly introspective expression can be misinterpreted. A bright countenance reflects confidence that you know where you're going and want others to follow.

Source: Based on Patricia Wallington, "The Ins and Outs of Personality," *CIO* (January 15, 2003), pp. 42, 44.

Personality Traits and Leader Behavior

Two specific personality attributes that have a significant impact on behavior and are thus of particular interest for leadership studies are locus of control and authoritarianism.

Locus of Control Some people believe that their actions can strongly affect what happens to them. In other words, they believe they are "masters of their own fate." Others feel that whatever happens to them in life is a result of luck, chance, or outside people and events; they believe they have little control over their fate. A person's **locus of control** defines whether he or she places the primary responsibility within the self or on outside forces.[12] People who believe their actions determine what happens to them have a high *internal* locus of control (internals), whereas those who believe outside forces determine what happens to them have a high *external* locus of control (externals).

Locus of control
defines whether a person places the primary responsibility for what happens to him or her within him/herself or on outside forces

Research on locus of control has shown real differences in behavior between internals and externals across a wide range of settings.[13] Internals in general are more self-motivated, are in better control of their own behavior, participate more in social and political activities, and more actively seek information. There is also evidence that internals are better able to handle complex information and problem solving, and that they are more achievement-oriented than externals. In addition, people with a high internal locus of control are more likely than externals to try to influence others, and thus more likely to assume or seek leadership opportunities. People with a high external locus of control typically prefer to have structured, directed work situations. They are better able than internals to handle work that requires compliance and conformity, but they are generally not as effective in situations that require initiative, creativity, and independent action. Therefore, since externals do best in situations where success depends on complying with the direction or guidance of others, they are less likely to enjoy or succeed in leadership positions.

Action Memo
Do you believe luck, chance, or the actions of other people play a major role in your life, or do you feel in control of your own fate? Learn more about your locus of control by completing the questionnaire in Leader's Self-Insight 4.2 on page 104.

Authoritarianism The belief that power and status differences *should* exist in an organization is called **authoritarianism**.[14] Individuals who have a high degree of this personality trait tend to adhere to conventional rules and values, obey established authority, respect power and toughness, judge others critically, and disapprove of the expression of personal feelings. A leader's degree of authoritarianism will affect how the leader wields and shares power. A highly authoritarian leader is likely to rely heavily on formal authority and unlikely to want to share power with subordinates. High authoritarianism is associated with the traditional, rational approach to management described in Chapter 1. The new leadership paradigm requires that leaders be less authoritarian, although people who rate high on this personality trait can be effective leaders as well. Leaders should also understand that the degree to which followers possess authoritarianism influences how they react to the leader's use of power and authority. When leaders and followers differ in their degree of authoritarianism, effective leadership may be more difficult to achieve.

Authoritarianism
the belief that power and status differences should exist in an organization

Action Memo
As a leader, you can improve your effectiveness by recognizing how traits such as authoritarianism and locus of control affect your relationships with followers. You can tone down a strong authoritarian or dogmatic personality to motivate others.

A trait that is closely related to authoritarianism is *dogmatism,* which refers to a person's receptiveness to others' ideas and opinions. A highly dogmatic person is closed-minded and not receptive to others' ideas. When in a leadership position, dogmatic individuals

For each of these ten questions, indicate the extent to which you agree or disagree using the following scale:

1 = Strongly disagree   5 = Slightly agree
2 = Disagree   6 = Agree
3 = Slightly disagree   7 = Strongly agree
4 = Neither agree or disagree

	Strongly disagree						Strongly agree
1. When I get what I want, it's usually because I worked hard for it.	1	2	3	4	5	6	7
2. When I make plans, I am almost certain to make them work.	1	2	3	4	5	6	7
3. I prefer games involving some luck over games requiring pure skill.	1	2	3	4	5	6	7
4. I can learn almost anything if I set my mind to it.	1	2	3	4	5	6	7
5. My major accomplishments are entirely due to my hard work and ability.	1	2	3	4	5	6	7
6. I usually don't set goals, because I have a hard time following through on them.	1	2	3	4	5	6	7
7. Competition discourages excellence.	1	2	3	4	5	6	7
8. Often people get ahead just by being lucky.	1	2	3	4	5	6	7
9. On any sort of exam or competition, I like to know how well I do relative to everyone else.	1	2	3	4	5	6	7
10. It's pointless to keep working on something that's too difficult for me.	1	2	3	4	5	6	7

Scoring and Interpretation

To determine your score, reverse the values you selected for questions 3, 6, 7, 8, and 10 (1 = 7, 2 = 6, 3 = 5, 4 = 4, 5 = 3, 6 = 2, 7 = 1). For example, if you strongly disagreed with the statement in question 3, you would have given it a value of 1. Change this value to a 7. Reverse the scores in a similar manner for questions 6, 7, 8, and 10. Now add the point values from all 10 questions together.

Your score:_____

This questionnaire is designed to measure locus of control beliefs. Researchers using this questionnaire in a study of college students found a mean of 51.8 for men and 52.2 for women, with a standard deviation of 6 for each. The higher your score on this questionnaire, the more you tend to believe that you are generally responsible for what happens to you; in other words, high scores are associated with internal locus of control. Low scores are associated with external locus of control. Scoring low indicates that you tend to believe that forces beyond your control, such as powerful other people, fate, or chance, are responsible for what happens to you.

Sources: Adapted from J. M. Burger, *Personality: Theory and Research* (Belmont, CA: Wadsworth, 1986), pp. 400–401, cited in D. Hellriegel, J. W. Slocum, Jr., and R. W. Woodman, *Organizational Behavior*, 6th ed. (St. Paul, MN: West Publishing Co., 1992), pp. 97–100. Original Source: D. L. Paulhus. "Sphere-Specific Measures of Perceived Control." *Journal of Personality and Social Psychology* 44 (1983), pp. 1253–1265.

often make decisions quickly based on limited information, and they are unreceptive to ideas that conflict with their opinions and decisions. Effective leaders, on the other hand, generally have a lower degree of dogmatism, which means they are open-minded and receptive to others' ideas.

Understanding how personality traits and dimensions affect behavior can be a valuable asset for leaders. Knowledge of individual differences gives leaders valuable insights into their own behavior as well as that of followers. It also offers a framework that leaders can use to diagnose situations and make changes to benefit the organization. For example, when Reed Breland became a team facilitator at Hewlett-Packard's financial services center in Colorado, he noticed immediately that one team was in constant turmoil. Breland's understanding of individual differences helped him recognize that two members of the team had a severe personality clash and could not see eye-to-eye on any issue. Although Breland tried to work things out within the team, after several months he simply dissolved the group and reassigned members to other areas. The team members all did fine in other assignments; the personality conflict between the two members was just too strong to overcome and it affected the team's productivity and effectiveness.[15]

Values and Attitudes

In addition to personality differences, people differ in the values and attitudes they hold. These differences affect the behavior of leaders and followers.

Instrumental and End Values

Values are fundamental beliefs that an individual considers to be important, that are relatively stable over time, and that have an impact on attitudes, perception, and behavior.[16] Values are what cause a person to prefer that things be done one way rather than another way. Whether we recognize it or not, we are constantly valuing things, people, or ideas as good or bad, pleasant or unpleasant, ethical or unethical, and so forth.[17] When a person has strong values in certain areas, these can have a powerful influence on behavior. For example, a person who highly values honesty and integrity might lose respect and lessen his commitment and performance for a leader who tells "little white lies."

One way to think about values is in terms of instrumental and end values.[18] Social scientist Milton Rokeach developed a list of 18 instrumental values and 18 end values that have been found to be more or less universal across cultures. **End values**, sometimes called *terminal values*, are beliefs about the kind of goals or outcomes that are worth trying to pursue. For example, some people value security, a comfortable life, and good health above everything else as the important goals to strive for in life. Others may place greater value on social recognition, pleasure, and an exciting life. **Instrumental values** are beliefs about the types of behavior that are appropriate for reaching goals. Instrumental values include such things as being helpful to others, being honest, or exhibiting courage.

Although everyone has both instrumental and end values, individuals differ in how they order the values into priorities, which accounts for tremendous variation among people. Part of this difference relates to culture. In the United States, independence is highly valued and is reinforced by many institutions, including schools, religious organizations, and businesses. Other cultures place less value on independence and more value on being part of a tightly knit community. A person's family background also influences his or her values. Values are learned, not inherited, but some values become incorporated into a person's thinking very early in life. Some leaders cite their parents as a primary source of their leadership abilities because they helped to shape their values.[19] Bill Farmer, president of the Jackson-Monroe (Mississippi) division of Time Warner Cable, says his mother instilled in him the importance of giving back to the community. Farmer voluteers as a guest reader at Jackson State University's Learning Center, has served on the boards of numerous non-profit organizations, and is actively

Values
fundamental beliefs that an individual considers to be important, that are relatively stable over time, and that have an impact on attitudes and behavior

End values
sometimes called terminal values, these are beliefs about the kind of goals or outcomes that are worth trying to pursue

Instrumental values
beliefs about the types of behavior that are appropriate for reaching goals

Action Memo
Complete the exercise in Leader's Self-Insight 4.3 on page 106 to see what you can learn about your own values and how they affect your decisions and actions. Were you surprised by any of your instrumental or end values?

In each column below, place a check mark by the five values that are most important to you. After you have checked five values in each column, rank order the checked values in each column from one to five, with 1 = most important and 5 = least important.

Rokeach's Instrumental and End Values

End Values		Instrumental Values	
A comfortable life	____	Ambition	____
Equality	____	Broad-mindedness	____
An exciting life	____	Capability	____
Family security	____	Cheerfulness	____
Freedom	____	Cleanliness	____
Health	____	Courage	____
Inner harmony	____	Forgiveness	____
Mature love	____	Helpfulness	____
National security	____	Honesty	____
Pleasure	____	Imagination	____
Salvation	____	Intellectualism	____
Self-respect	____	Logic	____
A sense of accomplishment	____	Ability to love	____
		Loyalty	____
Social recognition	____	Obedience	____
True friendship	____	Politeness	____
Wisdom	____	Responsibility	____
A world at peace	____	Self-control	____
A world of beauty	____		

NOTE: The values are listed in alphabetical order and there is no one-to-one relationship between the end and instrumental values.

Scoring and Interpretation

End values, according to Rokeach, tend to fall into two categories—personal and social. For example, mature love is a personal end value and equality is a social end value. Analyze the five end values you selected and their rank order, and determine whether your primary end values tend to be personal or social. What do your five selections together mean to you? What do they mean for how you make life decisions? Compare your end value selections with another person, with each of you explaining what you learned about your end values from this exercise.

Instrumental values also tend to fall into two categories—morality and competence. The means people use to achieve their goals might violate moral values (e.g., be dishonest) or violate one's personal sense of competence and capability (e.g., be illogical). Analyze the five instrumental values you selected, and their rank order, and determine whether your primary instrumental values tend to focus on morality or competence. What do the five selected values together mean to you? What do they mean for how you will pursue your life goals? Compare your instrumental value selections with another person and describe what you learned from this exercise.

Warning: The two columns shown to the left do *not* represent the full range of instrumental and end values. Your findings would change if a different list of values were provided. This exercise is for discussion and learning purposes only and is not intended to be an accurate assessment of your actual end and instrumental values.

Sources: Robert C. Benfari, *Understanding and Changing Your Management Style* (San Francisco: Jossey-Bass, 1999), pp. 178–183; and M. Rokeach, *Understanding Human Values* (The Free Press, 1979).

involved in local Chamber of Commerce initiatives designed to create a positive community environment.[20]

Our values are generally fairly well established by early adulthood, but a person's values can also change throughout life. This chapter's *Consider This* reflects on how the values that shape a leader's actions in a moment of crisis have been developed over time. Values may affect leaders and leadership in a number of ways.[21] For one thing, a leader's personal values affect his or her perception of situations and problems. Perception will be discussed in more detail in the following section. Values also affect how leaders relate to others. A leader who values obedience, conformity, and politeness may have a difficult time understanding and appreciating a follower who is self-reliant, independent, creative, and a bit rebellious. Consider the kind of values that contribute to successful leadership at Whole Foods Market.

Consider This!

Developing Character

"The character that takes command in moments of critical choices has already been determined. It has been determined by a thousand other choices made earlier in seemingly unimportant moments. It has been determined by all those 'little' choices of years past—by all those times when the voice of conscience was at war with the voice of temptation—whispering a lie that 'it doesn't really matter.' It has been determined by all the day-to-day decisions made when life seemed easy and crises seemed far away, the decisions that piece by piece, bit by bit, developed habits of discipline or of laziness; habits of self-sacrifice or self-indulgence; habits of duty and honor and integrity—or dishonor and shame."

Source: President Ronald Reagan, quoted in Norman R. Augustine, "Seven Fundamentals of Effective Leadership," an original essay written for the Center for the Study of American Business, Washington University in St. Louis, *CEO Series* Issue no. 27, (October 1998).

Wendy Steinberg, Whole Foods Market

Whole Foods Market started as one small health foods store in Austin, Texas in 1978. By 2006, it had grown to 187 locations with sales approaching $5 billion.

Wendy Steinberg, now an associate team leader at the Columbus Circle Store, recalls her first meeting with the company's founder and CEO, John Mackey: "I was on break in the break room. I hadn't been a team member more than six months, and there was this guy in the break room. He was sitting there, with his hands crossed . . . just checking things out. . . . He asked me a lot of questions. I had no idea who he was." Mackey's style is a reflection of the values that guide Whole Foods, even through its tremendous growth in recent years. As Mackey once put it, "We're creating an organization based on love instead of fear."

At Whole Foods, leaders from the top down have to be comfortable with extreme decentralization, a "no-secrets" management approach, and an egalitarian culture. The company's core values include a commitment to both "customer delight" and "team member happiness." Whole Foods' dress code is very liberal, allowing people to express their individuality, and each employee can take 20 hours of paid time each year to do volunteer work. Each store is divided into functional teams that make decisions about everything from what gets stocked on the shelves to who gets hired as a team member. People are hired onto a team provisionally; after four weeks, the team votes whether to keep the new employee permanently. It's a critical issue, since high performing teams earn additional money through profit-sharing. At headquarters, as well, the National Leadership Team makes decisions by majority vote. At the end of every business meeting, including those conducted by the CEO, participants do a round of "appreciations" in which they say something nice about the other people involved in the meeting.

In every Whole Foods store, there's a book that lists the pay of every employee, from the CEO on down. Executive pay is limited to no more than 14 times the average pay of frontline workers. Everyone qualifies for stock options (about 94 percent are currently held by non-management employees), and employees get to vote on such matters as what health insurance plan to adopt (Whole Foods pays 100 percent of the cost for full-time workers).

At the Columbus Circle store in Manhattan, long-time employees and leaders such as Steinberg provided the "starter culture" to instill the Whole Foods values into new workers. Many of the store's newcomers were "used to being trod on" by previous employers, says Barry Keenan, who works on the seafood team. "They have a lot more respect for you as a person here."[22]

To some, Whole Foods unwritten management rules seem eccentric. Certainly, a leader who highly values personal ambition, authoritarianism, status and power, and obedience would not feel comfortable working in an environment like that at Whole Foods. Recognizing value differences can help leaders find compatible job situations, as well as help them better understand and work with varied followers.

A third way in which values affect leadership is that they guide a leader's choices and actions. A leader who places high value on being courageous and standing up for what one believes in, for example, is much more likely to make decisions that may not be popular but which he believes are right. Values determine how leaders acquire and use power, how they handle conflict, and how they make decisions. A leader who values competitiveness and ambition will behave differently from one who places a high value on cooperativeness and forgiveness. Ethical values help guide choices concerning what is morally right or wrong. Values concerning end goals also help determine a leader's actions and choices in the workplace. Leaders can be more effective when they clarify their own values and understand how values guide their actions and affect their organizations. In addition, for many organizations today, clarifying and stating their corporate values, including ethical values, has become an important part of defining how the organization operates.

> **Action Memo**
>
> As a leader, you can clarify your values so you know what you stand for and how your values may conflict with others in the organization. You can cultivate positive attitudes toward yourself and others, and learn to expect the best from followers.

How Attitudes Affect Leadership

Values help determine the attitudes leaders have about themselves and about their followers. An **attitude** is an evaluation—either positive or negative—about people, events, or things. As we discussed in Chapter 2, an optimistic attitude or positive outlook on life is often considered a key to successful and effective leadership.

Attitude
an evaluation (either positive or negative) about people, events, or things

Behavioral scientists consider attitudes to have three components: cognitions (thoughts), affect (feelings), and behavior.[23] The cognitive component includes the ideas and knowledge a person has about the object of an attitude, such as a leader's knowledge and ideas about a specific employee's performance and abilities. The affective component concerns how an individual feels about the object of an attitude. Perhaps the leader resents having to routinely answer questions or help the employee perform certain tasks. The behavioral component of an attitude predisposes a person to act in a certain way. For example, the leader might avoid the employee or fail to include him or her in certain activities of the group. Although attitudes change more easily than values, they typically reflect a person's fundamental values as well as a person's background and life experiences. A leader who highly values forgiveness, compassion toward others, and helping others would have different attitudes and behave very differently toward the above-mentioned subordinate than one who highly values personal ambition and capability.

One consideration is a leader's attitudes about himself or herself. **Self-concept** refers to the collection of attitudes we have about ourselves and includes the element of self-esteem, whether a person generally has positive or negative feelings about himself. A person with an overall positive self-concept has high self-esteem, whereas one with a negative self-concept has low self-esteem. In general, leaders

Self-concept
the collection of attitudes we have about ourselves; includes self-esteem and whether a person generally has a positive or negative feeling about him/herself

What Got You Here Won't Get You There

by Marshall Goldsmith and Mark Reiter

Success, says executive coach Marshall Goldsmith, makes many people believe they must be doing eveything right. Therefore, they sabotage their continued effectiveness and career advancement by failing to recognize and correct the mistakes they make in interpersonal relationships. "All other things being equal, your people skills (or lack of them) become more pronounced the higher up you go," he writes in *What Got You Here Won't Get You There*. Goldsmith and his collaborator, Mark Reiter, identify 20 behavioral habits that damage organizational relationships and hold leaders back.

NOBODY'S PERFECT

Every leader has some habits or negative behaviors that can limit his or her effectiveness. Following are a few of the behavioral flaws Goldsmith and Reiter describe. Do you recognize any of these in your own behaviors?

- **Winning at all costs and in all situations.** We all know them—those people who feel like they have to win every argument and always be right. They want to win the big points, the small points, and everything in between. If they go along with another's idea that doesn't work out, they adopt an "I told you so" attitude. In the workplace, a leader's need to be right and to point out that he or she is right damages relationships and destroys teamwork.

- **Clinging to the past.** There's nothing wrong with looking at and understanding the past as a way to come to terms with it or learn from it. Too often, though, people cling to the past as a way to blame others for things that have gone wrong in their lives, using the past as a weapon to control others or punish them for not doing exactly what the leader wants.

- **Never being able to say you're sorry.** It's not true that "love means never having to say you're sorry." Apologizing is love in action. Refusing to apologize probably causes more ill will—whether it be in a romance, a family, or a work relationship—than any other interpersonal flaw. "People who can't apologize at work may as well be wearing a T-shirt that says: 'I don't care about you,'" Gladwell writes.

CHANGE IS POSSIBLE

Gladwell has spent his career helping leaders find and fix their behavioral blind spots. His prescription for success can benefit any leader who genuinely wants to improve his or her interpersonal relationships. The first step is to gather feedback that helps you identify the specific behaviors you need to change. Next, focus on fixing the problem by apologizing for your behavioral flaws, advertising your efforts to change, listening to the input of others, showing gratitude for others' contributions to your change process, and following up on your progress. When you acknowledge your dependence on others, Gladwell points out, they typically not only agree to help you be better person, they also try to become better people themselves.

What Got You Here Won't Get You There, by Marshall Goldsmith and Mark Reiter, is published by Hyperion Books.

with positive self-concepts are more effective in all situations. Leaders who have a negative self-concept, who are insecure and have low self-esteem, often create environments that limit other people's growth and development.[24] They may also sabotage their own careers. The Leader's Bookshelf further discusses how certain attitudes and behavior patterns can limit a leader's effectiveness and career development.

The way in which the leader relates to followers also depends significantly on his or her attitudes about others.[25] A leader's style is based largely on attitudes about human nature in general—ideas and feelings about what motivates people, whether people are basically honest and trustworthy, and about the extent to which people can grow and change. One theory developed to explain differences in style was developed by Douglas McGregor, based on his experiences as a manager and consultant and his training as a psychologist.[26] McGregor identified two sets of

Exhibit 4.2 Attitudes and Assumptions of Theory X and Theory Y

Assumptions of Theory X	Assumptions of Theory Y
• The average human being has an inherent dislike of work and will avoid it if possible.	• The expenditure of physical and mental effort in work is as natural as play or rest. The average human being does not inherently dislike work.
• Because of the human characteristic of dislike for work, most people must be coerced, controlled, directed, or threatened with punishment to get them to put forth adequate effort toward the achievement of organizational objectives.	• External control and the threat of punishment are not the only means for bringing about effort toward organizational objectives. A person will exercise self-direction and self-control in the service of objectives to which he or she is committed.
• The average human being prefers to be directed, wishes to avoid responsibility, has relatively little ambition, and wants security above all.	• The average human being learns, under proper conditions, not only to accept but to seek responsibility.
	• The capacity to exercise a relatively high degree of imagination, ingenuity and creativity in the solution of organizational problems is widely, not narrowly, distributed in the population.
	• Under the conditions of modern industrial life, the intellectual potentialities of the average human being are only partially utilized.

Source: Douglas McGregor, *The Human Side of Enterprise* (New York: McGraw-Hill, 1960), pp. 33–48.

Theory X
the assumption that people are basically lazy and not motivated to work and that they have a natural tendency to avoid responsibility

Theory Y
the assumption that people do not inherently dislike work and will commit themselves willingly to work that they care about

assumptions about human nature, called **Theory X** and **Theory Y**, which represent two very different sets of attitudes about how to interact with and influence subordinates. Exhibit 4.2 explains the fundamental assumptions of Theory X and Theory Y.

In general, Theory X reflects the assumption that people are basically lazy and not motivated to work and that they have a natural tendency to avoid responsibility. Thus, a supervisor who subscribes to the assumptions of Theory X believes people must be coerced, controlled, directed, or threatened to get them to put forth their best effort. In some circumstances, the supervisor may come across as bossy or overbearing, impatient with others, and unconcerned with people's feelings and problems. Referring back to Chapter 2, the Theory X leader would likely be task-oriented and highly concerned with production rather than people. Theory Y, on the other hand, is based on assumptions that people do not inherently dislike work and will commit themselves willingly to work that they care about. Theory Y also assumes that, under the right conditions, people will seek out greater responsibility and will exercise imagination and creativity in the pursuit of solutions to organizational problems. A leader who subscribes to the assumptions of Theory Y does not believe people have to be coerced and controlled in order to perform effectively. These leaders are more often people-oriented and concerned with relationships, although some Theory Y leaders can also be task- or production-oriented. McGregor believed Theory Y to be a more realistic and productive approach for viewing subordinates and shaping leaders' attitudes. Studies exploring the relationship between leader attitudes and leadership success in general support his idea, although this relationship has not been carefully explored.[27]

Social Perception and Attribution Theory

By **perception**, we mean the process people use to make sense out of their surroundings by selecting, organizing, and interpreting information. Values and attitudes affect perceptions, and vice versa. For example, a person might have developed the attitude that managers are insensitive and arrogant, based on a pattern of perceiving arrogant and insensitive behavior from managers over a period of time. If the person moves to a new job, this attitude will continue to affect the way he or she perceives superiors in the new environment, even though managers in the new workplace might take great pains to understand and respond to employees' needs. As another example, a leader who greatly values ambition and career success may perceive a problem or a subordinate's mistake as an impediment to her own success, whereas a leader who values helpfulness and obedience might see it as a chance to help a subordinate improve or grow.

Because of individual differences in attitudes, personality, values, interests, and experiences, people often "see" the same thing in different ways. Consider that a recent survey of nearly 2,000 workers in the United States found that 92 percent of managers think they are doing an "excellent" or "good" job managing employees, but only 67 percent of workers agree. As another example, in a survey of finance professionals, 40 percent of women said they perceive that women face a "glass ceiling" that keeps them from reaching top management levels, whereas only 10 percent of men share that perception.[28]

Perceptual Distortions

Of particular concern for leaders are **perceptual distortions**, errors in perceptual judgment that arise from inaccuracies in any part of the perceptual process. Some types of errors are so common that leaders should become familiar with them. These include stereotyping, the halo effect, projection, and perceptual defense. Leaders who recognize these perceptual distortions can better adjust their perceptions to more closely match objective reality.

Stereotyping is the tendency to assign an individual to a group or broad category (e.g., female, black, elderly or male, white, disabled) and then to attribute widely held generalizations about the group to the individual. Thus, someone meets a new colleague, sees he is in a wheelchair, assigns him to the category "physically disabled," and attributes to this colleague generalizations she believes about people with disabilities, which may include a belief that he is less able than other coworkers. However, the person's inability to walk should not be seen as indicative of lesser abilities in other areas. Indeed, the assumption of limitations may not only offend him, it also prevents the person making the stereotypical judgment from benefiting from the many ways in which this person can contribute. Stereotyping prevents people from truly knowing those they classify in this way. In addition, negative stereotypes prevent talented people from advancing in an organization and fully contributing their talents to the organization's success.

The **halo effect** occurs when the perceiver develops an overall impression of a person or situation based on one characteristic, either favorable or unfavorable. In other words, a halo blinds the perceiver to other characteristics that should be used in generating a more complete assessment. The halo effect can

Perception
the process people use to make sense out of the environment by selecting, organizing, and interpreting information

Perceptual distortions
errors in judgment that arise from inaccuracies in the perceptual process

Stereotyping
the tendency to assign an individual to a broad category and then attribute generalizations about the group to the individual

Halo effect
an overall impression of a person or situation based on one characteristic, either favorable or unfavorable

play a significant role in performance appraisal. For example, a person with an outstanding attendance record may be assessed as responsible, industrious, and highly productive; another person with less-than-average attendance may be assessed as a poor performer. Either assessment may be true, but it is the leader's job to be sure the assessment is based on complete information about all job-related characteristics and not just his or her preferences for good attendance.

Projection is the tendency of perceivers to see their own personal traits in other people; that is, they project their own needs, feelings, values, and attitudes into their judgment of others. A leader who is achievement oriented might assume that subordinates are as well. This might cause the manager to restructure jobs to be less routine and more challenging, without regard for employees' actual satisfaction. The best guards against errors based on projection are self-awareness and empathy.

Perceptual defense is the tendency of perceivers to protect themselves against ideas, objects, or people that are threatening. People perceive things that are satisfying and pleasant, but tend to disregard things that are disturbing and unpleasant. In essence, people develop blind spots in the perceptual process so that negative sensory data do not hurt them. For example, the director of a non-profit educational organization in Tennessee hated dealing with conflict because he had grown up with parents who constantly argued and often put him in the middle of their arguments. The director consistently overlooked discord among staff members until things would reach a boiling point. When the blow-up occurred, the director would be shocked and dismayed, because he had truly perceived that everything was going smoothly among the staff. Recognizing perceptual blind spots can help people develop a clearer picture of reality.

Attribution Theory

As people organize what they perceive, they often draw conclusions, such as about an object, event, or person. **Attribution theory** refers to how people explain the causes of events or behaviors. For example, many people contribute the success or failure of an organization to the top leader, when in reality there may be many factors that contribute to organizational performance. People also make attributions or judgments about what caused a person's behavior—something about the person or something about the situation. An *internal attribution* says characteristics of the person led to the behavior ("My subordinate missed the deadline because he's lazy and incompetent"). An *external attribution* says something about the situation caused the person's behavior ("My subordinate missed the deadline because he didn't have the team support and resources he needed"). Attributions are important because they help people decide how to handle a situation. In the case of a subordinate missing a deadline, a leader who blames the mistake on the employee's personal characteristics might reprimand the person or, more effectively, provide additional training and direction. A leader who blames the mistake on external factors will try to help prevent such situations in the future, such as making sure team members have the resources they need, providing support to remove obstacles, and insuring that deadlines are realistic.

Social scientists have studied the attributions people make and identified three factors that influence whether an attribution will be external or internal.[29] Exhibit 4.3 illustrates these three factors.

1. *Distinctiveness.* Whether the behavior is unusual for that person (in contrast to a person displaying the same kind of behavior in many situations). If the behavior is distinctive, the perceiver probably will make an *external* attribution.

Projection
the tendency to see one's own personal traits in other people

Perceptual defense
the tendency to protect oneself by disregarding ideas, situations, or people that are unpleasant

Attribution theory
how people draw conclusions about what caused certain behaviors or events

Exhibit 4.3 Factors Influencing Whether Attributions Are Internal or External

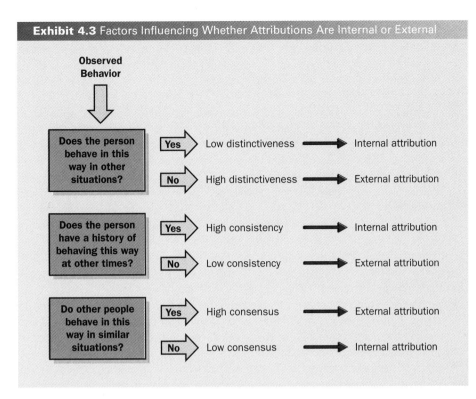

2. *Consistency.* Whether the person being observed has a history of behaving in the same way. People generally make *internal* attributions about consistent behavior.

3. *Consensus.* Whether other people tend to respond to similar situations in the same way. A person who has observed others handle similar situations in the same way will likely make an *external* attribution; that is, it will seem that the situation produces the type of behavior observed.

In addition to these general rules, people tend to have biases that they apply when making attributions. When evaluating others, we tend to underestimate the influence of external factors and overestimate the influence of internal factors. This tendency is called the **fundamental attribution error**. Consider the case of someone being promoted to CEO. Employees, outsiders, and the media generally focus on the characteristics of the person that allowed him or her to achieve the promotion. In reality, however, the selection of that person might have been heavily influenced by external factors, such as business conditions creating a need for someone with a strong financial or marketing background at that particular time.

Another bias that distorts attributions involves attributions we make about our own behavior. People tend to overestimate the contribution of internal factors to their successes and overestimate the contribution of external factors to their failures. This tendency, called the **self-serving bias**, means people give themselves too much credit for what they do well and give external forces too much blame when they fail. Thus, if a leader's subordinates say she doesn't listen well enough, and the leader thinks subordinates don't communicate well enough, the truth may actually lie somewhere in between. At Emerald Pakaging, Kevin Kelly examined his attributions and improved his leadership effectiveness by overcoming the self-serving bias.

Fundamental attribution error
the tendency to underestimate the influence of external factors on another's behavior and overestimate the influence of internal factors

Self-serving bias
the tendency to overestimate the influence of internal factors on one's successes and the influence of external factors on one's failures

Kevin Kelly, Emerald Packaging

As the top leader of his family's California company, Emerald Packaging—a maker of plastic bags for the food industry, Kevin Kelly thought of himself as on top of his game, chief architect of the company's growing sales and profits. When Emerald began to falter, Kelly blamed it on his managers' resistance to new ideas that could keep the business thriving. He thought everyone needed to change except him.

For some time, Kelly's leadership approach was to reprimand and complain, then let the matter drop, only to reprimand and complain again a few weeks or months later. Then, Kelly decided to look at things in a different way. Was it really all his managers' fault? Maybe there were other factors besides their personal shortcomings that were to blame. Realizing that everyone was under stress from several years of rapid growth, Kelly decided to hire a pack of new, young managers to reinforce his exhausted troops. Surprisingly, though, things just seem to get worse, with the new managers feeling adrift and the old-timers seeming even less focused than before. Then Kelly had to face an even harder truth: rather than being the one person in the organization who didn't need to change, as Kelly had previously thought, he realized he was a big part of the problem.

The idea both unnerved and excited him as Kelly realized that he needed to remake himself, becoming a mentor who could shape positive attitudes in others and knit the newcomers and long-time employees into a cohesive and productive team. Kelly sought out consultants and classes to help boost his people skills and began taking a more interested and understanding role in the problems his veteran managers had been facing on a daily basis. He began meeing regularly with the new hires as well, rather than expecting other managers to do all the work of integrating them into the team. By examining his attributions and shifting his perception of himself, the organizational situation, and his managers' abilities, Kelly made changes that successfully united the two groups into a cohesive team.[30]

Cognitive Differences

Cognitive style
how a person perceives, processes, interprets, and uses information

The final area of individual differences we will explore is cognitive style. **Cognitive style** refers to how a person perceives, processes, interprets, and uses information. Thus, when we talk about cognitive differences, we are referring to varying approaches to perceiving and assimilating data, making decisions, solving problems, and relating to others.[31] Cognitive approaches are *preferences* that are not necessarily rigid, but most people tend to have only a few preferred habits of thought. One of the most widely recognized cognitive differences is between what we call left-brained versus right-brained thinking patterns.

Patterns of Thinking and Brain Dominance

Neurologists and psychologists have long known that the brain has two distinct hemispheres. Furthermore, science has shown that the left hemisphere controls movement on the body's right side and the right hemisphere controls movement on the left. In the 1960s and 1970s, scientists also discovered that the distinct hemispheres influence thinking, which led to an interest in what has been called left-brained versus right-brained thinking patterns. The left hemisphere is associated with logical, analytical thinking and a linear approach to problem-solving, whereas the right hemisphere is associated with creative, intuitive, values-based thought processes.[32] A recent JC Penney television commercial provides a simple illustration. The commercial shows a woman whose right brain is telling her to go out and spend money to buy fun clothes, while the left brain is telling her to be

What's Your Thinking Style?

The following characteristics are associated with the four quadrants identified by Herrmann's whole brain model. Think for a moment about how you approach problems and make decisions. In addition, consider how you typically approach your work or class assignments and how you interact with others. Circle ten of the terms below that you believe best describe your own cognitive style. Try to be honest and select terms that apply to you as you are, not how you might like to be. There are no right or wrong answers.

A	B	C	D
Analytical	Organized	Friendly	Holistic
Factual	Planned	Receptive	Imaginative
Directive	Controlled	Enthusiastic	Intuitive
Rigorous	Detailed	Understanding	Synthesizing
Realistic	Conservative	Expressive	Curious
Intellectual	Disciplined	Empathetic	Spontaneous
Objective	Practical	Trusting	Flexible
Knowledgeable	Industrious	Sensitive	Open-Minded
Bright	Persistent	Passionate	Conceptual
Clear	Implementer	Humanistic	Adventurous

The terms in Column A are associated with logical, analytical thinking (Quadrant A); those in Column B with organized, detail-oriented thinking (Quadrant B); those in Column C with empathetic and emotionally based thinking (Quadrant C); and those in Column D with integrative and imaginative thinking (Quadrant D). Do your preferences fall primarily in one of the four columns, or do you have a more balanced set of preferences across all four? If you have a strong preference in one particular quadrant, were you surprised by which one?

---

logical and save money. As another simplified example, people who are very good at verbal and written language (which involves a linear thinking process) are using the left brain, whereas those who prefer to interpret information through visual images are more right-brained.

Although the concept of right-brained versus left-brained thinking is not entirely accurate physiologically (not all processes associated with left-brained thinking are located in the left hemisphere and vice versa), this concept provides a powerful metaphor for two very different ways of thinking and decision making. It is also important to remember that everyone uses both left-brained and right-brained thinking, but to varying degrees.

More recently, these ideas have been broadened to what is called the **whole brain concept**.[33] Ned Herrmann began developing his concept of whole brain thinking while he was a manager at General Electric in the late 1970s and has expanded it through many years of research with thousands of individuals and organizations. The whole brain approach considers not only a person's preference for right-brained versus left-brained thinking, but also for conceptual versus experiential thinking. Herrmann's whole brain model thus identifies four quadrants of the brain that are related to different thinking styles. Again, while not entirely accurate physiologically, the whole brain model is an excellent metaphor for understanding differences in thinking patterns. Some people strongly lean toward using one quadrant in most situations, whereas others rely on two, three, or even all four styles of thinking. An individual's preference

Action Memo
A simplified exercise to help you think about your own preferences appears in Leader's Self-Insight 4.4. Before reading further, follow the instructions and complete the exercise to get an idea about your dominant thinking style according to Herrmann's whole brain model. Then, read the descriptions of each quadrant below.

Whole brain concept
an approach that considers not only a person's preference for right-brained versus left-brained thinking, but also conceptual versus experiential thinking; identifies four quadrants of the brain related to different thinking styles

for each of the four styles is determined through a survey called the *Herrmann Brain Dominance Instrument (HBDI)*, which has been administered to hundreds of thousands of individuals.

The whole brain model provides a useful overview of an individual's mental preferences, which in turn affect patterns of communication, behavior, and leadership.

Quadrant A
the part of the brain associated in the whole brain model with logical thinking, analysis of facts, and processing numbers

Quadrant A is associated with logical thinking, analysis of facts, and processing numbers. A person who has a quadrant A dominance is rational and realistic, thinks critically, and likes to deal with numbers and technical matters. These people like to know how things work and to follow logical procedures. A leader with a predominantly A-quadrant thinking style tends to be directive and authoritative. This leader focuses on tasks and activities and likes to deal with concrete information and facts. Opinions and feelings are generally not considered as important as facts.

Quadrant B
the part of the brain associated in the whole brain model with planning, organizing facts, and careful detailed review

Quadrant B deals with planning, organizing facts, and careful detailed review. A person who relies heavily on quadrant B thinking is well-organized, reliable, and neat. These people like to establish plans and procedures and get things done on time. Quadrant-B leaders are typically conservative and highly traditional. They tend to avoid risks and strive for stability. Thus, they may insist on following rules and procedures, no matter what the circumstances are.

Quadrant C
the part of the brain associated in the whole brain model with interpersonal relationships and intuitive and emotional thought processes

Quadrant C is associated with interpersonal relationships and affects intuitive and emotional thought processes. C-quadrant individuals are sensitive to others and enjoy interacting with and teaching others. They are typically emotional and expressive, outgoing, and supportive of others. Leaders with a predominantly quadrant-C style are friendly, trusting, and empathetic. They are concerned with people's feelings more than with tasks and procedures and may put emphasis on employee development and training.

Quadrant D
the part of the brain associated in the whole brain model with conceptualizing, synthesizing, and integrating facts and patterns.

Quadrant D is associated with conceptualizing, synthesizing, and integrating facts and patterns, with seeing the big picture rather than the details. A person with a quadrant-D preference is visionary and imaginative, likes to speculate, break the rules, and take risks, and may be impetuous. These people are curious and enjoy experimentation and playfulness. The D-quadrant leader is holistic, imaginative, and adventurous. This leader enjoys change, experimentation and risk-taking, and generally allows followers a great deal of freedom and flexibility.

Exhibit 4.4 illustrates the model with its four quadrants and some of the mental processes associated with each. Each style has positive and negative results for leaders and followers. There is no style that is necessarily better or worse, though any of the styles carried to an extreme can be detrimental. It is important to remember that every individual, even those with a strong preference in one quadrant, actually has a coalition of preferences from each of the four quadrants.[34] Therefore, leaders with a predominantly quadrant-A style may also have elements from one or more of the other styles, which affects their leadership effectiveness. For example, a leader with a strong A-quadrant preference might also have preferences from quadrant C, the interpersonal area, which would cause her to have concern for people's feelings even though she is primarily concerned with tasks, facts, and figures.

In addition, Herrmann believes people can learn to use their "whole brain," rather than relying only on one or two quadrants. His research indicates that very few, if any, individuals can be wholly balanced among the four quadrants, but people can be aware of their preferences and engage in activities and experiences that help develop the other quadrants. Leaders who reach the top of organizations often have well-balanced brains, according to Herrmann's research. In fact, the

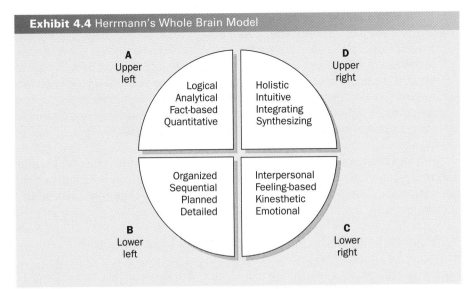

Exhibit 4.4 Herrmann's Whole Brain Model

Source: Ned Herrmann, *The Whole Brain Business Book,* (New York: McGraw-Hill, 1996), p. 15.

typical CEO has at least two, usually three, and often four strong preferences and thus has a wide range of thinking options available to choose from. A broad range of thinking styles is particularly important at higher levels of organizations because leaders deal with a greater variety and complexity of people and issues.[35]

Understanding that individuals have different thinking styles can also help leaders be more effective in interacting with followers. Some leaders act as if everyone responds to the same material and behavior in the same way, but this isn't true. Some people prefer facts and figures, whereas others want to know about relationships and patterns. Some followers prefer freedom and flexibility, whereas others crave structure and order. At Nissan Design International, Jerry Hirshberg used an understanding of cognitive differences to change how he leads.

Action Memo

As a leader, you can strive for "whole brain" thinking to deal effectively with a wide variety of people and complex issues. You can be aware of your natural thinking patterns and include other perspectives that help you develop a broader understanding.

IN THE LEAD

Jerry Hirshberg, Nissan Design International

Jerry Hirshberg is a predominantly D-quadrant leader. He likes thinking broadly and dreaming big, deriving ideas intuitively—and he abhors tight structure and control. He once assumed that his employees would as well. Hirshberg wanted his designers to have the freedom to be creative, to take risks, and to innovate. Therefore, he was surprised when he learned that a few of his followers actually wanted and needed more structure in order to perform at their best.

Hirshberg assumed his employees would react to information and ideas the same way he did. He would throw huge amounts of information at them and expect them to respond intuitively and creatively. Some people, however, always hesitated, which Hirschberg originally interpreted as a resistance to innovation and change. However, over time, he came to realize that some of his designers simply wanted and needed time to "process" the information and to develop more logical, analytical approaches to Hirschberg's intuitively derived ideas. When they were given this time, the employees returned with significant contributions and excellent plans that moved the project forward.

It didn't take Hirshberg long to recognize that the contributions of the more logical, analytical, and detail-oriented thinkers were just as critical to the success of a project as those of the intuitive, creative thinkers. Hirshberg turned his realization into a new approach to creativity at Nissan. He now hires designers in what he calls *divergent pairs*. He believes that by putting together two spectacularly gifted people who have different cognitive styles and see the world in different ways, he builds a creative tension that keeps the organization energized and provides unlimited potential for innovation. Essentially, Hirshberg mixes styles to create a "whole brain" company at Nissan Design International.[36]

As this example illustrates, leaders can shift their styles and behaviors to more effectively communicate with followers and to help them perform up to their full potential. Leaders can also recruit people with varied cognitive styles to help achieve goals.

Problem-Solving Styles: The Myers–Briggs Type Indicator

Another approach to cognitive differences grew out of the work of psychologist Carl Jung. Jung believed that differences in individual behavior resulted from preferences in how we go about gathering and evaluating information for solving problems and making decisions.[37] One of the most widely used personality tests in the United States, the **Myers–Briggs Type Indicator (MBTI)**, is one way of measuring how individuals differ in these areas.[38] The MBTI has been taken by millions of people around the world and can help individuals better understand themselves and others. Nearly 90 percent of Fortune 100 companies report using the MBTI to help leaders make hiring and promotion decisions.[39]

The MBTI uses four different pairs of attributes to classify people in 1 of 16 different personality types:

> **Myers–Briggs Type Indicator (MBTI)**
> personality test that measures how individuals differ in gathering and evaluating information for solving problems and making decisions

1. **Introversion versus extraversion:** This dimension focuses on where people gain interpersonal strength and mental energy. Extraverts (E) gain energy from being around others and interacting with others, whereas introverts (I) gain energy by focusing on personal thoughts and feelings.

2. **Sensing versus intuition:** This identifies how a person absorbs information. Those with a sensing preference (S) gather and absorb information through the five senses, whereas intuitive people (N) rely on less direct perceptions. Intuitives, for example, focus more on patterns, relationships, and hunches than on direct perception of facts and details.

3. **Thinking versus feeling:** This dimension relates to how much consideration a person gives to emotions in making a decision. Feeling types (F) tend to rely more on their values and sense of what is right and wrong, and they consider how a decision will affect other people's feelings. Thinking types (T) tend to rely more on logic and be very objective in decision making.

4. **Judging versus perceiving:** The judging versus perceiving dimension concerns an individual's attitudes toward ambiguity and how quickly a person makes a decision. People with a judging preference like certainty and closure. They enjoy having goals and deadlines and tend to make decisions quickly based on available data. Perceiving people, on the other hand, enjoy ambiguity, dislike deadlines, and may change their minds several times before making a final decision. Perceiving types like to gather a large amount of data and information before making a decision.

The various combinations of these preferences result in 16 unique personality types. There are a number of exercises available in print and on the Internet that can help people determine their preferences according to the MBTI. Individuals develop unique strengths and weaknesses as a result of their preferences for introversion versus extraversion, sensing versus intuition, thinking versus feeling, and judging versus perceiving. As with the whole brain approach, MBTI types should not be considered ingrained or unalterable. People's awareness of their preferences, training, and life experiences can cause them to change their preferences over time.

Leaders should remember that each type can have positive and negative consequences for behavior. By understanding their MBTI type, leaders can learn to maximize their strengths and minimize their weaknesses. John Bearden, chief executive of GMAC Home Services, took the MBTI and learned that he was an ENTJ (extraverted, intuitive, thinking, and judging). ENTJ types can be dynamic, inspiring, and self-confident in making tough decisions. However, they can also be overbearing, insensitve, and hasty in their judgments. Bearden said the MBTI was a "quantum leap" in his understanding of his strengths and weaknesses. He began consciously refining his leadership style, making a determined effort to give more consideration to hard data and listen more carefully to colleagues' opinions. Bearden put himself to the test at a recent national convention. "In the past, I would have gotten very much involved interjecting my own position very early on and probably biasing the process," he said. "But here I found myself quite content to allow their positions to be articulated and argued with creative tension. All I did was sit and absorb. It was a very satisfying process."[40]

> **Action Memo**
> Go to Leader's Self-Insight 4.5, on page 122 at the end of this chapter, to complete an exercise that will identify your MBTI personality type.

Application of the MBTI in leadership studies is increasing rapidly.[41] There is no "leader type," and all 16 of the MBTI types can function effectively as leaders. As with the four quadrants of the whole brain model, leaders can learn to use their preferences and balance their approaches to best suit followers and the situation. However, research reveals some interesting, although tentative, findings. For example, although extraversion is often considered an important trait for a leader, leaders in the real world are about equally divided between extraverts and introverts. In regard to the sensing versus intuition dimension, data reveal that sensing types are in the majority in fields where the focus is on the immediate and tangible (e.g., construction, banking, manufacturing). However, in areas that involve breaking new ground or long-range planning, intuitive leaders are in the majority. Thinking (as opposed to feeling) types are more common among leaders in business and industry as well as in the realm of science. In addition, thinking types appear to be chosen more often as managers even in organizations that value "feeling," such as counseling centers. Finally, one of the most consistent findings is that judging types are in the majority among the leaders studied.

Thus, based on the limited research, the two preferences that seem to be most strongly associated with successful leadership are thinking and judging. However, this doesn't mean that people with other preferences cannot be effective leaders. Much more research needs to be done before accurate conclusions can be reached about the relationship between MBTI types and leadership.

Matching Leaders with Roles

Leaders, like all individuals, can differ significantly in their personalities, attitudes, values, and thinking styles. These individual differences help in part to explain why a leader might succeed in some situations yet fail in others, despite appearing to have all the necessary skills and abilities for the job.

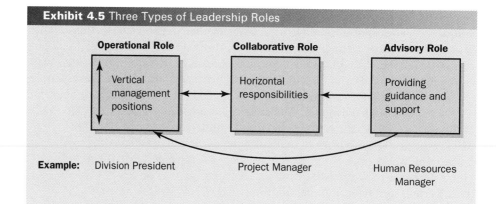

Exhibit 4.5 Three Types of Leadership Roles

Recent research suggests that different types of personalities and thinking styles might be better suited to different types of leadership roles.[42] Exhibit 4.5 illustrates three types of leadership roles identified in today's organizations by a team of experts at Hay Group, a global organizational and human resources consulting firm. The researchers found that, although there is a core set of competencies that all leaders need, there is significant variation in the cognitive skills, behaviors, and personalities that correlate with success in the different roles.

Operational Role This role is the closest to a traditional, vertically-oriented management role, where an executive has direct control over people and resources to accomplish results. Operational leaders fill traditional line and general management positions in a business, for example. They set goals, establish plans, and get things done primarily through the vertical hierarchy and the use of position power. Operations leaders are doggedly focused on delivering results. They tend to be assertive, always pushing forward and raising the bar. Successful operations leaders are typically analytical and knowledgeable, yet they also have the ability to translate their knowledge into a vision that others can become passionate about.

Collaborative Role This is a horizontal role and includes people such as project managers, matrix managers, and team leaders in today's more horizontally-organized companies. This role, which has grown tremendously in importance in recent years, is quite challenging. Leaders in collaborative roles typically don't have the strong position power of the operational role. They often work behind the scenes, using their personal power to influence others and get things done. Collaborative leaders need excellent people skills in order to network, build relationships, and obtain agreement through personal influence. They also are highly proactive and tenacious, and they exhibit extreme flexibility to cope with the ambiguity and uncertainty associated with the collaborative role.

Advisory Role Leaders in an advisory role provide guidance and support to other people and departments in the organization. Advisory leadership roles are found, for example, in departments such as legal, finance, and human resources. These leaders are responsible for developing broad organizational capabilities rather than accomplishing specific business results. Advisory leaders also need great people skills

Action Memo

As a leader, you can understand the type of leadership role in which your personality traits and thinking style would be most effective and satisfying. You can pursue an operational, collaborative, or advisory leadership role depending on your natural tendencies.

and the ability to influence through personal knowledge and influence. In addition, leaders in advisory roles need exceptionally high levels of honesty and integrity to build trust and keep the organization on solid ethical ground.

The Hay Group research findings shed new light on the types of roles leaders fill in today's organizations and emphasize that individual differences can influence how effective a leader might be in a particular role. Success as a leader involves more than mastering the knowledge and skills of a particular job. A leader's personality, values and attitudes, and thinking style also play a part.

Summary and Interpretation

This chapter explored some of the individual differences that affect leaders and the leadership process. Individuals differ in many ways, including personality, values and attitudes, and styles of thinking and decision making. One model of personality, the Big Five personality dimensions, examines whether individuals score high or low on the dimensions of extraversion, agreeableness, conscientiousness, emotional stability, and openness to experience. Although there is some indication that a high degree of each of the personality dimensions is associated with successful leadership, individuals who score low on various dimensions may also be effective leaders. Two specific personality traits that have a significant impact on leader behavior are locus of control and authoritarianism.

Values are fundamental beliefs that cause a person to prefer that things be done one way rather than another. One way to think about values is in terms of instrumental and end values. End values are beliefs about the kinds of goals that are worth pursuing, whereas instrumental values are beliefs about the types of behavior that are appropriate for reaching goals. Values also affect an individual's attitudes. A leader's attitudes about self and others influence how the leader behaves toward and interacts with followers. Two sets of assumptions called Theory X and Theory Y represent two very different sets of attitudes leaders may hold about people in general. Differences in personality, values, and attitudes influence perception, which is the process people use to select, organize, and interpret information. Perceptual distortions include stereotyping, the halo effect, projection, and perceptual defense. Attribution theory refers to how people explain the causes of events or behaviors. Based on their perception, people may make either internal or external attributions.

Another area of individual differences is cognitive style. The whole brain concept explores a person's preferences for right-brained versus left-brained thinking and for conceptual versus experiential thinking. The model provides a powerful metaphor for understanding differences in thinking styles. Individuals can learn to use their "whole brain" rather than relying on one thinking style. Another way of looking at cognitive differences is the Myers–Briggs Type Indicator, which measures an individual's preferences for introversion versus extraversion, sensing versus intuition, thinking versus feeling, and judging versus perceiving.

Finally, we talked about three types of leadership roles: operational roles, collaborative roles, and advisory roles. Recent studies suggest that different types of personalities and thinking styles are better suited to different types of leadership roles, and leaders can be more effective when they are in positions that best match their natural tendencies.

JUNG'S TYPOLOGY AND THE MYERS–BRIGGS TYPE INDICATOR

For each item below, circle either "a" or "b." In some cases, both "a" and "b" may apply to you. You should decide which is *more* like you, even if it is only slightly more true.

1. I would rather
   a. Solve a new and complicated problem
   b. Work on something that I have done before

2. I like to
   a. Work alone in a quiet place
   b. Be where "the action" is

3. I want a boss who
   a. Establishes and applies criteria in decisions
   b. Considers individual needs and makes exceptions

4. When I work on a project, I
   a. Like to finish it and get some closure
   b. Often leave it open for possible change

5. When making a decision, the most important considerations are
   a. Rational thoughts, ideas, and data
   b. People's feelings and values

6. On a project, I tend to
   a. Think it over and over before deciding how to proceed
   b. Start working on it right away, thinking about it as I go along

7. When working on a project, I prefer to
   a. Maintain as much control as possible
   b. Explore various options

8. In my work, I prefer to
   a. Work on several projects at a time, and learn as much as possible about each one
   b. Have one project that is challenging and keeps me busy

9. I often
   a. Make lists and plans whenever I start something and may hate to seriously alter my plans
   b. Avoid plans and just let things progress as I work on them

10. When discussing a problem with colleagues, it is easy for me
    a. To see "the big picture"
    b. To grasp the specifics of the situation

11. When the phone rings in my office or at home, I usually
    a. Consider it an interruption
    b. Don't mind answering it

12. The word that describes me better is
    a. Analytical
    b. Empathetic

13. When I am working on an assignment, I tend to
    a. Work steadily and consistently
    b. Work in bursts of energy with "down time" in between

14. When I listen to someone talk on a subject, I usually try to
    a. Relate it to my own experience and see if it fits
    b. Assess and analyze the message

15. When I come up with new ideas, I generally
    a. "Go for it"
    b. Like to contemplate the ideas some more

16. When working on a project, I prefer to
    a. Narrow the scope so it is clearly defined
    b. Broaden the scope to include related aspects

17. When I read something, I usually
    a. Confine my thoughts to what is written there
    b. Read between the lines and relate the words to other ideas

18. When I have to make a decision in a hurry, I often
    a. Feel uncomfortable and wish I had more information
    b. Am able to do so with available data

19. In a meeting, I tend to
    a. Continue formulating my ideas as I talk about them
    b. Only speak out after I have carefully thought the issue through

20. In work, I prefer spending a great deal of time on issues of
    a. Ideas
    b. People

21. In meetings, I am most often annoyed with people who
    a. Come up with many sketchy ideas
    b. Lengthen the meeting with many practical details

22. I tend to be
    a. A morning person
    b. A night owl

23. My style in preparing for a meeting is
    a. To be willing to go in and be responsive
    b. To be fully prepared and sketch out an outline of the meeting

24. In meetings, I would prefer for people to
    a. Display a fuller range of emotions
    b. Be more task-oriented

25. I would rather work for an organization where
    a. My job was intellectually stimulating
    b. I was committed to its goals and mission

26. On weekends, I tend to
    a. Plan what I will do
    b. Just see what happens and decide as I go along

27. I am more
    a. Outgoing
    b. Contemplative

28. I would rather work for a boss who is
    a. Full of new ideas
    b. Practical

Continued

In the following, choose the word in each pair that appeals to you more:

29. a. Social
    b. Theoretical

30. a. Ingenuity
    b. Practicality

31. a. Organized
    b. Adaptable

32. a. Activity
    b. Concentration

Scoring

Count one point for each item listed below that you circled in the inventory.

Score for I (Introversion)	Score for E (Extraversion)	Score for S (Sensing)	Score for N (Intuition)
2a	2b	1b	1a
6a	6b	10b	10a
11a	11b	13a	13b
15b	15a	16a	16b
19b	19a	17a	17b
22a	22b	21a	21b
27b	27a	28b	28a
32b	32a	30b	30a

Totals ____ ____   ____ ____

Circle the one with more points:
I or E
(If tied on I/E, don't count #11)

Circle the one with more points:
S or N
(If tied on S/N, don't count #16)

Score for T (Thinking)	Score for F (Feeling)	Score for J (Judging)	Score for P (Perceiving)
3a	3b	4a	4b
5a	5b	7a	7b
12a	12b	8b	8a
14b	14a	9a	9b
20a	20b	18b	18a
24b	24a	23b	23a
25a	25b	26a	26b
29b	29a	31a	31b

Totals ____ ____   ____ ____

Circle the one with more points:
T or F
(If tied on T/F, don't count #24)

Circle the one with more points:
J or P
(If tied on J/P, don't count #23)

Your Score Is: I or E _____ S or N _____ T or F _____ J or P _____

Your MBTI type is: _____ (example: INTJ; ESFP; etc.)

Scoring and Interpretation

The Myers–Briggs Type Indicator (MBTI), based on the work of psychologist Carl Jung, is the most widely used personality assessment instrument in the world. The MBTI, which was described in the chapter text, identifies 16 different "types," shown with their dominant characteristics in the following chart. Remember that no one is a pure type; however, each individual has preferences for introversion versus extraversion, sensing versus intuition, thinking versus feeling, and judging versus perceiving. Based on your scores on the survey, read the description of your type in the chart. Do you believe the description fits your personality?

Source: From *Organizational Behavior: Experience and Cases*, 4th edition by Dorothy Marcic. © 1995. Reprinted with permission of South-Western, a division of Thomson Learning: *http://www.thomsonrights.com*. Fax: 800-730-2215.

Continued

Characteristics Frequently Associated with Each Type

| | Sensing Types | | Intuitive Types | |

Introverts

ISTJ

Quiet, serious, earn success by thoroughness and dependability. Practical, matter-of-fact, realistic, and responsible. Decide logically what should be done and work toward it steadily, regardless of distractions. Take pleasure in making everything orderly and organized—their work, their home, their life. Value traditions and loyalty.

ISFJ

Quiet, friendly, responsible, and conscientious. Committed and steady in meeting their obligations. Thorough, painstaking, and accurate. Loyal, considerate, notice and remember specifics about people who are important to them, concerned with how others feel. Strive to create an orderly and harmonious environment at work and at home.

INFJ

Seek meaning and connection in ideas, relationships, and material possessions. Want to understand what motivates people and are insightful about others. Conscientious and committed to their firm values. Develop a clear vision about how best to serve the common good. Organized and decisive in implementing their vision.

INTJ

Have original minds and great drive for implementing their ideas and achieving their goals. Quickly see patterns in external events and develop long-range explanatory perspectives. When committed, organize a job and carry it through. Skeptical and independent, have high standards of competence and performance—for themselves and others.

ISTP

Tolerant and flexible, quiet observers until a problem appears, then act quickly to find workable solutions. Analyze what makes things work and readily get through large amounts of data to isolate the core of practical problems. Interested in cause and effect, organize facts using logical principles, value efficiency.

ISFP

Quiet, friendly, sensitive, and kind. Enjoy the present moment, what's going on around them. Like to have their own space and to work within their own time frame. Loyal and committed to their values and to people who are important to them. Dislike disagreements and conflicts, do not force their opinions or values on others.

INFP

Idealistic, loyal to their values and to people who are important to them. Want an external life that is congruent with their values. Curious, quick to see possibilities, can be catalysts for implementing ideas. Seek to understand people and to help them fulfill their potential. Adaptable, flexible, and accepting unless a value is threatened.

INTP

Seek to develop logical explanations for everything that interests them. Theoretical and abstract, interested more in ideas than in social interaction. Quiet, contained, flexible, and adaptable. Have unusual ability to focus in depth to solve problems in their area of interest. Skeptical, sometimes critical, always analytical.

Extraverts

ESTP

Flexible and tolerant, they take a pragmatic approach focused on immediate results. Theories and conceptual explanations bore them—they want to act energetically to solve the problem. Focus on the here-and-now, spontaneous, enjoy each moment that they can be active with others. Enjoy material comforts and style. Learn best through doing.

ESFP

Outgoing, friendly, and accepting. Exuberant lovers of life, people, and material comforts. Enjoy working with others to make things happen. Bring common sense and a realistic approach to their work, and make work fun. Flexible and spontaneous, adapt readily to new people and environments. Learn best by trying a new skill with other people.

ENFP

Warmly enthusiastic and imaginative. See life as full of possibilities. Make connections between events and information very quickly, and confidently proceed based on the patterns they see. Want a lot of affirmation from others, and readily give appreciation and support. Spontaneous and flexible, often rely on their ability to improvise and their verbal fluency.

ENTP

Quick, ingenious, stimulating, alert, and outspoken. Resourceful in solving new and challenging problems. Adept at generating conceptual possibilities and then analyzing them strategically. Good at reading other people. Bored by routine, will seldom do the same thing the same way, apt to turn to one new interest after another.

ESTJ

Practical, realistic, matter-of-fact. Decisive, quickly move to implement decisions. Organize projects and people to get things done, focus on getting results in the most efficient way possible. Take care of routine details. Have a clear set of logical standards, systematically follow them and want others to also. Forceful in implementing their plans.

ESFJ

Warmhearted, conscientious, and cooperative. Want harmony in their environment, work with determination to establish it. Like to work with others to complete tasks accurately and on time. Loyal, follow through even in small matters. Notice what others need in their day-by-day lives and try to provide it. Want to be appreciated for who they are and for what they contribute.

ENFJ

Warm, empathetic, responsive, and responsible. Highly attuned to the emotions, needs, and motivations of others. Find potential in everyone, want to help others fulfill their potential. May act as catalysts for individual and group growth. Loyal, responsive to praise and criticism. Sociable, facilitate others in a group, and provide inspiring leadership.

ENTJ

Frank, decisive, assume leadership readily. Quickly see illogical and inefficient procedures and policies, develop and implement comprehensive systems to solve organizational problems. Enjoy long-term planning and goal setting. Usually well informed, well read, enjoy expanding their knowledge and passing it on to others. Forceful in presenting their ideas.

Discussion Questions

1. Extraversion is often considered a "good" quality for a leader to have. Why might introversion be considered an equally positive quality?

2. What might be some reasons the dimension of "openness to experience" correlates so strongly with historians' ratings of the greatest U.S. presidents but has been less strongly associated with business leader success? Do you think this personality dimension might be more important for business leaders of today than it was in the past? Discuss.

3. Leaders in many of today's organizations use the results of personality testing to make hiring and promotion decisions. Discuss some of the pros and cons of this approach.

4. From Leader's Self-Insight 4.3, identify four or five values (instrumental or end values) that could be a source of conflict between leaders and followers. Explain.

5. How do a person's attitudes and assumptions about human nature in general affect his or her leadership approach? How might a leader's attitudes about him or herself alter or reinforce this approach?

6. Do you believe understanding your preferences according to the whole brain model can help you be a better leader? Discuss.

7. How can a leader use an understanding of brain dominance to improve the functioning of the organization?

8. Why do you think *thinking* and *judging* are the two characteristics from the Myers-Briggs Type Indicator that seem to be most strongly associated with effective leadership?

9. Do you believe a leader's success in a particular leadership role would be influenced more by personality characteristics or by the leader's thinking and decision-making style? Discuss. What type of leadership role would you feel most comfortable in? Discuss your reasons.

Leadership at Work

Past and Future

Draw a life line below that marks high and low experiences during your life. Think of key decisions, defining moments, peak experiences, and major disappointments that shaped who you are today. Draw the line from left to right, and identify each high and low point with a word or two.

Birth Year: Today's Date:

What made these valued experiences? How did they shape who you are today?

_____

_____

Now take the long view of your life. In 10-year increments, write below the leader experiences you want to have. Provide a brief past-tense description of each decade (e.g., next 10 years—big starting salary, bored in first job, promoted to middle management)

Next 10 years: _____
_____

Following 10 years: _____
_____

Following 10 years: _____
_____

Following 10 years: _____
_____

What personal skills and strengths will you use to achieve the future?
_____
_____

What is your core life purpose or theme as expressed in the life line and answers above?
_____
_____

What would your desired future self say to your present self?
_____
_____

How do your answers above relate to your scores on the Leader Self-Insight question-naires you completed in this chapter?
_____
_____

Leadership Development: Cases for Analysis

International Bank

Top executives and board members of a large international bank in New York are meeting to consider three finalists for a new position. The winning candidate will be in a high-profile job, taking charge of a group of top loan officers who have recently gotten the bank into some risky financial arrangements in Latin America. The bank had taken a financial bath when the Mexican peso collapsed, and the board voted to hire someone to directly oversee this group of loan officers and make sure the necessary due diligence is done on major loans before further commitments are made. Although the bank likes for decisions to be made as close to the action level as possible, they believe the loan officers have gotten out of hand and need to be reined in. The effectiveness of the person in this new position is considered to be of utmost importance for the bank's future. After care-fully reviewing resumés, the board selected six candidates for the first round of interviews, after which the list of finalists was narrowed to three. All three candidates seem to have the intellect and experience to handle the job. Before the second-round interview, the board has asked their regular consulting firm to review the candidates, conduct more extensive background checks, and administer personality tests. A summary of their reports on the three candidates follows:

A.M. This candidate has a relatively poor self-concept and exhibits a fear of the unknown. She is somewhat of an introvert and is uncomfortable using power openly and conspicuously. A.M.'s beliefs about others are that all people are inherently noble, kind, and disposed to do the right thing, and that it is possible to influence and modify the behavior of anyone through logic and reason. Once a person's shortcomings are pointed out to her, A.M. will try to help the person overcome them. She believes that all employees can be happy, content, and dedicated to the goals of the organization.

J.T. J.T. is an extravert with a strong drive for achievement and power. He likes new experiences and tends to be impulsive and adventurous. He is very self-assured and confident in his own abilities, but highly suspicious of the motives and abilities of others. J.T. believes the average person has an inherent dislike for work and will avoid responsibility when possible. He is very slow to trust others, but does have the ability over time to develop close, trusting relationships. In general, though, J.T. believes most people must be coerced, controlled, and threatened to get them to do their jobs well and to the benefit of the organization.

F.C. This candidate is also an extravert, but, although she is competitive, F.C. does not seem to have the strong desire for dominance that many extraverts exhibit. F.C. is also highly conscientious and goal-oriented, and will do whatever she believes is necessary to achieve a goal. F.C. has a generally positive attitude toward others, believing that most people want to do their best for the organization. F.C. does, though, seem to have a problem forming close, personal attachments. Her lively, outgoing personality enables her to make many superficial acquaintances, but she seems to distrust and avoid emotions in herself and others, preventing the development of close relationships.

Sources: This case is based on information in "Consultant's Report" in John M. Champion and Francis J. Bridges, *Critical Incidents in Management: Decision and Policy Issues*, 6th ed. (Homewood, IL: Irwin, 1989), pp. 55–60; and James Waldroop and Timothy Butler, "Guess What? You're Not Perfect," *Fortune*, (October 16, 2000), pp. 415–420.

QUESTIONS

1. Based only on the consultant's summary, which of the three candidates would you select as a leader for the group of loan officers? Discuss and defend your decision.

2. The selection committee is more divided than before on who would be best for the job. What additional information do you think you would need to help you select the best candidate?

3. How much weight do you think should be given to the personality assessment? Do you believe personality tests can be useful in predicting the best person for a job? Discuss.

The Deadlocked Committee

Ned Norman tried to reconstruct, in his own mind, the series of events that had culminated in this morning's deadlocked committee meeting. Each of the members had suddenly seemed to resist any suggestions that did not exactly coincide with his or her own ideas for implementing the program under consideration. This sort of "stubbornness," as Norman considered it, was not like the normal behavior patterns of most committee participants. Of course, the comment during last week's meeting about "old fashioned seat-of-the-pants decision making" had ruffled a few feathers, but Ned didn't think that was why things had bogged down today.

Ned recalled starting this morning's session by stating that the committee had discussed several of the factors connected with the proposed expanded services program, and now it seemed about time to make a decision about which way to go. Robert Romany had immediately protested that they had barely scratched the surface of the possibilities for implementing the program. Then, both Hillary Thomas and David Huntington, who worked in the statistics department of Division B, had sided with Romany and insisted that more time was needed for in-depth research. Walter Weston had entered the fray by stating that this seemed a little uncalled for, since previous experience has clearly indicated that expansion programs such as this one should be implemented through selected area district offices. This had sparked a statement from Susan Pilcher that experience was more often than not a lousy teacher, which was followed by Todd Tooley repeating his unfortunate statement about old-fashioned decision making! Robert Romany had further heated things up by saying that it was obviously far better to go a little slower in such matters by trying any new program in one area first, rather than having the committee look "unprogressive" by just "trudging along the same old cow paths"!

At this point, Ned had intuitively exercised his prerogative as chairman to stop the trend that was developing. However, things were obviously so touchy among the members that they simply refused to either offer suggestions or support any that Ned offered for breaking the deadlock. Ned decided to approach each of the division directors for whom the various committee members worked. In each area he visited, he learned that the directors were already aware of the problems, and each one had his or her own ideas as to what should be done:

Division A: The director stated that he was not much in sympathy with people who wanted to make a big deal out of every program that came along. He recalled a similar problem years ago when the company first introduced decision support software, which was hailed as the manager's replacement in decision making. He noted that the software was still in use but that he had probably made better decisions as a result of his broad background and knowledge than any computer ever could. "When I've served as chair of a deadlocked committee," he said, "I simply made the decision and solved the problem. If you're smart, you'll do the same. You can't worry about everybody's feelings on this thing."

Division B: "I know you'll want to use the best available information in estimating any program's potential performance," the director of Division B told Ned. She sided with Hillary Thomas and David Huntington that an investigative approach was the only way to go. After all, the director said, it logically followed that a decision could be no better than the research effort behind it. She also told Ned that she had told Thomas and Huntington to go ahead and collect the data they needed. "My division will be footing the bill for this, so nobody can gripe about the cost aspects." she said. "Any price would be cheap if it awakens some of the people around here to the tremendous value of a scientific approach."

Division C: The director of Division C bluntly told Ned that he didn't really care how the decision was made. However, he thought the best course of action would be to carefully develop a plan and implement it a piece at a time. "That way," he said, "you can evaluate how it looks without committing the company to a full-scale expansion. It doesn't take a lot of figuring to figure that one out!"

Division D: "We've got a time problem here," the director of Division D said. "The committee simply can't look at all possible angles. They need to synthesize the information and understandings they have and make a decision based on two or three possible solutions."

Source: This is a revised version of a case by W. D. Heier, "Ned Norman, Committee Chairman," in John E. Dittrich and Robert A. Zawacki, *People and Organizations: Cases in Management and Organizational Behavior* (Plano, TX: Business Publications, Inc., 1981), pp. 9–11.

QUESTIONS

1. Based on the whole brain concept, what different thinking styles are represented by the committee members and division directors? Do you believe they can ever be brought together? Discuss.

2. What personality characteristics do you think could help Norman resolve this dilemma and break the impasse? Discuss your reasons.

3. If you were the chairman of this committee, what would you do? Discuss.

References

1   Chip Cummins, "Workers Wear Feelings on Their Hard Hats and Show True Colors: On Oil Rigs and Assembly Lines, Sensitivity Training Pays Off," *The Wall Street Journal*, (November 7, 2000), p. A1.

2   J. M. Digman, "Personality Structure: Emergence of the Five-Factor Model," *Annual Review of Psychology* 41 (1990), pp. 417–440; M. R. Barrick and M. K. Mount, "Autonomy as a Moderator of the Relationships Between the Big Five Personality Dimensions and Job Performance," *Journal of Applied Psychology* (February 1993), pp. 111–118; J. S. Wiggins and A. L. Pincus, "Personality: Structure and Assessment," *Annual Review of Psychology* 43 (1992), pp. 473–504; and Carl Zimmer, "Looking for Personality in Animals, of All People," *The New York Times* (March 1, 2005), p. F1.

3   Del Jones, "Not All Successful CEOs Are Extroverts," *USA Today* (June 6, 2006), p. B1.

4 Anthony J. Mayo and Nitin Nohria, "Double-Edged Sword," *People Management* (October 27, 2005); Carol Hymowitz, "Rewarding Competitors Over Collaborators No Longer Makes Sense" (In the Lead column), *The Wall Street Journal* (February 13, 2006), p. B1; and Joseph Nocera, "In Business, Tough Guys Finish Last," *The New York Times* (June 18, 2005), p. C1.

5 Tim Sanders, *The Likeability Factor: How to Boost Your L-Factor and Achieve the Life of Your Dreams* (New York: Crown, 2005).

6 Ron Stodghill, "Boxed Out," *FSB* (April 2005), pp. 69–72.

7 Louisa Kamps, "Reinventing Real Estate," *More* (October 2006), pp. 75–76.

8 Carol Hymowitz, "Executives Who Make Their Leisure Time Inspiring and Useful" (In the Lead column), *The Wall Street Journal* (August 14, 2006), p. B1.

9. James B. Hunt, "Travel Experience in the Formation of Leadership: John Quincy Adams, Frederick Douglass, and Jane Addams," *The Journal of Leadership Studies* 7, no. 1 (2000), pp. 92–106.

10 R. T. Hogan, G. J. Curphy, and J. Hogan, "What We Know About Leadership: Effectiveness and Personality," *American Psychologist* 49, no. 6 (1994), pp. 493–504.

11 Randolph E. Schmid, "Psychologists Rate What Helps Make a President Great," *Johnson City Press* (August 6, 2000), p. 10; and "Personality and the Presidency" segment on NBC News with John Siegenthaler, Jr., August 5, 2000.

12 P. E. Spector, "Behavior in Organizations as a Function of Employee's Locus of Control," *Psychological Bulletin* (May 1982), pp. 482–497; and H. M. Lefcourt, "Durability and Impact of the Locus of Control Construct," *Psychological Bulletin* 112 (1992), pp. 411–414.

13 Ibid.; and J. B. Miner, *Industrial-Organizational Psychology* (New York: McGraw-Hill, 1992), p. 151.

14 T. W. Adorno, E. Frenkel-Brunswick, D. J. Levinson, and R. N. Sanford, *The Authoritarian Personality* (New York: Harper & Row, 1950).

15 Susan Caminiti, "What Team Leaders Need to Know," *Fortune* (February 20, 1995), pp. 93–100.

16 E. C. Ravlin and B. M. Meglino, "Effects of Values on Perception and Decision Making: A Study of Alternative Work Value Measures," *Journal of Applied Psychology* 72 (1987), pp. 666–673.

17 Robert C. Benfari, *Understanding and Changing Your Management Style* (San Francisco: Jossey-Bass, 1999), p. 172.

18 Milton Rokeach, *The Nature of Human Values* (New York: The Free Press, 1973); and M. Rokeach, *Understanding Human Values* (New York: The Free Press, 1979).

19 Carol Hymowitz, "For Many Executives, Leadership Lessons Started with Mom" (In the Lead column), *The Wall Street Journal* (May 16, 2000), p. B1.

20 Lynne Jeter, "Early Lessons Helped Form Leadership Skills," *The Mississippi Business Journal* (March 13, 2006), p. 23.

21 Based on G. W. England and R. Lee, "The Relationship between Managerial Values and Managerial Success in the United States, Japan, India, and Australia," *Journal of Applied Psychology* 59 (1974), pp. 411–419.

22 Charles Fishman, "The Anarchist's Cookbook," *Fast Company* (July 2004), pp. 70–78; and http://www.wholefoods.com

23 S. J. Breckler, "Empirical Validation of Affect, Behavior, and Cognition as Distinct Components of Attitudes," *Journal of Personality and Social Psychology* (May 1984), pp. 1191–1205; and J. M. Olson and M. P. Zanna, "Attitudes and Attitude Change," *Annual Review of Psychology* 44 (1993), pp. 117–154.

24 Parker J. Palmer, *Leading from Within: Reflections on Spirituality and Leadership* (Indianapolis: Indiana Office for Campus Ministries, 1990), and Diane Chapman Walsh, "Cultivating Inner Sources for Leadership," in *The Organization of the Future,* Frances Hesselbein, Marshall Goldsmith, and Richard Beckhard, eds. (San Francisco: Jossey-Bass, 1997), pp. 295–302.

25 Based on Richard L. Hughes, Robert C. Ginnett, and Gordon J. Curphy, *Leadership: Enhancing the Lessons of Experience* (Boston: Irwin McGraw-Hill, 1999), pp. 182–184.

26 Douglas McGregor, *The Human Side of Enterprise* (New York: McGraw-Hill, 1960).

27 J. Hall and S. M. Donnell, "Managerial Achievement: The Personal Side of Behavioral Theory," *Human Relations* 32 (1979), pp. 77–101.

28 Andrea Coombes, "Managers Rate Themselves High But Workers Prove Tough Critics," *The Wall Street Journal* (September 26, 2006), p. B8; Jaclyne Badal, "Surveying the Field: Cracking the Glass Ceiling," (sidebar in Theory & Practice column), *The Wall Street Journal* (June 19, 2006), p. B3.

29 H. H. Kelley, "Attribution in Social Interaction," in E. Jones et al. (eds.), *Attribution: Perceiving the Causes of Behavior* (Morristown, NJ: General Learning Press, 1972).

30 Kevin Kelly, "Branching Out," *FSB* (December 2005–January 2006), p. 39.

31 Dorothy Leonard and Susaan Straus, "Putting Your Company's Whole Brain to Work," *Harvard Business Review* (July–August 1997), pp. 111–121.

32 Henry Mintzberg, "Planning on the Left Side and Managing on the Right," *Harvard Business Review* (July–August 1976), pp. 49–57; Richard Restak, "The Hemispheres of the Brain Have Minds of Their Own," *The New York Times* (January 25, 1976); and Robert Ornstein, *The Psychology of Consciousness* (San Francisco: W. H. Freeman, 1975).

33 This discussion is based on Ned Herrmann, *The Whole Brain Business Book* (New York: McGraw Hill, 1996).

34 Herrmann, *The Whole Brain Business Book*, p. 103.

35 Herrmann, *The Whole Brain Business Book*, p. 179.

36 Leonard and Straus, "Putting Your Company's Whole Brain to Work"; and Katherine Mieszkowski, "Opposites Attract," *Fast Company* (December–January 1998), pp. 42, 44.

37 Carl Jung, *Psychological Types* (London: Routledge and Kegan Paul, 1923).

38 Otto Kroeger and Janet M. Thuesen, *Type Talk* (New York: Delacorte Press, 1988); Kroeger and Thuesen, *Type Talk at Work* (New York: Dell, 1992); "Conference Proceedings," The Myers–Briggs Type Indicator and Leadership: An International Research Conference, January 12–14, 1994; and S. K. Hirsch, *MBTI Team Member's Guide* (Palo Alto, Calif.: Consulting Psychologists Press, 1992).

39 Reported in Lisa Takeuchi Cullen, "SATS for J-O-B-S," *Time* (April 3, 2006), p. 89.

40 Coeli Carr, "Redesigning the Management Psyche," *The New York Times,* (May 26, 2002), Business Section, p. 14.

41 Based on Mary H. McCaulley, "Research on the MBTI and Leadership: Taking the Critical First Step," Keynote Address, The Myers–Briggs Type Indicator and Leadership: An International Research Conference, January 12–14, 1994.

42 This discussion is based heavily on "Towards a More Perfect Match: Building Successful Leaders by Effectively Aligning People and Roles," Hay Group Working paper (2004); and "Making Sure the 'Suit' Fits," Hay Group Research Brief (2004). Available from Hay Group, The McClelland Center, 116 Huntington Avenue, Boston, MA, 02116, or at http://www. haygroup.com.

Chapter 5

Your Leadership Challenge

After reading this chapter, you should be able to:

- Recognize how mental models guide your behavior and relationships.

- Engage in independent thinking by staying mentally alert, thinking critically, and being mindful rather than mindless.

- Break out of categorized thinking patterns and open your mind to new ideas and multiple perspectives.

- Begin to apply systems thinking and personal mastery to your activities at school or work.

- Exercise emotional intelligence, including being self-aware, managing your emotions, motivating yourself, displaying empathy, and managing relationships.

- Apply the difference between motivating others based on fear and motivating others based on love.

Leadership Mind and Heart

When Larry Walters took over at Qwest Communication's Idaho Falls call center, many people thought the situation was downright hopeless: Doors slamming. People crying on the phone to their friends. Rampant absenteeism. Rumors that the center would soon close.

Walters soon realized that most of the frontline supervisors at the center managed through fear and intimidation. One of his first moves was to tell them they were expected to help people be their best rather than bullying and harassing them in an effort to improve productivity. Four of the supervisors refused to go along with the new approach and were fired, sending a clear signal to employees that it was a new day in Idaho Falls. Walters set clear performance standards and posted the results so everyone would know how the center was doing compared to its peers. But he softened this strong focus on results by letting people know he genuinely cared about them. His first question to an employee in the morning wouldn't be "How are your numbers?" but "How was your son's Little League game?" or "Did you have a fun weekend?" Walters got out on the floor and got to know people by name. He listened to their frustrations and made changes to alleviate them where he could. He stood on a desk in the middle of the building and told people he loved them and believed they could accomplish great things.

Before long, people were accomplishing great things. The center buzzed with activity and enthusiasm as figures for sales and customer service consistently went up. Senior executives were so impressed that they decided to expand the center. Walters cried along with employees as the announcement was made. Down to just 65 people and with the lights out in half of the building when Walters arrived, within two years the Idaho Falls center employed around 400 in two buildings and was the largest Qwest call center in the country.[1]

Larry Walters created a new model for the Qwest Idaho Falls call center, one that puts a priority on people and relationships rather than treating employees like production machinery. In many of today's organizations, leaders are beginning to talk about building work relationships based on trust, caring, and respect. *Employee engagement* has become a motto for companies that want motivated and committed workers. In a study of companies trying to transform, Harvard researcher Christopher Bartlett found that the biggest obstacle was leaders' inability to engage employees and give them a sense of purpose and meaning in their jobs.[2] At West Point, where future Army leaders are trained, cadets are taught that the great leaders are those who genuinely care about their soldiers and never ask others to do anything they aren't willing to do themselves.[3] A former Yahoo executive even wrote a book titled *Love is the Killer App* to emphasize that compassion and empathy are essential characteristics for leadership in today's world.[4] Many leaders have a growing appreciation for the fact that the strength and quality of relationships with employees, customers, suppliers, and competitors is just as important as formal rules, contracts, plans, and even profits.

Making relationships rather than rules and schedules a priority is not easy for traditional managers who have been accustomed to thinking emotions should be left outside the company gate. However, smart leaders are aware that human emotion is the most basic force in organizations and that acknowledging and respecting employees as whole people can enhance organizational performance. People cannot be separated from their emotions, and it is through emotion that leaders generate a commitment to shared vision and mission, values and culture, and caring for the work and each other.

Noted leadership author and scholar Warren Bennis has said that "there's no difference between being a really effective leader and becoming a fully integrated person."[5] This chapter and the next examine current thinking about the importance of leaders becoming fully integrated people by exploring the full capacities of their minds and spirits. By doing so, they help others reach their full potential and contribute fully to the organization. We first define what we mean by leader capacity. Then we expand on some of the ideas introduced in the previous chapter to consider how the capacity to shift our thinking and feeling can help leaders alter their behavior, influence others, and be more effective. We discuss the concept of mental models, and look at how qualities such as independent thinking, an open mind, and systems thinking are important for leaders. Then we take a closer look at human emotion as illustrated in the concept of emotional intelligence and the emotions of love versus fear in leader–follower relationships. The next chapter will turn to spirit as reflected in moral leadership and courage.

Leader Capacity versus Competence

Traditionally, effective leadership, like good management, has been thought of as competence in a set of skills; once these specific skills are acquired, all one has to do to succeed is put them into action. However, as we all know from personal experience, working effectively with other people requires much more than practicing specific, rational skills; it often means drawing on subtle aspects of ourselves—our thoughts, beliefs, or feelings—and appealing to those aspects in others. Anyone who has participated on an athletic team knows how powerfully thoughts and emotions can affect performance. Some players are not as highly skilled from a technical standpoint but put forth amazing performances by playing with heart. Players who can help others draw on these positive emotions and thoughts usually emerge as team leaders.

In organizations, just like on the playing field, skills competence is important, but it is not enough. Although leaders have to attend to organizational issues such as production schedules, structure, finances, costs, profits, and so forth, they also tend to human issues, particularly in times of uncertainty and rapid change. Key issues include how to give people a sense of meaning and purpose when major shifts occur almost daily; how to make employees feel valued and respected in an age of downsizing and job uncertainty; and how to keep morale and motivation high in the face of uncertainty and the stress it creates.

In this chapter, rather than discussing competence, we explore a *person's capacity* for mind and heart. Whereas competence is limited and quantifiable, capacity is unlimited and defined by the potential for expansion and growth.[6] **Capacity** means the potential each of us has to be more than we are now. The U.S. Army's leadership expression "Be, Know, Do," coined more than 25 years ago, puts *Be* first because who a leader is as a person—his or her character, values, spirit, and ethical center—colors everything else.

Action Memo

As a leader, you can expand the capacity of your mind, heart, and spirit by consciously engaging in activities that use aspects of the whole self. You can reflect on your experiences to learn and grow from them.

Capacity
the potential each of us has to do more and be more than we are now

Developing leadership capacity goes beyond learning the skills for organizing, planning, or controlling others. It also involves something deeper and more subtle than the leadership traits and styles we discussed in Chapters 2 and 3. Living, working, and leading based on our capacity means using our whole selves, including intellectual, emotional, and spiritual abilities and understandings. A broad literature has emphasized that being a whole person means operating from mind, heart, spirit, and body.[7] Although we can't "learn" capacity the way we learn a set of skills, we can expand and develop leadership capacity. Just as the physical capacity of our lungs is increased through regular aerobic exercise, the capacities of the mind, heart, and spirit can be expanded through conscious development and regular use. In the previous chapter, we introduced some ideas about how individuals think, make decisions, and solve problems based on values, attitudes, and patterns of thinking. This chapter builds on some of those ideas to provide a broader view of the leadership capacities of mind and heart.

Mental Models

A mental model can be thought of as an internal picture that affects a leader's actions and relationships with others. **Mental models** are theories people hold about specific systems in the world and their expected behavior.[8] A system means any set of elements that interact to form a whole and produce a specified outcome. An organization is a system, as is a football team, a sorority pledge drive, a marriage, the registration system at a university, or the claims process at an insurance company. Leaders have many mental models that tend to govern how they interpret experiences and how they act in response to people and situations. For example, one mental model about what makes an effective team is that members share a sense of team ownership and feel that they have authority and responsibility for team actions and outcomes.[9] A leader with this mental model would likely push power, authority, and decision making down to the team level and strive to build norms that create a strong group identity and trust among members. However, a leader with a mental model that every group needs a strong leader to take control and make the decisions is less likely to encourage norms that lead to effective teamwork. Exhibit 5.1 shows the mental model that Google's top leaders use to keep the company on the cutting edge as its core business of search matures. At Google, risk-taking, a little craziness, and making mistakes is encouraged for the sake of innovation. Too much structure and control is considered death to the company.[10]

Mental models
theories people hold about specific systems in the world and their expected behavior

Action Memo
As a leader, you can become aware of your mental models and how they affect your thinking and behavior. You can learn to regard your assumptions as temporary ideas and strive to expand your mindset.

Exhibit 5.1 Google Leaders' Mental Model

- Stay uncomfortable
- Let failure coexist with triumph
- Use a little less "management" than you need
- Defy convention
- Move fast and figure things out as you go

Source: Based on Adam Lashinsky, "Chaos by Design," *Fortune* (October 2, 2006), pp. 86–98.

Leaders at Google, as well as other organizations, strive to create mental models that are aligned with organizational needs, goals, and values. However, personal values, attitudes, beliefs, biases, and prejudices can all affect one's mental model. A leader's assumptions play an important role in shaping his or her mental model, but leaders can examine their assumptions and shift mental models when needed to keep their organizations healthy.[11]

Assumptions

In the previous chapter, we discussed two very different sets of attitudes and assumptions that leaders may have about subordinates, called Theory X and Theory Y, and how these assumptions affect leader behavior. A leader's assumptions naturally are part of his or her mental model. Someone who assumes that people can't be trusted will act very differently in a situation than someone who has the assumption that people are basically trustworthy. Leaders have assumptions about events, situations, and circumstances as well as about people. Assumptions can be dangerous because people tend to accept them as "truth." A good example of faulty assumptions comes from Pets.com, a classic example of an early Internet company that was based on a flawed business model. Leaders assumed that people would start buying all their pet supplies online, but basic goods like dog food and cat litter are much easier to pick up at the local grocery store along with the regular shopping. In addition, the clever sock puppet commercials just didn't work. Leaders assumed that owners would "get" the idea of a puppet talking directly to their pets, since many owners see their pets as members of the family. But the approach of treating pets rather than people as the buyers flopped.[12] As another example, consider leaders at Ford Motor Company, who assumed that their way of doing business, which has kept the company profitable for decades, would continue to be successful in the twenty-first century. Finally accepting that the old way was no longer making money, Bill Ford resigned as CEO in the fall of 2006, acknowledging that the company needed someone with a new mental model based on different assumptions.[13] One organization that found success by bringing in a new leader with a different set of assumptions is Yahoo Inc.

Yahoo Inc.

Yahoo Inc. was started in 1994 by engineers Jerry Yang and David Filo while they were still graduate students at Stanford University. The company grew quickly and became a darling of the high-tech bubble of the late 1990s. But then the bubble burst. Like many Internet companies, Yahoo faced a crisis, and some observers even expected it to fold. That's when Yang asked Terry Semel to replace Tim Koogle as CEO of the struggling company.

Lots of people, both inside and outside the organization, thought it was a horrendous mistake. Up to that point, Yahoo, like other Internet start-ups, had been run by leaders under the assumption that the technology should come first. The company was run loosely, with little concern for structure or control. Semel came in with a mental model based on the assumption that solid business practices focused on distribution of content was what Yahoo needed most. As an "old media" executive whose most recent job was co-head of Warner Bros., Semel knew almost nothing about the digital world—he had barely even used a PC or surfed the Net. He didn't have a clue what a buddy list or a protocol was. He spent his first months on the job in marathon sessions just getting up to speed on the technology. Yet, while he understood that the technology had to be first-rate, Semel based his leadership on the assumption that Yahoo was a twenty-first century entertainment and media company, not a technology company. He set about methodically reorganizing Yahoo to meet the goal of entertaining and informing people in a new way. Semel said he approached running the business from the viewpoint of "a typical user who wants things to happen with ease and comfort," rather than from the viewpoint of a technology whiz.

The shift in mental models had a tremendous impact. From losing $100 million on $717 million in revenues the year Semel arrived, Yahoo went to earning $239 million on $1.4 billion in revenues 18 months later. By 2005, Yahoo earned $1.2 billion on sales of $5.3 billion, had the widest global reach of any Internet site, and owned the most-used e-mail, instant messaging, and music Web sites in the world.[14]

Mary Meeker, an analyst for Morgan Stanley, said Semel's mental model—"to keep the users growing and . . . keep growing usage"—made all the difference. "It sounds like mom and apple pie," she says, "but that was something a lot of people did not get in 2001." Recently, Yahoo's numbers have slipped as competition has increased. Semel may have to shift some of his assumptions to define priorities, bring focus, and keep the company strong as the online world continues to change.[15]

As the story of Yahoo illustrates, a mental model based on a certain set of assumptions might work great in some circumstances, yet be detrimental to success in other circumstances. It's important for leaders to regard their assumptions as temporary ideas rather than fixed truths. The more aware a leader is of his or her assumptions, the more the leader understands how assumptions guide behavior. In addition, the leader can question whether long-held assumptions fit the reality of the situation. Questioning assumptions can help leaders understand and shift their mental models.

Changing Mental Models

The mindset of the top leader has always played a key role in organizational success. A Harvard University study ranking the top 100 business leaders of the twentieth century found that they all shared what the researchers refer to as "contextual intelligence," the ability to sense the social, political, technological, and economic context of the times and adopt a mental model that helped their organizations best respond.[16] In today's world of rapid and discontinuous change, the greatest factor determining the success of leaders and organizations may be the ability to change one's mental model.[17]

For business leaders, the uncertainty and volatility of today's environment is reflected in a sharp increase in the number of companies that Standard & Poor's consider high risk. In 1985, 35 percent of companies were rated high risk, with 41 percent considered low risk. By 2006, only 13 percent were in the low-risk category, with a whopping 73 percent rated high risk. Considering this and other environmental factors, one business writer concluded: "The forecast for most companies is continued chaos with a chance of disaster."[18] Coping with this volatility requires a tremendous shift in mental models for most leaders. Yet leaders can become prisoners of their own assumptions and mindsets. They find themselves simply going along with the traditional way of doing things—whether it be managing a foundation, handling insurance claims, selling cosmetics, or coaching a basketball team—without even realizing they are making decisions and acting within the limited frame of their own mental model.[19]

A recent study by Stephan Lewandowsky, a psychology professor at the University of Western Australia, Crawley, demonstrates the tremendous power mental models can have on our thinking. Researchers showed more than 860 people in Australia, Germany, and the United States a list of events associated with the United States-led invasion of Iraq. Some were true, some were originally reported as fact by the media but later retracted, and some were completely invented for the study. After interepreting the results, reasearchers determined that people tended to believe the "facts" that fit with their mindset about the Iraqi war, even if those facts were clearly not true. People who accepted as valid the official U.S. justification for the war continued to believe reports that cast the United States in a good light and the Iraqi forces in a bad light, even if they knew the reports had been retracted. Those who were suspicious of U.S. motives easily discounted the misinformation. Lewandowsky says supporters of the war held fast to believing what they originally heard, even though they knew it had been retracted, "because it fits with their mental model, which people seek to retain whatever it takes." This is an important point: People tend to believe what they want to believe because doing otherwise "would leave their world view a shambles."[20]

Despite the mental discomfort and sense of disarticulation it might cause, leaders must allow their mental models to be challenged and even demolished. Successful global leaders, for example, have learned to expand their thinking by questioning assumptions about the "right" way to conduct business. They learn to appreciate and respect other values and methods, yet also look for ways to push beyond the limits of cultural assumptions and find opportunities to innovate.[21] Consider how acting based on limited assumptions hurt Swedish furniture maker Ikea when it first entered the U.S. market. Leaders duplicated traditional Swedish concepts such as no home delivery, a Swedish cafeteria, and beds made the way they were in Sweden (which conformed to Swedish rather than U.S. standards). They seemed almost blind to any other way to conduct business. The company's disappointing performance, however, quickly led leaders to reevaluate their ideas and assumptions and consider how acting from a "Swedish mindset" was posing a barrier to success in foreign markets.[22] Today, Ikea is a highly successful global company because leaders were able to shift to a global mindset.

Becoming aware of assumptions and understanding how they influence emotions and actions is the first step toward being able to shift mental models and see the world in new ways. Leaders can break free from outdated mental models. They can recognize that what worked yesterday may not work today. Following conventional wisdom about how to do things may be the surest route to failure. Effective leaders learn to continually question their own beliefs, assumptions, and perceptions in order to see things in unconventional ways and meet the challenge of the future head on.[23] Leaders also encourage others to question the status quo and look for new ideas. Getting others to shift their mental models is perhaps even more difficult than changing one's own, but leaders can use a variety of techniques to bring about a shift in thinking, as described in the Leader's Bookshelf.

Developing a Leader's Mind

How do leaders make the shift to a new mental model? The leader's mind can be developed beyond the non-leader's in four critical areas: independent thinking, open-mindedness, systems thinking, and personal mastery. Taken together, these

Leader's Bookshelf

Changing Minds: The Art and Science of Changing Our Own and Other People's Minds

by Howard Gardner

After about the age of 10, psychologist Howard Gardner asserts, people tend to retreat to old ideas rather than open up to new possibilities. "I'm not stating on small matters it's difficult to change people's minds," Gardner writes. "But on fundamental ideas of how the world works, about what your enterprise is about, about what your life goals are, about what it takes to survive—it's on these topics that it's very difficult. . . ." Why? Because, over time, as people gain more formal and informal knowledge, patterns of thought become engraved in our minds, making it tough to shift to fresh ways of thinking. Yet lasting change in mindset is achievable, Gardner believes, if leaders use specific mind-changing tools.

GETTING OTHERS TO SEE THINGS DIFFERENTLY

Based on decades of extensive psychological research and observation, Gardner details seven "levers of change" that can be used to shift people's mindsets. He advises leaders to "think of them as arrows in a quiver," that can be drawn upon and used in different combinations for different circumstances. Here are some of Gardner's lessons:

- *Take your time, and approach change from many vantage points.* To shift people's way of thinking, leaders get the message out many different times in many different ways, using a variety of approaches and symbols. Gardner calls this *representational redescription*, which means finding diverse ways to get the same desired mind change across to people. "Give your message in more than one way, arranging things so the [listener] has a different experience." For example, simply talking about something in a different setting, such as over coffee or a drink after work, can sometimes be effective because the usual assumptions and resistances may be diminished.

- *Don't rely on reason alone.* Using a rational approach complemented by research and statistical data can shore up your argument. But effective leaders know they have to touch people's emotions as well, which Gardner calls *resonance*. Using stories, imagery, and real-world events can be a highly effective way to bring about change. Gardner uses the example of former British Prime Minister Margaret Thatcher. Thatcher effectively shifted the mindset of her constituency toward the idea that Britain could re-emerge as a leading global power because her message resonated with people. As the daughter of a poor grocer, Thatcher worked her way through school and raised a family before she entered politics.

- *Don't underestimate how powerful resistances can be.* As head of Monsanto, Robert Shapiro strongly believed in the benefits of genetically altered foods, and he assumed that the rest of the world would gladly embrace them. He was wrong, and his company suffered greatly because of his failure to understand and effectively address the resistances he encountered. Gardner identifies several specific types of barriers and advises leaders to arm themselves as if for battle when trying to change minds.

LASTING CHANGE IS VOLUNTARY CHANGE

Some people tend to think secrecy and manipulation is the quickest way to bring about change, and Gardner admits that in the short run, deception is effective. However, he emphasizes that change doesn't stick unless people change voluntarily. Manipulation backfires. Leaders who want to effect lasting changes in mindset wage their change campaigns openly and ethically.

Changing Minds, by Howard Gardner, is published by Harvard Business School Press.

---

four disciplines provide a foundation that can help leaders examine their mental models and overcome blind spots that may limit their leadership effectiveness and the success of their organizations.

Independent Thinking

Independent thinking means questioning assumptions and interpreting data and events according to one's own beliefs, ideas, and thinking, not according to pre-established rules, routines, or categories defined by others. People who think independently are willing to stand apart, to have opinions, to say what they think,

Independent thinking
questioning assumptions and interpreting data and events according to one's own beliefs, ideas, and thinking, rather than pre-established rules or categories defined by others

and to determine a course of action based on what they personally believe rather than on what other people think or say. For example, at Yahoo, Terry Semel didn't let it bother him that many people thought his ideas for Yahoo would never work. Good leadership isn't about following the rules of others, but standing up for what you believe is best for the organization.

To think independently means staying mentally alert and thinking critically. Independent thinking is one part of what is called leader mindfulness.[24] **Mindfulness** can be defined as continuously reevaluating previously learned ways of doing things in the context of evolving information and shifting circumstances. Mindfulness involves independent thinking, and it requires leader curiosity and learning. Mindful leaders are open minded and stimulate the thinking of others through their curiosity and questions. Mindfulness is the opposite of *mindlessness,* which means blindly accepting rules and labels created by others. Mindless people let others do the thinking for them, but mindful leaders are always looking for new ideas and approaches.

In the world of organizations, everything is constantly changing. What worked in one situation may not work the next time. In these conditions, mental laziness and accepting others' answers can hurt the organization and all its members. Leaders apply critical thinking to explore a situation, problem, or question from multiple perspectives and integrate all the available information into a possible solution. When leaders think critically, they question all assumptions, vigorously seek divergent opinions, and try to give balanced consideration to all alternatives.[25] Leaders at today's best-performing organizations, for example, deliberately seek board members who can think independently and are willing to challenge senior management or other board members. Consider the board member at Medtronic who stood his ground against the CEO and 11 other members concerning an acquisition. The board approved the acquisition, but then-CEO Bill George was so persuaded by the dissenter's concerns that he reconvened the board by conference call. After hearing the dissenting board member's cogent argument that the deal would take Medtronic into an area it knew nothing about and divert attention from the core business, the board reconsidered and decided against the deal.[26]

Thinking independently and critically is hard work, and most of us can easily relax into temporary mindlessness, accepting black-and-white answers and relying on standard ways of doing things. Companies that have gotten into ethical and legal trouble in recent years often had executives and board members who failed to question enough or to challenge the status quo.

Leaders also encourage followers to be mindful rather than mindless. Bernard Bass, who has studied charismatic and transformational leadership, talks about the value of *intellectual stimulation*—arousing followers' thoughts and imaginations as well as stimulating their ability to identify and solve problems creatively.[27] People admire leaders who awaken their curiosity, challenge them to think and learn, and encourage openness to new, inspiring ideas and alternatives.

Open-Mindedness

One approach to independent thinking is to break out of the mental boxes, the categorized thinking patterns we have been conditioned to accept as correct. Leaders have to "keep their mental muscle loose."[28] John Keating, the private school teacher portrayed in the movie, *Dead*

Mindfulness
the process of continuously reevaluating previously learned ways of doing things in the context of evolving information and shifting circumstances

Action Memo
As a leader, you can train yourself to think independently. You can be curious, keep an open mind, and look at a problem or situation from multiple perspectives before reaching your conclusions.

Action Memo
Evaluate your skill in three dimensions of mindfulness, including intellectual stimulation, by completing the exercise in Leader's Self-Insight 5.1

Getty Images

Mindfulness

Think back to how you behaved toward others at work or in a group when you were in a formal or informal leadership position. Please respond to the following items based on how frequently you did each behavior. Indicate whether each item is Mostly False or Mostly True for you.

	Mostly False	Mostly True
1. Enjoyed hearing new ideas.	_____	_____
2. Challenged someone to think about an old problem in a new way.	_____	_____
3. Tried to integrate conversation points at a higher level.	_____	_____
4. Felt appreciation for the viewpoints of others.	_____	_____
5. Would ask someone about the assumptions underlying his or her suggestions.	_____	_____
6. Came to my own conclusion despite what others thought.	_____	_____
7. Was open about myself to others.	_____	_____
8. Encouraged others to express opposing ideas and arguments.	_____	_____
9. Fought for my own ideas.	_____	_____
10. Asked "dumb" questions.	_____	_____
11. Offered insightful comments on the meaning of data or issues.	_____	_____
12. Asked questions to prompt others to think more about an issue.	_____	_____
13. Expressed a controversial opinion.	_____	_____
14. Encouraged opposite points of view.	_____	_____
15. Suggested ways of improving my and others' ways of doing things.	_____	_____

Scoring and Interpretation

Give yourself one point for each Mostly True checked for items 1–8 and 10–15. Give yourself one point for checking Mostly False for item 9. A total score of 12 or higher would be considered a high level of overall mindfulness. There are three subscale scores that represent three dimensions of leader mindfulness. For the dimension of open or beginner's mind, sum your responses to questions 1, 4, 7, 9, and 14. For the dimension of independent thinking, sum your scores for questions 3, 6, 11, 13, and 15. For the dimension of intellectual stimulation, sum your scores for questions 2, 5, 8, 10, and 12.

My scores are:
Open or beginner's mind _____
Independent Thinking   _____
Intellectual Stimulation   _____

These scores represent three aspects of leader mindfulness—what is called open mind or beginner's mind, independent thinking, and intellectual stimulation. A score of 4.0 or above on any of these dimensions is considered high because many people do not practice mindfulness in their leadership or group work. A score of 3 is about average, and 2 or less would be below average. Compare your three subscale scores to understand the way you use mindfulness. Analyze the specific questions for which you did not get credit to see more deeply into your pattern of mindfulness strengths or weaknesses. Open mind, independent thinking, and intellectual stimulation are valuable qualities to develop for effective leadership.

Sources: The questions above are based on ideas from R. L. Daft and R. M. Lengel, *Fusion Leadership*, Chapter 4, (Berrett Koehler, 2000); B. Bass and B. Avolio, *Multifactor Leadership Questionnaire*, 2nd ed. (Mind Garden, Inc.); and P. M. Podsakoff, S. B. MacKenzie, R. H. Moorman, and R. Fetter, "Transformational Leader Behaviors and Their Effects on Followers' Trust in Leader, Satisfaction, and Organizational Citizenship Behaviors," *Leadership Quarterly* 1, no. 2 (1990), pp. 107–42.

Poets Society, urged his students to stand on their desks to get a new perspective on the world: "I stand on my desk to remind myself we must constantly look at things a different way. The world looks different from here."

The power of the conditioning that guides our thinking and behavior is illustrated by what has been called the Pike Syndrome. In an experiment, a northern pike is placed in one half of a large glass-divided aquarium, with numerous minnows placed in the other half. The hungry pike makes repeated attempts to

An Empty Sort of Mind

Reflecting on how Winnie the Pooh found Eeyore's missing tail:
"An Empty sort of mind is valuable for finding pearls and tails and things because it can see what's in front of it. An Overstuffed mind is unable to. While the clear mind listens to a bird singing, the Stuffed-Full-of-Knowledge-and-Cleverness mind wonders what *kind* of bird is singing. The more Stuffed Up it is, the less it can hear through its own ears and see through its own eyes. Knowledge and Cleverness tend to concern themselves with the wrong sorts of things, and a mind confused by Knowledge, Cleverness, and Abstract Ideas tends to go chasing off after things that don't matter, or that don't even exist, instead of seeing, appreciating, and making use of what is right in front of it."

Source: Benjamin Hoff, *The Tao of Pooh* (New York: E. P. Dutton, 1982), pp.146–147.

get the minnows, but succeeds only in battering itself against the glass, finally learning that trying to reach the minnows is futile. The glass divider is then removed, but the pike makes no attempt to attack the minnows because it has been conditioned to believe that reaching them is impossible. When people assume they have complete knowledge of a situation because of past experiences, they exhibit the Pike Syndrome, a trained incapacity that comes from rigid commitment to what was true in the past and a refusal to consider alternatives and different perspectives.[29]

Leaders have to forget many of their conditioned ideas to be open to new ones. This openness—putting aside preconceptions and suspending beliefs and opinions—can be referred to as "beginner's mind." Whereas the expert's mind rejects new ideas based on past experience and knowledge, the beginner's mind reflects the openness and innocence of a young child just learning about the world. The value of a beginner's mind is captured in the story told in this chapter's *Consider This*.

Nobel prize-winning physicist Richard Feynman, one of the most original scientific minds of the twentieth century, illustrates the power of the beginner's mind. Feynman's IQ was an unremarkable 125. The heart of his genius was a childlike curiosity and a belief that doubt was the essence of learning and knowing. Feynman was always questioning, always uncertain, always starting over, always resisting any authority that prevented him from doing his own thinking and exploring.[30]

Effective leaders strive to keep open minds and cultivate an organizational environment that encourages curiosity and learning. They understand the limitations of past experience and reach out for diverse perspectives. Rather than seeing any questioning of their ideas as a threat, these leaders encourage everyone throughout the organization to openly debate assumptions, confront paradoxes, question perceptions, and express feelings.[31]

Leaders can use a variety of approaches to help themselves and others keep an open mind. At McKinsey & Co., worldwide managing director Rajat Gupta reads poetry at the end of the partners' regular meetings. Poetry and literature, he says, "help us think in more well-rounded ways. . . . Poetry helps us reflect on the important questions: What is the purpose of our business? What are our values?

Poetry helps us recognize that we face tough questions and that we seldom have perfect answers."[32]

Systems Thinking

Systems thinking means the ability to see the synergy of the whole rather than just the separate elements of a system and to learn to reinforce or change whole system patterns.[33] Many people have been trained to solve problems by breaking a complex system, such as an organization, into discrete parts and working to make each part perform as well as possible. However, the success of each piece does not add up to the success of the whole. In fact, sometimes changing one part to make it better actually makes the whole system function less effectively. In recent years, new drugs have been a lifesaver for people living with HIV, for example, but the drop in mortality rates has led to a reduction in perceived risk and therefore more incidences of risky behavior. After years of decline, HIV infection rates began rising again, indicating that the system of HIV treatment is not well understood. California's partial deregulation of the electricity market was designed to lower costs to consumers, but poor understanding of the overall system contributed to rolling blackouts, record-high rates, and political and economic turmoil. Or consider a small city that embarked on a road building program to solve traffic congestion without whole-systems thinking. With new roads available, more people began moving to the suburbs. The solution actually increased traffic congestion, delays, and pollution by enabling suburban sprawl.[34]

It is the *relationship* among the parts that form a whole system—whether it be a community, an automobile, a non-profit agency, a human being, or a business organization—that matters. Systems thinking enables leaders to look for patterns of movement over time and focus on the qualities of rhythm, flow, direction, shape, and networks of relationships that accomplish the performance of the whole. Systems thinking is a mental discipline and framework for seeing patterns and interrelationships.

It is important to see organizational systems as a whole because of their complexity. Complexity can overwhelm leaders, undermining confidence. When leaders can see the structures that underlie complex situations, they can facilitate improvement. But it requires a focus on the big picture. Leaders can develop what David McCamus, former Chairman and CEO of Xerox Canada, calls "peripheral vision"—the ability to view the organization through a wide-angle lens, rather than a telephoto lens—so that they perceive how their decisions and actions affect the whole.[35]

An important element of systems thinking is to discern circles of causality. Peter Senge, author of *The Fifth Discipline,* argues that reality is made up of circles rather than straight lines. For example, Exhibit 5.2 shows circles of influence for producing new products. In the circle on the left, a high-tech firm grows rapidly by pumping out new products quickly. New products increase revenues, which enable the further increase of the R&D budget to add more new products.

But another circle of causality is being influenced as well. As the R&D budget grows, the engineering and research staff increases. The burgeoning technical staff becomes increasingly hard to manage. The management burden falls on senior engineers, who provide less of their time for developing new products, which slows product development time. The slowing of product development time has a negative impact on new products, the very thing

Systems thinking
the ability to see the synergy of the whole rather than just the separate elements of a system and to learn to reinforce or change whole system patterns

Action Memo
As a leader, you can cultivate an ability to analyze and understand the relationships among parts of a team, organization, family, or other system to avoid making changes that have unintended negative consequences.

Exhibit 5.2 Two Circles of Causality in an Organization

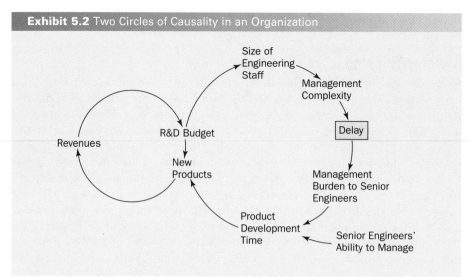

Source: From *The Fifth Discipline: The Art and Practice of the Learning Organization* by Peter M. Senge, p. 97. Copyright © 1990 by Peter M. Senge. Used by permission of Doubleday, a division of Bantam Doubleday Dell Publishing Group, Inc.

that created organizational success. Maintaining product development time in the face of increasing management complexity depends upon senior engineers' management ability. Thus, understanding the circle of causality enables leaders to allocate resources to the training and development of engineering leadership as well as directly to new products. Without an understanding of the system, top leaders would fail to understand why increasing R&D budgets can actually increase product development time and reduce the number of new products coming to market.

The other element of systems thinking is learning to influence the system with reinforcing feedback as an engine for growth or decline. In the example of new products, after managers see how the system works, they can allocate revenues to speed new products to market, either by hiring more engineers, or by training senior engineers in management and leadership skills. They can guide the system when they understand it conceptually. Without this kind of understanding, managers will hit blockages in the form of seeming limits to growth and resistance to change because the large complex system will appear impossible to manage. Systems thinking is a significant solution.

Personal Mastery

Another concept introduced by Senge is *personal mastery*, a term he uses to describe the discipline of personal growth and learning, of mastering yourself in a way that facilitates your leadership and achieves desired results.[36]

Personal mastery
the discipline of personal growth and learning and of mastering yourself; it embodies personal visions, facing reality, and holding creative tension

Personal mastery embodies three qualities—personal vision, facing reality, and holding creative tension. First, leaders engaged in personal mastery know and clarify what is important to them. They focus on the end result, the vision or dream that motivates them and their organization. They have a clear vision of a desired future, and their purpose is to achieve that future. One element of personal mastery, then, is the discipline of continually focusing and defining what one wants as their desired future and vision.

Second, facing reality means a commitment to the truth. Leaders are relentless in uncovering the mental models that limit and deceive them and are willing to challenge assumptions and ways of doing things. These leaders are committed to the truth, and will break through denial of reality in themselves and others. Their quest for truth leads to a deeper awareness of themselves and of the larger systems and events within which they operate. Commitment to the truth enables them to deal with reality, which increases the opportunity to achieve desired results.

Third, often there is a large gap between one's vision and the current situation. The gap between the desired future and today's reality, say between the dream of starting a business and the reality of having no capital, can be discouraging. But the gap is the source of creative energy. Acknowledging and living with the disparity between the truth and the vision, and facing it squarely, is the source of resolve and creativity to move forward. The effective leader resolves the tension by letting the vision pull reality toward it, in other words, by reorganizing current activities to work toward the vision. The leader works in a way that moves things toward the vision. The less effective way is to let reality pull the vision downward toward it. This means lowering the vision, such as walking away from a problem or settling for less than desired. Settling for less releases the tension, but it also engenders mediocrity. Leaders with personal mastery learn to accept both the dream and the reality simultaneously, and to close the gap by moving toward the dream.

All five elements of mind are interrelated. Independent thinking and open-mindedness improve systems thinking and enable personal mastery, helping leaders shift and expand their mental models. Since they are all interdependent, leaders working to improve even one element of their mental approach can move forward in a significant way toward mastering their minds and becoming more effective.

Emotional Intelligence—Leading with Heart and Mind

Psychologists and other researchers, as well as people in all walks of life, have long recognized the importance of cognitive intelligence, or IQ, in determining a person's success and effectiveness. In general, research shows that leaders score higher than most people on tests of cognitive ability, such as IQ tests, and that cognitive ability is positively associated with effective leadership.[37] Increasingly, leaders and researchers are recognizing the critical importance of emotional intelligence, or EQ, as well. Some have suggested that emotion, more than cognitive ability, drives our thinking and decision making, as well as our interpersonal relationships.[38] **Emotional intelligence** refers to a person's abilities to perceive, identify, understand, and successfully manage emotions in self and others. Being emotionally intelligent means being able to effectively manage ourselves and our relationships.[39]

Emotional understanding and skills impact our success and happiness in our work as well as our personal lives. Leaders can harness and direct the power of emotions to improve follower satisfaction, morale, and motivation, as well as to enhance overall organizational effectiveness. The U.S. Air Force started using EQ to select recruiters after learning that the best recruiters scored higher in EQ competencies. Leaders who score high in EQ are typically more effective and rated as more effective by peers and subordinates.[40]

Emotional intelligence
a person's abilities to perceive, identify, understand, and successfully manage emotions in self and others

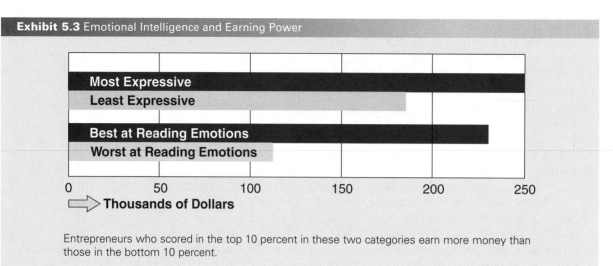

Exhibit 5.3 Emotional Intelligence and Earning Power

Entrepreneurs who scored in the top 10 percent in these two categories earn more money than those in the bottom 10 percent.

Source: Rensselaer Polytechnic Institute, Lally School of Management and Technology, as reported in *BusinessWeek Frontier* (February 5, 2001), p. F4.

Action Memo

As a leader, you can develop emotional intelligence and act as a positive role model by being optimistic and enthusiastic.

Moreover, in a study of entrepreneurs, researchers at Rensselaer Polytechnic Institute found that those who are more expressive of their own emotions and more in tune with the emotions of others make more money, as illustrated in Exhibit 5.3.

Some leaders act as if people leave their emotions at home when they come to work, but we all know this isn't true. Indeed, a key component of leadership is being emotionally connected to others and understanding how emotions affect working relationships and performance.

What Are Emotions?

There are hundreds of emotions and more subtleties of emotion than there are words to explain them. One important ability for leaders is to understand the range of emotions people have and how these emotions may manifest themselves. Many researchers accept eight categories or "families" of emotions, as illustrated in Exhibit 5.4.[41] These categories do not resolve every question about how to categorize emotions, and scientific debate continues. The argument for there being a set of core emotions is based partly on the discovery that specific facial expressions for four of them (fear, anger, sadness, and enjoyment) are universally recognized. People in cultures around the world have been found to recognize these same basic emotions when shown photographs of facial expressions. The primary emotions and some of their variations follow.

- *Anger:* fury, outrage, resentment, exasperation, indignation, animosity, annoyance, irritability, hostility, violence.
- *Sadness:* grief, sorrow, gloom, melancholy, self-pity, loneliness, dejection, despair, depression.
- *Fear:* anxiety, apprehension, nervousness, concern, consternation, wariness, edginess, dread, fright, terror, panic.
- *Enjoyment:* happiness, joy, relief, contentment, delight, amusement, pride, sensual pleasure, thrill, rapture, gratification, satisfaction, euphoria.

Exhibit 5.4 Eight Families of Emotions

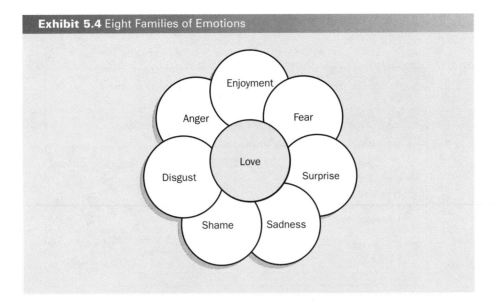

- *Love:* acceptance, respect, friendliness, trust, kindness, affinity, devotion, adoration, infatuation.
- *Surprise:* shock, astonishment, amazement, wonder.
- *Disgust:* contempt, disdain, scorn, abhorrence, aversion, distaste, revulsion.
- *Shame:* guilt, embarrassment, chagrin, remorse, humiliation, regret, mortification, contrition.

Leaders who are attuned to their own feelings and the feelings of others can use their understanding to enhance the organization. For example, studies of happiness in the workplace find that employee happiness can play a major role in organizational success. And a *Gallup Management Journal* survey emphasizes that leaders, especially frontline supervisors, have a lot to do with whether employees have positive or negative feelings about their work lives.[42]

The Components of Emotional Intelligence

The competencies and abilities of emotional intelligence are grouped into four fundamental categories, as illustrated in Exhibit 5.5.[43] It is important to remember that emotional intelligence can be learned and developed. Anyone can strengthen his or her abilities in these four categories.

Self-awareness might be considered the basis of all the other competencies. It includes the ability to recognize and understand your own emotions and how they affect your life and work. People who are in touch with their emotions are better able to guide their own lives. Leaders with a high level of self-awareness learn to trust their "gut feelings" and realize that these feelings can provide useful information about difficult decisions. Answers are not always clear as to whether to propose a major deal, let an employee go, reorganize a business, or revise job responsibilities. When the answers are not available from external sources, leaders have to rely on their own feelings. This component also includes the ability to accurately assess your own strengths and limitations, along with a healthy sense of self-confidence.

Self-management, the second key component, includes the ability to control disruptive, unproductive, or harmful emotions and desires. An interesting experiment from the 1960s sheds some light on the power of self-management. A group of

Self-awareness
the ability to recognize and understand your own emotions and how they affect your life and work

Self-management
the ability to control disruptive or harmful emotions

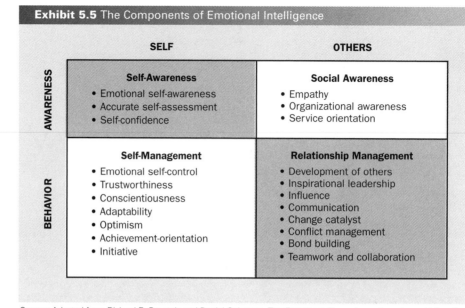

Exhibit 5.5 The Components of Emotional Intelligence

	SELF	**OTHERS**
AWARENESS	**Self-Awareness** • Emotional self-awareness • Accurate self-assessment • Self-confidence	**Social Awareness** • Empathy • Organizational awareness • Service orientation
BEHAVIOR	**Self-Management** • Emotional self-control • Trustworthiness • Conscientiousness • Adaptability • Optimism • Achievement-orientation • Initiative	**Relationship Management** • Development of others • Inspirational leadership • Influence • Communication • Change catalyst • Conflict management • Bond building • Teamwork and collaboration

Source: Adapted from Richard E. Boyatzis and Daniel Goleman, *The Emotional Competence Inventory—University Edition* (Boston, MA: The Hay Group, 2001).

four-year-olds and five-year-olds were offered a marshmallow, which the researcher placed in front of each child on the desk. Then, the children were told that if they could wait a few minutes while the researcher ran an errand, they would be given two marshmallows. Some children were unable to resist the temptation of a marshmallow "right now" and ate theirs immediately. Others employed all sorts of techniques, from singing or talking to themselves to hiding under the desk, to resist their impulses and earn the reward of two marshmallows instead of one. Researchers then followed the children over a period of 20 years and found some interesting results. As young men and women, the ones who had resisted the desire to eat the marshmallow revealed a much higher ability to handle stress and embrace difficult challenges. They also were more self-confident, trustworthy, dependable, and tenacious in pursuing goals.[44] The children who developed techniques for self-management early in life carried these with them into adulthood.

It is never too late for people to learn how to manage their emotions and impulses. Leaders learn to balance their own emotions so that worry, desire, anxiety, fear, or anger do not get in the way, thus enabling them to think clearly and be more effective. Managing emotions does not mean suppressing or denying them but understanding them and using that understanding to deal with situations productively.[45]

Other characteristics in this category include *trustworthiness,* which means consistently displaying honesty and integrity, *conscientiousness,* which means managing and honoring your responsibilities, and *adaptability,* which refers to the ability to adjust to changing situations and overcome obstacles. Showing initiative to seize opportunities and achieve high internal standards is also a part of self-management. Leaders skilled at self-management remain hopeful and optimistic despite obstacles, setbacks, or even outright failures. Martin Seligman, a professor of psychology at the University of Pennsylvania, once advised the MetLife insurance company to hire a special group of job applicants who tested high on optimism but failed the normal sales aptitude test. Compared to salespeople who passed the regular aptitude test but scored high on pessimism, the "optimistic" group made 21 percent more sales in their first year and 57 percent more in the second.[46]

Social awareness relates to one's ability to understand others. Socially aware leaders practice **empathy**, which means being able to put yourself in other people's shoes, sense their emotions, and understand their perspective. These leaders understand that effective leadership sometimes means pushing people beyond their comfort zone, and they are sensitive to the fear or frustration this can engender in followers. They learn to engage in "professional intimacy," which means they can display compassion and and concern for others without becoming so wrapped up in others' emotions that it clouds their judgment.[47] Socially aware leaders are also capable of understanding divergent points of view and interacting effectively with many different types of people and emotions. The related characteristic of *organizational awareness* refers to the ability to navigate the currents of organizational life, build networks, and effectively use political behavior to accomplish positive results. This component also includes a *service orientation,* which refers to the ability to recognize and serve the needs of employees, customers, or clients.

Relationship management refers to the ability to connect with others and build positive relationships. Leaders with high emotional intelligence treat others with compassion, sensitivity, and kindness.[48] This aspect of EQ encompasses developing others, inspiring others with a powerful vision, learning to listen and communicate clearly and convincingly, and using emotional understanding to influence others in positive ways. Leaders use their understanding of emotions to inspire change and lead people toward something better, to build teamwork and collaboration, and to resolve conflicts that inevitably arise. These leaders cultivate and maintain a web of relationships both within and outside the organization. As the new CEO of Disney, Bob Iger is winning praise for his skills at relationship management. Iger is known as a good listener with a calm, diplomatic, and collaborative approach to leadership. He is using his emotional intelligence to both build a more adaptive and collegial culture within the company as well as to mend relationships with partners such as Pixar Animation Studios.[49]

Taken together, the four components shown in Exhibit 5.5 build a strong base of emotional intelligence that leaders can use to more effectively guide teams and organizations. One research project suggests that all effective leadership styles arise from different components of emotional intelligence.[50] The best leaders combine styles or vary their styles, depending on the situation or problem at hand, by using all of the components. By being sensitive to their own and others' emotions, these leaders can recognize what effect they are having on followers and seamlessly adjust their approach to create a positive result. Consider how Mike Krzyzewski, coach of the Duke University Blue Devils, uses emotional intelligence to bring out the best in his players.

Social awareness
one's ability to understand and empathize with others

Empathy
being able to put yourself in someone else's shoes

Relationship management
the ability to connect with others and build positive relationships

Action Memo
As a leader, you can recognize and manage your own emotions so that negative feelings don't cloud your mind, distort your judgment, or cripple your ability to lead.

IN THE LEAD

Mike Krzyzewski, Duke Univeristy Blue Devils

Mike Krzyzewski doesn't think of himself as a basketball coach. He considers himself a leader who just happens to coach basketball. And for Krzyzewski, almost everything in leadership depends on one element: personal relationships.

Although he's a tough man with tough standards, Krzyzewski has been accused of "coaching like a girl" because of his interactive, emotionally-charged style. When the legendary coach of Duke University's Blue Devils recruits a player, for example, he tells him, "We're developing a relationship here, and if you're not interested, tell me sooner rather than later." The emphasis on relationships comes partly from Krzyzewski's years playing, and later coaching, at the U.S. Military Academy at West Point, which he calls the greatest leadership school in the world because it teaches officers how to bond soldiers together. As a coach, Krzyzewski emphasizes teamwork rather than individual performers, fosters a family feeling among players, and says he coaches "by feel." That is, he gets to know his players as individuals and learns how they can best interact to succeed. He builds such strong positive relationships among players that they communicate constantly and effortlessly on the court, sometimes without saying a word. Although Krzyzewski gives instructions during a time-out, the players then form their own huddle to talk things out for themselves, and they continually make decisions among themselves on the floor without looking to the bench for direction or approval. Krzyzewski believes that "hum" of personal connection and communication should permeate every game, even every practice.

Leading a basketball team, Krzyzewski believes, is just like leading a business, a military unit, a school, a volunteer group, or anything else: "You gotta get through all their layers and get right into their hearts."[51]

> **Action Memo**
> As a leader, you can empathize with others, treat people with compassion and sensitivity, build teamwork, and learn to listen, interpret emotions, and resolve interpersonal conflicts.

Mike Krzyzewski has created the kind of workplace that many of today's organizations need—one in which leaders are more interactive than command and control, where leadership and decision making is spread across all levels, and where individual goals are met through teamwork and collaboration. In an environment where relationships with employees and customers are becoming more important than technology and material resources, interest in developing leaders' emotional intelligence continues to grow. All leaders have to pay attention to the emotional climate in their organization. Recent world events have thrust emotions to the forefront for both individuals and organizations.

The Emotionally Competent Leader

How is emotional intelligence related to effective leadership? A high level of self-awareness, combined with the ability to manage one's own emotions, enables a leader to display self-confidence and earn the respect and trust of followers. In addition, the ability to manage or temporarily restrain one's emotions can enable a leader to objectively consider the needs of others over his or her own immediate feelings. Giving in to strong feelings of anger or depression, for example, may intensify a self-centered focus on one's own needs and limit the ability of the leader to understand the needs of others or see things from other perspectives.

A leader's emotional abilities and understandings play a key role in charismatic and transformational leadership behavior, which will be discussed in detail in Chapter 12.[52] Charismatic leaders generally hold strong emotional convictions and appeal to followers on an emotional basis. Transformational leaders project an inspiring vision for change and motivate followers to achieve it, which requires using all the components of emotional intelligence. Charismatic and transformational leaders typically exhibit self-confidence, determination, and persistence in the face of adversity, characteristics that result from emotional competence. Emotionally competent leaders are more resilient, more adaptable to ever-changing circumstances, more willing to step outside their comfort zone, and more open to the opinions and ideas of others.[53]

> **Action Memo**
> Evaluate your level of emotional intelligence by completing the questionnaire in Leader's Self-Insight 5.2.

Emotional Intelligence

For each item below, rate how well you display the behavior described. Before responding, try to think of actual situations in which you have had the opportunity to use the behavior. Indicate whether each item below is Mostly False or Mostly True for you.

	Mostly False	Mostly True
1. Associate different internal physiological cues with different emotions.		
2. Relax when under pressure in situations.		
3. Know the impact that your behavior has on others.		
4. Initiate successful resolution of conflict with others.		
5. Know when you are becoming angry.		
6. Recognize when others are distressed.		
7. Build consensus with others.		
8. Produce motivation when doing uninteresting work.		
9. Help others manage their emotions.		
10. Make others feel good.		
11. Identify when you experience mood shifts.		
12. Stay calm when you are the target of anger from others.		
13. Know when you become defensive.		
14. Follow your words with actions.		
15. Engage in intimate conversations with others.		
16. Accurately reflect people's feelings back to them.		

Scoring and Interpretation

Sum your Mostly True responses to the 16 questions to obtain your overall emotional intelligence score. Your score for self-awareness is the total of questions 1, 5, 11, and 13. Your score for self-management is the total of questions 2, 8, 12, and 14. Your score for social awareness is the sum of questions 3, 6, 9, and 15. Your score for relationship management is the sum of questions 4, 7, 10, and 16. This questionnaire provides some indication of your emotional intelligence. If you received a total score of 14 or more, you are certainly considered a person with high emotional intelligence. A score from 10 to 13 means you have a good platform of emotional intelligence from which to develop your leadership capability. A score of 7 to 9 would be moderate emotional intelligence. A score below 7 indicates that you realize that you are probably below average in emotional intelligence.

For each of the four components of emotional intelligence—self-awareness, self-management, social awareness, and relationship management—a score of 4 is considered high, whereas a score of two or less would be considered low. Review the discussion in this chapter about the four components of emotional intelligence and think about what you might do to develop those areas where you scored low. Compare your scores to those of other students. What can you do to improve your scores?

Source: Adapted from Hendrie Weisinger, *Emotional Intelligence at Work* (San Francisco: Jossey-Bass, 1998), pp. 214–215.

Emotional intelligence is also important for leaders because the emotional state of the leader impacts the entire group, department, or organization. Most of us recognize that we can "catch" emotions from others. If we're around someone who is smiling and enthusiastic, the positive emotions rub off on us. Conversely, someone in a bad mood can bring us down. This *emotional contagion*[54] means that leaders who are able to maintain balance and keep themselves motivated are positive role models to help motivate and inspire those around them. The energy level of the entire organization increases when leaders are optimistic and hopeful. The ability to empathize with others and to manage interpersonal relationships also contributes to motivation and inspiration because it helps leaders create feelings of unity and team spirit.

Perhaps most importantly, emotional intelligence enables leaders to recognize and respect followers as whole human beings with feelings, opinions, and ideas of their own. Leaders treat followers as individuals with unique needs, abilities, and dreams. They can use their emotional intelligence to help followers grow and develop, see and enhance their self-image and feelings of self-worth, and help meet their needs and achieve their personal goals.

Emotionally intelligent leaders have a positive impact on organizations by helping employees grow, learn, and develop; creating a sense of purpose and meaning; instilling unity and team spirit; and building relationships of trust and respect that allow each employee to take risks and fully contribute to the organization.

The Emotional Intelligence of Teams

Much of the work in today's organizations, even at top management levels, is done in teams rather than by individuals. Although most studies of emotional intelligence have focused on individuals, research is beginning to emerge concerning how emotional intelligence relates to teams. For example, one study found that untrained teams made up of members with high emotional intelligence performed as well as trained teams made up of members who rated low on emotional intelligence.[55] The high emotional intelligence of the untrained team members enabled them to assess and adapt to the requirements of teamwork and the tasks at hand.

Moreover, research has suggested that emotional intelligence can be developed as a *team* competency and not just an individual competency.[56] That is, teams themselves—not just their individual members—can become emotionally intelligent. Leaders build the emotional intelligence of teams by creating norms that support emotional development and influence emotions in constructive ways. Emotionally intelligent team norms are those that (1) create a strong group identity, (2) build trust among members, and (3) instill a belief among members that they can be effective and succeed as a team.

Leaders "tune in" to the team's emotional state and look for unhealthy or unproductive norms that inhibit cooperation and team harmony.[57] Building the emotional intelligence of the team means exploring unhealthy norms, deliberately bringing emotions to the surface, and understanding how they affect the team's work. Raising these issues can be uncomfortable, and a leader needs both courage and individual emotional intelligence to guide a team through the process. Only by getting emotions into the open can the team build new norms and move to a higher level of group satisfaction and performance. Leaders continue to build emotional intelligence by encouraging and enabling the team to explore and use emotion in its everyday work.

Leading with Love versus Leading with Fear

You wouldn't expect a high-ranking military officer to go around spouting talk about love, but that's exactly what Rear Admiral Albert Konetzni, now retired, often did. As commander of the U.S. Navy's Pacific submarine fleet, Konetzni's favorite phrase was, "I love you guys." He repeated variations of it dozens of times a day—to fellow admirals, sailors, and others he came in contact with. By genuinely caring about others and considering their needs and feelings, Konetzni transformed a toxic environment that had left the Navy facing a serious personnel shortage.[58] Konetzni's leadership approach, of course, reflected his own personality and style—not all leaders would feel comfortable with such an open approach. However, many leaders are learning that an environment that reflects care and respect for people is much more effective than one in which people are fearful.

Getty Images

Love or Fear?

The following items describe reasons why you work. *Answer the questions twice,* the first time for doing work (or homework) that is not your favorite, and the second time for doing a hobby or sports activity that you enjoy. *Consider each item thoughtfully and respond according to your inner motivation and experience.* Indicate whether each item below is Mostly False or Mostly True for you.

	Mostly False	Mostly True
1. I feel it is important to perform well so I don't look bad.	_____	_____
2. I have to force myself to complete the task.	_____	_____
3. I don't want to have a poor outcome or get a poor grade.	_____	_____
4. I don't want to embarrass myself or do less well than others.	_____	_____
5. The experience leaves me feeling relieved that it is over.	_____	_____
6. My attention is absorbed entirely in what I am doing.	_____	_____
7. I really enjoy the experience.	_____	_____
8. Time seems to pass more quickly than normal.	_____	_____
9. I am completely focused on the task at hand.	_____	_____
10. The experience leaves me feeling great.	_____	_____

Scoring and Interpretation

The items above reflect motivation shaped by either love or fear. Your "fear of failure" score is the number of Mostly True answers for questions 1–5. Your "love of task" score is the number of Mostly True answers for questons 6–10. A score of 4 or 5 would be considered high for either love or fear, and a score of 0–2 would be considered low. You would probably score more points for "love of task" for your hobby or sports activity than for homework.

Some people are motivated by high internal standards and fear of not meeting those standards. This may be called fear of failure, which often spurs people to great accomplishment. Love of task provides a great intrinsic pleasure but won't always lead to high achievement. Love of task is related to the idea of "flow" wherein people become fully engaged and derive great satisfaction from their activity. Would love or fear influence your choice to become a leader or how you try to motivate others? Discuss with other students the relative importance of love or fear motivation in your lives.

Love in the workplace means genuinely caring for others and sharing one's knowledge, understanding, and compassion to enable others to grow and succeed.

Traditionally, leadership in many organizations has been based on fear. An unspoken notion among many senior-level executives is that fear is a good thing and benefits the organization.[59] Indeed, fear can be a powerful motivator. When organizational success depended primarily on people mindlessly following orders, leading with fear often met the organization's needs. Today, however, success depends on the knowledge, mindpower, commitment, and enthusiasm of everyone in the organization. A fear-based organization loses its best people, and the knowledge they take with them, to other firms. In addition, even if people stay with the organization, they typically don't perform up to their real capabilities.

One major drawback of leading with fear is that it creates avoidance behavior, because no one wants to make a mistake, and this inhibits growth and change. Leaders can learn to bind people together for a shared purpose through more positive forces such as caring and compassion, listening, and connecting to others on a personal level. The emotion that attracts people to take risks, learn, grow, and move the organization forward comes from love, not fear.

Showing respect and trust not only enables people to perform better; it also allows them to feel emotionally connected with their

Action Memo
To learn about your own motivations concerning love versus fear, complete the exercise in Leader's Self-Insight 5.3.

work so that their lives are richer and more balanced. Leaders can rely on negative emotions such as fear to fuel productive work, but by doing so they may slowly destroy people's spirits, which ultimately is bad for employees and the organization.[60]

Fear in Organizations

The workplace can hold many kinds of fear, including fear of failure, fear of change, fear of personal loss, and fear of the boss. All of these fears can prevent people from doing their best, from taking risks, and from challenging and changing the status quo. Fear gets in the way of people feeling good about their work, themselves, and the organization. It creates an atmosphere in which people feel powerless, so that their confidence, commitment, enthusiasm, imagination, and motivation are diminished.[61]

Aspects of Fear A particularly damaging aspect of fear in the workplace is that it can weaken trust and communication. Employees feel threatened by repercussions if they speak up about work-related concerns. A survey of employees in 22 organizations around the country found that 70 percent of them "bit their tongues" at work because they feared repercussions. Twenty-seven percent reported that they feared losing their credibility or reputation if they spoke up. Other fears reported were lack of career advancement, possible damage to the relationship with their supervisor, demotion or losing their job, and being embarrassed or humiliated in front of others.[62] When people are afraid to speak up, important issues are suppressed and problems hidden. Employees are afraid to talk about a wide range of issues. These "undiscussables" can range from the poor performance of a coworker to concerns over benefits to suggestions for organizational improvement. However, by far the largest category of undiscussables is the behavior of executives, particularly their interpersonal and relationship skills. When fear is high, managers destroy the opportunity for feedback, blinding them to reality and denying them the chance to correct damaging decisions and behaviors.

Relationship with Leaders Leaders control the fear level in the organization. We all know from personal experience that it is easier to report bad news to some people than to others. A boss or teacher who is understanding and compassionate is much easier to approach than one who is likely to blow up and scream at us. The relationship between an employee and supervisor is the primary factor determining the level of fear experienced at work. The legacy of fear and mistrust associated with traditional hierarchies in which bosses gave orders and employees jumped to obey "or else" still colors organizational life. Leaders are responsible for creating a new environment that enables people to feel safe speaking their minds. Leaders can act from love rather than fear to free employees and the organization from the chains of the past.

Bringing Love to Work

When leaders act from their own fear, they create fear in others. Organizations have traditionally rewarded people for strong qualities such as rational thinking, ambition, and competitiveness. These qualities are important, but their overemphasis has left many organizational leaders out of touch with their softer, caring, creative capabilities, unable to make emotional connections with others and

Action Memo

As a leader, you can choose to lead with love, not with fear. You can show respect and trust toward followers and help people learn, grow, and contribute their best to achieve the organization's vision.

afraid to risk showing any sign of "weakness." A leader's fear can manifest itself in arrogance, selfishness, deception, unfairness, and disrespect for others.[63]

Leaders can learn to develop their capacity for the positive emotions of love and caring. Former General Electric chairman and CEO Jack Welch was known as something of a hard-nosed manager, but he was also a master at leading with love, and followers responded, contributing to growth and success for the organization. Jeffrey Immelt, who succeeded Welch as CEO, recalls the comment Welch made to him once when he'd had a terrible year: "I love you and I know you can do better."[64]

Most of us have experienced the power of love at some time in our lives. There are many different kinds of love—for example, the love of a mother for her child, romantic love, brotherly love, or the love of country, as well as the love some people feel for certain sports, hobbies, or recreational pursuits. Despite its power, the "L" word is often looked upon with suspicion in the business world.[65] However, there are a number of aspects of love that are directly relevant to work relationships and organizational performance.

Love as motivation is the force within that enables people to feel alive, connected, energized, and "in love" with life and work. Western cultures place great emphasis on the mind and the rational approach. However, it is the heart rather than the mind that powers people forward. Recall a time when you wanted to do something with all your heart, and how your energy and motivation flowed freely. Also recall a time when your head said you had to do a task, but your heart was not in it. Motivation is reduced, perhaps to the point of procrastination. There's a growing interest in helping people feel a genuine passion for their work.[66] People who are engaged rather than alienated from their work are typically more satisfied, productive, and successful. The best leaders are those who love what they do, because they infect others with their enthusiasm and passion. The founders of SVS Inc. started their company with passion as a guiding force.

IN THE LEAD

Paul Shirley, SVS Inc.

When Paul Shirley and two colleagues decided to start a company, they agreed to two things: It had to be fun and it had to make a difference. Later, the three added that, "Oh, by the way, it needs to make a profit." Thus, SVS was founded on the passion of its leaders, who believed in the company so much that two of them put second mortgages on their homes to keep it alive. Today, the company is a wholly-owned subsidiary of Boeing (Boeing-SVS Inc.) and is a world-class leader in precision acquisition, tracking, and targeting systems for the military.

When they started the company, Shirley and his partners also wanted to unlock the passion of their employees. To start with, they hired people who cared less about titles and money and more about the challenges and contributions of the work itself. Then, leaders asked people to write their life plans and talk with leaders about how their plans meshed with the company's goals. "I was amazed at what came up," Shirley said. The life plans gave leaders an understanding of what their employees were passionate about and how SVS could tap into that passion by helping them meet their personal goals.

Another aspect of building a passionate work environment was making people feel like part of a special community. Even in a company of scientists and technicians, Shirley believed, people would be happier and more energized if they felt strong personal connections to others. One symbolic gesture was having a company coffee cup made with the names of every employee and the date they were

IN THE LEAD

hired. And the organization chart of SVS didn't just show the company's 115 employees. It also showed spouses, children, and even grandchildren who were considered part of the corporate family.

By starting with passionate leadership and making a conscious effort to help others find their passion at work, SVS leaders built a strong company and a committed workforce.[67]

SVS also tapped into the aspect of love as feelings. *Love as feelings* involves attraction, fascination, and caring for people, work, or other things. This is what people most often think of as love, particularly in relation to romantic love between two people. However, love as feelings is also relevant in work situations. Feelings of compassion and caring for others are a manifestation of love, as are forgiveness, sincerity, respect, and loyalty, all of which are important for healthy working relationships. One personal feeling is a sense of *bliss,* best articulated for the general public by Joseph Campbell in his PBS television series and companion book with Bill Moyers, *The Power of Myth.*[68] Finding your bliss means doing things that make you light up inside, things you do for the joy of doing rather than for material rewards. Most of us experience moments of this bliss when we become so absorbed in enjoyable work activities that we lose track of time. This type of feeling and caring about work is a major source of charisma. Everyone becomes more charismatic to others when they pursue an activity they truly care about.

Love as action means more than feelings; it is translated into behavior. Stephen Covey points out that in all the great literature, love is a verb rather than a noun.[69] Love is something you do, the sacrifices you make and the giving of yourself to others. The feelings of compassion, respect, and loyalty, for example, are translated into acts of friendliness, teamwork, cooperation, listening, and serving others. Feelings of unity and cooperation in organizations by leaders or followers translate into acts of helping, sharing, and understanding. Sentiments emerge as action.

Why Followers Respond to Love

Most people yearn for more than a paycheck from their jobs. Leaders who lead with love have extraordinary influence because they meet five unspoken employee needs:

Hear and understand me.

Even if you disagree with me, please don't make me wrong.

Acknowledge the greatness within me.

Remember to look for my loving intentions.

Tell me the truth with compassion.[70]

When leaders address these subtle emotional needs directly, people typically respond by loving their work and becoming emotionally engaged in solving problems and serving customers. Enthusiasm for work and the organization increases. People want to believe that their leaders genuinely care. From the followers' point of view, love versus fear has different motivational potential.

Fear-based motivation
motivation based on fear of
losing a job

- **Fear-based motivation:** I need a job to pay for my basic needs (fulfilling lower needs of the body). You give me a job, and I will give you just enough to keep my job.

- **Love-based motivation:** If the job and the leader make me feel valued as a person and provide a sense of meaning and contribution to the community at large (fulfilling higher needs of heart, mind, and body), then I will give you all I have to offer.[71]

A good example comes from Southwest Airlines, the only major airline that remained profitable during the turmoil following the September 2001 terrorist attacks in the United States. Founder and former CEO Herb Kelleher built the organization based on love, and employees responded with amazing performance and acts of selflessness. After the attacks, most airlines asked their employees to donate portions of their pay back to the company, leading to strained union–management relations. At Southwest, which is also unionized, the employees themselves organized the give-back effort because of their positive feelings for the company.[72] Many examples throughout this book illustrate what happens when positive emotion is used. One management consultant went so far as to advise that finding creative ways to love could solve every imaginable leadership problem.[73] Rational thinking is important, but leading with love can build trust, stimulate creativity, inspire commitment, and unleash boundless energy.

Love-based motivation
motivation based on feeling valued in the job

Summary and Interpretation

Leaders use intellectual as well as emotional capabilities and understandings to guide organizations through a turbulent environment and help employees feel energized, motivated, and cared for in the face of rapid change, uncertainty, and job insecurity. Leaders can expand the capacities of their minds and hearts through conscious development and practice.

Leaders should be aware of how their mental models affect their thinking and may cause "blind spots" that limit understanding. Becoming aware of assumptions is a first step toward shifting one's mental model and being able to see the world in new and different ways. Four key issues important to expanding and developing a leader's mind are independent thinking, open-mindedness, systems thinking, and personal mastery.

Leaders should also understand the importance of emotional intelligence. Four basic components of emotional intelligence are self-awareness, self-management, social awareness, and relationship management. Emotionally intelligent leaders can have a positive impact on organizations by helping employees grow, learn, and develop; creating a sense of purpose and meaning; instilling unity and team spirit; and basing relationships on trust and respect, which allows employees to take risks and fully contribute to the organization. Most work in organizations is done in teams, and emotional intelligence applies to teams as well as to individuals. Leaders develop a team's emotional intelligence by creating norms that foster a strong group identity, building trust among members, and instilling a belief among members that they can be effective and succeed as a team.

Traditional organizations have relied on fear as a motivator. Although fear does motivate people, it prevents people from feeling good about their work and often causes avoidance behavior. Fear can reduce trust and communication so that important problems and issues are hidden or suppressed. Leaders can choose to lead with love instead of fear. Love can be thought of as a motivational force that enables people to feel alive, connected, and energized; as feelings of liking, caring, and bliss; and as actions of helping, listening, and cooperating. Each of these aspects of love has relevance for organizational relationships. People respond to love because it meets unspoken needs for respect and affirmation. Rational thinking is important to leadership, but it takes love to build trust, creativity, and enthusiasm.

Discussion Questions

1. How do you feel about developing the emotional qualities of yourself and other people in the organization as a way to be an effective leader? Discuss.

2. Do you agree that people have a capacity for developing their minds and hearts beyond current competency? Can you give an example? Discuss.

3. What are some specific reasons leaders need to be aware of their mental models?

4. Discuss the similarities and differences between mental models and open-mindedness.

5. What is the concept of personal mastery? How important is it to a leader?

6. Which of the four elements of emotional intelligence do you consider most essential to an effective leader? Why?

7. Consider fear and love as potential motivators. Which is the best source of motivation for soldiers during a war? For members of a new product development team? For top executives at a media conglomerate? Why?

8. Have you ever experienced love and/or fear from leaders at work? How did you respond?

9. Do you think it is appropriate for a leader to spend time developing a team's emotional intelligence? Why or why not?

10. Think about the class for which you are reading this text as a system. How might making changes without whole-systems thinking cause problems for students?

Leadership at Work

Mentors

Think of a time when someone reached out to you as a mentor or coach. This might have been a time when you were having some difficulty, and the person who reached out would have done so out of concern for you rather than for their own self interest.

Below, briefly describe the situation, who the mentor was, and what the mentor did for you.

Mentoring comes from the heart, is a generous act, and is usually deeply appreciated by the recipient. How does it feel to recall the situation in which a mentor assisted you?

Share your experience with one or more students. What are the common characteristics that mentors possess based on your combined experiences?

In Class: A discussion of experiences with mentors is excellent for small groups. The instructor can ask each group to identify the common characteristics that their mentors displayed, and each group's conclusions can be written on the board. From these lists of mentor characteristics, common themes associated with mentors can be defined. The instructor can ask the class the following key questions: What are the key characteristics of mentors? Based on the key mentor characteristics, is effective mentoring based more on a person's heart or mind? Will you (the student) reach out as a mentor to others in life, and how will you do it? What factors might prevent you from doing so?

Leadership Development: Cases for Analysis

The New Boss

Sam Nolan clicked the mouse for one more round of solitaire on the computer in his den. He'd been at it for more than an hour, and his wife had long ago given up trying to persuade him to join her for a movie or a rare Saturday night on the town. The mind-numbing game seemed to be all that calmed Sam down enough to stop agonizing about work and how his job seemed to get worse every day.

Nolan was Chief Information Officer at Century Medical, a large medical products company based in Connecticut. He had joined the company four years ago, and since that time Century had made great progress integrating technology into its systems and processes. Nolan had already led projects to design and build two highly successful systems for Century. One was a benefits-administration system for the company's human resources department. The other was a complex Web-based purchasing system that streamlined the process of purchasing supplies and capital goods. Although the system had been up and running for only a few months, modest projections were that it would save Century nearly $2 million annually. The new Web-based system dramatically cut the time needed for processing requests and placing orders. Purchasing managers now had more time to work collaboratively with key stakeholders to identify and select the best suppliers and negotiate better deals.

Nolan thought wearily of all the hours he had put in developing trust with people throughout the company and showing them how technology could not only save time and money but also support team-based work, encourage open information sharing, and give people more control over their own jobs. He smiled briefly as he recalled one long-term HR employee, 61-year-old Ethel Moore. She had been terrified when Nolan first began showing her the company's intranet, but she was now one of his biggest supporters. In fact, it had been Ethel who had first approached him with an idea about a Web-based job posting system. The two had pulled together a team and developed an idea for linking Century managers, internal recruiters, and job applicants using artificial intelligence software on top of an integrated Web-based system. When Nolan had presented the idea to his boss, executive vice president Sandra Ivey, she had enthusiastically endorsed it. Within a few weeks the team had authorization to proceed with the project.

But everything began to change when Ivey resigned her position 6 months later to take a plum job in New York. Ivey's successor, Tom Carr, seemed to have little interest in the project. During their first meeting, Carr had openly referred to the project as a waste of time and money. He immediately disapproved several new features suggested by the company's internal recruiters, even though the project team argued that the features could double internal hiring and save millions in training costs. "Just stick to the original plan and get it done. All this stuff needs to be handled on a personal basis anyway," Carr countered. "You can't learn more from a computer than you can talking to real people—and as for internal recruiting, it shouldn't be so hard to talk to people if they're already working right here in the company." Carr seemed to have no understanding of how and why technology was being used. He became irritated when Ethel Moore referred to the system as "Web-based." He boasted that he had never visited Century's intranet site and suggested that "this Internet fad" would blow over in a year or so anyway. Even Ethel's enthusiasm couldn't get through to him. "Technology is for those people in the IS department. My job is people, and yours should be too." Near the end of the meeting, Carr even jokingly suggested that the project team should just buy a couple of good filing cabinets and save everyone some time and money.

Nolan sighed and leaned back in his chair. The whole project had begun to feel like a joke. The vibrant and innovative human resources department his team had imagined now seemed like nothing more than a pipe dream. But despite his frustration, a new thought entered Nolan's mind: "Is Carr just stubborn and narrow-minded or does he have a point that HR is a people business that doesn't need a high-tech job posting system?"

Sources: Based on Carol Hildebrand, "New Boss Blues," *CIO Enterprise*, Section 2, (November 15, 1998), pp. 53–58; and Megan Santosus, "Advanced Micro Devices' Web-Based Purchasing System," *CIO*, Section 1 (May 15, 1998), p. 84. A version of this case originally appeared in Richard L. Daft, *Organization Theory and Design*, 7th ed. (Cincinnati, OH: South-Western, 2001), pp. 270–271.

QUESTIONS

1. Describe the two different mental models represented in this story.

2. What are some of the assumptions and perceptions that shape the mindset of Sam Nolan? Of Tom Carr?

3. Do you think it is possible for Carr to shift to a new mental model? If you were Sam Nolan, what would you do?

The USS Florida

The atmosphere in a Trident nuclear submarine is generally calm and quiet. Even pipe joints are cushioned to prevent noise that might tip off a pursuer. The Trident ranks among the world's most dangerous weapons—swift, silent, armed with 24 long-range missiles carrying 192 nuclear warheads. Trident crews are the cream of the Navy crop, and even the sailors who fix the plumbing exhibit a white-collar decorum. The culture aboard ship is a low-key, collegial one in which sailors learn to speak softly and share close quarters with an ever-changing roster of shipmates. Being subject to strict security restrictions enhances a sense of elitism and pride. To move up and take charge of a Trident submarine is an extraordinary feat in the Navy—fewer than half the officers qualified for such commands ever get them. When Michael Alfonso took charge of the USS *Florida*, the crew welcomed his arrival. They knew he was one of them—a career Navy man who joined up as a teenager and moved up through the ranks. Past shipmates remembered him as basically a loner, who could be brusque but generally pleasant enough. Neighbors on shore found Alfonso to be an unfailingly polite man who kept mostly to himself.

The crew's delight in their new captain was short-lived. Commander Alfonso moved swiftly to assume command, admonishing his sailors that he would push them hard. He wasn't joking—soon after the *Florida* slipped into deep waters to begin a postoverhaul shakedown cruise, the new captain loudly and publicly reprimanded those whose performance he considered lacking. Chief Petty Officer Donald MacArthur, chief of the navigation division, was only one of those who suffered Alfonso's anger personally. During training exercises, MacArthur was having trouble keeping the boat at periscope depth because of rough seas. Alfonso announced loudly, "You're disqualified." He then precipitously relieved him of his diving duty until he could be recertified by extra practice. Word of the incident spread quickly. The crew, accustomed to the Navy's adage of "praise in public, penalize in private," were shocked. It didn't take long for this type of behavior to have an impact on the crew, according to Petty Officer Aaron Carmody: "People didn't tell him when something was wrong. You're not supposed to be afraid of your captain, to tell him stuff. But nobody wanted to."

The captain's outbursts weren't always connected with job performance. He bawled out the supply officer, the executive officer, and the chief of the boat because the soda dispenser he used to pour himself a glass of Coke one day contained Mr. Pibb instead. He exploded when he arrived unexpected at a late-night meal and found the fork at his place setting missing. Soon, a newsletter titled *The Underground* was being circulated by the boat's plumbers, who used sophomoric humor to spread the word about the captain's outbursts over such petty matters. By the time the sub reached Hawaii for its "Tactical Readiness Evaluation," an intense week-long series of inspections by staff officers, the crew was almost completely alienated. Although the ship tested well, inspectors sent word to Rear Admiral Paul Sullivan that something seemed to be wrong on board, with severely strained relations between captain and crew. On the Trident's last evening of patrol, much of the crew celebrated with a film night—they chose *The Caine Mutiny* and *Crimson Tide*, both movies about Navy skippers who face mutinies and are relieved of command at sea. When Humphrey Bogart, playing the captain of the fictional USS *Caine*, exploded over a missing quart of strawberries, someone shouted, "Hey, sound familiar?"

When they reached home port, the sailors slumped ashore. "Physically and mentally, we were just beat into the ground," recalls one. Concerned about reports that the crew seemed "despondent," Admiral Sullivan launched an informal inquiry that eventually led him to relieve Alfonso of his command. It was the first-ever firing of a Trident submarine commander. "He had the chance of a lifetime to experience the magic of command, and he squandered it," Sullivan said. "Fear and intimidation lead to certain ruin." Alfonso himself seemed dumbfounded by Admiral Sullivan's actions, pointing out that the USS *Florida* under his command posted "the best-ever grades assigned for certifications and inspections for a postoverhaul Trident submarine."

Source: Thomas E. Ricks, "A Skipper's Chance to Run a Trident Sub Hits Stormy Waters," *The Wall Street Journal* (November 20, 1997), pp. A1, A6.

QUESTIONS

1. Analyze Alfonso's impact on the crew in terms of love versus fear. What might account for the fact that he behaved so strongly as captain of the USS *Florida*?

2. Which do you think a leader should be more concerned about aboard a nuclear submarine—high certification grades or high-quality interpersonal relationships? Do you agree with Admiral Sullivan's decision to fire Alfonso? Discuss.

3. Discuss Commander Alfonso's level of emotional intelligence in terms of the four components listed in the chapter. What advice would you give him?

References

1   Rodd Wagner, "Becoming the Best at Qwest," *Gallup Management Journal* (January 13, 2005). Retrieved March 8, 2007, from: http://gmj.gallup.com/content/default.aspx?ci=14593&pg=3.

2   Christopher Bartlett, quoted in Betsy Morris, "The New Rules," *Fortune* (July 24, 2006), pp. 70–87.

3   Keith H. Hammonds, "'You Can't Lead Without Making Sacrifices,'" *Fast Company* (June 2001), pp. 106–116.

4   Tim Sanders, *Love is the Killer App* (New York: Crown, 2002).

5   Warren Bennis, quoted in Tricia Bisoux, "What Makes Great Leaders," *BizEd* (September–October 2005), pp. 40–45.

6   Robert B. French, "The Teacher as Container of Anxiety: Psychoanalysis and the Role of Teacher," *Journal of Management Education* 21, no. 4 (November 1997), pp. 483–495.

7   This basic idea is found in a number of sources, among them: Jack Hawley, *Reawakening the Spirit in Work* (San Francisco: Berrett-Koehler, 1993); Aristotle, *The Nicomachean Ethics*, trans. by the Brothers of the English Dominican Province, rev. by Daniel J. Sullivan (Chicago: Encyclopedia Britannica, 1952); Alasdair MacIntyre, *After Virtue: A Study in Moral Theory* (Notre Dame, IN: University of Notre Dame Press, 1984); and Stephen Covey, *The Seven Habits of Highly Effective People: Powerful Lessons in Personal Change* (New York: Fireside Books/Simon & Schuster, 1990).

8   Vanessa Urch Druskat and Anthony T. Pescosolido, "The Content of Effective Teamwork Mental Models in Self-Managing Teams: Ownership, Learning, and Heedful Interrelating," *Human Relations*

55, no. 3 (2002), pp. 283–314; and Peter M. Senge, *The Fifth Discipline: The Art and Practice of the Learning Organization* (New York: Doubleday, 1990).

9   Druskat and Pescosolido, "The Content of Effective Teamwork Mental Models."

10 Adam Lashinsky, "Chaos by Design," *Fortune* (October 2, 2006), pp. 86–98.

11 This discussion is based partly on Robert C. Benfari, *Understanding and Changing Your Management Style* (San Francisco: Jossey-Bass, 1999), pp. 66–93.

12 Dave Marcum, Steve Smith, and Mahan Khalsa, "The Marshmallow Conundrum," *Across the Board* (March–April 2004), pp. 26–30.

13 Geoffrey Colvin, "Managing in Chaos," *Fortune* (October 2, 2006), pp. 76–82.

14 Richard Siklos, "When Terry Met Jerry, Yahoo!" *The New York Times* (January 29, 2006), Section 3 p.1 and Fred Vogelstein, "Bringing Up Yahoo," *Fortune* (April 5, 2004), pp. 221–228.

15 Siklos, "When Terry Met Jerry, Yahoo!"; and Kevin J. Delaney, "Spreading Change: As Yahoo Falters, Executive's Memo Calls for an Overhaul," *The Wall Street Journal* (November 18–19, 2006), pp. A1, A7.

16 Anthony J. Mayo and Nitin Nohria, *In Their Time: The Greatest Business Leaders of the 20th Century* (Boston: Harvard Business School Press, 2005).

17 Geoffrey Colvin, "The Most Valuable Quality in a Manager," *Fortune* (December 29, 1997), pp. 279–280; and Marlene Piturro, "Mindshift," *Management Review* (May 1999), pp. 46–51.

18 Colvin, "Managing In Chaos."

19 Gary Hamel, "Why . . . It's Better to Question Answers Than to Answer Questions," *Across the Board* (November–December 2000), pp. 42–46; Jane C. Linder and Susan Cantrell, "It's All in the Mind(set)," *Across the Board* (May–June 2002), pp. 39–42.

20 Reported in Sharon Begley, "People Believe a 'Fact' That Fits Their Views, Even If It's Clearly False," (Science Journal column), *The Wall Street Journal* (February 4, 2005), p. A8.

21 Anil K. Gupta and Vijay Govindarajan, "Cultivating a Global Mindset," *Academy of Management Executive* 16, no. 1 (2002), pp. 116–126.

22 Ibid.

23 Hamel, "Why . . . It's Better to Question Answers Than to Answer Questions;" and Colvin, "Managing in Chaos."

24 Ellen Langer and John Sviokla, "An Evaluation of Charisma from the Mindfulness Perspective," unpublished manuscript, Harvard University. Part of this discussion is also drawn from Richard L. Daft and Robert H. Lengel, *Fusion Leadership: Unlocking the Subtle Forces that Change People and Organizations* (San Francisco: Berrett-Koehler, 1998).

25 T. K. Das, "Educating Tomorrow's Managers: The Role of Critical Thinking," *The International Journal of Organizational Analysis* 2, no. 4 (October 1994), pp. 333–360.

26 Carol Hymowitz, "Building a Board That's Independent, Strong, and Effective," (In the Lead column), *The Wall Street Journal* (November 19, 2002), p. B1.

27 Bernard M. Bass, *Leadership and Performance Beyond Expectations* (New York: The Free Press, 1985); and *New Paradigm Leadership: An Inquiry into Transformational Leadership* (Alexandria, VA: U.S. Army Research Institute for the Behavioral and Social Sciences, 1996).

28 Leslie Wexner, quoted in Rebecca Quick, "A Makeover That Began at the Top," *The Wall Street Journal* (May 25, 2000), pp. B1, B4.

29 The Pike Syndrome has been discussed in multiple sources.

30 James Gleick, *Genius: The Life and Science of Richard Feynman* (New York: Pantheon Books, 1992).

31 Chris Argyris, *Flawed Advice and the Management Trap* (New York: Oxford University Press, 2000); and Eileen C. Shapiro, "Managing in the Cappuccino Economy" (review of *Flawed Advice*), *Harvard Business Review* (March–April 2000), pp. 177–183.

32 Rajat Gupta, quoted in *Fast Company* (September 1999), p. 120.

33 This section is based on Peter M. Senge, *The Fifth Discipline: The Art and Practice of the Learning Organization* (New York: Doubleday,

1990); John D. Sterman, "Systems Dynamics Modeling: Tools for Learning in a Complex World," *California Management Review* 43, no. 4 (Summer, 2001), pp. 8–25; and Ron Zemke, "Systems Thinking," *Training* (February 2001), pp. 40–46.

34 These examples are cited in Sterman, "Systems Dynamics Modeling."

35 Peter M. Senge, Charlotte Roberts, Richard B. Ross, Bryan J. Smith, and Art Kleiner, *The Fifth Discipline Fieldbook* (New York: Currency/Doubleday, 1994), p. 87.

36 Senge, *The Fifth Discipline.*

37 Timothy A. Judge, Amy E. Colbert, and Remus Ilies, "Intelligence and Leadership: A Quantitative Review and Test of Theoretical Propositions," *Journal of Applied Psychology* (June 2004), pp. 542–552.

38 Daniel Goleman, *Emotional Intelligence: Why It Can Matter More Than IQ* (New York: Bantam Books, 1995); John D. Mayer and David Caruso, "The Effective Leader: Understanding and Applying Emotional Intelligence," *Ivey Business Journal* (November–December 2002); Pamela Kruger, "A Leader's Journey," *Fast Company* (June 1999), pp. 116–129; Hendrie Weisinger, *Emotional Intelligence at Work* (San Francisco: Jossey-Bass, 1998).

39 Based on Goleman, *Emotional Intelligence;* Goleman, "Leadership That Gets Results," *Harvard Business Review* (March–April 2000), pp. 79–90; J. D. Mayer, D. R. Caruso, and P. Salovey, "Emotional Intelligence Meets Traditional Standards for an Intelligence," *Intelligence* 27, no. 4 (1999), pp. 266–298; Neal M. Ashkanasy and Catherine S. Daus, "Emotion in the Workplace: The New Challenge for Managers," *Academy of Management Executive* 16, no.1 (2002), pp. 76–86; and Weisinger, *Emotional Intelligence at Work.*

40 Studies reported in Stephen Xavier, "Are You At the Top of Your Game? Checklist for Effective Leaders," *Journal of Business Strategy* 26, no. 3 (2005), pp. 35–42.

41 This section is based largely on Daniel Goleman, *Emotional Intelligence: Why It Can Matter More Than IQ* (New York: Bantam Books, 1995), pp. 289–290.

42 Jerry Krueger and Emily Killham, "At Work, Feeling Good Matters," *Gallup Management Journal* (December 8, 2005).

43 Goleman, "Leadership that Gets Results"; and Richard E. Boyatzis and Daniel Goleman, *The Emotional Competence Inventory— University Edition,* The Hay Group, 2001.

44 Marcum, et al., "The Marshmallow Conundrum."

45 Hendrie Weisinger, *Emotional Intelligence at Work* (San Francisco: Jossey-Bass, 1998).

46 Alan Farnham, "Are You Smart Enough to Keep Your Job?" *Fortune* (January 15, 1996), pp. 34–47.

47 Peter J. Frost, "Handling the Hurt: A Critical Skill for Leaders," *Ivey Management Journal* (January–February 2004).

48 Rolf W. Habbel, "The Human[e] Factor: Nurturing a Leadership Culture," *Strategy & Business* 26 (First Quarter 2002), pp. 83–89.

49 Marc Gunther, "Is Bob Iger Ready for His Close-Up?" *Fortune* (April 4, 2005), pp. 76–78.

50 Research study results reported in Goleman, "Leadership that Gets Results."

51 Michael Sokolove, "Follow Me," *The New York Times Magazine* (February 2006), p. 96.

52 Lara E. Megerian and John J. Sosik, "An Affair of the Heart: Emotional Intelligence and Transformational Leadership," *The Journal of Leadership Studies* 3, no. 3 (1996), pp. 31–48; and Ashkanasy and Daus, "Emotion in the Workplace."

53 Xavier, "Are You at the Top of Your Game?"

54 E. Hatfield, J. T. Cacioppo, and R. L. Rapson, *Emotional Contagion* (New York: Cambridge University Press, 1994).

55 P. J. Jordan, N. M. Ashkanasy, C. E. J. Härtel, and G. S. Hooper, "Workgroup Emotional Intelligence: Scale Development and Relationship to Team Process Effectiveness and Goal Focus," *Human Resource Management Review* 12, no. 2 (Summer 2002), pp. 195–214.

56 This discussion is based on Vanessa Urch Druskat and Steven B. Wolf, "Building the Emotional Intelligence of Groups," *Harvard Business Review* (March 2001), pp. 81–90.

57 Daniel Goleman, Richard Boyatzis, and Annie McKee, "The Emotional Reality of Teams," *Journal of Organizational Excellence* (Spring 2002), pp. 55–65.

58 Greg Jaffe, "How Admiral Konetzni Intends to Mend Navy's Staff Woes," *The Wall Street Journal* (July 6, 2000), pp. A1, A6.

59 Kathleen D. Ryan and Daniel K. Oestreich, *Driving Fear Out of the Workplace: How to Overcome the Invisible Barriers to Quality, Productivity, and Innovation* (San Francisco: Jossey-Bass, 1991).

60 David E. Dorsey, "Escape from the Red Zone," *Fast Company*, (April/May 1997), pp. 116–127.

61 This section is based on Ryan and Oestreich, *Driving Fear Out of the Workplace;* and Therese R. Welter, "Reducing Employee Fear: Get Workers and Managers to Speak Their Minds," *Small Business Report* (April 1991), pp. 15–18.

62 Ryan and Oestreich, *Driving Fear Out of the Workplace,* p. 43.

63 Donald G. Zauderer, "Integrity: An Essential Executive Quality," *Business Forum* (Fall 1992), pp. 12–16.

64 Geoffrey Colvin, "What's Love Got to Do with It?" *Fortune* (November 12, 2001), p. 60.

65 Jack Hawley, *Reawakening the Spirit at Work* (San Francisco: Berrett-Koehler, 1993), p. 55; and Rodney Ferris, "How Organizational Love Can Improve Leadership," *Organizational Dynamics,* 16, no. 4 (Spring 1988), pp. 40–52.

66 Barbara Moses, "It's All About Passion," *Across the Board* (May–June 2001), pp. 55–58.

67 Michael Kroth and Patricia Boverie, "Leading with Passion," *Leader to Leader* (Winter 2003), pp. 44–50.

68 Joseph Campbell with Bill Moyers, *The Power of Myth* (New York: Doubleday, 1988).

69 Stephen R. Covey, *The Seven Habits of Highly Effective People: Powerful Lessons in Personal Change* (New York: Fireside/Simon & Schuster, 1990), p. 80.

70 Hyler Bracey, Jack Rosenblum, Aubrey Sanford, and Roy Trueblood, *Managing from the Heart* (New York: Dell Publishing, 1993), p. 192.

71 Madan Birla with Cecilia Miller Marshall, *Balanced Life and Leadership Excellence* (Memphis, TN: The Balance Group, 1997), pp. 76–77.

72 Colvin, "What's Love Got to Do with It?"

73 Ferris, "How Organizational Love Can Improve Leadership."

Chapter 6

Your Leadership Challenge

After reading this chapter, you should be able to:

- Combine a rational approach to leadership with a concern for people and ethics.

- Recognize your own stage of moral development and ways to accelerate your moral maturation.

- Know and use mechanisms that enhance an ethical organizational culture.

- Apply the principles of stewardship and servant leadership.

- Recognize courage in others and unlock your own potential to live and act courageously.

Courage and Moral Leadership

Washington, DC; February 23, 2003. After a brilliant 38-year military career, four-star General Eric Shinseki did something many considered shocking, if not downright foolish. While testifying before a U.S. Senate Armed Services Committee hearing on the impending war in Iraq, Shinseki told the senators it would take several hundred thousand soldiers to keep the peace in postwar Iraq. Just a simple, candid answer, but one that was in direct opposition to what Shinseki's civilian boss, U.S. Secretary of Defense Donald Rumsfeld, wanted him to say. Rumsfeld had been working hard to convince Congress that the war would require relatively few ground forces, and here was the U.S. Army chief of staff telling them from his experience that it would instead require massive manpower. The Department of Defense response was quick and unforgiving, with both Rumsfeld and Deputy Secretary of Defense Paul Wolfowitz publicly repudiating Shinseki's comments.

Chagrined by Shinseki's refusal to toe the party line and his support of the Crusader artillery system, which civilian leaders opposed, Rumsfeld later took the unprecedented step of naming Shinseki's replacement more than a year before the end of his term. Neither Rumsfeld nor Wolfowitz attended Shinseki's retirement ceremony, a major breach of protocol that reflected their disdain for the general.

By mid-2006, half a dozen generals had publicly expressed doubts over Rumsfeld's handling of the war and called for him to step down, but only after they had safely retired. Rumsfeld resigned later that year. Shinseki had the courage to express his concerns at the beginning of the war, despite the potential damage to his own reputation and career. In discussing the general's willingness to stand alone among the top brass in bucking the higher ups, a professor of management at the Wharton School of Business said, "This is someone who at the height of his professional career . . . in the name of disclosure and truthfulness chose to take the ultimate hit." Shinseki himself just sees it as honoring his responsibility to the young people that the United States "asks to stand up and do the unthinkable." Shinseki knows that when there aren't enough soldiers, too many people are going to die. "I made it a point to remind myself that I was first, last, and always a soldier," he said.[1]

Eric Shinseki had the courage to say what he believed. Whether one agrees or disagrees with U.S. policies in Iraq and Donald Rumsfeld's performance as Secretary of Defense is beside the point in this case. Shinseki was willing to disagree with his bosses because he felt a moral responsibility to do so, even though it might cause personal suffering.

Being a real leader means learning who you are and what you stand for, and then having the courage to act. Leaders demonstrate confidence and commitment in what they believe and what they do. A deep devotion to a cause or a purpose larger than one's self sparks the courage to act, as it did for General Shinseki. In addition, Shinseki's story demonstrates that leadership has less to do with using other people than with serving other people. Placing others ahead of oneself is a key to successful leadership, whether in politics, war, education, sports, social services, or business.

This chapter explores ideas related to courage and moral leadership. In the previous chapter, we discussed mind and heart, two of the three elements that come together for successful leadership. This chapter focuses on the third element, spirit—on the ability to look within, to contemplate the human condition, to think about what is right and wrong, to see what really matters in the world, and to have the courage to stand up for what is worthy and right. We begin by examining the situation in which most organizations currently operate, the dilemma leaders face in the modern world, and the kinds of behaviors that often contribute to an unethical organizational climate. Next we explore how leaders can act in a moral way, examine a model of personal moral development, and look at the importance of stewardship and servant leadership. The final sections of the chapter explore what courage means and how leaders develop the courage for moral leadership to flourish.

Moral Leadership Today

Every decade sees its share of political, social, and corporate villains, but the pervasiveness of ethical lapses in recent years has been astounding. In the political arena, U.S. Representative Mark Foley resigned amid allegations that he engaged in sexually explicit online chats with congressional pages. Russia's telecom minister is on the hot seat over charges that he owns huge chunks of the industry he oversees, having surreptitiously converted telecom businesses from state ownership.[2] The U.S. Army is still dealing with the fallout from the Abu Ghraib prisoner abuse scandal, and the U.S. Air Force has canceled a $26 billion deal to lease tankers from Boeing Corp. after learning that a former procurement officer favored Boeing in contracts in order to get hired by the aerospace company.[3] The names of once-revered corporations have become synonymous with greed, deceit, and financial chicanery: Enron, Adelphia, Arthur Andersen, HealthSouth, WorldCom, Tyco. Recently, the CEO of giant health insurer UnitedHealth Group resigned under pressure after an outside probe found that he was involved in issuing millions of backdated stocks that benefitted himself and other executives.[4] No wonder a CBS poll found that 79 percent of respondents believe questionable business practices are widespread and less than one-third think most CEOs are honest.[5] Harvard Business School professor and author Shoshana Zuboff describes the impact of these public sentiments: "The chasm between individuals and organizations is marked by frustration, mistrust, disappointment, and even rage."[6]

The Ethical Climate in U.S. Business

Ethical lapses occur at all levels of organizations, but top leaders in particular are facing closer scrutiny in light of recent unethical and illegal actions. What's going on at the top trickles down through organizations and society. When leaders fail to set and live up to high ethical standards, organizations, employees, shareholders, and the general public suffer. Unethical and illegal behavior can lead to serious consequences for organizations. For one thing, companies have a hard time attracting good employees. Evidence shows that the recent wave of scandals has prompted job seekers to go to great lengths to check out companies' ethical standards.[7] When current employees lose trust in leaders, morale, commitment, and performance suffer. Customers who lose trust in the organization will bolt, as evidenced by the mass desertion of Arthur Andersen after the firm was found guilty

Action Memo

As a leader, you can put moral values into action and set the example you want followers to live by. You can resist pressures to act unethically just to avoid criticism or achieve short-term gains.

of obstruction of justice for destroying tons of documents related to Enron. Investors may also withdraw their support from the company—or even file suit if they believe they've been lied to and cheated.

Leaders at all levels carry a tremendous responsibility for setting the ethical climate and can act as role models for others. Dale Prows had such a role model early in his career. Now serving as vice president of global purchasing for a leading chemical company, Prows says he always considers the impact his decisions and actions have on others because he admired that consistent quality in a previous supervisor.[8] However, leaders face many pressures that challenge their ability to do the right thing. The most dangerous obstacles for leaders are personal weakness and self-interest rather than full-scale corruption.[9] Pressures to cut costs, increase profits, meet the demands of vendors or business partners, and look successful can all contribute to ethical lapses. During the stock market bubble of the late 1990s, for example, many leaders simply got caught up in the overriding emphasis on fast profits and ever-growing stock prices. The practice of rewarding managers with stock options, originally intended to align the interests of managers with those of shareholders, caused basic human greed to get out of hand during this period.[10] *The New York Times* represents another example of ethical lapses resulting from subtle pressures. After reporter Jayson Blair was discovered to be fabricating research on top stories such as the rescue of Jessica Lynch in Iraq, there were indications that top executives knew something was wrong long before the scandal broke. They ignored the signs because they didn't want to either believe or admit that a newspaper of the *Times'* reputation could be associated with that kind of dishonesty and irresponsibility.[11] Most people want to be liked, and they want their organizations to appear successful. Leaders sometimes do the wrong thing just so they will look good to others. The question for leaders is whether they can summon the fortitude to do the right thing despite outside pressures. "Life is lived on a slippery slope," says Harvard Business School's Richard Tedlow. "It takes a person of character to know what lines you don't cross."[12]

What Leaders Do to Make Things Go Wrong

What actions of leaders contribute to a dearth of integrity within the organization? Recall from Chapter 2 that integrity means adhering to moral principles and acting based on those beliefs. Leaders signal what matters through their behavior, and when leaders operate from principles of selfishness and greed, many employees come to see unethical behavior as okay. At Enron, for example, senior executives were openly arrogant and ambitious for personal successes, and they blatantly flouted the rules and basic standards of fairness and honor to achieve personal gain. As one young Enron employee said, "It was easy to get into, 'Well, everybody else is doing it, so maybe it isn't so bad.'"[13]

Exhibit 6.1 compares unethical and ethical leadership by looking at ten things leaders do that make things go wrong for the organization from a moral standpoint. The behaviors listed in column 1 contribute to an organizational climate ripe for ethical and legal abuses. Column 2 lists the opposite behaviors, which contribute to a climate of trust, fairness, and doing the right thing.[14]

As we discussed in Chapter 1, the leader as hero is an outdated notion, but some executives are preoccupied with their own importance and take every opportunity to feed their greed or nourish their own egos. They focus on having a huge salary, a big office, and other symbols of status rather than on what is good for the

Action Memo
Go to Leader's Self-Insight 6.1 on page 166 and complete the questions to learn your Mach score and how you might fit into an Enron-type environment.

Leaders differ in how they view human nature and the tactics they use to get things done through others. Answer the questions below based on how you view others. Think carefully about each question and be honest about what you feel inside. Please answer whether each item below is Mostly False or Mostly True for you.

	Mostly False	Mostly True
1. Overall, it is better to be humble and honest than to be successful and dishonest.	_____	_____
2. If you trust someone completely, you are asking for trouble.	_____	_____
3. A leader should take action only when it is morally right.	_____	_____
4. A good way to handle people is to tell them what they like to hear.	_____	_____
5. There is no excuse for telling a white lie to someone.	_____	_____
6. It makes sense to flatter important people.	_____	_____
7. Most people who get ahead as leaders have led very moral lives.	_____	_____
8. It is better to not tell people the real reason you did something unless it benefits you to do so.	_____	_____
9. The vast majority of people are brave, good, and kind.	_____	_____
10. It is hard to get to the top without sometimes cutting corners.	_____	_____

Scoring and Interpretation

To compute your Mach score, give yourself one point for each Mostly False answer to items 1, 3, 5, 7, and 9, and one point for each Mostly True answer to items 2, 4, 6, 8, and 10. These items were drawn from the works of Niccolo Machiavelli, an Italian political philosopher who wrote *The Prince* in 1513 to describe how a prince can retain control of his kingdom. From 8–10 points suggests a high Machiavellian score. From 4–7 points indicates a moderate score, and 0–3 points would indicate a low "Mach" score. Successful political intrigue at the time of Machiavelli was believed to require behaviors that today would be considered ego centered and manipulative, which is almost the opposite of ethical leadership. A high Mach score today does not mean a sinister or vicious person, but probably means the person has a cool detachment, sees life as a game, and is not personally engaged with people. Discuss your results with other students, and talk about whether politicians in local or federal government, or top executives in a company like Enron, would likely have a high or a low Mach score.

Source: Adapted from R. Christie and F. L. Geis, *Studies in Machiavellianism* (New York: Academic Press, 1970.)

organization. These leaders typically pay more attention to gaining benefits for themselves rather than for the organization or larger society. Top executives who expect big salaries and perks at the same time the company is struggling and laying off thousands of workers are not likely to create an environment of trust and integrity.[15]

Unethical leaders are dishonest with employees, partners, customers, vendors, and shareholders, and they regularly fail to honor their agreements or commitments to others. In a *USA Today* survey, 82 percent of CEOs said they lied about their golf scores. Sure, it's a small thing, but little by little, dishonesty can become a way of life and business.[16] Unethical leaders also frequently treat people unfairly, perhaps by giving special favors or privileges to followers who flatter their egos or by promoting people based on favoritism rather than concrete business results. For example, at Morgan Stanley, former CEO Philip Purcell has been accused of brutally dismissing managers who fell out of favor

Exhibit 6.1 Comparing Unethical Versus Ethical Leadership

The Unethical Leader	The Ethical Leader
Is arrogant and self-serving	Possesses humility
Excessively promotes self-interest	Maintains concern for the greater good
Practices deception	Is honest and straightforward
Breaches agreements	Fulfills commitments
Deals unfairly	Strives for fairness
Shifts blame to others	Takes responsibility
Diminishes others' dignity	Shows respect for each individual
Neglects follower development	Encourages and develops others
Withholds help and support	Serves others
Lacks courage to confront unjust acts	Shows courage to stand up for what is right

Source: Based on Donald G. Zauderer, "Integrity: An Essential Executive Quality," *Business Forum* (Fall 1992), pp. 12–16.

and promoting his own favored executives rather than basing advancement on merit.[17]

Unethical leaders tend to take all the credit for successes, but they blame others when things go wrong. By taking credit for followers' accomplishments, failing to allow others to have meaningful participation in decision making, and generally treating people with discourtesy and disrespect, they diminish the dignity of others. They see followers as a means to an end, and they show little concern for treating people as individuals or helping followers develop their own potential. Whereas ethical leaders serve others, unethical leaders focus on their own personal needs and goals.

Finally, one of the primary ways leaders contribute to an unethical and potentially corrupt organization is by failing to speak up against acts they believe are wrong. A leader who holds his tongue in order to "fit in with the guys" when colleagues are telling sexually offensive jokes is essentially giving his support for that type of behavior. If a leader knows someone is being treated unfairly by a colleague and does nothing, the leader is setting a precedent for others to behave unfairly as well. Peers and subordinates with lax ethical standards feel free to act as they choose. It is often hard to stand up for what is right, but this is a primary way in which leaders create an environment of integrity.

Acting Like a Moral Leader

Many leaders forget that business is about *values*, not just economic performance. Moral leadership doesn't mean ignoring profit and loss, stock price, production costs, and other hard measurable facts. But it does require recognizing the importance of moral values, human meaning, quality, and higher purpose.[18] Henry Ford's century-old comment seems tailor-made for today's poor ethical climate: "For a long time people believed that the only purpose of industry was to make a profit. They are wrong. Its purpose is to serve the general welfare."[19]

Despite the corporate realities of greed, competition, and the drive to achieve goals and profits, leaders can act from moral values and encourage others to develop and use moral values in the workplace. *The single most important factor in ethical decision making in organizations is whether leaders show a commitment to ethics in their talk and especially their behavior.* Employees learn

Exhibit 6.2 How to Act Like a Moral Leader

1. Develop, articulate, and uphold high moral principles.
2. Focus on what is right for the organization as well as all the people involved.
3. Set the example you want others to live by.
4. Be honest with yourself and others.
5. Drive out fear and eliminate undiscussibles.
6. Establish and communicate ethics policies.
7. Develop a backbone—show zero tolerance for ethical violations.
8. Reward ethical conduct.
9. Treat everyone with fairness, dignity, and respect, from the lowest to the highest level of the organization.
10. Do the right thing in both your private and professional life—even if no one is looking.

Sources: Based on Linda Klebe Treviño, Laura Pincus Hartman, and Michael Brown, "Moral Person and Moral Manager: How Executives Develop a Reputation for Ethical Leadership," *California Management Review* 42, no. 4 (Summer 2000), pp. 128–142; Christopher Hoenig, "Brave Hearts," *CIO* (November 1, 2000), pp. 72–74; and Patricia Wallington, "Honestly?!" *CIO* (March 15, 2003), pp. 41–42.

about the values that are important in the organization by watching leaders. "The CEO sets the tone for an organization's [values]." says Alfred P. West, the founder and CEO of SEI Investments, a financial services firm. West is careful to espouse and model values that build integrity, accountability, and trustworthiness into the organization's culture. He answers his own phone and has the same open-plan office space as everyone else at SEI's headquarters. He doesn't take stock options, pays himself a modest salary, and shuns the perks that are demanded by many top executives. He believes if you separate yourself from employees with corporate jets, enormous stock options, and other special benefits, it sends the wrong message. West also emphasizes open information, which he believes improves performance as well as makes it easier for employees to report ethical lapses or unfair practices.[20]

Action Memo

As a leader, you can drive fear out of the organization so that followers feel comfortable reporting problems or ethical abuses. You can establish clear ethics policies, reward ethical conduct, and show zero tolerance for violations.

Leaders like Alfred West put values into action. Exhibit 6.2 lists some specific ways leaders act to build an environment that allows and encourages people to behave ethically and morally. Leaders create organizational systems and policies that support ethical behavior, such as creating open-door policies that encourage employees to talk about anything without fear, establishing clear ethics codes, rewarding ethical conduct, and showing zero tolerance for violations. After a series of scandals rocked aerospace giant Boeing Co., new CEO Jim McNerney is trying to ingrain ethical behavior into the fabric of the organization. McNerney has instituted new ethics training for employees worldwide and is tying managers' compensation to ethical leadership.[21] Companies such as Computer Associates, KPMG, and Marsh McLennan have hired high-level chief compliance officers to police managers and employees.[22] Most companies have established codes of ethics to guide employee behavior, such as the clear, concise statement used by Trans World Entertainment, shown in Exhibit 6.3. Each of the key points in Trans World's general statement of policy is described in detail in the company's complete code of ethics. However, an ethics code alone is not enough. Most importantly, leaders articulate and uphold high moral standards, and they do the right thing even if they think no one is looking. If leaders cut corners or bend

Exhibit 6.3 Trans World Entertainment Corporation Code of Ethics

General Statement of Policy

- Honesty and candor in our activities, including observance of the spirit, as well as the letter of the law;
- Avoidance of conflicts between personal interests and the interests of the Company, or even the appearance of such conflicts;
- Avoidance of Company payments to candidates running for government posts, or government officials;
- Compliance with generally accepted accounting principles and controls;
- Maintenance of our reputation and avoidance of activities which might reflect adversely on the Company; and
- Integrity in dealing with the Company's assets.

Source: Trans World Entertainment Corporation Code of Ethics. n.d. Retrieved February 7, 2007, from http://www.twec.com/corpsite/corporate/code.cfm.

the rules when they think they won't get caught, they and their organizations will ultimately suffer the consequences.

Moreover, leaders realize that what they do in their personal lives carries over to the professional arena. Leaders are a model for the organization twenty-four hours a day, seven days a week. Consider Mike Price, who was fired as the University of Alabama's football coach before he ever coached a game. While in Florida participating in a golf tournament, Price spent hundreds of dollars on drinks and tips for exotic dancers, spent the night with a woman other than his wife, and ran up a $1,000 room-service bill. The university administration fired Price as a clear signal that the "boys-will-be-boys" mindset in the athletic department would no longer be tolerated. A visible leadership position entails the responsibility for conducting both one's personal and professional life in an ethical manner. Leaders build ethical organizations by demonstrating the importance of serving people and society, as well as winning football games or increasing business profits. Consider how capitalism and service go hand-in-hand for Jeffrey Swartz, CEO of Timberland.

IN THE LEAD

Jeffrey Swartz, Timberland Co.

Jeffrey Swartz, the third-generation CEO whose grandfather founded the Timberland Co. in 1952, says he is "desperately" proud of the high-quality boots, shoes, and other outdoor gear his company makes. But what keeps him going is the larger purpose of helping to solve the world's problems. Swartz has built a culture of service at Timberland that is unparalleled in the corporate world.

Timberland employees get 40 paid hours of leave annually to pursue volunteer activities, which can be projects the company supports or those of their own choosing. The local offices of City Year, a non-profit organization that puts young people into public service for a year, is housed entirely at Timberland's headquarters. And each year, Timberland holds a day-long "Serv-a-palooza," when the company shuts down and employees around the world participate in volunteer work. In 2005, Serv-a-palooza hosted 170 service projects in 27 countries, representing about 45,000 volunteer hours.

In 1995, when Timberland was facing a financial crisis, a banker told Swartz he needed to "cut the country-club crap out." Instead of heeding that advice, Swartz doubled the amount of paid service time for employees and managed to turn the company around. Since then, Timberland has seen growing sales and profits. Swartz is an avowed capitalist and has no desire to pursue his social objectives through a nonprofit. He believes commerce and justice should go hand in hand and he's using Timberland as a living laboratory to prove it.

People like working for a company that puts its values into action. "I love my job," says staff attorney Michael Moody. "The core values are humanity, humility, integrity, and excellence, and I see those values used as a touchstone in all conversations."[23]

Leaders like Jeffrey Swartz illustrate that leaders can run successful organizations based on moral principles. There is some evidence that doing right by employees, customers, and the community, as well as by shareholders, is good business. One study by Governance Metrics International, an independent corporate governance ratings agency in New York, found that the stocks of companies that are run on more selfless principles perform better than those run in a self-serving manner. Top-ranked companies such as Pfizer, Johnson Controls, and Sunoco also outperformed lower-ranking companies in measures like return on assets, return on investment, and return on capital.[24]

Becoming a Moral Leader

Moral leadership
distinguishing right from wrong and doing right; seeking the just, honest, and good in the practice of leadership

Leadership is not merely a set of practices with no association with right or wrong. All leadership practices can be used for good or evil and thus have a moral dimension. Leaders choose whether to act from selfishness and greed to diminish others or in ways that serve and motivate others to develop to their full potential as employees and as human beings.[25] **Moral leadership** is about distinguishing right from wrong and doing right, seeking the just, the honest, the good, and the right conduct in its practice. Leaders have great influence over others, and moral leadership gives life to others and enhances the lives of others. Immoral leadership takes away from others in order to enhance oneself.[26] Leaders who would do evil toward others, such as Hitler, Stalin, or Cambodia's Pol Pot, are immoral. The following historical example illustrates the height of moral leadership.

Raoul Wallenberg

During the waning months of World War II, a young man climbed atop the roof of a train ready to start for Auschwitz. Ignoring shouts—and later bullets—from Nazis and soldiers of the Hungarian Arrow Cross, he began handing fake Swedish passports to the astonished Jews inside and ordering them to walk to a caravan of cars marked in Swedish colors. By the time the cars were loaded, the soldiers were so dumbfounded by the young man's actions that they simply stood by and let the cars pass, carrying to safety dozens of Jews who had been headed for the death camps.

Virtually alone in Hungary, one of the most perilous places in Europe in 1944, Raoul Wallenberg worked such miracles on a daily basis, using as his weapons courage, self-confidence, and his deep, unwavering belief in the rightness of his mission. No one knows how many people he directly or indirectly saved from certain death, though it is estimated at more than 100,000.

Wallenberg was 32 years old in 1944, a wealthy, politically connected, upperclass Swede from a prominent, well-respected family. When asked by the U.S. War Refugee Board to enter Hungary and help stop Hitler's slaughter of innocent civilians, Wallenberg had everything to lose and nothing to gain. Yet he left his life of safety and comfort to enter Hungary under cover as a diplomat, with the mission of saving as many of Hungary's Jews as possible. Wallenberg never returned, but apparently was captured as a suspected anti-Soviet spy, and died in a Soviet prison. He gave his life fighting for a cause he believed in, and his actions made a real difference in the world.[27]

Raoul Wallenberg emerged from a dismal period in human history as a courageous leader who made the ultimate sacrifice for what he believed Most leaders never have the opportunity to save lives, and few leaders help as many people as Wallenberg did, but the principles of moral leadership he demonstrated are valuable to anyone who aspires to make a positive difference in the world. Moral leadership uplifts people, enabling them to be better than they were without the leader. Leaders are responsible for building a foundation that strengthens and enriches the lives of organization members.

Specific personality characteristics such as ego strength, self-confidence, and a sense of independence may enable leaders to behave morally in the face of opposition. This chapter's Leader's Bookshelf argues that confidence is a key requirement of moral courage, because it moves leaders from contemplating what is right to acting on their moral values. Moreover, leaders can develop these characteristics through their own hard work. People have choices about whether to behave morally. Consider the following remembrance of Viktor Frankl, who was in one of the death camps in Nazi Germany.

> We who lived in concentration camps can remember the men who walked through the huts comforting the others, giving away their last piece of bread. They may have been few in number, but they offer sufficient proof that everything can be taken from a man but one thing: the last of the human freedoms—to choose one's attitude in any given set of circumstances. To choose one's own way.
>
> And there were always choices to make. Every day, every hour, offered the opportunity to make a decision, a decision which determined whether you would or would not submit to those powers which threatened to rob you of your very self, your inner freedom. . . .[28]

A leader's capacity to make moral choices is related to the individual's level of moral development.[29] Exhibit 6.4 shows a simplified illustration of one model

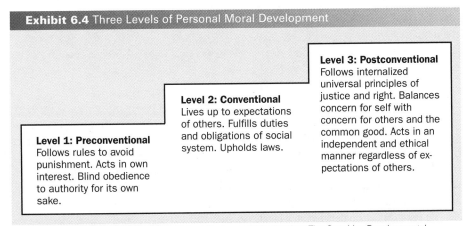

Exhibit 6.4 Three Levels of Personal Moral Development

Level 3: Postconventional
Follows internalized universal principles of justice and right. Balances concern for self with concern for others and the common good. Acts in an independent and ethical manner regardless of expectations of others.

Level 2: Conventional
Lives up to expectations of others. Fulfills duties and obligations of social system. Upholds laws.

Level 1: Preconventional
Follows rules to avoid punishment. Acts in own interest. Blind obedience to authority for its own sake.

Sources: Based on Lawrence Kohlberg, "Moral Stages and Moralization: The Cognitive-Developmental Approach," in *Moral Development and Behavior: Theory, Research, and Social Issues,* ed. Thomas Likona (Austin, TX: Holt, Rinehart and Winston, 1976), pp. 31–53; and Jill W. Graham, "Leadership, Moral Development, and Citizenship Behavior," *Business Ethics Quarterly* 5, No. 1 (January 1995), pp. 43–54.

Moral Courage: Taking Action When Your Values Are Put to the Test

by Rushworth M. Kidder

Despite the broad diversity in the world, Rushworth Kidder, founder and president of the Institute for Global Ethics, says five core principles define morality everywhere: honesty, responsibility, respect, fairness, and compassion. Many leaders agree that living by these values is the right thing to do, yet standing up for moral principles can sometimes be difficult, carrying the risks of humiliation, ridicule, loss of reputation, or even unemployment. In his thought-provoking new book, Kidder defines *moral courage* as the willingness to uphold these core values even when doing so involves significant personal risk. He wrote *Moral Courage: Taking Action When Your Values Are Put to the Test* to give people a structure they can use to better identify and exemplify moral courage.

THE THREE CIRCLES OF MORAL COURAGE

Moral courage exists at the intersection of three domains: a commitment to moral principles, an awareness of the dangers involved in supporting those principles, and a willingness to endure the risks.

- **Principles.** When faced with a choice, leaders can assess the situation to determine whether it requires moral courage, and then determine the specific values that need to be upheld. The first step in behaving with moral courage, Kidder says, is to focus on one or two key values that fit the situation. He uses the example of a human resources manager at a manufacturing company in a small rural town, who noticed some odd expenditures while working on the annual budget and discovered that the boss had charged champagne for his daughter's wedding to the company. The manager knew her job would be on the line if she brought her concerns into the open, but her commitment to principles of fairness and honestly compelled her to act.

- **Danger.** The second key to moral courage lies in accurately assessing the degree of risk. Leaders need to carefully consider what the potential negative consequences of their actions might be and make a conscious decision that standing up for their convictions is worth the risks. In addition, leaders don't want to overestimate the risks, which could make their actions seem like mere bluster and bravado.

- **Endurance.** This is where the rubber meets the road. A leader can understand what key values are at stake, assess the risks involved, and believe in upholding moral principles, yet still lack the courage to act. Leaders need confidence to move from contemplation to action, to be willing to endure the hardships that moral courage requires. They can find this confidence in several areas: their experience and skills; their character and the values and virtues that sustain them emotionally; spiritual insight or faith in a higher power; and their gut feelings about what is the right thing to do.

CHECKPOINTS FOR FINDING MORAL COURAGE

Throughout the book, Kidder illustrates how the three elements of moral courage intersect, using numerous modern and historical examples (of both courage and the lack of it) from business, politics, sports, and other aspects of life. These stories make the book interesting to read at the same time they provide a solid grounding in what it means to act with moral courage. In addition, each chapter ends with a "Moral Courage Checklist" that offers practical advice and guidelines.

Moral Courage: Taking Action When Your Values Are Put to the Test, by Rushworth M. Kidder, is published by William Morrow.

Preconventional level
the level of personal moral development in which individuals are egocentric and concerned with receiving external rewards and avoiding punishments

of personal moral development. At the **preconventional level**, individuals are egocentric and concerned with receiving external rewards and avoiding punishments. They obey authority and follow rules to avoid detrimental personal consequences or satisfy immediate self-interests. The basic orientation toward the world is one of taking what one can get. Someone with this orientation in a leadership position would tend to be autocratic toward others and use the position for personal advancement.

At level two, the **conventional level**, people learn to conform to the expectations of good behavior as defined by colleagues, family, friends, and society. People at this level follow the rules, norms, and values in the corporate culture. If the rules are to not steal, cheat, make false promises, or violate regulatory laws, a person at the conventional level will attempt to obey. They adhere to the norms of the larger social system. However, if the social system says it is okay to inflate bills to the government or make achieving the bottom line more important than integrity, people at the conventional level will usually go along with that norm also. Often, when organizations do something illegal, many managers and employees are simply going along with the system.[30]

At the post-conventional or **principled level**, leaders are guided by an internalized set of principles universally recognized as right or wrong. People at this level may even disobey rules or laws that violate these principles. These internalized values become more important than the expectations of other people in the organization or community. A leader at this level is visionary, empowering, and committed to serving others and a higher cause.

Most adults operate at level two of moral development, and some have not advanced beyond level one. Only about 20 percent of American adults reach the third, post-conventional level of moral development, although most of us have thecapacity to do so. People at level three are able to act in an independent, ethical manner regardless of expectations from others inside or outside the organization, and despite the risk to their own reputation or safety. The U.S. media has reported acts of post-conventional moral courage occurring during the war in Iraq, such as the January 2007 *ABC News* report of 19-year-old Ross McGuinness, who went against his training and jumped into a tank to absorb the impact of a grenade, losing his own life but saving four fellow soldiers.

Impartially applying universal standards to resolve moral conflicts balances self-interest with a concern for others and for the common good. Research has consistently found a direct relationship between higher levels of moral development and more ethical behavior on the job, including less cheating, a tendency toward helpfulness to others, and the reporting of unethical or illegal acts, known as whistleblowing.[31] Leaders can use an understanding of these stages to enhance their own and followers' moral development and to initiate ethics training programs to move people to higher levels of moral reasoning. When leaders operate at level three of moral development, they focus on higher principles and encourage others to think for themselves and expand their understanding of moral issues.

Servant Leadership

What is a leader's moral responsibility toward followers? Is it to limit and control them to meet the needs of the organization? Is it to pay them a fair wage? Or is it to enable them to grow and create and expand themselves as human beings?

Much of the thinking about leadership today implies that moral leadership encourages change toward turning followers into leaders, thereby developing their potential rather than using a leadership position to control or limit people. The ultimate expression of this leadership approach is called *servant leadership*, which can best be understood by comparing it to other approaches. Exhibit 6.5 illustrates a continuum of leadership thinking and practice. Traditional organizations were based on the idea that the leader is in charge of subordinates and the success of the organization depends on leader control over followers. In the first stage, subordinates are passive—not expected to think for themselves but simply to do as they are told. Stage two in the continuum involves subordinates more actively in their own work. Stage three is stewardship, which represents a significant shift in mindset by moving responsibility and authority from leaders to followers.

Conventional level
the level of personal moral development in which people learn to conform to the expectations of good behavior as defined by colleagues, family, friends, and society

Principled level
the level of personal moral development in which leaders are guided by an internalized set of principles universally recognized as right or wrong

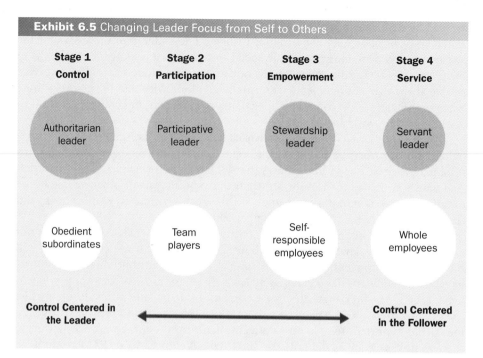

Exhibit 6.5 Changing Leader Focus from Self to Others

Stage 1 Control	Stage 2 Participation	Stage 3 Empowerment	Stage 4 Service
Authoritarian leader	Participative leader	Stewardship leader	Servant leader
Obedient subordinates	Team players	Self-responsible employees	Whole employees

Control Centered in the Leader ←——————————→ Control Centered in the Follower

Servant leadership represents a stage beyond stewardship, where leaders give up control and make a choice to serve employees. Along the continuum, the focus of leadership shifts from leader to followers. In the following sections, we will discuss each stage of this leadership continuum in more detail.

Authoritarian Management

The traditional understanding of leadership is that leaders are good managers who direct and control their people. Followers are obedient subordinates who follow orders. In Chapter 2, we discussed the autocratic leader, who makes the decisions and announces them to subordinates. Power, purpose, and privilege reside with those at the top of the organization. At this stage, leaders set the strategy and goals, as well as the methods and rewards for attaining them. Organizational stability and efficiency are paramount, and followers are routinized and controlled along with machines and raw materials. Subordinates are given no voice in creating meaning and purpose for their work and no discretion as to how they perform their jobs. This leadership mindset emphasizes tight top-down control, employee standardization and specialization, and management by impersonal measurement and analysis.

Participative Management

Since the 1980s, many organizations have made efforts to actively involve employees. Leaders have increased employee participation through employee suggestion programs, participation groups, and quality circles. Teamwork has become an important part of how work is done in many organizations. One study, sponsored by the Association for Quality and Participation, revealed that more than 70 percent of the largest U.S. corporations have adopted some kind of employee participation program. However, most of these programs do not redistribute power and authority to lower-level workers.[32] The mindset is still paternalistic in that top leaders determine purpose and goals, make final decisions, and decide rewards. Employees are expected to make suggestions for quality improvements, act as team players, and take greater responsibility for their own jobs, but they are not allowed to be true partners in the enterprise. Leaders are responsible for outcomes, and they may act as mentors and coaches. They have given up some of their control, but they are still responsible for the morale, emotional well-being, and performance of subordinates, which can lead to treating followers as if they are not able to think for themselves.[33]

Stewardship

Stewardship is a pivotal shift in leadership thinking. Followers are empowered to make decisions and they have control over how they do their own jobs. Leaders give followers the power to influence goals, systems, and structures and become leaders themselves. **Stewardship** supports the belief that leaders are deeply accountable to others as well as to the organization, without trying to control others, define meaning and purpose for others, or take care of others.[34] In fact, stewardship has been called an alternative to leadership because the spotlight is on the people actually doing the work, making the product, providing the service, or working directly with the customer. Four principles provide the framework for stewardship.

Stewardship
a belief that leaders are deeply accountable to others as well as to the organization, without trying to control others, define meaning and purpose for others, or take care of others

1. *Reorient toward a partnership assumption.* Partnership can happen only when power and control shift away from formal leaders to core workers. Partners have a right to say "no" to one another. They are totally honest with one another, neither hiding information nor protecting the other from bad news. In addition, partners (leaders and followers) are jointly responsible for defining vision and purpose and jointly accountable for outcomes.

2. *Localize decisions and power to those closest to the work and the customer.* Decision-making power and the authority to act should reside right at the point where the work gets done. This means reintegrating the "managing" and the "doing" of work, so that everyone is doing some of the core work of the organization part of the time. Nobody gets paid simply to plan and manage the work of others.

3. *Recognize and reward the value of labor.* The reward systems tie everyone's fortunes to the success of the enterprise. Stewardship involves redistributing wealth by designing compensation so that core workers can make significant gains when they make exceptional contributions. Everyone earns his or her pay by delivering real value, and the organization pays everyone as much as possible.

4. *Expect core work teams to build the organization.* Teams of workers who make up the core of the organization or division define goals, maintain controls, create a nurturing environment, and organize and reorganize themselves to respond to a changing environment and the marketplace they serve.

Stewardship leaders guide the organization without dominating it and facilitate followers without controlling them. Stewardship allows for a relationship between leaders and followers in which each makes significant, self-responsible contributions to organizational success. In addition, it gives followers a chance to use their minds, bodies, and spirits on the job, thereby allowing them to be whole human beings.

Stewardship leaders can help organizations thrive in today's complex environment because they tap into the energy and commitment of followers. Although the ideas we have discussed may sound new, an

Action Memo
As a leader, you can apply the principles of stewardship and treat followers as true partners by sharing power and authority for setting goals, making decisions, and maintaining control over their own work and performance.

early management thinker, Mary Parker Follett, captured the spirit of stewardship 80 years ago when she described the type of leader who motivated her.

> *The skillful leader, then, does not rely on personal force; he controls his group not by dominating but by expressing it. He stimulates what is best in us; he unifies and concentrates what we feel only gropingly and scatteringly, but he never gets away from the current of which we and he are both an integral part. He is a leader who gives form to the inchoate energy in every man. The person who influences me most is not he who does great deeds but he who makes me feel I can do great deeds.[35]*

The Servant Leader

Servant leadership takes stewardship assumptions about leaders and followers one step further. Robert Wood Johnson, who built Johnson & Johnson from a small private company into one of the world's greatest corporations, summarized his ideas about management in the expression "to serve." In a statement called "Our Management Philosophy," Johnson went on to say, "It is the duty of the leader to be a servant to those responsible to him."[36] Johnson died more than 30 years ago, but his beliefs about the moral responsibility of a leader are as fresh and compelling (and perhaps as controversial) today as they were when he wrote them.

Servant leadership

leadership in which the leader transcends self-interest to serve the needs of others, help others grow, and provide opportunities for others to gain materially and emotionally

    Servant leadership is leadership upside-down. Servant leaders transcend self-interest to serve the needs of others, help others grow and develop, and provide opportunity for others to gain materially and emotionally. In organizations, these leaders' top priority is service to employees, customers, shareholders, and the general public. In their minds, the purpose of their existence is to serve; leadership flows out of the act of service because it enables other people to grow and become all they are capable of being.[37] There has been an explosion of interest in the concept of leader as servant in recent years because of the emphasis in organizations on empowerment, participation, shared authority, and building a community of trust.[38]

    Servant leadership was first described by Robert Greenleaf in his book, *Servant Leadership*. Greenleaf began developing his ideas after reading Hermann Hesse's novel, *Journey to the East*. The central character of the story is Leo, who appears as a servant to a group of men on a journey. Leo performs the lowliest, most menial tasks to serve the group, and he also cheers them with his good spirits and his singing. All goes well until Leo disappears, and then the journey falls into disarray. Years later, when the narrator is taken to the headquarters of the Order that had sponsored the original journey, he encounters Leo again. There, he discovers that Leo is in fact the titular head of the Order, a great leader.[39] Hesse's fictional character is the epitome of the servant leader, and some doubt whether real human beings functioning in the real world of organizations can ever achieve Leo's level of selflessness in service to others. However, many organizational leaders have shown that it is possible to operate from the principles of servant leadership, even in the business world. For example, when Robert Townsend took over as head of the investment department at American Express, he made it his mission to stay out of his employees' way and invest his time and energy in getting them the pay, titles, and recognition they deserved from the organization.[40] After PeopleSoft lost its bitter battle against Oracle's takeover, PeopleSoft founder and former CEO David Duffield offered $10,000 of his own money to each employee who lost his or her job, a sharp contrast to many of today's top leaders who grab the rewards for themselves and show little concern for followers who have been hurt.[41]

Action Memo

As a leader, you can put the needs, interests, and goals of others above your own and use your personal gifts to help others achieve their potential. Complete the questionnaire in Leader's Self-Insight 6.2 to evaluate your leadership approach along the dimensions of authoritarian leadership, participative leadership, stewardship, and servant leadership.

Think about situations in which you were in a formal or informal leadership role in a group or organization. Imagine using your personal approach as a leader. To what extent does each of the following statements characterize your leadership? Please answer whether each item below is Mostly False or Mostly True for you.

	Mostly False	Mostly True
1. My actions meet the needs of others before my own.	_____	_____
2. I explicitly enable others to feel ownership for their work.	_____	_____
3. I like to consult with people when making a decision.	_____	_____
4. I'm a perfectionist.	_____	_____
5. I like to be of service to others.	_____	_____
6. I try to learn the needs and perspectives of others.	_____	_____
7. I consciously utilize the skills and talents of others.	_____	_____
8. I am assertive about the right way to do things.	_____	_____
9. I give away credit and recognition to others.	_____	_____
10. I believe that others have good intentions.	_____	_____
11. I quickly inform others of developments that affect their work.	_____	_____
12. I tend to automatically take charge.	_____	_____
13. I encourage the growth of others, expecting nothing in return.	_____	_____
14. I value cooperation over competition as a way to energize people.	_____	_____
15. I involve others in planning and goal setting.	_____	_____
16. I put people under pressure when needed.	_____	_____

Scoring and Interpretation

There are four subscale scores that represent four dimensions of leadership. For the dimension of authoritarian leadership, give yourself one point for each "Mostly True" response to questions 4, 8, 12, and 16. For the dimension of participative leadership, give yourself one point for each "Mostly True" response to questions 2, 6, 10, and 14. For the dimension of stewardship, give yourself one point for each "Mostly True" response to questions 3, 7, 11, and 15. For the dimension of servant leadership, give yourself one point for each "Mostly True" response to questions 1, 5, 9, and 13.

My leadership scores are:

Authoritarian _____.
Participative _____.
Stewardship _____.
Servant _____.

These scores represent the four aspects of leadership called authoritarian, participative, stewardship, and servant as described in the text and illustrated in Exhibit 6.5. A score of 3–4 on any of these dimensions would be considered above average, and a score of 0–1 is below average. Compare your four scores to each other to understand your own approach to stewardship and servant leadership. On which of the four dimensions would you like to have the highest score? The lowest? Study the specific questions on which you scored Mostly True or Mostly False to analyze your pattern of strengths and weaknesses. It is not possible to display all four dimensions of leadership simultaneously, so you should think about the dimension you want to emphasize to reflect your leader ideal.

There are four basic precepts in Greenleaf's servant leadership model:[42]

1. *Put service before self-interest.* Servant leaders make a conscious choice to use their gifts in the cause of change and growth for other individuals and for the organization. The desire to help others takes precedence over the desire to achieve a formal leadership position or to attain power and control over others. The servant leader calls for doing what is good and right for others,

even if it does not "pay off" financially. In this view, the organization exists as much to provide meaningful work to the person as the person exists to perform work for the organization.

2. *Listen first to affirm others.* The servant leader doesn't have answers; he asks questions. One of the servant leader's greatest gifts to others is listening, fully understanding the problems others face, and affirming his confidence in others. The servant leader tries to figure out the will of the group and then further it however he can. The leader doesn't impose his or her will on others. By understanding others, the leader can contribute to the best course of action.

3. *Inspire trust by being trustworthy.* Servant leaders build trust by doing what they say they will do, being totally honest with others, giving up control, and focusing on the well-being of others. They share all information, good and bad, and they make decisions to further the good of the group rather than their own interests. In addition, trust grows from trusting others to make their own decisions. Servant leaders gain trust because they give everything away—power, control, rewards, information, and recognition. Trust allows others to flourish.

4. *Nourish others and help them become whole.* Servant leaders care about followers' spirits as well as their minds and bodies, and they believe in the unique potential of each person to have a positive impact on the world. Servant leaders help others find the power of the human spirit and accept their responsibilities. This requires an openness and willingness to share in the pain and difficulties of others. Being close to people also means leaders make themselves vulnerable to others and are willing to show their own pain and humanity.

Servant leadership can mean something as simple as encouraging others in their personal development and helping them understand the larger purpose in their work. When Linda Burzynski became president of Molly Maid International, she learned about servant leadership from one of her cleaners. Posing as a new member of the cleaning crew, Burzynski entered a home with her partner, Dawn, to find dishes piled high, food spilled on countertops, clothes and magazines strewn about, and pet hair everywhere. Surveying the mess, Burzynski was ready to walk out, but Dawn explained that the woman who owned the house was going through a divorce and dealing with three rebellious teenage sons. "She's barely hanging on," said Dawn, and having a clean house gave her a sense of order and control. Burzynski noticed that Dawn seemed to take extra care because she knew she was helping the woman with more than just her household chores. Burzynski says she learned that day about the power of being a servant to her employees and helping them find larger meaning in their difficult jobs.[43] Another example of a leader who puts service to workers first is William Pollard, chairman of ServiceMaster.

C. William Pollard, ServiceMaster

ServiceMaster is a successful, dynamic company that cleans and maintains hospitals, schools, and other buildings. It's not a glamorous industry, and many of the jobs are menial—cleaning toilets, scrubbing floors, and killing bugs. But ServiceMaster has instilled in its employees a sense of dignity, responsibility, and meaningfulness, thanks largely to the servant leadership of chairman C. William Pollard.

Pollard believes it is immoral to take away an employee's right to make decisions and take action. He sees leaders as having a moral responsibility to help employees develop to their full potential, which means giving them the skills, information, tools, and authority they need to act independently. Pollard describes himself as a "leader who leads with a servant's heart," and he encourages others to lead in the same manner. Leaders throughout the organization don't see their jobs as just getting people to perform at work. Instead, their role is to help employees become well-rounded people—enabling them to grow as individuals who contribute not only at work but also at home and in their communities. They care how employees feel about themselves, about their work, and about the people they interact with. ServiceMaster also insists that leaders keep an open-door policy and make themselves available to listen to any concern.

To Pollard, the real leader is not the "person with the most distinguished title, the highest pay, or the longest tenure . . . but the role model, the risk taker, the servant; not the person who promotes himself or herself, but the promoter of others."[44]

For leaders like William Pollard, Linda Burzynski, Robert Townsend, and David Duffield, leadership contains a strong moral component. Servant leaders truly value and respect others as human beings, not as objects of labor. To fully trust others relies on an assumption that we all have a moral duty to one another.[45] To make the choice for service requires a belief in a purpose higher than acquiring more material goods for oneself. Organizational leaders can act from moral values rather than from greed, selfishness, and fear. Indeed, Greenleaf believed that many people have the capacity for servant leadership. He said the greatest enemy to organizations and to society is fuzzy thinking on the part of good, intelligent, vital people who "have the potential to lead but do not lead, or who choose to follow a nonservant."[46]

Leadership Courage

Throughout this chapter, you have probably noticed words like *backbone, guts,* and *fortitude*. No doubt about it, doing the right thing requires courage. Leaders sometimes have to reach deep within themselves to find the strength and courage to resist temptations or to stand up for moral principles when others may ridicule them.

Some would say that without courage, leadership can't exist. However, for many leaders, particularly those working in large organizations, the importance of courage is easily obscured—the main thing is to get along, fit in, and do whatever brings promotions and pay raises. In a world of stability and abundance, it was easy to forget even the *meaning* of courage, so how can leaders know where to find it when they need it? In the following sections, we will examine the nature of leadership courage and discuss some ways courage is expressed in organizations. The final section of the chapter will explore the sources of leadership courage.

What Is Courage?

Many people know intuitively that courage can carry you through deprivation, ridicule, and rejection and enable you to achieve something about which you care deeply. Courage is both a moral and a practical matter for leaders. A lack of courage is what allows greed and self-interest to overcome concern for the common good.[47] Years of stability and abundance misled American businesses into thinking that courage isn't needed in the business world. The lesson executives learned to advance in their careers was "Don't fail. Let someone else take the risk. Be careful. Don't make mistakes." Such a philosophy is no longer beneficial. Indeed, the courage to take risks has always been important for living a full,

Consider This!

Is It Worth the Risk?

To *laugh* . . . is to risk appearing the fool.

To *weep* . . . is to risk appearing sentimental.

To *reach out* . . . is to risk involvement.

To *expose feelings* . . . is to risk exposing your true self.

To *place your ideas and dreams before a crowd* . . . is to risk rejection.

To *love* . . . is to risk not being loved in return.

To *live* . . . is to risk dying.

To *hope* . . . is to risk despair.

To *try* . . . is to risk failure.

But risks must be taken, because the greatest hazard in life is to risk nothing.

Those who risk nothing do nothing and have nothing.

They may avoid suffering and sorrow,

But they cannot learn, feel, change, grow, or love.

Chained by their certitude, they are slaves; they have forfeited their freedom.

Only one who risks is free.

© Janet Rand

rewarding life, as discussed in the *Consider This* box. For today's organizations, things are constantly changing, and leaders thrive by solving problems through trial and error. They create the future by moving forward in the face of uncertainty, by taking chances, by acting with courage.[48] The defining characteristic of **courage** is the ability to step forward through fear. Courage doesn't mean the absence of doubt or fear, but the ability to act in spite of them. As U.S. Senator John McCain puts it, "Fear is the opportunity for courage, not proof of cowardice."[49]

In fact, if there were no fear or doubt, courage would not be needed. People experience all kinds of fears, including fear of death, mistakes, failure, embarrassment, change, loss of control, loneliness, pain, uncertainty, abuse, rejection, success, and public speaking. It is natural and right for people to feel fear when real risk is involved, whether the risk be losing your life, losing your job, losing the acceptance of peers, or losing your reputation. Consider that Charles Darwin put off publishing his *Origin of Species* for two decades because he feared public scorn and ridicule from his peers.[50] But many fears are learned and prevent people from doing what they want. True leaders step through these learned fears to accept responsibility, take risks, make changes, speak their minds, and fight for what they believe.

Courage means accepting responsibility. Leaders make a real difference in the world when they are willing to step up and take personal responsibility. Some people just let life happen to them; leaders make things happen. Courageous leaders create opportunities to make a difference in their organizations and communities. One societal example is Barbara Johns, an ordinary 16-year-old who made an extraordinary difference during the Civil Rights movement in the South. Johns led students of her segregated high school on a 2-week strike after a bus full of white students refused to pick her up. The NAACP stepped in and helped the young people sue for an integrated school. The Johns family home was burned the same year. Other young people took a stand too, with some children as young as grade school being jailed for protesting the segregation of lunch counters, community centers, or sports leagues.[51]

Leaders also demonstrate courage by openly taking responsibility for their failures and mistakes, rather than avoiding blame or shifting it to others. David

Courage
the ability to step forward through fear

Pottruck was fired as CEO of Charles Schwab, and he admits that he had to resist a strong urge to blame everyone else for the downfall. Yet Pottruck found the courage to publicly accept responsibility for his mistakes rather than pointing the finger at others, which allowed him to reflect on the experience more calmly and move ahead with his life and career.[52] The acceptance of responsibility in many of today's large, bureaucratic organizations seems nonexistent. In one large agency of the federal government, the slightest mistake created a whirlwind of blaming, finger pointing, and extra effort to avoid responsibility. The absence of courage froze the agency to the point that many employees were afraid to even do their routine tasks.[53]

Courage often means nonconformity. Leadership courage means going against the grain, breaking traditions, reducing boundaries, and initiating change. Leaders are willing to take risks for a larger, ethical purpose, and they encourage others to do so. Consider the following example.

Clive Warrilow, Volkswagen of America Inc.

When Clive Warrilow took over as president of Volkswagen AG's Americas division, the subsidiary was a mess, with sluggish sales and a demoralized workforce. For many Volkswagen executives, it looked like a situation that called for a strong hand at the top. As a company, Volkswagen has long favored strict hierarchy and control, but Warrilow had come to believe that style no longer worked so well.

After years of climbing the corporate hierarchy, Warrilow had the courage to risk his career by challenging the status quo. Whereas area managers previously had to ask headquarters for permission to make even the smallest decision, Warrilow allowed them to approach their jobs in their own individual ways. If a manager wanted to cut back on advertising and use the money for bonuses, for example, he had the freedom to do so, no questions asked. Warrilow also changed the relationship with dealers. Rather than reprimanding, ridiculing, or terminating dealers who missed their sales targets, he would ask what they could learn from the situation that would enable them to do things better in the future.

Warrilow emphasized trust as the foundation of his leadership, and he encouraged other managers to build good relationships with their subordinates. He even took three busloads of executives to a farm in Solvang, California, where they watched Monty Roberts, the "Horse Whisperer," create an environment for a wild horse to learn, rather than breaking the animal's spirit in the traditional way. It was a metaphor for the type of management Warrilow wanted his executives to practice, a style that emphasizes winning people over rather than bossing them around.

Volkswagen of America made an impressive comeback, thanks in large part to the courage Warrilow showed in instituting a new style of leadership. Nevertheless, VW's top German executives remained wary of the more relaxed approach. "I have empathy for what Warrilow does," one said. "But sometimes I am afraid. Business is tough."[54]

After 4 years leading Volkswagen of America, Warrilow was replaced by top management and decided to retire, leaving the company in a stronger position than he'd found it. It isn't clear if his management style had anything to do with his dismissal, but Warrilow likely would have made the same choice no matter what. He had the courage to go against the grain and do what he believed was best for the company, even if it might not be best for his own career.

Going against the status quo is difficult. It's often easier to stay with what is familiar, even if it will lead to certain failure, than to initiate bold change. A naval aviator once said that many pilots die

> **Action Memo**
> As a leader, you can develop the backbone to accept personal responsibility for achieving desired outcomes, going against the status quo, and standing up for what you believe. You can learn to push beyond your comfort zone and break through the fear that limits you.

because they choose to stay with disabled aircraft, preferring the familiarity of the cockpit to the unfamiliarity of the parachute.[55] Similarly, many leaders hurt their organizations and their own careers by sticking with the status quo rather than facing the difficulty of change. Most leaders initiating change find some cooperation and support, but they also encounter resistance, rejection, loneliness, and even ridicule. Taking chances means making mistakes, enduring mockery or scorn, being outvoted by others, and sometimes failing miserably.

Courage means pushing beyond the comfort zone. To take a chance and improve things means leaders have to push beyond their comfort zone. When people go beyond the comfort zone, they encounter an internal "wall of fear." A social experiment from thirty years ago illustrates the wall of fear that rises when people push beyond their comfort zone. To explore the web of unwritten rules that govern people's behavior on New York City subways, Dr. Stanley Milgram asked his first-year graduate students to board a crowded train and ask someone for a seat. Milgram's focus of interest soon shifted to the students themselves, as the seemingly simple assignment proved to be extremely difficult, even traumatic. Most students found it decidedly uncomfortable to bluntly ask someone for a seat. One now says of the experiment: "I was afraid I was going to throw up."[56] People may encounter the internal wall of fear when about to ask someone for a date, confront the boss, break off a relationship, launch an expensive project, or change careers. Facing the internal wall of fear is when courage is needed most.

Courage means asking for what you want and saying what you think. Leaders have to speak out to influence others. However, the desire to please others—especially the boss—can sometimes block the truth. Everyone wants approval, so it is difficult to say things when you think others will disagree or disapprove. Author and scholar Jerry Harvey tells a story of how members of his extended family in Texas decided to drive 40 miles to Abilene for dinner on a hot day when the car air conditioning did not work. They were all miserable. Talking about it afterward, each person admitted they had not wanted to go, but went along to please the others. The **Abilene Paradox** is the name Harvey uses to describe the tendency of people to not voice their true thoughts because they want to please others.[57] Courage means speaking your mind even when you know others may disagree with you and may even deride you. Courage also means asking for what you want and setting boundaries. It is the ability to say no to unreasonable demands from others, as well as the ability to ask for what you want to help achieve the vision.

Abilene Paradox
the tendency of people to resist voicing their true thoughts or feelings in order to please others and avoid conflict

Courage means fighting for what you believe. Courage means fighting for valued outcomes that benefit the whole. Leaders take risks, but they do so for a higher purpose. Kailash Satyarthi, head of the South Asian Coalition on Child Servitude, receives regular threats and two of his coworkers have been killed, but Satyarthi continues striving to free India's millions of children forced to work in bonded labor.[58] He doesn't risk his life just for the thrill of it. He does so for a cause he deeply believes in—the dignity of all human beings. Taking risks that do not offer the possibility of valuable and ethical outcomes is at best foolish and at worst evil. Leaders at Enron, for example, pushed risk to the limits, but they did so for selfish and unethical reasons. Courage doesn't mean doing battle to destroy the weak, feed one's own ego, or harm others. It means doing what you believe is right, even when this goes against the status quo and possibly opens you to failure and personal sacrifice.

Action Memo
Assess your level of leadership courage by completing the exercise in Leader's Self-Insight 6.3.

How Does Courage Apply to Moral Leadership?

There are many people working in organizations who have the courage to be unconventional, to do what they think is right, to dare to treat employees and customers as whole human beings who deserve respect. Balancing profit with

Assess Your Moral Courage

Think about situations in which you either assumed or were given a leadership role in a group or organization. Imagine using your own courage as a leader. To what extent does each of the following statements characterize your leadership? Please answer whether each item below is Mostly False or Mostly True for you.

	Mostly False	Mostly True
1. I risk substantial personal loss to achieve the vision.	_____	_____
2. I take personal risks to defend my beliefs.	_____	_____
3. I say no even if I have a lot to lose.	_____	_____
4. I consciously link my actions to higher values.	_____	_____
5. I don't hesitate to act against the opinions and approval of others.	_____	_____
6. I quickly tell people the truth, even when it is negative.	_____	_____
7. I feel relaxed most of the time.	_____	_____
8. I speak out against organizational injustice.	_____	_____
9. I stand up to people if they make offensive remarks.	_____	_____
10. I act according to my conscience even if it means I lose status and approval.	_____	_____

Scoring and Interpretation

Each question above pertains to some aspect of displaying courage in a leadership situation. Add up your points for Mostly True answers: _____. If you received a score of 7 or higher, you have real potential to act as a courageous leader. A score below 3 indicates that you avoid difficult issues or have not been in situations that challenge your moral leadership. Is your score consistent with your understanding of your own courage? Look at the individual questions for which you scored Mostly False or Mostly True and think about your specific strengths and weaknesses. Compare your score to that of other students. How might you increase your courage as a leader? Do you want to?

people, self-interest with service, and control with stewardship requires individual moral courage.

Acting Like a Moral Leader Requires Personal Courage To practice moral leadership, leaders have to know themselves, understand their strengths and weaknesses, know what they stand for, and often be nonconformists. Honest self-analysis can be painful, and acknowledging one's limitations in order to recognize the superior abilities of others takes personal strength of character. In addition, moral leadership means building relationships, which requires sharing yourself, listening, having significant personal experiences with others, and making yourself vulnerable—qualities that frighten many people. Yet finding emotional strength requires people to overcome their deepest fears and accept emotions as a source of strength rather than weakness. True power lies in the emotions that connect people. By getting close and doing what is best for others—sharing the good and the bad, the pain and anger as well as the success and the joy—leaders bring out the best qualities in others.[59]

An example of this in practice is when William Peace had to initiate a layoff as general manager of the Synthetic Fuels Division of Westinghouse. To make the division attractive to buyers, executives made a painful decision to cut any jobs not considered essential. Peace had the courage to deliver the news about layoffs personally. He took some painful blows in the face-to-face meetings he held with the workers to be laid off, but he believed that allowing people to vent their grief and anger at him and the situation was the moral thing to do. His action sent a message to the remaining workers that, even though layoffs were necessary, leaders valued each of them as human beings with feelings. Because the workers recognized that layoffs were a last resort and the executive team was doing everything they could to save as many jobs as possible, they rededicated themselves to helping save the division. A buyer was found and the company had the opportunity to rehire half of those who had been laid off. Everyone contacted agreed to come back because the humane way they had been treated overcame negative feelings about the layoff.[60] For Peace, the courage to practice moral leadership gained respect, renewed commitment, and higher performance, even though he suffered personally in the short run.

Whistleblowing
employee disclosure of illegal, immoral, or unethical practices in the organization

Opposing Unethical Conduct Requires Courage Whistleblowing means employee disclosure of illegal, immoral, or unethical practices in the organization.[61] One recent example of courage in this area is Colleen Rowley, the Minneapolis FBI staff attorney whose whistleblowing letter called attention to agency shortcomings that may have contributed to the September 11, 2001, terrorist tragedy. A colleague of Rowley's said, "She always does what is right, even when no one is watching."[62]

Whistleblowing has become widespread in recent years, but it is still highly risky for employees, who may lose their jobs, be ostracized by coworkers, or be transferred to undesirable positions. Consider David Windhauser, the former controller of Trane, a heating and cooling company owned by American Standard, who was fired after reporting that managers were fraudulently reporting expenses on financial statements. The 2002 Sarbanes-Oxley Act provides some safety for whistleblowers like Windhauser. People who have been fired for reporting wrongdoing can file a complaint under the law and are eligible to get back pay, attorney's fees, and a chance to get their old job back, as Windhauser did. Yet Trane fought the court order for months and finally settled with the former employee out of court. Many whistleblowers, like Windhauser, fear that they will experience even more hostility if they return to the job after winning a case under Sarbanes-Oxley.[63]

Most whistleblowers realize they may suffer financially and emotionally from their willingness to report unethical conduct on the part of bosses or coworkers. They step forward to tell the truth despite a jumble of contradictory emotions and fears. Choosing to act courageously means conflicting emotions—whistleblowers may feel an ethical obligation to report the wrongdoing but may also feel disloyal to their bosses and coworkers. Some may do battle within themselves about where their responsibility lies.[64] As a result of widespread corporate scandals in recent years, smart companies are beginning to see whistleblowing as a benefit rather than a threat, however. One survey found that 88 percent of respondents agreed that whistleblowing is good for business. Many companies, such as Marvin Windows and Doors, use new whistleblowing software, which allows employees to anonymously report wrongdoing to top executives or outside board members. Marvin's leaders "want the company to do the right thing," says manager Steve Tourek. "And we want to give our employees a place to tell us when we aren't."[65]

Finding Personal Courage

How does a leader find the courage to step through fear and confusion, to act despite the risks involved? All of us have the potential to live and act courageously, if we can push through our own fears. Most of us have learned fears that limit our comfort zones and stand in the way of being our best and accomplishing our goals. We have been conditioned to follow the rules, not rock the boat, to go along with things we feel are wrong so others will like and accept us. There are a number of ways people can unlock the courage within themselves, including committing to causes they believe in, connecting with others, welcoming failure as a natural and beneficial part of life, and harnessing anger.

Believe in a Higher Purpose Courage comes easily when we fight for something we really believe in. Leaders who have a strong emotional commitment to a larger vision or purpose find the courage to step through fear. In 1968, Eleanor Josaitis cofounded Focus: HOPE as a food program to serve pregnant women, new mothers, and their children in Detroit. Soon realizing that hunger was just a symptom of a larger problem, she expanded the organization as a civil rights group to try to bridge the economic and racial divides in the city. Over the years, Josaitis has received tons of hate mail, had her offices firebombed, and been threatened regularly with bodily harm, but it only makes her more determined. The higher purpose overshadows concerns about her own self-interests.[66] In business organizations, too, courage depends on belief a higher vision. Lawrence Fish, chairman, president, and CEO of Citizens Bank, has built his organization into the eighth largest commercial banking company in the United States, but he says, "If we just make money, we'll fail." Fish is known for his volunteer efforts and commitment to the community, and his unconventional approach to operating a bank efficiently but with heart has created a banking powerhouse. In his career, Fish has experienced both tremendous success and downright failure, but he has maintained the courage to pursue a vision that business is as much about doing good in the world as it is about making money.[67]

> **Action Memo**
> As a leader, you can find your personal courage by committing to something you deeply believe in. You can welcome potential failure as a means of growth and development and build bonds of caring and mutual support with family, friends, and colleagues to reduce fear.

Draw Strength from Others Caring about others and having support from others is a potent source of courage in a topsy-turvy world. Love is a strong ingredient of courage, because it makes us willing to sacrifice.[68] Consider a caring parent who will risk his or her own life to save a child. Leaders who genuinely care about the people they work with will take risks to help those people grow and succeed. Having the support of others is also a source of courage, and the best leaders aren't afraid to lean on others when they need to. People who feel alone in the world take fewer risks because they have more to lose.[69] Being part of an organizational team that is supportive and caring, or having a loving and supportive family at home, can reduce the fear of failure and help people take risks they otherwise wouldn't take. Consider the example of Daniel Lynch, CEO of ImClone. When he took over the top job, things were about as bad as they could get. Founder Sam Waksal had been hauled off in handcuffs for alleged insider trading, the financial state of the company was in a shambles, and the company's application for Food and Drug Administration (FDA) approval of a key cancer drug had just been rejected. Over a 2-year period, Lynch led a remarkable turnaround by focusing on getting the financial house in order, restoring trust among employees, and getting approval for Erbitux, which he believed could dramatically help people with colorectal cancer. Lynch didn't hesitate to tell people he needed their help, and managers and employees rose to the challenge. For 2 years, bad news just kept coming, but people pulled together and kept pushing forward even though many of them said they sometimes felt like running away. According to chief financial officer Michael Howerton, the camaraderie that emerged as people struggled through the difficulties together gave them the courage to keep putting one foot in front of the other, no matter how bad things looked.[70]

Welcome Failure Walt Disney, who had a business venture go bankrupt before he went on to achieve major success, once said, "It's important to have a good hard failure when you're young."[71] Today, many people want success to come without difficulties, problems, or struggles. However, accepting—even welcoming—failure enables courage. Failure can play a creative role in work and in life because people and organizations can learn valuable lessons from things that go wrong. Leaders can redefine failure away from its negative associations and see it as an important first step toward success.[72]

When people accept failure and are at peace with the worst possible outcome, they find they have the fortitude to move forward. Leaders know that failure can lead to success and that the pain of learning strengthens individuals and the organization. Sharon McCollick was hired for a top sales and planning position at a hot software startup partly because she had started a business and failed. Company leaders liked the fact that she had been willing to take the risks associated with starting a business and then move forward after the failure. Even people who invested in her business and lost money say they'd do it again. "She tried and failed and so what?" said one backer. "The next time, my bet's on her."[73] McCollick believes that having hit rock bottom and survived has given her greater courage. In addition, she radiates self-confidence because she is no longer terrified of failure. There is evidence that with repeated practice, people can overcome fears such as a fear of flying or fear of heights. Practice also enables people to overcome fear of risk-taking in their work. Every time you push beyond your comfort zone, every time you fail and try again, you build psychological strength and courage.

Harness Frustration and Anger If you have ever been really angry about something, you know that it can cause you to forget about fear of embarrassment or fear that others won't like you. In organizations, we can also see the power of frustration and anger. Glenn McIntyre used his anger and frustration to start a new life and a new business. After he was paralyzed in a motorcycle accident, McIntyre first used his anger to overcome thoughts of suicide and begin intensive physical therapy. Later, frustration over how poorly hotels served handicapped guests led him to start a consulting firm, Access Designs. The firm helps hotels such as Quality Suites and Renaissance Ramada redesign their space to be more usable for disabled travelers.[74] Another example comes from Nigeria, where anger and frustration play a key role in Nuhu Ribadu's courage in cracking down on oil smugglers and crooked politicians. Death threats against Ribadu, head of the new Economic and Financial Crimes Commission, are common, but he is committed to ridding Nigeria, and ultimately all of Africa, of fraud and corruption. His determination comes partly from the frustration he felt as a student in the 1980s, as he watched a democratically elected government crumble due to rampant fraud, and the anger he still feels as he sees Nigeria's people suffer from an unethical and dysfunctional political system.[75]

People in organizations can harness their anger to deal with difficult situations. When someone has to be fired for just cause, a supervisor may put if off until some incident makes her angry enough to step through the fear and act. Sometimes, outrage over a perceived injustice can give a mild-mannered person the courage to confront the boss head on.[76] In addition, getting mad at yourself may be the motivation to change. Anger, in moderate amounts, is a healthy emotion that provides energy to move forward. The challenge is to harness anger and use it appropriately.

Summary and Interpretation

This chapter explored a number of ideas concerning moral leadership and leadership courage. People want honest and trustworthy leaders. However, the ethical climate in many organizations is at a low point. Leaders face pressures that challenge their ability to do the right thing—pressures to cut costs, increase profits, meet the demands of various stakeholders, and look successful. Creating an ethical organization requires that leaders act based on moral principles. Leaders cause things to go wrong in the organization when they excessively promote self-interest, practice deception and breach agreements, and when they lack the courage to confront unjust acts. Ethical leaders are humble, honest, and straightforward. They maintain a concern for the greater good, strive for fairness, and demonstrate the courage to stand up for what is right. Acting as a moral leader means demonstrating the importance of serving people and society as well as increasing profits or personal gain.

One personal consideration for leaders is the level of moral development. Leaders use an understanding of the stages of moral development to enhance their own as well as followers' moral growth. Leaders who operate at higher stages of moral development focus on the needs of followers and universal moral principles.

Ideas about control versus service between leaders and followers are changing and expanding, reflected in a continuum of leader–follower relationships. The continuum varies from authoritarian managers to participative managers to stewardship to servant leadership. Leaders who operate from the principles of stewardship and servant leadership can help build ethical organizations.

The final sections of the chapter discussed leadership courage and how leaders can find their own courage. Courage means the ability to step forward through fear, to accept responsibility, to take risks and make changes, to speak your mind, and to fight for what you believe. Two expressions of courage in organizations are moral leadership and ethical whistleblowing. Sources of courage include belief in a higher purpose, connection with others, experience with failure, and harnessing anger.

Discussion Questions

1. If you were in a position similar to Raoul Wallenberg (page 170), what do you think you would do? Why?

2. What are some pressures you face as a student that challenge your ability to do the right thing? Do you expect to face more or fewer pressures as a leader? Discuss what some of these pressures might be.

3. If most adults are at a conventional level of moral development, what does this mean for their potential for moral leadership?

4. Do you feel that the difference between authoritarian leadership and stewardship should be interpreted as a moral difference? Discuss.

5. Should serving others be placed at a higher moral level than serving oneself? Discuss.

6. If you find yourself avoiding a situation or activity, what can you do to find the courage to move forward? Explain.

7. If it is immoral to prevent those around you from growing to their fullest potential, are you being moral?

8. Do you have the courage to take a moral stand that your peers and even authority figures will disagree with? Why?

9. Do you agree that it is important for leaders to do the right thing even if no one will ever know about it? Why or why not?

10. A consultant recently argued that the emphasis on corporate governance and social responsibility has distracted leaders from key business issues such as serving customers and beating competitors. Do you agree? Should leaders put business issues first or ethical issues first?

Leadership at Work

Scary Person

Think of a person in your life right now who is something of a scary person for you. Scary people are those you don't really know but who are scary to you because you anticipate that you won't like them, perhaps because you don't like the way they act or look from a distance, and hence you avoid building relationships with them. A scary person might be a student at school, someone at work, a neighbor, or someone you are aware of in your social circle.

Scary people trigger a small amount of fear in us—that is why we avoid them and don't really get to know them. A test of courage is whether you can step through your fear. You will experience fear many times as a leader.

For this exercise, your assignment is to reach out to one or more scary persons in your life. Invite the person for lunch or just walk up and introduce yourself and start a conversation. Perhaps you can volunteer to work with the person on an assignment. The key thing is to step through your fear and get to know this person well enough to know what he or she is really like.

After you have completed your assignment, share what happened with another person. Were you able to reach out to the scary person? What did you discover about the scary person? What did you discover about yourself by doing this activity? If you found the exercise silly and refused to do it, you may have let fear get the better of you by rationalizing that the assignment has little value.

In Class: The instructor can give this assignment to be done prior to a specific class. During class it is a good exercise for students to discuss their scary person experiences among themselves in small groups. The instructor can ask students to report to their groups about the scary person, revealing as many details as they are comfortable with, explaining how they summoned the courage to reach out, and the result. After the groups have finished their exchange, the instructor can ask a couple of student volunteers to report their experiences to the entire class. Then students can be asked questions such as: Looking back on this experience, what is courage? How was it expressed (or not) in this exercise? How will fear and courage be part of organizational leadership?

Leadership Development: Cases for Analysis

Young Leaders Council

Gehan Rasinghe was thrilled to be appointed to the Young Leaders Council at Werner & Burns, a large consulting and financial management firm located in Boston. When Rasinghe had first joined the firm he'd had a hard time fitting in, with his accented English and quiet manner. However, through hard work and persistence, he had overcome many obstacles, made many friends, and worked his way up in the organization. He had been in a leadership position as an account manager for 2 years, and he particularly loved working with new employees and helping them find their niches in the company and develop greater skills and confidence. His employee evaluations by both superiors and subordinates had been exceptional, and Rasinghe himself was pleased with his success as a leader.

Now, this! The purpose of the Young Leaders Council was to provide a training ground for young executives at Werner & Burns and help them continue to improve their leadership skills. In addition, top executives and the Board used the Council as a way to evaluate the potential of young managers for higher-level positions. Everyone knew that a good showing on the Council often resulted in a promotion. Typically, an appointment to the Council was for a 1-year period, with new members added every 6 months on a rotating basis. Occasionally, some members would stay an additional 6 months, based on the results of an appraisal process personally introduced by the CEO. The process involved each member of the Council being rated by each of the other members on four criteria: (1) general intelligence and knowledge of the business; (2) creativity and innovativeness; (3) cooperation and team spirit; and (4) adherence to company values.

Rasinghe was attending his fifth monthly meeting when several members of the Council raised a concern about the rating system. They felt that it was being forced on the group, was controlled by top management, and was not used as a fair and accurate rating of each member's abilities but just as a way "to pat your buddies on the back," as his colleague Cathy Patton put it. Most of the other members seemed to agree with their arguments, at least to some degree. Rasinghe agreed that the system was flawed, but he was surprised by their suggestion for a solution. One member made an informal motion that in the next appraisal every member of the Council should simply give every other member the highest rating in each category.

Rasinghe quickly considered what to do as the chairman called for a show of hands from those in favor of the motion. His gut feeling is that such a "solution" to the problem of the rating system would be dishonest and unethical, but he remembers what it felt like to be an "outsider," and he doesn't want to be there again.

Source: Based on "Junior Board," in John M. Champion and Francis J. Bridges, *Critical Incidents in Management,* rev. ed., (Homewood, IL: Irwin, 1969), pp. 106–107.

QUESTIONS

1. What personal and organizational factors might influence Rasinghe's decision?
2. Do you believe it would take courage for Rasinghe to vote against the motion? What sources of courage might he call upon to help him vote his conscience?
3. What do you think about the current rating system? If you were in Rasinghe's position, what would you do? Discuss.

The Boy, the Girl, the Ferryboat Captain, and the Hermits

There was an island, and on this island there lived a girl. A short distance away there was another island, and on this island there lived a boy. The boy and the girl were very much in love with each other.

The boy had to leave his island and go on a long journey, and he would be gone for a very long time. The girl felt that she must see the boy one more time before he went away. There was only one way to get from the island where the girl lived to the boy's island, and that was on a ferryboat that was run by a ferryboat captain. And so the girl went down to the dock and asked the ferryboat captain to take her to the island where the boy lived. The ferryboat captain agreed and asked her for the fare. The girl told the ferryboat captain that she did not have any money. The ferryboat captain told her that money was not necessary: "I will take you to the other island if you will stay with me tonight."

The girl did not know what to do, so she went up into the hills on her island until she came to a hut where a hermit lived. We will call him the first hermit. She related the whole story to the hermit and asked for his advice. The hermit listened carefully to her story, and then told her, "I cannot tell you what to do. You must weigh the alternatives and the sacrifices that are involved and come to a decision within your own heart."

And so the girl went back down to the dock and accepted the ferryboat captain's offer.

The next day, when the girl arrived on the other island, the boy was waiting at the dock to greet her. They embraced, and then the boy asked her how she got over to his island, for he knew she did not have any money. The girl explained the ferryboat captain's offer and what she did. The boy pushed her away from him and said, "We're through. That's the end. Go away from me. I never want to see you again," and he left her.

The girl was desolate and confused. She went up into the hills of the boy's island to a hut where a second hermit lived. She told the whole story to the second hermit and asked him what she should do. The hermit told her that there was nothing she could do, that she was welcome to stay in his hut, to partake of his food, and to rest on his bed while he went down into the town and begged for enough money to pay the girl's fare back to her own island.

When the second hermit returned with the money for her, the girl asked him how she could repay him. The hermit answered, "You owe me nothing. We owe this to each other. I am only too happy to be of help." And so the girl went back down to the dock and returned to her own island.

QUESTIONS

1. List in order the characters in this story that you like, from most to least. What values governed your choices?

2. Rate the characters on their level of moral development. Explain.

3. Evaluate each character's level of courage. Discuss.

References

1 Jennifer Reingold, "Soldiering On," *Fast Company* (September 2004), p. 72; and Evan Thomas and John Barry, "Anatomy of a Revolt," *Newsweek,* (April 24, 2006). Retrieved March 9, 2007, from http://www.msnbc.msn.com/id/12335719/site/newsweek.

2 Gregory L. White, David Crawford, and Glenn R. Simpson, "Russian Connection; Why Putin's Telecom Minister Is in Investigators' Sights Abroad," *The Wall Street Journal* (October 17, 2006), p. A1.

3 Christopher Graveline, "The Unlearned Lessons of Abu Ghraib," *The Washington Post* (October 19, 2006), p. A29; David S. Cloud, "Air Force Seeks $13 Billion to Start Replacing Tankers," *The New York Times* (October 13, 2006), p. C2.

4 James Bandler and Charles Forelle, "CEO to Leave Under Pressure at UnitedHealth," *The Wall Street Journal* (October 16, 2006), p. A1.

5 Patricia "Wallington, "Honestly?!" *CIO* (March 15, 2003), pp. 41–42.

6 Brian Cronin, "After Enron: The Ideal Corporation," *BusinessWeek* (August 26, 2002), pp. 8–74.

7 Kris Maher, "Wanted: Ethical Employer," *The Wall Street Journal* (July 9, 2002), pp. B1, B8.

8 Gary R. Weaver, Linda Klebe Treviño, and Bradley Agle, "'Somebody I Look Up To:' Ethical Role Models in Organizations," *Organizational Dynamics* 34, no. 4 (2005), pp. 313–330.

9 Chuck Salter, paraphrasing Bill George, former CEO of Medtronic, in "Mr. Inside Speaks Out," *Fast Company* (September 2004), pp. 92–93.

10 David Wessel, "Venal Sins: Why the Bad Guys of the Boardroom Emerged en Masse," *The Wall Street Journal* (June 20, 2002), pp. A1, A6.

11 Sydney Finkelstein, "Jayson Blair, Meet Nicholas Leeson," (Manager's Journal column), *The Wall Street Journal* (May 20, 2003), p. B2.

12 Wessel, "Venal Sins."

13 John A. Byrne with Mike France and Wendy Zellner, "The Environment Was Ripe for Abuse," *BusinessWeek* (February 25, 2002), pp. 118–120.

14 This section is based on Donald G. Zauderer, "Integrity: An Essential Executive Quality," *Business Forum* (Fall, 1992), pp. 12–16.

15 Jerry Useem, "Have They No Shame?" *Fortune* (April 28, 2003), pp. 56–64.

16 Wallington, "Honestly?!"

17 Emily Thornton, "How Purcell Lost His Way," *BusinessWeek* (July 11, 2005), pp. 68–70.

18 Al Gini, "Moral Leadership and Business Ethics," *The Journal of Leadership Studies* 4, no. 4 (Fall 1997), pp. 64–81.

19 Henry Ford, Sr., quoted by Thomas Donaldson, *Corporations and Morality* (Prentice Hall, Inc., 1982), p. 57 in Al Gini, "Moral Leadership and Business Ethics."

20 John A. Bryne, "After Enron: The Ideal Corporation," *BusinessWeek* (August 26, 2002), pp. 68–74; and Nancy D. Holt, "Alfred P. West Jr., SEI Investments," (Workspaces column), *The Wall Street Journal* (February 19, 2003), p. B10.

21 J. Lynn Lynsford, "Piloting Boeing's New Course," *The Wall Street Journal* (June 13, 2006), p. B1, B3; and Kathryn Kranhold, "U.S. Firms Raise Ethics Focus," *The Wall Street Journal* (November 28, 2005), p. B4.

22 Joseph Weber, "The New Ethics Enforcers," *BusinessWeek* (February 13, 2006), pp. 76–77.

23 Jennifer Reingold, "Walking the Walk," *Fast Company* (November 2005), pp. 81–85.

24 Gretchen Morgenson, "Shares of Corporate Nice Guys Can Finish First," *New York Times* (April 27, 2003), p. 1.

25 Donald G. Zauderer, "Integrity: An Essential Executive Quality," *Business Forum* (Fall 1992), pp. 12–16.

26 James M. Kouzes and Barry Z. Posner, *Credibility: How Leaders Gain and Lose It, Why People Demand It* (San Francisco: Jossey-Bass, 1993), p. 255.

27 John C. Kunich and Richard I. Lester, "Profile of a Leader: The Wallenberg Effect," *The Journal of Leadership Studies* 4, no. 3 (Summer 1997), pp. 5–19.

28 Viktor E. Frankl, *Man's Search for Meaning* (New York: Pocket Books, 1959), p. 104.

29 Lawrence Kolhberg, "Moral Stages and Moralization: The Cognitive Developmental Approach," in Thomas Likona, ed. *Moral Development and Behavior: Theory, Research, and Social Issues* (Austin, TX: Holt, Rinehart and Winston, 1976), pp. 31–53; Jill W. Graham, "Leadership, Moral Development, and Citizenship Behavior," *Business Ethics Quarterly* 5, no. 1 (January 1995), pp. 43–54; James Weber, "Exploring the Relationship between Personal Values and Moral Reasoning," *Human Relations* 46, no. 4 (April 1993), pp. 435–463; and Duane M. Covrig, "The Organizational Context of Moral Dilemmas: The Role of Moral Leadership in Administration in Making and Breaking Dilemmas," *The Journal of Leadership Studies* 7, no. 1 (2000), pp. 40–59.

30 Tom Morris, *If Aristotle Ran General Motors* (New York: Henry Holt, 1997).

31 James Weber, "Exploring the Relationship Between Personal Values and Moral Reasoning," *Human Relations* 46, no. 4 (April 1993), pp. 435–463.

32 Peter Block, "Reassigning Responsibility," *Sky* (February 1994), pp. 26–31; and David P. McCaffrey, Sue R. Faerman, and David W. Hart, "The Appeal and Difficulty of Participative Systems," *Organization Science* 6, no. 6 (November–December 1995), pp. 603–627.

33 Block, "Reassigning Responsibility."

34 This discussion of stewardship is based on Peter Block, *Stewardship: Choosing Service Over Self-Interest* (San Francisco: Berrett-Koehler Publishers, 1993), pp. 29–31; and Block, "Reassigning Responsibility."

35 Mary Parker Follett, from *The New State* (1918), as quoted in David K. Hurst, "Thoroughly Modern—Mary Parker Follett," *Business Quarterly* 56, no. 4 (Spring 1992), pp. 55–58.

36 Lawrence G. Foster, *Robert Wood Johnson—The Gentleman Rebel* (Lemont, PA: Lillian Press, 1999); and John Cunniff, "Businessman's Honesty, Integrity Lesson for Today," *Johnson City Press* (May 28, 2000).

37 Sen Sendjaya and James C. Sarros, "Servant Leadership: Its Origin, Development, and Application in Organizations," *Journal of Leadership and Organizational Studies* 9, no. 2 (2002), pp. 57–64.

38 Ibid.; examples include B. M. Bass, "The Future of Leadership in Learning Organizations," *The Journal of Leadership Studies* 7, no. 3 (2000), pp. 18–40; I. H. Buchen, "Servant Leadership: A Model for Future Faculty and Future Institutions," *The Journal of Leadership Studies* 5, no. 1 (1998), p. 125; Y. Choi and R. R. Mai-Dalton, "On the Leadership Function of Self-Sacrifice," *Leadership Quarterly* 9, no. 4 (1998), pp. 475–501; R. F. Russel, "The Role of Values in Servant Leadership," *Leadership and Organizational Development Journal* 22, no. 2 (2001), pp. 76–83.

39 Robert K. Greenleaf, *Servant Leadership: A Journey into the Nature of Legitimate Power and Greatness* (Mahwah, NJ: Paulist Press, 1977), p. 7.

40 Robert Townsend, "Leader at Work," *Across the Board* (January 2001), pp. 13–14.

41 "The Courageous Few: 2004–2005 Edition," *Fast Company* (September 2005), pp. 54–55.

42 The following is based on Greenleaf, *Servant Leadership;* Walter Kiechel III, "The Leader as Servant," *Fortune* (May 4, 1992), pp. 121–122; and Mary Sue Polleys, "One University's Response to the Anti-Leadership Vaccine: Developing Servant Leaders," *The Journal of Leadership Studies* 8, no. 3 (2002), pp. 117–130.

43 Marcia Heroux Pounds, "Execs Should Head For Trenches to Find Out How Business Works," *The Tennessean* (May 9, 1999), p. 2H.

44 C. William Pollard, "The Leader Who Serves," in *The Leader of the Future,* Frances Hesselbein, Marshall Goldsmith, and Richard Beckhard, eds. (San Francisco: Jossey-Bass, 1996), pp. 241–248; and C. W. Pollard, "The Leader Who Serves," *Strategy and Leadership* (September–October 1997), pp. 49–51.

45 LaRue Tone Hosmer, "Trust: The Connecting Link between Organizational Theory and Philosophical Ethics," *Academy of Management Review* 20, no. 2 (April 1995), pp. 379–403.

46 Greenleaf, *Servant Leadership,* p. 45.

47 John McCain, "In Search of Courage," *Fast Company* (September 2004), pp. 53–56.

48 Richard L. Daft and Robert H. Lengel, *Fusion Leadership: Unlocking the Subtle Forces that Change People and Organizations* (San Francisco: Berrett-Koehler, 1998).

49 McCain, "In Search of Courage."

50 Reported in Nando Pelusi, "The Right Way to Rock the Boat," *Psychology Today* (May–June 2006), pp. 60–61.

51 Jeffrey Zaslow, "Kids on the Bus: The Overlooked Role of Teenagers in the Civil-Rights Era," *The Wall Street Journal* (November 11, 2005), p. D1.

52 Jennifer Reingold, "My Brilliant Failure: The Fall and Rise of David Pottruck," *Fast Company* (September 2005), pp. 56–62.

53 Daft and Lengel, *Fusion Leadership,* p. 155.

54 Ann Marsh, "The Man Who Listens to Horses," *Forbes* (May 4, 1998), p. 122; and Larraine Segil, "Leading Fearlessly," *Leader to Leader* (Winter 2003), pp. 38–43.

55 Reported in Nido R. Qubein, *Stairway to Success: The Complete Blueprint for Personal and Professional Achievement* (New York: John Wiley & Sons, 1997).

56 Michael Luo, "Revisiting a Social Experiment, and the Fear That Goes with It," *The New York Times* (September 14, 2004), Section B. p. 1.

57 Jerry B. Harvey, *The Abilene Paradox and Other Meditations on Management* (Lexington, MA: Lexington Books, 1988), pp. 13–15.

58 Kerry Kennedy Cuomo, "'Courage Begins with One Voice,'" *Parade Magazine* (September 24, 2000), pp. 6–8.

59 A. J. Vogl, "Risky Work," an interview with Max DuPree, *Across the Board* (July/August 1993): pp. 27–31.

60 William H. Peace, "The Hard Work of Being a Soft Manager," *Harvard Business Review,* (November–December 1991), pp. 40–47.

61 Janet P. Near and Marcia P. Miceli, "Effective Whistle-Blowing," *Academy of Management Review* 20, no. 3 (1995), pp. 679–708.

62 Wallington, "Honestly?!"

63 Jayne O'Donnell, "Some Whistle-blowers Don't Want Lost Jobs," *USA Today* (August 1, 2005), p. B2.

64 Hal Lancaster, "Workers Who Blow the Whistle on Bosses Often Pay a High Price," *The Wall Street Journal* (July 18, 1995), p. B1; Richard P. Nielsen, "Changing Unethical Organizational Behavior," *The Executive* (May 1989), pp. 123–130; and Barbara Ettorre, "Whistleblowers: Who's the Real Bad Guy?" *Management Review* (May 1994), pp. 18–23.

65 Darren Dahl, "Learning to Love Whistleblowers," *Inc. Magazine* (March 2006), pp. 21–23.

66 Alison Overholt, "The Housewife Who Got Up Off the Couch," *Fast Company* (September 2004), p. 94.

67 Joseph Rebello, "Radical Ways of Its CEO Are a Boon to Bank," *The Wall Street Journal* (March 20, 1995), p. B1.

68 McCain, "In Search of Courage."

69 James M. Kouzes and Barry Z. Posner, *The Leadership Challenge: How to Get Extraordinary Things Done in Organizations* (San Francisco: Jossey-Bass, 1988).

70 Linda Tischler, "The Trials of ImClone," *Fast Company* (September 2004), pp. 88–89.

71 Quoted by Michael Eisner, interviewed by Laura Rich in "Talk About Failure," *The Industry Standard* (July 30, 2001), pp. 41–47.

72 Mark D. Cannon and Amy C. Edmondson, "Failing to Learn and Learning to Fail (Intelligently): How Great Organizations Put Failure to Work to Innovate and Improve," *Long Range Planning* 38, Issue 3 (June 2005), pp. 299–319.

73 Thomas Petzinger Jr. "She Failed. So What? An Entrepreneur Finds Her Prestige Rising" (The Front Lines column), *The Wall Street Journal* (October 31, 1997), p. B1.

74 Michael Warshaw, ed., "Great Comebacks," *Success* (July/August 1995), pp. 33–46.

75 Chip Cummins, "Crude Theft; A Nigerian Cop Cracks Down on a Vast Black Market in Oil," *The Wall Street Journal* (April 13, 2005), pp. A1, A15.

76 Ira Cheleff, *The Courageous Follower: Standing Up To and For Our Leaders* (San Francisco: Berrett-Koehler, 1995).

Chapter 7

Followership

Five hours into her shift, four harried customers line up at Dawn Marshall's cash register at the Pathmark supermarket in Upper Derby, Pennsylvania. Eight minutes and 27 bags later, they're all out the door with smiles on their faces. Few people would think Marshall has a glamourous or influential job—but she treats it like the most significant job in the world.

In a society that is rapidly going self-service, Marshall specializes in giving people a little bit of luxury in the mundane chore of grocery shopping. She's a good cashier, but her forte is bagging. Marshall knows how to pack the flimsy plastic bags so that eggs don't get broken, bread doesn't get squashed, and ground beef doesn't leak all over the cereal boxes. She even won a National Grocers Association contest as the best bagger in America, based on speed, bag-building technique, style, and attitude. "I believe it's an art that should be taken seriously," Marshall says of her work. Many Pathmark customers agree. They're tired of cashiers and baggers who simply throw the stuff in bags without giving a care for the customer's convenience or needs. One customer admits that she shops at Pathmark rather than a store closer to her home because of Marshall. "I like her attitude," says the customer. "Clone her."

Even though Marshall works on her feet all day and often has to put up with rude or insensitive customers, she handles whatever comes her way with a positive attitude. For Marshall, her job is not bagging groceries, but making people's lives easier. Thus, she approaches her work with energy and enthusiasm, striving to do her best in every encounter. She doesn't need close supervision or someone pushing her to work harder. The busier it is, the better she likes it.[1]

At Pathmark, Dawn Marshall has taken what some would consider a boring, low-paying job and imbued it with meaning and value. She accepts responsibility for her own personal fulfillment and finds ways to expand her potential and use her capacities to serve the needs of others and the organization. These are the hallmarks of both good followers and good leaders.

Leadership and followership are closely intertwined. As a Pathmark cashier, Dawn Marshall is a follower, but she acts as a leader by setting an example for others and using her positive attitude to inspire and uplift other people. She is capable of self-management rather than needing someone else to tell her how to approach her work, and she strives to create a positive impact rather than dwelling on the negative aspects of her job. Effective followers like Dawn Marshall are essential to the success of any endeavor, whether it be running a supermarket, winning a football game, completing a class assignment, or organizing a United Way fund drive.

In this chapter, we examine the important role of followership, including the nature of the follower's role, the different styles of followership that individuals express, and how effective followers behave. The chapter also explores sources of power available to followers and how followers develop their personal potential to be more effective. Finally, we look at the leader's role in developing effective followers and how followers can work with leaders to build a sense of community within their organizations.

The Role of Followers

Followership is important in the discussion of leadership for several reasons. First, without followers, there are no leaders. Leadership and followership are fundamental roles that individuals shift into and out of under various conditions. Everyone—leaders included—is a follower at one time or another. Indeed, most individuals, even those in positions of authority, have some kind of boss or supervisor. Individuals are more often followers than leaders.[2]

Second, recall that the definition of a leader from Chapter 1 referred to an influence relationship among leaders and followers. This means that in a position of leadership, an individual is influenced by the actions and the attitudes of followers. In fact, the contingency theories introduced in Chapter 3 are based on how leaders adjust their behavior to fit situations, especially their followers. Thus, the nature of leader–follower relationships involves reciprocity, the mutual exchange of influence.[3] The followers' influence upon a leader can enhance the leader or underscore the leader's shortcomings.[4]

Third, many of the qualities that are desirable in a leader are the same qualities possessed by an effective follower. In addition to demonstrating initiative, independence, commitment to common goals, and courage, a follower can provide enthusiastic support of a leader, but not to the extent that the follower fails to challenge a leader who is unethical or threatens the values or objectives of the organization.[5] One corporate governance consultant, for example, points out that ineffective followers are as much to blame for the recent wave of ethical and legal scandals as are crooked leaders.[6] Followers have a responsibility to speak up when leaders do things wrong.

Both leader and follower roles are proactive; together they can achieve a shared vision. The military often provides insight into the interaction of leadership and followership. A performance study of U.S. Navy personnel found that the outstanding ships were those staffed by followers who supported their leaders but also took initiative and did not avoid raising issues or concerns with their superiors. D. Michael Abrashoff, former commander of the USS *Benfold*, recognized as one of the best ships in the Navy, always encouraged his followers to speak up. To Abrashoff, the highest boss should be the sailor who does the work—the follower—not the person with the most stripes on his or her uniform.[7] In any organization, leaders can help develop effective followers, just as effective followers develop better leaders. The performance of followers, leaders, and the organization are variables that depend on one another.

Styles of Followership

Critical thinking
thinking independently and being mindful of the effects of one's own and other people's behavior on achieving the organization's vision

Uncritical thinking
failing to consider possibilities beyond what one is told; accepting the leader's ideas without thinking

Despite the importance of followership and the critical role followers play in the success of any endeavor, research on the topic is limited. One theory of followership was proposed by Robert E. Kelley, who conducted extensive interviews with leaders and followers and came up with five styles of followership.[8] These followership styles are categorized according to two dimensions, as illustrated in Exhibit 7.1. The first dimension is the quality of independent, **critical thinking** versus dependent, **uncritical thinking**. Independent thinking recalls our discussion of mindfulness in Chapter 5; independent critical thinkers are mindful of the effects of people's behavior on achieving organizational goals. They are aware of the significance of their own actions and the actions of others. They can weigh the impact of decisions on the vision set forth by a leader and offer constructive criticism, creativity, and innovation. Conversely, a dependent, uncritical thinker

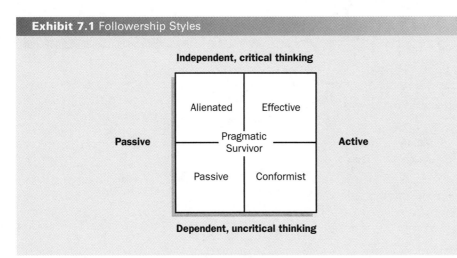

Exhibit 7.1 Followership Styles

Independent, critical thinking

Alienated | Effective

Pragmatic Survivor

Passive — — — **Active**

Passive | Conformist

Dependent, uncritical thinking

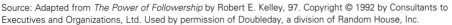

Source: Adapted from *The Power of Followership* by Robert E. Kelley, 97. Copyright © 1992 by Consultants to Executives and Organizations, Ltd. Used by permission of Doubleday, a division of Random House, Inc.

does not consider possibilities beyond what he or she is told, does not contribute to the cultivation of the organization, and accepts the leader's ideas without thinking.

According to Kelley, the second dimension of followership style is active versus passive behavior. An active individual participates fully in an organization, engages in behavior that is beyond the limits of the job, demonstrates a sense of ownership, and initiates problem solving and decision making. A passive individual is characterized by a need for constant supervision and prodding by superiors. Passivity is often regarded as laziness; a passive person does nothing that is not required and avoids added responsibility.

The extent to which one is active or passive and is a critical, independent thinker or a dependent, uncritical thinker determines whether he or she is an alienated follower, a passive follower, a conformist, a pragmatic survivor, or an effective follower, as shown in Exhibit 7.1.

The **alienated follower** is a passive, yet independent, critical thinker. Alienated followers are often effective followers who have experienced setbacks and obstacles, perhaps promises broken by superiors. Thus, they are capable, but they focus exclusively on the shortcomings of the organization and other people. Often cynical, alienated followers are able to think independently, but they do not participate in developing solutions to the problems or deficiencies they see. For example, Barry Paris spent more than 10 years writing on and off for the *Pittsburgh Post-Gazette*, where he was known for his bad attitude and lack of enthusiasm and teamwork. Eventually Paris realized that he wasted that time ruminating over what he perceived as the hypocrisy of journalistic objectivity. "I could never resign myself to it," says Paris. Thus, rather than doing his best and trying to help others maintain standards of integrity and objectivity, he allowed hostility and cynicism to permeate his work.[9]

The **conformist** participates actively in the organization but does not utilize critical thinking skills in his or her task behavior. In other words, a conformist typically carries out any and all orders regardless of the nature of those tasks. The conformist participates willingly, but without considering the consequences of what he or she is being asked to do—even at the risk of contributing to a harmful endeavor. A conformist is concerned only with avoiding conflict. Indeed, this style often results from

Alienated follower
a person in the organization who is a passive, yet independent, critical thinker

Conformist
a follower who participates actively in the organization but does not utilize critical thinking skills in his or her task behavior

Getty Images

For each statement below, please answer whether each item below is Mostly False or Mostly True for you. Think of a specific but typical followership situation and how you acted.

	Mostly False	Mostly True
1. Does your work help you fulfill some higher societal or personal goal that is important to you?	_____	_____
2. Are you highly committed to and energized by your work and organization, giving them your best ideas and performance?	_____	_____
3. Does your enthusiasm also spread to and energize your co-workers?	_____	_____
4. Instead of waiting for or merely accepting what the leader tells you, do you personally figure out the most critical activities for achieving the organization's priority goals?	_____	_____
5. Do you actively develop a distinctive competence in those critical activities so that you become more valuable to the leader and the organization?	_____	_____
6. When starting a new job or assignment, do you quickly build a record of successes in tasks that are important to the leader?	_____	_____
7. Do you take the initiative to seek out and successfully complete assignments that go above and beyond your job?	_____	_____
8. When you are not the leader of a group project, do you still contribute at a high level, often doing more than your share?	_____	_____

	Mostly False	Mostly True
9. Do you independently think up and champion new ideas that will contribute significantly to the leader's or the organization's goals?	_____	_____
10. Do you try to solve the tough problems (technical or organizational), rather than look to the leader to do it?	_____	_____
11. Do you help out your co-workers, making them look good even when you do not get any credit?	_____	_____
12. Do you help the leader or group see both the upside potential and downside risks of ideas or plans, playing the devil's advocate if need be?	_____	_____
13. Do you understand the leader's needs, goals, and constraints, and work hard to meet them?	_____	_____
14. Do you actively and honestly own up to your strengths and weaknesses rather than put off evaluation?	_____	_____
15. Do you act on your own ethical standards rather than the leader's or the group's standards?	_____	_____
16. Do you assert your views on important issues, even though it might mean conflict with your group or reprisals from the leader?	_____	_____

Scoring and Interpretation

Questions 1, 4, 9, 10, 12, 14, 15, and 16 measure "independent thinking." Sum the number of Mostly True answers checked and write your score below.

Questions 2, 3, 5, 6, 7, 8, 11, and 13 measure "active engagement." Sum the number of Mostly True answers checked and write your score below.

Independent Thinking Total Score = _____
Active Engagement Total Score = _____

Continued

These two scores indicate how you carry out your followership role. A score of 2 or below is considered low. A score of 6 or higher is considered high. A score of 3–5 is in the middle. Based on whether your score is high, middle, or low, assess your followership style below.

Followership Style	Independent Thinking Score	Active Engagement Score
Effective	High	High
Alienated	High	Low
Conformist	Low	High
Pragmatist	Middling	Middling
Passive	Low	Low

How do you feel about your followership style? Compare your style to others. What might you do to be more effective as a follower?

Source: From Robert E. Kelley, *The Power of Followership: How to Create Leaders People Want to Follow and Followers Who Lead Themselves*, pp. 89–97. Copyright © 1992 by Consultants to Executives and Organizations, Ltd. Used by permission of Doubleday, a division of Random House, Inc.

rigid rules and authoritarian environments in which leaders perceive subordinate recommendations as a challenge or threat. When Kelley, the author who developed the two dimensions of followership, was consulted about how to improve employee creativity and innovation for an oil company, he discovered that each office was virtually identical, owing to strict company policies that prohibited individual expression. This is specifically the kind of environment that suppresses effective followership and creates conformists.[10]

The **pragmatic survivor** has qualities of all four extremes—depending on which style fits with the prevalent situation. This type of follower uses whatever style best benefits his or her own position and minimizes risk. Pragmatic survivors often emerge when an organization is going through desperate times, and followers find themselves doing whatever is needed to get themselves through the difficulty. Within any given company, some 25 to 35 percent of followers tend to be pragmatic survivors, avoiding risks and fostering the status quo, often for political reasons. Government appointees often demonstrate this followership style because they have their own agendas and a short period of time in which to implement them. They may appeal to the necessary individuals, who themselves have a limited time to accomplish goals, and are therefore willing to do whatever is necessary to survive in the short run.[11]

The **passive follower** exhibits neither critical, independent thinking nor active participation. Being passive and uncritical, these followers display neither initiative nor a sense of responsibility. Their activity is limited to what they are told to do, and they accomplish things only with a great deal of supervision. Passive followers leave the thinking to their leaders. Often, however, this style is the result of a leader who expects and encourages passive behavior. Followers learn that to show initiative, accept responsibility, or think creatively is not rewarded, and may even be punished by the leader, so they grow increasingly passive. Passive followers are often the result of leaders who are overcontrolling of others and who punish mistakes.[12]

The **effective follower** is both a critical, independent thinker and active in the organization. Effective followers behave the same toward everyone, regardless

Action Memo
Complete the questionnaire in Leader's Self-Insight 7.1 to evaluate how well you carry out a followership role.

Pragmatic survivor
a follower who has qualities of all four extremes (alienated, effective, passive, conformist), depending on which style fits with the prevalent situation

Passive follower
a person in an organization who exhibits neither critical, independent thinking nor active participation

Effective follower
a critical, independent thinker who actively participates in the organization

of their positions in the organization. They do not try to avoid risk or conflict. Rather, effective followers have the courage to initiate change and put themselves at risk or in conflict with others, even their leaders, to serve the best interest of the organization.

Characterized by both mindfulness and a willingness to act, effective followers are essential for an organization to be effective. They are capable of self-management, they discern strengths and weaknesses in themselves and in the organization, they are committed to something bigger than themselves, and they work toward competency, solutions, and positive impact. Effective followers are far from powerless—and they know it. Therefore, they do not despair in their positions, nor do they resent or manipulate others. This chapter's *Consider This* provides highlights from a speech given by Nelson Mandela that underscores his meaning of effective followership.

> **Action Memo**
> As a leader, you can also be an effective follower. You can think independently and critically instead of blindly accepting what your superiors tell you. Rather than dwelling on the shortcomings of others, you can look for solutions.

Demands on the Effective Follower

Effective followership is not always easy. The discussion of courage and integrity in Chapter 6 applies to followers as well as leaders. Indeed, followers sometimes experience an even greater need for these qualities because of their subordinate position. To be effective, followers have to know what they stand for and be willing to express their own ideas and opinions to their leaders, even though this might mean risking their jobs, being demeaned, or feeling inadequate.[13] Effective followers have the courage to accept responsibility, serve the needs of the organization, challenge authority, participate in change, and leave the organization when necessary.[14]

The Courage to Assume Responsibility The effective follower feels a sense of personal responsibility and ownership in the organization and its mission. Thus, the follower assumes responsibility for his or her own behavior and its impact on the organization. Effective followers do not presume that a leader or an organization will provide them with security, permission to act, or personal growth. Instead, they initiate the opportunities through which they can achieve personal fulfillment, exercise their potential, and provide the organization with the fullest extent of their capabilities. Emiliana "Millie" Barela has been cleaning rooms for 32 years at Antlers at Vail, a Colorado ski lodge. She takes pride in her work and sees her job as an important part of creating a good experience for guests. Barela takes it upon herself to get to know guests and put their interests and needs first.[15]

The Courage to Serve An effective follower discerns the needs of the organization and actively seeks to serve those needs. Just as leaders can serve others, as discussed in the previous chapter, so can followers. A follower can provide strength to the leader by supporting the leader's decisions and by contributing to the organization in areas that complement the leader's position. By displaying the will to serve others over themselves, followers act for the common mission of the organization with a passion that equals that of a leader. Timothy D. Cook, who is second in command at Apple, is known as an exceptional follower.

> **Action Memo**
> As a follower, you can assume responsibility for your own personal development, behavior, and work performance. You can look for opportunities to make a difference, seek to meet organizational needs, serve others, and work toward the common good.

IN THE LEAD

Timothy D. Cook, Apple Inc.

As CEO, Steve Jobs provides the pizzazz at Apple for employees and the public alike. But it is Timothy Cook who makes sure things run smoothly behind the scenes. "He's the story behind the story," says one former Apple executive.

Cook was originally hired in 1998 as a senior vice president of operations and has made a steady climb up the ranks to now serve as chief operating officer (COO) and second-in-command. Cook counters the CEO's quick, unpredictable temper with his quiet, thoughtful manner. Jobs can concentrate on the big picture and ideas for snazzy new products because he knows Cook is taking care of the nuts and bolts of the business. Far from being a "yes-man," Cook has his own ideas about how things should be done, and industry insiders see his stamp on the company. Yet he is content to play "Spock" to Steve Jobs' "Captain Kirk," using his analytical and detail-oriented mind to offset Jobs' more intuitive, emotional approach. Like Spock supporting Captain Kirk, Cook doesn't hesitate to push Jobs' boundaries to help him, and the organization, become better. And just as Kirk never hesitated to beam down to a planet and leave Spock in charge, Jobs confidently placed the company in the hands of Cook while he was recovering from surgery for pancreatic cancer several years ago.

For now, Cook is content to keep a low profile but have a high impact at Apple. Yet his contributions have caught the attention of other technology companies, and he is routinely solicited for CEO jobs. If Cook takes the step to top leader, he can hope to have a second-in-command who is as courageous in serving as he has been at Apple.[16]

The Courage to Challenge Although effective followers serve and support others, they don't sacrifice their personal integrity or the good of the organization in order to maintain harmony. If a leader's actions and decisions contradict the best interests of the organization, effective followers take a stand. Obedience is considered a high virtue in military organizations, for example, but the U.S. Army teaches soldiers that they have a duty to disobey illegal or immoral orders.[17] Good leaders want followers who are willing to challenge them for the good of the organization. When he was CEO of IBM, Lou Gerstner hired Larry Ricciardi as senior vice president and corporate counsel even though he knew Ricciardi would challenge his thinking and decisions.[18] Leaders are human and make mistakes. Effective leaders depend on followers who have the courage to challenge them.

The Courage to Participate in Transformation Effective followers view the struggle of corporate change and transformation as a mutual experience shared by all members of the organization. When an organization undergoes a difficult transformation, effective followers support the leader and the organization. They are not afraid to confront the changes and work toward reshaping the organization. David Chislett, of Imperial Oil's Dartmouth, Nova Scotia refinery, was faced with this test of courage. The refinery was the least efficient in the industry and the Board of Directors gave management 9 months to turn things around. Chislett's bosses asked him to give up his management position and return to the duties of a wage earner as part of an overall transformation strategy. He agreed to the request, thereby contributing to the success of the refinery's transformation.[19]

The Courage to Leave Sometimes organizational or personal changes create a situation in which a follower must withdraw from a particular leader–follower relationship. People might know they need new challenges, for example, even though it is hard to leave a job where they have many friends and valued colleagues. If followers are faced with a leader or an organization unwilling to make necessary changes, it is time to take their support elsewhere. Sometimes followers and leaders have such strong differences of opinion that the follower can no longer support the leader's decisions and feels a moral obligation to leave. U.S. General John Batiste turned down a promotion and resigned because he felt he could no longer support civilian leaders' decisions regarding Iraq. The role of military officers is to advise civilian leaders and then carry out orders even when they disagree. Gen. Batiste spent weeks torn between his sense of duty and respect for the chain of command and a feeling that he owed it to his soldiers to speak out against leaders' decisions. Ultimately, believing he could no longer serve his leaders as he should, the general had the courage to leave the job, even though it meant the end of a lifelong career he highly valued.[20]

Developing Personal Potential

How do followers expand their potential to be critical, independent thinkers who make active contributions to their organizations? Later in this chapter, we'll discuss the crucial role of leaders in developing effective followers. However, followers can expand their own capabilities by developing and applying personal leadership qualities in both their private and work lives. One well-known and widely acclaimed approach to helping people deal courageously with life's changes and challenges is Stephen Covey's *The 7 Habits of Highly Effective People*.[21] Covey defines a habit as the intersection of knowledge, skill, and desire. His approach to personal and interpersonal effectiveness includes seven habits arranged along a maturity continuum, from dependence to independence to interdependence, as

Exhibit 7.2 The Maturity Continuum®

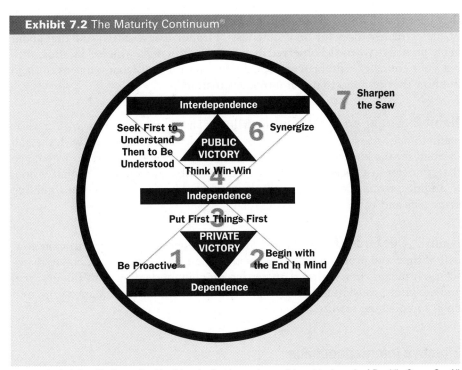

illustrated in Exhibit 7.2. Each habit builds on the previous one so that individuals grow further along the maturity continuum as they develop these personal effectiveness habits.

In organizations, many people fall into a mindset of dependency, expecting someone else to take care of everything and make all the decisions. The *dependent* person is comparable to the passive follower we described earlier, displaying neither initiative nor a sense of personal responsibility. Dependent people expect someone else to take care of them and blame others when things go wrong. An *independent* person, on the other hand, has developed a sense of self-worth and an attitude of self-reliance. Independent people accept personal responsibility and get what they want through their own actions. To be a truly effective follower—or leader—requires a further step to *interdependence*, the realization that the best things happen by working cooperatively with others, that life and work are better when one experiences the richness of close interpersonal relationships.

From Dependence to Independence

Covey's first three habits deal with self-reliance and self-mastery. Covey calls these *private victories* because they involve only the individual follower growing from dependence to independence, not the follower in relationship with others.[22]

Action Memo
As a leader or follower, you can expand your potential by consciously developing and applying leadership qualities in your personal and work life. You can move from dependence and passivity toward greater self-reliance and interdependence based on positive, productive relationships with others.

Habit 1: Be Proactive® Being proactive means more than merely taking initiative; it means being responsible for your own life. Proactive people recognize that they have the ability to choose and to act with integrity. They don't blame others or life's circumstances for their outcomes. Eleanor Roosevelt was talking about being proactive when she observed that, "No one can make you feel inferior without your consent."[23] Proactive people know that it is not what happens to them but how they respond to it that ultimately matters.

Habit 2: Begin with the End in Mind® This means to start with a clear mental image of your destination. For each individual, beginning with the end in mind means knowing what you want, what is deeply important to you, so that you can live each day in a way that contributes to your personal vision. In addition to clarifying goals and plans, this habit entails establishing guiding principles and values for achieving them.

Habit 3: Put First Things First® This habit encourages people to gain control of time and events by relating them to their goals and by managing themselves. It means that, rather than getting tangled up dealing with things, time, and activities, we should focus on preserving and enhancing *relationships* and on accomplishing *results*.

Effective Interdependence

The first three habits build a foundation of independence, from which one can move to interdependence—caring, productive relationships with others—which Covey calls *public victories*. Moving to effective interdependence involves open communication, effective teamwork, and building positive relationships based on trust, caring, and respect, topics that are discussed throughout this book. No matter what position you hold in the organization, when you move to interdependence, you step into a leadership role.

Habit 4: Think Win–Win® To think win–win means understanding that without cooperation, the organization cannot succeed. When followers understand this, they cooperate in ways that ensure their mutual success and allow everyone to come out a winner. Win–win is a frame of mind and heart that seeks agreements or solutions that are mutually beneficial and satisfying.

Habit 5: Seek First to Understand, Then to Be Understood® This principle is the key to effective communication. Many people don't listen with the intent to understand; they are too busy thinking about what they want to say. Seeking first to understand requires being nonjudgmental and able to empathize with the other person's situation. *Empathetic listening* gets inside another person's frame of reference so that you can better understand how that person feels. Chapter 9 discusses communication in detail.

Habit 6: Synergize® Synergy is the combined action that occurs when people work together to create new alternatives and solutions. In addition, the greatest opportunity for synergy occurs when people have different viewpoints, because the differences present new opportunities. The essence of synergy is to value and respect differences and take advantage of them to build on strengths and compensate for weaknesses.

Habit 7: Sharpen the Saw® This habit encompasses the previous six—it is the habit that makes all the others possible. "Sharpening the saw" is a process of using and continuously renewing the physical, mental, spiritual, and social aspects of your life. To be an effective follower or an effective leader requires living a balanced life. For example, John Barr founded Barr Devlin, an investment bank that specializes in utility mergers. He's also a writer who has published four volumes of poetry.[24] Larry Ricciardi of IBM, introduced earlier, is an avid traveler and voracious reader who likes to study art, literature, and history. He once spent 18 months learning everything he could about the Ottoman Empire just because he "realized he knew nothing about the Ottoman Empire." He also likes to read tabloids in addition to his daily fare of *The Wall Street Journal*. On business trips, he scouts out side trips to exotic or interesting sites, and he likes to take adventurous vacations with his family and friends. Ricciardi loves his job, but he also loves exploring other aspects of life.[25]

Sources of Follower Power

Another issue of concern is how followers gain and use power in organizations. Formal leaders typically have more power than followers do. Nevertheless, effective followers participate fully in organizations by culling power from the available sources. Even the lowest-level follower has personal and position-based sources of power that can be used to generate upward influence, thereby impacting the organization and establishing a mutually beneficial relationship with leaders.[26] Personal sources of power include knowledge, expertise, effort, and persuasion. Position sources of power include location, information, and access.

Personal Sources

A knowledgeable follower has skills and talents that are a valuable resource to the leader and to the organization. Such a follower is of real value, and his or her departure would be a loss. *Knowledge* is a source of upward influence. In addition, a follower who has a demonstrated record of performance often develops *expertise* and in this way can influence decisions. A record of successes and a history of contributions can garner expert status for followers, from which followers can derive the power to influence operations and establish themselves as a resource to the leader. The power to influence is also associated with the *effort* put forth by a follower. By demonstrating a willingness to learn, to accept difficult or undesirable projects, and to initiate activities beyond the scope of expected effort, a follower can gain power in an organization.[27] Tim Chapman was hired by Spartan Motors during his senior year of high school. By age 20, he was the head electrical engineer, troubleshooting and consorting with key vendors. "I guess I'm willing to learn," says Chapman.[28]

Followers can also use persuasion as a source of personal power. *Persuasion* refers to the direct appeal to leaders in an organization for desired outcomes.[29] In addition to being direct, speaking truthfully to a leader can be a source of power for effective followers.[30] Rob Hummel, head of international post-production at Dreamworks SKG, once promoted an employee who was known for being "difficult" because he always challenged his superiors. The fact that this follower was willing to speak truthfully to higher-ups based on his own knowledge and creative brilliance gave him increased power.[31] Power doesn't always come from titles or seniority in the organization; sometimes it comes from one's knowledge and contributions.

Position Sources

Often the formal position of a follower in an organization can provide sources of power. For example, the location of a follower can render him or her *visible* to numerous individuals. A *central location* provides influence to a follower, because the follower is known to many and contributes to the work of many. Similarly, a position that is key to the *flow of information* can establish that position and the follower in it as critical—thus, influential—to those who seek the information. Access to people and information in an organization provides the follower in the position a means to establish relationships with others. With a *network of relationships*, a follower has greater opportunity to persuade others and to make contributions to numerous organizational processes.

Strategies for Managing Up

Action Memo
Leader's Self-Insight 7.2 gives you a chance to see if you're guilty of being an annoying follower.

There is growing recognition that how followers manage their leaders is just as important as how their leaders manage them.[32] Most followers at some point complain about the leader's deficiencies, such as the leader's failure to listen, to encourage, or to recognize followers' efforts.[33] Effective followers, however, transform the leader–follower relationship by striving to improve their leaders rather than just criticizing them. To be effective, followers develop a meaningful, task-related relationship with their bosses that enables them to add value to the organization even when their ideas disagree with those of the bosses.[34] You might have experienced this with a special teacher or coach. For example, students who are especially interested in a class sometimes challenge the professor on a topic as a way to expand the professor's thinking and enhance the learning experience for everyone.

Followers should also be aware of behaviors that can annoy leaders and interfere with building a quality relationship. A business magazine recently interviewed powerful people about their pet peeves and identified 30 misdemeanors that followers often commit without being aware of it.

Most relationships between leaders and followers are characterized by some emotion and behavior based on authority and submission. Leaders are authority figures and may play a disproportionately large role in the mind of a follower. Followers may find themselves being overcritical of their leaders, or rebellious, or passive. Irvin D. Yalom, a professor of psychiatry and author of the novels *Lying on the Couch* and *When Nietzsche Wept,* once had a patient in group therapy who ranted at great length about her boss who never listened and refused to pay her any respect. Interestingly, this woman's complaints persisted through three different jobs and three different bosses.[35] The relationships between leaders and followers are not unlike those between parents and children, and individuals may engage old family patterns when entering into leader–follower relationships.[36] Effective followers, conversely, typically perceive themselves as the equals of their leaders, not inherently subordinate.[37] Exhibit 7.3 illustrates the strategies that enable followers to overcome the authority-based relationship and develop an effective, respectful relationship with their leaders.

1. If you think there might be a mistake in something you've done, what do you do?
   A. Fess up. It's better to share your concerns up front so your boss can see if there is a problem and get it corrected before it makes him look bad.
   B. Try to hide it. Maybe there isn't really a problem, so there's no use in making yourself look incompetent.

2. How do you handle a criticism from your boss?
   A. Poke your head in her door or corner her in the cafeteria multiple times to make sure everything is okay between the two of you.
   B. Take the constructive criticism, make sure you understand what the boss wants from you, and get on with your job.

3. You're in a crowded elevator with your boss after an important meeting where you've just landed a million-dollar deal. You:
   A. Celebrate the victory by talking to your boss about the accomplishment and the details of the meeting.
   B. Keep your mouth shut or talk about non–business-related matters.

4. Your boss has an open-door policy and wants people to feel free to drop by her office any time to talk about anything. You pop in just after lunch and find her on the phone. What do you do?
   A. Leave and come back later.
   B. Wait. You know most of her phone calls are quick, so she'll be free in a few minutes.

5. You've been called to the boss's office and have no idea what he wants to talk about.
   A. You show up on time, empty-handed, and ask the boss what you need to bring with you.
   B. You show up on time with a pen, paper, and your calendar or PDA.

6. You've been trying to get some face time with your boss for weeks and luckily catch him or her in the bathroom. You:
   A. Take care of personal business and get out of there.
   B. Grab your chance to schmooze with the boss. You might not get another any time soon.

Here are the appropriate follower behaviors:

1. **A.** Honest self-assessment and fessing up to the boss builds mutual confidence and respect. Nothing destroys trust faster than incompetence exposed after the fact.

2. **B.** David Snow, former president and COO of Empire Blue Cross and Blue Shield, refers to insecure, thin-skinned people who have to check in frequently after a criticism as *door swingers.* Door swingers are annoying in both our personal and work lives. Just get on with things.

3. **B.** You have no idea who else is in the elevator. Keep your mouth shut. You can crow about the new deal later in private.

4. **A.** There's nothing worse than having someone hovering while you're trying to carry on a phone conversation. Leave a note with your boss's assistant or come back later.

5. **B.** You can usually be safe in assuming your boss hasn't called you in for idle chit-chat. Never show up without a pen and paper to make notes.

6. **A.** At best, to use the bathroom as a place to try to impress the boss makes you look desperate. It also shows a lack of tact and judgment.

Most of these seem obvious, but based on interviews with leaders, subordinates commit these sins over and over in the workplace. Keep these missteps in mind so you don't become an annoying follower.

Source: Based on William Speed Weed, Alex Lash, and Constance Loizos, "30 Ways to Annoy Your Boss," *MBA Jungle* (March–April 2003), pp. 51–55.

Be a Resource for the Leader

Effective followers align themselves to the purpose and the vision of the organization. They ask the leader about vision and goals and help achieve them. In this way, followers are a resource of strength and support for the leader. This alignment involves understanding the leader's goals, needs, strengths and weaknesses, and organizational constraints. An effective follower can complement the leader's weaknesses with the follower's own strengths,[38] as we saw earlier in the

Exhibit 7.3 Ways to Influence Your Leader

Be a Resource for the Leader Determine the leader's needs. Zig where leader zags. Tell leader about you. Align self to team purpose/vision.	**Help the Leader Be a Good Leader** Ask for advice. Tell leader what you think. Find things to thank leader for.
Build a Relationship Ask about leader at your level/position. Welcome feedback and criticism, such as "What experience led you to that opinion?" Ask leader to tell you company stories.	**View the Leader Realistically** Give up idealized leader expectations. Don't hide anything. Don't criticize leader to others. Disagree occasionally.

example of Timothy Cook and Steve Jobs at Apple. Similarly, effective followers indicate their personal goals and the resources they bring to the organization. Effective followers inform their leaders about their own ideas, beliefs, needs, and constraints. The more leaders and followers can know the day-to-day activities and problems of one another, the better resources they can be for each other. For example, one group of handicapped workers took advantage of a board meeting to issue rented wheelchairs to the members, who then tried to move around the factory in them. Realizing what the workers faced, the board got the factory's ramps improved, and the handicapped workers became a better resource for the organization.[39]

Help the Leader Be a Good Leader

Good followers seek the leader's counsel and look for ways the leader can help them improve their skills, abilities, and value to the organization. They help their leaders be good leaders by simply saying what they need in order to be good followers. If a leader believes a follower values his or her advice, the leader is more likely to give constructive guidance rather than unsympathetic criticism.

A leader can also become a better leader when followers compliment the leader and thank him or her for behavior that followers appreciate, such as listening, rewarding followers' contributions, and sharing credit for accomplishments.[40] If a leader knows what followers appreciate, the leader is more likely to repeat that behavior. One employee working for a micromanaging boss who was always negative found that the key to helping him be a better leader was to model the behavior she wanted from the boss. Rather than pushing back when he micromanaged, she was cheerful and helpful. Rather than complaining, she started acting like he was "the world's best boss with the world's best employee." This approach gradually influenced the boss's behavior in such a way that he displayed greater trust toward the employee and

Action Memo
As a leader, you can use strategies for managing up to create an equitable and respectful relationship with your superiors. You can help your supervisor be the best he or she can be by getting beyond submissive feelings and behaviors, recognizing that leaders are fallible, and being a resource for the leader.

began treating her in a more equitable manner.[41] Sometimes, however, effective followers have to find diplomatic ways to let leaders know when their behavior is counterproductive.

Asking for advice, thanking the leader for helpful behaviors, modeling the behavior you want, and being honest about areas that need improvement are important ways followers can affect the conduct of leaders and help them be better leaders.

Build a Relationship with the Leader

Effective followers work toward a genuine relationship with their leaders, which includes developing trust and speaking honestly on the basis of that trust.[42] By building a relationship with a leader, a follower makes every interaction more meaningful to the organization. Furthermore, the relationship is imbued with mutual respect rather than authority and submission. Wes Walsh used mindful initiatives to create a relationship with his boss that maximized his own upward influence.

IN THE LEAD

Wes Walsh

When Wes Walsh came under an autocratic manager, his position predecessor warned him to either stay away from the infamously autocratic boss, or else be prepared to give up any influence over the unit operations. Walsh decided to ignore this advice. Instead, he started dropping by his boss's office on a regular basis to discuss production progress. Walsh also sought approval on very small matters because they were virtually impossible for his boss to oppose. Walsh continued these frequent, informal interactions over a lengthy period of time before moving on to more consequential matters.

Eventually, major projects had to be addressed. For example, an increase in the volume of materials processed had rendered Walsh's unit too slow and too limited to adequately serve the increased production. In response, Walsh first requested his boss to devote a couple of hours to him at some designated point in the near future. When the appointed time arrived, Walsh took his boss on a lengthy tour of the plant, pointing out the volume of material scattered about waiting to be processed. He supplemented this visual evidence with facts and figures.

The boss was compelled to acknowledge the problem. Thus, he asked for Walsh's proposal, which Walsh had carefully prepared beforehand. Although the boss had rejected identical proposals from Walsh's predecessor, this time the boss almost immediately approved the sum of $150,000 for updating the unit equipment.[43]

Walsh's conscious effort to interact and get his boss comfortable saying yes on small matters set a precedent for a pattern of respect that was not lost even on his autocratic superior.

Followers can generate respect by asking questions about the leader's experiences in the follower's position, actively seeking feedback, and clarifying the basis for specific feedback and criticism from the leader. Followers can also ply the leader for company stories.[44] By doing so, followers are getting beyond submissive behavior by asking leaders to be accountable for their criticism, to have empathy for the followers' position, and to share history about something both parties have in common—the organization.

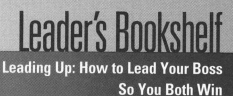
Getty Images

Michael Useem, professor of management and director of the Center for Leadership and Change Management at the Wharton School of the University of Pennsylvania, puts a new twist on leadership advice by stressing that leadership has to come from below as well as from above. "We have all known a supervisor or president, a coach or minister, an officer or director who should have made a difference but did not," Useem writes. "We privately complained, we may even have quit, but we rarely stepped forward to help them transcend their limitations and be the best boss they could be." In *Leading Up: How to Lead Your Boss So You Both Win,* Useem offers lessons in leading up by examining both positive and negative real-life examples.

EXAMPLES OF LEADING UP

Here are a few real life successes and failures that bring the concept of upward leadership to life:

- Civil War commanders on both the Union and Confederate sides openly disrespected and often misinformed their commanders-in-chief, which contributed to tragic consequences for both sides. For example, Union General George McClellan didn't even try to disguise his contempt for President Abraham Lincoln and eventually alienated every member of Lincoln's cabinet. Two days before the Peninsula Campaign in mid-spring 1862, Lincoln relieved McClellan from his position. Lesson: Disdain and contempt for your superior will be returned in kind. To build your superior's confidence in you, give your confidence to the leader.
- U.S. Marine Corps general Peter Pace had to report to six bosses with varying agendas, but he successfully

brought together conflicting priorities by keeping everyone informed of what he was recommending to all the others. In addition, Pace was willing to challenge his superiors when their proposals or policies were at odds with his own informed judgment. Lesson: Total honesty and frequent face-to-face discussions are a must for communicating what the boss needs to know and maintaining the trust that is essential to good leader-follower relationships.

- Eight climbers died on Mount Everest in May of 1996 partly because the mountaineers failed to question their guides' flawed and inconsistent instructions and decisions. The surviving climbers admit they might have protected themselves and others from harm if they had been willing to rise up when their leaders were faltering. Lesson: Although respect for and confidence in your superior is vital, good followers know that nobody is invincible or faultless. "Biding your time and deferring to authority serves no one well when it's clear that the boss would fare far better with your upward help."

ANSWERING THE CALL TO UPWARD LEADERSHIP

Useem uses heroic accounts and moments of crisis as examples because he believes they are the best teachers. However, he points out that opportunities for leading up come to all of us in many different situations. Without effective followers who act as upward leaders to offer information, guidance, insight, and initiative—and to challenge their superiors when necessary—leadership is an incomplete and impotent exercise.

Leading Up: How To Lead Your Boss So You Both Win, by Michael Useem, is published by Crown Business.

View the Leader Realistically

Unrealistic follower expectations is one of the biggest barriers to effective leader–follower relationships. To view leaders realistically means to give up idealized images of them. Understanding that leaders are fallible and will make many mistakes leads to acceptance and the potential for an equitable relationship. The way in which a follower perceives his or her boss is the foundation of their relationship. It helps to view leaders as they really are, not as followers think they should be.[45]

Similarly, effective followers present realistic images of themselves. Followers do not try to hide their weaknesses or cover their mistakes, nor do they criticize their leaders to others.[46] Hiding things is symptomatic of conforming and passive followers. Criticizing leaders to others merely bolsters alienation and reinforces the mindset of an alienated follower. These kinds of alienated and passive behaviors can have negative—and sometimes disastrous—consequences for leaders, followers, and the organization, as illustrated by the stories in this chapter's Leader's Bookshelf. Only positive things about a leader should be shared with others. It is an alienated follower who complains without engaging in constructive action. Instead of criticizing a leader to others, it is far more constructive to directly disagree with a leader on matters relevant to the department's or organization's work.

What Followers Want

Throughout much of this chapter, we've been talking about demands on followers and how followers can become more effective and powerful in the organization. However, the full responsibility doesn't fall on the follower. To have good followers, the requirements and obligations of those in a leadership role should be reexamined as well.[47] Leaders have a duty to create a leader–follower relationship that engages whole people rather than treats followers as passive sheep who should blindly follow orders and support the boss.

Research indicates that followers have expectations about what constitutes a desirable leader.[48] Exhibit 7.4 shows the top four choices in rank order based on surveys of followers about what they desire in leaders and colleagues.

Followers want their leaders to be honest, forward-thinking, inspiring, and competent. A leader must be worthy of trust, envision the future of the organization, inspire others to contribute, and be capable and effective in matters that will affect the organization. In terms of competence, leadership roles may shift from the formal leader to the person with particular expertise in a given area.

Action Memo

As a leader, you can learn to give and receive feedback that contributes to growth and improvement rather than fear and hard feelings.

Followers want their fellow followers to be honest and competent, but also dependable and cooperative. Thus, desired qualities of colleagues share two qualities with leaders—honesty and competence. However, followers themselves want other followers to be dependable and cooperative, rather than forward-thinking and inspiring. The hallmark that distinguishes the role of leadership from the role of followership, then, is not authority, knowledge, power, or other conventional notions of what a follower is not. Rather, the distinction lies in the clearly defined leadership activities of fostering a vision and inspiring others to achieve that vision. Chapter 13 discusses vision in detail. Organizations that can boast of effective

---

Exhibit 7.4 Rank Order of Desirable Characteristics

Desirable Leaders Are	Desirable Colleagues (Followers) Are
Honest	Honest
Forward thinking	Cooperative
Inspiring	Dependable
Competent	Competent

Source: Adapted from James M. Kouzes and Barry Z. Posner, *Credibility: How Leaders Gain and Lose It, Why People Demand It* (San Francisco, CA: Jossey-Bass Publishers, 1993), p. 255.

Feedback
using evaluation and communication to help individuals and the organization learn and improve

Observations
visible occurrences, such as a follower's behavior on a job

Assessment
the interpretation of observed behaviors; an evaluation of the results in terms of vision and goals

Consequence
the outcome of what was observed; can include both actual consequences and the consequences possible if no change takes place

Development
the sustainment or improvement of follower behaviors

Action Memo
Before reading on, answer the questions in Leader's Self-Insight 7.3 to learn how you may manage performance feedback from your boss.

followers tend to have leaders who deal primarily with change and progress.[49] The results in Exhibit 7.4 also underscore the idea that behaviors of effective leaders and followers often overlap. Followers do not want to be subjected to leader behavior that denies them the opportunity to make valued contributions. Leaders have a responsibility to enable followers to fully contribute their ideas and abilities.

Using Feedback to Develop Followers

Giving and receiving feedback is often difficult for both leaders and followers. At annual review time in many organizations, for example, bosses worry that even the slightest criticism will provoke anger or tears, while employees are terrified that they'll hear nothing but complaints. Thus, people often say as little as possible, and both followers and leaders lose a valuable opportunity. Feedback should be seen as a route to improvement and development, not as something to dread or fear.[50] A survey of managers by McKinsey & Company calls attention to the problem of poor feedback for organizations. When asked what factors contributed to their growth and development, respondents ranked "candid, insightful feedback" as one of the most important elements; however, most also indicated that their supervisors did not do a good job of providing such feedback.[51]

Feedback occurs when a leader uses evaluation and communication to help individuals and the organization learn and improve.[52] The feedback process involves four elements, as illustrated in Exhibit 7.5. **Observations** are visible occurrences, such as a follower's behavior on the job. An **assessment** is the interpretation of observed behaviors, an evaluation of the results in terms of vision and goals. A **consequence** refers to the outcome of what was observed, and can include both actual consequences and the consequences possible if no change takes place. **Development** refers to the sustainment or improvement of behaviors. Leaders communicate what they observe, how they assess it, what consequences it has, and how to

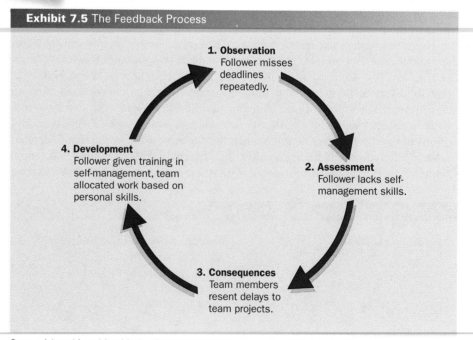

Exhibit 7.5 The Feedback Process

1. Observation
Follower misses deadlines repeatedly.

2. Assessment
Follower lacks self-management skills.

3. Consequences
Team members resent delays to team projects.

4. Development
Follower given training in self-management, team allocated work based on personal skills.

Source: Adapted from Mary Mavis, "Painless Performance Evaluations," *Training and Development* (October 1994), pp. 40–44.

Receiving Feedback

The following items describe ways you might act toward receiving feedback from a supervisor. Think about a job you had, or just imagine how you would behave if you had a job, and answer the questions below. Indicate whether each item below is Mostly False or Mostly True for you.

	Mostly False	Mostly True
1. After performing a task well, I would cheerfully greet my supervisor hoping that this would lead to a conversation about my work.	_____	_____
2. After performing poorly, I might try to schedule outside appointments or take a sick day to avoid my supervisor.	_____	_____
3. I would confess about my poor performance to my supervisor immediately, but have several solutions prepared to show that I would not make the same mistake twice.	_____	_____
4. After performing well, I might display my excellent work to my co-workers and hope they might relay some positive remarks to my supervisor.	_____	_____
5. After performing poorly, I might go the other way when I saw my supervisor coming or otherwise avoid contact for awhile.	_____	_____
6. I would inform my boss that I wasn't able to complete my assignment on time but that I would stay late that night to finish it.	_____	_____
7. After performing well, I would ask my supervisor about my performance to draw his/her attention to my success.	_____	_____
8. After performing poorly, I would try to avoid eye contact with my supervisor so that he/she didn't start a conversation with me about my performance.	_____	_____
9. After performing poorly, I would immediately show my supervisor that I was taking responsibility for my performance by taking corrective measures.	_____	_____

Scoring and Interpretation

Most followers want to perform well and receive appropriate recognition, and most followers sometimes experience poor performance. The questions above provide some indication of how you manage feedback from your supervisor. Questions 1, 4, and 7 indicate your "feedback seeking" behavior and indicate the extent to which you want your boss to know about your good work and provide you with positive feedback. Questions 2, 5, and 8 indicate your "feedback avoiding" behavior when your performance is poor. Questions 3, 6, and 9 indicate your "feedback mitigating" behavior to correct the outcome when your performance is poor. Record the number of Mostly True responses below for each set of questions. A score of 3 would be considered high, and a score of 0 or 1 would be low for each type of behavior.

Feedback seeking (1, 4, 7) _____ "Feedback seeking" is a personal preference because good performance serves your supervisor well, and whether you want feedback from your boss is up to you. A high score indicates you want feedback, but any score indicates appropriate followership.

Feedback avoiding (2, 5, 8) _____ In terms of followership, "feedback avoiding" behavior is perhaps least effective for serving your boss. Avoiding poor performance feedback means you may have trouble confronting reality and fear negative evaluation. A low score here is characteristic of a good follower.

Feedback mitigating (3, 6, 9) _____ "Feedback mitigating" behavior is very effective follower behavior because you take personal responsibility to correct poor outcomes and keep your boss informed. A high score indicates good followership.

Source: Adapted from Sherry E. Moss, Enzo R. Valenzi, and William Taggart, "Are You Hiding from Your Boss? The Development of a Taxonomy and Instrument to Assess the Feedback Management Behaviors of Good and Bad Performers." *Journal of Management* 29, no. 4 (2003), pp. 487–510. Used with permission.

effectively address the observed behavior and consequence. Each element is communicated from the leader to the individual or organization.[53] Furthermore, the development becomes an observation in the next feedback loop. For example, a leader who observes development and assesses it positively may consequently promote the responsible follower.

Leaders can use these four elements to provide feedback that facilitates growth for followers and the organization. For example, when he was senior vice-president of Dell, Kevin Rollins changed the culture by asking every manager to submit to 360-degree feedback from followers and colleagues. Rollins himself received stinging comments. He was said to be aloof, a poor listener, unapproachable, icy cold, argumentative, and even bullheaded. Rollins welcomed the feedback, and stood before 50 other top executives and acknowledged his need to grow as a manager. "I could give the cold, calculating answer, but I really wanted to be a more inspriational leader," Rollins said. "Maybe I can't be George Washington . . . but I can always do better." Honest feedback was the trigger for Rollins's growth.[54]

Yet most people face significant challenges in giving and receiving feedback.[55] For one thing, the feedback process is usually characterized by high levels of emotion, and many traditionally trained managers have been accustomed to thinking that emotions have no place in the organization. They thus find it both exhausting and uncomfortable to confront the strong emotions that may arise in a feedback situation. A second drawback to effective feedback is that leaders and followers may have different cognitive styles, as described in Chapter 4, and may see things in very different ways, which can lead to misunderstandings, disagreements, and communication breakdowns.

There are several ways leaders can optimize the use of feedback and minimize the conflict and fear that often accompanies it. Giving good feedback requires emotional intelligence, as described in Chapter 5, courage, as discussed in Chapter 6, and an understanding of different personalities and thinking styles, as discussed in Chapter 4. *Empathy* is one of the leader's most powerful tools during the feedback process. The leader must be able to put him or herself in the follower's shoes and understand what the follower might be feeling. Empathy helps the leader approach feedback in a way that reflects a genuine concern for the follower. Here are some other tips for using feedback to develop effective followers:

- *Make regular feedback a habit.* Feedback should be an ongoing process. Leaders should not save everything up for an annual performance review. In addition, by tying feedback to specific goals and objectives, leaders make criticisms and suggestions for improvement concrete to the follower. The leader can also provide illustrations or examples to clarify what behavior is considered ineffective and what actions the leader wants from the follower.

- *Use elements of storytelling.* Followers as well as leaders usually learn a lot more from examining the *story* of how and why something happened than they do from conventional evaluations that might seem like a "chewing out from the boss."[56] This is one of the most powerful approaches to feedback because investigating what happened and why typically puts the leader and follower on an equal footing. Both people are involved in examining their roles and responsibilities in the problem. Chapter 9 discusses communication and using metaphor and story in detail.

- *Be generous with positive feedback.* Too many leaders offer feedback only when something goes wrong. They should remember to congratulate behaviors that support the organization's vision and goals, while at the same time working to improve the behaviors that do not. When feedback is limited to moments of shortcoming, followers can become discouraged and demoralized. The best leaders look for opportunities to provide positive feedback to even the weakest performers.

- *Train followers to view feedback as an opportunity for development.* Followers can learn to think of feedback as a positive rather than a negative process. When people recognize and acknowledge their emotions in response to criticisms, they can then "reframe" the feedback to their own advantage. That is, followers can see feedback as a way to advance their own interests. One follower who practiced the technique of reframing feedback discovered that he wasn't really happy doing the tasks that were required of him. After requesting a transfer to another department, he became much more satisfied and successful.[57]

Action Memo

As a leader, you can make feedback a regular habit and remember to include positive comments and praise. As a follower, you can view feedback as a chance to improve yourself. Reframe negative feedback in a way that helps you take positive action toward what you want out of your work and life.

Leading Others to Lead Themselves

One of the most important steps a leader can take to develop effective followers is to accept and acknowledge his or her own limitations and, indeed, his or her inability to accomplish anything without the help of followers.[58] The leader who tries to do it all alone never gets very far. By acknowledging imperfections and limitations, leaders open the door for followers to contribute their own unique competencies.

Good leaders strive toward a collaborative relationship with followers. One approach proposed by Charles Manz and Henry Sims is **self-management leadership**, which means leading others to lead themselves.[59] Self-management leadership calls for leaders to share power and responsibility in such a way that anyone can become a leader, depending on the circumstances of the situation. The organization becomes a community where anyone who is capable and willing can assume a leadership role. Formal leaders act as coaches and mentors, show trust in others, remove barriers to learning, offer encouragement and support, and provide constructive feedback. Leaders develop followers by providing them with opportunities to gain new experience and understandings. However, followers and leaders are active partners who are continually learning, growing, and changing.[60]

Leaders who practice self-management leadership do not try to control employee behavior in traditional ways, but coach employees to think critically about their own performance and judge how well they are accomplishing tasks and achieving goals. Leaders also make sure employees have the information they need to perform effectively and an understanding of how their jobs are relevant to attaining the organization's vision. By linking individual jobs with larger organizational goals, employees have a framework within which to act. Self-management leadership hinges on providing employees with this directed autonomy.[61]

Empowerment of frontline employees, participative management, and other forms of democratic practice are growing trends in organizations. Thus, there are more situations that call for self-management leadership. However, there has been little research to test the effectiveness of this new approach. As with other styles of leadership, it is likely that self-management leadership is effective for some, but not all, situations. Yet all leaders can act in ways that encourage followers to think independently and be willing to take risks, challenge unproductive or unethical norms, and initiate change for the benefit of the organization. Consider how West Point trains future military leaders by emphasizing the importance of followership.

Self-management leadership
leading others to lead themselves

U.S. Military Academy, West Point

At West Point, everyone leads and everyone follows. It's a 24-hour leadership laboratory where people learn that leadership and followership are two sides of the same whole. An important lesson is that leaders are nothing without followers. "You learn from the beginning that you're not in a position of leadership because you're smarter or better," says cadet Joe Bagaglio. "As soon as you think you know it all, you get burned."

Each spring, West Point graduates nearly 1,000 men and women who leave with a bachelor's degree and a commission as second lieutenant in the U. S. Army. After a 6-week leave, these new graduates take their first jobs as military officers in places like Kosovo, Germany, Guam, Afghanistan, or Iraq. Most of us think of West Point as a place of rules, rigidity, structure, and conformity, and to a great extent, it is. Cadets have to learn to subordinate their self-interest for the good of the whole, because that's what they'll be called upon to do when they graduate. However, there's another side to the story, one that instills creativity and flexibility into students who might someday have to make rapid decisions in the chaos of a battlefield. Cadets learn to rely on the competencies of followers and their own judgment. They learn that everyone is part of the team and no one individual—no matter his or her rank—is more important than the mission of the whole. The entire community relies on this interdependence.

At West Point, everyone is evaluated all the time, and every action is an opportunity to learn, to gain new experience, and to grow in understanding. Formal leaders are continually pushing people—including themselves—to get out of their comfort zone so that they expand their capacity for leadership. "Everyone's a teacher," says cadet Chris Kane, a platoon leader in Company C-2 at West Point. "That's what I love about this place. We're all teachers."[62]

Building a Community of Followers

Together, followers and leaders provide the dependability, cooperation, and commitment to build a sense of community and interdependence in the organization. When there is a sense of community, as at West Point, people feel a strong commitment to the whole and feel that they are important to others in the group. You may have felt this in your personal life as a member of a social club, a religious organization, or a sports team. Community provides a spirit of connection that sustains effective relationships and commitment to purpose. People in a community accomplish shared goals through trust and teamwork.[63] In a community, people are able to communicate openly with one another, maintain their uniqueness, and be firmly committed to something larger than selfish interests. In short, a group of effective followers provides the basis for community. It is not by coincidence that effective followers and effective community members share certain characteristics. Historically, communities of all sorts were based on service, informed participation, and individual contributions.[64]

Action Memo
As a leader, you can work cooperatively with others to build a sense of community, interdependence, and common purpose. You can contribute to a positive culture and a spirit of equality by practicing inclusivity and respect.

Characteristics of Community

Successful communities share a number of important characteristics. In effective communities, members practice inclusivity, a positive culture, conversation, caring and trust, and shared leadership.[65]

Inclusivity In a community, everyone is welcome and feels a sense of belonging. Divergent ideas and different points of view are encouraged, as a true community cannot exist without diversity.[66] However, community focuses on the whole rather than the parts, and people emphasize what binds them together. People can speak honestly when their convictions differ from others. This courage often stems from the belief in the inherent equality between themselves, other followers, and their leaders—that is, wholeness.

Positive Culture Leaders and followers perceive the organization as a community with shared norms and values. Members care about newcomers and work to socialize them into the culture. In addition, effective communities are not insular. They encourage adaptive values that help the group or organization interact effectively with a dynamic environment.

Conversation Conversation is how people make and share the meanings that are the basis of community. One special type of communication, **dialogue**, means that each person suspends his attachment to a particular viewpoint so that a deeper level of listening, synthesis, and meaning evolves from the whole community. Individual differences are acknowledged and respected, but the group searches for an expanded collective perspective.[67] Chapter 9 explains dialogue more thoroughly. Only through conversation can people build collaboration and collective action so they move together on a common path.

Dialogue
a type of communication in which each person suspends his attachment to a particular viewpoint so that a deeper level of listening, synthesis, and meaning evolves from the whole community

Caring and Trust Members of a community genuinely care about one another. People consider how their actions affect others and the community as a whole. In addition, members accept others and help them grow without trying to control them, strive to understand others' viewpoints and problems, and have empathy for others. Trust is developed from caring relationships and an emphasis on ethical behavior that serves the interests of the whole.

Shared Leadership In a community, a leader is one among many equals. People do not try to control others, and anyone can step forward as a leader. There is a spirit of equality, and everyone has an opportunity to make a valued contribution. Like plugs of zoysia grass planted far apart that eventually meld together into a beautiful carpet of lawn, leaders and followers who join in a true community meld together to make good things happen.[68]

Communities of Practice

One way in which people can build a sense of community in organizations is by enabling and supporting communities of practice. Communities of practice often form spontaneously in organizations as people gravitate toward others who share their interests and face similar problems.

Communities of practice are made up of individuals who are informally bound to one another through exposure to a similar set of problems and a common pursuit of solutions.[69] For example, a community of practice might be customer service technicians at Dell Computer Corp. who share tips around the water cooler, a district sales office that has a goal of being the top district office in the country, or people located in various departments of a social services agency who share an interest in computer games. Communities of practice are similar to professional societies—people join them and stay in them *by choice,* because they think they have something to learn and something to contribute. Communities of practice are, by their nature, informal and voluntary. However, anyone can spur the creation of a community of practice simply by purposefully developing personal relationships and facilitating relationships among others throughout the organization who share common interests or goals.

Communities of practice
made up of individuals who are informally bound to one another through exposure to a similar set of problems and a common pursuit of solutions

Both leaders and followers can encourage and support these groups to help people find meaning and purpose and build the relationships needed to move the whole organization forward. However, followers are typically in a better position than formal leaders to enable communities of practice. If a formal leader tries to establish such a group, it might be perceived by others as obligatory, which destroys the voluntary nature of the community. Followers who are willing to assume responsibility and serve others can be highly effective in pulling together communities of practice based on common interests, problems, needs, and objectives. By facilitating relationships across boundaries, communities of practice move both leadership and followership to new levels.

Summary and Interpretation

Leadership doesn't happen without followers, and the important role of followership in organizations is increasingly recognized. People are followers more often than leaders, and effective leaders and followers share similar characteristics. An effective follower is both independent and active in the organization. Being an effective follower depends on not becoming alienated, conforming, passive, nor a pragmatic survivor.

Effective followership is not always easy. Effective followers display the courage to assume responsibility, to serve, to challenge, to participate in transformation, and to leave the organization when necessary. Followers also are aware of their own power and its sources, which include personal and position sources. Strategies for being an effective follower include being a resource, helping the leader be a good leader, building a relationship with the leader, and viewing the leader realistically.

Followers want both their leaders and their colleagues to be honest and competent. However, they want their leaders also to be forward-thinking and inspirational. The two latter traits distinguish the role of leader from follower. Followers want to be led, not controlled. Leaders play an important role by creating an environment that enables people to contribute their best. Leaders can use feedback to develop effective followers by making regular feedback a habit, using elements of storytelling, being generous with positive feedback, and helping followers see feedback as an opportunity. They further expand followers' potential and contributions through self-management leadership, which calls for leaders to share power and responsibility in such a way that anyone can become a leader.

Together, leaders and followers forge a sense of interdependence and community in the organization. Community is characterized by inclusivity, a positive culture, conversation, caring, trust, and shared leadership. Communities of practice are an important tool for building community in the organization. Because they are voluntary by nature, communities of practice are created and sustained primarily by followers rather than by leaders.

Discussion Questions

1. Discuss the role of a follower. Why do you think so little emphasis is given to followership compared to leadership in organizations?
2. Compare the alienated follower with the passive follower. Can you give an example of each? How would you respond to each if you were a leader?

3. Do you think self-management leadership should be considered a leadership style? Why or why not?

4. Which of the five demands on effective followers do you feel is most important? Least important? How does a follower derive the courage and power to be effective? Discuss.

5. Do you think you would respond better to feedback that is presented using elements of storytelling rather than with a traditional performance review format? Discuss. How might using story and metaphor help followers reframe negative feedback?

6. Describe the strategy for managing up that you most prefer. Explain.

7. What do the traits followers want in leaders and in other followers tell us about the roles of each? Discuss.

8. How might the characteristics of effective followership contribute to building community? Discuss.

9. Is the will to leave a job the ultimate courage of a follower, compared to the will to participate in transformation? Which would be hardest for you?

Leadership at Work

Follower Role Play

You are a production supervisor at Hyperlink Systems. Your plant produces circuit boards that are used in Nokia cell phones and IBM computers. Hyperlink is caught in a competitive pricing squeeze, so senior management hired a consultant to study the production department. The plant manager, Sue Harris, asked that the consultant's recommendations be implemented immediately. She thought that total production would increase right away. Weekly production goals were set higher than ever. You don't think she took into account the time required to learn new procedures, and plant workers are under great pressure. A handful of workers have resisted the new work methods because they can produce more circuit boards using the old methods. Most workers have changed to the new methods, but their productivity has not increased. Even after a month, many workers think the old ways are more efficient, faster, and more productive.

You have a couple of other concerns with Harris. She asked you to attend an operations conference, and at the last minute sent another supervisor instead, without any explanation. She has made other promises of supplies and equipment to your section, and then has not followed through. You think she acts too quickly without adequate implementation and follow-up.

You report directly to Harris and are thinking about your responsibility as a follower. Write below specifically how you would handle this situation. Will you confront her with the knowledge you have? When and where will you meet with her? What will you say? How will you get her to hear you?

_____

_____

_____

What style—Effective, Conformist, Passive, Alienated—best describes your response to this situation? Referring to Exhibit 7.3, which strategy would you like to use to assist Harris?

_____

_____

_____

In Class: The instructor can ask students to volunteer to play the role of the plant manager and the production supervisor. A few students can take turns role-playing the production supervisor in front of the class to show different approaches to being a follower. Other students can be asked to provide feedback on each production supervisor's effectiveness and on which approach seems more effective for this situation.

Source: Based on K.J. Keleman, J.E. Garcia, and K.J. Lovelace, *Management Incidents: Role Plays for Management Development*, (Kendall Hunt Publishing Company, 1990), pp. 73–75, 83.

Leadership Development: Cases for Analysis

General Products Britain

Carl Mitchell was delighted to accept a job in the British branch office of General Products, Inc., a multinational consumer products corporation. Two months later, Mitchell was miserable. The problem was George Garrow, the general manager in charge of the British branch, to whom Mitchell reported.

Garrow had worked his way to the general manager position by "keeping his nose clean" and not making mistakes, which he accomplished by avoiding controversial and risky decisions.

As Mitchell complained to his wife, "Any time I ask him to make a decision, he just wants us to dig deeper and provide 30 more pages of data, most of which are irrelevant. I can't get any improvements started."

For example, Mitchell believed that the line of frozen breakfasts and dinners he was in charge of would be more successful if prices were lowered. He and his four product managers spent weeks preparing graphs and charts to justify a lower price. Garrow reviewed the data but kept waffling, asking for more information. His latest request for weather patterns that might affect shopping habits seemed absurd.

Garrow seemed terrified of departing from the status quo. The frozen breakfast and dinner lines still had 1970s-style packaging, even though they had been reformulated for microwave ovens. Garrow would not approve a coupon program in March because in previous years coupons had been run in April. Garrow measured progress not by new ideas or sales results but by hours spent in the office. He arrived early and shuffled memos and charts until late in the evening and expected the same from everyone else.

After 4 months on the job, Mitchell made a final effort to reason with Garrow. He argued that the branch was taking a big risk by avoiding decisions to improve things. Market share was slipping. New pricing and promotion strategies were essential. But Garrow just urged more patience and told Mitchell that he and his product managers would have to build a more solid case. Soon after, Mitchell's two best product managers quit, burned out by the marathon sessions analyzing pointless data without results.

QUESTIONS

1. How would you evaluate Mitchell as a follower? Evaluate his courage and style.

2. If you were Mitchell, what would you do now?

3. If you were Garrow's boss and Mitchell came to see you, what would you say?

Trams Discount Store

"Things are different around here" were the first words Jill heard from her new manager. Mr. Tyler was welcoming Jill back to another summer of working at Trams, a nationwide discount store. Jill was not at all thrilled with the prospect of another summer at Trams, but jobs were hard to find.

Reluctantly, Jill had returned to work the 6:00 P.M. to 10:00 P.M. shift at Trams, where she worked in the ladies' and children's apparel department. Her job consisted of folding clothes, straightening up the racks, and going to the registers for "price checks." Jill's stomach tied in knots as she remembered her previous work experience at Trams. She was originally hired because management had found that college students work hard, and work hard Jill did. Her first boss at Trams was Ms. Williams, who had strict rules that were to be adhered to or else you were fired. There was to be no talking between employees, or to friends and family who entered the store. Each of the four clerks who worked the night shift was assigned a section of the department and was held responsible for it. With the clientele and the number of price checks, it was almost impossible to finish the work, but each night Jill would race against the clock to finish her section. Ms. Williams was always watching through a one-way mirror, so everyone was alert at all times. It seemed there wasn't a minute to breathe—her 20-minute break (and not a minute more!) was hardly enough to recover from the stress of trying to beat the clock.

As Jill talked to Mr. Tyler, she sensed that things really were different. She was introduced to the other employees she'd be working with and, to her surprise, they all seemed to know one another well and enjoy working at Trams. Mr. Tyler then left a little after 6 P.M., leaving the night shift with no supervision! One of the girls explained that they all worked as a team to get the work done. There was constant chatter, and her co-workers seemed eager to get to know her and hear about her experiences at college. It was hard for Jill at first, but she gradually became used to talking and working. The others teased her a bit for working so hard and fast and rushing back to the department at the end of her allotted 20 minutes of break time.

At first, Jill was appalled by the amount of goofing off the clerks did, but as time passed she began to enjoy it and participate. After all, the work got done with time to spare. Maybe things weren't quite as neat as before—and the store manager had alerted the department that sales were down—but no one had asked the workers to change their behavior. Everyone, including Jill, began taking longer and longer breaks. Some of the clerks even snacked on the sales floor, and they were becoming sloppier and sloppier in their work. Jill liked the relaxed atmosphere, but her work ethic and previous training made it hard for her to accept this. She felt responsible for the decline in sales, and she hated seeing the department so untidy. She began to make a few suggestions, but the other workers ignored her and began excluding her from their bantering. She even talked to Mr. Tyler, who agreed that her suggestions were excellent, but he never said anything to the others. Their behavior grew more and more lax. None of the clerks did their job completely, and breaks often stretched to an hour long. Jill knew the quality of her own work went down as well, but she tried hard to keep up with her own job and the jobs of the others. Again, Trams became a nightmare.

The final straw came when her co-worker Tara approached Jill and asked her to change the price tag on a fashionable tank top to $2 and then "back her up" at the register. Jill replied that the tag said $20, not $2. Tara explained that she worked hard, did her job, and never received any reward. The store owed her this "discount." Jill adamantly refused. Tara changed the price tag herself, went to the register to ring it up, and called Jill a college snob. Jill knew it was time for her to act.

Source: Adapted from "Things Are Different Around Here," prepared by Ann Marie Calacci, with the assistance of Frank Yeandel, in John E. Dittrich and Robert A. Zawacki, *People and Organizations: Cases in Management and Organizational Behavior* (Plano, TX: Business Publications, Inc., 1981), pp. 72–75.

QUESTIONS

1. What types of "follower courage" does Jill need in this situation?

2. If you were Jill, what action would you take first? If that didn't produce results, what would you do second? Third?

3. How might Jill use this experience to develop her personal potential?

References

1 Melanie Trottman, "Baggers Get the Sack, But Dawn Marshall Still Excels as One," *The Wall Street Journal* (May 2, 2003), pp. A1, A6.

2 Robert E. Kelley, "In Praise of Followers," *Harvard Business Review* (November/December 1988), pp. 142–148.

3 Bernard M. Bass, *Bass & Stodgill's Handbook of Leadership,* 3rd ed. (New York: Free Press, 1990).

4 Ira Chaleff, *The Courageous Follower: Standing Up To and For Our Leaders* (San Francisco, CA: Berrett-Koehler, 1995).

5 Ira Chaleff, "Learn the Art of Followership," *Government Executive* (February 1997), p. 51.

6 Del Jones, "What Do These 3 Photos Have in Common? They Show Leaders and Their Followers, Winning Combos," *USA Today* (December 10, 2003), p. 1B.

7 D. E. Whiteside, *Command Excellence: What It Takes to Be the Best!,* Department of the Navy, Washington, DC: Naval Military Personnel Command, 1985; Polly LaBarre, "'The Most Important Thing a Captain Can Do Is to See the Ship From the Eyes of the Crew,'" *Fast Company* (April 1999), pp. 115–126.

8 Robert E. Kelley, *The Power of Followership* (New York: Doubleday, 1992).

9 Ibid., 101.

10 Ibid., 111–112.

11 Ibid., 117–118.

12 Ibid., 123.

13 David N. Berg, "Resurrecting the Muse: Followership in Organizations," presented at the 1996 International Society for the Psychoanalytic Study of Organizations (ISPSO) Symposium, New York, NY, June 14–16, 1996.

14 Chaleff, *The Courageous Follower: Standing Up To and For Our Leaders.*

15 Jones, "What Do These 3 Photos Have in Common?"

16 Nick Wingfield, "Apple's No. 2 Has Low Profile, High Impact," *The Wall Street Journal* (October 16, 2006), pp. B1, B9.

17 Major (General Staff) Dr. Ulrich F. Zwygart, "How Much Obedience Does an Officer Need? Beck, Tresckow, and Stauffenberg—Examples of Integrity and Moral Courage for Today's Officer." Combat Studies Institute; U.S. Army Command and General Staff College, Fort Leavenworth, Kansas. Accessed March 29, 2007 at http://www.cgsc.army.mil/carl/resources/csi/Zwygart/zwygart.asp.

18 Ira Sager with Diane Brady, "Big Blue's Blunt Bohemian," *BusinessWeek* (June 14, 1999), pp. 107–112.

19 Merle MacIsaac, "Born Again Basket Case," *Canadian Business* (May 1993), pp. 38–44.

20 Greg Jaffe, "The Two-Star Rebel; For Gen. Batiste, a Tour in Iraq Turned a Loyal Soldier Into Rumsfeld's Most Unexpected Critic," *The Wall Street Journal* (May 13, 2006), p. A1.

21 Stephen R. Covey, *The 7 Habits of Highly Effective People: Powerful Lessons in Personal Change* (New York: Simon & Schuster 1989).

22 This discussion of the seven habits is based on Covey, *The 7 Habits of Highly Effective People;* and Don Hellriegel, John W. Slocum, Jr., and Richard Woodman, *Organizational Behavior,* 8th ed. (Cincinnati, OH: South-Western College Publishing, 1998), pp. 350–352.

23 Stephen R. Covey, *The 7 Habits of Highly Effective People* (New York: Fireside edition/Simon & Schuster, 1990), p. 72.

24 Jia Lynn Yang and Jerry Useem, "Cross-Train Your Brain," *Fortune* (October 30, 2006), pp. 135–136.

25 Sager with Brady, "Big Blue's Blunt Bohemian."

26 David C. Wilson and Graham K. Kenny, "Managerially Perceived Influence Over Interdepartmental Decisions," *Journal of Management Studies* 22 (1985), pp. 155–173; Warren Keith Schilit, "An Examination of Individual Differences as Moderators of Upward Influence Activity in Strategic Decisions," *Human Relations* 39 (1986), pp. 933–953; David Mechanic, "Sources of Power of Lower Participants in Complex Organizations," *Administrative Science Quarterly* 7 (1962), pp. 349–364.

27 Peter Moroz and Brian H. Kleiner, "Playing Hardball in Business Organizations," *IM* (January/February 1994), pp. 9–11.

28 Edward O. Welles, "The Shape of Things to Come," *Inc.* (February 1992), pp. 66–74.

29 Warren Keith Schilit and Edwin A. Locke, "A Study of Upward Influence in Organizations," *Administrative Science Quarterly* 27 (1982), pp. 304–316.

30 Chaleff, *The Courageous Follower: Standing Up To and For Our Leaders.*

31 "Open Mouth, Open Career," sidebar in Michael Warshaw, "Open Mouth, Close Career?" *Fast Company* (December 1998), p. 240ff.

32 David K. Hurst, "How to Manage Your Boss," *Strategy + Business,* Issue 28 (Third Quarter 2002), pp. 99–103; Joseph L. Badaracco, Jr., *Leading Quietly: An Unorthodox Guide to Doing the Right Thing* (Boston: Harvard Business School Press, 2002); Michael Useem, *Leading Up: How to Lead Your Boss So You Both Win* (New York: Crown Business, 2001).

33 Len Schlesinger, "It Doesn't Take a Wizard to Build a Better Boss," *Fast Company* (June/July 1996), pp. 102–107.

34 Hurst, "How to Manage Your Boss."

35 Irvin D. Yalom, M.D., with Ben Yalom, "Mad About Me," *Inc.* (December 1998), pp. 37–38.

36 Judith Sills, "When You're Smarter Than Your Boss," *Psychology Today* (May–June 2006), pp. 58–59; and Frank Pittman, "How to Manage Mom and Dad," *Psychology Today* (November/December 1994), pp. 44–74.

37 Kelley, "In Praise of Followers."

38 Chaleff, *The Courageous Follower: Standing Up To and For Our Leaders;* and John J. Gabarro and John P. Kotter, "Managing Your Boss," *Harvard Business Review* "Best of HBR," (January 2005), pp. 92–99.

39 Christopher Hegarty, *How to Manage Your Boss* (New York: Ballantine 1985), p. 147.

40 Ibid.

41 Robert McGarvey, "And You Thought Your Boss Was Bad," *American Way* (May 1, 2006), pp. 70–74.

42 Chaleff, *The Courageous Follower: Standing Up To and For Our Leaders.*

43 Peter B. Smith and Mark F. Peterson, *Leadership, Organizations and Culture* (London: Sage Publications, 1988), pp. 144–145.

44 Pittman, "How to Manage Mom and Dad."

45 Hegarty, *How to Manage Your Boss.*

46 Pittman, "How to Manage Mom and Dad."

47 Berg, "Resurrecting the Muse."

48 James M. Kouzes and Barry Z. Posner, *Credibility: How Leaders Gain and Lose It, Why People Demand It* (San Francisco: Jossey-Bass, 1993).

49 Kelley, "In Praise of Followers."

50 Jay M. Jackman and Myra H. Strober, "Fear of Feedback," *Harvard Business Review* (April 2003), pp. 101–108.

51 McKinsey & Company's *War for Talent 2000 Survey,* reported in E. Michaels, H. Handfield-Jones, and B. Axelrod, *The War for Talent* (Boston: Harvard Business School Press, 2001), p. 100.

52 John C. Kunich and Richard I. Lester, "Leadership and the Art of Feedback: Feeding the Hands That Back Us," *The Journal of Leadership Studies* 3, no. 4 (1996), pp. 3–22.

53 Mary Mavis, "Painless Performance Evaluations," *Training & Development* (October 1994), pp. 40–44.

54 Gary Rivlin, "He Naps. He Sings. And He Isn't Michael Dell," *The New York Times* (September 11, 2005), pp. 3–1, 3–7.

55 Based on Mark D. Cannon and Robert Witherspoon, "Actionable Feedback: Unlocking the Power of Learning and Performance Improvement," *Academy of Management Executive* 19, no. 2 (2005), pp. 120–134.

56 Thomas A. Stewart, "The Cunning Plots of Leadership," *Fortune* (September 7, 1998), pp. 165–166.

57 Jackman and Strober, "Fear of Feedback."

58 Berg, "Resurrecting the Muse."

59 Charles C. Manz and Henry P. Sims, Jr., "Leading Workers to Lead Themselves: The External Leadership of Self-Managing Work Teams," *Administrative Science Quarterly* (March 1987), pp. 106–129; and Charles C. Manz, *Mastering Self-Leadership: Empowering Yourself for Personal Excellence* (Englewood Cliffs, NJ: Prentice Hall, 1992).

60 Iain L. Densten and Judy H. Gray, "The Links Between Followership and the Experiential Learning Model: Followership Coming of Age," *The Journal of Leadership Studies* 8, no. 1 (2001), pp. 70–76.

61 Robert C. Ford and Myron D. Fottler, "Empowerment: A Matter of Degree," *Academy of Management Executive* 9 (1995), pp. 21–31.

62 Keith H. Hammonds, "You Can't Lead Without Making Sacrifices," *Fast Company* (June 2001), pp. 106–116.

63 Susan Komives, Nance Lucas, and Timothy R. McMahon, *Exploring Leadership* (San Francisco: Jossey-Bass, 1998), p. 229.

64 Juanita Brown and David Isaacs, "Building Corporations as Communities: The Best of Both Worlds," in *Community Building: Renewing Spirit & Learning in Business,* Kazimierz Gozdz, ed. (San Francisco: Sterling & Stone, Inc., 1995), pp. 69–83.

65 These are based on M. Scott Peck, *The Different Drum: Community Making and Peace* (New York: Touchstone, 1987); J. W. Gardner, *On Leadership* (New York: The Free Press), pp. 116–118; and Komives, et al., *Exploring Leadership.*

66 W. B. Gudykunst, *Bridging Differences: Effective Intergroup Communication* (Newbury Park, CA: Sage, 1991), p. 146.

67 Brown and Isaacs, "Building Corporations as Communities"; Glenna Gerard and Linda Teurfs, "Dialogue and Organizational Transformation," in Kazimierz Gozdz, ed., *Community Building* (San Francisco: Sterling & Stone, Inc., 1995), pp. 142–153; and Edgar G. Schein, "On Dialogue, Culture, and Organizational Learning," *Organizational Dynamics* (Autumn 1993), pp. 40–51.

68 Brown and Isaacs, "Building Corporations as Communities."

69 Verna Allee, *The Knowledge Evolution* (Oxford: Butterworth-Heinemann, 1997), pp. 218–219; Thomas A. Stewart, *Intellectual Capital* (New York: Bantam Books, 1998), pp. 96–100; and W. H. Drath and C. J. Palus, *Making Common Sense: Leadership as Meaning-Making in a Community of Practice* (Greensboro, NC: Center for Creative Leadership, 1994).

PART 4
The Leader as a Relationship Builder

Getty Images

Chapter 8

Motivation and Empowerment

Not so long ago, Kwik-Fit Financial Services was struggling. Morale at the Lanarkshire, Scotland-based insurance intermediary was dismal. People didn't want to come to work, and most of those who showed up at the call center found it hard to slog through the day. The company was having a hard time recruiting workers to make up for a 52 percent staff turnover rate, and top managers had doubts about the firm's future profitability.

Managing Director Martin Oliver and Human Resource Director Keren Edwards embarked on a campaign to make Kwik-Fit "a fantastic place to work." The two leaders started by listening, and they learned that most employees felt like the company didn't care about them. So, Edwards led a series of workshops that involved every employee in examining life at the call center and how to make it better. In all, 32 workshops generated more than six thousand ideas. The company then charged teams made up of managers and rank-and-file volunteers with the task of implementing selected ideas. As a result, Kwik-Fit employees now work in a completely renovated building and enjoy bonuses, performance-based pay, flextime, flexible benefits, and onsite day care. In addition, they counter job stress by taking advantage of the free corporate gym; a cheerful "chill-out room" complete with TV, pool tables and computer games; yoga and tai chi classes; and a massage service. And then there's Rob Hunter, the company's first "minister of fun," who organizes special theme days, social evenings, annual sales awards, and the holiday party. "Staff needs to work hard and play hard to be motivated and productive," Hunter observes.

Kwik-Fit has gone from being perceived as a company that doesn't care about its workers to one where employees feel a sense of ownership, belonging, and engagement. By 2006, absenteeism had declined significantly, turnover was down 22 percent, and 80 percent of employees said they would recommend Kwik-Fit as a great place to work. Moreover, 2005 profits rose by 50 percent, thanks to improved customer service. As Oliver said, "You cannot give good customer service if your employees don't feel good about coming to work."[1]

Martin Oliver and Keren Edwards improved motivation at Kwik-Fit by creating an environment where people feel that they matter. Rewards such as bonuses and performance-based pay, and amenities such as the corporate gym and a massage service, contribute to employee satisfaction, but they are only part of the story. Equally important to motivation at Kwik-Fit is that employees feel that managers genuinely care about them and are willing to listen to their needs and concerns.

Many other leaders have found that creating an environment where people feel valued is a key to high motivation. This chapter explores motivation in organizations and examines how leaders can bring out the best in followers. We examine the difference between intrinsic and extrinsic rewards and discuss how these rewards meet the needs of followers. Individuals have both lower and higher needs, and there are different methods of motivation to meet those needs. The chapter presents several theories of motivation, with particular attention to the differences between leadership and conventional management methods for creating a motivated workforce. The final sections of the chapter explore empowerment and other recent motivational tools that do not rely on traditional reward and punishment methods.

Leadership and Motivation

Most of us get up in the morning, go to school or work, and behave in ways that are predictably our own. We usually respond to our environment and the people in it with little thought as to why we work hard, enjoy certain classes, or find some recreational activities so much fun. Yet all these behaviors are motivated by something. **Motivation** refers to the forces either internal or external to a person that arouse enthusiasm and persistence to pursue a certain course of action. Employee motivation affects productivity, and so part of a leader's job is to channel followers' motivation toward the accomplishment of the organization's vision and goals.[2] The study of motivation helps leaders understand what prompts people to initiate action, what influences their choice of action, and why they persist in that action over time.

Exhibit 8.1 illustrates a simple model of human motivation. People have basic needs, such as for food, recognition, or monetary gain, which translate into an internal tension that motivates specific behaviors with which to fulfill the need. To the extent that the behavior is successful, the person is rewarded when the need is satisfied. The reward also informs the person that the behavior was appropriate and can be used again in the future.

The importance of motivation, as illustrated in Exhibit 8.1, is that it can lead to behaviors that reflect high performance within organizations. Studies have found that high employee motivation and high organizational performance and profits go hand in hand.[3] An extensive survey by the Gallup organization, for example, found that when all of an organization's employees are highly motivated and performing at their peak, customers are 70 percent more loyal, turnover drops by 70 percent, and profits jump 40 percent.[4] Leaders can use motivation theory to help satisfy followers' needs and simultaneously encourage high work performance. When workers are not motivated to achieve organizational goals, the fault is often with the leader.

Intrinsic and Extrinsic Rewards

Rewards can be either intrinsic or extrinsic, systemwide, or individual. Exhibit 8.2 illustrates the categories of rewards, combining intrinsic and extrinsic rewards with those that are applied systemwide or individually.[5] **Intrinsic rewards** are the internal satisfactions a person receives in the process of performing a particular action. Solving a problem to benefit others may fulfill a personal mission, or the completion of a complex task may bestow a pleasant feeling of accomplishment. An intrinsic reward is internal and under the control of the individual, such as to engage in task behavior to satisfy a need for competency and self-determination. Consider the motivation of Oprah Winfrey. Winfrey is an Emmy award-winning

Motivation
the forces either internal or external to a person that arouse enthusiasm and persistence to pursue a certain course of action

Intrinsic rewards
internal satisfactions a person receives in the process of performing a particular action

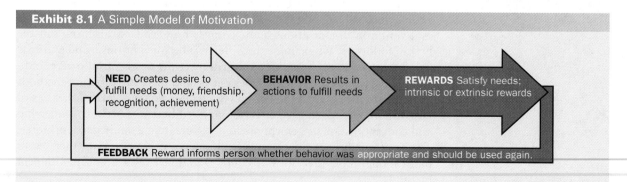

Exhibit 8.1 A Simple Model of Motivation

NEED Creates desire to fulfill needs (money, friendship, recognition, achievement)

BEHAVIOR Results in actions to fulfill needs

REWARDS Satisfy needs; intrinsic or extrinsic rewards

FEEDBACK Reward informs person whether behavior was appropriate and should be used again.

Exhibit 8.2 Examples of Intrinsic and Extrinsic Rewards

	Extrinsic	Intrinsic
Individual	Large merit increase	Feeling of self-fulfillment
System-wide	Insurance benefits	Pride in being part of a "winning" organization

Source: Adapted from Richard M. Steers, Lyman W. Porter, and Gregory A. Bigley, *Motivation and Leadership at Work*, 6th ed. (New York: McGraw-Hill, 1996), p. 498. Reprinted with permission of the McGraw-Hill Companies.

television talk show host and is personally worth an estimated $1.5 billion. Yet Winfrey says she has never been motivated by money or a desire for power and prestige. Instead, she is driven to high performance by a personal mission to serve others by uplifting, enlightening, encouraging, and transforming how people see themselves.[6]

Conversely, **extrinsic rewards** are given by another person, typically a supervisor, and include promotions and pay increases. Extrinsic rewards at United Scrap Metal, for example, include annual bonuses, a 401(k) plan, and an annual $2,000 tuition-reimbursement program.[7] Because they originate externally as a result of pleasing others, extrinsic rewards compel individuals to engage in a task behavior for an outside source that provides what they need, such as money to survive in modern society. Think about the difference in motivation for polishing a car if it belongs to you versus if you work at a car wash. Your good feelings from making your own car shine would be intrinsic. However, buffing a car that is but one of many in a day's work requires the extrinsic reward of a paycheck.[8]

Rewards can be given systemwide or on an individual basis. **Systemwide rewards** apply the same to all people within an organization or within a specific category or department. **Individual rewards** may differ among people within the same organization or department. An extrinsic, systemwide reward could be insurance benefits or vacation time available to an entire organization or category of people, such as those who have been with the organization for six months or more. An intrinsic, systemwide reward would be the sense of pride that comes from within by virtue of contributing to a "winning" organization. An extrinsic, individual reward is a promotion or a bonus check. An intrinsic, individual reward would be a sense of self-fulfillment that an individual derives from his or her work.

Although extrinsic rewards are important, leaders work especially hard to help followers achieve intrinsic rewards—both individually and systemwide. We all know that people voluntarily invest significant time and energy in activities they enjoy, such as hobbies, charitable causes, or community projects. Similarly, employees who get intrinsic satisfaction from their jobs often put forth increased effort. In addition, leaders genuinely care about others and want them to feel good about their work. Leaders create an environment that brings out the best in people.

Extrinsic rewards
rewards given by another person, typically a supervisor, such as pay increases and promotions

Systemwide rewards
rewards that apply the same to all people within an organization or within a specific category or department

Individual rewards
rewards that differ among individuals within the same organization or department

On the job, people may always have to perform some activities they don't particularly like, but leaders try to match followers with jobs and tasks that provide individual intrinsic rewards. They also strive to create an environment where people feel valued and feel that they are contributing to something worthwhile, helping followers achieve systemwide intrinsic rewards. In *Fortune* magazine's annual list of "100 Best Companies to Work For," one of the primary characteristics shared by best companies is that they are *purpose-driven;* that is, people have a sense that what they do matters and makes a positive difference in the world.[9] One example is Les Schwab Tire Centers, where employees feel like partners united toward a goal of making people's lives easier. Stores fix flats for free, and some have been known to install tires hours before opening time for an emergency trip. Employees frequently stop to help stranded motorists. Schwab rewards people with a generous profit-sharing plan for everyone and promotes store managers solely from within. These external rewards supplement the intrinsic rewards people get from their work, leading to extremely high motivation.[10]

Action Memo

As a leader, you can provide extrinsic rewards, such as promotions, pay raises, and praise, but also help followers achieve intrinsic rewards and meet their higher-level needs for accomplishment, growth, and fulfillment.

Higher Versus Lower Needs

Intrinsic rewards appeal to the "higher" needs of individuals, such as for accomplishment, competence, fulfillment, and self-determination. Extrinsic rewards appeal to the "lower" needs of individuals, such as for material comfort and basic safety and security. Exhibit 8.3 outlines the distinction between conventional management and leadership approaches to motivation based on people's needs. Conventional

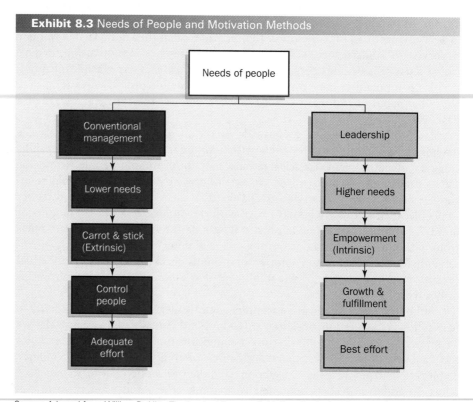

Exhibit 8.3 Needs of People and Motivation Methods

Source: Adapted from William D. Hitt, *The Leader-Manager: Guidelines for Action* (Columbus, OH: Battelle Press, 1988), p. 153.

management approaches often appeal to an individual's lower, basic needs and rely on extrinsic rewards and punishments—carrot-and-stick methods—to motivate subordinates to behave in desired ways. These approaches are effective, but they are based on controlling the behavior of people by manipulating their decisions about how to act. The higher needs of people may be unmet in favor of utilizing their labor in exchange for external rewards. Under conventional management, people perform adequately to receive the "carrot," or avoid the "stick," because they will not necessarily derive intrinsic satisfaction from their work.

The leadership approach strives to motivate people by providing them with the opportunity to satisfy higher needs and become intrinsically rewarded. For example, employees in companies that are infused with a social mission, and that find ways to enrich the lives of others, are typically more highly motivated because of the intrinsic rewards they get from helping other people.[11] Leaders at any company can enable people to find meaning in their work. At FedEx, for example, many employees take pride in getting people the items they need on time, whether it be a work report that is due, a passport for a holiday trip to Jamaica, or an emergency order of medical supplies.[12] Remember, however, that the source of an intrinsic reward is internal to the follower. Thus, what is intrinsically rewarding to one individual may not be so to another. One way in which leaders try to enable all followers to achieve intrinsic rewards is by giving them more control over their own work and the power to affect outcomes. When leaders empower others, allowing them the freedom to determine their own actions, subordinates reward themselves intrinsically for good performance. They may become creative, innovative, and develop a greater commitment to their objectives. Thus motivated, they often achieve their best possible performance.

Ideally, work behaviors should satisfy both lower and higher needs, as well as serve the mission of the organization. Unfortunately, this is often not the case. The leader's motivational role, then, is to create a situation that integrates the needs of people—especially higher needs—and the fundamental objectives of the organization.

Needs-Based Theories of Motivation

Needs-based theories emphasize the needs that motivate people. At any point in time, people have basic needs such as those for monetary reward or achievement. These needs are the source of an internal drive that motivates behavior to fulfill the needs. An individual's needs are like a hidden catalog of the things he or she wants and will work to get. To the extent that leaders understand worker needs, they can design the reward system to reinforce employees for directing energies and priorities toward attainment of shared goals.

Hierarchy of Needs Theory

Probably the most famous needs-based theory is the one developed by Abraham Maslow.[13] Maslow's **hierarchy of needs theory** proposes that humans are motivated by multiple needs and those needs exist in a hierarchical order, as illustrated in Exhibit 8.4, wherein the higher needs cannot be satisfied until the lower needs are met. Maslow identified five general levels of motivating needs.

- **Physiological** The most basic human physiological needs include food, water, and oxygen. In the organizational setting, these are reflected in the needs for adequate heat, air, and base salary to ensure survival.

Hierarchy of needs theory
Maslow's theory proposes that humans are motivated by multiple needs and those needs exist in a hierarchical order

Exhibit 8.4 Maslow's Hierarchy of Needs

Need Hierarchy	Fulfillment on the Job
Self-actualization Needs	Opportunities for advancement, autonomy, growth, creativity
Esteem Needs	Recognition, approval, high status, increased responsibilities
Belongingness Needs	Work groups, clients, co-workers, supervisors
Safety Needs	Safe work, fringe benefits, job security
Physiological Needs	Heat, air, base salary

- **Safety** Next is the need for a safe and secure physical and emotional environment and freedom from threats—that is, for freedom from violence and for an orderly society. In an organizational workplace, safety needs reflect the needs for safe jobs, fringe benefits, and job security.

- **Belongingness** People have a desire to be accepted by their peers, have friendships, be part of a group, and be loved. In the organization, these needs influence the desire for good relationships with co-workers, participation in a work team, and a positive relationship with supervisors.

- **Esteem** The need for esteem relates to the desires for a positive self-image and for attention, recognition, and appreciation from others. Within organizations, esteem needs reflect a motivation for recognition, an increase in responsibility, high status, and credit for contributions to the organization.

- **Self-actualization** The highest need category, self-actualization, represents the need for self-fulfillment: developing one's full potential, increasing one's competence, and becoming a better person. Self-actualization needs can be met in the organization by providing people with opportunities to grow, be empowered and creative, and acquire training for challenging assignments and advancement.

According to Maslow's theory, physiology, safety, and belonging are deficiency needs. These low-order needs take priority—they must be satisfied before higher-order, or growth needs, are activated. The needs are satisfied in sequence: Physiological needs are satisfied before safety needs, safety needs are satisfied before social needs, and so on. A person desiring physical safety will devote his or her efforts to securing a safer environment and will not be concerned with esteem or self-actualization. Once a need is satisfied, it declines in importance and the next higher need is activated. When a union wins good pay and working conditions for its members, for example, basic needs will be met and union members may then want to have social and esteem needs met in the workplace.

Action Memo

You can evaluate your current or a previous job according to Maslow's needs theory and Herzberg's two-factor theory by answering the questions in Leader's Self-Insight 8.1 on page 232.

Two-Factor Theory

Frederick Herzberg developed another popular needs-based theory of motivation called the *two-factor theory*.[14] Herzberg interviewed hundreds of workers about times when they were highly motivated to work and other times when they were dissatisfied and unmotivated to work. His findings suggested that the work characteristics associated with dissatisfaction were quite different from those pertaining to satisfaction, which prompted the notion that two factors influence work motivation.

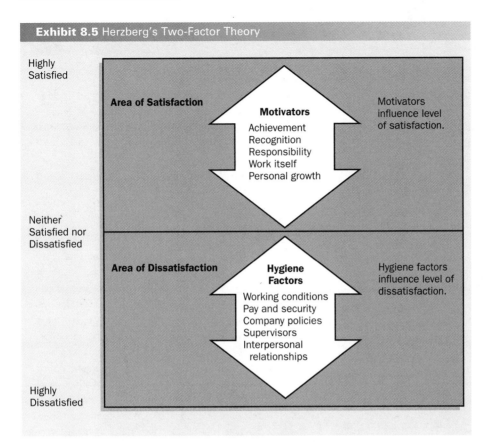

Exhibit 8.5 Herzberg's Two-Factor Theory

Highly Satisfied

Area of Satisfaction

Motivators
Achievement
Recognition
Responsibility
Work itself
Personal growth

Motivators influence level of satisfaction.

Neither Satisfied nor Dissatisfied

Area of Dissatisfaction

Hygiene Factors
Working conditions
Pay and security
Company policies
Supervisors
Interpersonal relationships

Hygiene factors influence level of dissatisfaction.

Highly Dissatisfied

Exhibit 8.5 illustrates the two-factor theory. The center of the scale is neutral, meaning that workers are neither satisfied nor dissatisfied. Herzberg believed that two entirely separate dimensions contribute to an employee's behavior at work. The first dimension, called **hygiene factors**, involves the presence or absence of job dissatisfiers, such as working conditions, pay, company policies, and interpersonal relationships. When hygiene factors are poor, work is dissatisfying. This is similar to the concept of deficiency needs described by Maslow. Good hygiene factors remove the dissatisfaction, but they do not in themselves cause people to become highly satisfied and motivated in their work.

The second set of factors does influence job satisfaction. **Motivators** fulfill high-level needs such as needs for achievement, recognition, responsibility, and opportunity for growth. Herzberg believed that when motivators are present, workers are highly motivated and satisfied. Thus, hygiene factors and motivators represent two distinct factors that influence motivation. Hygiene factors work in the area of lower-level needs, and their absence causes dissatisfaction. Unsafe working conditions or a noisy work environment will cause people to be dissatisfied, but their correction will not cause a high level of work enthusiasm and satisfaction. Higher-level motivators such as challenge, responsibility, and recognition must be in place before employees will be highly motivated to excel at their work.

The implication of the two-factor theory for leaders is clear. People have multiple needs, and the leader's role is to go beyond the removal of dissatisfiers to the use of motivators to meet higher-level needs and propel employees toward greater enthusiasm and satisfaction. At steel-maker Nucor, leaders have created one of the most motivated and dynamic workforces in the United States by incorporating motivators to meet people's higher level needs.

Hygiene factors
the first dimension of Herzberg's two-factor theory; involves working conditions, pay, company policies, and interpersonal relationships

Motivators
the second dimension of Herzberg's two-factor theory; involves job satisfaction and meeting higher-level needs such as achievement, recognition, and opportunity for growth

Action Memo
As a leader, you can use good working conditions, satisfactory pay, and comfortable relationships to reduce job dissatisfaction. To spur greater follower satisfaction and enthusiasm, you can employ motivators— challenge, responsibility, and recognition.

Think of a specific job (current or previous) you have held. If you are a full-time student, think of your classes and study activities as your job. Please answer the questions below about those work activities. Indicate whether each item below is Mostly False or Mostly True for you.

	Mostly False	Mostly True
1. I feel physically safe at work.	_____	_____
2. I have good health benefits.	_____	_____
3. I am satisfied with what I'm getting paid for my work.	_____	_____
4. I feel that my job is secure as long as I want it.	_____	_____
5. I have good friends at work.	_____	_____
6. I have enough time away from my work to enjoy other things in life.	_____	_____
7. I feel appreciated at work.	_____	_____
8. People at my workplace respect me as a professional and expert in my field.	_____	_____
9. I feel that my job allows me to realize my full potential.	_____	_____
10. I feel that I am realizing my potential as an expert in my line of work.	_____	_____
11. I feel I'm always learning new things that help me to do my work better.	_____	_____
12. There is a lot of creativity involved in my work.	_____	_____

Scoring and Interpretation

Compute the Number of Mostly True responses for the questions that represent each level of Maslow's hierarchy, as indicated below, and write your score where indicated:

Questions 1–2: Physiological and health needs. Score = _____

Questions 3–4: Economic and safety needs. Score = _____

Questions 5–6: Belonging and social needs. Score = _____

Questions 7–8: Esteem needs. Score = _____

Questions 9–12: Self-actualization needs. Score = _____

These five scores represent how you see your needs being met in the work situation. An average score for overall need satisfaction (all 12 questions) is typically 6, and the average for lower level needs tends to be higher than for higher level needs. Is that true for you? What do your five scores say about the need satisfaction in your job? Which needs are less filled for you? How would that affect your choice of a new job? In developed countries, lower needs are often taken for granted, and work motivation is based on the opportunity to meet higher needs. Compare your scores to those of another student. How does that person's array of five scores differ from yours? Ask questions about the student's job to help explain the difference in scores.

Re-read the 12 questions. Which questions would you say are about the *motivators* in Herzberg's Two-Factor Theory? Which questions are about *hygiene factors?* Calculate the average points for the motivator questions and the average points for the hygiene factor questions. What do you interpret from your scores on these two factors compared to the five levels of needs in Maslow's hierarchy?

Source: These questions are taken from *Social Indicators Research* 55 (2001), pp. 241–302, "A New Measure of Quality of Work Life (QWL) based on Need Satisfaction and Spillover Theories," M. Joseph Sirgy, David Efraty, Phillip Siegel and Dong-Jin Lee. Copyright © and reprinted with kind permission of Kluwer Academic Publishers.

IN THE LEAD

Daniel R. DiMicco, Nucor

Since Daniel R. DiMicco took over at Nucor in 2000, sales have jumped from $4.6 billion to $12.7 billion, income has grown from $311 million to $1.3 billion, and the company shipped more steel in 2005 than any other company in the United States. Those results speak for the extraordinary effort made by Nucor's highly motivated employees. As top executive of the Charlotte, North Carolina-based minimill, DiMicco follows the employee-centered, egalitarian management philosophy of Nucor's legendary former CEO, the late F. Kenneth Iverson.

At Nucor, rewarding people richly, treating them with respect, and giving them real power sparks amazing motivation and performance. Employees are organized into teams in a decentralized, flattened, four-level organization. With most decision-making authority pushed down to the division level, employees run their part of the business as if it were their own. It's not unusual for front-line workers to take it upon themselves to work 20-hour shifts to get a disabled plant up and running, for example. As Iverson once put it, "Instead of telling people what to do and then hounding them to do it, our managers focus on shaping an environment that frees employees to determine what they can do and should do, to the benefit of themselves and the business. We've found that their answers drive the progress of our business faster than our own."

Base pay at Nucor is relatively low, but under the company's performance-based compensation system, weekly bonuses can average 80 to 150 percent of a steelworker's base pay. Even though base pay starts at around $10 an hour, the average Nucor steelworker took home around $100,000 in 2005. In a bad year, everyone—the CEO included—shares the pain. The financial incentives are important, but motivation at Nucor relies more on leaders' determined focus on creating an environment where front-line workers can thrive. It's an environment that long-time employees have called "magical."[15]

Leaders at Nucor have successfully applied the two-factor theory to provide both hygiene factors and motivators, thus meeting employees higher as well as lower needs. It's a formula that has created happy, engaged employees and a successful organization.

Acquired Needs Theory

Another needs-based theory was developed by David McClelland. The **acquired needs theory** proposes that certain types of needs are acquired during an individual's lifetime. In other words, people are not born with these needs, but may learn them through their life experiences.[16] For example, the parents of Bill Strickland, who founded and runs a highly successful non-profit organization, always encouraged him to follow his dreams. When he wanted to go south to work with the Freedom Riders in the 1960s, they supported him. His plans for tearing up the family basement and making a photography studio were met with equal enthusiasm. Strickland thus developed a *need for achievement* that enabled him to accomplish amazing results later in life.[17] You will learn more about Bill Strickland's leadership approach in Chapter 12. Three needs most frequently studied are the need for achievement, need for affiliation, and need for power.

Acquired needs theory
McClelland's theory that proposes that certain types of needs (achievement, affiliation, power) are acquired during an individual's lifetime

- *Need for achievement*—the desire to accomplish something difficult, attain a high standard of success, master complex tasks, and surpass others.

- *Need for affiliation*—the desire to form close personal relationships, avoid conflict, and establish warm friendships.

- *Need for power*—the desire to influence or control others, be responsible for others, and have authority over others.

For more than 20 years, McClelland studied human needs and their implications for management. People with a high need for achievement tend to enjoy work that is entrepreneurial and innovative. People who have a high need for affiliation are successful "integrators," whose job is to coordinate the work of people and departments.[18] Integrators include brand managers and project managers, positions that require excellent people skills. A high need for power is often associated with successful attainment of top levels in the organizational hierarchy. For example, McClelland studied managers at AT&T for 16 years and found that those with a high need for power were more likely to pursue a path of continued promotion over time.

In summary, needs-based theories focus on underlying needs that motivate how people behave. The hierarchy of needs theory, the two-factor theory, and the acquired needs theory all identify the specific needs that motivate people. Leaders can work to meet followers' needs and hence elicit appropriate and successful work behaviors.

Other Motivation Theories

Three additional motivation theories, the reinforcement perspective, expectancy theory, and equity theory, focus primarily on extrinsic rewards and punishments. Relying on extrinsic rewards and punishments is sometimes referred to as the "carrot-and-stick" approach.[19] The behavior that produces a desired outcome is rewarded with "carrots," such as a pay raise or a promotion. Conversely, undesirable or unproductive behavior brings the "stick," such as a demotion or withholding a pay raise. Carrot-and-stick approaches tend to focus on lower needs, although higher needs can sometimes also be met.

Reinforcement Perspective on Motivation

The reinforcement approach to employee motivation sidesteps the deeper issue of employee needs described in the needs-based theories. **Reinforcement theory** simply looks at the relationship between behavior and its consequences by changing or modifying followers' on-the-job behavior through the appropriate use of immediate rewards or punishments.

Behavior modification is the name given to the set of techniques by which reinforcement theory is used to modify behavior.[20] The basic assumption underlying behavior modification is the **law of effect**, which states that positively reinforced behavior tends to be repeated, and behavior that is not reinforced tends not to be repeated. **Reinforcement** is defined as anything that causes a certain behavior to be repeated or inhibited. Four ways in which leaders use reinforcement to modify or shape employee behavior are: positive reinforcement, negative reinforcement, punishment, and extinction.

Positive reinforcement is the administration of a pleasant and rewarding consequence following a behavior. A good example of positive reinforcement is immediate praise for an employee who arrives on time or does a little extra in his or her work. The pleasant consequence will increase the likelihood of the excellent work behavior occurring again. Studies have shown that positive reinforcement does help to improve performance. In addition, non-financial reinforcements such as positive feedback, social recognition, and attention are just as effective as financial rewards.[21] Indeed, many people consider factors other than money to be more important. Nelson Motivation Inc. conducted a survey of 750 employees across various industries to assess the value they placed on various rewards. Cash and other monetary awards came in dead last. The most valued rewards involved praise and manager support and involvement.[22]

Negative reinforcement is the withdrawal of an unpleasant consequence once a behavior is improved. Sometimes referred to as *avoidance learning*, negative reinforcement means people learn to perform the desired behavior by avoiding unpleasant situations. A simple example would be when a supervisor stops reprimanding an employee for tardiness once the employee starts getting to work on time.

Reinforcement theory
a motivational theory that looks at the relationship between behavior and its consequences by changing or modifying followers' on-the-job behavior through the appropriate use of immediate rewards or punishments

Behavior modification
the set of techniques by which reinforcement theory is used to modify behavior

Law of effect
states that positively reinforced behavior tends to be repeated and behavior that is not reinforced tends not to be repeated

Reinforcement
anything that causes a certain behavior to be repeated or inhibited

Positive reinforcement
the administration of a pleasant and rewarding consequence following a behavior

Negative reinforcement
the withdrawal of an unpleasant consequence once a behavior is improved

Punishment is the imposition of unpleasant outcomes on an employee. Punishment typically occurs following undesirable behavior. For example, a supervisor may berate an employee for performing a task incorrectly. The supervisor expects that the negative outcome will serve as a punishment and reduce the likelihood of the behavior recurring. The use of punishment in organizations is controversial and often criticized because it fails to indicate the correct behavior.

Extinction is the withdrawal of a positive reward, meaning that behavior is no longer reinforced and hence is less likely to occur in the future. If a perpetually tardy employee fails to receive praise and pay raises, he or she will begin to realize that the behavior is not producing desired outcomes. The behavior will gradually disappear if it is continually not reinforced.

A *New York Times* reporter wrote a humorous article about how she learned to stop nagging and instead use reinforcement theory to shape her husband's behavior after studying how professionals train animals.[23] When her husband did something she liked, such as throw a dirty shirt in the hamper, she would use *positive reinforcement,* thanking him or giving him a hug and a kiss. Undesirable behaviors, such as throwing dirty clothes on the floor, on the other hand, were simply ignored, applying the principle of *extinction.*

Leaders can also apply reinforcement theory to influence the behavior of followers. They can reinforce behavior after each and every occurrence, which is referred to as *continuous reinforcement,* or they can choose to reinforce behavior intermittently, which is referred to as *partial reinforcement.* Some of today's companies use a continuous reinforcement schedule by offering people cash, game tokens, or points that can be redeemed for prizes each time they perform the desired behavior. Leaders at LDF Sales & Distributing, for example, tried a program called "The Snowfly Slots," developed by management professor Brooks Mitchell, to cut inventory losses. Workers received tokens each time they double-checked the quantity of a shipment. Since LDF started using Snowfly, inventory losses have fallen by 50 percent, saving the company $31,000 a year.[24]

With partial reinforcement, the desired behavior is reinforced often enough to make the employee believe the behavior is worth repeating, even though it is not rewarded every time it is demonstrated. Continuous reinforcement can be very effective for establishing new behaviors, but research has found that partial reinforcement is more effective for maintaining behavior over extended time periods.[25]

Some leaders have applied reinforcement theory very effectively to shape followers' behavior. Garry Ridge, CEO of WD-40 Company, which makes the popular lubricant used for everything from loosening bolts to removing scuff marks from floors, wanted to encourage people to talk about their failures so the company could learn from them. He offered prizes to anyone who would e-mail and share their "learning moments," and each respondent would have the chance to win an all-expenses paid vacation. The positive reinforcement, combined with the company's "blame-free" policy, motivated people to share ideas that have helped WD-40 keep learning and growing.[26]

Expectancy Theory

Expectancy theory suggests that motivation depends on individuals' mental expectations about their ability to perform tasks and receive desired rewards. Expectancy theory is associated with the work of Victor Vroom, although a number of scholars have made contributions in this area.[27] Expectancy theory is concerned not with understanding types of needs, but with the thinking process that individuals use to achieve rewards.

Punishment
the imposition of unpleasant outcomes on an employee following undesirable behavior

Extinction
the withdrawal of a positive reward, meaning that behavior is no longer reinforced and hence is less likely to occur in the future

Expectancy theory
a theory that suggests that motivation depends on individuals' mental expectations about their ability to perform tasks and receive desired rewards

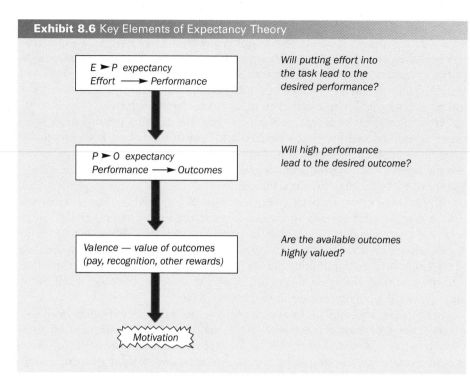

Exhibit 8.6 Key Elements of Expectancy Theory

Expectancy theory is based on the relationship among the individual's effort, the possibility of high performance, and the desirability of outcomes following high performance. Exhibit 8.6 illustrates these elements and the relationships among them. The $E > P$ expectancy is the probability that putting effort into a task will lead to high performance. For this expectancy to be high, the individual must have the ability, previous experience, and necessary tools, information, and opportunity to perform. The $P > O$ expectancy involves whether successful performance will lead to the desired outcome. If this expectancy is high, the individual will be more highly motivated. Valence refers to the value of outcomes to the individual. If the outcomes that are available from high effort and good performance are not valued by an employee, motivation will be low. Likewise, if outcomes have a high value, motivation will be higher. A simple example to illustrate the relationships in Exhibit 8.6 is Alfredo Torres, a salesperson at Diamond Gift Shop. If Alfredo believes that increased selling effort will lead to higher personal sales, his $E > P$ expectancy would be considered high. Moreover, if he also believes that higher personal sales will lead to a promotion or pay raise, the $P > O$ expectancy is also high. Finally, if Alfredo places a high value on the promotion or pay raise, valence is high and he will be highly motivated. For an employee to be highly motivated, all three factors in the expectancy model must be high.[28]

Like the path–goal theory of leadership described in Chapter 3, expectancy theory is personalized to subordinates' needs and goals. A leader's responsibility is to help followers meet their needs while attaining organizational goals. One employee may want to be promoted to a position of increased responsibility, and another may want a good relationship with peers. To increase motivation, leaders can increase followers' expectancy by clarifying individual needs, providing the desired outcomes, and ensuring that individuals have the ability and support needed

Action Memo
As a leader, you can change follower behavior through the appropriate use of rewards and punishments. To establish new behaviors quickly, you can reinforce the desired behavior after each and every occurrence. To sustain the behaviors over a long time period, try reinforcing the behaviors intermittently.

to perform well and attain their desired outcomes. One interesting illustration of the use of expectancy theory is the Pathways to Rewards program, sponsored by non-profit organization Project Match as a way to help poor people improve their lives.

Project Match, Pathways to Rewards

It's a perpetual problem for social service agencies working with the poor: How do you get people who feel tired and beaten down to pull themselves up and take positive steps toward improving their lives? A few small, experimental programs around the United States are using incentives to motivate poor people to look for jobs, enroll in literacy classes, keep their houses clean, or pay their rent on time.

One such program, Pathways to Rewards, sponsored by Project Match, has doled out about $19,000 in prizes such as DVD players, bicycles, clothing, or food certificates in a low-income area near Chicago. Participants in the program meet with counselors to establish goals and then pick the rewards they'd like to work toward. One woman, who has struggled with depression, uses the program to motivate herself to keep her doctor's appointments, get her children dressed for school, and do volunteer work to get out of the house. When the person accumulates the number of points needed for the desired item, the counselor arranges for a gift certificate or check written to the store for the purchase. Those who reach their goals are also recognized at an awards banquet, where their names and point totals are displayed on a big screen as they are honored on stage. "They flash the lights and take your picture and make you feel like you're a star," said one participant. The recognition for many is just as important a reward as the prizes.

Programs such as Pathways to Rewards aren't a cure-all, but many experts think the use of incentives holds great potential for changing some of the behaviors that keep people tied to poverty. "We're saying, 'Look, every single person can make progress,'" says Toby Herr, executive director of Project Match. "We're asking you to tell us what you're good at and offer you a broad enough array of goals [and rewards] so you can keep succeeding."[29]

Participants in the Pathways to Rewards program work with counselors to set goals that they believe they can achieve if they put forth effort; they know that achieving the goal will lead to reward and recognition; and they have the opportunity to pick the type of rewards they desire. Thus, all three elements of the expectancy theory model illustrated in Exhibit 8.6 are high, which leads to high motivation. As soon as people show that they can consistently meet a goal, counselors work with them to set more ambitious ones in order to keep receiving rewards points. Within the first 18 months of the program, about 80 percent of those enrolled had met their goals.

Action Memo

Expectancy theory and reinforcement theory are widely used in all types of organizations and leadership situations. The questionnaire in Leader's Self-Insight 8.2 on page 238 gives you the opportunity to see how effectively you apply these motivational ideas in your own leadership.

Equity Theory

Sometimes employees' motivation is affected not only by their expectancies and the rewards they receive, but also by their perceptions of how fairly they are treated in relation to others. **Equity theory** proposes that people are motivated to seek social equity in the rewards they receive for performance.[30] According to the theory, if people perceive their rewards as equal to what others receive for similar contributions, they will believe they are treated fairly and will be more highly motivated. When they believe they are not being treated fairly and equitably, motivation will decline.

Equity theory
a theory that proposes that people are motivated to seek social equity in the rewards they expect for performance

Think about situations in which you were in a formal or informal leadership role in a group or organization. Imagine using your personal approach as a leader, and answer the questions below. Indicate whether each item below is Mostly False or Mostly True for you.

	Mostly False	Mostly True
1. I ask the other person what rewards they value for high performance.	_____	_____
2. I find out if the person has the ability to do what needs to be done.	_____	_____
3. I explain exactly what needs to be done for the person I'm trying to motivate.	_____	_____
4. Before giving somebody a reward, I find out what would appeal to that person.	_____	_____
5. I negotiate what people will receive if they accomplish the goal.	_____	_____
6. I make sure people have the ability to achieve performance targets.	_____	_____
7. I give special recognition when others' work is very good.	_____	_____
8. I only reward people if their performance is up to standard.	_____	_____
9. I use a variety of rewards to reinforce exceptional performance.	_____	_____
10. I generously praise people who perform well.	_____	_____
11. I promptly commend others when they do a better-than-average job.	_____	_____
12. I publicly compliment others when they do outstanding work.	_____	_____

Scoring and Interpretation

These questions represent two related aspects of motivation theory. For the aspect of expectancy theory, sum the points for Mostly True to questions 1–6. For the aspect of reinforcement theory, sum the points for Mostly True for questions 7–12.

The scores for my approach to motivation are:

My use of expectancy theory _____
My use of reinforcement theory _____

These two scores represent how you see yourself applying the motivational concepts of expectancy and reinforcement in your own leadership style. Four or more points on *expectancy theory* means you motivate people by managing expectations. You understand how a person's effort leads to performance and make sure that high performance leads to valued rewards. Four or more points for *reinforcement theory* means that you attempt to modify people's behavior in a positive direction with frequent and prompt positive reinforcement. New managers often learn to use reinforcements first, and as they gain more experience are able to apply expectancy theory.

Exchange information about your scores with other students to understand how your application of these two motivation theories compares to other students. Remember, leaders are expected to master the use of these two motivation theories. If you didn't receive an average score or higher, you can consciously do more with expectations and reinforcement when you are in a leadership position.

Sources: The questions above are based on D. Whetten and K. Cameron, *Developing Management Skills*, 5th ed. (Prentice-Hall, 2002), pp. 302–303; and P.M. Podsakoff, S.B. Mackenzie, R.H. Moorman, and R. Fetter, "Transformational Leader Behaviors and Their Effects on Followers' Trust in Leader, Satisfaction, and Organizational Citizenship Behaviors," *Leadership Quarterly* 1, no. 2 (1990), pp. 107–142.

People evaluate equity by a ratio of inputs to outcomes. That is, employees make comparisons of what they put into a job and the rewards they receive relative to those of other people in the organization. Inputs include such things as education, experience, effort, and ability. Outcomes include pay, recognition, promotions, and other rewards. A state of equity exists whenever the ratio of one person's outcomes to inputs equals the ratio of others' in the work group. Inequity occurs when the input/outcome ratios are out of balance, such as when an employee with a high level of experience and ability receives the same salary as a new, less-educated employee. Consider Deb Allen, an employee who went into the office on a weekend to catch up on work and found a document accidentally left on the copy machine. When she saw that some new hires were earning thousands more than their counterparts (including Allen) with more experience, and that "a noted screw-up" was making more than some highly competent people, Allen began questioning why she was working on weekends for less pay than many others were receiving. She became so demoralized by the perceived state of inequity that she quit her job three months later.[31]

This discussion provides only a brief overview of equity theory. The theory's practical use has been criticized because a number of key issues are unclear. However, the important point of equity theory is that, for many people, motivation is influenced significantly by relative as well as absolute rewards. The concept reminds leaders that they should be cognizant of the possible effects of perceived inequity on follower motivation and performance.

Action Memo

As a leader, you can clarify the rewards a follower desires and ensure that he or she has the knowledge, skills, resources, and support to perform and obtain the desired rewards. You can keep in mind that perceived equity or inequity in rewards also influences motivation.

The Carrot-and-Stick Controversy

Reward and punishment motivational practices dominate organizations. According to the Society for Human Resource Management, 84 percent of all companies in the United States offer some type of monetary or non-monetary reward system, and 69 percent offer incentive pay, such as bonuses, based on an employee's performance.[32] However, in other studies, more than 80 percent of employers with incentive programs have reported that their programs are only somewhat successful or not working at all.[33]

When used appropriately, financial incentives can be quite effective. For one thing, giving employees pay raises or bonuses can signal that leaders value their contributions to the organization. Some researchers argue that using money as a motivator almost always leads to higher performance.[34] However, despite the testimonies of numerous organizations that enjoy successful incentive programs, the arguments against the efficacy of carrot-and-stick methods are growing. Critics argue that extrinsic rewards are neither adequate nor productive motivators and may even work against the best interests of organizations. Reasons for this criticism include the following:

1. *Extrinsic rewards diminish intrinsic rewards.* The motivation to seek an extrinsic reward, whether a bonus or professional approval, leads people to focus on the reward rather than on the work they do to achieve it.[35] Reward-seeking of this type necessarily diminishes the intrinsic satisfaction people receive from the process of working. Numerous studies have found that giving people extrinsic rewards undermines their interest in the work itself.[36] When people lack intrinsic rewards in their work, their performance levels out; it stays just adequate to reach the reward. In the worst case, people perform hazardously, such as covering up an on-the-job accident to get a bonus based on a safety target. In addition, with extrinsic rewards, individuals tend to attribute their behavior to extrinsic rather than intrinsic factors, diminishing their own contributions.[37]

2. *Extrinsic rewards are temporary.* Bestowing outside incentives on people might ensure short-term success, but not long-term quality.[38] The success of reaching immediate goals is quickly followed by the development of unintended consequences. Because people are focusing on the reward, the work they do holds no interest for them, and without interest in their work, the potential for exploration, innovation, and creativity disappears.[39] The current deadline may be met, but better ways of working will not be discovered.

3. *Extrinsic rewards assume people are driven by lower needs.* The perfunctory rewards of praise and pay increases tied to performance presumes that the primary reason people initiate and persist in actions is to satisfy lower needs. However, behavior is also based on yearning for self-expression, and on self-esteem, self-worth, feelings, and attitudes. A survey of employees at *Fortune*'s "100 Best Companies to Work For" found that the majority mentioned intrinsic rather than extrinsic rewards as their motivation. Although many of these workers had been offered higher salaries elsewhere, they stayed where they were because of such motivators as a fun, challenging work environment; flexibility that provided a balance between work and personal life; and the potential to learn, grow, and be creative.[40] Offers of an extrinsic reward do not encourage the myriad behaviors that are motivated by people's need to express elements of their identities. Extrinsic rewards focus on the specific goals and deadlines delineated by incentive plans rather than enabling people to facilitate their vision for a desired future, that is, to realize their possible higher need for growth and fulfillment.[41]

4. *Organizations are too complex for carrot-and-stick approaches.* The current organizational climate is marked by uncertainty and high interdependence among departments and with other organizations. In short, the relationships and the accompanying actions that are part of organizations are overwhelmingly complex.[42] By contrast, the carrot-and-stick plans are quite simple, and the application of an overly simplified incentive plan to a highly complex operation usually creates a misdirected system.[43] It is difficult for leaders to interpret and reward all the behaviors that employees need to demonstrate to keep complex organizations successful over the long term. Thus, extrinsic motivators often wind up rewarding behaviors that are the opposite of what the organization wants and needs. Although managers may espouse long-term growth, for example, they reward quarterly earnings; thus, workers are motivated to act for quick returns for themselves. In recent years, numerous scandals have erupted because the practice of rewarding executives with stock options unintentionally encouraged managers to push accounting rules to the limits in order to make their financial statements look good and push up the stock prices.[44] This chapter's *Consider This* further examines how incentives can end up motivating the wrong behaviors.

5. *Carrot-and-stick approaches destroy people's motivation to work as a group.* Extrinsic rewards and punishments create a culture of competition versus a culture of cooperation.[45] In a competitive environment, people see their goal as individual victory, as making others appear inferior. Thus, one person's success is a threat to another's goals. Furthermore, sharing problems and solutions is out of the question when co-workers may use your weakness to undermine you, or when a supervisor might view the need for assistance as a disqualifier for rewards. The organization is less likely to achieve excellent performance from employees who are mistrustful and threatened by one another. In contrast, replacing the carrot-and-stick with methods based on meeting higher *as well as* lower needs enables a culture of collaboration marked by compatible goals; all the members of the organization are trying to achieve a shared vision. Without the effort to control behavior individually through rigid rewards, people can see co-workers as part of their success. Each person's success is mutually enjoyed because every success benefits the organization. When leaders focus on higher needs, they can make everyone feel valued, which facilitates excellent performance.

Consider This!

On the Folly of Rewarding A While Hoping for B

Managers who complain about the lack of motivation in workers might do well to examine whether the reward system encourages behavior different from what they are seeking. People usually determine which activities are rewarded and then seek to do those things, to the virtual exclusion of activities not rewarded. Nevertheless, there are numerous examples of fouled-up systems that reward unwanted behaviors, whereas the desired actions are not being rewarded at all.

In sports, for example, most coaches stress teamwork, proper attitude, and one-for-all spirit. However, rewards are usually distributed according to individual performance. The college basketball player who passes the ball to teammates instead of shooting will not compile impressive scoring statistics and will be less likely to be drafted by the pros. The big-league baseball player who hits to advance the runner rather than to score a home run is less likely to win the titles that guarantee big salaries. In universities, a primary goal is the transfer of knowledge from professors to students, yet professors are rewarded primarily for research and publication, not for their commitment to good teaching. Students are rewarded for making good grades, not necessarily for acquiring knowledge, and may resort to cheating rather than risk a low grade on their college transcript.

In business, there are often similar discrepancies between the desired behaviors and those rewarded. For example, see the following table.

What do a majority of managers see as the major obstacles to dealing with fouled-up reward systems?

1. The inability to break out of old ways of thinking about reward and recognition. This includes entitlement mentality in workers and resistance by management to revamp performance review and reward systems.
2. Lack of an overall systems view of performance and results. This is particularly true of systems that promote subunit results at the expense of the total organization.
3. Continuing focus on short-term results by management and shareholders.

Motivation theories must be sound because people do what they are rewarded for. But when will organizations learn to reward what they say they want?

Sources: Steven Kerr, "An Academy Classic: On the Folly of Rewarding A, While Hoping for B," and "More on the Folly," *Academy of Management Executive* 9, no. 1 (1995), pp. 7–16.

Managers Hope For	But They Reward
Teamwork and collaboration	The best individual performers
Innovative thinking and risk taking	Proven methods and not making mistakes
Development of people skills	Technical achievements and accomplishment
Employee involvement and empowerment	Tight control over operations and resources
High achievement	Another year's routine effort
Commitment to quality	Shipping on time, even with defects
Long-term growth	Quarterly earnings

Managers' difficulty getting people to cooperate and share knowledge at Blackmer/Dover Resources Inc. illustrates some of the problems associated with carrot-and-stick approaches.

Blackmer/Dover Inc.

Bill Fowler is one of the fastest and most accurate workers at the Blackmer/Dover factory in Grand Rapids, Michigan, where the 24-year plant veteran cuts metal shafts for heavy-duty industrial pumps. It's a precision task that requires a high level of skill, and managers would love to know Fowler's secrets so they could improve other workers and the manufacturing process. But Fowler refuses to share his tricks of the trade, even with his closest fellow workers. According to another employee, machinist Steve Guikema, Fowler "has hardly ever made a suggestion for an improvement" in the plant.

One reason is that Fowler believes managers could use his ideas and shortcuts to speed production and ultimately make his job harder. Another is that his knowledge has given him power, increased status, and a bigger paycheck. Until recently, workers could earn a premium on top of their hourly wage based on the number of pumps or pump parts they produced. That practice gave people a strong incentive to keep their output-enhancing tricks secret from fellow workers. A revised compensation system has done away with such incentives, but a long tradition of hoarding knowledge means there are still an estimated 10 to 20 percent of workers who refuse to cooperate with either managers or fellow employees. The culture of competition and hoarding knowledge is too entrenched.

These workers, like Fowler, see their expertise and accumulated experience as their only source of power. If other workers gained the same knowledge, they would no longer enjoy a superior status. New leaders at Blackmer/Dover Resources are looking for motivational tools that will encourage another kind of behavior: greater cooperation, knowledge sharing, and collaboration between workers and management to improve the plant and help it weather the economic slump. Revising compensation is the first step in establishing a system that will focus on meeting higher as well as lower-level needs.[46]

Action Memo

As a leader, you can avoid total reliance on carrot-and-stick motivational techniques. You can acknowledge the limited effects of extrinsic rewards and appeal to people's higher needs for intrinsic satisfaction.

Incentive programs can be successful, especially when people are actually motivated by money and lower needs. However, individual incentives are rarely enough to motivate behaviors that benefit the organization as a whole. One way for leaders to address the carrot-and-stick controversy is to understand a program's strengths and weaknesses and acknowledge the positive but limited effects of extrinsic motivators. A leader also appeals to people's higher needs, and no subordinate should have work that does not offer some self-satisfaction as well as a yearly pay raise. Furthermore, rewards can be directly linked to behavior promoting the higher needs of both individuals and the organization, such as rewarding quality, long-term growth, or a collaborative culture.[47]

Empowering People to Meet Higher Needs

A significant way in which leaders can meet the higher motivational needs of subordinates is to shift power down from the top of the organizational hierarchy and share it with subordinates. They can decrease the emphasis on incentives designed to affect and control subordinate behavior and instead attempt to share power with organizational members to achieve shared goals. One of the problems at the Blackmer/Dover factory, for example, is that workers are accustomed to hoarding knowledge and expertise because they feel powerless otherwise. They have no motivation to help others, because they don't feel a sense of responsibility and commitment toward shared goals.

Empowerment refers to power sharing, the delegation of power or authority to subordinates in the organization.[48] Many leaders are shifting from efforts to control behavior through carrot-and-stick approaches to providing people with the power, information, and authority that enables them to find greater intrinsic satisfaction with their work. Leaders provide their followers with an understanding of how their jobs are important to the organization's mission and performance, thereby giving them a direction within which to act freely.[49] Consider how an empowered workforce at Mississippi Power restored electricity in only 12 days after Hurricane Katrina knocked the lights out in Mississippi.

Empowerment
power sharing; the delegation of power or authority to subordinates in the organization

Melvin Wilson, Mississippi Power

One day, Melvin Wilson was reviewing next year's advertising campaign. A day later, he was responsible for coordinating the feeding, housing, and health care of 11,000 repairmen from around the country. "My day job did not prepare me for this," said the marketing manager of the chaos and confusion that ensued when Hurricane Katrina hit the state in August of 2005, wiping out 1,000 miles of power lines, destroying 65 percent of the company's transmission and distribution facilities, damaging 300 transmission towers, and knocking out power for all 195,000 customers. Mississippi Power's corporate headquarters was totally destroyed, its disaster response center flooded and useless.

Amazingly, employees got the job done smoothly and efficiently, restoring electricity in just 12 days, thus meeting the bold target of getting power back on by the symbolic date of September 11. The tale of how they did it is a lesson for leaders in how much can be accomplished quickly when people are empowered to think and act on their own initiative and understanding. Rather than running hurricane response from the top down, decision making at Mississippi Power is pushed far down to the level of the substation, and employees are empowered to act within certain guidelines to accomplish a basic mission: "Get the power on."

The corporate culture, based on values of unquestionable trust, superior performance, and total commitment, supports individual initiative and management confidence that people will respond with quick action and on-the-spot innovation. During the disaster recovery, even out-of-state crews working unsupervised were empowered to engineer their own solutions to problems in the field. Everyone at Mississippi Power, from linemen to accountants, is encouraged to experiment, innovate, share knowledge, and solve problems.[50]

As at Mississippi Power, the autonomy of empowered employees can create flexibility and motivation that is an enormous advantage for a company.[51] Empowering workers enables leaders to create a unique organization with superior performance capabilities.[52]

For one thing, empowerment provides strong motivation because it meets the higher needs of individuals. Research indicates that individuals have a need for *self-efficacy*, which is the capacity to produce results or outcomes, to feel they are effective.[53] Most people come into an organization with the desire to do a good job, and empowerment enables leaders to release the motivation already there. Increased responsibility motivates most people to strive to do their best.

Action Memo
As a leader, you can give employees greater power and authority to help meet higher motivational needs. You can implement empowerment by providing the five elements of information, knowledge, discretion, significance, and rewards.

In addition, leaders greatly benefit from the expanded capabilities that employee participation brings to the organization. This enables them to devote more attention to vision and the big picture. It also takes the pressure off of leaders when subordinates are able to respond better and more quickly to the markets they serve.[54] Frontline workers often have a better understanding than do leaders of how to improve a work process, satisfy a customer, or solve a production problem.

Elements of Empowerment

Typically, increased power and responsibility leads to greater motivation, increased employee satisfaction, and decreased turnover and absenteeism. In one survey, for example, empowerment of workers, including increased job responsibility, authority to define their work, and power to make decisions, was found to be the most dramatic indicator of workplace satisfaction.[55]

The first step toward effective empowerment is effective hiring and training. At Reflexite, a company that makes reflective material, components for motion sensors, and films for screens of mobile phones and laptops, leaders use a 16-step hiring process because they want people who have the ability and desire to make a genuine contribution to the organization.[56] In addition to hiring the right people, organizations provide them with the training and resources they need to excel. However, having a team of competent employees isn't enough. Five elements must be in place before employees can be truly empowered to perform their jobs successfully: information, knowledge, discretion, meaning, and rewards.[57]

1. *Employees receive information about company performance.* In companies where employees are fully empowered, no information is secret. At KI, an office furniture maker, everyone is taught to think like a business owner. Each month, managers share business results for each region, customer segment, and factory with the entire workforce so that everyone knows what product lines are behind or ahead, which operations are struggling, and what they can do to help the company meet its goals.[58]

2. *Employees receive knowledge and skills to contribute to company goals.* Companies train people to have the knowledge and skills they need to personally contribute to company performance. Knowledge and skills lead to competency—the belief that one is capable of accomplishing one's job successfully.[59] For example, when DMC, which makes pet supplies, gave employee teams the authority and responsibility for assembly line shut downs, it provided extensive training on how to diagnose and interpret line malfunctions, as well as the costs related to shut-down and start-up. Employees worked through case studies to practice line shut-downs so they would feel they had the skills to make good decisions in real-life situations.[60]

3. *Employees have the power to make substantive decisions.* Many of today's most competitive companies give workers the power to influence work procedures and organizational direction through quality circles and self-directed work teams. Teams of tank house workers at BHP Copper Metals in San Manuel, Arizona, identify and solve production problems and determine how best to organize themselves to get the job done. In addition, they can even determine the specific hours they need to handle their own workloads. For example, an employee could opt to work for four hours, leave, and come back to do the next four.[61]

4. *Employees understand the meaning and impact of their jobs.* Empowered employees consider their jobs important and meaningful, see themselves

as capable and influential, and recognize the impact their work has on customers, other stakeholders, and the organization's success.[62] Understanding the connection between one's day-to-day activities and the overall vision for the organization gives people a sense of direction, an idea of what their jobs mean. It enables employees to fit their actions to the vision and have an active influence on the outcome of their work.[63]

5. *Employees are rewarded based on company performance.* Studies have revealed the important role of fair reward and recognition systems in supporting empowerment. By affirming that employees are progressing toward goals, rewards help to keep motivation high.[64] Leaders are careful to examine and redesign reward systems to support empowerment and teamwork. Two ways in which organizations can financially reward employees based on company performance are through profit sharing and employee stock ownership plans (ESOPs). Through an ESOP at Reflexite, for example, three-quarters of the equity of the company is in the hands of employees, including managers, professional staff members, and factory floor workers.[65] At W. L. Gore and Associates, makers of Gore-Tex, compensation takes three forms—salary, profit sharing, and an associate stock ownership program.[66] Unlike traditional carrot-and-stick approaches, these rewards focus on the performance of the group rather than individuals. As Joe Cabral, CEO of Chatsworth Products Inc., says, an ESOP "gets everyone pulling in the same direction. Everybody wants the company to do the best it possibly can."[67] Furthermore, rewards are just one component of empowerment rather than the sole basis of motivation.

Empowerment Applications

Many of today's organizations are implementing empowerment programs, but they are empowering workers to varying degrees. At some companies, empowerment means encouraging employee ideas, whereas managers retain final authority for decisions; at others it means giving frontline workers almost complete power to make decisions and exercise initiative and imagination.[68]

Current methods of empowering workers fall along a continuum as shown in Exhibit 8.7. The continuum runs from a situation where frontline workers have no discretion (such as on a traditional assembly line) to full empowerment where workers even participate in formulating organizational strategy. An example of full empowerment is when self-directed teams are given the power to hire, discipline, and dismiss team members and to set compensation rates. Few organizations have moved to this level of empowerment. One that has is Semco, a $160 million South American company involved in manufacturing, services, and e-business. Majority owner Ricardo Semler believes that people will act in their own, and by extension, the organization's best interests if they're given complete freedom. Semco allows its 1,300 employees to choose what they do, where and when they do it, and even how they get paid for it. Semco has remained highly successful and profitable under a system of complete empowerment for more than 20 years.[69]

Empowerment programs can be difficult to implement in established organizations because they destroy hierarchies and upset the familiar balance of power. A study of *Fortune* 1000 companies found that the empowerment practices that have diffused most widely are those that redistribute power and authority the least, for example, quality circles or job enrichment. Managers can keep decision

Action Memo
Have you felt empowered in a job you have held? Take the quiz in Leader's Self-Insight 8.3 on page 247 to evaluate your empowerment experience and compare it to the experience of other students.

Exhibit 8.7 The Empowerment Continuum

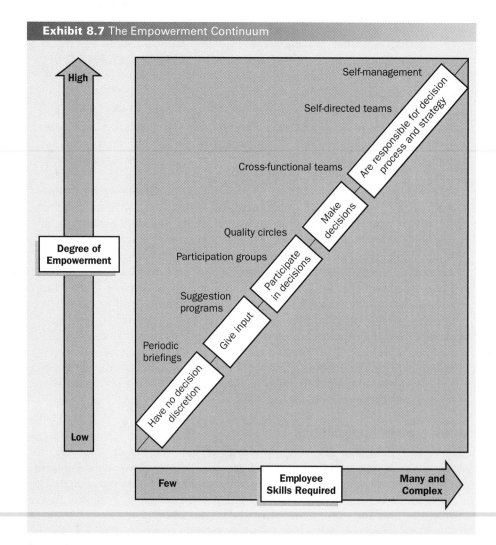

Sources: Based on Robert C. Ford and Myron D. Fottler, "Empowerment: A Matter of Degree," *Academy of Management Executive* 9, no. 3 (1995), pp. 21–31; Lawrence Holpp, "Applied Empowerment," *Training* (February 1994), pp. 39–44; and David P. McCaffrey, Sue R. Faerman, and David W. Hart, "The Appeal and Difficulties of Participative Systems," *Organization Science* 6, no. 6 (November–December 1995), pp. 603–627.

authority and there is less chance that workers will resist because of the added responsibilities that full empowerment brings.[70]

Organizationwide Motivational Programs

Leaders can motivate people using other recent ideas that are more than the carrot-and-stick approaches described earlier in this chapter, but may be less than full empowerment. One approach is to foster an organizational environment that helps people find true value and meaning in their work. A second approach is to implement organization-wide programs such as employee ownership, job enrichment, or new types of incentive plans.

Giving Meaning to Work Through Engagement

Throughout this chapter, we have talked about the importance of intrinsic rewards to high motivation. One way people get intrinsic rewards at work is when they feel

Are You Empowered?

Think of a job—either current or previous job—that was important to you, and then answer the questions below with respect to the managers above you in that job. Indicate whether each item below is Mostly False or Mostly True for you.

In general, my supervisor/manager:

	Mostly False	Mostly True
1. Gave me the support I needed to do my job well.	_____	_____
2. Gave me the performance information I needed to do my job well.	_____	_____
3. Explained top management's strategy and vision for the organization.	_____	_____
4. Gave me many responsibilities.	_____	_____
5. Trusted me.	_____	_____
6. Allowed me to set my own goals.	_____	_____
7. Encouraged me to take control of my own work.	_____	_____
8. Used my ideas and suggestions when making decisions.	_____	_____
9. Made me responsible for what I did.	_____	_____
10. Encouraged me to figure out the causes and solutions to problems.	_____	_____

Scoring and Interpretation

Add one point for each Mostly True answer to the 10 questions to obtain your total score. The questions represent aspects of empowerment that an employee may experience in a job. If your score was 6 or above, you probably felt empowered in the job for which you answered the questions. If your score was 3 or below, you probably did not feel empowered. Did you feel highly motivated in that job, and was your motivation related to your empowerment? What factors explained the level of empowerment you felt? Was empowerment mostly based on your supervisor's leadership style? The culture of the organization? Compare your scores with another student. Each of you take a turn describing the job and the level of empowerment you experienced. Do you want a job in which you are fully empowered? Why or why not?

Sources: These questions were adapted from Bradley L. Kirkman and Benson Rosen, "Beyond Self-management: Antecedents and Consequences of Team Empowerment," *Academy of Management Journal* 42, no. 1 (February 1999), pp. 58–74; and Gretchen M. Spreitzer, "Psychological Empowerment in the Workplace: Dimensions, Measurements, and Validation," *Academy of Management Journal* 38, no. 5 (October 1995), pp. 1442–1465.

a deep sense of importance and meaningfulness, such as people who work for a social cause or mission. However, people can find a sense of meaning and importance no matter what type of organization they work in if leaders build an environment in which people can flourish. Researchers have found that highly successful factories in less-developed countries, such as Morocco or Mexico, for example, have leaders who treat people with care and respect, engender a culture of mutual trust, and build on local values to create a community of meaning.[71] When people feel that they're a part of something special, they are more highly motivated and committed to the success of the organization and all its members. One path to meaning is through *employee engagement*, which researchers have found contributes to stronger organizational performance. An engaged employee is one who is emotionally connected to the organization, who is fully involved in and enthusiastic about his or her work, and who cares about the success of the organization.[72]

A Gallup Organization study found that the single most important variable in whether employees are engaged is the relationship between employees and their direct supervisor.[73] A leader's role is not to control others, but to organize the workplace in such a way that each person can learn, contribute, and grow. Good leaders create an organizational climate that allows people to become fully engaged and committed to helping the organization accomplish its goals. The Gallup researchers developed a metric called the Q12, a list of 12 questions that provides a way to evaluate how leaders are doing in creating an environment that provides intrinsic rewards by meeting higher-level needs. The Q12 evaluates characteristics such as whether employees know what is expected of them, whether they have opportunities to learn and grow, whether they have a friend at work, and whether they feel that their opinions are important. The full list of questions on the Q12 survey can be found in the book, *First Break All the Rules,* by researchers Marcus Cunningham and Curt Coffman.[74] When a majority of employees can answer the Q12 questions positively, the organization enjoys a highly motivated, engaged, and productive workforce. Buckingham has since written a new book, discussed in the Leader's Bookshelf, which takes a more in-depth look at what constitutes superior leadership.

> **Action Memo**
>
> As a leader, you can build an environment that unleashes employee potential and allows people to find meaning in their work. You can also apply ideas, such as employee ownership, job enrichment, and new incentives, to motivate people toward greater cooperation and teamwork.

Organizations where employees give high marks on the Q12 enjoy reduced turnover, are more productive and profitable, and enjoy greater employee and customer loyalty.[75] Unfortunately, Gallup's semi-annual Employee Engagement Index reveals that employee engagement is at a low level. The most recent results found that only 29 percent of U.S. employees are actively engaged. A similar Towers Perrin global survey reflects even more dismal results, with only 14 percent of employees worldwide showing high engagement levels.[76]

Leaders can identify the level of engagement in their organizations and implement strategies to facilitate full engagement and improve organizational performance. Consider how the Medical Center of Plano (Texas) used the Q12 to spark a turnaround.

Medical Center of Plano

IN THE LEAD

"You can't make a profit in this business unless you're a quality provider of health care," says Jerry McMorrough, vice president of human resources at the Medical Center of Plano. The 427-bed Hospital Corporation of America (HCA) facility competes with 29 other world-class hospitals in the Dallas-Fort Worth, Texas, area, all with great location, state-of-the-art technology, and sophisticated public relations.

Leaders knew that getting and staying ahead of the pack required getting the very best from every employee. Unfortunately, the Medical Center had high turnover and low morale, and leaders couldn't put their finger on the reasons why. They decided to use the Gallup Q12 as a way to measure employee expectations and how well the organization was meeting them. The results were shocking: only 18 percent of employees were engaged, 55 percent were not engaged, and 27 percent were actively disengaged, meaning that they were actively undermining the hospital's success.

CEO Harvey Fishero and other leaders guided their transformation of the Medical Center by focusing on each element of the Q12, which includes such questions as *At work, do I have the opportunity to do what I do best every day?; Does my supervisor seem to care about me as a person?,* and *Do I have the materials and equipment that I need in order to do my work right?*

Within five years, the percentage of actively disengaged employees at the Medical Center of Plano dropped to 9 percent, whereas the percentage of engaged employees jumped to 61 percent. The facility went from ranking near the bottom of all HCA hospitals on employee engagement to ranking the second highest of all HCA's 191 facilities. In addition, turnover has declined, customer satisfaction has improved, costs have gone down, and profits have gone up as employee engagement levels have risen.[77]

Leader's Bookshelf

The One Thing You Need to Know ... About Great Managing, Great Leading, and Sustained Individual Success

by Marcus Buckingham

Marcus Buckingham has spent two decades, including 17 years with the Gallup Organization, studying managers and leaders and how they build effective workplaces. His most recent book, *The One Thing You Need to Know ... About Great Managing, Great Leading, and Sustained Individual Success,* brings together his thoughts in a well-written and engaging format. Buckingham points out that: "A leader's job is to rally people toward a better future." The problem, though, is that motivation can flag because most people fear the future. So how do leaders "find a way to make people excited and confident about what comes next"?

DO ONE THING: BE CLEAR

Clarity, Buckingham contends, it the most effective way to turn fear into confidence and motivation. Leaders define the future in such clear and vivid terms—through their actions, their stories, their heroes, their images, their measurements, and their rewards—that everyone can see where the organization is, where it wants to go, and how they can take it there. He offers four points of clarity that leaders address:

- *Who do we serve?* Leaders let followers know precisely whom they are trying to please. General Manager Denny Clements, for example makes clear that the only people Toyota's Lexus Group is trying to serve are customers for whom time is their most precious commodity. Leaders don't always have to be right, Buckingham says, because there are often no right answers. They just have to be focused.
- *What is our core strength?* People know competition is tough. If leaders expect followers to feel confidence about the future, they need to tell them why they're going to win. For Best Buy CEO Brad Anderson, this core strength is the quality of frontline store employees, so people get the training they need to better serve customers.
- *What is our core measurement?* Rather than looking at 15 different metrics, leaders identify the one score that will track people's progress toward the future. At Best Buy, the core measurement is employee engagement, based on the Gallup Q12 survey (discussed in this textbook).
- *What actions can we take right now?* Leaders highlight a few carefully selected actions they can take to show followers the way to the future. Some actions are symbolic and demonstrate the leader's vision of the future. Others are systemic and compel people to do things differently.

THREE DISCIPLINES OF LEADERS

"Effective leaders don't have to be passionate or charming or brilliant," says Buckingham. "What they must be is clear." To find that clarity, leaders develop three disciplines. First, they take the time to reflect so they can distill complexity into a vivid path to the future. Next, they practice the key words, images, and stories they will use to describe where they want followers to go. The third discipline involves selecting and celebrating heroes in the organization who visibly embody the future. By mastering these three disciplines, leaders can provide clarity for followers and engender confidence, motivation, and creativity to move toward the desired future.

The One Thing You Need to Know, by Marcus Buckingham, is published by Free Press.

By conscientiously implementing changes designed to meet the needs of employees based on the Q12, leaders dramatically boosted engagement and helped turn the Medical Center into the leader of Plano's medical institution pack. However, they know long-term success depends on continually looking for ways to maintain high employee motivation. In addition, leaders are expanding their efforts to measure and increase patient satisfaction and engagement as well.

Other Approaches

There are a number of other approaches to improving organization-wide motivation. Some of the most common are job enrichment programs, employee ownership, gainsharing, paying for knowledge, and paying for performance. Variable compensation and various forms of "at risk" pay are key motivational tools today and are becoming more common than fixed salaries at many companies.

Employee ownership
giving employees real and psychological ownership in the organization; as owners, people are motivated to give their best performance

Employee ownership occurs on two levels. First, empowerment can result in a psychological commitment to the mission of an organization, whereby members act as "owners" rather than employees. Second, by owning stock in the companies for which they work, individuals are motivated to give their best performances.

Hot Dog on a Stick is wholly owned by its 1,300 employees, 85 percent of whom are women and 92 percent of whom are under the age of 25. "They schedule their locations, order the food, look at the profit-and-loss statements," says CEO Fredrica Thode. "It's like being CEO of their own store."[78] Giving all employees ownership is a powerful way to motivate people to work for the good of the entire company. Employee ownership also signals that leaders acknowledge each person's role in reaching corporate goals. Employee ownership programs are usually supported by *open book management,* which enables all employees to see and understand how the company is doing financially and how their actions contribute to the bottom line.

Gainsharing
motivational approach that encourages people to work together rather than focus on individual achievements and rewards; ties additional pay to improvements in overall employee performance

Gainsharing is another approach that motivates people to work together rather than focus on individual achievements and rewards. Gainsharing refers to an employee involvement program that ties additional pay to improvements in total employee performance.[79] Employees are asked to actively search for ways to make process improvements, with any resulting financial gains divided among employees. One example is a gainsharing program at Meritor. Since it rewards employees for improvements in their own unit as well as companywide, the program has proven to be a powerful incentive for teamwork.[80]

Pay for knowledge
programs that base an employee's pay on the number of skills he or she possesses

Pay for knowledge programs base an employee's salary on the number of task skills he or she possesses. If employees increase their skills, they get paid more. A workforce in which individuals skillfully perform numerous tasks is more flexible and efficient. At BHP Copper Metals, for example, leaders devised a pay-for-skills program that supported the move to teamwork. Employees can rotate through various jobs to build their skills and earn a higher pay rate. Rates range from entry-level workers to lead operators. Lead operators are those who have demonstrated a mastery of skills, the ability to teach and lead others, and effective self-directed behavior.[81]

Pay for performance
a program that links at least a portion of employees' monetary rewards to results or accomplishments

Pay for performance, which links at least a portion of employees' monetary rewards to results or accomplishments, is a significant trend in today's organizations.[82] Gainsharing is one type of pay for performance. Other examples include profit sharing, bonuses, and merit pay. In addition to the potential for greater income, pay for performance can give employees a greater sense of control over the outcome of their efforts. At Semco, described earlier, employees choose how they are paid based on 11 compensation options, which can be combined in various ways. Exhibit 8.8 lists Semco's 11 ways to pay. Semco leaders indicate that the flexible pay plan encourages innovation and risk-taking and motivates people to perform in the best interest of the company as well as themselves.

Job enrichment
a motivational approach that incorporates high-level motivators into the work, including job responsibility, recognition, and opportunities for growth, learning, and achievement

Job enrichment incorporates high-level motivators into the work, including job responsibility, recognition, and opportunities for growth, learning, and achievement. In an enriched job, the employee controls resources needed to perform well and makes decisions on how to do the work. One way to enrich an oversimplified job is to enlarge it, that is, to extend the responsibility to cover several tasks instead of only one.

Leaders at Ralcorp's cereal manufacturing plant in Sparks, Nevada, enriched jobs by combining several packing positions into a single job and cross-training employees to operate all of the packing line's equipment. Employees were given both the ability and the responsibility to perform all the various functions in their department, not just a single task. In addition, line employees are responsible for all screening and interviewing of new hires as well as training and advising one another. They also manage the production flow to and from their upstream and downstream partners—they understand the entire production process so they can

Exhibit 8.8 Semco's 11 Ways to Pay

Semco, a South American company involved in manufacturing, services, and e-business, lets employees choose how they are paid based on 11 compensation options:

1. Fixed salary
2. Bonuses
3. Profit sharing
4. Commission
5. Royalties on sales
6. Royalties on profits
7. Commission on gross margin
8. Stock or stock options
9. IPO/sale warrants that an executive cashes in when a business unit goes public or is sold
10. Self-determined annual review compensation in which an executive is paid for meeting self-set goals
11. Commission on difference between actual and three-year value of the company

Source: Ricardo Semler, "How We Went Digital Without a Strategy," *Harvard Business Review*, (September–October 2000), pp. 51–58.

see how their work affects the quality and productivity of employees in other departments. Ralcorp invests heavily in training to be sure employees have the needed operational skills as well as the ability to make decisions, solve problems, manage quality, and contribute to continuous improvement. Enriched jobs have improved employee motivation and satisfaction, and the company has benefited from higher long-term productivity, reduced costs, and happier employees.[83]

Summary and Interpretation

This chapter introduced a number of important ideas about motivating people in organizations. Individuals are motivated to act to satisfy a range of needs. The leadership approach to motivation tends to focus on the higher needs of employees. The role of the leader is to create a situation in which followers' higher needs and the needs of the organization can be met simultaneously.

Needs-based theories focus on the underlying needs that motivate how people behave. Maslow's hierarchy of needs proposes that individuals satisfy lower needs before they move on to higher needs. Herzberg's two-factor theory holds that dissatisfiers must be removed and motivators then added to satisfy employees. McClelland asserted that people are motivated differently depending on which needs they have acquired. Other motivation theories, including the reinforcement perspective, expectancy theory, and equity theory, focus primarily on extrinsic rewards and punishments, sometimes called *carrot-and-stick* methods of motivation. The reinforcement perspective proposes that behavior can be modified by the use of rewards and punishments. Expectancy theory is based on the idea that a person's motivation is contingent upon his or her expectations that a given behavior will result in desired rewards. Equity theory proposes that individuals' motivation is affected not only by the rewards they receive, but also by their perceptions of how fairly they are treated in relation to others. People are motivated to seek social equity in the rewards they expect for performance.

Although carrot-and-stick methods of motivation are pervasive in North American organizations, many critics argue that extrinsic rewards undermine intrinsic rewards, bring about unintended consequences, are too simple to capture organizational realities, and replace workplace cooperation with unhealthy competition.

An alternative approach to carrot-and-stick motivation is that of empowerment, by which subordinates know the direction of the organization and have the autonomy to act as they see fit to go in that direction. Leaders provide employees with the knowledge to contribute to the organization, the power to make consequential decisions, and the necessary resources to do their jobs. Empowerment typically meets the higher needs of individuals. Empowerment is tied to the trend toward helping employees find value and meaning in their jobs and creating an environment where people can flourish. When people are fully engaged with their work, satisfaction, performance, and profits increase. Leaders create the environment that determines employee motivation and satisfaction. One way to measure how engaged people are with their work is the Q12, a list of 12 questions about the day-to-day realities of a person's job. Other current organization-wide motivational programs include employee ownership, gainsharing, pay for knowledge, pay for performance, and job enrichment.

Discussion Questions

1. Describe the kinds of needs that people bring to an organization. How might a person's values and attitudes, as described in Chapter 4, influence the needs he or she brings to work?

2. What is the relationship among needs, rewards, and motivation?

3. What do you see as the leader's role in motivating others in an organization?

4. What is the carrot-and-stick approach? Do you think that it should be minimized in organizations? Why?

5. What are the features of the reinforcement and expectancy theories that make them seem like carrot-and-stick methods for motivation? Why do they often work in organizations?

6. Why is it important for leaders to have a basic understanding of equity theory? Can you see ways in which some of today's popular compensation trends, such as gainsharing or pay for performance, might contribute to perceived inequity among employees? Discuss.

7. What are the advantages of an organization with empowered employees? Why might some individuals *not* want to be empowered?

8. Do you agree that hygiene factors, as defined in Herzberg's two-factor theory, cannot provide increased satisfaction and motivation? Discuss.

9. Discuss whether you believe it is a leader's responsibility to help people find meaning in their work. How might leaders do this for employees at a fast-food restaurant? How about for employees who clean restrooms at airports?

10. If you were a leader at a company like Blackmer/Dover, discussed on page 242 of the chapter, what motivational techniques might you use to improve cooperation and teamwork?

Leadership at Work

Should, Need, Like, Love

Think of a school or work task that you feel an obligation or commitment to complete, but you don't really want to do it. Write the task here:

_____

_____

_____

Think of a school or work task you do because you need to, perhaps to get the benefit, such as money or credit. Write the task here:

_____

_____

_____

Think of a school or work task you like to do because it is enjoyable or fun. Write the task here:

_____

_____

_____

Think of a task you love to do—one in which you become completely absorbed and from which you feel a deep satisfaction when finished. Write the task here:

_____

_____

_____

Now reflect on those four tasks and what they mean to you. How motivated (high, medium, low) are you to accomplish each of these four tasks? How much mental effort (high, medium, low) is required from you to complete each task?

_____

_____

_____

Now estimate the percentage of your weekly tasks that you would rate as *should, need, like, love*. The combined estimates should total 100%.

Should _____%
Need _____%
Like _____%
Love _____%

If your *should* and *need* percentages are substantially higher than your *like* and *love* categories, what does that mean for you? Does it mean that you are forcing yourself to do tasks you find unpleasant? Why? Why not include more *like* and *love* tasks in your life? Might you grow weary of the *should* and *need* tasks at some point and select a new focus or job in your life? Think about this and discuss your percentages with another student in the class.

Tasks you *love* connect you with the creative spirit of life. People who do something they love have a certain charisma, and others want to follow their lead. Tasks you *like* typically are those that fit your gifts and talents and are tasks for which you can make a contribution. Tasks you do because of *need* are typically practical in the sense that they produce an outcome you want, and these tasks often do not provide as much satisfaction as the *like* and *love* tasks. Tasks you do strictly because you *should*, and which contain no *love, like*, or *need*, may be difficult and distasteful and require great effort to complete. You are unlikely to become a leader for completing *should* tasks.

What does the amount of each type of task in your life mean to you? How do these tasks relate to your passion and life satisfaction? Why don't you have more *like* and *love* tasks? As a leader, how would you increase the *like* and *love* tasks for people who report to you? Be specific.

_____

_____

_____

In Class: The instructor can have students talk in small groups about their percentages and what the percentages mean to them. Students can be asked how the categories of *should*, *need*, *like*, and *love* relate to the theories of motivation in the chapter. Do leaders have an obligation to guide employees toward tasks they like and love, or is it sufficient at work for people to perform need and should tasks?

The instructor can write student percentages on the board so students can see where they stand compared to the class. Students can be asked to interpret the results in terms of the amount of satisfaction they receive from various tasks. Also, are the percentages related to the students' stage of life?

Leadership Development: Cases for Analysis

The Parlor

The Parlor, a local franchise operation located in San Francisco, serves sandwiches and small dinners in an atmosphere reminiscent of the "roaring twenties." Period fixtures accent the atmosphere and tunes from a mechanically driven, old-time player piano greet one's ears upon entering. Its major attraction, however, is a high-quality, old-fashioned soda fountain that specializes in superior ice cream sundaes and sodas. Fresh, quality sandwiches are also a popular item. Business has grown steadily during the seven years of operation.

The business has been so successful that Richard Purvis, owner and manager, decided to hire a parlor manager so that he could devote more time to other business interests. After a month of quiet recruitment and interviewing, he selected Paul McCarthy, whose prior experience included the supervision of the refreshment stand at one of the town's leading burlesque houses.

The current employees were unaware of McCarthy's employment until his first day on the job, when he walked in unescorted (Purvis was out of town) and introduced himself.

During the first few weeks, he evidenced sincere attempts at supervision and seemed to perform his work efficiently. According to his agreement with Purvis, he is paid a straight salary plus a percentage of the amount he saves the business monthly, based on the previous month's operating expenses. All other employees are on a straight hourly rate.

After a month on the job, McCarthy single-mindedly decided to initiate an economy program designed to increase his earnings. He changed the wholesale meat supplier and lowered both his cost and product quality in the process. Arbitrarily, he reduced the size and portion of everything on the menu, including those fabulous sundaes and sodas. He increased the working hours of those on minimum wage and reduced the time of those employed at a higher rate. Moreover, he eliminated the fringe benefit of a one-dollar meal credit for employees who work longer than a five-hour stretch, and he cut out the usual 20 percent discount on anything purchased by the employees.

When questioned by the owner about the impact of his new practices, McCarthy swore up and down that there would be no negative effect on the business. Customers, though, have begun to complain about the indifferent service of the female waitresses and the sloppy appearance of the male soda fountain clerks—"Their hair keeps getting in the ice cream." And there has been almost a complete turnover among the four short-order cooks who work two to a shift.

Ron Sharp, an accounting major at the nearby university, had been a short-order cook on the night shift for five months prior to McCarthy's arrival. Conscientious and ambitious, Ron enjoys a fine work record, and even his new boss recognizes Ron's superiority over the other cooks—"The best we got."

Heavy customer traffic at the Parlor has always required two short-order cooks working in tandem on each shift. The work requires a high degree of interpersonal cooperation in completing the food orders. An unwritten and informal policy is that each cook would clean up his specific work area at closing time.

One especially busy night, Ron's fellow cook became involved in a shouting match with McCarthy after the cook returned five minutes late from his shift break. McCarthy fired him right on the spot and commanded him to turn in his apron. This meant that Ron was required to stay over an extra half-hour to wash the other fellow's utensils. He did not get to bed until 3 A.M. But McCarthy wanted him back at the store at 9 A.M. to substitute for a daytime cook whose wife reported him ill. Ron was normally scheduled to begin at 4 P.M. However, when Ron arrived somewhat sleepily at 10 A.M. (and after an 8 A.M. accounting class), McCarthy was furious. He thereupon warned Ron, "Once more and you can look for another job. If you work for me, you do things my way or you don't work here at all." "Fine with me," fired back Ron as he slammed his apron into the sink. "You know what you can do with this job!"

The next day, McCarthy discussed his problems with the owner. Purvis was actually very upset. "I can't understand what went wrong. All of a sudden, things have gone to hell."

Source: Bernard A. Deitzer and Karl A. Schillif, *Contemporary Incidents in Management* (Columbus, OH: Grid, Inc., 1977), pp. 167–168. Reprinted by permission of John Wiley & Sons, Inc.

QUESTIONS

1. Contrast the beliefs about motivation held by Purvis and McCarthy.

2. Do you consider either Purvis or McCarthy a leader? Discuss.

3. What would you do now if you were in Purvis's position? Why?

Cub Scout Pack 81

Things certainly have changed over the past six years for Cub Scout Pack 81. Six years ago, the pack was on the verge of disbanding. There were barely enough boys for an effective den, and they had been losing membership for as long as anyone could remember. The cub master was trying to pass his job onto any parent foolish enough to take the helm of a sinking ship, and the volunteer fire department that sponsored the pack was openly considering dropping it.

But that was six years ago. Today the pack has one of the largest memberships of any in the Lancaster/Lebanon Council. It has started its own Boy Scout troop, into which the Webelos can graduate, and it has received a presidential citation for its antidrug program. The pack consistently wins competitions with other packs in the Council, and the fire department is very happy about its sponsorship. Membership in the pack is now around 60 cubs at all levels, and they have a new cub master.

"Parents want their boys to be in a successful program," says Cub Master Mike Murphy. "Look, I can't do everything. We depend on the parents and the boys to get things done. Everybody understands that we want to have a successful program, and that means we all have to participate to achieve that success. I can't do it all, but if we can unleash the energy these boys have, there isn't anything in the Cub Scout Program we can't do!"

It was not always like that. "About five years ago we placed fourth for our booth in the Scout Expo at the mall," says Mike. "Everybody was surprised! Who was Pack 81? We were all elated! It was one of the best things to happen to this pack in years. Now, if we don't win at least something, we're disappointed. Our kids expect to win, and so do their parents."

Fourth place at the Scout Expo eventually led to several first places. Success leads to success, and the community around Pack 81 knows it.

"Last year, we made our annual presentation to the boys and their parents at the elementary school. We were with several other packs, each one trying to drum up interest in their program. When everyone was finished, the boys and their parents went over to the table of the pack that most interested them. We must have had well over half of the people at our table. I was embarrassed! They were standing six or seven deep in front of our table, and there was virtually nobody in front of the others."

Source: "Case IV: Cub Scout Pack 81," in *2001–02 Annual Editions: Management*, Fred H. Maidment, ed. (Guilford, CT: McGraw-Hill/Dushkin, 2001), p. 130.

QUESTIONS

1. What are some of Mike Murphy's basic assumptions about motivation?
2. Why do you think he has been so successful in turning the organization around?
3. How would you motivate people in a volunteer organization such as the Cub Scouts?

References

1 Lou Prendergast, "Kwik As You Like; Employees Rate Kwik-Fit Financial Serivces' Call Centre As a Wonderful Place to Work," *Daily Record* (March 24, 2005), p. 8; Jonathan Rennie, "Small Firms 'Have Woken Up and Smelt the Coffee'; Scots Business Leads Way in Employer-Employee Relations," *Evening Times* (March 14, 2006), p. 45; Steve Crabb, "You Can't Get Better,"*People Management* (November 10, 2005), pp. 28–30; "Meet the Winner," CIPD Web Page, www.onrec.com/content2/news.asp?ID=9527; and "Kwik-Fit Financial Services," *The Sunday Times* (March 06, 2005): http://business.timesonline.co.uk/article/0,,12190-1501501,00.html.

2 Michael West and Malcolm Patterson, "Profitable Personnel," *People Management* (January 8, 1998), pp. 28–31; Richard M. Steers and Lyman W. Porter, eds. *Motivation and Work Behavior,* 3rd ed. (New York: McGraw-Hill, 1983); Don Hellriegel, John W. Slocum, Jr., and Richard W. Woodman, *Organizational Behavior,* 7th ed. (St. Paul, MN: West Publishing Co., 1995), p. 170; and Jerry L. Gray and Frederick A. Starke, *Organizational Behavior: Concepts and Applications,* 4th ed. (New York: Macmillan, 1988), pp. 104–105.

3 Linda Grant, "Happy Workers, High Returns," *Fortune* (January 12, 1998), p. 81; Elizabeth J. Hawk and Garrett J. Sheridan, "The Right Staff," *Management Review,* (June 1999), pp. 43–48; and West and Patterson, "Profitable Personnel."

4 Anne Fisher, "Why Passion Pays," *FSB* (September 2002), p. 58; and Curt Coffman and Gabriel Gonzalez-Molina, *Follow This Path: How the World's Greatest Organizations Drive Growth by Unleashing Human Potential* (New York: Warner Books, 2002.)

5 Richard M. Steers, Lyman W. Porter, and Gregory A. Bigley, *Motivation and Leadership at Work,* 6th ed. (New York: McGraw-Hill, 1996), pp. 496–498.

6 Martha Lagace, "Oprah: A Case Study Comes Alive," (Lessons from the Classroom) *HBS Working Knowledge* (February 20, 2006), Harvard Business School, accessed at http://hbswk.hbs.edu/item/5214.html on April 2, 2007.

7 Arlyn Tobias Gajilan, "Scrap Mettle," *FSB* (December 2005–January 2006), pp. 95–96.

8 Steven Bergals, "When Money Talks, People Walk," *Inc.* (May 1996), pp. 25–26.

9 Geoff Colvin, "The 100 Best Companies to Work For 2006," *Fortune* (January 23, 2006), p. 71ff.

10 Cheryl Dahle, "Four Tires, Free Beef," *Fast Company* (September 2003), p. 36.

11 Rosabeth Moss Kanter, "How to Fire Up Employees Without Cash or Prizes," *Business 2.0* (June 2002), pp. 134–152.

12 Colvin, "The 100 Best Companies to Work For"; Levering and Moskowitz, "And the Winners Are . . ." *Fortune* (January 23, 2006) p. 89ff; and Daniel Roth, "Trading Places," *Fortune* (January 23, 2006), pp. 120–128.

13 Abraham F. Maslow, "A Theory of Human Motivation," *Psychological Review* 50 (1943), pp. 370–396.

14 Frederick Herzberg, "One More Time: How Do You Motivate Employees?" *Harvard Business Review* (January–February 1968), pp. 53–62.

15 Nanette Byrnes with Michael Arndt, "The Art of Motivation," *Business Week* (May 1, 2006), p. 57; "About Us," Nucor Steel Web Page, http://www.nucor.com/; Patricia Panchak, "Putting Employees First Pays Off," *Industry Week,* (June 2002), 14; and "Nucor CEO: Instill Your Culture, Empower Workers to Reach Goal," *Charlotte Business Journal* (November 22, 2002). Accessed April 2, 2007, from http://charlotte.bizjournals.com/charlotte/stories/2002/11/25/editorial2.html.

16 David C. McClelland, *Human Motivation* (Glenview, IL: Scott Foresman, 1985).

17 John Brant, "What One Man Can Do," *Inc. Magazine* (September 2005), pp. 145–153.

18 David C. McClelland, "The Two Faces of Power," in *Organizational Psychology,* D. A. Colb, I. M. Rubin, and J. M. McIntyre, eds. (Englewood Cliffs, NJ: Prentice-Hall, 1971), pp. 73–86.

19 Alfie Kohn, "Why Incentive Plans Cannot Work," *Harvard Business Review* (September–October 1993): 54–63; A. J. Vogl, "Carrots, Sticks, and Self-Deception," (an interview with Alfie Kohn), *Across the Board,* (January 1994), 39–44; and Alfie Kohn, "Challenging Behaviorist Dogma: Myths about Money and Motivation," *Compensation and Benefits Review* (March–April 1998), pp. 27, 33–37.

20 H. Richlin, *Modern Behaviorism* (San Francisco: Freeman, 1970); B. F. Skinner, *Science and Human Behavior* (New York: Macmillan, 1953); Alexander D. Stajkovic and Fred Luthans, "A Meta-Analysis of the Effects of Organizational Behavior Modification on Task Performance 1975–1995," *Academy of Management Journal* (October 1997), pp. 1122–1149; F. Luthans and R. Kreitner, *Organizational Behavior Modification and Beyond,* 2nd ed. (Glenview, IL: Scott Foresman, 1985).

21 Alexander D. Stajkovic and Fred Luthans, "A Meta-Analysis of the Effects of Organizational Behavior Modification on Task Performance, 1975–1995," *Academy of Management Journal* (October 1997), pp. 1122–1149; and Fred Luthans and Alexander D. Stajkovic, "Reinforce for Performance: The Need to Go Beyond Pay and Even Rewards," *Academy of Management Executive* 13, no. 2 (1999), pp. 49–57.

22 Reported in Charlotte Garvey, "Meaningful Tokens of Appreciation," *HR Magazine* (August 2004), pp. 101–105.

23 Amy Sutherland, "What Shamu Taught Me About a Happy Marriage," *The New York Times* (June 25, 2006). Accessed April 2, 2007 at http://www.nytimes.com/2006/06/25/fashion/25love.html?ex=1175659200&en=4c3d257c4d16e70d&ei=5070.

24 Jaclyn Badal, "New Incentives for Workers Combine Cash, Fun" (Theory & Practice column), *The Wall Street Journal* (June 19, 2006), p. B3.

25 Luthans and Kreitner, *Organizational Behavior Modification and Beyond;* L. M. Saari and G. P. Latham, "Employee Reaction to Continuous and Variable Ratio Reinforcement Schedules Involving a Monetary Incentive," *Journal of Applied Psychology* 67 (1982), pp. 506–508; and R. D. Pritchard, J. Hollenback, and P. J. DeLeo, "The Effects of Continuous and Partial Schedules of Reinforcement on Effort, Performance, and Satisfaction," *Organizational Behavior and Human Performance* 25 (1980), pp. 336–353.

26 Gwendolyn Bounds, "Boss Talk: No More Squeaking By—WD-40 CEO Garry Ridge Repackages a Core Product," *The Wall Street Journal* (May 23, 2006), p. B1.

27 Victor H. Vroom, *Work and Motivation* (New York: Wiley, 1969); B. S. Gorgopoulos, G. M. Mahoney, and N. Jones, "A Path–Goal Approach to Productivity," *Journal of Applied Psychology* 41 (1957), pp. 345–353; and E. E. Lawler III, *Pay and Organizational Effectiveness: A Psychological View* (New York: McGraw-Hill, 1981).

28 Richard M. Daft and Richard M. Steers, *Organizations: A Micro/Macro Approach* (Glenview, IL: Scott, Foresman, 1986).

29 Jonathen Eig, "Poverty: The New Search for Solutions; Extra Credit: Poverty Program Gives Points to Do the Right Thing," *The Wall Street Journal* (July 7, 2006), p. A1.

30 J. Stacy Adams, "Injustice in Social Exchange," in *Advances in Experimental Social Psychology,* 2nd ed., L. Berkowitz, ed. (New York: Academic Press, 1965); and J. Stacy Adams, "Toward an Understanding of Inequity," *Journal of Abnormal and Social Psychology* (November 1963), pp. 422–436.

31 Jared Sandberg, "Why You May Regret Looking at Papers Left on the Office Copier" (Cubicle Culture column), *The Wall Street Journal* (June 20, 2006), p. B1.

32 Amy Joyce, "The Bonus Question; Some Managers Still Strive to Reward Merit," *The Washington Post* (November 13, 2005), p. F6.

33 Survey results from WorldatWork and Hewitt Associates, reported in Karen Kroll, "Benefits: Paying for Performance," *Inc.* (November 2004), p. 46; and Kathy Chu, "Firms Report Lackluster Results from Pay-for-Performance Plans," *The Wall Street Journal* (June 15, 2004), p. D2.

34 Nina Gupta and Jason D. Shaw, "Let the Evidence Speak: Financial Incentives *Are* Effective!!" *Compensation and Benefits Review* (March/April 1998), pp. 26, 28–32.

35 Vogl, "Carrots, Sticks, and Self-Deception," 40; and Alfie Kohn, "Incentives Can Be Bad for Business," *Inc.,* (January 1998), pp. 93–94.

36 Kohn, "Challenging Behaviorist Dogma."

37 Jerry L. Gray and Frederick A. Starke, *Organizational Behavior: Concepts and Applications,* 4th ed. (New York: Merrill, 1988).

38 Richard M. Steers, Lyman W. Porter, and Gregory A. Bigley, *Motivation and Leadership at Work,* 6th ed. (New York: McGraw-Hill, 1996), p. 512.

39 Steers, Porter, and Bigley, *Motivation and Leadership at Work,* 517; Vogl, "Carrots, Sticks, and Self-Deception," p. 40.

40 Steers, Porter, and Bigley, *Motivation and Leadership at Work,* 154–157; Anne Fisher, "The 100 Best Companies to Work for in America," *Fortune* (January 12, 1998), pp. 69–70.

41 William D. Hitt, *The Leader-Manager: Guidelines for Action* (Columbus, OH: Battelle Press, 1988), p. 153.

42 Steers, Porter, and Bigley, *Motivation and Leadership at Work,* pp. 520–525.

43 Vogl, "Carrots, Sticks, and Self-Deception," p. 43.

44 Greg Hitt and Jacob M. Schlesinger, "Perk Police: Stock Options Come Under Fire in Wake of Enron's Collapse," *The Wall Street Journal* (March 26, 2002), pp. A1, A8.

45 James M. Kouzes and Barry Z. Posner, *The Leadership Challenge,* (San Francisco, CA: Jossey-Bass), p. 153.

46 Timothy Aeppel, "Tricks of the Trade: On Factory Floors, Top Workers Hide Secrets to Success," *The Wall Street Journal* (July 1, 2002), pp. A1, A10.

47 Kouzes and Posner, *The Leadership Challenge,* p. 282.

48 Edwin P. Hollander and Lynn R. Offerman, "Power and Leadership in Organizations," *American Psychology* 45 (February 1990), pp. 179–189.

49 Robert C. Ford and Myron D. Fottler, "Empowerment: A Matter of Degree," *Academy of Management Executive* 9 (1995), pp. 21–31.

50 Dennis Cauchon, "The Little Company That Could," *USA Today* (October 9, 2005), http://www.usatoday.com/money/companies/management/2005-10-09-mississippi-power-usat_x.htm.

51 David P. McCaffrey, Sue R. Faerman, and David W. Hart, "The Appeal and Difficulties of Participative Systems," *Organization Science* 6, no. 6 (November–December 1995), pp. 603–627.

52 David E. Bowen and Edward E. Lawler III, "Empowering Service Employees," *Sloan Management Review* (Summer 1995), pp. 73–84.

53 Jay A. Conger and Rabindra N. Kanungo, "The Empowerment Process: Integrating Theory and Practice," *Academy of Management Review* 13 (1988), pp. 471–482.

54 McCaffrey, Faerman and Hart, "The Appeal and Difficulties of Participative Systems."

55 "Great Expectations?" *Fast Company* (November 1999), pp. 212–224.

56 William C. Taylor, "Under New Management; These Workers Act Like Owners (Because They Are)," *The New York Times* (May 21, 2006), http://select.nytimes.com/gst/abstract.html?res=F60C1EFC385A0C728EDDAC0894DE404482.

57 Bowen and Lawler, "Empowering Service Employees."

58 Taylor, "These Workers Act Like Owners."

59 Gretchen Spreitzer, "Social Structural Characteristics of Psychological Empowerment," *Academy of Management Journal* 39, no. 2 (April 1996), pp. 483–504.

60 Russ Forrester, "Empowerment: Rejuvenating a Potent Idea," *Academy of Management Executive* 14, no. 3 (2000), pp. 67–80.

61 Glenn L. Dalton, "The Collective Stretch," *Management Review* (December 1998), pp. 54–59.

62 Bradley L. Kirkman and Benson Rosen, "Powering Up Teams," *Organizational Dynamics* (Winter 2000), pp. 48–66; and Gretchen M. Spreitzer, "Psychological Empowerment in the Workplace: Dimensions, Measurement, and Validation," *Academy of Management Journal* 38, no. 5 (October 1995), p. 1442.

63 Spreitzer, "Social Structural Characteristics of Psychological Empowerment."

64 Roy C. Herrenkohl, G. Thomas Judson, and Judith A. Heffner, "Defining and Measuring Employee Empowerment," *The Journal of Applied Behavioral Science* 35, no. 3 (September 1999), pp. 373–389.

65 Taylor, "These Workers Act Like Owners."

66 Frank Shipper and Charles C. Manz, "Employee Self-Management Without Formally Designated Teams: An Alternative Road to Empowerment," *Organizational Dynamics* (Winter 1992), pp. 48–61.

67 Steve Kaufman, "ESOPs' Appeal on the Increase," *Nation's Business* (June 1997), pp. 43–44.

68 Ford and Fottler, "Empowerment: A Matter of Degree."

69 Lawrence Fisher, "Ricardo Semler Won't Take Control," *Strategy + Business* (Winter 2005), pp. 78–88; and Ricardo Semler, "How We Went Digital Without a Strategy," *Harvard Business Review* (September–October 2000), pp. 51–58.

70 McCaffrey, Faerman, and Hart, "The Appeal and Difficulties of Participative Systems."

71 Philippe d'Iribarne, "Motivating Workers in Emerging Countries: Universal Tools and Local Adaptations," *Journal of Organizational Behavior* 23 (2002), pp. 243–256.

72 Gerard H. Seijts and Dan Crim, "What Engages Employees the Most, or The Ten C's of Employee Engagement," *Ivey Business Journal* (March–April 2006).

73 This discussion is based on Tony Schwartz, "The Greatest Sources of Satisfaction in the Workplace are Internal and Emotional," *Fast Company* (November 2000), pp. 398–402; and Marcus Buckingham and Curt Coffman, *First, Break All the Rules: What the World's Greatest Managers Do Differently* (New York: Simon & Schuster, 1999).

74 Buckingham and Coffman, *First, Break All the Rules.*

75 Polly LaBarre, "Marcus Buckingham Thinks Your Boss Has an Attitude Problem" *Fast Company* (August 2001), pp. 88–98.

76 Survey results reported in Seijts and Crim, "What Engages Employees the Most."

77 Jennifer Robison, "This HCA Hospital's Healthy Turnaround," *Gallup Management Journal* (January 13, 2005).

78 Taylor, "These Workers Act Like Owners."

79 Michael J. Gaudioso, "How a Successful Gainsharing Program Arose from an Old One's Ashes at Bell Atlantic (Now Verizon) Directory Graphics," *Journal of Organizational Excellence* (Winter 2000), pp. 11–18.

80 Hawk and Sheridan, "The Right Staff."

81 Dalton, "The Collective Stretch."

82 Christopher Caggiano, "The Right Way to Pay," *Inc.* (November 2002), pp. 84–92.

83 Dalton, "The Collective Stretch."

Chapter 9

Your Leadership Challenge

After reading this chapter, you should be able to:

- Act as a communication champion rather than just as an information processor.

- Use key elements of effective listening and understand why listening is important to leader communication.

- Recognize and apply the difference between dialogue and discussion.

- Select an appropriate communication channel for your leadership message.

- Use communication to influence and persuade others.

- Effectively communicate during times of stress or crisis.

Leadership Communication

Kent Thiery, CEO of DaVita, the nation's number two dialysis-treatment operator, has been hearing nothing but positive news from employees about the recent merger with Gambro Healthcare. That feels good, considering the mess DaVita was in when Thiery took over. The El Segundo, California company was in default on its bank loans and barely able to make payroll. Turnover was 45 percent a year.

Then Thiery reminds himself what pulled DaVita out of the quagmire—it wasn't his brilliant strategies and plans but rather a vigorous seeking and acting on honest feedback from front-line workers. So, when employees at an annual staff gathering agree with him that integrating DaVita and Gambro is "fun," Thiery challenges them: "Either you're all on drugs or better than me because integrations are a god-awful nightmare." He then reminds workers that he depends on their frank feedback to "keep from messing up."

Thiery is striving to build open communication into the DNA of DaVita. Managers get plenty of data via monthly reports, but Thiery knows written reports don't tell them what's really going on in the company. Every manager spends a week working in a dialysis center to see firsthand the challenges and stresses technicians and nurses face. Thiery holds about 20 town-hall style meetings a year and asks other top managers to convene a truth-telling session any time they are with at least seven employees (now called teammates). He wants people to think of the company as "a village with shared responsibility," and he routinely revises procedures or practices that employees say aren't working or could be improved.

Companies like DaVita in the healthcare industry face many challenges, from stiff competition to tough government regulations. Thanks to Thiery's encouragement of open and honest communication, DaVita has cut employee turnover to around 20 percent, increased revenues to more than $5 billion, and achieved the dialysis industry's best clinical outcomes.[1]

In the previous chapter, we discussed motivation and reviewed some of the ways in which leaders motivate followers toward the accomplishment of the organization's goals. As this story illustrates, motivation depends greatly on a leader's ability to communicate effectively, which includes the critical role of listening to followers. People look to leaders for direction and inspiration, but they also want to have their ideas and opinions heard.

Leadership cannot happen without effective communication. Recall that leadership means influencing people to bring about change toward a vision, or desirable future for the organization. Leaders communicate to share the vision with others, inspire and motivate them to strive toward the vision, and build the values and trust that enable effective working relationships and goal accomplishment.

Successful leader communication also includes deceptively simple components, such as asking questions, paying attention to nonverbal communication, and actively listening to others. Today's fast-paced environment does not always provide time for the listening and reflection that good communication requires.[2] Surveys of managers typically reveal that they consider communication their most important skill and one of their top responsibilities. However, one study found that fewer than half bother to tailor their messages to employees, customers, or suppliers, and even fewer seek feedback from those constituencies. Furthermore, in many cases investors appear to have a better idea of the vision and mission of companies than do employees.[3] Research shows that some senior executives in particular are not investing the time and energy to be effective communicators, which can leave the entire organization floundering for direction or prevent top leaders from adequately responding to problems or opportunities. Many top managers, for example, resist employee feedback, because they don't want to hear negative information. Without feedback, though, leaders often make decisions and plans that are out of alignment with employee perceptions, making smooth implementation less likely.[4]

This chapter describes tools and skills that can be used to overcome the communication deficit pervading today's organizations and the broader social world. We also examine how leaders use communication skills to make a difference in their organizations and the lives of followers.

How Leaders Communicate

We have all had both positive and negative experiences with communication in our personal as well as our work lives. Have you ever had a supervisor or instructor whose communication skills were so poor that you didn't have any idea what was expected of you or how to accomplish the job you were asked to do? On the other hand, have you experienced the communication flair of a teacher, boss, or coach who "painted a picture in words" that both inspired you and clarified how to achieve an objective?

Leadership means communicating with others in such a way that they are influenced and motivated to perform actions that further common goals and lead toward desired outcomes. **Communication** is a process by which information and understanding are transferred between a sender and a receiver, such as between a leader and an employee, an instructor and a student, or a coach and a football player. Exhibit 9.1 shows the key elements of the communication process. The leader initiates a communication by *encoding* a thought or idea, that is, by selecting symbols (such as words) with which to compose and transmit a message. The message is the tangible formulation of the thought or idea sent to the receiver, and the *channel* is the medium by which the message is sent. The channel

Communication
a process by which information and understanding are transferred between a sender and a receiver

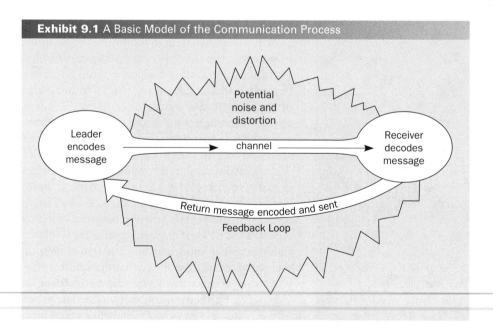

Exhibit 9.1 A Basic Model of the Communication Process

could be a formal report, a telephone call, an e-mail or text message, or a face-to-face conversation. The receiver *decodes* the symbols to interpret the meaning of the message. Encoding and decoding can sometimes cause communication errors because individual differences, knowledge, values, attitudes, and background act as filters and may create "noise" when translating from symbols to meaning. Employees and supervisors, husbands and wives, parents and children, friends and strangers all have communication breakdowns because people can easily misinterpret messages. *Feedback* is the element of the communication process that enables someone to determine whether the receiver correctly interpreted the message. Feedback occurs when a receiver responds to a leader's communication with a return message. Without feedback, the communication cycle is incomplete. Effective communication involves both the transference and the mutual understanding of information.[5] The process of sending, receiving, and feedback to test understanding underlies both management and leadership communication.

Management Communication

The traditional role of a manager is that of "information processor." Managers spend some 80 percent of each working day in communication with others.[6] In other words, 48 minutes of every hour are spent in meetings, on the telephone, or talking informally with others. Managers scan their environments for important written and personal information, gathering facts, data, and ideas, which in turn are sent to subordinates and others who can use them. A manager then receives subordinate messages and feedback to see if "noise" interfered with translation, and determines whether to modify messages for accuracy.

> **Action Memo**
> Networking is a vital part of leadership information sharing. Answer the questions in Leader's Self-Insight 9.1 on page 262 to learn whether you network with other people similar to what successful leaders do.

Managers have a huge communication responsibility directing and controlling an organization. Communication effectiveness lies in accuracy of formulation, with less "noise" as one determinant of success. Managers communicate facts, statistics, and decisions. Effective managers establish themselves at the center of information networks to facilitate the completion of tasks. Leadership communication, however, serves a different purpose.

Leader Communication

Although leadership communication also includes the components of sending, receiving, and feedback, it is different from management communication. Leaders often communicate the big picture—the vision, as defined in Chapter 1—rather than facts and pieces of information. A leader can be seen as a communication champion.[7]

A **communication champion** is philosophically grounded in the belief that communication is essential to building trust and gaining commitment to the vision. Leaders use communication to inspire and unite people around a common sense of purpose and identity. A communication champion enables followers to "live" the vision in their day-to-day activities.[8] This chapter's *Consider This* box highlights the importance of this aspect of leader communication. People need a vision to motivate them toward the future. Learning, problem solving, decision making, and strategizing are all oriented around and stem from the vision. Furthermore, communication champions visibly and symbolically engage in communication-based activities. Whether they walk around asking questions or thoughtfully listen to a subordinate's problem, the actions of champions convey a commitment to communication. Communication isn't just about occasional meetings, formal speeches, or presentations. Leaders actively communicate through both words

Communication champion
a person who is philosophically grounded in the belief that communication is essential to building trust and gaining commitment to a vision

Leader's Self-Insight 9.1

Think about your current life as an employee or as a student. Indicate whether each item below is Mostly False or Mostly True for you.

	Mostly False	Mostly True
1. I learn early on about changes going on in the organization that might affect me or my job.		
2. I have a clear belief about the positive value of active networking.		
3. I am good at staying in touch with others.		
4. I network as much to help other people solve problems as to help myself.		
5. I am fascinated by other people and what they do.		
6. I frequently use lunches to meet and network with new people.		
7. I regularly participate in charitable causes.		
8. I maintain a list of friends and colleagues to whom I send holiday cards.		
9. I build relationships with people of different gender, race, and nationality than myself.		
10. I maintain contact with people from previous organizations and school groups.		
11. I actively give information to subordinates, peers, and my boss.		
12. I know and talk with peers in other organizations.		

Scoring and Interpretation

Add the number of Mostly True answers above for your score: _____. A score of 9 or above indicates that you are excellent at networking and can be a networking leader. A score of 3 or below would suggest that you need to focus more on building networks, perhaps work in a slow moving occupation or organization, or not put yourself in a position of leadership. A score of 4–8 would be about average.

Networking is the active process of building and managing productive relationships. Networking builds social, work, and career relationships that facilitate mutual understanding and mutual benefit. Leaders accomplish much of their work through networks rather than formal hierarchies.

Source: The ideas for this self-insight questionnaire were drawn primarily from Wayne E. Baker, *Networking Smart: How to Build Relationships for Personal and Organizational Success* (McGraw-Hill, 1994).

and actions every day. Regular communication is essential for building personal relationships with followers.

Exhibit 9.2 shows the leader-as-communication-champion model. By establishing an open communication climate, asking questions, actively listening to others, learning to discern underlying messages, and applying the practice of dialogue, leaders facilitate and support *strategic conversations* that help move the organization forward. Leader communication is *purpose-directed* in that it directs everyone's attention toward the vision, values, and desired outcomes of the group or organization and persuades people to act in a way to help achieve the vision.

Leaders use many communication methods, including selecting rich channels of communication, stories, metaphors, and informal communication. For example, in communicating his message about the federal budget, President Ronald Reagan spoke of a trillion dollars in terms of stacking it next to the Empire State Building. Framed this way, the message redefined the meaning of a trillion dollars, and took on a new reality for the audience. Historical

Action Memo

As a leader, you can be a communication champion. You can use verbal, nonverbal, and symbolic communication to unite people around a common vision, facilitate strategic conversations, and build trust.

Getty Images

and contemporary leaders as diverse as Reagan, Martin Luther King, Jr., Oprah Winfrey, Steve Jobs, Aung San Suu Kyi, Bono, and Meg Whitman all share the ability to powerfully communicate their messages to followers and others.

Leading Strategic Conversations

Strategic conversation refers to people talking across boundaries and hierarchical levels about the group or organization's vision, critical strategic themes, and the values that can help achieve desired outcomes. Leaders facilitate strategic conversations by (1) asking questions and actively listening to others to understand their attitudes and values, needs, personal goals, and desires; (2) setting the agenda for conversation by underscoring the key strategic themes that are linked to

Strategic conversation
communication that takes place across boundaries and hierarchical levels about the group or organization's vision, critical strategic themes, and values that can help achieve desired outcomes

Exhibit 9.2 The Leader as Communication Champion

Internal and External Sources →

Strategic Conversation
Open climate
Asking questions
Listening
Discernment
Dialogue →

Leader as Communication Champion →

Purpose Directed
Direct attention to vision/values, desired outcomes; use persuasion

Methods
Use rich channels
Stories and metaphors
Informal communication

organizational success; and (3) selecting the right communication channels and facilitating dialogue.[9] An example of strategic conversation comes from Royal Philips Electronics, Europe's largest electronics outfit. President Gerard Kleisterlee outlined four key technology themes that he believes should define Philips' future in the industry: display, storage, connectivity, and digital video processing. These themes intentionally cross technology boundaries and require people to communicate and collaborate across departments and divisions. A strategic conversation for each theme begins with a one-day summit that brings together everyone who has relevant information to contribute—regardless of rank or job position—so that people can together gain a clear sense of goals and establish cooperative working relationships.[10]

Five key components necessary for strategic conversations are an open communication climate, asking questions, active listening, discernment, and dialogue.

Creating an Open Communication Climate

Open communication
leaders sharing all types of information throughout the company and across all levels

Open communication means sharing all types of information throughout the organization, especially across functional and hierarchical boundaries. Open communication runs counter to the traditional flow of selective information downward from supervisors to subordinates. But leaders want communication to flow in all directions. People throughout the organization need a clear direction and an understanding of how they can contribute.[11] A recent survey of U.S. employees reveals that people genuinely want open and honest communication from their leaders, including the bad news as well as the good. Yet when these employees were asked to evaluate how well their leaders were doing on a scale of zero to 100, the average score was 69.[12]

To build an open communication climate, leaders break down conventional hierarchical and departmental boundaries that may be barriers to communication, enabling them to convey a stronger awareness of and commitment to organizational vision, goals, and values. In an open climate, a leader's communication of the vision "cascades" through an organization, as explained in Exhibit 9.3. Consistent and frequent communication brings follower acceptance and understanding. Smart executives also recognize the critical role of open communication in building trust.[13] Trust is an essential element in effective leader-follower relationships because it inspires collaboration and commitment to common goals.[14]

Exhibit 9.3 Why Open the Communication Climate?

An open climate is essential for cascading vision, and cascading is essential because:

Natural Law 1: You Get What You Talk About

A vision must have ample 'air time' in an organization. A vision must be shared and practiced by leaders at every opportunity.

Natural Law 2: The Climate of an Organization Is a Reflection of the Leader

A leader who doesn't embody the vision and values doesn't have an organization that does.

Natural Law 3: You Can't Walk Faster Than One Step at a Time

A vision is neither understood nor accepted overnight. Communicating must be built into continuous, daily interaction so that over time followers will internalize it.

Source: Based on Bob Wall, Robert S. Slocum, and Mark R. Sobol, *Visionary Leader* (Rocklin, CA: Prima Publishing, 1992), pp. 87–89.

Another important outcome of an open communication climate is that employees understand how their actions interact with and affect others in the organization. Open communication encompasses the trend toward *open-book management*, which means sharing financial information with all employees to engender an attitude of employee ownership. Recall from the previous chapter that when employees feel a sense of ownership in the company, they are more highly motivated to achieve goals. In addition, when people have access to complete information, they make decisions that are good for the company. At Tampa-based AmeriSteel, opening the books and training all employees to understand the numbers helped cut the cost of converting a ton of scrap steel into a ton of finished steel from $145 to $127.[15] The open-book management program helped workers understand how every decision and action affects organizational success.

Communication across traditional boundaries enables leaders to hear what followers have to say, which means the organization gains the benefit of all employees' minds. The same perspectives batted back and forth between top executives don't lead to effective change, the creation of a powerful shared vision, or the network of personal relationships that keep organizations thriving. New voices and continuous conversation involving a broad spectrum of people revitalize and enhance communication.[16] Leaders at Boeing, which was hit hard in recent years by a series of ethical and political scandals, are using blogs as part of their strategy to create an open communication climate and rebuild trust among customers, employees, and the public.

IN THE LEAD

James F. Albaugh, Boeing Integrated Defense Systems

"I've always been a big believer in open and honest dialogue that gets the issues on the table," says James Albaugh, the chief executive of Boeing Integrated Defense Systems. Yet Albaugh's view hasn't always been shared by other Boeing executives. Indeed, defense contractors and aerospace companies in general aren't known for their openness. Yet after a series of scandals rocked the giant company, Boeing leaders are embracing a new approach to communication.

One aspect of the once-secretive company's attempt to build an open communication climate is the use of both external and internal blogs. Randy Baseler, vice president for marketing at Boeing Commercial Airplanes, for example, started a public blog to share the company's view on products and marketing strategies—and comments are welcome. The blog has exposed Boeing to some stinging criticism, but leaders believe the openness will lead to more constructive dialogue with customers and the public. Employees, too, are seeing a more open approach to communication. Internal blogs, such as one used by Albaugh, get conversations going and enable people to raise issues or point out problems anonymously.

It's too soon to say whether Boeing executives' use of blogs and other strategies will result in a more productive, open communication climate. Operating in an industry built on security clearances and classified government projects, secrecy is woven into the fibre of the organization. Some issues may always require secrecy, yet leaders are making a sincere effort to break down walls where possible, be more open with employees and the public, prevent the kind of ethical lapses that have occurred in recent years., and restore trust.[17]

Action Memo
As a leader, you can create an open communication climate by sharing both good and bad information, and you can facilitate communication across groups, departments, and hierarchical levels.

Leaders at Boeing, as at other organizations, want an open communication climate, because it can help to alleviate tension and conflict between departments, build trust, reaffirm employee commitment to a shared vision, and make the company more competitive.

Asking Questions

Managers typically think they should be the people with the right answers. After all, aren't people rewarded from grade school through college and in their first jobs for having answers? Leadership, though, is more about being the person with the right *questions*. Questions encourage people to think and empower them to find answers. Many leaders—indeed, most people in general—are unaware of the amazing power of questions. In our society, we're conditioned to come up with answers. Very young children are typically full of questions, but from an early age they're discouraged from asking them.[18] Children may be told that questioning adults is rude or disrespectful. Students are expected to hold up their hands in class to give the right answer, and they're often chastised for an incorrect response. Leaders often assume that if someone comes to them with a problem, their job is to solve it with the correct answer. They mistakenly fear that not having an answer means followers will lose respect for them. When leaders do ask questions, they typically focus on specific issues or problems, such as why a project is behind schedule or when a report will be finished. They don't use questioning as a way to develop new insights into work processes or to spur critical thinking by others.

Asking the right kinds of questions can benefit both leaders and followers in many ways.[19] Questioning leads to a free flow of ideas and information that is so important in today's changing organizations. With advances in technology and communications, no one person can master all the data and information needed to meet the challenges most organizations face. In addition, asking questions shows that leaders value the knowledge of others and are open to new ideas, which helps to build trusting, respectful relationships. Leadership questioning serves as a role model to let followers know that asking questions is not a sign of weakness but an opportunity for learning. Asking the right questions can also develop critical thinking skills. One study found that 99 percent of top managers surveyed believe that critical thinking skills at all levels are crucial to the success of their organizations.[20] As the best teachers have long known, using the Socratic method—asking questions rather than giving answers—provokes critical thought and leads to deeper, more lasting learning. The late management scholar Peter Drucker, who prided himself on asking "dumb questions," once said: "The leader of the past was a person who knew how to tell. The leader of the future will be a person who knows how to ask." Good leaders are willing to be vulnerable, and they have the courage to ask questions that others might not want to hear.[21]

What are the important questions for leaders to ask? There are two basic approaches to leader questioning. The traditional purpose of questioning is *leader-centered,* in that it seeks to inform the leader about specific issues, investigate problems or opportunities, and gather information, ideas, or insights. This type of questioning is important because it helps leaders tap into the expertise and ideas of followers. Yet leaders also use questions for another purpose. This approach is *follower-centered,* in that it seeks to encourage critical thinking, expand people's awareness, and stimulate learning. This type of questioning empowers followers and helps to build positive attitudes and follower self-confidence, as well.

Listening

Just as important as asking questions is sincerely listening to the answers. One of the most important tools in a leader's communication tool kit is listening, both to followers and customers. Many leaders now believe that important information flows from the bottom up, not top down, and that a crucial component of leadership is to listen effectively.[22] It is only by listening that leaders can identify strategic themes and understand how to influence others to achieve desired outcomes. Listening helps create an open communication climate, because people are willing to share their ideas, suggestions, and problems when they think someone is listening and genuinely values what they have to say.

Listening involves the skill of grasping and interpreting a message's genuine meaning. Remember that message reception is a vital link in the communication process. However, many people do not listen effectively. They concentrate on formulating what they're going to say next rather than on what is being said to them. Our listening efficiency, as measured by the amount of material understood and remembered by subjects 48 hours after listening to a 10-minute message, is, on average, no better than 25 percent.[23]

What constitutes good listening? Exhibit 9.4 gives 10 keys to effective listening and illustrates a number of ways to distinguish a bad listener from a good one. A key to effective listening is focus. A good listener's total attention is focused on the message; he isn't thinking about an unrelated problem in the purchasing department, how much work is piled up on his desk, or what to have for lunch. A good listener also listens actively, finds areas of interest, is flexible, works hard at listening, and uses thought speed to mentally summarize, weigh, and anticipate what the speaker says.

Effective listening is engaged listening. Good leaders ask lots of questions, force themselves to get out of their office and mingle with others, set up listening forums where people can say whatever is on their minds, and provide feedback to let people know they have been heard.[24]

Listening
the skill of grasping and interpreting a message's genuine meaning

Action Memo
Evaluate your listening skills by answering the questions in Leader's Self-Insight 9.2 on page 268.

Exhibit 9.4 Ten Keys to Effective Listening

Keys	Poor Listener	Good Listener
1. Listen actively	Is passive, laid back	Asks questions; paraphrases what is said
2. Find areas of interest	Tunes out dry subjects	Looks for opportunities, new learning
3. Resist distractions	Is easily distracted	Fights distractions; tolerates bad habits; knows how to concentrate
4. Capitalize on the fact that thought is faster than speech	Tends to daydream with slow speakers	Challenges, anticipates, summarizes; listens between lines to tone of voice
5. Be responsive	Is minimally involved	Nods; shows interest, positive feedback
6. Judge content, not delivery	Tunes out if delivery is poor	Judges content; skips over delivery errors
7. Hold one's fire	Has preconceptions; argues	Does not judge until comprehension is complete
8. Listen for ideas	Listens for facts	Listens to central themes
9. Work at listening	No energy output; faked attention	Works hard; exhibits active body state, eye contact
10. Exercise one's mind	Resists difficult material in favor of light, recreational material	Uses heavier material as exercise for the mind

Sources: Adapted from Sherman K. Okum, "How to Be a Better Listener," *Nation's Business* (August 1975), p. 62; and Philip Morgan and Kent Baker, "Building a Professional Image: Improving Listening Behavior," *Supervisory Management* (November 1985), pp. 34–38.

Go through the following questions, answering No or Yes next to each question. Mark each as truthfully as you can in light of your behavior in the last few meetings or social gatherings you attended.

	No	Yes
1. I frequently attempt to listen to several conversations at the same time.		
2. I like people to give me the facts and then let me make my own interpretation.		
3. I sometimes pretend to pay attention to people.		
4. I pay attention to nonverbal communications.		
5. I usually know what another person is going to say before he or she says it.		
6. I usually respond immediately when someone has finished talking.		
7. I evaluate what is being said while it is being said.		
8. I usually formulate a response while the other person is still talking.		
9. I notice the speaker's "delivery" style which may distract me from the content.		
10. I often ask people to clarify what they have said rather than guess at the meaning.		
11. I make a concerted effort to understand other people's points of view.		
12. People feel that I have understood their point of view even when we disagree.		

Scoring and Interpretation

The correct answers according to communication theory are as follows: No for questions 1, 2, 3, 5, 6, 7, 8, and 9. Yes for questions 4, 10, 11, and 12.

If you missed only two or three questions, you strongly approve of your own listening habits and you are on the right track to becoming an effective listener in your role as a leader. If you missed four or five questions, you have uncovered some doubts about your listening effectiveness, and your knowledge of how to listen has some gaps. If you missed six or more questions, you probably are not satisfied with the way you listen, and your followers and co-workers might feel that you are not paying attention when they speak. Work on improving your active listening skills.

Being a good listener expands a leader's role in the eyes of others and enhances the leader's influence. Consider the example of Patrick Charmel, CEO of Griffin Hospital in Derby, Connecticut. When Charmel took the top job, he knew that actively listening to employees and patients was key to helping the community hospital survive against larger, more aggressive competitors. Charmel implemented virtually every requested change, including installing wooden rather than steel handrails in hallways, banning fluorescent bulbs in favor of soft, indirect lighting, and adding cozy, home-style kitchens within easy access of all patient rooms. In addition, every patient now takes part in a detailed "case conference" with doctors, nurses, and other caregivers. They're encouraged to look at their medical charts and given detailed literature about their condition. Employees throughout the hospital are authorized to make decisions and take actions within their area of expertise based on the best interest of the patient.[25] By listening to the needs of patients and employees, and subsequently responding to those needs, Charmel transformed Griffin Hospital—as well as the relationships between leaders and employees and between employees and patients. This kind of transformation is what leader listening—indeed, communication—is all about.

Active listening is a daily, ongoing part of a leader's communication. The connection between personal satisfaction and being listened to, whether one is a customer or an employee, is not a mystery. We all know that few things are as maddening as not being listened to, whether we're talking to a doctor, a sales clerk, a partner, a customer service representative, a parent, or our boss. When people sense that they have been heard, they simply feel better. Dr. Robert Buckman, a cancer specialist who teaches other doctors, as well as businesspeople, how to break bad news, says you have to start by listening. "The trust that you build just by letting people say what they feel is incredible," Buckman says.[26] In the business world, customers are often infuriated when their requests are ignored or they are told they can't be accommodated, signals that nobody is listening to their needs. Furthermore, when leaders fail to listen to employees, it sends the signal, "you don't matter," which decreases commitment and motivation.

Action Memo

As a leader, you can learn to be a better listener. You can focus your total attention on what the other person is saying and work hard to listen—use eye contact; ask questions and paraphrase the message; and offer positive feedback.

Discernment

One of the most rewarding kinds of listening involves **discernment**. By this kind of listening, a leader detects the unarticulated messages hidden below the surface of spoken interaction, complaints, behavior, and actions. A discerning leader pays attention to patterns and relationships underlying the organization and those it serves.

Companies such as Kimberly-Clark and Procter & Gamble that live or die on new products have discovered the importance of discernment. Customers are frequently unable to articulate to market researchers exactly what they want, but some companies have become experts at discerning unspoken desires. For example, in an effort to discover what customers really value, Procter & Gamble recently sent researchers into women's homes to chart their emotional reactions to home hair coloring. They found that people get a huge psychological boost from dying their hair but a corresponding downslide when the color fades and roots start to show. Yet most women put off coloring because of the time and hassle of the process. P&G introduced Clairol's Nice & Easy Root Touch-Up, which allows people to do an easy, 10-minute stop-gap application, as well as introduced new formulas that cling to the hair but take less time and effort. The new products are sliding off the shelves.[27]

Effective communication with followers also depends on discernment. One leader dealing with a problem employee in the kitchen at an upscale restaurant got nowhere by asking outright why her sous chef had gone from consistently good performance to frequently being tardy or absent. After several days working almost full-time in the kitchen and keeping her eyes and ears open, the restaurant manager discerned that the quiet, introverted employee felt insecure and inadequate since a new head chef with a flamboyant personality had been hired. With this understanding, she got the two employees together and was able to solve the problem. As another example, leaders who are trying to implement major changes frequently have to use discernment to detect problems or deep-seated reasons for employee resistance. CEO Aylwin B. Lewis is applying discernment in his efforts to lead a turnaround at Sears Holdings Corp., which was formed from the recent merger of Kmart and Sears Roebuck & Co.

Discernment
listening in which a leader detects unarticulated messages hidden below the surface of spoken interaction

Aylwin B. Lewis, Sears Holdings Corp.

"Our worst stores are dungeons!" Aylwin Lewis shouts to a group of Kmart managers attending a dinner meeting, sounding for all the world like a Southern Baptist preacher. "Well, who wants to work in a dungeon? Who wants to shop in a dungeon? Who wants to walk into an environment that is so dull and lifeless that it is sucking the air out of your body?" The managers give their new CEO a standing ovation. They've been waiting for someone to recognize how demoralizing their work environment has become and speak the truth.

Lewis is using his superb communication skills in an effort to overhaul the giant corporation's dysfunctional culture and put both Sears and Kmart back on the road to profitability. A big part of his job is discerning the unspoken feelings of employees and determining why they are resistant to some of the changes Lewis and chairman Edward S. "Eddie" Lampert want to make. In addition, he needs to understand the company's problems from the customer's viewpoint. To accomplish that, Lewis spends Thursday through Saturday visiting stores, staying about three to four hours at each one. He's also changing the discernment of others by requiring that all managers and headquarters staff spend a day working in a store, and he's redesigning jobs so that store employees spend less time in back rooms and more time interacting with customers. Traditionally, both Sears and Kmart have had insular cultures that are more inward-looking than focused on the customer. Lewis is hoping the increased interaction among managers, employees, and customers will build a framework for a new, customer-focused culture.

"Make no mistake, we have to change," Lewis tells 500 leaders and potential leaders who participate 40 at a time in a day-long course called "Sowing the Seeds of Our Culture." The change won't be easy—some even say it's impossible—but Lewis's communication skills, including discernment, give him an edge. He's tapped into the feelings of store managers and employees by discerning that they are tired of feeling like losers and want leaders who are willing to tell the truth about the company's problems. Now he has to find a way to help them be winners again.[28]

Discernment is a critical skill for leaders such as Aylwin Lewis, because it enables them to tap into the unarticulated, often deep-seated needs, fears, desires, and hopes of followers and customers. A discerning leader hears the undercurrents that have yet to emerge.[29]

Dialogue
active sharing and listening in which people explore common ground and grow to understand each other and share a world view

Dialogue

When a group of people are actively listening to one another and paying attention to unspoken undercurrents, an amazing type of communication, referred to as dialogue, occurs. The "roots of dialogue" are *dia* and *logos,* which can be thought of as *stream of meaning.* In **dialogue**, people together create a stream of shared meaning that enables them to understand each other and share a view of the world.[30] People may start out as polar opposites, but by actively listening and talking authentically to one another, they discover their common ground, common issues, and common dreams on which they can build a better future.

Most of us have a tendency to infuse everything we hear with our own opinions rather than being genuinely open to what others are saying. In addition, traditional business values in the United States and most other Western countries reward people for forcefully asserting their own ideas and opinions and trying to discredit or contradict others.[31] But people can engage in dialogue only when they come to a conversation free of prejudgments, personal agendas, and "right" answers.

Action Memo
As a leader, you can use dialogue to help people create a shared sense of meaning and purpose. You can enable people to express their hopes and fears, suspend their convictions and explore assumptions, and become motivated to search for common ground.

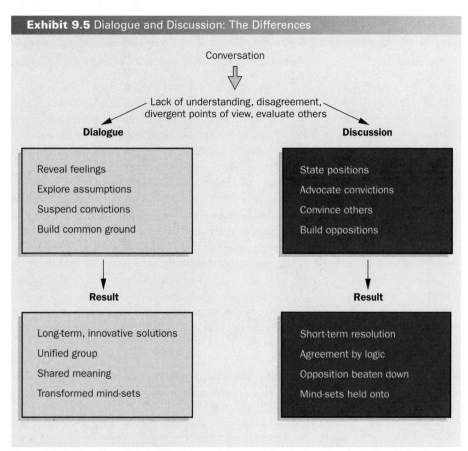

Exhibit 9.5 Dialogue and Discussion: The Differences

Conversation

Lack of understanding, disagreement, divergent points of view, evaluate others

Dialogue

- Reveal feelings
- Explore assumptions
- Suspend convictions
- Build common ground

Result

- Long-term, innovative solutions
- Unified group
- Shared meaning
- Transformed mind-sets

Discussion

- State positions
- Advocate convictions
- Convince others
- Build oppositions

Result

- Short-term resolution
- Agreement by logic
- Opposition beaten down
- Mind-sets held onto

Source: Adapted from Edgar Schein, "On Dialogue, Culture, and Organizational Learning," *Organizational Dynamics* (Autumn 1993), p. 46.

Participants in a dialogue do not presume to know the outcome, nor do they sell their convictions.

One way to understand the distinctive quality of dialogue is to contrast it with discussion.[32] Exhibit 9.5 illustrates the differences between a dialogue and a discussion. Typically, the intent of a discussion is to present one's own point of view and persuade others in the group to adopt it. A discussion is often resolved by logic or by "beating down" opposing viewpoints. Dialogue, on the other hand, requires that participants suspend their attachments to a particular point of view so that a deeper level of listening, synthesis, and meaning can emerge from the group. A dialogue's focus is to reveal feelings and build common ground, with the emphasis on inquiry rather than advocacy. As discussed in the Leader's Bookshelf, dialogue is particularly useful for conversations about difficult and emotionally charged issues. Henry Bertolon, cofounder and CEO of NECX, an online marketplace that was acquired by Converge, introduced dialogue to improve communication after a period of rapid growth led to internal tensions. "We'd have meetings that just melted down," he says. "Everyone would scream at each other and then leave." Bertolon hired Wil Calmas, a psychologist with an MBA, to lead a series of programs to get people talking—and listening—to one another on a deeper, authentic level. People were encouraged to express fear, hostility, frustration, secret wishes, whatever feelings were affecting their lives and work. The dialogue sessions created a safe environment for people to reveal their feelings, explore ideas, and build common ground. Bertolon also believed it helped employees be loose, flexible, and open to new ideas—ready to respond to the rapid changes taking place all around them.[33]

by Kerry Patterson, Joseph Grenny, Ron McMillan, and Al Switzler

Almost all of us have experienced the discomfort of a *crucial conversation*, which refers to a discussion where emotions run strong, opinions vary, and the stakes are high. Crucial conversations are conversations about tough issues that may cause conflict. Some examples that occur in the workplace include confronting a co-worker who makes suggestive comments or behaves offensively, approaching a boss who is breaking his own safety rules, or talking to a team member who isn't keeping commitments. For most of us, the more crucial the conversation, the less likely we are to handle it well. The authors of *Crucial Conversations: Tools for Talking When Stakes Are High* take a step-by-step approach to explore tools leaders can use to help create the conditions, within themselves and others, for effectively dealing with difficult issues.

THE LEADER'S ROLE IN CRUCIAL CONVERSATIONS

Leaders use the technique of dialogue to keep themselves and others calm and focused when discussions turn into crucial conversations. Here are a few guidelines:

- *Encourage a free flow of information.* When it comes to controversial, risky, and emotional conversations, effective leaders find a way to get all relevant information from themselves and others into the open. At the core of every successful crucial conversation is the free flow of information and ideas, with people feeling safe enough to openly and honestly express their opinions, feelings, and theories.
- *Start with heart.* A key principle of dialogue is that the leader starts with getting his or her own heart right. In a high-risk conversation, the leader has to start with the right motives and stay calm and focused no matter what happens. To stay focused, leaders have to know what they want for themselves, for others, and for the relationship.
- *When people are at cross purposes, think CRIB.* **C**ommit to seek a mutual purpose; **R**ecognize the purpose behind the strategy; **I**nvent a mutual purpose; **B**rainstorm new strategies. When people are poles apart on what they want, leaders can use this tool to bring people back to dialogue. They first get people to commit to finding some agreement, strive to discern the true purpose behind one another's words; find broader goals that can serve as a basis for mutual purpose; and, with a mutual purpose as a grounding, brainstorm ideas for meeting each person's individual needs.

COMMUNICATING WHEN IT MATTERS MOST

When we're angry, upset, frustrated, anxious, or otherwise influenced by strong emotions, conversation often deteriorates into *violence* or *silence,* verbally attacking the other person or verbally withdrawing. These are the times when dialogue is most important. *Crucial Conversations* offers ideas for thinking about and preparing for difficult conversations, along with specific tips and tools that can help leaders say and do the right thing.

Source: *Crucial Conversations: Tools for Talking When Stakes Are High,* by Kerry Patterson, Joseph Grenny, Ron McMillan, and Al Switzler, is published by McGraw-Hill.

Both forms of communication, dialogue and discussion, can result in organizational change. However, the result of a discussion is limited to a specific topic being deliberated, whereas the result of dialogue is characterized by group unity, shared meaning, and transformed mindsets. This kind of result is far-reaching. A new, common mindset is not the same thing as agreement, because it creates a reference point from which subsequent communication can start. As new and deeper solutions are developed, a trusting relationship is built among communicators, which is important to all communication episodes that follow. Dialogue thus transforms communication and, by extension, the organization.

The Leader as Communication Champion

To act as a communication champion, as described earlier in this chapter, leaders don't communicate just to convey information, but to persuade and influence others. They use communication skills to sell others on the vision and influence them to behave in ways that achieve goals and help accomplish the vision.

The ability to persuade others is more critical today than ever before. The command-and-control mindset of managers telling workers what to do and how to do it is gone. Employees don't just want to know *what* they should do but *why* they should do it. Leaders can follow four steps to practice the art of persuasion:[34]

1. *Establish credibility.* A leader's credibility is based on the leader's knowledge and expertise as well as his or her relationships with others. When leaders have demonstrated that they make well-informed, sound decisions, followers have confidence in their expertise. Leaders also build credibility by establishing good relationships and showing that they have others' best interests at heart.

2. *Build goals on common ground.* To be persuasive, leaders describe how what they're requesting will benefit others as well as the leader. For example, to get fast food franchisees to support new pricing discounts desired by headquarters, one leader cited research showing that the new pricing policies improved franchisees' profits.[35] When people see how they will personally benefit from doing something, they're usually eager to do it. When leaders can't find common advantages, it's a good signal that they need to adjust their goals and plans.

3. *Make your position compelling to others.* Leaders appeal to others on an emotional level by using symbols, metaphors, and stories to express their messages, rather than relying on facts and figures alone. By tapping into the imaginations of their followers, leaders can inspire people to accomplish amazing results.

4. *Connect emotionally.* Recall the discussion of emotional intelligence from Chapter 5. Good leaders sense others' emotions and adjust their approach to match the audience's ability to receive their message. Leaders use their emotional understanding to influence others in positive ways. In addition, by looking at how people have interpreted and responded to past events in the organization, leaders can get a better grasp on how followers may react to their ideas and proposals.

Persuasion is a valuable communication process that individuals can use to lead others to a shared solution or commitment. Karen Tse, founder and director of International Bridges to Justice, provides an excellent example of a persuasive leader. She was just 37 years old when she founded an organization that would change the lives of thousands of prisoners in places like China, Cambodia, and Vietnam by training public defenders and raising awareness of human rights abuses. Tse persuades by connecting emotionally to people, whether it is a businessman she's asking for a donation or a prison guard she's encouraging to allow prisoners daily exercise. Rather than fighting against the "bad," Tse says she tries to find the good in each person and work with that part of them to make changes. One Cambodian prison director who initially told Tse he would beat prisoners down "like rats" eventually worked with her to improve the prison's dark, dank cells, build a garden, and implement exercise classes for prisoners and guards.[36]

Action Memo
As a leader, you can increase your credibility by becoming knowledgeable and building positive relationships with others. You can show how your plans will benefit followers and tap into their imagination and emotions to inspire support.

To be persuasive and act a communication champion, leaders must communicate frequently and easily with others in the organization. Yet for some individuals, communication experiences are unrewarding, so they may consciously or unconsciously

The questions below are about your feelings toward communication with other people. Indicate whether each item below is Mostly False or Mostly True for you. There are no right or wrong answers. Many of the statements are similar to other statements. Do not be concerned about this. Work quickly and just record your first impressions.

	Mostly False	Mostly True
1. I look forward to expressing myself at meetings.	_____	_____
2. I hesitate to express myself in a group.	_____	_____
3. I look forward to an opportunity to speak in public.	_____	_____
4. Although I talk fluently with friends, I am at a loss for words on the platform.	_____	_____
5. I always avoid speaking in public if possible.	_____	_____
6. I feel that I am more fluent when talking to people than most other people are.	_____	_____
7. I like to get involved in group discussions.	_____	_____
8. I dislike to use my body and voice expressively.	_____	_____
9. I'm afraid to speak up in a conversation.	_____	_____
10. I would enjoy presenting a speech on a local television show.	_____	_____

Scoring and interpretation

Give yourself 1 point for each Mostly False answer to questions 2, 4, 5, 8, and 9. Give yourself 1 point for each Mostly True answer to questions 1, 3, 6, 7, and 10.

Your total points _____

This personal assessment provides an indication of how much apprehension (fear or anxiety) you feel in a variety of communication settings. Total scores may range from 0 to 10. A score of 3 or less indicates that you are more apprehensive about communication than the average person. A score of 8 or above indicates a low level of communication apprehension. Scores between 4 and 7 indicate average apprehension.

Individual questions above pertain to four common situations—public speaking, meetings, group discussions, and interpersonal conversations. Study the individual questions to see which situations create more apprehension for you. To be an effective communication champion, you should work to overcome communication anxiety. Interpersonal conversations create the least apprehension for most people, followed by group discussions, larger meetings, and then public speaking. Compare your scores with another student. What aspect of communication creates the most apprehension for you? How do you plan to improve it?

Source: Adapted from J. C. McCroskey, "Validity of the PRCA as an Index of Oral Communication Apprehension," *Communication Monographs* 45 (1978), pp. 192–203. Used with permission.

Action Memo

Complete the questions in Leader's Self-Insight 9.3 to learn your level of communication apprehension.

avoid situations where communication is required.[37] The term *communication apprehension* describes this avoidance behavior, and is defined as "an individual's level of fear or anxiety associated with either real or anticipated communication with another person or persons."[38]

To be effective communication champions, leaders pay attention to the channels of communication they use, employ aspects of storytelling and metaphor to enrich their communications, and use informal as well as formal communication techniques.

Selecting Rich Communication Channels

Channel
a medium by which a communication message is carried from sender to receiver

A **channel** is a medium by which a communication message is carried from sender to receiver. Leaders have a choice of many channels through which to communicate to subordinates. A leader may discuss a problem face-to-face, use the telephone, write a memo or letter, use e-mail, send a text message, or put an item in a newsletter, depending on the nature of the message. New communication media such as Web pages, blogs, intranets, and extranets have expanded leaders' options for communicating to followers as well as the organization's customers, clients, or shareholders.

The Continuum of Channel Richness

Research has attempted to explain how leaders select communication channels to enhance communication effectiveness.[39] Studies have found that channels differ in their capacity to convey information. Just as a pipeline's physical characteristics limit the kind and amount of liquid that can be pumped through it, a communication channel's physical characteristics limit the kind and amount of information that can be conveyed among people. The channels available to leaders can be classified into a hierarchy based on information richness. **Channel richness** is the amount of information that can be transmitted during a communication episode. Exhibit 9.6 illustrates the hierarchy of channel richness.

> **Channel richness**
> the amount of information that can be transmitted during a communication episode

The richness of an information channel is influenced by three characteristics: (1) the ability to handle multiple cues simultaneously; (2) the ability to facilitate rapid, two-way feedback; and (3) the ability to establish a personal focus for the communication. Face-to-face discussion is the richest medium, because it permits direct experience, multiple information cues, immediate feedback, and personal focus. Face-to-face discussions facilitate the assimilation of broad cues and deep, emotional understanding of the situation. For example, Tony Burns, former CEO of Ryder System, Inc., says he prefers to handle things face-to-face: "You can look someone in the eyes. You can tell by the look in his eyes or the inflection of his voice what the real problem or question or answer is."[40]

Telephone conversations are next in the richness hierarchy. Eye contact, gaze, posture, and other body language cues are missing, but the human voice still carries a tremendous amount of emotional information. Electronic messaging, or e-mail, which lacks both visual and verbal cues, is increasingly being used for communications that were once handled over the telephone. E-mail has improved the

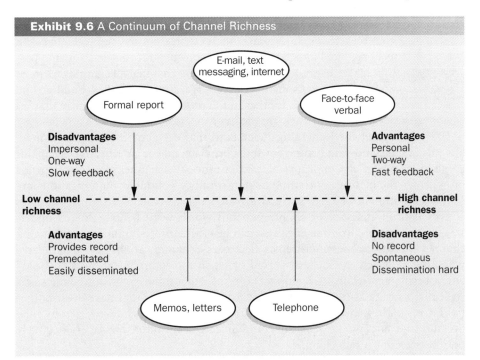

Exhibit 9.6 A Continuum of Channel Richness

speed and reduced the cost of long-distance communication in particular. Rather than playing "phone tag," a leader or employee can send an e-mail message to communicate necessary information. A recent survey by Ohio State University researchers found that about half of the respondents reported making fewer telephone calls since they began using e-mail. However, respondents also said they preferred the telephone or face-to-face conversations for expressing affection, giving advice, or communicating difficult news.[41]

Some studies have found that e-mail, instant messaging, and other forms of electronic communication can enable reasonably rich communication if the technology is used appropriately.[42] However, the proliferation of electronic media has contributed to *poorer* communication in many organizations. Employees who work in offices down the hall from one another will often send e-mail rather than communicating face to face. One employee reported that he was fired via e-mail—by a manager who sat five feet away in the same office.[43]

Other forms of electronic communication, such as video conferencing, recognize the need for channel richness, allowing for voice as well as body language cues. A lower level of richness is offered by the World Wide Web and company intranets, but these have opened new avenues for keeping in touch with employees and customers. An intranet enables leaders to disseminate certain types of information to a huge number of employees simultaneously, such as a traditional company newsletter might. Company Web pages and Web logs, or blogs, are increasingly being used to keep in closer touch with customers, suppliers, employees, and partners, and unlike print media, the Web allows for rapid feedback.

Written media such as notes and letters can be personalized, but they convey only the cues written on paper and are slow to provide feedback. Impersonal written media, including fliers, bulletins, and standard computer reports, are the lowest in richness. The channels are not focused on a single receiver, use limited information cues, and do not permit feedback. Paul Stevenson, president and CEO of ATI Medical, Inc., banned the practice of writing memos to encourage employees to use rich communication channels. He felt that memos substituted for human interaction and wasted valuable decision-making time. Stevenson attributes the company's yearly increase in sales to the productive and timely personal interactions that have resulted from the no-memo policy.[44] Lacking memos as a communication channel, ATI employees must communicate in person to get their ideas out, and they build strong relationships with one another in the process. Leaders recognize that innovation and teamwork are the byproducts of using rich channels.

It is important for leaders to understand that each communication channel has advantages and disadvantages, and that each can be an effective means of communication in the appropriate circumstances.[45] Channel selection depends on whether the message is routine or non-routine. Routine communications are simple and straightforward, such as a product price change. Routine messages convey data or statistics or simply put into words what people already understand and agree on. Routine messages can be efficiently communicated through a channel lower in richness. Written or electronic communications also are effective when the audience is widely dispersed or when the communication is "official" and a permanent record is required.[46] On the other hand, non-routine messages typically concern issues of change, conflict, or complexity that have great potential for misunderstanding. Non-routine messages often are characterized by time pressure and surprise. Leaders can communicate non-routine messages effectively only by selecting a rich channel.

Action Memo

As a leader, you can choose rich forms of communication, such as face to face or the telephone, when an issue is complex, emotionally charged, or especially important. For a routine, straightforward message, you can use a written or electronic form of communication.

Consider a CEO trying to work out a press release with public relations people about a plant explosion that injured 15 employees. If the press release must be ready in three hours, the communication is truly non-routine and forces a rich information exchange. The group will meet face-to-face, brainstorm ideas, and provide rapid feedback to resolve disagreement and convey the correct information. If the CEO has three days to prepare the release, less information capacity is needed. The CEO and public relations people might begin developing the press release with an exchange of telephone calls and e-mail messages.

The key is to select a channel to fit the message. During a major acquisition, one firm chose to send senior executives to all major work sites, where 75 percent of the acquired workforce met the officials in person. The results were well worth the time and expense of the personal appearances. Participating leaders claimed that the workers saw them as understanding and willing to listen—people they would not mind working for.[47] On the other hand, consider the executive who addressed a letter "Dear Team" to inform employees in his department that they would be required to make significant changes to achieve a new corporate quality goal of zero defects. Although the letter indicated that the supervisor realized this would "not be welcome news," it directs employees to renew their commitment to quality and pull together as a team. The letter concludes with a P.S.: "As of tomorrow, I will be on vacation in Hawaii for the next four weeks and out of reach." If you were a member of this supervisor's team, how would you feel about such a communication? Most leader communication by its very nature is comprised of non-routine messages. Although leaders maximize the use of all channels, they don't let anything substitute for the rich face-to-face channel when important issues are at stake.

Effectively Using Electronic Communication Channels

Virtual communication through voice mail, e-mail, video conferencing, and text messaging has become a fact of life in today's organizations. The U.S. Army uses electronic technology to rapidly transmit communications about weather conditions, the latest intelligence on the enemy, and so forth to lieutenants on the battlefield. Companies such as Celanese Chemicals use wireless text messaging to keep in touch with salespeople in the field and help them close deals faster.[48] These new tools provide highly efficient ways of communicating, and they can be particularly useful for routine messages. Text messaging, which allows people to share short-hand messages instantly, has rapidly grown in use and is becoming more common than e-mail in some organizations.[49] Many leaders find that text messaging helps them get responses faster and collaborate with people more smoothly. "It's just like having my office next to any of [my employees] and being able to stick my head in and ask a question," says Jim McCain, president of sales consulting firm McCain and Associates, which has employees scattered from Tallahassee, Florida, to Hyderabad, India.[50]

Action Memo
As a leader, you can avoid letting electronic communications become a complete substitute for human interactions. You can resist the urge to criticize or complain in an electronic message, and never send an e-mail when you are angry or upset.

Electronic communication has many advantages, but there are disadvantages as well. For one thing, electronic methods increase the potential for communication errors. People often come across as sounding cold, arrogant, or insensitive when they attempt to discuss delicate issues via e-mail, for example. Things that might be handled smoothly in a face-to-face conversation or over the phone turn into massive problems by fostering resentment, bitterness, and hard feelings.[51]

Another equally disturbing concern, one psychiatrist argues, is that the growing use of technology for communicating has created hidden problems for both individuals and organizations by depriving people of the "human moments" that are needed to energize people, inspire creativity, and support emotional well-being.[52] People need to interact with others in physical space to build the connections that create great organizations. Electronic communication is here to stay, and has brought tremendous advantages. The key for leaders is to benefit from the efficiencies of new technologies while preventing their unintended problems. Here are some tips for effectively using electronic communication:

- *Combine high-tech and high-touch.* Never allow electronic communication to take the place of human connections. People who work together should meet face to face on a regular basis, and leaders should get to know their followers in real as well as virtual space. Many companies that use virtual workers require that they come into the office at least once a month for unstructured face time.[53] A real-estate developer in Boston set up a free-pizza day once a week when widely scattered workers could come by the office, sit around the table in his office, and just talk.[54]

- *Consider the circumstances.* People who know one another well and have worked together a long time can typically communicate about more complex issues via e-mail or instant messaging than can people who have a new working relationship.[55] When people have a long-term working relationship, there is less potential for misunderstandings and hard feelings. In addition, when all parties involved have a good grasp of the issues being discussed, e-mail can be used effectively. A leader of a long-standing, well-functioning team could thus use e-mail more extensively than the leader of a team that has just been formed.

- *Read twice before you hid the "Send" button.* Never send an e-mail or instant message without reading it at least twice. You wouldn't send a letter without reading it over to make sure it says what you meant to say and checking the grammar and spelling. Give the same attention to your electronic messages. Make sure you use the niceties, like saying please and thank you, and signing your name. Be as courteous to the receiver as if you were delivering the message in person. Another important point is to never send an electronic message when you are angry or upset. This is a situation that definitely calls for richer communication channels.

- *Know what's off limits.* Select richer channels of communication as well for important, complex, or sensitive messages. Layoffs, firings, and reprimands should always be given face-to-face, or at least via telephone. In addition, never use e-mail to complain about or ridicule your boss or colleagues. A human resources employee at CNN tells of writing an e-mail calling her boss all sorts of evil names, intending to send it to a friend in another department. Only too late did she realize she'd sent the e-mail to the boss instead.[56] It's easy to do. Be careful what you write. Exhibit 9.7 lists some further dos and don'ts concerning subjects appropriate for electronic mail.

Using Stories and Metaphors

The Ute Indians of Utah, as well as many other native tribes, made the best storytellers their tribal leaders.[57] Why? Because storytelling is a powerful means of persuasion and influence. Stories enable leaders to connect with people on an emotional as well as an intellectual level. In addition, telling stories helps people

Exhibit 9.7 Dos and Don'ts of Electronic Mail

Do

- Use e-mail to set up meetings, to recap spoken conversations, or to follow up on information already discussed face to face.
- Keep e-mail messages short and to the point. Many people read e-mail on hand-held devices, which have small screens.
- Use e-mail to prepare a group of people for a meeting. For example, it is convenient to send the same documents to a number of people and ask them to review the materials before the meeting.
- Use e-mail to transmit standard reports.
- Act like a newspaper reporter. Use the subject line to quickly grab the reader's attention, much like a newspaper headline. Put the most important information in the first paragraph. Answer any questions—who, what, when, where, why, and how—that are pertinent.

Don't

- Use e-mail to discuss something with a colleague who sits across the aisle or down the hall from you. Take the old-fashioned approach of speaking to each other.
- Lambast a friend or colleague via e-mail—and especially don't copy others on the message.
- Use e-mail to start or perpetuate a feud. If you get an e-mail that tempts you to respond in a scathing manner, stop yourself. You may be misinterpreting the message. Even if you're not, take the high road.
- Write anything in an e-mail you wouldn't want published in a newspaper. E-mail with sensitive or potentially embarrassing information has an uncanny way of leaking out.

Sources: Based on "15 Dos and Don'ts" box in Andrea C. Poe, "Don't Touch that 'Send' Button," *HR Magazine* (July 2001), pp. 74–80; and Michael Goldberg, "The Essential Elements of E-Mail," *CIO* (June 1, 2003), p. 24.

make sense of complex situations, inspires action, and brings about change in ways that other forms of communication cannot.

Leaders have to be conscious of the language they use in all situations. Just being aware of the terminology they choose and the definitions and context they create is one way leaders enhance communications with others. Even simple language choices make a tremendous difference for leadership. However, it is by using language rich in metaphor and storytelling that leaders can create a deep and lasting effect on others. For example, at National Grange Mutual, a property-casualty insurance company, leaders in the claims unit picked up on a statement made by one of the company's independent agents. When discussing how the claims unit should relate to customers, the agent said, "I want my customers to feel your arm go around them when they have a claim." Leaders used this evocative image to focus employees on reengineering the claims process to provide better, faster, more caring service.[58]

A study of the speeches of U.S. presidents found that those who used imagery to convey their messages were rated higher in both personal charisma and historical greatness, suggesting that a leader's ability to achieve a vision is related to the ability to paint followers a verbal picture of what can be accomplished if everyone pulls together.[59] A leader is responsible for directing followers' attention to a vision and the values that can help attain it, for defining the meaning of situations and objectives, and for presenting messages in ways that make them palpable and meaningful to organizational members. People seek meaning in their daily work and want to understand their role in the larger context of the organization. It is up to leaders to provide that context for followers, to frame activity with discrete meaning.[60] By using language rich in metaphor and storytelling, leaders can make sense of situations in ways that will be understood similarly throughout the organization.

Action Memo

As a leader, you can use stories and metaphors to help people connect emotionally with your message and the key values you want to instill. You can symbolize important messages through your appearance, body language, facial expressions, and daily actions.

Stories need not be long, complex, or carefully constructed. A story can be a joke, a metaphor, or a verbal snapshot of something from the leader's past experience.[61] Jean-Pierre Garnier, CEO of GlaxoSmithKline, used the metaphor of a snake to encourage his 100,000 employees to stamp out bureaucracy and work smarter and faster: "Say you're in a plant and there's a snake on the floor," Garnier said in his year-end address. "What are you going to do? Call a consultant? Get a meeting together?" Instead, Garnier said people should do "one thing: You walk over there and step on the friggin snake." Garnier's image has people talking in a more colorful way about his request that they simplify processes and "don't accept that every time something comes up you have to get a whole team of people to discuss it."[62]

Some believe that the true impact of a leader depends primarily on the stories he or she tells and how followers receive them.[63] Storytelling is a powerful way to relay a message because a story evokes both visual imagery and emotion, which helps people connect with the message and the key values. People are almost always able to apply some aspect of the story to themselves, and a story is often much more convincing and more likely to be remembered than a simple directive or a batch of facts and figures.[64]

Evidence for the compatibility of stories with human thinking was demonstrated by a study at the Stanford Business School.[65] The point was to convince MBA students that a company practiced a policy of avoiding layoffs. For some students, only a story was used. For others, statistical data were provided that showed little turnover compared to competitors. For other students, statistics and stories were combined, and yet other students were shown the company's policy statement. Of all these approaches, students presented with the story alone were most convinced about the avoiding layoffs policy.

Informal Communication

Leaders don't just communicate stories in words. They also *embody* the stories in the way that they live their lives and what they seek to inspire in others.[66] Leaders are watched, and their appearance, behavior, actions, and attitudes are symbolic to others. Even the selection of a communication channel can convey a symbolic message. In other words, members of an organization attach meaning to the channel itself. Reports and memos typically convey formality and legitimize a message. Personal visits from a leader are interpreted as a sign of teamwork and caring.[67] The very modes of communication are symbolic, such as when students gauge the importance of a topic by the amount of time a professor spends talking about it, or when an individual experiences indignation at receiving a "Dear John" letter instead of having a relationship terminated in person.

Symbols are a powerful informal tool for communicating what is important. Many people don't realize that they are communicating all the time, without saying a word, by their facial expressions, body language, and actions.[68] Leaders strive to be aware of what they signal to others in addition to verbal messages.

Indeed, **nonverbal communication**, that is, messages transmitted through action and behavior, accounts for over one half of the entire message received in a personal encounter.[69] People interpret leader actions as symbols, just as they attach meaning to words.

In interpreting a leader's nonverbal cues, followers determine the extent to which a leader's actions correspond with his or her verbal messages. If a leader talks about customer service, but spends no time with customers, followers would likely place little value on service. Research suggests that if there is a discrepancy between a person's verbal and nonverbal communication, the nonverbal is granted more weight by the interpreter.[70] Consider how a plant manager symbolized the importance of cost-cutting when he took over at a struggling factory. He noticed that when most of the management team had to travel, they flew first class. Rather than issuing a directive that first-class travel was not allowed, the plant manager always flew coach. Soon, everyone throughout the company was flying coach.[71] Leaders use actions to symbolize their vision and draw attention to specific values and ideas.

Informal communication is built into an open communication climate and includes interactions that go beyond formal, authorized channels. One example of informal communication is "management by wandering around (MBWA)."[72] MBWA means that leaders leave their offices and speak directly to employees as they work. These impromptu encounters send positive messages to followers. In addition, the communication is richer, and therefore likely to make a lasting impression in both directions. When E. Grady Bogue became interim chancellor at Louisiana State University, one of the first things he did was walk through the departments on campus. He wound up in the biology building, where he enjoyed an extended tour of the facility by a faculty member he ran across. Bogue remarked that he learned an enormous amount about the university operations and the strengths, weaknesses, and needs of the biology program that was "more direct, personal and meaningful than any written communication might have conveyed."[73] Thus, both leaders and followers benefit from informal communications.

Nonverbal communication
messages transmitted through action and behavior

Action Memo
As a leader, you can be more effective by using informal communication and management by wandering around. You can get out and mingle with followers and customers to learn about their ideas, problems, and needs through informal observation and conversation.

Communicating in a Crisis

A leader's skill at communicating becomes even more crucial during times of rapid change, uncertainty, or crisis. Over the past few years, the sheer number and scope of crises—everything from terrorist attacks, school shootings, and major natural disasters such as Hurricane Katrina and the Asian tsunami, to corporate accounting scandals and ethical lapses—have made communication a more demanding role for leaders. Organizations face small crises every day, such as the loss of computer data, charges of racial discrimination, a factory fire, or a flu epidemic. Moreover, incidents of intentional evil acts such as bombings and kidnappings continue to increase, with the impact on people and organizations rivaling that of major natural disasters.[74]

Communicating in a crisis has always been part of a leader's job, but the world has become so fast, interconnected, and complex that unexpected events happen more frequently and often with greater and more painful consequences. As a former governor of California put it in referring to California's 2000–2001 energy crisis, ". . . extraordinary times . . . require extraordinary leadership."[75] To be prepared, leaders can develop four skills for communicating in a crisis.[76]

1. *Stay calm; listen harder.* A leader's emotions are contagious, so leaders have to stay calm and focused. Perhaps the most important part of a leader's job in a crisis situation is to absorb people's fears and uncertainties, which means listening is more important than ever. Leaders also tailor their messages to reflect hope and optimism at the same time they acknowledge the danger and difficulties, thus giving comfort, inspiration, and hope to others. "You do not pass uncertainty down to your team members," said Eugene Kranz, the NASA flight director charged with returning the crippled *Apollo 13* spacecraft safely to earth in 1970. "No matter what is going on around you, you have to be cooler than cool."[77]

2. *Be visible.* When people's worlds have become ambiguous and uncertain, they need to feel that someone is in control. Many leaders underestimate just how important their presence is during a crisis.[78] They have a tendency to want to hide, gather information, think things through, deal with their own emotions, and develop a strategy for tackling the problem. However, being a leader means stepping out immediately, both to reassure followers and respond to public concerns. Face-to-face communication with followers during difficult times is crucial for good leadership. People want to know that their leaders care about them and what they're going through. After Hurricane Katrina destroyed Valero's St. Charles oil refinery near New Orleans, CEO Bill Greehey got special permission to fly into New Orleans' closed airport so he could visit the facility and talk face-to-face with employees about their experiences and what they needed from the company.[79]

3. *Tell the truth.* Leaders gather as much information from as many diverse sources as they can, do their best to determine the facts, and then "get the awful truth out" to employees and the public as soon as possible.[80] Rumor control is critical. Consider what happened at Duke University Hospital after doctors there made one of the worst mistakes in modern medical history—transplanting the wrong heart and lungs into 17-year-old Jesica Santillan, who later died. Although the story was already out, it took nine days for Duke leaders to fully admit the hospital's mistake. By that time, the organization's image was severely damaged, and rumors of unauthorized medical experiments and doctors pulling the plug against the family's wishes were rampant. To counteract the damage, Duke's health chief and the surgeons involved in the transplant went on CBS's *60 Minutes* to tell the whole story and offer a mournful public apology.[81]

4. *Communicate a vision for the future.* Although leaders should first deal with the physical and emotional needs of people, they also need to get back to work as soon as possible. The group, organization, or community has to keep going, and most people want to be a part of the rebuilding process, to feel that they have something to look forward to. Moments of crisis present excellent opportunities for leaders to communicate a vision for the future that taps into people's emotions and desires for something better.

The following example illustrates how a new CEO effectively applied these crisis communication skills to lead a turnaround at Xerox.

Anne Mulcahy, Xerox Corp.

Anne Mulcahy, a Xerox veteran who began her career as a copier salesperson, says she was probably a last-resort choice for CEO of the company, but Mulcahy has saved the giant corporation from almost certain death. When she took over, Xerox was in a mess: $19 billion in debt, revenues falling by double digits, the stock price sliding, and the Securities and Exchange Commission investigating the company for possible fraud.

Previous leaders had often pretended that things were getting better at the giant company, but Mulcahy took a different approach. Five months after she became CEO, Mulcahy bluntly told Wall Street analysts that the company's business model was unsustainable. She'd been warned that the market would react badly—and indeed, Xerox stock fell 60 percent within hours—but Mulcahy believed it was important to tell the truth about the company's dire situation. She was equally straight with employees, spending three months traveling the globe listening to employees and customers tell her what they thought had gone wrong and sharing with them her plans for revitalizing the company, which included massive layoffs and outsourcing. When she made the difficult decision to close the struggling personal computer division, Mulcahy personally walked the halls to tell people she was sorry and let them vent their anger. To remaining managers and employees, she reportedly "looked people in the eye and said, 'This is going to be one of the most stressful situations of your life, so if your heart isn't in it, please don't stay.'"

Her courage in telling the truth gained Mulcahy the respect and commitment of employees. In addition, she showed that she genuinely cared about people. She hid her own fears and insecurities and, even during the darkest days, refused to consider bankruptcy, choosing instead to focus people on her vision that Xerox could once again be a great company if everyone pulled together. Her willingness to work with employees on the front lines expanded her credibility and enabled her to energize people who had been demoralized and hopeless. "She was leading by example," said one of Xerox's creditors. "Everybody at Xerox knew she was working hard, and that she was working hard for them."[82]

Anne Mulcahy didn't hide in her office and send out pink slips while pretending things were okay at Xerox. She emphasized face-to-face communication and keeping employees up to date on the company's problems. People rallied around her and rose to the challenge she put before them. By mid-2006, Xerox was growing again, debt had been slashed significantly, the stock price had quadrupled, and *Fortune* magazine named Anne Mulcahy the second most powerful woman in business.[83]

Summary and Interpretation

Effective communication is an essential element of leadership. Leaders are communication champions who inspire and unite people around a common sense of purpose and identity. They lead strategic conversations that get people talking across boundaries about the vision, key strategic themes, and the values that can help the group or organization achieve desired outcomes. Five elements necessary for strategic conversations are an open communication climate, asking questions, active listening, discernment, and dialogue. Open communication is essential for building trust, and it paves the way for more opportunities to communicate with followers, thus enabling the organization to gain the benefits of all employees' minds. However, leaders must be active listeners and must learn to discern the hidden undercurrents that have yet to emerge. It is through listening and discernment, both with followers and customers, that leaders identify strategic issues and build productive relationships that help the organization succeed. When active listening spreads throughout a group, a type of communication referred to as dialogue occurs. Through dialogue, people discover common ground and together create a shared meaning that enables them to understand each other and share a view of the world.

Leader communication is purpose-directed, and an important element is persuading others to act in ways that achieve goals and accomplish the vision. Four steps for practicing the art of persuasion are to establish credibility, build goals on common ground, make your position compelling, and connect with others on an emotional level. Leaders use rich communication channels, communicate through stories and metaphors, and rely on informal as well as formal communication. Electronic communication channels present new challenges for leader communication. Electronic channels can be very advantageous if used appropriately, but their use increases the potential for communication errors, and these channels are not effective for complex or sensitive messages. The final point emphasized in this chapter is that effective communication becomes even more crucial during times of rapid change and crisis. Four critical skills for communicating in a crisis are to remain calm, be visible, "get the awful truth out," and communicate a vision for the future.

Discussion Questions

1. How do you think leadership communication differs from conventional management communication?

2. If you were to evaluate an organization based on the degree of open communication climate, what things would you look for? Discuss.

3. A manager in a communication class remarked, "Listening seems like minimal intrusion of oneself into the conversation, yet it also seems like more work." Do you agree or disagree? Discuss.

4. How does dialogue differ from discussion? Give an example of each from your experience.

5. Some senior executives believe they should rely on written information and computer reports because these yield more accurate data than face-to-face communications do. Do you agree? Discuss.

6. Why is *management by wandering around* (MBWA) considered effective communication?

7. If you were to communicate symbolically with your team to create a sense of trust and team work, what would you do?

8. How do leaders use communication to influence and persuade others? Think of someone you have known who is skilled in the art of persuasion. What makes this person an effective communicator?

9. Why is storytelling such a powerful means of communication for a leader? Can you give examples from your own experience of leaders who have used metaphor and story? What was the effect on followers?

10. Think about a recent crisis, such as the shootings at Virginia Tech University or the detection of radiation on British Airways planes, and discuss how you think leaders handled crisis communication.

Leadership at Work

Listen Like a Professional

The fastest way to become a great listener is to act like a professional listener, such as a clinical psychologist who uses listening to heal another person. Therapists drop their own point of view to concentrate on the patient's point of view. The therapist listens totally, drawing out more information rather than thinking about a response.

The next time you are in a conversation in which the other person talks about some problem or concern practice professional listening by doing the following:

1. Hold a steady gaze on the person's left eye (not the nose or face, but the left eye)—use a soft gaze, not a hard stare.

2. Remove your thoughts and opinions from the conversation—quell your mind chatter and your desire to say something in response.

3. Suspend judgment—rather than critically analyzing what is being said, feel empathy as if you are walking in the other person's shoes.

4. Draw out the other person's thoughts with brief questions and paraphrasing. Repeat the professional listening approach at least three times with different people to get comfortable with it.

List your thoughts on how the other people responded to your listening, and what it felt like to you.

Other person responded:

1. _____

_____

_____

2. _____

_____

_____

3. _____

_____

_____

What I felt:

1. _____

_____

_____

2. _____

_____

_____

3. _____

_____

_____

In Class: The instructor can divide students into pairs—listener and speaker—in class to practice this exercise. The "speaking" students can be asked to talk about some small problem or annoyance they encountered in the previous day or two. The "listening" students can be given instructions to not speak during the first trial, and instead just maintain a soft gaze into the speaker's left eye and respond only with body language (facial expressions and nods). The speaking student should continue until they have no more to say or until they feel an emotional shift and the problem seems to have disappeared. After students switch roles and play both speaker and listener, the instructor can ask the class for perceptions of what happened and what they were feeling during the conversation.

It works well to have the students choose a second pairing, and redo the exercise with a new problem. The only difference the second time is that the "listener" role is given fewer restrictions, so the listener can make brief comments such as to paraphrase or ask a short question. The listeners, however, should keep spoken comments to a minimum and definitely should not offer their own ideas or point of view. After the students finish, the instructor can gather opinions about what the experience was like for both the speaker and the listener. Key questions include the following: What did it feel like to listen rather than respond verbally to what another person said? What is the value of this professional listening approach? In what situations is professional listening likely to be more or less effective? If the instructor desires, the exercise can be done a third time to help students get more comfortable with a true listening role.

Source: Adapted from Michael Ray and Rochelle Myers, *Creativity in Business* (Broadway Books, 2000), pp. 82–83.

Leadership Development: Cases for Analysis

The Superintendent's Directive

Educational administrators are bombarded by possible innovations at all educational levels. Programs to upgrade math, science, and social science education, state accountability plans, new approaches to administration, and other ideas are initiated by teachers, administrators, interest groups, reformers, and state regulators. In a school district, the superintendent is the key leader; in an individual school, the principal is the key leader.

In the Carville City School District, Superintendent Porter has responsibility for 11 schools—eight elementary, two junior high, and one high school. After attending a management summer course, Porter sent an e-mail directive to principals stating that every teacher in their building was required to develop a set of performance objectives for each class they taught. These objectives were to be submitted one month after the school opened, and copies were to be forwarded to the superintendent's office. Porter also wrote that he had hired the consultant who taught the summer management course to help teachers write objectives during their annual opening in-service day of orientation work.

Mr. Weigand, Principal of Earsworth Elementary School, sent his teachers the following memo: "Friends, Superintendent Porter has asked me to inform you that written performance objectives for your courses must be handed in one month from today. This afternoon at the in-service meeting, you will receive instruction in composing these objectives."

In response, one teacher sent a note asking, "Is anything wrong with our teaching? Is this the reason we have to spend hours writing objectives?"

Another teacher saw Weigand in the hall and said, "I don't see how all this objectives business will improve my classroom. It sounds like an empty exercise. In fact, because of the time it will take me to write objectives, it may hurt my teaching. I should be reading on new developments and working on lesson plans."

In response to these and other inquiries, Principal Weigand announced to the teachers with a follow-up memo, "I was told to inform all of you to write performance objectives. If you want to talk about it, contact Dr. Porter."

Source: Based on Robert C. Mills, Alan F. Quick, and Michael P. Wolfe, *Critical Incidents in School Administration* (Midland, MI: Pendell Publishing Co., 1976).

QUESTIONS

1. Evaluate the communications of Porter and Weigand. To what extent do they communicate as leaders? Explain.

2. How would you have handled this if you were Superintendent Porter?

3. How would you have handled the communication if you were the principal of Earsworth Elementary School? Why?

Imperial Metal Products

Imperial Metal Products, a mid-sized manufacturing company located in the southeast, makes wheel rims for automobiles. With 42 furnaces on the production floor, the temperature often reaches well over 100 degrees Fahrenheit. Even employees who work in the lab complain of the heat, because they have to venture onto the production floor numerous times a day to take metal samples from the furnaces.

A year ago, the top executive team recommended to the board that the employee lounge, located at the far end of the production floor near the plant manager's office, be air-conditioned. Company profits had been good, and the managers wanted to do something to show appreciation for employees' good work. The board enthusiastically approved the proposal and the work was completed within a month.

At the end of the fiscal year, the top management team met to review the company's operations for the past year. Profits were higher than ever, and productivity for the past year had been excellent. The team unanimously agreed that the employees deserved additional recognition for their work, and they considered ways to show management's appreciation. Robb Vaughn suggested that it might be interesting to see what workers thought about the action managers took last year to have the lounge air-conditioned. Everyone agreed, and the human resources director, Amy Simpkins, was instructed to send a questionnaire to a sample of employees to get their reaction to the air-conditioned lounge. The team agreed to meet in six weeks and review the results.

Simpkins mailed a simple form to 100 randomly selected employees with the following request: "Please state your feelings about the recently air-conditioned employee lounge." The response rate was excellent, with 96 forms being returned. Simpkins classified the responses into the following categories and presented her report to the top management team:

1. I thought only managers could use the lounge.	25
2. I didn't know it was air-conditioned.	21
3. If management can spend that kind of money, they should pay us more.	21
4. The whole plant should be air-conditioned.	10
5. I never use the lounge anyway.	8
6. OK	8
7. Miscellaneous comments	3

Top managers were shocked by the responses. They had expected a majority of the employees to be grateful for the air conditioning. One of the managers suggested that it was useless to do anything else for employees, because it wouldn't be appreciated anyway. Another argued, however, that top managers just needed to communicate better with plant workers. She suggested posting flyers on the bulletin boards announcing that the lounge was now air-conditioned, and perhaps putting a memo in with employees' next paycheck. "They slave away eight or nine hours a day in that heat; at least we need to let them know they have a cool place to take a break or eat lunch!" she pointed out. "And if we plan to do another 'employee appreciation' project this year, maybe we should send out another questionnaire and ask people what they want."

Source: Based on "The Air Conditioned Cafeteria," in John M. Champion and John H. James, *Critical Incidents in Management: Decision and Policy Issues*, 6th ed. (Homewood, IL: Irwin, 1989), pp. 280–281.

QUESTIONS

1. How would you rate the communication climate at Imperial Metal Products?

2. What channels do you think top managers should use to improve communications and both keep employees informed as well as learn about what they are thinking?

3. If you were a top manager at Imperial, what is the first step you would take? Why?

References

1 Carol Hymowitz, "Executives Who Build Truth-Telling Cultures Learn Fast What Works" (In the Lead column), *The Wall Street Journal* (June 12, 2006), p. B1.

2 Cynthia Crossen, "Blah, Blah, Blah: The Crucial Question for These Noisy Times May Just Be: 'Huh?'" *The Wall Street Journal* (July 10, 1997), p. A1; Paul Roberts, "Live! From Your Office! It's . . ." *Fast Company,* (October 1999), pp. 151–170; and Cathy Olofson, "Can We Talk? Put Another Log on the Fire," *Fast Company,* (October 1999), p. 86.

3 Eric Berkman, "Skills," *CIO,* (March 1, 2002), pp. 78–82; Peter Lowry and Byron Reimus, "Ready, Aim, Communicate," *Management Review* (July 1996).

4 Studies from The Elliot Leadership Institute, reported in Louise van der Does and Stephen J. Caldeira, "Effective Leaders Champion Communication Skills," *Nation's Restaurant News* (March 27, 2006), p. 20; and Dennis Tourish, "Critical Upward Communication: Ten Commandments for Improving Strategy and Decision Making," *Long Range Planning* 38 (2005), pp. 485–503.

5 Bernard M. Bass, *Bass & Stogdill's Handbook of Leadership,* 3rd ed. (New York: The Free Press, 1990).

6 Henry Mintzberg, *The Nature of Managerial Work* (New York: Harper & Row, 1973).

7 Mary Young and James E. Post, "Managing to Communicate, Communicating to Manage: How Leading Companies Communicate with Employees," *Organizational Dynamics* (Summer 1993), pp. 31–43; and Warren Bennis and Burt Nanus, *Leaders: The Strategies for Taking Charge* (New York: Harper & Row, 1985).

8 Colin Mitchell, "Selling the Brand Inside," *Harvard Business Review* (January 2002), pp. 99–105.

9 Phillip G. Clampitt, Laurey Berk, and M. Lee Williams, "Leaders as Strategic Communicators," *Ivey Business Journal* (May–June 2002), pp. 51–55.

10 Ian Wylie, "Can Philips Learn to Walk the Talk?" *Fast Company* (January 2003), pp. 44–45.

11 John Luthy, "New Keys to Employee Performance and Productivity," *Public Management* (March 1998), pp. 4–8.

12 Reported in Van Der Does and Caldeira, "Effective Leaders Champion Communication Skills."

13 "What Is Trust," results of a survey by Manchester Consulting, reported in Jenny C. McCune, "That Elusive Thing Called Trust," *Management Review* (July–August 1998), pp. 10–16.

14 Mirta M. Martin, "Trust Leadership," *The Journal of Leadership Studies* 5, no. 3 (1998), pp. 41–49.

15 Julie Carrick Dalton, "Between the Lines: The Hard Truth About Open-Book Management," *CFO* (March 1999), pp. 58–64.

16 Gary Hamel, "Killer Strategies That Make Shareholders Rich," *Fortune* (June 23, 1997), pp. 70–84.

17 Stanley Holmes, "Into the Wild Blog Yonder," *BusinessWeek* (May 22, 2006), pp. 84, 86.

18 This discussion is based on "The Power of Questions," (Practical Wisdom column), *Leadership: The Journal of the Leader to Leader Institute* (Spring 2005), pp. 59–60.

19 Based on "The Power of Questions" and Quinn Spitzer and Ron Evans, "The New Business Leader: Socrates with a Baton," *Strategy & Leadership* (September–October 1997), pp. 32–38.

20 Reported in Spitzer and Evans, "Socrates with a Baton."

21 Geoffrey Colvin, "The Wisdom of Dumb Questions," *Fortune* (June 27, 2005), p. 157.

22 C. Glenn Pearce, "Doing Something About Your Listening Ability," *Supervisory Management* (March 1989), pp. 29–34; and Tom Peters, "Learning to Listen," *Hyatt Magazine* (Spring 1988), pp. 16–21.

23 Gerald M. Goldhaber, *Organizational Communication,* 4th ed. (Dubuque, IA: Wm. C. Brown, 1980), p. 189.

24 Tom Peters, "Learning to Listen."

25 David H. Freedman, "Intensive Care," *Inc.* (February 1999), pp. 72–80.

26 Curtis Sittenfeld, "Good Ways to Deliver Bad News," *Fast Company* (April 1999), pp. 58, 60.

27 Deborah Ball and Ellen Byron, "Getting to the Root of the Problem," *The Wall Street Journal* (November 11–12, 2006), pp. A1, A8.

28 Robert Berner, "At Sears, a Great Communicator," *BusinessWeek* (October 31, 2005), pp. 50, 52.

29 Joseph Jaworski, *Synchronicity: the Inner Path of Leadership* (San Francisco, CA.: Berrett-Koehler, 1996).

30 David Bohm, *On Dialogue* (Ojai, CA: David Bohm Seminars, 1989).

31 Bill Isaacs, *Dialogue and the Art of Thinking Together* (New York: Doubleday, 1999); and "The Art of Dialogue," column in Roberts, "Live! From Your Office!"

32 Based on Glenna Gerard and Linda Teurfs, "Dialogue and Organizational Transformation," in *Community Building: Renewing Spirit and Learning in Business,* Kazimierz Gozdz, ed. (New Leaders Press, 1995).

33 Scott Kirsner, "Want to Grow? Hire a Shrink!" *Fast Company* (December–January 1998), pp. 68, 70.

34 This section is based heavily on Jay A. Conger, "The Necessary Art of Persuasion," *Harvard Business Review* (May–June 1998), pp. 84–95.

35 Conger, "The Necessary Art of Persuasion."

36 Elizabeth Weiss Green, "The Power of Persuasion," *U.S. News and World Report* (August 7, 2006), pp. 60, 62.

37 J. C. McCroskey and V. P. Richmond, "The Impact of Communication Apprehension on Individuals in Organizations, *Communication Quarterly,* 27 (1979), pp. 55–61.

38 J. C. McCroskey, "The Communication Apprehension Perspective," in J. C. McCroskey & J. A. Daly, eds. *Avoiding Communication: Shyness, Reticence, and Communication Apprehension* (London: Sage Publications Inc., 1984), pp. 13–38.

39 Robert H. Lengel and Richard L. Daft, "The Selection of Communication Media as an Executive Skill," *Academy of Management Executive* 2 (August 1988), pp. 225–232; and Richard L. Daft and Robert Lengel, "Organizational Information Requirements, Media Richness and Structural Design," *Managerial Science* 32 (May 1986), pp. 554–572.

40 Ford S. Worthy, "How CEOs Manage Their Time," *Fortune* (January 18, 1988), pp. 88–97.

41 "E-mail Can't Mimic Phone Calls," *Johnson City Press* (September 17, 2000), p. 31.

42 John R. Carlson and Robert W. Zmud, "Channel Expansion Theory and the Experiential Nature of Media Richness Perceptions," *Academy of Management Journal* 42, no. 2 (1999), pp. 153–170; R. Rice and G. Love, "Electronic Emotion," *Communication Research* 14 (1987), pp. 85–108.

43 Anne Fisher, "Readers Weigh in on Rudeness and Speechmaking" (Ask Annie column), *Fortune* (January 10, 2000), p. 194.

44 "Enforcing a No-Memo Policy," *Small Business Report* (July 1988), pp. 26–27.

45 Ronald E. Rice, "Task Analyzability, Use of New Media, and Effectiveness: A Multi-Site Exploration of Media Richness," *Organizational Science* 3, no. 4 (November 1994), pp. 502–527.

46 Richard L. Daft, Robert H. Lengel, and Linda Klebe Treviño, "Message Equivocality, Media Selection and Manager Performance: Implications for Information Systems," *MIS Quarterly* 11 (1987), pp. 355–368.

47 Young and Post, "Managing to Communicate, Communicating to Manage."

48 Greg Jaffe, "Tug of War: In the New Military, Technology May Alter Chain of Command," *The Wall Street Journal* (March 30, 2001), pp. A3, A6; Susanna Patton, "The Wisdom of Starting Small," *CIO* (March 15, 2001), pp. 80–86.

49 Daniel Nasaw, "Instant Messages Are Popping Up All Over," *The Wall Street Journal* (June 12, 2003), p. B4.

50 Scott Kirsner, "IM Is Here. RU Prepared?" *Darwin Magazine* (February 2002), pp. 22–24.

51 Edward M. Hallowell, "The Human Moment at Work" *Harvard Business Review* (January–February 1999), pp. 58–66; Andrea C. Poe, "Don't Touch That 'Send' Button!" *HR Magazine* (July 2003), pp. 74–80.

52 Hallowell, "The Human Moment at Work."

53 Hallowell, "The Human Moment at Work"; Deborah L. Duarte and Nancy Tennant Snyder, *Mastering Virtual Teams: Strategies, Tools, and Techniques That Succeed* (San Francisco: Jossey-Bass, 2000).

54 Hallowell, "The Human Moment."

55 Carlson and Zmud, "Channel Expansion Theory and the Experiential Nature of Media Richness Perceptions."

56 Jared Sandberg, "Workplace E-Mail Can Turn Radioactive in Clumsy Hands," *The Wall Street Journal* (February 12, 2003), p. B1.

57 David M. Boje, "Learning Storytelling: Storytelling to Learn. Management Skills," *Journal of Management Education* 15, no. 3 (August 1991), pp. 279–294.

58 John Guaspari, "A Shining Example," *Across the Board* (May–June 2002), pp. 67–68.

59 Cynthia G. Emrich, Holly H. Brower, Jack M. Feldman, and Howard Garland, "Images in Words: Presidential Rhetoric, Charisma, and Greatness," *Administrative Science Quarterly* 46 (2001), pp. 527–557.

60 Linda Smircich and Gareth Morgan, "Leadership: The Management of Meaning," *Journal of Applied Behavioral Science* 18 (November 3, 1982), pp. 257–273.

61 Bill Birchard, "Once Upon a Time," *Strategy + Business,* Issue 27 (Second Quarter 2002), pp. 99–104.

62 Carol Hymowitz, "Smart Executives Shed Some Traditional Tasks to Focus on Key Areas," (In the Lead column), *The Wall Street Journal* (June 10, 2006), p. B1.

63 Howard Gardner, *Leading Minds: An Anatomy of Leadership* (New York: Basic Books, 1995).

64 Robert F. Dennehy, "The Executive as Storyteller," *Management Review* (March 1999), pp. 40–43.

65 J. Martin and M. Powers, "Organizational Stories: More Vivid and Persuasive than Quantitative Data," in B. M. Staw, ed., *Psychological Foundations of Organizational Behavior* (Glenview, IL: Scott Foresman, 1982), pp. 161–168.

66 Gardner, *Leading Minds.*

67 Jane Webster and Linda Klebe Treviño, "Rational and Social Theories as Complementary Explanations of Communication Media Choices: Two Policy Capturing Studies," *Academy of Management Journal* (December 1995), pp. 1544–1572.

68 Mac Fulfer, "Nonverbal Communication: How To Read What's Plain As the Nose . . . or Eyelid . . . or Chin . . . On Their Faces," *Journal of Organizational Excellence* (Spring, 2001), pp. 19–27.

69 Albert Mehrabian, *Silent Messages* (Belmont, CA: Wadsworth, 1971); and Albert Mehrabian, "Communicating Without Words," *Psychology Today* (September 1968), pp. 53–55.

70 I. Thomas Sheppard, "Silent Signals," *Supervisory Management* (March 1986), pp. 31–33.

71 Linda Klebe Treviño, Laura Pincus Hartman, and Michael Brown, "Moral Person and Moral Manager: How Executives Develop a Reputation for Ethical Leadership," *California Management Review* 42, no. 4 (Summer 2000), pp. 128–142.

72 Thomas H. Peters and Robert J. Waterman, Jr., *In Search of Excellence* (New York: Harper & Row, 1982); and Tom Peters and Nancy Austin, *A Passion for Excellence: The Leadership Difference* (New York: Random House, 1985).

73 Grady Bogue, *Leadership by Design: Strengthening Integrity in Higher Education* (San Francisco, CA: Jossey-Bass, Inc., 1994), p. 81.

74 Ian I. Mitroff and Murat C. Alpaslan, "Preparing for Evil," *Harvard Business Review* (April 2003), pp. 109–115.

75 Quoted in James Sterngold, "Power Crisis Abates, But It Hounds Gov. Davis," *The New York Times* (October 5, 2001), p. A16.

76 This section is based on Leslie Wayne and Leslie Kaufman, "Leadership, Put to a New Test," *The New York Times* (September 16, 2001), Section 3, pp. 1, 4; Jerry Useem, "What It Takes," *Fortune* (November 12, 2001), pp. 126–132; Andy Bowen, "Crisis Procedures That Stand the Test of Time," *Public Relations Tactics* (August 2001), p. 16; and Matthew Boyle, "Nothing Really Matters," *Fortune* (October 15, 2001), pp. 261–264.

77 Useem, "What It Takes."

78 Stephen Bernhut, "Leadership, with Michael Useem," (Leader's Edge interview), *Ivey Business Journal* (January–February 2002), pp. 42–43.

79 Janet Guyon, "The Soul of a Moneymaking Machine," *Fortune* (October 3, 2005), pp. 113–120.

80 Ian I. Mitroff, "Crisis Leadership," *Executive Excellence* (August 2001), p. 19.

81 Allison Fass, "Duking It Out," *Forbes* (June 9, 2003), pp. 74–76.

82 Betsy Morris, "The Accidental CEO," *Fortune* (June 23, 2003), pp. 58–67; Kevin Maney, "Mulcahy Traces Steps of Xerox's Comeback," *USA Today* (September 21, 2006), p. B4; and Carol Hymowitz, "Should CEOs Tell Truth About Being in Trouble, Or Is That Foolhardy?" (In the Lead column), *The Wall Street Journal* (February 15, 2005), p. B1.

83 The 50 Most Powerful Women in Business," *Fortune* (October 16, 2006), pp. 145–154.

Chapter 10

Your Leadership Challenge

After reading this chapter, you should be able to:

- Turn a group of individuals into a collaborative team that achieves high performance through shared mission and collective responsibility.

- Understand and handle the stages of team development, and design an effective team in terms of size, diversity, and levels of interdependence.

- Develop and apply the personal qualities of effective team leadership for traditional, virtual, and global teams.

- Handle conflicts that inevitably arise among members of a team.

Chapter Outline

Leading Teams

It's 5:45 A.M. and 50-year-old Charles Pope is bending and stretching along with nearly 200 other Seagate Technology staff members in the dark of a New Zealand park. It's the start of another day at the sixth annual Eco Seagate. The event, dreamed up by CEO Bill Watkins, is an intense week of team-building that will be topped off by an adventure race in which teams made up of people from a dozen or so countries will kayak, hike, bike, swim, and rappel down a cliff. Eco Seagate is one way the company's leaders strive to break down barriers, boost confidence, and build a sense of teamwork among Seagate's 45,000 employees spread around the world. People are chosen to reflect a mix of disciplines, hierarchical levels, countries, and ages.

After the morning stretch, the CEO or another top leader gives an unscripted talk about a key attribute of a strong team, such as trust, healthy conflict, or shared responsibility. Then teams head out to learn the skills they'll need to compete in the final race. They earn points for various activities that they can use on race day to buy better maps, skip a checkpoint, or use a bridge over a frigid river. One of Pope's team members with a fear of heights won extra points for her team by volunteering to rappel off a bridge, something she did because the team's success became more important than her own fear. Throughout the week, and particularly during the race itself, people have to rely on one another and be willing to ask for and give help as needed to accomplish the team's mission. To get a head start, some teams started their team-building before they ever arrived in New Zealand, by e-mailing or calling back and forth to establish good communication and bonds of trust.

Pope, who is chief financial officer, once pooh-poohed Eco Seagate as a waste of money—the 2006 event cost $1.8 million—until he attended one and became a believer. "I consider this an investment," Pope says, now indicating it would be one of the last things he'd cut from the budget.

Despite the fun, Eco Seagate "isn't a vacation," Pope says, and leaders follow up to ask employees what they learned from the event and how it has made them do things differently.[1]

From the classroom to the battlefield, from the assembly line to the executive suite, and from giant corporations such as Seagate, the world's largest maker of hard drives, to small companies like plantscaping firm Growing Green and non-profit organizations like Parkland Memorial Hospital, teams are becoming the basic building block of organizations. The ability to inspire and support teamwork is critical to effective leadership.

The use of teams has increased dramatically in response to new competitive pressures, the need for greater flexibility and speed, and a desire to give people more opportunities for involvement and decision making. Many organizations have reported great success with teams, including increased productivity, quality improvements, greater innovation, and higher employee satisfaction. At Xerox, for example, production plants using teams reported a 30 percent increase in productivity. Federal Express cut service problems such as incorrect bills or lost packages by 13 percent by using teams.[2] A recent study of team-based organizations in Australia supports the idea that teams provide benefits for both organizations and employees through higher labor productivity, a flatter management structure, and lower employee turnover.[3]

Leader's Bookshelf
The Five Dysfunctions of a Team

by Patrick Lencioni

According to Patrick Lencioni, author of *The Five Dysfunctions of a Team,* building an effective team requires behaviors that are remarkably simple yet extremely difficult to put into practice day after day. "For all the attention that it has received over the years . . . teamwork is as elusive as it has ever been within most organizations," Lencioni writes. "The fact remains that teams, because they are made up of imperfect human beings, are inherently dysfunctional." To accomplish results, Lencioni argues that teams must overcome five specific dysfunctions.

THE FIVE DYSFUNCTIONS

Lencioni says leaders can enable team members to embody the behaviors described below to help them surmount each of the dysfunctions.

1. *Absence of Trust.* Members of great teams trust one another on a deep emotional level and are comfortable being vulnerable with one another. People feel free to openly share their hopes, fears, mistakes, and ideas.
2. *Fear of Conflict.* Trust enables people to engage in passionate dialogue about issues and decisions. Team members don't hesitate to disagree with, question, or challenge one another in the interest of finding the best approach to a problem or task.
3. *Lack of Commitment.* When team members are open with one another and can effectively disagree, they are able to obtain genuine commitment around important decisions. Because everyone has had a say, there are no unresolved issues.

4. *Avoidance of Accountability.* Members of effective teams also hold one another accountable. They don't rely on the leader or other managers as the primary source of accountability. Team leaders and followers are mutually accountable to one another for outcomes.
5. *Inattention to Results.* In an effective team, individual members set aside their own needs and agendas to focus on what is best for the team. Collective results, not individual performance or status, defines success.

A ROADMAP FOR OVERCOMING THE DYSFUNCTIONS

Lencioni begins his exploration of teamwork with a story about a leader in a realistic but fictional organization, which allows readers to lose themselves in interesting characters and situations. He then outlines the five dysfunctions in detail, concluding with a self-assessment and some suggested tools for overcoming teamwork problems. Taken together, these elements of *The Five Dysfunctions of a Team* provide an interesting and effective guide for leaders attempting to build effective teams in today's real world of pressures, deadlines and distractions. Although the book was originally intended for business leaders, it has also gained attention from several NFL coaches who use the book to help them maximize teamwork in organizations made up of high-performing individuals.

Source: *The Five Dysfunctions of a Team,* by Patrick Lencioni, is published by John Wiley & Sons.

However, teams present greater leadership challenges than does the traditional hierarchical organization. This chapter's Leader's Bookshelf examines five specific problems associated with teams in organizations and offers tips for how leaders can overcome them. In a team, every member has to develop some leadership capability. And for some companies, team members may be spread all over the world, as they are at Seagate, which intensifies the leadership challenge. This chapter explores team leadership in today's organizations. We define various types of teams, look at how teams develop, and examine characteristics such as size, interdependence, and diversity that can influence team effectiveness. The chapter then explores topics such as cohesiveness and performance, task and socioemotional roles of team members, and the leader's personal impact on building effective teams. The new challenge of leading virtual and global teams is also discussed. The final part of the chapter looks at how leaders manage team conflict, including using negotiation.

Teams in Organizations

More and more companies are recognizing that the best way to meet the challenges of higher quality, faster service, and total customer satisfaction is through an aligned, coordinated, and committed effort by all employees,[4] and organizing people into teams helps meet this objective. The concept of teamwork is a fundamental change in the way work is organized. Consider the Ralston Foods Sparks, Nevada, plant, which produces cereal. The plant's 150 or so workers are organized into six operating work groups, which are in turn divided into small teams. Many of the teams function without designated leaders and handle all issues and problems that arise, including hiring and firing, scheduling, quality, budget management, and disciplinary problems. The top leaders of Cirque du Soleil, including the CEO, chief operating officer, chief financial officer, and vice president of creation, function as a team to coordinate, develop, and oversee 13 acrobatic troupes that travel to 100 cities on four continents. And at Massachusetts General Hospital, the emergency trauma team performs so smoothly that the team switches leaders seamlessly, depending on the crisis at hand. With each new emergency, direction may come from a doctor, intern, nurse, or technician—whoever is particularly experienced with the problem.[5]

Yet, teams are not right for every organizational situation. Some tasks by their very nature are better performed by individuals. In addition, organizations frequently fail to realize the benefits of teams because they have a hard time balancing authority between leaders and teams, fail to provide adequate training or support for teamwork, or continue to manage people as a collection of individuals rather than on a team level.[6] Effective teams have leaders who consciously build a team identity, actively involve all members, act as coaches and facilitators rather than bosses, and invest time and resources for team learning.[7]

What Is a Team?

A **team** is a unit of two or more people who interact and coordinate their work to accomplish a shared goal or purpose.[8] This definition has three components. First, teams are made up of two or more people. Teams can be large, but most have fewer than 15 people. Second, people in a team work together regularly. People who do not interact regularly, such as those waiting in line at the company cafeteria or riding together in the elevator, do not compose a team. Third, people in a team share a goal, whether it is building a car, placing mentally challenged clients in job training, or writing a textbook. Today's students are frequently assigned to complete assignments in teams. In this case, the shared goal is to complete the task and receive an acceptable grade. However, in many cases, student teams are given a great deal of structure in terms of team roles and responsibilities, time frame, activities, and so forth. In a work setting, these elements are typically much more ambiguous and have to be worked out within the team.

A team is a group of people, but the two are not one and the same. A professor, coach, or employer can put together a *group* of people and never build a *team*. The sports world is full of stories of underdog teams that have won championships against a group of players who were better individually but did not make up a better team.[9] For example, the 2004 U.S. Olympic basketball team was made up entirely of superstar players, yet the members never coalesced as a team, instead functioning as a group of individual players. The team came in third and lost to Lithuania. In contrast, the 1980 U.S. hockey team that beat the Soviets to win gold at the Lake Placid Olympics consisted of a bunch of no-name players.

Team
a unit of two or more people who interact and coordinate their work to accomplish a shared goal or purpose

Lessons from Geese

Fact 1: As each goose flaps its wings, it creates an "uplift" for the birds that follow. By flying in a "V" formation, the whole flock adds 71 percent greater flying range than if each bird flew alone.

Lesson: People who share a common direction and sense of community can get where they are going quicker and easier because they are traveling on the thrust of one another.

Fact 2: When a goose falls out of formation, it suddenly feels the drag and resistance of flying alone. It quickly moves back into formation to take advantage of the lifting power of the bird immediately in front of it.

Lesson: If we have as much sense as a goose, we stay in formation with those headed where we want to go. We are willing to accept their help and give our help to others.

Fact 3: When the lead goose tires, it rotates back into the formation and another goose flies to the point position.

Lesson: It pays to take turns doing the hard tasks and sharing leadership. Like geese, people are interdependent on each other's skills, capabilities, and unique arrangements of gifts, talents, or resources.

Fact 4: The geese flying in formation honk to encourage those up front to keep up their speed.

Lesson: We need to make sure our honking is encouraging. In groups where there is encouragement, the production is much greater. The power of encouragement (to stand by one's heart or core values and encourage the heart and core of others) is the quality of honking we seek.

Fact 5: When a goose gets sick, wounded, or shot down, two geese drop out of the formation and follow it down to help and protect it. They stay until it dies or is able to fly again. Then, they launch out with another formation or catch up with the flock.

Lesson: If we have as much sense as geese, we will stand by each other in difficult times as well as when we are strong.

Source: 1991 Organizational Development Network. Original author unknown.

Coach Herb Brooks picked players based on their personal chemistry—how they worked together as a team—rather than on their individual abilities and egos.[10] Only when people sublimate their individual needs and desires and synthesize their knowledge, skills, and efforts toward accomplishment of a communal goal do they become a team. This chapter's *Consider This* illustrates the spirit and power of teamwork.

Exhibit 10.1 lists the primary differences between a group and a team. A team achieves high levels of performance through shared leadership, a sense of purpose, and collective responsibility by all members working toward a common goal. Teams are characterized by equality; in the best teams, there are no individual "stars" and everyone sublimates individual ego to the good of the whole.

All organizations are made up of groups of people who work together to accomplish specific goals. Although not all organizations use teams as they are defined in Exhibit 10.1, many of the leadership ideas presented in this chapter can also be applied in leading other types of groups.

Exhibit 10.1	Differences Between Groups and Teams

Group	Team
Has a designated, strong leader	Shares or rotates leadership roles
Individual accountability	Mutual and individual accountability (accountable to each other)
Identical purpose for group and organization	Specific team vision or purpose
Performance goals set by others	Performance goals set by team
Works within organizational boundaries	Not inhibited by organizational boundaries
Individual work products	Collective work products
Organized meetings, delegation	Mutual feedback, open-ended discussion, active problem-solving

Sources: Based on Jon R. Katzenbach and Douglas K. Smith, "The Discipline of Teams," *Harvard Business Review* (March–April 1995), pp. 111–120; and Milan Moravec, Odd Jan Johannessen, and Thor A. Hjelmas, "Thumbs Up for Self-Managed Teams," *Management Review* (July–August 1997), pp. 42–47 (chart on 46).

How Teams Develop

Smoothly functioning teams don't just happen. They are built by leaders who take specific actions to help people come together as a team. One important point is for leaders to understand that teams go through distinct stages of development.[11] New teams are different from mature teams. If you have participated in teams to do class assignments, you probably noticed that the team changed over time. In the beginning, members have to get to know one another, establish some order, divide responsibilities, and clarify tasks. These activities help members become part of a smoothly functioning team. The challenge for leaders is to recognize the stages of development and help teams move through them successfully.

Research suggests that teams develop over several stages. Exhibit 10.2 shows one model of the stages of team development. These four stages typically occur in sequence, although there can be overlap. Each stage presents team members and leaders with unique problems and challenges.

Action Memo

As a leader, you can guide your team through its stages of development. Early on, you can help members know one another, and then encourage participation and common purpose, followed by clarifying goals and expectations. Finally, you can concentrate on helping the team achieve high performance.

Forming The **forming** stage of development is a period of orientation and getting acquainted. Team members find out what behavior is acceptable to others, explore friendship possibilities, and determine task orientation. Uncertainty is high, because no one knows what the ground rules are or what is expected of them. Members will usually accept whatever power or authority is offered by either formal or informal leaders. The leader's challenge at this stage of development is to facilitate communication and interaction among team members to help them get acquainted and establish guidelines for how the team will work together. It is important at this stage that the leader try to make everyone feel comfortable and like a part of the team. Leaders can draw out shy or quiet team members to help them establish relationships with others.

Forming
stage of team development that includes orientation and getting acquainted

Storming During the **storming** stage, individual personalities emerge more clearly. People become more assertive in clarifying their roles. This stage is marked by conflict and disagreement. Team members may disagree over their perceptions of the team's mission or goals. They may jockey for position or form subgroups based

Storming
stage of team development in which individual personalities and conflicts emerge

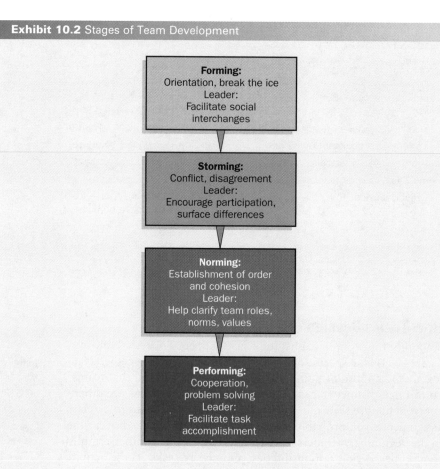

Exhibit 10.2 Stages of Team Development

on common interests. The team is characterized by a general lack of unity and cohesiveness. It is essential that teams move beyond this stage or they will never achieve high performance. The leader's role is to encourage participation by each team member and help them find their common vision and values. Members need to debate ideas, surface conflicts, disagree with one another, and work through the uncertainties and conflicting perceptions about team tasks and goals.

Norming At the **norming** stage, conflict has been resolved and team unity and harmony emerge. Consensus develops as to who the natural team leaders are, and members' roles are clear. Team members come to understand and accept one another. Differences are resolved and members develop a sense of cohesiveness. This stage typically is of short duration and moves quickly into the next stage. The team leader should emphasize openness within the team and continue to facilitate communication and clarify team roles, values, and expectations.

Performing During the **performing** stage, the major emphasis is on accomplishing the team's goals. Members are committed to the team's mission. They interact frequently, coordinate their actions, and handle disagreements in a mature, productive manner. Team members confront and resolve problems in the interest of task accomplishment. At this stage, the team leader should concentrate on facilitating high task performance and helping the team self-manage to reach its goals.

Norming
stage of team development in which conflicts have been resolved and team unity emerges

Performing
stage of team development in which the major emphasis is on accomplishing the team's goals

Leaders at McDevitt Street Bovis, one of the country's largest construction management firms, strive to accelerate the stages of team development to help put teams on a solid foundation.

McDevitt Street Bovis

McDevitt Street Bovis credits its team-building process for quickly and effectively unifying teams, circumventing damaging and time-consuming conflicts, and preventing lawsuits related to major construction projects. The goal is to take the team to the performing stage as quickly as possible by giving everyone an opportunity to get to know one another, explore the ground rules, and clarify roles, responsibilities and expectations.

Rather than the typical construction project characterized by conflicts, frantic scheduling, and poor communications, Bovis wants its collection of contractors, designers, suppliers, and other partners to function like a true team—putting the success of the project ahead of their own individual interests. The team is first divided into separate groups that may have competing objectives—such as the clients in one group, suppliers in another, engineers and architects in a third, and so forth—and asked to come up with a list of their goals for the project. Although interests sometimes vary widely in purely accounting terms, there are almost always common themes. By talking about conflicting goals and interests, as well as what all the groups share, facilitators help the team gradually come together around a common purpose and begin to develop shared values that will guide the project. After jointly writing a mission statement for the team, each party says what it expects from the others, so that roles and responsibilities can be clarified. The intensive team-building session helps take members quickly through the forming and storming stages of development, but meetings continue all the way through the project to keep relationships strong and to keep people on target toward achieving the team mission. "We prevent conflicts from happening," says facilitator Monica Bennett. Leaders at McDevitt Street Bovis believe building better teams builds better buildings.[12]

As at McDevitt Street Bovis, personal contact and face-to-face communication is important for building individuals into a team.

Team Types and Characteristics

In the following sections, we will look at various types of teams that have traditionally been used in organizations and examine some characteristics that are important to team dynamics and performance. Later in the chapter, we will discuss the new challenge of leading virtual and global teams.

Traditional Types of Teams

There are three fundamental types of teams used in today's organizations: functional teams, cross-functional teams, and self-directed teams. Exhibit 10.3 illustrates these types of teams.

Functional Teams A **functional team** is part of the traditional vertical hierarchy. This type of team is made up of a supervisor and his or her subordinates in the formal chain of command. Sometimes called a *vertical team* or a *command team*, the functional team can include three or four levels of hierarchy within a department. Typically, a functional team makes up a single department in the organization. For example, the quality control department at Blue Bell Creameries in

Functional team
team made up of a supervisor and subordinates in the formal chain of command

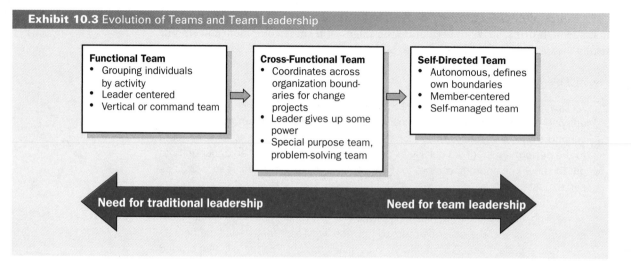

Exhibit 10.3 Evolution of Teams and Team Leadership

Brenham, Texas, is a functional team that tests all incoming ingredients to make sure only the best products go into the company's ice cream. A financial analysis department, a human resources department, and a sales department are all functional or vertical teams. Each is created by the organization within the vertical hierarchy to attain specific goals through members' joint activities.

Cross-Functional Teams As the name implies, **cross-functional teams** are made up of members from different functional departments within the organization. Employees are generally from about the same hierarchical level in the organization, although cross-functional teams sometimes cross vertical as well as horizontal boundaries. Cross-functional teams typically have a specific team leader and coordinate across boundaries to lead change projects, such as creating a new product in a manufacturing organization or developing an interdisciplinary curriculum in a middle school. Cross-functional teams are generally involved in projects that affect several departments and therefore require that many views be considered.

Cross-functional teams facilitate information sharing across functional boundaries, generate suggestions for coordinating the departments represented, develop new ideas and solutions for existing organizational problems, and assist in developing new practices or policies. The members of one type of cross-functional team, the *problem-solving* or *process-improvement* team, meet voluntarily to discuss ways to improve quality, efficiency, and the work environment. Their recommendations are proposed to top executives for approval.

Another frequent application of cross-functional teams is for change projects, especially new product innovation, because effectively developing new products and services requires coordination across many departments. IBM uses cross-functional "swat teams" that work directly with clients such as Wal-Mart, Charles Schwab, and the Mayo Clinic to design products and services to solve specific problems. At Charles Schwab, for example, the company's extensive portfolio analysis using Forecaster software was supposed to inspire more trading and higher commissions, but it was so slow that it was turning customers off. An IBM team of hardware, software, research, strategy, and sales people came up with the idea of organizing all of Schwab's computers into a so-called "grid" that functions

Cross-functional team
team made up of members from different functional departments within an organization

Action Memo
As a leader, you can create a cross-functional team to handle a change project, such as product innovation, that requires coordination across departmental boundaries. Use a problem-solving or process-improvement team to initiate ideas for improving quality and efficiency.

as one giant computer. That way, Forecaster could grab the computing power it needed from anywhere in the company rather than relying on dedicated servers that would bog down at busy times. As a result, a broker could get recommendations from Forecaster in 20 seconds that might have taken two days in the past. The grid idea has since been applied to solve similar problems in other commercial enterprises.[13]

Evolution to Self-Directed Teams Cross-functional teams may gradually evolve into self-directed teams, which represent a fundamental change in how work is organized. Exhibit 10.3 illustrates the evolution of teams and team leadership. The functional team represents grouping individuals by common skill and activity within the traditional structure. Leadership is based on the vertical hierarchy. In cross-functional teams, members have more freedom from the hierarchy, but the team typically is still leader-centered and leader-directed. The leader is most often assigned by the organization and is usually a supervisor or manager from one of the departments represented on the team. Leaders do, however, have to give up some of their control and power at this stage in order for the team to function effectively.

In the next stage of evolution, team members work together without the direction of managers, supervisors, or assigned team leaders.[14] **Self-directed teams** are member- rather than leader-centered and directed. Hundreds of companies, including Consolidated Diesel, Industrial Light and Magic, the Mayo Clinic, and Edy's Grand Ice Cream, are using self-directed teams, which can enable workers to feel challenged, find their work meaningful, and develop a strong sense of identity with the organization.[15]

Self-directed teams typically consist of 5 to 20 members who rotate jobs to produce an entire product or service or at least one complete aspect or portion of a product or service (for example, engine assembly or insurance claims processing).[16] Self-directed teams often are long-term or permanent in nature, although many of today's fast-moving companies also use temporary self-directed teams that come together to work on a specific project and then disband when their work is done. Self-directed teams typically include three elements:

1. The team includes workers with varied skills and functions, and the combined skills are sufficient to perform a major organizational task, thereby eliminating barriers among departments and enabling excellent coordination.

2. The team is given access to resources such as information, financial resources, equipment, machinery, and supplies needed to perform the complete task.

3. The team is empowered with decision-making authority, which means that members have the freedom to select new members, solve problems, spend money, monitor results, and plan for the future.

In self-directed teams, members take over duties such as scheduling work or vacations, ordering materials, and evaluating performance. Teams work with minimum supervision, and members are jointly responsible for conflict resolution and decision making. Many self-directed teams elect one of their own to serve as team leader, and the leader may change each year. Some teams function without a designated leader, so anyone may play a leadership role depending on the situation. In either case, equality and empowerment are key values in organizations based on self-directed teams.

Action Memo
As a leader, you can use a self-directed team when members are capable of working without active supervision. Give the team access to the money, equipment, supplies, and information needed to perform its project or task, and empower the team with decision-making authority.

Self-directed teams
teams made up of members who work with minimum supervision and rotate jobs to produce a complete product or service

Understanding Team Characteristics

One of a leader's most important jobs is to get the team designed right by considering such characteristics as size, diversity, and interdependence. The quality of team design has a significant impact on the success of teams.[17]

Size More than 30 years ago, psychologist Ivan Steiner examined what happened each time the size of a team increased, and he proposed that team performance and productivity peaked at about five—a quite small number. He found that adding additional members beyond five caused a decrease in motivation, an increase in coordination problems, and a general decline in performance.[18] Since then, numerous studies have found that smaller teams perform better, though most researchers say it's impossible to specify an optimal team size. One recent investigation of team size based on data from 58 software development teams found that the five best-performing teams ranged in size from three to six members.[19] Results of a recent Gallup poll in the United States show that 82 percent of employees agree that small teams are more productive.[20]

Teams should be large enough to take advantage of diverse skills, yet small enough to permit members to feel an intimate part of a community. In general, as a team increases in size it becomes harder for each member to interact with and influence the others. A summary of research on size suggests that small teams show more agreement, ask more questions, and exchange more opinions. Members want to get along with one another. Small teams report more satisfaction and enter into more personal discussions, and members feel a greater sense of cohesiveness and belonging. Large teams (generally defined as 12 or more members) tend to have more disagreements and differences of opinion. Subgroups often form and conflicts among them may occur. Demands on leaders are greater in large teams, because there is less member participation. Large teams also tend to be less friendly and members do not feel that they are part of a cohesive community.[21] As a general rule, it is more difficult to satisfy members' needs in large teams, forcing leaders to work harder to keep members focused and committed to team goals.

Diversity Because teams require a variety of skills, knowledge, and experience, it seems likely that heterogeneous teams would be more effective because members bring diverse abilities and information to bear on a project or problem. In general, research supports this idea, showing that heterogeneous teams produce more innovative solutions to problems than do homogeneous teams.[22] Diversity within a team can be a source of creativity. One international business consultant uses the 1960s rock sensation The Beatles to illustrate the importance of diversity to creative teamwork, pointing out how personality differences, distinct abilities, and collegial competition among the four band members contributed to their phenomenal success.[23] Within organizations, too, diversity can contribute to a healthy level of conflict that leads to better decision making. Some conflict helps to prevent "groupthink," in which people are so committed to a cohesive team that they are reluctant to express contrary opinions. Among top management teams, for example, low levels of conflict are associated with poor decision making. Furthermore, many of these low-conflict teams reflect little diversity among members.[24] Consider the example of Mark IV Transportation & Logistics.

Jerry Giampaglia, Mark IV Transportation & Logistics

Members of the top management team of Mark IV Transportation and Logistics don't have much interest in socializing together on weekends. They are so different in their lifestyles and interests that they can't seem to find much to talk about outside of work. But that's just fine with CEO Jerry Giampaglia, who has seen this diverse team accomplish amazing results, driving revenue from $3 million to $20 million in five years. "We're nothing alike when we're outside this company," Giampaglia says, "but when we walk through those doors, we're clicking."

For a decade, Mark IV was run by a tightly-knit group of friends and family, mostly men, who thought alike, acted alike, and often met for drinks or sporting events after work. It was an agreeable and satisfying work environment. The trouble was, Mark IV was in a rut, providing the same three basic services as every other courier service in town and unable to push past the $3 million mark in revenues. Giampaglia had an insight that things were likely to stay the same as long as the company was run by the same homogeneous top management team. So he started filling open positions with a more diverse mix of people that he likely would have shunned in the past.

Now, meetings are often raucous and consensus isn't easy to achieve. People argue opinions back and forth and challenge one another's assumptions. The disagreements have sparked new ideas and new ways of thinking. Mark IV now customizes its services to meet the needs of clients. Revenue has increased more than six-fold. "In the old company, the challenges found us and we sweated them out," Giampaglia says. "Now, we create challenges and love finding solutions."[25]

Jerry Giampaglia discovered what many leaders now know: team diversity can provide a healthy level of disagreement that sparks innovation and leads to better decision making. However, despite the value of some conflict, conflict that is too strong or is not handled appropriately can limit team members' satisfaction and performance. For example, a new product team at a company that manufactures and sells upscale children's furniture found their differing perspectives and working styles to be a significant source of conflict during crunch times. Members who needed peace and quiet were irked at those who wanted music playing in the background. Compulsively neat members found it almost impossible to work with those who liked working among stacks of clutter. Fortunately, this team was able to overcome these divisive issues for the sake of the project.[26]

Diversity can provide fertile ground for disagreements and disputes that may be based on personal rather than team issues.[27] In particular, racial and national differences can interfere with team interaction and performance, particularly in the short term.[28] Teams made up of racially and culturally diverse members tend to have more difficulty learning to work well together, but, with effective leadership and conflict resolution, the problems seem to dissipate over time. The benefits and challenges of diversity will be discussed in detail in the next chapter.

Interdependence Interdependence means the extent to which team members depend on each other for information, resources, or ideas to accomplish their tasks. Tasks such as performing surgery or directing military operations, for example, require a high degree of interaction and exchange, whereas tasks such as assembly-line manufacturing require very little.[29]

Three types of interdependence can affect teams: pooled, sequential, and reciprocal.[30] In **pooled interdependence,** the lowest form of interdependence, members are fairly independent of one another in completing their work, participating on a team, but not *as* a team.[31] They may share a machine or a common secretary, but most of their work is done independently. An example might be a sales team, with each salesperson responsible for his or her own sales area and customers, but sharing the same appointment secretary. Salespersons need not interact to accomplish their work and little day-to-day coordination is needed.[32]

Interdependence
the extent to which team members depend on each other for information, resources, or ideas to accomplish their tasks

Pooled interdependence
the lowest form of team interdependence; members are relatively independent of one another in completing their work

Sequential interdependence
serial form of interdependence in which the output of one team member becomes the input to another team member

Sequential interdependence is a serial form wherein the output of one team member becomes the input to another team member. One member must perform well in order for the next member to perform well, and so on. Because team members have to exchange information and resources and rely upon one another, this is a higher level of interdependence. An example might be an engine assembly team in an automobile plant. Each team member performs a separate task, but his work depends on the satisfactory completion of work by other team members. Regular communication and coordination is required to keep work running smoothly.

The highest level of interdependence, **reciprocal interdependence**, exists when team members influence and affect one another in reciprocal fashion. The output of team member A is the input to team member B, and the output of team member B is the input back again to team member A. Reciprocal interdependence characterizes most teams performing knowledge-based work. Writing a technical manual, for example, rarely moves forward in a logical, step-by-step fashion. It is more like "an open-ended series of to-and-fro collaborations, iterations, and reiterations" among team members.[33] On reciprocal teams, each individual member makes a contribution, but only the team as a whole "performs." The team that developed the Ford Escape Hybrid SUV provides an example of reciprocal interdependence.

> **Action Memo**
> As a leader, you can improve team effectiveness by paying attention to the size, diversity, and interdependence of your team. When interdependence among members is high, empower team members to make decisions and initiate action together.

Reciprocal interdependence
highest form of team interdependence; members influence and affect one another in reciprocal fashion

Ford Motor Company's Escape Hybrid SUV

When Ford Motor Company vowed to be the first auto manufacturer to come out with a hybrid SUV, managers knew they needed a new approach to product development to do it. The vehicle was a dramatically different vehicle for Ford and the most technically advanced model the company had ever made, involving the development of nine new technologies.

Researchers and engineers hadn't worked closely together at Ford—in fact, they were located in different buildings a half a mile apart. Work was organized sequentially, with one department passing work on to the next. Meeting the demanding schedule for the Escape Hybrid, however, called for a new approach—a team of research scientists and product engineers working side by side, creating and building hardware and software together and then working with production personnel to bring their creation to life. Whereas in the past, problems were "tossed over the wall," they were now ironed out collaboratively within the team.

To support the high level of interdependence in the Escape Hybrid team, members were all located on the same floor at headquarters. Problems were often solved in hallway chats or over lunch in the nearby cafeteria. Top managers gave the team nearly complete autonomy so that decisions could be made fast. Getting the Escape Hybrid SUV right required hundreds of back-and-forth discussions and thousands of adjustments to the hardware, software, and wiring of the vehicle.

As Mary Ann Wright, who led the team through the launch phase, told team members: "If one person is struggling, we're all struggling." That's why the team met the demanding schedule and introduced the Escape Hybrid SUV right on time.[34]

Leaders are responsible for facilitating the degree of coordination and communication needed among team members, depending on the level of team interdependence. Top executives at Ford created the conditions to support a high level of interdependence for the team developing the Escape Hybrid SUV, enabling members to complete an extraordinarily complex project on a tight time schedule. Although Ford is currently struggling, the vehicle was a resounding success when it was introduced in 2005, and applying the hybrid technologies developed during the project is key to Ford's turnaround plans.[35]

When team interdependence is high, true team leadership, which involves empowering the team to make decisions and take action, is especially important to high performance. However, for teams with low interdependence, traditional leadership, individual rewards, and granting authority and power to individuals rather than the team may be appropriate.[36]

Leadership and Team Effectiveness

Team effectiveness can be defined as achieving four performance outcomes— innovation/adaptation, efficiency, quality, and employee satisfaction.[37] *Innovation/ adaptation* means the degree to which teams affect the organization's ability to learn and to rapidly respond to environmental needs and changes. *Efficiency* pertains to whether the team helps the organization attain goals using fewer resources. *Quality* refers to achieving fewer defects and exceeding customer expectations. *Satisfaction* pertains to the team's ability to maintain employee commitment and enthusiasm by meeting the personal needs of its members. Three areas related to understanding team effectiveness are team cohesiveness and performance; team task and socioemotional roles; and the personal impact of the team leader.

> **Team effectiveness**
> the extent to which a team achieves four performance outcomes: innovation/ adaptation, efficiency, quality, and employee satisfaction

Team Cohesiveness and Effectiveness

Team cohesiveness is defined as the extent to which members stick together and remain united in the pursuit of a common goal.[38] Members of highly cohesive teams are committed to team goals and activities, feel that they are involved in something significant, and are happy when the team succeeds. Members of less cohesive teams are less concerned about the team's welfare.

> **Team cohesiveness**
> the extent to which members stick together and remain united in the pursuit of a common goal

Determinants of Cohesiveness
Leaders can use several factors to influence team cohesiveness. One is team *interaction*. The greater the amount of contact between team members and the more time they spend together, the more cohesive the team. Through frequent interaction, members get to know one another and become more devoted to the team. Another factor is *shared mission and goals*. When team members agree on purpose and direction, they will be more cohesive. The most cohesive teams are those that feel they are involved in something immensely relevant and important—that they are embarking on a journey together that will make the world better in some way. An aerospace executive, recalling his participation in an advanced design team, put it this way: "We even walked differently than anybody else. We felt we were way out there, ahead of the whole world."[39] A third factor is *personal attraction* to the team, meaning members find their common ground and enjoy being together. Members like and respect one another.

> **Action Memo**
> Cohesiveness is generally considered an attractive feature of teams. Leader's Self-Insight 10.1 on page 304 gives you a chance to measure the cohesiveness of a team you have been involved in at school or work.

The organizational context can also affect team cohesiveness. When a team is in moderate *competition* with other teams, its cohesiveness increases as it strives to win. Finally, *team success* and the favorable evaluation of the team's work by outsiders add to cohesiveness. When a team succeeds and others in the organization recognize this success, members feel good and their commitment to the team will be higher.

Consequences of Team Cohesiveness
The consequences of team cohesiveness can be examined according to two categories: morale and performance. As

Think of a specific team of which you are or were recently a part, either at work or school, and answer the following questions about your perception of the team. Indicate whether each item below is Mostly False or Mostly True for you.

	Mostly False	Mostly True
1. Members are proud to tell others they are part of the team.	_____	_____
2. Members are willing to put a great deal of effort into their work for the team to be successful.	_____	_____
3. Members sometimes try to make other team members look bad.	_____	_____
4. Members are willing to "talk up" the team's work with other employees as being good for the organization.	_____	_____
5. Members seem to take personal advantage of each other's mistakes.	_____	_____
6. Members really care about the success of the team.	_____	_____
7. Members feel there is not much to be gained by sticking with this team's project.	_____	_____
8. Members of this team really like spending time together.	_____	_____

Scoring and Interpretation

Give yourself 1 point for each Mostly False answer to questions 3, 5, and 7 and 1 point for each Mostly True answer to questions 1, 2, 4, 6, and 8. Sum your points for the 8 questions: _____. These questions pertain to team cohesion—the extent to which team members like, trust, and respect one another and are united toward a common goal. These questions were originally designed to assess the commitment of hospital upper management teams to joint strategic decisions. If your score is 6 or higher, your team would be considered high in cohesion—members are committed to one another and the team's goal. A score of 0–2 indicates below-average team cohesion.

Source: Adapted from Robert S. Dooley and Gerald E. Fryxell, "Attaining Decision Quality and Commitment from Dissent: The Moderating Effects of Loyalty and Competence in Strategic Decision-Making Teams," *Academy of Management Journal* 42, no. 4 (1999), pp. 389–402.

Action Memo

As a leader, you can facilitate team cohesiveness by providing members with opportunities to interact and know one another. You can use friendly competition with other teams to increase cohesion, and work with top leaders to develop high performance norms for the team.

a general rule, employee *morale* is much higher in cohesive teams because of increased communication, a friendly atmosphere, loyalty, and member participation in decisions and activities. High team cohesiveness has almost uniformly positive effects on the satisfaction and morale of team members.[40]

With respect to team *performance*, it seems that cohesiveness and performance are generally positively related, although research results are mixed. Cohesive teams can sometimes unleash enormous amounts of employee energy and creativity. One explanation for this is the research finding that working in a team increases individual motivation and performance. *Social facilitation* refers to the tendency for the presence of other people to enhance an individual's motivation and performance. Simply interacting with others has an energizing effect.[41] In relation to this, one study found that cohesiveness is more closely related to high performance when team interdependence is high, requiring frequent interaction, coordination, and communication, as discussed earlier in this chapter.[42]

Another factor influencing performance is the relationship between teams and top leadership. One study surveyed more than 200 work teams and correlated job performance with cohesiveness.[43] Highly cohesive teams were more productive when team members felt supported by organizational leaders and less productive when they sensed hostility and negativism from leaders. Similarly, a study of cross-division teams of managers set up to encourage learning and collaboration between divisions at BP found that top management support was a key factor in determining team effectiveness.[44] The support of top leaders contributes to the development of high performance norms, whereas hostility or indifference leads to team norms and goals of low performance. Consider the performance norms and effectiveness of the team that created the Motorola RAZR.

Motorola's 'Thin Clam' Team

The mood inside Motorola was bleak. Managers and engineers alike knew the company needed a hot new product to regain its reputation—and maybe even some of its lost market share. In the concept phone unit, engineers started talking about building an impossibly thin clamshell phone that would be as beautiful as a piece of fine jewelry and just as desirable—and they wanted it done in a year.

Engineer Roger Jellicoe aggressively promoted himself to lead the team and quickly put together a group of engineers, designers, and other specialists who were fired up by the ambitious project. The "thin clam" team, as they came to be known, rapidly became viewed almost as a rebellious cult within Motorola. The team worked at a facility 50 miles from Motorola's central research unit and kept the details of the project top-secret, even from their colleagues within the company. The need for secrecy and speed, as well as the relative isolation, contributed to the quick, tight bond that developed among team members. Time and again, the thin clam team flouted Motorola's rules for developing new products and followed their own instincts. Top management looked the other way. They wanted the team to have the freedom to be creative and take chances. Because Motorola badly needed a hit, money was not an object; top management gave the team whatever they needed in terms of support and resources to accomplish their goal.

The result was the RAZR, named as such based on the team's humorous reference to it as *siliqua patula,* Latin for razor clam. Unlike any other cellphone the world had seen, the RAZR wowed the industry and consumers alike—and rejuvenated the company in the process.[45]

At Motorola, a combination of team cohesiveness and management support that created high performance norms led to amazing results. The phone wasn't originally conceived to be a blockbuster, but it proved to be just that. Between the time the RAZR was launched in late 2004 and mid-2006, the stylish phone sold almost as many units as the red-hot Apple iPod.[46]

Meeting Task and Socioemotional Needs

Another important factor in team effectiveness is ensuring that the needs for both task accomplishment and team members' socioemotional well-being are met. Recall from Chapter 2 the discussion of task-oriented and people-oriented leadership behaviors. Task-oriented behavior places primary concern on tasks and production and is generally associated with higher productivity, whereas people-oriented behavior emphasizes concern for followers and relationships and is associated with higher employee satisfaction.

For a team to be successful over the long term, it must both maintain its members' satisfaction and accomplish its task. These requirements are met through two types of team leadership roles, as illustrated in Exhibit 10.4. A *role* might be thought of as a set of behaviors expected of a person occupying a certain

Exhibit 10.4 Two Types of Team Leadership Roles

Task-Specialist Behavior	Socioemotional Behavior
Propose solutions and initiate new ideas	Encourage contributions by others; draw out others' ideas by showing warmth and acceptance
Evaluate effectiveness of task solutions; offer feedback on others' suggestions	Smooth over conflicts between members; reduce tension and help resolve differences
Seek information to clarify tasks, responsibilities, and suggestions	Be friendly and supportive of others; show concern for members' needs and feelings
Summarize ideas and facts related to the problem at hand	Maintain standards of behavior and remind others of agreed-upon norms and standards for interaction
Energize others and stimulate the team to action	Seek to identify problems with team interactions or dysfunctional member behavior; ask for others' perceptions

Sources: Based on Robert A. Baron, *Behavior in Organizations,* 2nd ed. (Boston: Allyn & Bacon, 1986); Don Hellriegel, John W. Slocum, Jr., and Richard W. Woodman, *Organizational Behavior,* 8th ed. (Cincinnati, OH: South-Western, 1998), p. 244; and Gary A. Yukl, *Leadership in Organizations,* 4th ed. (Upper Saddle River, NJ: Prentice Hall, 1998), pp. 384–387.

Task-specialist role
team leadership role associated with initiating new ideas, evaluating the team's effectiveness, seeking to clarify tasks and responsibilities, summarizing facts and ideas for others, and stimulating others to action

Socioemotional role
team leadership role associated with facilitating others' participation, smoothing conflicts, showing concern for team members' needs and feelings, serving as a role model, and reminding others of standards for team interaction

position, such as that of team leader. The **task-specialist role** is associated with behaviors such as initiating new ideas or different ways of considering problems; evaluating the team's effectiveness by questioning the logic, facts, or practicality of proposed solutions; seeking information to clarify tasks, responsibilities, and suggestions; summarizing facts and ideas for others; and stimulating others to action when energy and interest wane. The **socioemotional role** includes behaviors such as facilitating the participation of others and being receptive to others' ideas; smoothing over conflicts between team members and striving to reduce tensions; showing concern for team members' needs and feelings; serving as a role model and reminding others of agreed-upon standards for interaction and cooperation; and seeking to identify problems with team interactions or dysfunctional member behaviors.[47]

The importance of these roles can be seen on a movie set, which can often become a pressure cooker with creative people struggling with technical specialists to meet both time and artistic goals. The unit production manager and the assistant directors are often considered the backbone of the team because they are primarily responsible for filling the vital task and socioemotional roles. The unit production manager coordinates all the intricate details of the production schedule, monitors work progress, and makes sure technical specialists and other team members deliver results on time. The assistant director, on the other hand, needs to have superb relationship skills in order to solve interpersonal disputes and diffuse tensions within the team.[48]

Ideally, a team leader plays both task-specialist and socioemotional roles to some extent. By satisfying both types of needs, the leader gains the respect and admiration of others. However, a leader might find it necessary to put more emphasis on one role over another. For example, if many members of the team are highly task-oriented, the leader might put more emphasis on meeting socioemotional needs.

Action Memo
As a leader, you can make sure that both the task and socioemotional needs of team members are met so that people experience both friendly support and goal accomplishment.

On the other hand, when most members seem to emphasize relationships, the leader will need to be more task-oriented to ensure that the team performs its tasks and meets its goals. It is the leader's responsibility to make sure both types of needs are met, whether through the leader's own behaviors or through the actions and behaviors of other team members. A well-balanced team does best over the long term because it is personally satisfying for members and also promotes the successful accomplishment of team tasks and goals.

The Team Leader's Personal Role

Successful teams begin with confident and effective team leaders. For example, Harvard Business School professors studying surgery teams have found that the attitude and actions of the team leader, and the quality of the leader's interactions with team members, are crucial to team effectiveness and the success of the surgery.[49] However, leading a team requires a shift in mindset and behavior for those who are accustomed to working in traditional organizations where managers make the decisions.

Most people can learn the new skills and qualities needed for team leadership, but it is not always easy. To be effective team leaders, people have to be willing to change themselves, to step outside their comfort zone and let go of many of the assumptions that have guided their behavior in the past. Here we will discuss three specific changes leaders can make to develop a foundation for effective team leadership.[50]

> **Action Memo**
>
> Complete the exercise in Leader's Self-Insight 10.2 on page 308 to evaluate your capacity for team leadership.

Recognize the Importance of Shared Purpose and Values Team leaders have to articulate a clear and compelling vision so that everyone is moving in the same direction. Moreover, good leaders help people feel that their work is meaningful and important. A study of cross-functional teams at Hewlett–Packard's Medical Products Group, for example, found that the most successful teams were those that had a clear sense of their mission and goals and believed their work was essential to the success of the company.[51] Similarly, Prabhaker Patil, leader of the Ford Escape Hybrid team described earlier, united members around what he called "the nobility of the cause," a chance to make a difference for customers, the company, and the environment. At heart, building a team means creating a community united by shared values and commitment. Leaders may use ritual, stories, ceremonies and other symbolism to create a sense of community, shared purpose, and meaning for team members.

Admit Your Mistakes The best team leaders are willing to make themselves vulnerable by admitting they don't know everything. Being an effective team leader means enabling everyone to contribute their unique skills, talents, and ideas. Leaders can serve as a *fallibility model* by admitting their ignorance and mistakes and asking for help, which lets people know that problems, errors, and concerns can be discussed openly without fear of appearing incompetent.[52] When Bruce Moravec was asked to lead a team to design a new fuselage for the Boeing 757, he had to gain the respect and confidence of people who worked in areas he knew little about. "You don't want to pretend you're more knowledgeable about subjects other people know more about," Moravec says. "That dooms you to failure. . . . They're the experts."[53]

> **Action Memo**
>
> As a leader, you can articulate a clear and compelling vision for the team to help members see their work as meaningful and important. You can make room for everyone to contribute and provide them with the training, support, and coaching they need to excel.

Leader's Self-Insight 10.2

Assess Your Team Leadership Skills

Answer the following questions based on what you have done as a team leader, or think you would do, related to the team situations and attitudes described. Check either Mostly False or Mostly True for each question.

	Mostly False	Mostly True
1. An important part of leading a team is to keep members informed almost daily of information that could affect their work.	_____	_____
2. I love communicating online to work on tasks with team members.	_____	_____
3. Generally, I feel somewhat tense while interacting with team members from different cultures.	_____	_____
4. I nearly always prefer face-to-face communications with team members over e-mail.	_____	_____
5. I enjoy doing things in my own way and in my own time.	_____	_____
6. If a new member were hired, I would expect the entire team to interview the person.	_____	_____
7. I become impatient when working with a team member from another culture.	_____	_____
8. I suggest a specific way each team member can make a contribution to the project.	_____	_____
9. If I were out of the office for a week, most of the important work of the team would get accomplished anyway.	_____	_____
10. Delegation is hard for me when an important task has to be done right.	_____	_____
11. I enjoy working with people with different accents.	_____	_____
12. I am confident about leading team members from different cultures.	_____	_____

Scoring and Interpretation

The answers for effective team leadership are as follows: Give yourself 1 point for each Mostly True answer to questions 1, 2, 6, 8, 9, 11, and 12. Give yourself 1 point for each Mostly False answer to questions 3, 4, 5, 7, and 10. If your score is 9 or higher, you certainly understand the ingredients to be a highly effective team leader. If your score is 3 or lower, you might have an authoritarian approach to leadership, or are not comfortable with culturally diverse team membership or virtual team communications, such as e-mail.

Questions 1, 5, 6, 8, 9, and 10 pertain to authoritarian versus participative team leadership. Questions 3, 7, 11, and 12 pertain to cultural differences. Questions 2 and 4 pertain to virtual team communications. Which aspects of team leadership reflect your leader strengths? Which reflect your weaknesses? Team leadership requires that the leader learn to share power, information, and responsibility, be inclusive of diverse members, and be comfortable with electronic communications.

Source: Adapted from "What Style of Leader Are You or Would You Be?" in Andrew J. DuBrin, *Leadership: Research Findings, Practice, and Skills*, 3rd ed. (Boston: Houghton Mifflin Company, 2001), pp. 126–127; and James W. Neuliep and James C. McCroskey, "The Development of Intercultural and Interethnic Communication Apprehension Scales," *Communication Research Reports*, 14, no. 2 (1997), pp. 145–156.

Provide Support and Coaching to Team Members Good team leaders make sure people get the training, development opportunities, and resources they need and that they are adequately rewarded for their contributions to the organization.

Rather than always thinking about oneself and how to get the next promotion or salary increase, effective team leaders spend their time taking care of team members. Most team members share the critically important needs for recognition and support. Leaders frequently overlook how important it is for people to feel that their contribution is valued, and they may especially forget to acknowledge the contributions of lower-level support staff. One woman who has held the same secretarial position for many years attributes her high enthusiasm to her team leader: "For the last several years, our team of four has reported to him. At the end of each day—no matter how hectic or trying things have been—he comes by each of our desks and says, 'Thank you for another good day.'"[54]

The Leader's New Challenge: Virtual and Global Teams

Being a team leader is even more challenging when people are scattered in different geographical locations and may be separated by language and cultural differences as well. Virtual and global teams are a reality for many of today's leaders. Exhibit 10.5 illustrates the primary differences between conventional types of teams and today's virtual and global teams. Conventional types of teams discussed earlier in this chapter meet and conduct their interactions face to face in the same physical space. Team members typically share similar cultural backgrounds and characteristics. The key characteristics of virtual and global teams, on the other hand, are (1) spatial distance limits face-to-face interaction, and (2) the use of technological communication is the primary means of connecting team members.[55] Members of virtual and global teams are scattered in different locations, whether it be different offices and business locations around the country or around the world. Most communication is handled via telephone, fax, e-mail, instant messaging, virtual document sharing, videoconferencing, and other media. In some virtual teams, members share the same dominant culture, but global teams are often made up of members whose cultural values vary widely. The leadership challenge is thus highest for global teams because of the increased potential for misunderstandings and conflicts.

Virtual Teams

A **virtual team** is made up of geographically or organizationally dispersed members who share a common purpose and are linked primarily through advanced information and telecommunications technologies.[56] Team members use e-mail, voice mail, videoconferencing, Internet and intranet technologies, and various forms of collaboration software to perform their work rather than meeting face to face.

Uses of Virtual Teams Virtual teams, sometimes called *distributed teams,* may be temporary cross-functional teams that work on specific projects, or they may be long-term, self-directed teams. Virtual teams sometimes include customers, suppliers, and even competitors to pull together the best minds to complete a project. For example, three of the top men's magazines—*Esquire, Men's Health,* and *Rolling Stone*—are fierce competitors, and leaders from the three organizations once barely spoke to one another. Several years ago, however, the three put together a

Virtual team
a team made up of geographically or organizationally dispersed members who share a common purpose and are linked primarily through advanced information technologies

Type of Team	Spatial Distance	Communications	Member Cultures	Leader Challenge
Conventional	Colocated	Face to face	Same	High
Virtual	Scattered	Mediated	Same	Higher
Global	Widely scattered	Mediated	Different	Very High

Exhibit 10.5 Differences Between Conventional, Virtual, and Global Teams

virtual team to develop a successful joint proposal for a major Haggar advertising campaign. Without this collaboration, it is unlikely that any of the companies could have competed against *Sports Illustrated*, a magazine with a circulation equal to that of the other three combined.[57]

Using virtual teams allows organizations to use the best people for a particular job, no matter where they are located, thus enabling a fast response to competitive pressures. When IBM needs to staff a project, it gives a list of skills needed to the human resources department, which provides a pool of people who are qualified. The team leader then puts together the best combination of people for the project, which often means pulling people from many different locations. IBM estimates that about a third of its employees participate in virtual teams.[58]

> **Action Memo**
>
> As a leader, you can help a virtual team perform even with limited control and supervision. You can select members who thrive in a virtual environment, arrange opportunities for periodic face-to-face meetings, and ensure that members understand the goals and performance standards.

Leading the Virtual Team Despite their potential benefits, there is growing evidence that virtual teams are typically less effective than teams whose members meet face-to-face.[59] The team leader can make a tremendous difference in how well a virtual team performs, but virtual teams bring significant leadership challenges.[60] Leaders of conventional teams can monitor how team members are doing and if everything is on track, but virtual team leaders can't see when or how well people are working. Virtual team leaders have to trust people to do their jobs without constant supervision, and they learn to focus more on results than on the process of accomplishing them. Too much control can kill a virtual team, so leaders have to give up most of their control and yet at the same time provide guidance, encouragement, support, and development. The ideas presented earlier regarding the team leader's personal role are applicable to virtual teams as well. In addition, to be successful, virtual team leaders can master the following skills:

- *Select the right team members.* Effective virtual team leaders put a lot of thought into getting the right mix of people on the team. Team members need to have the technical knowledge, skills, and personalities to work effectively in a virtual environment. When people are highly skilled and professional, they don't need to be monitored or supervised in a traditional way. As with other types of teams, small virtual teams tend to be more cohesive and work together more effectively. However, diversity of views and experiences is also important to the success of a virtual team. Diversity is usually built into virtual teams because when leaders can pick the right people for the job, no matter where they are located, members usually reflect diverse backgrounds and viewpoints.[61]

- *Build trust by building connections.* No matter how effective team members are as individuals, unless they can come together as a team, virtual teamwork will fail. Virtual team leaders work hard to establish connections among people, from which trust can grow. There simply is no substitute for initial face-to-face interaction for building trust quickly. At Mobil Corp., leaders bring virtual team members together in one location at the beginning of a project so they can begin to build personal relationships and gain an understanding of their goals and responsibilities.[62] These intense meetings allow the team to rapidly go through the *forming* and *storming* stages of development, as discussed earlier in this chapter. Studies of virtual teams suggest these processes are best accomplished at the same time and in the same place.[63]

- *Agree on ground rules.* At the beginning of the team's work, all team members need to explicitly understand both team and individual goals, deadlines, and expectations for participation and performance. It is important that leaders define a clear context so that people can make decisions, monitor their own performance, and regulate their behavior to accomplish goals.[64] Teams should work together to choose the collaboration software and other communications technologies they will use and then immediately practice using the new technology together.[65] Agreeing on communications etiquette is also essential. The team has to agree on issues such as whether good-natured flaming is okay or off limits, whether there are time limits on responding to voice mail or e-mail, and so forth.

- *Effectively use technology.* Communication can be a tremendous problem for virtual teams, and the ideas for using electronic communication channels in Chapter 9 can help virtual team leaders be more effective. When possible, leaders should use face-to-face communication sessions when rich communication is needed, such as for problem solving or whenever misunderstandings and frustration threaten the team's work.[66] Leaders can also schedule regular times for people to interact online and be sure all team members are trained in how to effectively use electronic communications. For example, leaders find that everything needs to be made more explicit online. Experienced virtual workers have learned how to "verbalize" to colleagues online when they're shifting mental gears or need more feedback.

Global Teams

Virtual teams are frequently also global teams, which means people are working together not only across spatial distances but across time barriers and cultural and language differences as well. The use of global teams is rapidly increasing. A survey of 103 firms found that nearly half now use global teams for new product development. Moreover, one out of every five teams in these companies is likely to be global.[67] **Global teams** are work teams made up of culturally diverse members who live and work in different countries and coordinate some part of their activities on a global basis.[68] For example, global teams of software developers at Tandem Services Corporation coordinate their work electronically so that the team is productive around the clock. Team members in London code a project and transmit the code each evening to members in the United States for testing. U.S. team members then forward the code they've tested to Tokyo for debugging. The next morning, the London team members pick up with the code debugged by their Tokyo colleagues, and another cycle begins.[69] In some organizations, such as open-source software maker MySQL, most employees are scattered around the world and never see one another face-to-face.

Global teams
teams made up of culturally diverse members who live and work in different countries and coordinate some part of their activities on a global basis

> **IN THE LEAD**
>
> *MySQL*
>
> How to instill esprit de corps in a far-flung virtual team is a challenge leaders at MySQL, a Swedish software maker, face daily. MySQL, which produces a database management system used in Web applications, employs around 320 people scattered in 25 countries. The majority of them work from home.
>
> For MySQL, building an effective global team begins with hiring the right people. Leaders look for people with the right technical skills and a passion for their work, and then find ways to keep them connected and motivated. Thomas

Basil, MySQL's director of support, works in a basement office next to his family's washing machine, so he knows from experience that people working virtually can feel isolated. When he signs in to the MySQL chatroom each day, he greets each support team member by name. Basil even staged on online Christmas party, gathering staffers from places like Russia, England, and Germany into a cyber get-together, where he played Santa and dispensed virtual drinks and gifts. "When a company is as spread out as this one," he points out, "you have to think of virtual ways to imitate the dynamics of what goes on in a more familiar work situation." Occasionally, top executives get the entire MySQL staff together online through a system dubbed "Radio Sakila," which combines a typical conference call with instant messaging.

MySQL managers have built in numerous communication channels to keep people talking across time and space. Team leaders recognize the limitations of text-based electronic communication, such as how easily miscommunication can occur in the absence of nonverbal cues. It's their responsibility to help people develop and follow guidelines for communication. As Basil has found, there are times when an old-fashioned telephone conversation works best. "Voice is more personal than text and more helpful in building real understanding," he points out.[70]

MySQL is a fledgling example of a new form of organization, one with which most leaders have little experience. Some researchers suggest that as companies strive for better ways to harness knowledge and respond more quickly on a global basis, many, like SQL, will come to resemble amoebas—collections of people connected electronically who are divided into ever-changing teams that can best exploit the organization's unique resources, capabilities, and core competencies.[71]

Why Global Teams Often Fail All of the challenges of virtual teamwork are magnified in the case of global teams because of the added problem of language and cultural barriers.[72] Building trust is an even greater challenge when people bring different norms, values, attitudes, and patterns of behavior to the team. Members from different cultures often have different beliefs about such things as authority, decision making, and time orientation. For example, some cultures, such as the United States, are highly focused on "clock time," and tend to follow rigid schedules, whereas many other cultures have a more relaxed, cyclical concept of time. These different cultural attitudes toward time can affect work pacing, team communications, and the perception of deadlines.[73] Members from different countries may also have varied attitudes about teamwork itself. In Mexico, U.S. companies trying to use teams have run into trouble, because the concept of shared leadership conflicts with traditional values that there should be status and power differences in organizations.[74]

Communication barriers can be formidable. Not only do global teams have to cope with different time zones and conflicting schedules, but members often speak different languages. Even when members can communicate in the same language, differences such as accent, tone of voice, dialect, and semantics can present problems. A survey found that senior leaders consider building trust and overcoming communication barriers as the two most important—but also the two most difficult—leader tasks related to the success of global teams.[75]

Leading the Global Team If managed correctly, global teams have many advantages. Increasingly, the expertise and knowledge needed to complete a project

Action Memo

As a leader, you can provide language and cross-cultural training for a global team and guide members to set aside their preconceived ideas and assumptions for behavior.

is scattered around the world. In addition, as discussed earlier, diversity can be a powerful stimulus for creativity and the development of better alternatives for problem solving. All of the guidelines for leading traditional and virtual teams apply to global teams as well. For example, a strong sense of shared purpose can help bridge language and culture gaps. In addition, global team leaders can improve success by incorporating the following ideas:[76]

- *Manage language and culture.* Organizations using global teams can't skimp on training. Language and cross-cultural education can help overcome linguistic and cultural hurdles. Language training encourages more direct and spontaneous communication by limiting the need for translators. Understanding one another's cultures can also enrich communications and interpersonal relationships. For the team to succeed, all team members have to gain an appreciation of cultural values and attitudes that are different from their own.

- *Stretch minds and behavior.* As team members learn to expand their thinking and embrace cultural differences they also learn to develop a shared team culture. In global teams, all members have to be willing to deviate somewhat from their own values and norms and establish new norms for the team.[77] Leaders can work with team members to set norms and guidelines for acceptable behavior. These guidelines can serve as a powerful self-regulating mechanism, enhance communications, enrich team interactions, and help the team function as an integrated whole.

Handling Team Conflict

As one would expect, there is an increased potential for conflict among members of global and virtual teams because of the greater chances for miscommunication and misunderstandings. Studies of virtual teams indicate that how they handle internal conflicts is critical to their success, yet conflict within virtual teams tends to occur more frequently and take longer to resolve. Moreover, people in virtual teams tend to engage in more inconsiderate behaviors such as name-calling or insults than do people who work face-to-face.[78] People in virtual teams may also show a greater propensity for shirking their duties or giving less than their full effort, which can lead to team conflicts.[79] Cultural value differences, little face-to-face interaction, and lack of on-site monitoring make it harder to build team identity and commitment.

Whenever people work together in teams, some conflict is inevitable. Whether leading a virtual team or a team whose members work side-by-side, bringing conflicts out into the open and effectively resolving them is one of the team leader's most challenging jobs.

Conflict refers to hostile or antagonistic interaction in which one party attempts to thwart the intentions or goals of another. Conflict is natural and occurs in all teams and organizations. It can arise between members of a team or between teams. Too much conflict can be destructive, tear relationships apart, and interfere with the healthy exchange of ideas and information needed for team development and cohesiveness.[80] High-performing teams typically have lower levels of conflict, and the conflict is more often associated with tasks than with interpersonal relationships. In addition, teams that reflect healthy patterns of conflict are usually characterized by high levels of trust and mutual respect.[81]

Conflict
antagonistic interaction in which one party attempts to thwart the intentions or goals of another

Causes of Conflict

Leaders can be aware of several factors that cause conflict among individuals or teams. Whenever teams compete for scarce resources, such as money, information, or supplies, conflict is almost inevitable. Conflicts also emerge when task responsibilities are unclear. People might disagree about who has responsibility for specific tasks or who has a claim on resources, and leaders help members reach agreement. Another reason for conflict is simply because individuals or teams are pursuing conflicting goals. For example, individual salespeople's targets may put them in conflict with one another and with the sales manager. Finally, it sometimes happens that two people simply do not get along with one another and will never see eye to eye on any issue. Personality clashes are caused by basic differences in personality, values, and attitudes, as described in Chapter 4, and can be particularly difficult to deal with. Sometimes, the only solution is to separate the parties and reassign them to other teams where they can be more productive.

Styles to Handle Conflict

Teams as well as individuals develop specific styles for dealing with conflict, based on the desire to satisfy their own concerns versus the other party's concerns. Exhibit 10.6 describes five styles of handling conflict. How an individual approaches conflict is measured along two dimensions: *assertiveness* and *cooperation*. Effective leaders and team members vary their style to fit a specific situation, as each style is appropriate in certain cases.[82]

1. The *competing style,* which reflects assertiveness to get one's own way, should be used when quick, decisive action is vital on important issues or unpopular actions, such as during emergencies or urgent cost cutting.

Exhibit 10.6 A Model of Styles to Handle Conflict

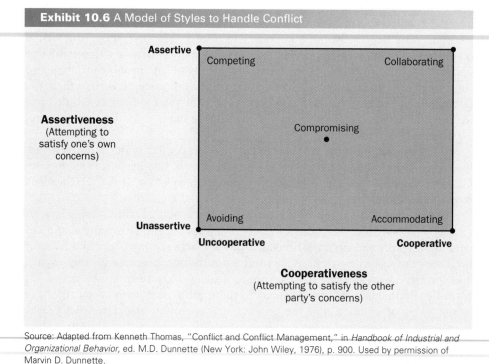

Source: Adapted from Kenneth Thomas, "Conflict and Conflict Management," in *Handbook of Industrial and Organizational Behavior,* ed. M.D. Dunnette (New York: John Wiley, 1976), p. 900. Used by permission of Marvin D. Dunnette.

2. The *avoiding style,* which reflects neither assertiveness nor cooperativeness, is appropriate when an issue is trivial, when there is no chance of winning, when a delay to gather more information is needed, or when a disruption would be costly.

3. The *compromising style* reflects a moderate amount of both assertiveness and cooperativeness. It is appropriate when the goals on both sides are equally important, when opponents have equal power and both sides want to split the difference, or when people need to arrive at temporary or expedient solutions under time pressure.

4. The *accommodating style* reflects a high degree of cooperativeness, which works best when people realize that they are wrong, when an issue is more important to others than to oneself, when building social credits for use in later discussions, or when maintaining cohesiveness is especially important.

5. The *collaborating style* reflects both a high degree of assertiveness and of cooperativeness. This style enables both parties to win, although it may require substantial dialogue and negotiation. The collaborating style is important when both sets of concerns are too important to be compromised, when insights from different people need to be merged into an overall solution, or when the commitment of both sides is needed for a consensus.

Each approach can be successful, depending on the people involved and the situation. In a study of conflict in virtual teams, researchers found that the competing and collaborating styles had a positive effect on team performance.[83] The effectiveness of the competing style might be related to the use of electronic communication, in that team members don't interpret the individual's approach as being aggressive and are more willing to accept a quick resolution.

Other Approaches

The various styles of handling conflict illustrated in Exhibit 10.6 are especially effective for an individual to use when he or she disagrees with another. But what can a team leader do when conflict erupts among others? Research suggests several techniques that help resolve conflicts among people or teams.

Action Memo
Which conflict-handling style do you tend to use most frequently? Answer the questions in Leader's Self-Insight 10.3 on page 316 to find out. Try to think of conflict situations you've been involved in where each of the styles might be appropriate.

Vision A compelling vision can pull people together. A vision is for the whole team and cannot be attained by one person. Its achievement requires the cooperation of conflicting parties. To the extent that leaders can focus on a larger team or organizational vision, conflict will decrease because the people involved see the big picture and realize they must work together to achieve it.

Bargaining/Negotiating Bargaining and negotiating mean that the parties engage one another and use logical problem solving in an attempt to systematically reach a solution. Using this approach to conflict management, people engage in give-and-take discussions and consider various alternatives to reach a joint decision that is acceptable to both parties. Conflicting parties may embark upon negotiation from different perspectives and with different intentions, reflecting either an *integrative* approach or a *distributive* approach. **Integrative negotiation** is based on a win-win assumption, in that all parties want to come up with a creative solution that can benefit both sides of the conflict. Rather than viewing the conflict as a win-lose situation, people look at the issues from multiple angles, consider trade-offs, and try to "expand the pie" rather than divide it. With integrative

Integrative negotiation
a cooperative approach to negotiation in which conflicting parties attempt to reach a win-win solution

Think of some disagreements you have had with a team member, a student group, manager, friend, or co-worker. Then answer the questions below based on how frequently you engage in each behavior. There are no right or wrong answers. Indicate whether each item below is Mostly False or Mostly True for you.

	Mostly False	Mostly True
1. I shy away from topics that might cause a dispute.	_____	_____
2. I strongly assert my opinion in a disagreement.	_____	_____
3. I suggest solutions that combine others' points of view.	_____	_____
4. I give in a little when other people do the same.	_____	_____
5. I avoid a person who wants to discuss a topic of disagreement.	_____	_____
6. I combine arguments into a new solution from the ideas raised in a dispute.	_____	_____
7. I will split the difference to reach a settlement.	_____	_____
8. I am quick to agree when someone I am arguing with makes a good point.	_____	_____
9. I keep my views to myself rather than argue.	_____	_____
10. I try to include other people's ideas to create a solution they will accept.	_____	_____
11. I offer trade-offs to reach solutions in a disagreement.	_____	_____
12. I try to smooth over disagreements by making them seem less serious.	_____	_____
13. I hold my tongue rather than argue with another person.	_____	_____
14. I raise my voice to get other people to accept my position.	_____	_____
15. I stand firm in expressing my viewpoints during a disagreement.	_____	_____

Scoring and Interpretation

Five categories of conflict-handling strategies are measured in this instrument: competing, avoiding, compromising, accommodating, and collaborating. By comparing your scores on the following five scales, you can see your preferred conflict-handling strategy.

To calculate your five scores, give yourself 1 point for each Mostly True for the three items indicated.

Competing: Items 2, 14, 15: _____
Avoiding: Items 1, 5, 9: _____
Compromising: Items 4, 7, 11: _____
Accommodating: Items 8, 12, 13: _____
Collaborating: Items 3, 6, 10: _____

Briefly review the text material (pages 314 and 315) about these five strategies for handling conflict. Which of the five strategies do you use the most? Which strategy do you find the most difficult to use? How would your strategy differ if the other person was a family member rather than a team member? Are there some situations where a strategy in which you are weak might be more effective? Explain your scores to another student and listen to the explanation for his or her scores. How are your conflict-handling strategies similar or different?

Source: Adapted from "How Do You Handle Conflict?" in Robert E. Quinn et al., *Becoming a Master Manager* (New York: Wiley, 1990), pp. 221–223.

Distributive negotiation
adversarial negotiation in which conflicting parties compete to win the most resources and give up as little as possible

negotiation, conflicts are managed through cooperation and compromise, which fosters trust and positive long-term relationships. **Distributive negotiation**, on the other hand, assumes there is a "fixed pie" and each party attempts to get as much of it as they can. One side wants to win, which means the other side must lose. With this win-lose approach, distributive negotiation is competitive and adversarial rather than collaborative, and does not typically lead to positive long-term relationships.[84] Most experts emphasize the value of integrative negotiation for today's collaborative business environment. That is, the key to effectiveness is to see negotiation not as a zero-sum game, but as a process for reaching a creative solution that benefits everyone.[85]

Mediation Using a third party to settle a dispute involves mediation. A mediator could be a supervisor, another team leader, someone from the human resources department, or an outside ombudsman. The mediator can discuss the conflict with each party and work toward a solution. For example, Alan Siggia and Richard Passarelli, cofounders of Sigmet, which designs data processors that turn weather radar signals into graphic displays used by meteorologists, were feeling overwhelmed dealing with the interpersonal conflicts within their small company. The leaders contracted with WorkWellTogether, a Boston consulting firm, to send in a mediator who listens to employee problems and helps leaders devise solutions to conflicts.[86] If a solution satisfactory to all parties cannot be reached, the parties may be willing to turn the conflict over to the mediator and abide by his or her solution.

Action Memo

As a leader, you can use techniques, such as bargaining and negotiation, third-party mediation, facilitating communication, and focusing people on a common vision, to aid in resolving a conflict.

Facilitating Communication One of the most effective ways to reduce conflict is to help conflicting parties communicate openly and honestly. As conflicting parties exchange information and learn more about one another, suspicions diminish and teamwork becomes possible. A particularly promising avenue for reducing conflict is through dialogue, as discussed in Chapter 9. Dialogue asks that participants suspend their attachments to their own viewpoint so that a deeper level of listening, synthesis, and meaning can evolve from the interaction. Individual differences are acknowledged and respected, but rather than trying to figure out who is right or wrong, the parties search for a joint perspective.

Each of these approaches can be helpful in resolving conflicts between individuals or teams. Effective leaders use a combination of these on a regular basis—such as articulating a larger vision and continuously facilitating communication—to keep conflict at a minimum while the team moves forward.

Summary and Interpretation

Teams are a reality in most organizations, and leaders are called upon to facilitate teams rather than manage direct-report subordinates. Functional teams typically are part of the traditional organization structure. Cross-functional teams, including problem-solving teams, process-improvement teams, and change teams, often represent an organization's first move toward greater team participation. Cross-functional teams may evolve into self-directed teams, which are member- rather than leader-centered and directed. Two recent types of teams—virtual teams and global teams—have resulted from advances in technology, changing employee expectations, and the globalization of business. New technology both supports teamwork and increases the pressures on organizations to expand opportunities for employee participation and the widespread sharing of information.

Teams go through stages of development and change over time. Guiding a team through these stages is an important part of team leadership. In addition, leaders have to get the team designed right by considering such factors as size, diversity, and interdependence and ensuring that task and socioemotional roles are filled. These considerations help to determine team effectiveness. The leader's personal role is also crucial. People typically have to change themselves to become good team leaders. Three principles that provide a foundation for team leadership are to recognize the importance of shared purpose and values, admit your mistakes, and provide support and coaching to team members.

These principles apply to virtual and global teams as well. However, being a team leader is even more challenging when people are scattered in different geographic locations and may be separated by language and cultural differences. To create effective, smoothly functioning virtual teams, leaders build trust by building connections in both physical and virtual space, select team members who have the skills and temperaments to work virtually, agree on ground rules for the team, and ensure that all team members effectively use technology. For global teams, leaders also have to manage language and cultural differences and guide people to stretch their minds and behavior to establish a shared culture for the team.

Virtual and global teams increase the potential for misunderstanding, disagreements, and conflicts. However, all teams experience some conflict because of scarce resources, faulty communication, goal conflicts, power and status differences, or personality clashes. Leaders use varied styles to handle conflict. In addition, they employ the following techniques to help resolve conflicts: unite people around a shared vision, use bargaining and negotiation, bring in a mediator, and help conflicting parties communicate openly and honestly, particularly through dialogue.

Discussion Questions

1. What is the difference between a "team" and a "group"? Describe your personal experience with each.

2. Discuss the differences between a cross-functional team and a self-directed team.

3. Why do you think organizations are increasingly using virtual and global teams? Would you like to be a member or leader of a virtual global team? Why or why not?

4. Why might a person need to go through significant personal changes to be an effective team leader? What are some of the changes required?

5. Describe the three levels of interdependence and explain how they affect team leadership.

6. Which is more important to team effectiveness—the task-specialist role or the socioemotional role? Discuss.

7. What are the stages of team development? How can a team leader best facilitate the team at each stage?

8. Discuss the relationship between team cohesiveness and performance.

9. What style of handling conflict do you typically use? Can you think of instances where a different style might have been more productive?

Leadership at Work

Team Feedback

Think back to your most recent experience working in a team, either at work or school. Write down your answers to the following questions about your role in the team.

What did the team members appreciate about you?

_____

_____

_____

What did the team members learn from you?

_____

_____

_____

What could the team members count on you for?

_____

_____

_____

How could you have improved your contribution to the team?

_____

_____

_____

Evaluate your answers. What is the overall meaning of your answers? What are the implications for your role as a team member? As a team leader?

_____

_____

_____

In Class: Team Feedback is an excellent exercise to use for student feedback to one another after a specific team class project or other activities done together during the class. If there were no assigned team activities, but students have gotten to know each other in class, they can be divided into groups and provide the information with respect to their participation in the class instead of in the student team.

The instructor can ask the student groups to sit in a circle facing one another. Then one person will volunteer to be the focal person, and each of the other team members will tell that team member the following:

- What I appreciate about you
- What I learned from you
- What I could count on you for
- My one suggestion for improvement as a team leader/member

When the team members have given feedback to the focal person, another team member volunteers to hear feedback, and the process continues until each person has heard the four elements of feedback from every other team member.

The key questions for student learning are: "Are you developing the skills and behaviors to be a team leader?" If not, what does that mean for you? If you are now providing team leadership, how can you continue to grow and improve as a team leader?

Source: Thanks to William Miller for suggesting the questions for this exercise.

Leadership Development: Cases for Analysis

Valena Scientific Corporation

Valena Scientific Corporation (VSC) is a large manufacturer of health care products. The health care market includes hospitals, clinical laboratories, universities, and industries. Clinical laboratories represent 52 percent of VSC's sales. Laboratories are located in hospitals and diagnostic centers where blood tests and urine analyses are performed for physicians. Equipment sold to laboratories can range from a five-cent test tube to a $195,000 blood analyzer.

By 1980, the industry experienced a move into genetic engineering. Companies such as Genentech Corporation and Cetus Scientific Laboratories were created and staffed with university microbiologists. These companies were designed to exploit the commercial potential for gene splicing.

Senior executives at VSC saw the trend developing and decided to create a Biotech Research Program. Skilled microbiologists were scarce, so the program was staffed with only nine scientists. Three scientists were skilled in gene splicing, three in recombination, and three in fermentation. The specialties reflected the larger departments to which they were assigned. However, they were expected to work as a team on this program. Twenty technicians were also assigned to the program to help the scientists.

Senior management believed that the biotech research program could be self-managed. For the first 18 months of operation, everything went well. Informal leaders emerged among the scientists in gene splicing, recombination, and fermentation. These three informal leaders coordinated the work of the three groups, which tended to stay separate. For example, the work typically started in the gene-splicing group, followed by work in recombination, and then in fermentation. Fermentation was used to breed the bacteria created by the other two groups in sufficient numbers to enable mass production.

During the summer of 1983, the biotech research program was given a special project. Hoffman-LaRoche was developing leukocyte interferon to use as a treatment against cancer. VSC contracted with Hoffman-LaRoche to develop a technique for large-scale interferon production. VSC had only six months to come up with a production technology. Scientists in each of the subgroups remained in their own geographical confines and began immediately to test ideas relevant to their specialty. In September, the informal group leaders met and discovered that each group had taken a different research direction. Each of the subgroups believed their direction was best and the informal leaders argued vehemently for their positions, rather than change to another direction. Future meetings were conflict-laden and did not resolve the issues. When managers became aware of the crisis, they decided to appoint a formal leader to the program.

On November 15, a Stanford professor with extensive research experience in recombinant DNA technology was hired. His title was chief biologist for the Biotech Research Program, and all project members reported to him for the duration of the interferon project.

The chief biologist immediately took the nine scientists on a two-day retreat. He assigned them to three tables for discussions, with a member from each subgroup at each table, so they had to talk across their traditional boundaries. He led the discussion of their common ground as scientists, and of their hopes and vision for this project. After they developed a shared vision, the group turned to scientific issues and in mixed groups discussed the ideas that the VSC subgroups had developed. Gradually, one approach seemed to have more likelihood of success than the others. A consensus emerged, and the chief biologist adopted the basic approach that would be taken in the interferon project. Upon their return to VSC, the technicians were brought in and the scientists explained the approach to them. At this point, each subgroup was assigned a set of instructions within the overall research plan. Firm deadlines were established based on group interdependence. Weekly progress reports to the chief biologist were required from each group leader.

Dramatic changes in the behavior of the scientists were observed after the two-day retreat. Communication among groups became more common. Problems discovered by one group were communicated to other groups so that effort was not expended needlessly. Subgroup leaders coordinated many solutions among themselves. Lunch and coffee gatherings that included several members of the subgroups began to appear. Group leaders and members often had daily discussions and cooperated on research requirements. Enthusiasm for the department and the interferon project was high, and cohesion seemed especially strong.

Source: From *Organization Theory and Design*, 5th edition, by Daft © 1995. Reprinted with permission of South-Western, a division of Thomson Learning; http://www.thomsonrights.com, fax 800-730-2215.

QUESTIONS

1. Was the research program a group or a team? If a team, what type of team was it (functional, cross-functional, self-directed)? Explain.

2. Did the interdependence among the subgroups change with the interferon project? What were the group norms before and after the retreat?

3. What factors account for the change in cohesiveness after the chief biologist took over?

Burgess Industries

Managers at Burgess Industries, one of the few remaining garment manufacturing companies in eastern North Carolina, are struggling to improve productivity and profits. If things don't get better, they and their 650 employees will be out of work. Top executives have been evaluating whether to close the plant, which makes pants for several different clothing companies, and move production to Mexico. However, everyone hopes to keep the North Carolina factory going. The latest effort to turn things around is a shift to teamwork.

Top executives directed managers to abandon the traditional assembly system, where workers performed a single task, such as sewing zippers or attaching belt loops. In the new team system, teams of 30 to 35 workers coordinate their activities to assemble complete garments. People were given training to help master new machinery and also attended a brief team-building and problem-solving seminar prior to the shift to teamwork. Approximately 50 workers at a time were taken off the production floor for an afternoon to attend the seminars, which were spread over a month's time. As an introduction to the seminar, employees were told that the new team system would improve their work lives by giving them more autonomy, eliminating the monotony of the old assembly system and reducing the number of injuries people received from repeating the same task over and over.

The pay system was also revised. Previously, workers were paid based on their total output. A skilled worker could frequently exceed his or her quota of belt loops or fly stitching by 20 percent or more, which amounted to a hefty increase in pay. In the new system, people are paid based on the total output of the team. In many cases, this meant that the pay of top performers went down dramatically because the productivity of the team was adversely affected by slower, inexperienced, or inefficient team members. Skilled workers were frustrated having to wait for slower colleagues to complete their part of the garment, and they resented having to pitch in and help out the less-skilled workers to speed things up. Supervisors, unaccustomed to the team system, provided little direction beyond telling people they needed to resolve work flow and personality issues among themselves. The idea was to empower employees to have more control over their own work.

So far, the experiment in teamwork has been a dismal failure. The quantity of garments produced per hour has actually declined 25 percent from pre-team levels. Labor costs have gone down, but morale is terrible. Threats and insults are commonly heard on the factory floor. One seamstress even had to restrain a coworker who was about to throw a chair at a team member who constantly griped about "having to do everyone else's work."

Source: Based on information reported in N. Munk, "How Levi's Trashed a Great American Brand," *Fortune* (April 12, 1999), pp. 83–90; and R. King, "Levi's Factory Workers Are Assigned to Teams, and Morale Takes a Hit," *The Wall Street Journal,* (May 20, 1998), pp. A1, A6.

QUESTIONS

1. Why do you think the experiment in teamwork at Burgess Industries has been unsuccessful? Consider the definition of teams, team characteristics and team dynamics, and issues of leadership.

2. If you were a consultant to Burgess, what would you recommend managers do to promote more effective teamwork?

3. How would you alleviate the conflicts that have developed among employees?

References

1 Sarah Max, "Seagate's Morale-athon," *BusinessWeek* (April 3, 2006), pp. 110–112.

2 J. D. Osburn, L. Moran, E. Musselwhite, and J. H. Zenger, *Self-Directed Work Teams: The New American Challenge* (Homewood, IL.: Business One Irwin, 1990).

3 Linda I. Glassop, "The Organizational Benefit of Teams," *Human Relations* 55, no. 2 (2002), pp. 225–249.

4 Jeffrey Pfeffer, "Producing Sustainable Competitive Advantage through the Effective Management of People," *Academy of Management Executive* 9, no. 1 (1995), pp. 55–72.

5 Daniel R. Kibbe and Jill Casner-Lotto, "Ralston Foods: From Greenfield to Maturity in a Team-Based Plant," *Journal of Organizational Excellence* (Summer 2002), pp. 57–67; Telis Demos, "Cirque du Balancing Act," *Fortune* (June 12, 2006), p. 114.; Kenneth Labich, "Elite Teams Get the Job Done," *Fortune* (February 19, 1996), pp. 90–99.

6 J. Richard Hackman, "Why Teams Don't Work," in *Theory and Research on Small Groups*, R. Scott Tindale, et al., eds. (New York: Plenum Press, 1998).

7 Avan R. Jassawalla and Hemant C. Sashittal, "Strategies of Effective New Product Team Leaders," *California Management Review* 42, no. 2 (Winter 2000), pp. 34–51.

8 Carl E. Larson and Frank M. J. LaFasto, *Team Work* (Newbury Park, CA: Sage, 1989); and C. P. Aldefer, "Group and Intergroup Relations," in *Improving Life at Work*, J. R. Hackman and J. S. Suttle, eds., (Santa Monica, CA: Goodyear, 1977).

9 Lee G. Bolman and Terrence E. Deal, "What Makes a Team Work?" *Organizational Dynamics* (August 1992), pp. 34–44.

10 Geoffrey Colvin, "Why Dream Teams Fail," *Fortune* (June 12, 2006), pp. 87–92.

11 Kenneth G. Koehler, "Effective Team Management," *Small Business Report* (July 19, 1989), pp. 14–16; Connie J. G. Gersick, "Time and Transition in Work Teams: Toward a New Model of Group Development," *Academy of Management Journal* 31 (1988), pp. 9–41; and John Beck and Neil Yeager, "Moving Beyond Myths," *Training & Development* (March 1996), pp. 51–55.

12 Thomas Petzinger Jr., "Bovis Team Helps Builders Construct a Solid Foundation" (The Front Lines column), *The Wall Street Journal* (March 21, 1997), p. B1.

13 David Kirkpatrick, "Inside Sam's $100 Billion Growth Machine," *Fortune* (June 14, 2004), pp. 80–98.

14 Pierre van Amelsvoort and Jos Benders, "Team Time: A Model for Developing Self-Directed Work Teams," *International Journal of Operations and Production Management* 16, no. 2 (1996), pp. 159–170.

15 Jeanne M. Wilson, Jill George, and Richard S. Wellins, with William C. Byham, *Leadership Trapeze: Strategies for Leadership in Team-Based Organizations* (San Francisco: Jossey-Bass, 1994).

16 Patricia Booth, "Embracing the Team Concept," *Canadian Business Review* (Autumn 1994), pp. 10–13.

17 Ruth Wageman, "Critical Success Factors for Creating Superb Self-Managing Teams," *Organizational Dynamics* (Summer 1997), pp. 49–61.

18 Reported in Jia Lynn Yang, "The Power of Number 4.6," part of a special series, "Secrets of Greatness: Teamwork," *Fortune* (June 12, 2006), p. 122.

19 Martin Hoegl, "Smaller Teams—Better Teamwork: How to Keep Project Teams Small," *Business Horizons* 48 (2005), pp. 209–214.

20 Reported in "Vive La Difference," box in Julie Connelly, "All Together Now," *Gallup Management Journal* (Spring 2002), pp. 13–18.

21 For research findings on group size, see M. E. Shaw, *Group Dynamics,* 3rd ed. (New York: McGraw-Hill, 1981); G. Manners, "Another Look at Group Size, Group Problem-Solving and Member Consensus," *Academy of Management Journal* 18 (1975), pp. 715–724; and Albert V. Carron and Kevin S. Spink, "The Group Size-Cohesion Relationship in Minimal Groups," *Small Group Research* 26, no. 1 (February 1995), pp. 86–105.

22 Warren E. Watson, Kamalesh Kumar, and Larry K. Michaelsen, "Cultural Diversity's Impact on Interaction Process and Performance: Comparing Homogeneous and Diverse Task Groups," *Academy of Management Journal* 36 (1993), pp. 590–602; Gail Robinson and Kathleen Dechant, "Building a Business Case for Diversity," *Academy of Management Executive* 11, no. 3 (1997), pp. 21–31; R. A. Guzzo and G. P. Shea, "Group Performance and Intergroup Relations in Organizations," in M. D. Dunnette and L. M. Hough, eds., *Handbook of Industrial & Organizational Psychology,* 2nd ed., vol. 3 (Palo Alto, CA: Consulting Psychologists Press, 1992), pp. 288–290; and David A. Thomas and Robin J. Ely, "Making Differences Matter: A New Paradigm for Managing Diversity," *Harvard Business Review* (September–October 1996), pp. 79–90.

23 Andrew Sobel, "The Beatles Principles," *Strategy + Business* Issue 42 (Spring 2006), pp. 32–35.

24 Kathleen M. Eisenhardt, Jean L. Kahwajy, and L. J. Bourgeois III, "Conflict and Strategic Choice: How Top Management Teams Disagree," *California Management Review* 39, no. 2 (Winter 1997), pp. 42–62.

25 Dee Gill, "Dealing with Diversity," *Inc. Magazine* (November 2005), pp. 37–40.

26 Linda A. Hill, "A Note for Analyzing Work Groups," Harvard Business Online, (August 28, 1995; revised April 3, 1998), Product # 9-496-026, ordered at http://www.hbsp.harvard.edu

27 Dora C. Lau and J. Keith Murnighan, "Demographic Diversity and Faultlines: The Compositional Dynamics of Organizational Groups," *Academy of Management Review* 23, no. 2 (1998), pp. 325–340; and K. A. Jehn, "A Multimethod Examination of the Benefits and Detriments of Intragroup Conflict," *Administrative Science Quarterly* 40 (1995), pp. 256–282.

28 Watson, Kumar, and Michaelsen, "Cultural Diversity's Impact on Interaction Process and Performance."

29 Stanley M. Gully, Dennis J. Devine, and David J. Whitney, "A Meta-Analysis of Cohesion and Performance: Effects of Level of Analysis and Task Interdependence," *Small Group Research* 26, no. 4 (November 1995), pp. 497–520.

30 James Thompson, *Organizations in Action* (New York: McGraw-Hill, 1967).

31 Peter F. Drucker, *Managing in a Time of Great Change* (New York: Truman Talley Books/Dutton, 1995), p. 98.

32 Ibid.

33 Thomas A. Stewart, "The Great Conundrum—You vs. the Team," *Fortune* (November 25, 1996), pp. 165–166.

34 Chuck Salter, "Ford's Escape Route," *Fast Company* (October 2004), pp. 106–110.

35 Bernard Simon, "Ford Aims to Build on Escape Hybrid's Success," *National Post* (January 26, 2005), pp. FP-10; and Amy Wilson, "Ford Escape Hybrid: OK, But It's No Prius," *Automotive News* (March 13, 2006), p. 6.

36 Robert C. Liden, Sandy J. Wayne, and Lisa Bradway, "Connections Make the Difference," *HR Magazine* (February 1996), p. 73.

37 Dexter Dunphy and Ben Bryant, "Teams: Panaceas or Prescriptions for Improved Performance," *Human Relations* 49, no. 5 (1996), pp. 677–699; Susan G. Cohen, Gerald E. Ledford, and Gretchen M. Spreitzer, "A Predictive Model of Self-Managing Work Team Effectiveness," *Human Relations* 49, no. 5 (1996), pp. 643–676; Martin Hoegl and Hans Georg Gemuenden, "Teamwork Quality and the Success of Innovative Projects: A Theoretical Concept and Empirical Evidence," *Organization Science* 12, no. 4 (July–August 2001), pp. 435–449; Ruth Wageman, J. Richard Hackman and Erin Lehman, "Team Diagnostic Survey: Development of an Instrument," *The Journal of Applied Behavioral Science* 41, no. 4 (December 2005), pp. 373–398; and Hill, "A Note for Analyzing Work Groups."

38 Carron and Spink, "The Group Size-Cohesion Relationship in Minimal Groups."

39 Harold J. Leavitt and Jean Lipman-Blumen, "Hot Groups," *Harvard Business Review* (July–August 1995), pp. 109–116.

40 Dorwin Cartwright and Alvin Zander, *Group Dynamics: Research and Theory,* 3rd ed. (New York: Harper & Row, 1968); Eliot Aronson, *The Social Animal* (San Francisco: W. H. Freeman, 1976); and Thomas Li-Ping Tang and Amy Beth Crofford, "Self-Managing Work Teams," *Employment Relations Today* (Winter 1995/96), pp. 29–39.

41 Tang and Crofford, "Self-Managing Work Teams."

42 Gully, Devine, and Whitney, "A Meta-Analysis of Cohesion and Performance: Effects of Level of Analysis and Task Interdependence."

43 Stanley E. Seashore, *Group Cohesiveness in the Industrial Work Group* (Ann Arbor, MI: Institute for Social Research, 1954).

44 Michael Goold, "Making Peer Groups Effective: Lessons from BP's Experience," *Long Range Planning* 38 (2005), pp. 429–443.

45 Adam Lashinsky, "RAZR's Edge," *Fortune* (June 12, 2006), pp. 124–132.

46 Ibid.

47 Based on Robert A. Baron, *Behavior in Organizations,* 2nd ed. (Boston: Allyn & Bacon, 1986); Don Hellriegel, John W. Slocum, Jr., and Richard W. Woodman, *Organizational Behavior,* 8th ed. (Cincinnati: South-Western, 1998), p. 244; and Gary A. Yukl, *Leadership in Organizations,* 4th ed. (Upper Saddle River, NJ: Prentice Hall, 1998), pp. 384–387.

48 This example is from Angus Strachan, "Lights, Camera, Interaction," *PeopleManagement* (September 16, 2004), accessed from http://www.peoplemanagement.co.uk.

49 Studies reported in Amy Edmondson, Richard Bohmer, and Gary Pisano, "Speeding Up Team Learning," *Harvard Business Review* (October 2001), pp. 125–132; and Scott Thurm, "Theory & Practice: Teamwork Raises Everyone's Game – Having Everyone Bond Benefits Companies More Than Promoting Stars," *The Wall Street Journal* (November 7, 2005), p. B8.

50 This section is based on Mark Sanborn, *Team Built: Making Teamwork Pay* (New York: MasterMedia Limited, 1992); Wilson, et al. *Leadership Trapeze;* J. Richard Hackman and R. E. Walton, "Leading Groups in Organizations," in *Designing Effective Work Groups,* P.S. Goodman and Associates, eds. (San Fransicso: Jossey-Bass, 1986); and Bolman and Deal, "What Makes a Team Work?"

51 Thomas L. Legare, "How Hewlett-Packard Used Virtual Cross-Functional Teams to Deliver Healthcare Industry Solutions," *Journal of Organizational Excellence* (Autumn 2001), pp. 29–38.

52 Edmondson, Bohmer, and Pisano, "Speeding Up Team Learning."

53 Eric Matson, "Congratulations, You're Promoted. (Now What?)," *Fast Company* (June–July 1997), pp. 116–130.

54 Mark Sanborn, *TeamBuilt: Making Teamwork Pay* (New York: MasterMedia Limited, 1992), p. 100.

55 Bradford W. Bell and Steve W. J. Kozlowski, "A Typology of Virtual Teams: Implications for Effective Leadership," *Group and Organization Management* 27, no. 1 (March 2002), pp. 14–49.

56 The discussion of virtual teams is based on Anthony M. Townsend, Samuel M. DeMarie, and Anthony R. Hendrickson, "Virtual Teams: Technology and the Workplace of the Future," *Academy of Management Executive* 12, no. 3 (August 1998), pp. 17–29; Deborah L. Duarte and Nancy Tennant Snyder, *Mastering Virtual Teams* (San Francisco: Jossey-Bass, 1999); and Jessica Lipnack and Jeffrey Stamps, "Virtual Teams: The New Way to Work," *Strategy & Leadership* (January–February 1999), pp. 14–18.

57 Lipnack and Stamps, "Virtual Teams."

58 Carla Joinson, "Managing Virtual Teams," *HR Magazine* (June 2002), pp. 69–73.

59 Stacie A. Furst, Martha Reeves, Benson Rosen, and Richard S. Blackburn, "Managing the Life Cycle of Virtual Teams" *Academy of Management Executive* 18, no. 2 (2004), pp. 6–20; R.E. Potter and P.A. Balthazard, "Understanding Human Interaction and Performance in the Virtual Team," *Journal of Information Technology Theory and Application* 4 (2002), pp. 1–23; and Kenneth W. Kerber and Anthony F. Buono, "Leadership Challenges in Global Virtual Teams: Lessons from the Field," *SAM Advanced Management Journal* (Autumn 2004), pp. 4–10.

60 The discussion of these challenges is based on Bradford S. Bell and Steve W. J. Kozlowski, "A Typology of Virtual Teams: Implications for Effective Leadership," *Group & Organization Management* 27, no. 1 (March 2002), pp. 14–49; Lipnack and Stamps, "Virtual Teams: The New Way to Work"; Joinson, "Managing Virtual Teams"; and Jon R. Katzenbach and Douglas K. Smith, "The Discipline of Virtual Teams," *Leader to Leader* (Fall 2001), pp. 16–25.

61 Terri L. Griffith and Margaret A. Neale, "Information Processing in Traditional, Hybrid, and Virtual Teams: From Nascent Knowledge to Transactive Memory," *Research in Organizational Behavior* 23 (2001), pp. 379–421.

62 Solomon, "Building Teams Across Borders."

63 Ron Young, "The Wide-Awake Club," *People Management* (February 5, 1998), pp. 46–49.

64 Kerber and Buono, "Leadership Challenges in Global Virtual Teams."

65 Katzenbach and Smith, "The Discipline of Virtual Teams."

66 Griffith and Neale, "Information Processing in Traditional, Hybrid, and Virtual Teams."

67 Edward F. McDonough III, Kenneth B. Kahn, and Gloria Barczak, "An Investigation of the Use of Global, Virtual, and Colocated New Product Development Teams," *The Journal of Product Innovation Management* 18 (2001), pp. 110–120.

68 Mary O'Hara-Devereaux and Robert Johansen, *Globalwork: Bridging Distance, Culture, and Time* (San Francisco: Jossey-Bass, 1994); Charles C. Snow, Scott A. Snell, Sue Canney Davison, and Donald C. Hambrick, "Use Transnational Teams to Globalize Your Company," *Organizational Dynamics* 24, no. 4 (Spring 1996), pp. 50–67; Vijay Govindarajan and Anil K. Gupta, "Building an Effective Global Business Team," *MIT Sloan Management Review* (Summer, 2001), pp. 63–71; and McDonough, et al., "An Investigation of the Use of Global, Virtual, and Colocated New Product Development Teams."

69 Carol Saunders, Craig Van Slyke, and Douglas R. Vogel, "My Time or Yours? Managing Time Visions in Global Virtual Teams," *Academy of Management Executive* 18, no. 1 (2004), pp. 19–31.

70 Josh Hyatt, "The Soul of a New Team," *Fortune* (June 12, 2006), pp. 134–143; and Victoria Murphy Barret, "A Chat With . . . Oracle's New Enemy," *Forbes.com* (February 15, 2006), accessed at http://www.forbes.com/technology/2006/02/15/oracle-yahoo-google-cz_vmb_0215Mysql.html

71 R. Duane Ireland and Michael A. Hitt, "Achieving and Maintaining Strategic Competitiveness in the 21st Century: The Role of Strategic Leadership," *Academy of Management Executive* 13, no. 1 (1999), pp. 43–57.

72 This section is based on Govindarajan and Gupta, "Building an Effective Global Business Team."

73 Saunders, et al., "My Time or Yours?"

74 Chantell E. Nicholls, Henry W. Lane, and Mauricio Brehm Brechu, "Taking Self-Managed Teams to Mexico," *Academy of Management Executive* 13, no. 2 (1999), pp. 15–27.

75 Govindarajan and Gupta, "Building an Effective Global Business Team."

76 Ibid.

77 Sylvia Odenwald, "Global Work Teams," *Training and Development* (February 1996), pp. 54–57; and Debby Young, "Team Heat," *CIO,* Section 1 (September 1, 1998), pp. 43–51.

78 Yuhyung Shin, "Conflict Resolution in Virtual Teams," *Organizational Dynamics* 34, no. 4 (2005), pp. 331–345.

79 Debra L. Shapiro, Stacie A. Furst, Gretchen M. Spreitzer, and Mary Ann Von Glinow, "Transnational Teams in the Electronic Age: Are Team Identity and High Performance at Risk?" *Journal of Organizational Behavior* 23 (2002), pp. 455–467.

80 Koehler, "Effective Team Management"; and Dean Tjosvold, "Making Conflict Productive," *Personnel Administrator* 29 (June 1984), p. 121.

81 Karen A. Jehn and Elizabeth A. Mannix, "The Dynamic Nature of Conflict: A Longitudinal Study of Intragroup Conflict and Group Performance," *Academy of Management Journal* 44, no. 2 (2001), pp. 238–251.

82 This discussion is based on K. W. Thomas, "Towards Multidimensional Values in Teaching: The Example of Conflict Behaviors," *Academy of Management Review* 2 (1977), p. 487.

83 Mitzi M. Montoya-Weiss, Anne P. Massey, and Michael Song, "Getting It Together: Temporal Coordination and Conflict Management in Global Virtual Teams," *Academy of Management Journal* 44, no. 6 (2001), pp. 1251–1262.

84 "The Negotiation Process: The Difference Between Integrative and Distributive Negotiation," La Piana Associates Inc., accessed from http://www.lapiana.org/resources/tips/negotiations.

85 Rob Walker, "Take It Or Leave It: The Only Guide to Negotiating You Will Ever Need," *Inc.,* (August 2003), pp. 75–82.

86 Jennifer Gill, "Squelching Office Conflicts," *Inc. Magazine* (November 2005), pp. 40–41.

Chapter 11

Your Leadership Challenge

After reading this chapter, you should be able to:

- Understand and reduce the difficulties faced by minorities in organizations.

- Apply an awareness of the dimensions of diversity and multicultural issues in your everyday life.

- Encourage and support diversity to meet organizational needs.

- Consider the role of cultural values and attitudes in determining how to deal with employees from different cultures or ethnic backgrounds.

- Break down your personal barriers that may stand in the way of enhancing your level of diversity awareness and appreciation.

Chapter Outline

Developing Leadership Diversity

India-born Indra Nooyi recently got a promotion. Already one of the most powerful women in business, in October of 2006 Nooyi became the first female CEO of PepsiCo. It's a clear reflection of the emphasis the company puts on providing equal opportunities for everyone. But Nooyi cautions that "the full potential of diversity is not realized without an inclusive culture," which means that people have to "become comfortable being uncomfortable" so they are willing to confront difficult diversity issues.

Getting people comfortable being uncomfortable is one reason Nooyi's predecessor, chairman and former CEO Steve Reinemund, gave several members of his top leadership team an unusual assignment. Reinemund named eight of his top managers as "executive sponsor" for a specific employee group, including African-Americans, Latinos, Asians, women, women of color, white males, disabled, and gay/lesbian/transgendered. In most assignments, the leaders would be different from the people they were sponsoring: white men are sponsored by African-American Larry Thompson, for example, and Irene Rosenfeld, a white female, sponsors African-Americans. The executives are expected to understand their group members' needs, identify key talent, and personally mentor at least three people from the group. It's an innovative way to give people experience in dealing with differences at the same time it develops minority talent for future leadership roles.

Both Reinemund and Nooyi know that the goal of inclusion is tough and elusive. Consider the reminder Reinemund got in an e-mail after addressing a group of African-American employees from the patio steps at Pepsi headquarters. He thought his closing remarks had been well received. The writer of the e-mail, however, said it reminded her of a plantation owner lecturing his slaves from on high.[1]

Steve Reinemund and Indra Nooyi, like many of today's leaders, know that diversity sparks innovation, leads to better decision making, and spurs growth. In one recent year, Pepsi attributed one percentage point of its 7.4 percent revenue growth to new products inspired by diversity efforts.[2] These benefits of diversity are one reason the face of America's organizations is beginning to change, with women and minorities, such as Nooyi, slowly moving into upper-level leadership positions. However, as also illustrated by the story at PepsiCo, there are still many challenges for creating diverse organizations. One of the most important roles for leaders in the coming years will be developing a solid base of diverse leadership talent. "In any organization in America, you will see diversity at the bottom of the house," says Roberta (Bobbi) Gutman, vice president and director of global diversity at Motorola. "But to get it higher up takes the clout and the wingspan of company leadership."[3]

Successful leaders in an increasingly diverse world have a responsibility to acknowledge and value cultural differences and understand how diversity affects organizational operations and outcomes.[4] This chapter explores the topic of diversity and multiculturalism. First, we look at the difficulties leaders encounter in leading people who are different from themselves and the challenges minorities face in organizations. Then, we explore the value of diversity for organizations and look at some new styles of leadership that support a more inclusive work environment. Next, the chapter takes a closer look at global diversity and how leaders can develop cultural intelligence. Finally, we discuss the personal stages of leader diversity awareness and the personal qualities for leading diverse workplaces.

Leading People Who Aren't Like You

You've recently gotten the promotion you've longed for, worked for, and know you deserve. The job of managing the New England district office of Allyn & Freeson Investments required relocating, but your family enthusiastically made the move. Your children seem to be adjusting well to their new school and your wife likes her job at the local bank. If only things were as smooth at Allyn & Freeson. The all-white staff seems to be throwing up roadblocks in every direction. Nobody seems to even talk to you unless they're asked a direct question or forced to make a response to your greeting of "Good morning." Traveling to the branch offices isn't much better, and many of the local managers have inexplicably stopped sending in their weekly reports. You knew being the first African-American district manager in the area was going to be a bit of a challenge, but the sense of isolation you feel is more powerful than you anticipated. Even in the branch offices, you've met only two other African-Americans, and they're in low-level clerical positions. "Even Noah's ark had two animals that were exactly alike," you moan to your wife over dinner one evening.[5]

Welcome to the real world of diverse leadership. As more women and minorities move up the management hierarchy, they're often finding it a lonely road to travel. Even for those who have experienced a degree of racism or sexism at lower organizational levels, stepping into positions of higher authority can be a real eye-opener. Racism and sexism in the workplace often show up in subtle ways—the disregard by a subordinate for an assigned chore; a lack of urgency in completing an important assignment; the ignoring of comments or suggestions made at a team meeting. Many minority leaders struggle daily with the problem of delegating authority and responsibility to employees who show them little respect.

How does an African-American or Hispanic manager lead an all-white workforce, or a female manager lead a workforce of mostly males? What happens when a 32-year-old is promoted to a position of authority over a group of mostly 50- to 60-year-old middle managers? These questions are being asked more and more often in today's diverse organizations. Consider Stanley O'Neal, CEO of Merrill Lynch, the only African-American running a major Wall Street company; Rachelle Hood, the African-American woman hired to transform Denny's Restaurants from an icon of racism after a series of discrimination lawsuits; or Donna Dennison, who in 2006 was elected the first ever female sheriff in the state of Maine and leads a largely male department. These leaders face enormous challenges. In many organizations, people who fall outside the traditional U.S. model of the middle-aged white male manager have a hard time being successful because the organizational climate doesn't genuinely support and value diversity. By the end of this chapter, we hope you will better understand some of the challenges, as well as some leadership strategies that can help make organizations more inclusive and provide a better working environment for all people.

Action Memo

Complete the exercise in Leader's Self-Insight 11.1 to learn about the values you will bring to leading people who are diverse and not like you.

Challenges Minorities Face

Valuing diversity and enabling all individuals to develop their unique talents is difficult to achieve. Most people, including leaders, have a natural tendency toward **ethnocentrism**, which refers to the belief that one's own culture and subculture are inherently superior to other cultures.[6] Many leaders relate to people in

Ethnocentrism
the belief that one's own culture and subculture are inherently superior to other cultures

Values Balancing

For each pair of values below, select the one that is most descriptive of you. Even if both qualities describe you, you must choose one.

1. Analytical	_____	Compassionate	_____
2. Collaborative	_____	Decisive	_____
3. Competitive	_____	Sociable	_____
4. Loyal	_____	Ambitious	_____
5. Resourceful	_____	Adaptable	_____
6. Sensitive to others	_____	Independent	_____
7. Self-reliant	_____	Uniting	_____
8. Helpful	_____	Persistent	_____
9. Risk-taker	_____	Contented	_____
10. Interested	_____	Knowledgeable	_____
11. Responsible	_____	Encouraging	_____
12. Tactful	_____	Driven	_____
13. Forceful	_____	Gentle	_____
14. Participating	_____	Achievement-oriented	_____
15. Action-oriented	_____	Accepting	_____

Scoring and Interpretation

The words above represent two leadership values: "capacity for collaboration" and "personal initiative." "Personal initiative" is represented by the first word in the odd-numbered rows and the second word in the even-numbered rows. "Capacity for collaboration" is represented by the first word in the even numbered rows and by the second word in the odd numbered rows. Add the number of words circled that represent each value and record the number below:

Personal Initiative: _____
Capacity for Collaboration: _____

Capacity for collaboration represents feminine values in our culture, and if you circled more of these items, you may be undervaluing your personal initiative. Personal initiative represents masculine values, and more circled words here may mean you are undervaluing your capacity for collaboration. How balanced are your values? How will you lead someone with values very different from yours?

Gender is a trait of diversity. How prevalent in organizations are feminine and masculine values? Read the rest of this chapter to learn which values are associated with successful leadership.

Source: Donald J. Minnick and R. Duane Ireland, "Inside the New Organization: A Blueprint for Surviving Restructuring, Downsizing, Acquisitions and Outsourcing." *Journal of Business Strategy* 26 (2005), pp. 18–25; and A. B. Heilbrun, "Measurement of Masculine and Feminine Sex Role Identities as Independent Dimensions." *Journal of Consulting and Clinical Psychology* 44 (1976), pp. 183–190.

---

the organization as if everyone shares similar values, beliefs, motivations, and attitudes about work and life. This assumption is typically false even when dealing with people who share the same ethnic or cultural background. Ethnocentric viewpoints combined with a standard set of cultural assumptions and practices create a number of challenges for minority employees and leaders.

Unequal Expectations/Difference as Deficiency One significant problem in many organizations is a mind-set that views difference as deficiency or dysfunction.[7] A survey by Korn Ferry International found that 59 percent of minority managers surveyed had observed a racially motivated double standard in the delegation of assignments.[8] Their perceptions are supported by a study that showed minority managers spend more time in the "bullpen" waiting for their chance and then have to prove themselves over and over again with each new assignment. Another recent study found that white managers gave more negative performance ratings to African-American leaders and white subordinates and more positive ratings to white leaders and African-American subordinates, affirming the widespread acceptance of these employees in their stereotypical roles.[9] The perception by many minorities is that no matter how many college degrees they earn, how many hours they work, how they dress, or how much effort and enthusiasm they invest, they are never considered to "have the right stuff." One Hispanic executive, in discussing the animosity he felt, said, "The fact that I graduated first in my class didn't make as much difference as the fact that I looked different."[10] If the standard of quality were based, for instance, on being white and male, anything else would be seen as deficient. This dilemma is often difficult for white men to understand because many of them are not intentionally racist and sexist. As one observer points out, you would need to be non-white to understand what it is like to have people assume a subordinate is your superior simply because he is white, or to lose a sale after the customer sees you in person and finds out you're not Caucasian.[11]

These attitudes are deeply rooted in our society as well as in our organizations. Sociologist William Bielby proposes that people have innate biases and, left to their own devices, they will automatically discriminate.[12] *Unconscious bias theory* suggests that white males, for example, will inevitably slight women and minorities because people unknowingly revert to stereotypes when making decisions. Indeed, passive, and sometimes unconscious, bias is a bigger problem than blatant discrimination in most organizations. Consider a recent report from the National Bureau of Economic Research, entitled *Are Greg and Emily More Employable than Lakisha and Jamal?*, which shows that employers often unconsciously discriminate against job applicants based solely on the Afrocentric or African-American–sounding names on their resume. In interviews prior to the research, most human resource managers surveyed said they expected only a small gap and some expected to find a pattern of reverse discrimination. The results showed instead that white-sounding names got 50 percent more callbacks than African-American–sounding names, even when skills and experience were equal.[13]

It takes conscious leadership to change the status quo. Leaders can establish conditions that limit the degree of unconscious bias that goes into hiring and promotion decisions. Corporations such as BP and Becton Dickinson & Co. are now using tools to measure unconscious as well as conscious bias in their diversity training programs.[14]

> **Action Memo**
> Take the quiz in Leader's Self-Insight 11.2 to evaluate your personal degree of passive bias and think about ways you can become more diversity-aware.

Living Biculturally Research on differences between whites and African-Americans has focused on issues of biculturalism and how it affects employees' access to information, level of respect and appreciation, and relation to superiors and subordinates. **Biculturalism** can be defined as the sociocultural skills and attitudes used by racial minorities as they move back and forth between the dominant culture and their own ethnic or racial culture.[15] More than 90 years ago, W. E. B. DuBois referred to this as a "double-consciousness. . . . One always feels his twoness—an American, a Negro; two souls, two thoughts, two unreconciled strivings. . . ."[16] In general, African-Americans feel less accepted in their organizations, perceive themselves to have less discretion on their jobs, receive lower ratings on job performance, experience lower levels of job satisfaction, and reach career plateaus earlier than whites.

Eula Adams, head of card operations for First Data, recalls the feeling of loneliness that can come from living biculturally. Adams began his career in 1972 at Touche Ross, the accounting firm that is today known as Deloitte & Touche, and became the firm's first African-American partner in 1983. "The loneliness, especially in the early days, was the hardest," Adams now says. "I lived in two worlds. I'd leave work and go home to one world and then wake up and go back to work in that other world."[17] Glenn D. Capel, the only African-American financial adviser in a Merrill Lynch office in Greensboro, North Carolina, knows the feeling well. Despite the fact that Merrill Lynch is

Biculturalism
the sociocultural skills and attitudes used by racial minorities as they move back and forth between the dominant culture and their own ethnic or racial culture

Check either NO or Yes for each question below.

No Yes

1. What you notice first about people around you are the characteristics that make them different from you. _____ _____

2. You make it a general rule never to discuss the subjects of race, ethnicity, politics, age, religion, gender, and sexuality when you are at work. _____ _____

3. When others make bigoted remarks or jokes, you either laugh or say nothing because you don't want to seem sensitive or self-righteous. _____ _____

4. When you see publications that are targeted at an ethnic, gender, or religious group that you do not represent, you usually ignore them. _____ _____

5. When you look for a mentor or protégé, you pick someone like yourself. _____ _____

6. If someone tells you about a cultural difference that you have never heard of, you don't ask questions about it. _____ _____

7. You are affiliated with organizations that practice subtle discrimination, but you say nothing because you didn't create the rules. _____ _____

8. Before you hire someone for a position, you have a vague picture in mind of what the ideal candidate would look like. _____ _____

9. Your conversations make use of phrases like "you people" or "our kind." _____ _____

10. You avoid talking about cultural differences when dealing with people different from you because you're afraid of saying the wrong thing. _____ _____

11. When complimenting someone from a different background, you might tell them, "You are nothing like the others" or "I really don't think of you as a _____." _____ _____

12. There are people in your organization whom you like and respect but whom you would feel uncomfortable introducing to your family or close friends. _____ _____

Scoring and Interpretation

Give yourself five points for each "yes" answer. The appropriate score for today's world is "0." However, if you scored less than 20, you're probably making a good attempt to eliminate personal passive bias. A score of 20 to 40 means you need to watch it—you reveal passive bias that is inappropriate in organizations and society. If you scored more than 40, your level of bias could get you into trouble. You should definitely consider ways to become more diversity-aware and culturally sensitive.

Source: Adapted from Lawrence Otis Graham, *Proversity: Getting Past Face Values and Finding the Soul of People* (New York: John Wiley & Sons, 1997). Used with permission of Lawrence Otis Graham.

now run by African-American Stanley O'Neal, Capel and other African-American brokers have charged in a race-discrimination suit that the company systematically limits opportunities for African-Americans to succeed and maintains a work environment where only whites are comfortable.[18] Other minority groups may struggle with biculturalism as well. They find themselves striving to adopt behaviors and attitudes that will help them be successful in the white-dominated corporate world while at the same time maintaining their ties to their racial or ethnic community and culture. Many minorities feel they have a chance for career advancement only by becoming bicultural or abandoning their native cultures altogether.

Glass ceiling
an invisible barrier that
separates women and minorities
from top leadership positions

The Glass Ceiling Another issue is the **glass ceiling**, an invisible barrier that separates women and minorities from top leadership positions. They can look up through the ceiling, but prevailing attitudes are invisible obstacles to their own advancement. Research has also suggested the existence of "glass walls" that serve as invisible barriers to important lateral movement within the organization. Glass walls bar experience in areas such as line supervision or general management that would enable women and minorities to advance to senior-level positions.[19]

Although a few women and minorities have recently moved into highly visible top leadership positions, such as Kenneth Chenault at American Express or Indra Nooyi at Pepsi-Co, most women and minorities are still clustered at the bottom of the organizational hierarchy. Women, for instance, have made significant strides in recent years, but they still represent less than 16 percent of corporate officers in America's 500 largest companies.[20] In 2006, only eight *Fortune* 500 companies had female CEOs. And both male and female African-Americans and Hispanics continue to hold only a small percentage of all management positions in the United States.[21] Leaders in other countries are struggling with similar diversity issues. A report on executive talent in the United Kingdom, for example, indicates that although employees on the front lines "reflect the rich diversity of 21st century Britain," the executive suite is overwhelmingly "white, male, able-bodied, and of a certain age—[with] a photo of their wife and kids . . . on the desk."[22] Japanese companies, too, face mounting criticism about the scarcity of women in management positions. In Japan, women make up 41 percent of the workforce but occupy less than 3 percent of high-level management positions.[23]

Action Memo

As a leader, you can fight ethnocentric attitudes. You can create an environment in which people value diverse ways of thinking, dressing, or behaving, and you can help break down the barriers of unequal expectations, stereotypes, unequal pay, and the glass ceiling. You can close the opportunity gap so minorities have an equal chance to succeed.

Many women and minorities feel that they are not evaluated by the same standards as their male counterparts. For example, where having a family is often considered a plus for a male executive, it can be perceived as a hindrance for a woman who wants to reach the top. One term heard frequently is the *mommy track,* which implies that a woman's commitment to her children limits her commitment to the company or her ability to handle the rigors of corporate leadership.[24] Indeed, women leaders frequently do give up personal time, outside friendships, or hobbies because they still do most of the child care and housework in addition to their business responsibilities. Exhibit 11.1 shows the discrepancy between high-achieving men and women in terms of the time they devote to domestic duties, based on one survey.

Some women get off the fast track before they ever encounter the glass ceiling, which has been referred to as the *opt-out trend.* In a survey of nearly 2,500 women and 653 men, 37 percent of highly qualified women report that they have voluntarily left the workforce at some point in their careers, compared to only 24 percent of similarly qualified men.[25] Although some women voluntarily leave the fast track, there are many who genuinely want to move up the corporate ladder but find their paths blocked. Fifty-five percent of executive women surveyed by Catalyst said they aspire to senior leadership levels.[26] In addition, a survey of 103 women voluntarily leaving executive jobs in Fortune 1000 companies found that corporate culture was cited as the number one reason for leaving.[27] The greatest disadvantages of women leaders stem largely from prejudicial attitudes and a heavily male-oriented corporate culture.[28] Some years ago, when Procter & Gamble asked the female executives it considered "regretted losses" (that is, high performers the company wanted to retain) why they left their jobs, the most common answer was that they didn't feel valued by the company.[29]

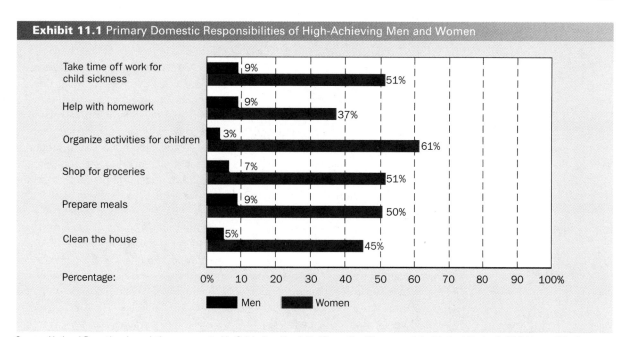

Exhibit 11.1 Primary Domestic Responsibilities of High-Achieving Men and Women

Source: National Parenting Association, as reported in Sylvia Ann Hewlett, "Executive Women and the Myth of Having It All," *Harvard Business Review* (April 2002), pp. 66–73.

Most top-level corporate cultures have evolved around white, heterosexual, American males, who tend to hire and promote people who look, act, and think like them. Many organizations were originally created by and for men, and the prevailing work practices and patterns of social interaction tend to privilege men and disadvantage women, often in subtle ways.[30] One study supports the idea that in organizations with strong male hierarchies, women are less likely than men to advance to higher-level positions. In addition, women are more likely to advance if they demonstrate traits associated with masculinity, such as assertiveness, achievement-orientation, and focus on material success.[31] Compatibility in thought and behavior plays an important role at higher levels of organizations. Among women who have managed to break through the glass ceiling, fully 96 percent said adapting to a predominantly white male culture was necessary for their success.[32]

The Opportunity Gap In some cases, people fail to advance to higher levels in organizations because they don't have the necessary education and skills. A final challenge is the lack of opportunities for many minorities to obtain the same level of education as white, American-born individuals. Only 62 percent of Hispanics, the fastest growing segment of the U.S. population, complete high school. Both African-Americans and Hispanics lag behind whites in college attendance, and only 10 percent of adults with disabilities have graduated from college.[33] Eric Adolphe, president and CEO of Optimus Corporation, who managed to stay in college because of a scholarship from the National Association Council for Minorities in Engineering, recalls many of the kids he grew up with in New York City: "There are a lot of people more gifted than myself who never made it—not because of their lack of ability, but because of their lack of opportunity."[34] Some companies and leaders are taking the lead to ensure that minorities get the education, skills, and opportunities they need to participate fully in today's economy. Consider the example of Ernst & Young.

Ernst & Young LLP

Ernst & Young's commitment to "building an inclusive environment" has been recognized with a number of awards, including eight consecutive years as one of *Hispanic Business* magazine's Top 50 Companies for Hispanics, *Fortune*'s 100 Best Companies to Work For, and *DiversityInc* magazine's Top 50 Companies for Diversity.

More than a decade ago, leaders launched two diversity initiatives aimed at increasing the recruitment and retention of women and minorities and began investing heavily in training, mentoring, and career development. These programs have had a positive impact, leading to a 79 percent increase in the firm's percentage of minority employees between 1995 and 2005 and a 100 percent rise in the number of diverse partners and principles. In mid-2006, Ernst & Young (E & Y) took the groundbreaking step of inviting Mitchell & Titus, the nation's largest African-American–owned accounting company, to join the Ernst & Young global firm.

What is equally important is that E & Y is aiming toward the future by giving minority high school and college students greater opportunities. E & Y has provided more than $1 million in scholarships for undergraduate and graduate minority students majoring in accounting, information technology, engineering, finance, and other disciplines. An innovative program called Your Master Plan (YMP) gives recent college graduates a chance to work at E & Y while they pursue a master's degree in accounting, paid for by the firm. For several years, *Black Collegian,* a magazine and career Web site for students of color, has recognized Ernst & Young as one of its Top 100 Diversity Employers. [35]

In an industry that is one of the least racially-diverse in the nation, Ernst & Young is taking solid steps to build a pipeline of minority candidates to be the leaders of tomorrow. In addition, E & Y is striving to create a corporate environment where all people have equal opportunities and are treated with respect, dignity, and fairness.

Diversity Today

Attitudes toward diversity are changing partly because they have to as leaders respond to significant changes in our society, including globalization and the changing workforce.[36] The average worker is older now, and white males now make up less than half the U.S. workforce, with many more women, people of color, and immigrants seeking employment opportunities.[37] The U.S. Bureau of Labor Statistics projects that women and minorities will make up 70 percent of new entrants to the workforce by 2008.[38]

The other factor contributing to increased acceptance of diversity is globalization. Leaders are emphasizing cross-cultural understanding so that people can work smoothly across borders. Some large multinational corporations, including Canada's Northern Telecom, U.S.-based Coca-Cola, Switzerland's Nestlé, and France's Carrefour, all get a large percentage of their sales from outside their home countries. Companies like Starbucks and MTV Networks are finding that the only potential for growth lies overseas. These organizations need diversity of leadership and sometimes find that U.S. managers don't have the broad experience needed to succeed in a global environment. An unprecedented number of foreign-born CEOs now run major companies in the United States, Britain, and several other countries.[39] Employees with global experience and cultural sensitivity are in high demand in many industries, and almost every employee is dealing with a wider range of cultures than ever before.

Definition of Diversity

Workforce diversity means a workforce made up of people with different human qualities or who belong to various cultural groups. From the perspective of individuals, **diversity** refers to differences among people in terms of dimensions such as age, ethnicity, gender, race, or physical ability. It is important to remember that diversity includes everyone, not just racial or ethnic minorities. Generational diversity, for example is a key concern for managers in many of today's companies, with four generations working side-by-side, each with a different mindset and different expectations.[40]

Exhibit 11.2 illustrates several important dimensions of diversity. This *diversity wheel* shows the myriad combinations of traits that make up diversity. The inside wheel represents primary dimensions of diversity, which include inborn differences or differences that have an impact throughout one's life.[41] Primary dimensions are core elements through which people shape their self-image and world view. These dimensions are age, race, ethnicity, gender, mental or physical abilities, and sexual orientation. Turn the wheel and these primary characteristics match up with various secondary dimensions of diversity.

Secondary dimensions can be acquired or changed throughout one's lifetime. These dimensions tend to have less impact than those of the core but nevertheless affect a person's self-definition and world view and have an impact on how the person is viewed by others. For example, veterans of the war in Iraq may have been profoundly affected by their military experience and may be perceived differently from other people. An employee living in a public housing project will be perceived differently from one who lives in an affluent part of town. Women with children are perceived differently in the work environment than those without children. Secondary dimensions such as work style, communication style, and educational or skill level are particularly relevant in the organizational setting.[42] One challenge for organizational leaders is to recognize that each person can bring value and strengths to the workplace based on his or her own combination of diversity characteristics. Organizations establish workforce diversity programs to promote the hiring, inclusion, and promotion of diverse employees and to ensure that differences are accepted and respected in the workplace.

Workforce diversity
a workforce made up of people with different human qualities or who belong to various cultural groups

Diversity
differences among people in terms of age, ethnicity, gender, race, or other dimensions

---

Exhibit 11.2 The Diversity Wheel

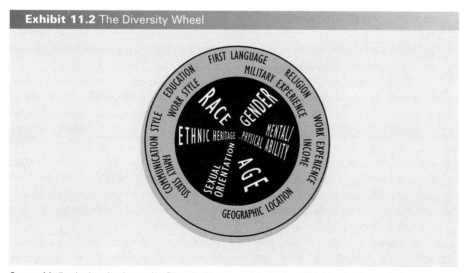

Source: Marilyn Loden, *Implementing Diversity* (Homewood, IL: Irwin, 1996). Used with permission.

The Value of Organizational Diversity

There is no question that the workforce is changing and organizations have to change to reflect the new workforce composition. However, there are a number of other reasons leaders want to incorporate diversity.

Recent research supports the idea that diversity adds value to organizations and can contribute to a firm's competitive advantage.[43] For one thing, leaders can use internal diversity to meet the needs of diverse customers. Culture plays an important part in determining the goods, entertainment, social services, and household products that people use and buy, so organizations are recruiting minority employees who can understand how diverse people live and what they want and need. Diverse employees can also help an organization build better relationships with customers by making them feel connected to the organization. When customers see and interact with people like themselves, they feel better about doing business with the company. An astute leader at Pepsi-Cola recognized this as early as the 1940s and embarked on an experiment that proved the economic value of diversity, as described in the Leader's Bookshelf. Allstate Insurance Company has built its success on the principle that the organization should be inclusive rather than exclusive. Allstate launched its first diversity program in 1969 and today ties 25 percent of managers' bonus pay to diversity performance.

IN THE LEAD

Allstate Insurance Company

You've probably seen the commercials: a popular African-American actor promising you that Allstate won't raise your rates just because of an accident, or telling you the company will give you $100 off your deductible for each year you go without having one. It's part of the diverse face that the leading insurance company for minorities presents to the world. "Being in a relationship business, how can you not look like and sound like your clients?" asks a vice president of sales for Allstate Insurance. "It's an obvious competitive advantage when you can mirror the clients that you serve."

Of the nearly 39,000 people working for Allstate, more than half are women and nearly 30 percent are minorities. Among officers and managers, 40 percent are women and nearly 20 percent are from minority groups. Allstate's diversity initiatives have earned the company a string of awards, including being named the No. 1 employer for African Americans in 2006 by *DiversityInc*. They have also led to some solid business results. A study by Simmons Research Group found that Allstate is the number one life and auto insurer among African-Americans and the number one homeowner's and life insurance firm among Hispanic Americans. Allstate's internal measurement systems show a steady increase in the customer base and growing levels of customer satisfaction.

The company's diverse workforce has helped Allstate establish solid relationships with culturally and ethnically diverse communities. At the Sunnyside neighborhood office in Queens, New York, one of the most ethnically diverse communities in the country, customers often relate to sales reps like members of their family, consulting them on problems that might have no relation to insurance. Mike Kalkin, the agent who heads up the office (and who is himself from an immigrant family), often recruits employees from within the community because they understand the local population's unique needs. A different situation exists at a northwestern Arkansas office, where a growing retired population means placing more emphasis on serving the needs of older customers.

Diversity at Allstate is a business strategy that provides us a competitive advantage," says Anise Wiley-Little, an African-American woman who serves as the company's Director of Diversity. At Allstate, the best human talent is diverse because the customers are.[44]

Leader's Bookshelf

The Real Pepsi Challenge: The Inspirational Story of Breaking the Color Barrier in American Business

Getty Images

by Stephanie Capparell

The rivalry between Pepsi and Coke was as hot in the 1940s as it is today. Pepsi's then-president Walter Mack decided he could gain an edge by hiring an all African-American sales team to actively pursue the untapped African-American consumer market. In her eye-opening and sometimes disturbing book, *The Real Pepsi Challenge: The Inspirational Story of Breaking the Color Barrier in American Business,* Stephanie Capparell commends Mack for hiring these dozen or so African-American executives at a time when job opportunities for African-Americans were limited primarily to the kitchen and the clean-up crew. Yet the real heroes of her tale are the salesmen themselves.

THE TEAM THAT FOUGHT AND WON

Things aren't always easy for African-American leaders in today's organizations. But imagine what it must have been like in the mid-1940s, when African-American Edward Boyd and his sales team went to work at Pepsi-Cola. Not only did they face prejudice within the organization, but traveling the country during the days of segregation and open bigotry, team members experienced humiliation, ridicule, and scorn. Yet they stood up to the challenge, buoyed by the respect and admiration they got from African-American communities and a chance to pave the way for future generations. In her book, Capparell highlights both the accomplishments of the team and the trials team members faced. Here are a few:

- Team members were more qualified than many of their white counterparts, with all having college degrees (one had an MBA), yet they were consistently paid less. They worked a grueling schedule, often working morning and night 7 days a week, visiting bottlers, churches, "ladies groups," insurance conferences, schools, YMCAs, community centers, and various other organizations.

- The team boosted sales of Pepsi in every geographical area they targeted, and during the four years the team operated, they consistently surpassed their profit goals.
- The marketing campaigns developed by Boyd and his team defined the concept of niche marketing and changed the way African-Americans were portrayed in advertising. Instead of stereotypes or offensive caricatures, Pepsi ads showed stylish, middle-class consumers. One campaign featured "leaders in their field," such as United Nations diplomat Ralph Bunche. Another featured top African-American university students.

THE LONG ROAD TO AN INCLUSIVE CULTURE

Despite their success, most team members never became fully accepted and integrated members of Pepsi's culture. After Mack retired, the new president of Pepsi-Cola fired Boyd and broke up the team. Most soon quit as a result of the frustrations of trying to succeed in a white-dominated corporation. One member, Harvey Russell, stayed and in 1962 became the first African-American vice president of a major U.S. corporation. Most team members went on to remarkable second careers, continuing to break color barriers along the way. Boyd joined the international aid agency CARE in the Middle East. Of his work at Pepsi, he says, "It was a contribution to progress. I didn't make that much of a dollar. I wasn't paid on the basis of other executives. It was at the beginning."

Source: *The Real Pepsi Challenge: The Inspirational Story of Breaking the Color Barrier in American Business,* by Stephanie Capparell, is published by Free Press.

Diversity at Allstate also helps to develop employee and organizational potential. When organizations support diversity, people feel valued for what they can bring to the organization, which leads to higher morale. A story from furniture manufacturer Herman Miller, told in the *Consider This* box, illustrates that each of us has unique talents and gifts. People can build better relationships at work when they develop the skills to understand and accept cultural differences. Allstate's diversity training emphasizes that employees can expect to be treated with respect and dignity,

Action Memo

As a leader, you can hire and promote people from diverse cultures and with diverse human characteristics. You can use organizational diversity to improve creativity and decision making, better serve customers, and enhance organizational flexibility.

Consider This!

Honoring Our Diversity of Gifts

One day the millwright died.

My father, being a young manager at the time, did not particularly know what he should do when a key person died, but thought he ought to go visit the family. He went to the house and was invited to join the family in the living room. There was some awkward conversation—the kind with which many of us are familiar.

The widow asked my father if it would be all right if she read aloud some poetry. Naturally, he agreed. She went into another room, came back with a bound book, and for many minutes, read selected pieces of beautiful poetry. When she finished, my father commented on how beautiful the poetry was and asked who wrote it. She replied that her husband, the millwright, was the poet.

It is now nearly sixty years since the millwright died, and my father and many of us at Herman Miller continue to wonder: Was he a poet who did millwright's work, or was he a millwright who wrote poetry?

* * *

Understanding diversity enables us to see that each of us is needed. . . .

The simple act of recognizing diversity in corporate life helps us to connect the great variety of gifts that people bring to the work and service of the organization. Diversity allows each of us to contribute in a special way, to make our special gift a part of the corporate effort.

Source: From *Leadership Is an Art*, by Max DePree, copyright © 1987 by Max DePree. Used with permission of Doubleday, a division of Random House, Inc.

but they are also expected to treat others the same way and to cultivate their business as well as relationship skills to help Allstate succeed.

Finally, diversity develops greater organizational flexibility. For one thing, by seriously recruiting and valuing individuals without regard to race, nationality, gender, age, sexual preference, or physical ability, organizations can attract and retain the best human talent. In addition, diversity within an organization provides a broader and deeper base of experience for problem solving, creativity, and innovation. Bell Atlantic CEO Ivan Seidenberg promotes diversity at his company primarily because he believes diverse groups make better decisions and bring the creativity and innovation needed to keep pace with massive changes in technology and competition. "If everybody in the room is the same," Seidenberg says, "you'll get a lot fewer arguments and a lot worse answers."[45] Referring back to our discussion of team diversity in the previous chapter, diverse groups tend to be more creative than homogeneous groups in part because of the different perspectives people can bring to the problem or issue. According to the results of one study, companies that are high on creativity and innovation have a higher percentage of women and non-white male employees than less innovative companies.[46]

One aspect of diversity that is of particular interest in organizations today is the way in which women's style of leadership may differ from men's. As women move into higher positions in organizations, it has been observed that they often use a style of leadership that is highly effective in today's turbulent, culturally diverse environment.[47]

Ways Women Lead

There is some evidence that men may become less influential in the U.S. work-force, with women becoming dominant players, because women's approach is more attuned to the needs and values of a multicultural environment. For example, there's a stunning gender reversal in U.S. education, with girls taking over almost every leadership role from kindergarten to graduate school. Women of all races and ethnic groups are outpacing men in earning bachelor's and master's degrees. In mid-2006, women made up 58 percent of undergraduate college students.[48] Among 25- to 29-year-olds, 32 percent of women have college degrees, compared to 27 percent of men. Women are rapidly closing the M.D. and Ph.D. gap, and they make up about half of all U.S. law students, half of all undergraduate business majors, and about 30 percent of MBA candidates. In addition, studies show that women students are more achievement-oriented, less likely to skip classes, spend more time studying, and typically earn higher grades.[49] Overall, women's participation in both the labor force and civic affairs has steadily increased since the mid-1950s, whereas men's participation has slowly but steadily declined.[50]

Women as Leaders

According to James Gabarino, an author and professor of human development at Cornell University, women are "better able to deliver in terms of what modern society requires of people—paying attention, abiding by rules, being verbally competent, and dealing with interpersonal relationships in offices."[51] His observation is supported by the fact that female managers are typically rated higher by subordinates on interpersonal skills as well as on factors such as task behavior, communication, ability to motivate others, and goal accomplishment.[52] As illustrated in Exhibit 11.3, one survey of followers rated women leaders significantly higher than men on several characteristics that are crucial for developing fast, flexible, adaptive organizations. Female leaders were rated as having more idealized

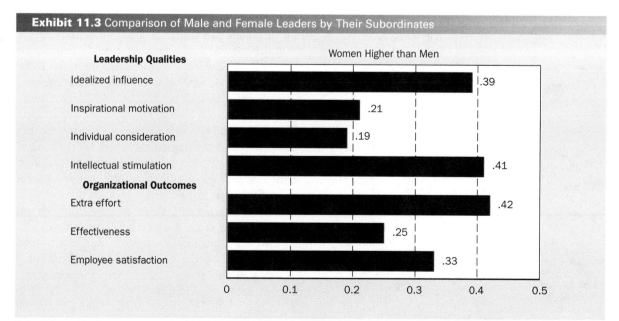

Exhibit 11.3 Comparison of Male and Female Leaders by Their Subordinates

Note: *Ratings of leaders were on a scale of 1–5. Women leaders were rated higher, on average, by the amount indicated for each item.*

Source: Based on Bernard M. Bass and Bruce J. Avolio, "Shatter the Glass Ceiling: Women May Make Better Managers," *Human Resource Management* 33, no. 4 (Winter 1994), pp. 549–560.

influence, providing more inspirational motivation, being more individually considerate, and offering more intellectual stimulation.[53] *Idealized influence* means that followers identify with and want to emulate the leader; the leader is trusted and respected, maintains high standards, and is considered to have power because of who she is rather than what position she holds. *Inspirational motivation* is derived from the leader who appeals emotionally and symbolically to employees' desire to do a good job and help achieve organizational goals. *Individual consideration* means each follower is treated as an individual but all are treated equitably; individual needs are recognized, and assignments are delegated to followers to provide learning opportunities. *Intellectual stimulation* means questioning current methods and challenging employees to think in new ways. In addition, women leaders were judged by subordinates as more effective and satisfying to work for and were considered able to generate extra levels of effort from employees.

Recent research has also found a correlation between balanced gender composition in companies (that is, roughly equal male and female representation) and higher organizational performance. Moreover, a study by Catalyst indicates that organizations with the highest percentage of women in top management financially outperform, by about 35 percent, those with the lowest percentage of women in higher-level jobs.[54]

Is Leader Style Gender-Driven?

As more women have moved into highly visible management positions, the question of whether women lead differently than men has gained increasing attention. Several researchers have looked at the differences between male and female leaders. Leadership traits traditionally associated with white, American-born males include aggressiveness or assertiveness, rational analysis, and a "take charge" attitude. Male leaders tend to be competitive and individualistic and prefer working in vertical hierarchies. They rely on formal authority and position in their dealings with subordinates.

Of course, women may also demonstrate these traits. Indeed, the 2006 hit movie *The Devil Wears Prada,* in which Meryl Streep plays an aggressive, authoritative boss who enjoys humiliating her subordinates, reminds people that some women can be tyrants in a leadership role, just as some men can. However, research has found that, in general, women prefer less competitive environments than men, tend to be more collaborative, and are more concerned with relationship building, inclusiveness, participation, and caring.[55] Female leaders such as Deborah Kent, the first woman to head a vehicle assembly plant for Ford Motor Co., or Terry Kelly, CEO of W.L. Gore & Associates, are often more willing to share power and information, to encourage employee development, and to strive to enhance others' feelings of self-worth. "It does no good to have a diverse workforce if you don't listen to their opinions and thoughts," says Kent. "I treat people the way I want to be treated."[56]

Professor and author Judy B. Rosener has called women's approach to leadership **interactive leadership**.[57] The leader favors a consensual and collaborative process, and influence derives from relationships rather than position power and authority. Some psychologists have suggested that women may be more relationship-oriented than men because of different psychological needs stemming from early experiences. This difference between the relationship orientations of men and women has sometimes been used to suggest that women cannot lead effectively because they fail to exercise power. However, whereas male leaders may

Action Memo

As a leader, you can choose to employ an interactive, collaborative leadership style. You can develop personal relationships with your followers and make everyone feel like an important part of things.

Interactive leadership
a leadership style in which people develop personal relationships with followers, share power and information, empower employees, and strive to enhance others' feelings of self-worth

associate effective leadership with a top-down command-and-control process, women's interactive leadership seems appropriate for the future of diversity and learning organizations. The following example describes how one female leader drew on her experience working with theater productions to provide interactive leadership that enabled her organization to be more creative and adaptable.

Linda St. Clair

"When I was at my best in the corporation, I helped the people who reported to me get what they needed to be effectively creative," Linda St. Clair says. St. Clair, who served as a successful personnel manager for manufacturing in a major technology firm, is profiled in *Leadership Can Be Taught,* published by Harvard Business School Press.

St. Clair's experience as a corporate leader relied on the same qualities she used as an artist-director of theater productions. Both required working effectively within a dynamic field of relationships and the ability to "give the work back to the group." Effective leaders, she believes, know when to let go and allow people to make critical decisions, acting not as a commander but rather as a coach, guide, mentor, and ally. She applied the idea of rehearsal and practice to encourage people to try out "what ifs" and have fun with their work.

At the same time, St. Clair paid attention to managing the interactions of everyone on the team. Just as in a theater production, "all must create something new," she says of corporate work. "While helping each part to move in a common direction, the director [leader] needs to be as creative as possible, honoring everyone's artistic power—and all the conflicts thereof. Tough decisions have to be made, and the [leader] must be willing to do so—jointly when possible—which means a lot of interaction . . . ."[58]

Although the values associated with interactive leadership, such as inclusion, relationship building, and caring, are generally considered "feminine" values, interactive leadership is not gender-specific. These values are becoming increasingly valuable for both male and female leaders. Today's flatter, team-based organizations are no longer looking for top-down authority figures but for more collaborative and inclusive approaches to leadership.[59]

Again, the interactive leadership style is not exclusive to women. Any leader can learn to adopt a more inclusive style by paying attention to nonverbal behavior and developing skills such as listening, empathy, cooperation, and collaboration.[60]

Global Diversity

One of the most rapidly increasing sources of diversity in North American organizations is globalization, which means that leaders are confronting diversity issues across a broader stage than ever before. To handle the challenges of global diversity, leaders can become aware of the sociocultural environment and develop cultural intelligence to know how to behave appropriately.

The Sociocultural Environment

For organizations operating globally, social and cultural differences may provide more potential for difficulties and conflicts than any other source. For instance, cultural factors have created problems for managers in some U.S. corporations trying to transfer their diversity policies and practices to European divisions. Policies designed to address diversity issues in the United States don't take into consideration the complex social and cultural systems in Europe. Even the meaning of the term *diversity* presents problems. In many European languages, the closest word implies separation rather than the inclusion sought by U.S. diversity programs.[61] Foreign firms doing business in the United States face similar challenges understanding and dealing with diversity issues. For example, Japanese leaders at Toyota Motor Company seriously bungled the handling of a sexual harassment complaint in the company's North American division, leading to a lawsuit. When Sayaka Kobayashi sent a letter to Dennis Cuneo, senior vice president of Toyota North America, saying she had endured months of romantic and sexual advances from her boss, Cuneo told her he would discuss the issue with the boss, Hideaki Otaka. However, Cuneo allegedly said that he didn't want to offend the man (a cultural norm), so he planned to say it was Kobayashi's boyfriend who was upset about the overtures. European companies have also been tripped up because of a lack of understanding of the American concept of sexual harassment, according to employment lawyer Wayne N. Outten. "There are some European countries where a certain degree of what we would consider over-the-line . . . is more the norm in the culture," Outten says.[62]

National cultures are intangible, pervasive, and difficult to comprehend. However, it is imperative that leaders in international organizations learn to understand local cultures and deal with them effectively. As C.R. "Dick" Shoemate, chairman and CEO of Bestfoods, says, "It takes a special kind of leadership to deal with the differences in a multicountry, multicultural organization. . . ." Bestfoods uses cross-border assignments and extensive individual coaching to train people to lead in different cultures.[63] One approach to understanding other cultures is to look at how social value systems differ.

Social Value Systems

Research done by Geert Hofstede on IBM employees in 40 countries discovered that mind-set and cultural values on issues such as individualism versus collectivism strongly influence organizational and employee relationships and vary widely among cultures.[64] Exhibit 11.4 shows examples of how countries rate on four significant dimensions.

- *Power distance.* High **power distance** means people accept inequality in power among institutions, organizations, and individuals. Low power distance means people expect equality in power. Countries that value high power distance are Malaysia, the Philippines, and Panama. Countries that value low power distance include Denmark, Austria, and Israel.

- *Uncertainty avoidance.* High **uncertainty avoidance** means that members of a society feel uncomfortable with uncertainty and ambiguity and thus support beliefs and behaviors that promise certainty and conformity. Low uncertainty avoidance means that people have a high tolerance for the unstructured, the unclear, and the unpredictable. High uncertainty avoidance cultures include Greece, Portugal, and Uruguay. Singapore and Jamaica are two countries with low uncertainty avoidance values.

- *Individualism and collectivism.* **Individualism** reflects a value for a loosely knit social framework in which individuals are expected to take care of themselves. **Collectivism** is a preference for a tightly knit social framework in which people look out for one another and organizations protect their members' interests. Countries with individualist values include the United States, Great Britain, and Canada. Countries with collectivist values are Guatemala, Ecuador, and Panama.

Action Memo

Social value differences can significantly affect leadership, working relationships, and organizational functioning. Answer the questions in Leader's Self-Insight 11.3 to better understand the social values of your classmates or coworkers.

Power distance
how much people accept equality in power; high power distance reflects an acceptance of power inequality among institutions, organizations, and individuals. Low power distance means people expect equality in power

Uncertainty avoidance
the degree to which members of a society feel uncomfortable with uncertainty and ambiguity and thus support beliefs and behaviors that promise certainty and conformity

Individualism
a value for a loosely knit social framework in which individuals are expected to take care of themselves

Collectivism
a preference for a tightly knit social framework in which people look out for one another and organizations protect their members' interests

Social Values

Instructions: Different social groups (work colleagues, family, professional groups, and national, religious, and cultural groups) are all around us. Focus on the group of individuals whom you consider to be your colleagues (e.g., team members, coworkers, classmates). Respond to each of the following statements and indicate its level of importance to your colleague group on the scale of (1) Not at all important to (5) Very important.

How Important Is It:	Not at all important				Very important
1. To compromise one's wishes to act together with your colleagues?	1	2	3	4	5
2. To be loyal to your colleagues?	1	2	3	4	5
3. To follow norms established by your colleagues?	1	2	3	4	5
4. To maintain a stable environment rather than "rock the boat"?	1	2	3	4	5
5. To not break the rules?	1	2	3	4	5
6. To be a specialist or professional rather than a manager?	1	2	3	4	5
7. To have an opportunity for high earnings?	1	2	3	4	5
8. To have an opportunity for advancement to higher level jobs?	1	2	3	4	5
9. To work with people who cooperate well with one another?	1	2	3	4	5
10. To have a good working relationship with your manager?	1	2	3	4	5
11. To have a manager that gives detailed instructions?	1	2	3	4	5
12. To avoid disagreement with a manager?	1	2	3	4	5

Scoring and Interpretation

There are four subscale scores that measure the four social values described by Hofstede. For the dimension of individualism–collectivism, compute your average score based on responses to questions 1, 2, and 3. For the dimension of uncertainty avoidance, compute your average score based on responses to questions 4, 5, and 6. For the dimension of masculinity–femininity, reverse score your responses to questions 9 and 10 (5 = 1, 4 = 2, 2 = 4, and 1 = 5) and then compute your average score for questions 7, 8, 9, and 10. For the dimension of power distance, compute the average score for questions 11 and 12.

My average social value scores are:

Individualism–collectivism (I–C) _____.
Uncertainty avoidance (UA) _____.
Masculinity–femininity (M–F) _____.
Power distance (PD) _____.

An average score of 4 or above on the I–C scale means that *collectivism* is a social value in your colleague group, and a score of 2 or below means that the value of *individualism* dominates. A score of 4 or above on the UA scale means that your group values the absence of ambiguity and uncertainty (*high uncertainty avoidance*), and a score below 2 means that uncertainty and unpredictability are preferred. A score of 4 or above on the M–F scale means that *masculinity* is a social value in your colleague group, and a score of 2 or below means that the value of *femininity* dominates. A score of 4 or above on the PD scale means that *high power distance*, or hierarchical differences, is a social value in your colleague group, and a score of 2 or below means that the value of *low power distance*, or equality, dominates.

Compare your four scores to one another to understand your perception of the different values. On which of the four values would you like to score higher? Lower? Analyze the specific questions on which you scored higher or lower to analyze the pattern of your group's social values. Show your scores to a student from another country and explain what they mean. How do your social values differ from the social values of the international student? How do these social values differ across the nationalities represented in your class?

Source: Adapted from Geert Hofstede, *Culture's Consequences* (London: Sage Publications, 1984); and D. Matsumoto, M. D. Weissman, K. Preston, B. R. Brown, and C. Kupperbausch, "Context-specific Measurement of Individualism–Collectivism on the Individual Level: The Individualism-Collectivism Interpersonal Assessment Inventory," *Journal of Cross-Cultural Psychology* 28, no. 6 (1997), pp. 743–767.

Exhibit 11.4 Rank Orderings of 10 Countries Along Four Dimensions of National Value System

Country	Power[a]	Uncertainty[b]	Individualism[c]	Masculinity[d]
Australia	7	7	2	5
Costa Rica	8	2 (tie)	10	9
France	3	2 (tie)	4	7
India	2	9	6	6
Japan	5	1	7	1
Mexico	1	4	8	2
Sweden	10	10	3	10
Thailand	4	6	9	8
United States	6	8	1	4

[a] 1 = highest power distance; 10 = lowest power distance
[b] 1 = highest uncertainty avoidance; 10 = lowest uncertainty avoidance
[c] 1 = highest individualism; 10 = highest collectivism
[d] 1 = highest masculinity; 10 = highest femininity

Source: From Dorothy Marcic, *Organizational Behavior and Cases,* 4th ed. (St. Paul, MN: West, 1995). Based on Geert Hofstede, *Culture's Consequences* (London: Sage Publications, 1984); and *Cultures and Organizations: Software of the Mind* (New York:McGraw-Hill, 1991).

Masculinity
a preference for achievement, heroism, assertiveness, work centrality, and material success

Femininity
a preference for relationships, cooperation, group decision making, and quality of life

- *Masculinity and femininity.* **Masculinity** reflects a preference for achievement, heroism, assertiveness, work centrality, and material success. **Femininity** reflects the values of relationships, cooperation, group decision making, and quality of life. Japan, Austria, and Mexico are countries with strong masculine values. Countries with strong feminine values include Sweden, Norway, Denmark, and the former Yugoslavia. Both men and women subscribe to the dominant value in masculine or feminine cultures.

Terry Neill, a managing partner at a London-based change management practice, uses Hofstede's findings in his work with companies. Based on his experiences with global companies such as Unilever PLC, Shell Oil, and BP, Neill points out that the Dutch, Irish, Americans, and British are generally quite comfortable with open argument. However, Japanese and other Asian employees often feel uneasy or even threatened by such directness.[65] In many Asian countries, leaders perceive the organization as a large family and emphasize cooperation through networks of personal relationships. In contrast, leaders in Germany and other central European countries typically strive to run their organizations as impersonal well-oiled machines.[66] How leaders handle these and other cultural differences can have tremendous impact on the satisfaction and effectiveness of diverse employees.

Developing Cultural Intelligence

Although understanding the sociocultural environment and social value differences is crucial, a person cannot expect to know everything necessary to be prepared for every conceivable situation. Thus, in a multicultural environment, leaders will be most successful if they are culturally flexible and able to easily adapt to new situations and ways of doing things. In other words, they need cultural intelligence. **Cultural intelligence (CQ)** refers to a person's ability to use reasoning and observation skills to interpret unfamiliar gestures and situations and devise appropriate behavioral responses.[67] Developing a high level of CQ enables a person

Cultural intelligence
the ability to use reasoning and observation to interpret unfamiliar situations and devise appropriate behavioral responses

to interpret unfamiliar situations and adapt quickly. Rather than a list of global "dos and don'ts," CQ is a practical learning approach that enables a person to ferret out clues to a culture's shared understandings and respond to new situations in culturally appropriate ways.

Cultural intelligence includes three components that work together: cognitive, emotional, and physical.[68] The cognitive component involves a person's observational and learning skills and the ability to pick up on clues to understanding. The emotional aspect concerns one's self-confidence and self-motivation. A leader has to believe in his or her ability to understand and assimilate into a different culture. Difficulties and setbacks are triggers to work harder, not a cause to give up.

The third component of CQ, the physical, refers to a person's ability to shift his or her speech patterns, expressions, and body language to be in tune with people from a different culture. Most people aren't equally strong in all three areas, but maximizing cultural intelligence requires that they draw upon all three facets. In a sense, CQ requires that the head, heart, and body work in concert.

High CQ also requires that a leader be open and receptive to new ideas and approaches. One study found that people who adapt to global management most easily are those who have grown up learning how to understand, empathize, and work with others who are different from themselves. For example, Singaporeans consistently hear English and Chinese spoken side by side. The Dutch have to learn English, German, and French, as well as Dutch, to interact and trade with their economically dominant neighbors. English Canadians must not only be well-versed in American culture and politics, but they also have to consider the views and ideas of French Canadians, who, in turn, must learn to think like North Americans, members of a global French community, Canadians, and Quebecois.[69] People in the United States who have grown up without this kind of language and cultural diversity typically have more difficulties with foreign assignments, but willing managers from any country can learn to open their minds and appreciate other viewpoints.

> **Action Memo**
> As a leader, you can develop cultural intelligence. You can study other languages and cultures and form relationships with people from different countries. You can learn to be sensitive to differences in social value systems, and find creative ways to address delicate diversity issues.

Leadership Implications

A study of executives in five countries found that although the globalization of business seems to be leading to a convergence of managerial values and attitudes, executives in different countries differ significantly in some areas, which can create problems for leadership.[70] To lead effectively in a diverse global environment, leaders should be aware of cultural and subcultural differences. Chapter 3 examined contingency theories of leadership that explain the relationship between leader style and a given situation. It is important for leaders to recognize that culture affects both style and the leadership situation. For example, in cultures with high uncertainty avoidance, a leadership situation with high task structure as described in Chapter 3 is favorable, but those in low uncertainty avoidance cultures prefer less-structured work situations.

In addition, how behavior is perceived differs from culture to culture. To criticize a subordinate in private directly is considered appropriate behavior in individualistic societies such as the United States. However, in Japan, which values collectivism over individualism, the same leader behavior would be seen as inconsiderate. Japanese employees lose face if they are criticized directly by a supervisor. The expectation is that people will receive criticism information from peers rather than directly from the leader.[71] Research into how the contingency models apply to cross-cultural situations is sparse. However, all leaders need to be aware of the impact that culture may have and consider cultural values in their dealings with employees.

Stages of Personal Diversity Awareness

One goal for today's global organizations is to ensure that *all* employees and customers—women, ethnic and racial minorities, gay people, the disabled, the elderly, as well as white males—are given equal opportunities and treated with fairness and respect.[72] Strong, culturally sensitive leadership can move organizations toward diversity, where all individuals are valued and respected for the unique abilities they can bring to the workplace.

Leaders vary in their sensitivity and openness to other cultures, attitudes, values, and ways of doing things. Exhibit 11.5 shows a model of five stages of individual diversity awareness and actions.[73] The continuum ranges from a defensive, ethnocentric attitude, in which leaders meet the minimum legal requirements regarding affirmative action and sexual harassment, to a complete understanding and acceptance of people's differences, in which leaders value diversity as an inherent part of the organizational culture.

Exhibit 11.5 Stages of Personal Diversity Awareness

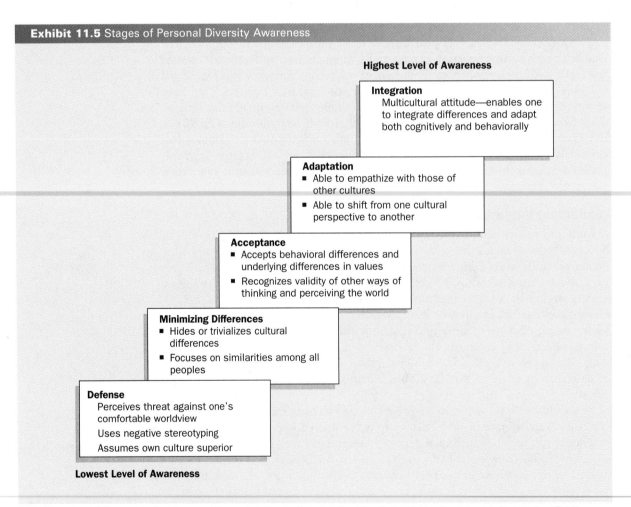

Source: Based on M. Bennett, "A Developmental Approach to Training for Intercultural Sensitivity, " *International Journal of Intercultural Relations* 10 (1986), pp. 179–196.

People at stage 1 see differences as a threat against their own comfortable world view and frequently use negative stereotyping or express prejudicial attitudes. Leaders at this stage of diversity awareness consider themselves successful if their legal record is good. They may view women and minorities as a "problem" that must be dealt with. Typically, these leaders promote a few minorities to executive-level jobs to meet legal requirements. At stage 2, people attempt to minimize differences and focus on the similarities among all people. This is the stage where unconscious and subtle bias is most evident, because people have moved beyond openly prejudicial attitudes. Leaders don't adequately recognize or respond to the challenges minorities and women face in the organization. When an individual moves to stage 3 of diversity awareness, he or she accepts cultural differences and recognizes the validity of other ways of thinking and doing things. Here, leaders become proactive and acknowledge that addressing issues of gender, race, disability, and so forth is important not just for the minority employees but for the health of the organization. They recognize that women and minorities can bring needed insight into developing and marketing products for new customers, so they look for ways to attract and retain high-quality minority employees. In stage 3 organizations, more women and minorities make it to high-level positions, and leaders begin providing diversity training to all employees.

When people reach stage 4, they are able to empathize with people who are different from themselves and can comfortably shift from one cultural perspective to another. Leaders at this stage make a strong commitment to broad equality and community and rectify the undervaluation and underutilization of women and minorities. Leaders make a genuine attempt to develop policies and practices that are inclusive rather than exclusive. At stage 5 of diversity awareness, people are capable of integrating differences and adapting both cognitively and behaviorally. It is at this stage where leaders can create organizations that are gender- and color-blind. All employees are judged on their competence, and stereotypes and prejudices are completely erased. No group of employees feels different or disadvantaged.

Stage 5 represents the ideal leader and organization. Although it may seem unreachable, many of today's best leaders are striving to achieve this stage of diversity awareness and acceptance. Each year, Diversity Best Practices and the Business Women's Network recognize top corporate leaders who show a deep commitment to diversity and inclusion. In 2006, the top winner was Edward M. Liddy, CEO of Allstate Insurance, described earlier in this chapter. Other 2006 winners included Reuben Mark of Colgate Palmolive, James Turley of Ernst & Young, Dale Gifford of Hewitt Associates, Bob Nardelli, former CEO of Home Depot, Patricia Russo of Lucent Technologies, Richard Parsons of Time Warner, and Steven Rogel of Weyerhaeuser Company.[74] The commitment of top leaders is critical to building organizations that embrace diversity in all aspects of the business.

Action Memo
As a leader, you can advance to higher stages of diversity awareness and action. You can commit to valuing diversity and providing equal opportunities for everyone.

Personal Qualities for Leading Diverse People

To be more effective leading in diverse organizations, leaders can develop personal characteristics that support diversity. Four characteristics have been identified as important for inclusive leadership.[75]

- *A personal, long-range vision that recognizes and supports a diverse organizational community*. Leaders should have long-term plans to include employees of various ethnic and cultural groups, races, ages, and so on at all levels of the organization. In addition, they express the vision through symbols and rituals that reinforce the value of a diverse workforce.

- *A broad knowledge of the dimensions of diversity and awareness of multicultural issues.* Leaders need a basic knowledge of the primary dimensions of diversity as discussed earlier in this chapter: age, race, ethnicity, gender, mental or physical abilities, and sexual orientation, as well as some understanding of secondary dimensions. Knowledge is also put into action through the use of inclusive language and showing respect for differences.

- *An openness to change themselves.* Leaders in diverse organizations encourage feedback from their employees, can accept criticism, and are willing to change their behavior. It is leaders' behavior that has the most impact on whether diversity is truly valued within the organization. At Baxter Healthcare Corp., for example, Chairman and CEO Harry Jansen Kraemer, Jr. writes a newsletter called *CEO Update* for the company intranet. Rather than just talking about business issues, he includes a section updating people on his family life. For women who are juggling career and family, it is a clear signal that the company values family and considers work/life balance important.[76]

- *Mentoring and empowerment of diverse employees.* Leaders take an active role in creating opportunities for all employees to use their unique abilities. They also offer honest feedback and coaching as needed, and they reward those in the organization who show respect to all individuals.

Once leaders examine and change themselves, they can lead change in the organization. Diversity presents many challenges, yet it also provides leaders with an exciting opportunity to build organizations as integrated communities in which all people feel encouraged, respected, and committed to common purposes and goals. Consider how leaders at Denny's Restaurants have improved diversity awareness to transform the company from an icon of racism to a paragon of diversity.

Action Memo

As a leader, you can create a personal vision for a diverse community. You can use words, symbols, and leadership actions to create an organizational culture that includes the participation of all people regardless of race, age, gender, cultural or ethnic group, or physical ability.

Denny's Restaurants

It was a spring morning in 1993 when six African-American Secret Service agents sat waiting for their food at Denny's for more than an hour while their white colleagues ate. Their meals arrived just before they had to leave. The highly publicized incident led to other revelations of discrimination against African-American customers and employees—and to a series of racial discrimination lawsuits. Thirteen years later, a Denny's executive received the "We Share the Dream Award" at the 18th annual Dr. Martin Luther King Jr. Awards Dinner, and the company was showing up on several "best companies for minorities" lists, including being ranked at the top of *Black Enterprise* magazine's 2006 "Best 40 Companies for Diversity." How did Denny's go from worst to first? It comes down to top leader commitment and some serious training to improve diversity awareness and behavior.

After settling the discrimination lawsuits in 1994, Denny's hired Rachelle Hood as its first chief diversity officer. Hood got the company to hire more than 100 diversity trainers and implemented training at every level. Every single person at Denny's—not just managers, dishwashers, and servers, but also media planners and leased security guards—attends diversity training with specific guidelines on how to apply diversity understanding and sensitivity to working in the restaurant business. In the "We Can" training program, for example, employees learn a three-step model: (1) *prevention,* such as how to behave in order to reduce the possibility of a guest or fellow employee feeling that he or she has been discriminated against; (2) *intervention,* which teaches people to "acknowledge, apologize, and act" when something goes wrong; and (3) *managing escalation,* in which employees learn how to genuinely listen, show empathy, and reduce the anger and frustration level. Denny's spends several million dollars a year on building awareness, and its diversity training system is one of the most comprehensive in the industry.

Hood cemented diversity awareness by working with managers to increase supplier diversity, developing marketing campaigns targeting minority customers, and tying bonus pay to meeting diversity goals. In 1993, only one of the chain's franchises was minority-owned, the company had no minority suppliers, and the board was made up primarily of white males. Today, however, things are very different:

- Forty-three percent of Denny's franchises are owned by minorities.

- Between 1995 and 2006, Denny's contracted nearly $1 billion for goods and services with minority suppliers, with African-Americans accounting for 48 percent of the business. That represents around 18 percent of the company's contracts, as compared to a national average of 3 to 4 percent.

- Fifty-six percent of the board of directors is composed of women and people of color.

- At the senior management level, 50 percent are women and people of color. Minority employees represent 32 percent of Denny's overall management and 51 percent of the workforce.[77]

Denny's turnaround is one of the best examples of how far and how fast a company can progress with strong leadership and an aggressive approach to culture change.

Summary and Interpretation

One main point of this chapter is that diversity is a fact of life in today's world, and leaders can create change in organizations to keep up. The U.S. population, the workforce, and the customer base are changing. In addition, people of different national origins, races, and religions are no longer willing to be assimilated into the mainstream culture. Organizations are also operating in an increasingly global world, which means dealing with diversity on a broader stage than ever before.

Today's leaders face significant challenges leading people who are different from themselves. The first step for leading diverse people is understanding the hardships that people who do not fit the mainstream white, U.S.-born, male culture often endure. These include unequal expectations, the need to live biculturally, the glass ceiling, and the opportunity gap. Another important issue is global diversity. Leaders can be aware of the impact culture may have, understand social and cultural value differences, and develop cultural intelligence.

Dimensions of diversity are both primary, such as age, gender, and race, and secondary, such as education, marital status, and religion. There are several reasons why organizations are recognizing the need to value and support diversity. Diversity helps organizations build better relationships with diverse customers and helps develop employee potential. Diversity provides a broader and deeper base of experience for creativity and problem solving, which is essential to building learning organizations. One aspect of diversity of particular interest is women's style of leadership, referred to as interactive leadership. The values associated with interactive leadership, such as inclusion, relationship building, and caring, are emerging as valuable qualities for both male and female leaders in the twenty-first century.

People differ in their level of diversity awareness and their sensitivity to other cultures, values, and ways of doing things. Leaders evolve through stages of personal diversity awareness and action, ranging from minimum efforts to meet affirmative action guidelines to valuing diversity as an integral part of organizational culture. Strong, culturally sensitive leadership is the only way organizations can become inclusive. Leaders first change themselves by developing personal characteristics that support diversity. They use these personal characteristics to change the organization. The ultimate goal for leaders in the twenty-first century is to build organizations as integrated communities in which all people feel encouraged, respected, and committed to common purposes and goals.

Discussion Questions

1. How might a leader's role and responsibility change as a company becomes more diverse? Explain.

2. How might diversity within the organization ultimately lead to better problem solving and greater creativity?

3. What is interactive leadership, and why might this approach be increasingly important in the twenty-first century?

4. Discuss ways in which low power distance as a social value among followers could affect their interaction with a leader who displays high power distance.

5. Why do you think the glass ceiling persists in organizations?

6. How would you lead a group of people who are different from you?

7. Why is it important for today's leaders to develop cultural intelligence? Do you think a leader who has never had experience with people different from him or herself can develop the ability to smoothly adapt to culturally different ways of thinking and behaving? Discuss.

8. Recall a leader you worked for. At what stage of personal diversity awareness (refer to Exhibit 11.5) was this leader? Explain. At what stage of diversity awareness are you?

9. Do you think people and organizations can ever become gender and color-blind? Discuss.

Leadership at Work

Personal Diversity

Each of us feels different in many ways from the average behavior or expectations that other people seem to value. This reflects our own feelings of diversity. The differences you feel compared to others could be about your physical characteristics (height, age, skin color), but also could reflect a difference in your thinking style, feelings, personality or behavior, especially when you feel different from what other people expect or what you perceive are the social norms. Write in the list below six ways you feel different from others:

1. _____   4. _____

2. _____   5. _____

3. _____   6. _____

Now answer the following questions with respect to your perceived diversity.
What are your feelings about being different?

_____

_____

_____

Which elements of diversity are you proud of? Why?

_____

_____

_____

What element would you like to change to be less diverse? Why?

_____

_____

_____

How do your differences contribute to a student team or work organization?

_____

_____

_____

In Class: This exercise can be adapted for group discussion in class about underlying
diversity. The instructor can ask students to sit in teams of 3 to 5 members in a circle facing
each other. A student (focal person) then volunteers to describe the way he or she feels different
from others based on the list above. Other students take turns providing feedback to the focal
person on what the perceived differences mean to them with respect to team or class contributions. Each student takes a turn as the focal person, describing their feelings of being different
and hearing feedback from others on the perception and impact of those differences.

Here are the key questions for this exercise: What did you learn about perceived
diversity and interpersonal relations? What does it mean when our differences appear
larger to ourselves than they appear to others? How does personal diversity affect team
or organizational performance?
(A list can be written on the board.)

Leadership Development: Cases for Analysis

Northern Industries

Northern Industries asked you, a consultant in organizational change and diversity management, to help them resolve some racial issues that, according to president Jim Fisher,
are "festering" in their manufacturing plant in Springfield, Massachusetts. Northern
Industries is a family owned enterprise that manufactures greeting cards and paper and
plastic holiday decorations. It employs 125 people full time, including African-Americans
and Asians. About 80 percent of the full-time workforce is female. During the peak production months of September and January (to produce orders primarily for Christmas/
Hanukah and Mother's Day), the company runs a second shift and adds about 50 part-
time workers, most of whom are women and minorities.

All orders are batch runs made to customer specifications. In a period of a week, it
is not unusual for 70 different orders to be filled requiring different paper stocks, inks,

plastics, and setups. Since these orders vary greatly in size, the company has a long-term policy of giving priority to high-volume customers and processing other orders on a first-come first-served basis. Half a dozen of the company's major customers have been doing business with Northern for more than 20 years, having been signed on by Jim Fisher's father (now retired).

To begin your orientation to the company, Fisher asks his production manager, Walter Beacon, to take you around the plant. Beacon points out the production areas responsible for each of the various steps in the manufacture of a greeting card, from purchasing to printing to quality control and shipping. The plant is clean, but the two large printing rooms, each the workplace for about 25 workers, are quite noisy. You catch snatches of the employees' conversations there, but you cannot figure out what language they are speaking. In the shipping and receiving department you notice that most workers are African-American. Beacon confirms that 8 out of 10 of the workers in that department are African-American males, and that their boss, Adam Wright, is also African-American.

It has been previously arranged that you would attend a meeting of top management in order to get a flavor of the organizational culture. The president introduces you as a diversity consultant and notes that several of his managers have expressed concerns about potential racial problems in the company. He says, "Each of the minority groups sticks together. The African Americans and Orientals rarely mix. Recently there has been a problem with theft of finished product, especially on the second shift, and we had to fire a Thai worker." Fisher has read a lot lately about "managing diversity" and hopes you will be able to help the company. Several managers nod their heads in agreement.

Fisher then turns his executive team to its daily business. The others present are the general manager, personnel manager (the only woman), sales manager, quality control manager, production manager (Beacon), and the shipping and receiving manager (the only non-white manager). Soon an angry debate ensues between the sales and shipping/receiving managers. It seems that orders are not being shipped quickly enough, according to the sales manager, and several complaints have been received from smaller customers about the quality of the product. The shipping/receiving manager argues that he needs more hands to do the job, and that the quality of incoming supplies is lousy. While this debate continues, the other managers are silent and seemingly uncomfortable. Finally one of them attempts to break up the argument with a joke about his wife. Fisher and the other men laugh loudly, and the conversation shifts to other topics.

Source: Copyright 1991 by Rae Andre of Northeastern University. Used with permission.

QUESTIONS

1. What recommendations would you make to Northern's leaders to help them move toward successfully managing diversity issues?

2. If you were the shipping and receiving or personnel manager, how do you think you would feel about your job? Discuss some of the challenges you might face at Northern.

3. Refer to Exhibit 11.5. Based on the information in the case, at what stage of personal diversity awareness do leaders at Northern seem to be? Discuss.

The Trouble with Bangles

Leela Patel was standing by her machine, as she had for eight hours of each working day for the past six years. Leela was happy; she had many friends among the 400 or so women at the food processing plant. Most of them were of Indian origin like herself, although Asian women formed less than a fifth of the female workforce. Leela was a member of a five-woman team that reported to supervisor Bill Evans.

Leela saw Evans approaching now, accompanied by Jamie Watkins, the shop steward. "Hello, Leela; we've come to explain something to you," Evans began. "You must have heard about the accident last month when one of the girls caught a bangle in the machine and cut her wrist. Well, the Safety Committee has decided that no one will be allowed to wear any bangles, engagement rings, earrings, or necklaces at work—only wedding rings, sleepers for pierced ears, and wristwatches will be allowed. So I'm afraid you'll have to remove your bangles." Leela, as was her custom, was wearing three bangles, one steel, one plastic, and one gold. All the married Asian women wore bangles, and many of the English girls had also begun wearing them. Leela explained that she was a Hindu wife and the bangles were important to her religion.

"Don't make a fuss, Leela," Evans said between clenched teeth. "I've already had to shout at Hansa Patel and Mira Desai. Why can't you all be like Meena Shah? She didn't mind taking her bangles off; neither did the English girls." Leela could see that Evans was very angry, so, almost in tears, she removed the bangles. When the two had moved off, however, she replaced the gold bangle and carried on with her work.

Within two or three days, the plant manager, Sam Jones, noticed that all the Asian women were wearing their bangles again—some, in fact, were wearing more than ever before. "I'm staggered by the response which this simple, common-sense restriction on the wearing of jewelry has brought," Jones remarked to the regional race relations employment advisor. "I have had several deputations from the Asian women protesting the ban, not to mention visits by individuals on the instruction of their husbands. In addition, I've just had a letter from something called the Asian Advisory Committee, asking that the ban be lifted until we meet with their representatives. The strength of this discontent has prompted me to talk to you. Jewelry constitutes both a safety and a hygiene hazard on this site, so it must be removed. And I'm afraid if I talk to this Asian Committee, they'll turn out to be a bunch of militants who'll cause all sorts of trouble. At the same time, we can't afford any work stoppages. What do you suggest?"

Several days later, the advisor had arranged for Mr. Singh from the local Council for Community Relations to talk to Jones and other managers. Singh explained that in his opinion there were no obstacles arising from *religious* observance that prevented implementation of the ban on bangles. However, he pointed out, the bangles do have a custom base which is stronger than the English tradition base for wedding rings. "The bangles are a mark not only of marriage but of the esteem in which a wife is held by her husband. The more bangles and the greater their value, the higher her esteem and the greater her social standing. The tradition also has religious overtones, since the wearing of bangles by the wife demonstrates that each recognizes the other as "worthy" in terms of the fulfillment of their religious obligations. This position is further complicated in that women remove their bangles if they are widowed, and some fear that the removal of the bangles may lead to their husbands' deaths."

Source: Adapted from "Bangles," in Allan R. Cohen, Stephen L. Fink, Herman Gadon, and Robin D. Willits, *Effective Behavior in Organizations: Cases, Concepts, and Student Experiences,* 7th ed. (Burr Ridge, IL: McGraw-Hill Irwin, 2001), pp. 413–414.

QUESTIONS

1. What is your initial reaction to this story? Why do you think you had this reaction?

2. Based on this limited information, how would you rate this organization in terms of developing leadership diversity? Discuss.

3. If you were a top manager at this company, how would you handle this problem?

References

1   Chad Terhune, "Pepsi, Vowing Diversity Isn't Just Image Polish, Seeks Inclusive Culture," (In the Lead column), *The Wall Street Journal* (April 19, 2005), p. B1; and Chad Terhune and Joann S. Lublin, "Pepsi's New CEO Doesn't Keep Her Opinions Bottled Up," *The Wall Street Journal* (August 15, 2006), p. B1.

2   Terhune, "Pepsi, Vowing Diversity Isn't Just Image Polish, Seeks Inclusive Culture."

3   "Diversity in the New Millennium," *Working Woman* (September 2000): Special Advertising Section.

4   Frances J. Milliken and Luis I. Martins, "Searching for Common Threads: Understanding the Multiple Effects of Diversity in Organizational Groups," *Academy of Management Review* 21, no. 2 (1996), pp. 402–433.

5   The quote is from Glenn D. Capel, the only black financial advisor in a Merrill Lynch office in Greensboro, North Carolina, reported in Patrick McGeehan, "Blacks Speak of Isolation, But Merrill Says It's Trying to Change," *The New York Times* (July 14, 2006), p. C1.

6   G. Haight, "Managing Diversity," *Across the Board* 27, No. 3 (1990), pp. 22–29.

7   Judy Rosener, *America's Competitive Secret: Women Managers* (New York: Oxford University Press, 1995), pp. 33–34.

8   Roy Harris, "The Illusion of Inclusion," *CFO* (May 2001), pp. 42–50.

9   Jennifer L. Knight, Michelle R. Hebl, Jessica B. Foster, and Laura M. Mannix, "Out of Role? Out of Luck: The Influence of Race and Leadership Status on Performance Appraisals," *The Journal of Leadership and Organizational Studies* 9, no. 3 (2003), pp. 85–93.

10 Ann Morrison, *The New Leaders: Guidelines on Leadership Diversity in America* (San Francisco: Jossey-Bass, 1992), p. 37.

11 Stephanie N. Mehta, "What Minority Employees Really Want," *Fortune* (June 10, 2000), pp. 181–186.

12 Reported in Michael Orey, "White Men Can't Help It," *BusinessWeek* (May 15, 2006), pp. 54, 57.

13 Marianne Bertrand, "Racial Bias in Hiring: Are Emily and Brendan More Employable than Lakisha and Jamal?" *Capital Ideas* (February 2005), pp. 7–9; and Marianne Bertrand and Sendhil Mullainathan, *Are Emily and Greg More Employable than Lakisha and Jamal?* National Bureau of Economic Research report, as reported in L. A. Johnson, "What's in a Name: When Emily Gets the Job Over Lakisha," *The Tennessean* (January 4, 2004), p. 14A.

14 Johnson, "What's in a Name: When Emily Gets the Job Over Lakisha."

15 Robert Hooijberg and Nancy DiTomaso, "Leadership in and of Demographically Diverse Organizations," *Leadership Quarterly* 7, no. 1 (1996), pp. 1–19.

16 W. E. B. DuBois, *The Souls of Black Folks* (Chicago: Chicago University Press, 1903), quoted in Hooijberg and DiTomaso, "Leadership in and of Demographically Diverse Organizations."

17 Cora Daniels, "The Most Powerful Black Executives in America," *Fortune* (July 22, 2002), pp. 60–80.

18 McGeehan, "Blacks Speak of Isolation, But Merrill Says It's Trying to Change."

19 Debra E. Meyerson and Joyce K. Fletcher, "A Modest Manifesto for Shattering the Glass Ceiling," *Harvard Business Review* (January–February 2000), pp. 127–136; Julie Amparano Lopez, "Study Says Women Face Glass Walls as Well as Glass Ceiling," *The Wall Street Journal* (March 3, 1992), pp. B1, B2; and Joann S. Lublin, "Women at Top Still Are Distant from CEO Jobs," *The Wall Street Journal* (February 28, 1996), pp. B1, B8.

20 Catalyst survey results reported in Jason Forsythe, "Winning with Diversity," special advertising supplement to *The New York Times Magazine* (March 28, 2004), pp. 65–72.

21 Barbara Reinhold, "Smashing Glass Ceilings: Why Women *Still* Find It Tough to Advance to the Executive Suite," *Journal of Organizational Excellence* (Summer 2005), pp. 43–55; Jory Des Jardins, "I Am Woman (I Think)," *Fast Company* (May 2005), 25–26; Lisa Belkin, "The Opt-Out Revolution," *The New York Times Magazine* (October 26, 2003), pp. 43–47, 58; and Meyerson and Fletcher, "A Modest Manifesto for Shattering the Glass Ceiling."

22 Anat Arkin, "Hidden Talents," *People Management* (July 14, 2006).

23 Ginny Parker Woods, "Japan's Diversity Problem," *The Wall Street Journal* (October 24, 2005), pp. B1, B4.

24 Deborah L. Jacobs, "Back from the Mommy Track," *The New York Times* (October 9, 1994), pp. F1, F6; Lisa Cullen, "Apple Pie, My Eye," *Working Woman* (May–June 2001), pp. 19–20; Ann Crittenden, *The Price of Motherhood* (New York: Metropolitan Books 2001); and Michelle Conlin, "The New Debate over Working Moms," *BusinessWeek* (September 18, 2000), pp. 102–104.

25 Sylvia Ann Hewlett and Carolyn Buck Luce, "Off-Ramps and On-Ramps; Keeping Talented Women on the Road to Success," *Harvard Business Review* (March 2005), pp. 43–54.

26 Sheila Wellington, Marcia Brumit Kropf, and Paulette R. Gerkovich, "What's Holding Women Back?" *Harvard Business Review* (June 2003), pp. 18–19.

27 The Leader's Edge/Executive Women Research 2002 survey, reported in "Why Women Leave," *Executive Female* (Summer 2003), p. 4.

28 Reinhold, "Smashing Glass Ceilings"; Des Jardins, "I Am Woman (I Think); and Alice H. Eagly and Linda L. Carli, "The Female Leadership Advantage: An Evaluation of the Evidence," *The Leadership Quarterly* 14 (2003), pp. 807–834.

29 Claudia H. Deutsch, "Behind the Exodus of Executive Women: Boredom," *USA Today* (May 2, 2005).

30 Robin J. Ely and Debra E. Meyerson, "Theories of Gender in Organizations: A New Approach to Organizational Analysis and Change," *Research in Organizational Behaviour* 22 (2000), pp. 103–151.

31 Phyllis Tharenou, "Going Up? Do Traits and Informal Social Processes Predict Advancing in Management?" *Academy of Management Journal* 44, no. 5 (2001), pp. 1005–1017.

32 C. Soloman, "Careers under Glass," *Personnel Journal* 69, no. 4 (1990), pp. 96–105; and Belle Rose Ragins, Bickley Townsend, and Mary Mattis, "Gender Gap in the Executive Suite: CEOs and Female Executives Report on Breaking the Glass Ceiling," *Academy of Management Executive* 12, no. 1 (1998), pp. 28–42.

33 U.S. Department of Labor, *Futurework: Trends and Challenges for Work in the 21st Century*.

34 "Diversity: Developing Tomorrow's Leadership Today," *BusinessWeek* (December 20, 1999): Special Advertising Section.

35 "Ernst & Young Ranks 24 on the 2006 *DiversityInc.* Top 50 Companies for Diversity List," *PR Newswire* (April 24, 2006); Paula Fagerberg, "Ernst & Young: Strong, Flexible Leadership and the Freedom to Create Your Own Space," *The Black Collegian Online* available at http://www.black-collegian.com; Elissa Silverman, "Accounting Firms Seek to Diversify Image," *The Washington Post* (June 29, 2005), D-04; and Ernst & Young's "Delivering on Diversity: A Firm Commitment," and "Maintaining a Diverse Culture" available at http://www.ey.com.

36 C. Keen, "Human Resource Management Issues in the '90s," *Vital Speeches* 56, no. 24 (1990), pp. 752–754.

37 Richard W. Judy and Carol D'Amico, *Workforce 2020: Work and Workers in the 21st Century* (Indianapolis, IN: Hudson Institute, 1997).

38 Reported in C. J. Prince, "Doing Diversity: The Question Isn't Why to Do It—But How. Here Are a Few Savvy Strategies That Really Work," *Chief Executive* (April 2005), p. 46ff.

39 G. Pascal Zachary, "Mighty is the Mongrel," *Fast Company* (July 2000), 270–284.

40 Lee Smith, "Closing the Gap," special adversiting feature, *Fortune* (November 14, 2005), prepared by the Society for Human Resource Management.

41 Marilyn Loden and Judy B. Rosener, *Workforce America!* (Homewood, IL: Business One Irwin, 1991); and Marilyn Loden, *Implementing Diversity* (Homewood, IL: Irwin, 1996).

42 Milliken and Martins, "Searching for Common Threads."

43 Orlando C. Richard, "Racial Diversity, Business Strategy, and Firm Performance: A Resource-Based View," *Academy of Management Journal* 43, no. 2 (2000), pp. 164–177.

44 "Diversity Proves to Be Important to Allstate," *The Sacramento Observer* (November 10–November 16, 2005), p. 31; Louisa Wah, "Diversity at Allstate: A Competitive Weapon," *Management Review* (July–August 1999), pp. 24–30; "Allstate Top Company for Diversity; Best Company for African Americans," *Business Wire* (April 18, 2006), p. 1; and information on the company available at http://www.allstate.com.

45 Geoffrey Colvin, "The 50 Best Companies for Asians, Blacks, and Hispanics," *Fortune* (July 19, 1999), pp. 53–58.

46 Taylor H. Cox, *Cultural Diversity in Organizations* (San Francisco: Berrett-Koehler, 1994).

47 Rosener, *America's Competitive Secret: Women Managers;* Judy B. Rosener, "Ways Women Lead," *Harvard Business Review* (November–December 1990), pp. 119–125; Sally Helgesen, *The Female Advantage: Women's Ways of Leadership* (New York: Currency/Doubleday, 1990); Joline Godfrey, "Been There, Doing That," *Inc.* (March 1996), pp. 21–22; Chris Lee, "The Feminization of Management," *Training* (November 1994), pp. 25–31; and Bernard M. Bass and Bruce J. Avolio, "Shatter the Glass Ceiling: Women May Make Better Managers," *Human Resource Management* 33, no. 4 (Winter 1994), pp. 549–560.

48 Reported in Tamar Lewin, "The New Gender Divide: At Colleges, Women Are Leaving Men in the Dust," *The New York Times* (July 9, 2006), Section 1, p. 1; and Mary Beth Marklein, "College Gender Gap Widens: 57% Are Women," *USA Today* (October 20, 2005), p. A1.

49 Lewin, "At Colleges, Women Are Leaving Men in the Dust."

50 Michelle Conlin, "The New Gender Gap," *BusinessWeek* (May 26, 2003), pp. 74–82.

51 Quoted in Conlin, "The New Gender Gap."

52 Kathryn M. Bartol, David C. Martin, and Julie A. Kromkowski, "Leadership and the Glass Ceiling: Gender and Ethnic Group Influences on Leader Behaviors at Middle and Executive Managerial Levels," *The Journal of Leadership and Organizational Studies* 9, no. 3 (2003), pp. 8–19; Bernard M. Bass and Bruce J. Avolio, "Shatter the Glass Ceiling: Women May Make Better Managers," *Human Resource Management* 33, no. 4 (Winter 1994), pp. 549–560; and Rochelle Sharpe, "As Leaders, Women Rule," *BusinessWeek* (November 20, 2002), pp. 75–84.

53 Bass and Avolio, "Shatter the Glass Ceiling."

54 Dwight D. Frink, Robert K. Robinson, Brian Reithel, Michelle M. Arthur, Anthony P. Ammeter, Gerald R. Ferris, David M. Kaplan, and Hubert S. Morrisette, "Gender Demography and Organization Performance: A Two-Study Investigation with Convergence," *Group & Organization Management* 28, no. 1 (March 2003), pp. 127–147; Catalyst research project cited in Reinhold, "Smashing Glass Ceilings."

55 The study on competitiveness was reported in Hal R. Varian, "The Difference Between Men and Women, Revisited: It's About Competition," *The New York Times* (March 9, 2006), p. C3. For recent reviews and analyses of the research on gender differences in leadership, see Nicole Z. Stelter, "Gender Differences in Leadership: Current Social Issues and Future Organizational Implications," *The Journal of Leadership Studies* 8, no. 4 (2002), pp. 88–99; and Alice H. Eagly, Mary C. Johannesen-Schmidt, and Marloes L. van Engen, "Transformational, Transactional, and Laissez-Faire Leadership Styles: A Meta-Analysis Comparing Women and Men," *Psychological Bulletin* 129, no. 4 (July 2003), p. 569ff.

56 Lena Williams, "A Silk Blouse on the Assembly Line? (Yes, the Boss's)," *The New York Times* (February 5, 1995) Business Section, p. 7.

57 Based on Rosener, *America's Competitive Secret,* pp. 129–135.

58 Sharon Daloz Parks, "What Artists Know About Leadership," (November 7, 2005), an excerpt from *Leadership Can Be Taught,* published by Harvard Business School Press, accessed on April 5, 2007 at http://hbswk.hbs.edu/archive/5076.html

59 Susan J. Wells, "A Female Executive Is Hard to Find," *HR Magazine* (June 2001), pp. 40–49; and Helgesen, *The Female Advantage.*

60 M. Fine, F. Johnson, and M. S. Ryan, "Cultural Diversity in the Workforce," *Public Personnel Management* 19 (1990), pp. 305–319; and Dawn Hill, "Women Leaders Doing It Their Way," *New Woman* (January 1994), p. 78.

61 Helen Bloom, "Can the United States Export Diversity?" *Across the Board* (March/April 2002), pp. 47–51.

62 Michael Orey, "Trouble at Toyota," *BusinessWeek* (May 22, 2006), pp. 46–48.

63 "Molding Global Leaders," *Fortune* (October 11, 1999), p. 270.

64 Geert Hofstede, "The Interaction between National and Organizational Value Systems," *Journal of Management Studies* 22 (1985), pp. 347–357; and Hofstede, "The Cultural Relativity of the Quality of Life Concept," *Academy of Management Review* 9 (1984), pp. 389–398.

65 Debby Young, "Team Heat," *CIO,* Section 1 (September 1, 1998), pp. 43–51.

66 Geert Hofstede, "Cultural Constraints in Management Theories," excerpted in Dorothy Marcic and Sheila M. Puffer, *Management International: Cases, Exercises, and Readings* (St. Paul, MN: West Publishing, 1994), p. 24.

67 The discussion of cultural intelligence is based on P. Christopher Earley and Elaine Mosakowski, "Cultural Intelligence," *Harvard Business Review* (October 2004), p. 139; Ilan Alon and James M. Higgins, "Global Leadership Success Through Emotional and Cultural Intelligence," *Business Horizons* 48 (2005), pp. 501–512; P. C. Earley and Soon Ang, *Cultural Intelligence: Individual Actions Across Cultures* (Stanford, CA: Stanford Business Books); and David C. Thomas and Kerr Inkson, *Cultural Intelligence: People Skills for Global Business* (San Francisco: Berrett-Koehler, 2004).

68 These components are from Earley and Mosakowski, "Cultural Intelligence."

69 Karl Moore, "Great Global Managers," *Across the Board* (May–June 2003), pp. 40–43.

70 Alison M. Konrad, Roger Kashlak, Izumi Yoshioka, Robert Waryszak, and Nina Toren, "What Do Managers *Like* to Do?" *Group and Organization Management* 26, no. 4 (December 2001), pp. 401–433.

71 Harry C. Triandis, "The Contingency Model in Cross-Cultural Perspective," in Martin M. Chemers and Roya Ayman, eds., *Leadership Theory and Research: Perspectives and Directions* (San Diego, CA: Academic Press, Inc., 1993), pp. 167–188; and Peter B. Smith and Mark F. Peterson, *Leadership, Organizations, and Culture: An Event Management Model* (London: Sage, 1988).

72 Renee Blank and Sandra Slipp, "The White Male: An Endangered Species?" *Management Review* (September 1994), pp. 27–32; and Sharon Nelton, "Nurturing Diversity," *Nation's Business* (June 1995), pp. 25–27.

73 Based on M. Bennett, "A Developmental Approach to Training for Intercultural Sensitivity," *International Journal of Intercultural Relations* 10 (1986), pp. 179–196.

74 "Allstate CEO Receives Top Diversity Honors," *Business Wire* (October 30, 2006).

75 Martin M. Chemers and Roya Ayman, *Leadership Theory and Research: Perspectives and Directions* (San Diego, CA: Academic Press, 1993), p. 209.

76 Susan J. Wells, "Smoothing the Way," *HR Magazine* (June 2001), pp. 52–58.

77 Irwin Speizer, "Diversity on the Menu," *Workforce Management* (November 2004), p. 41ff; Daniel Valentine, "King Award Given to Denny's Executive," *Capital* (January 15, 2006), p. D1; Jim Adamson, "How Denny's Went from Icon of Racism to Diversity Award Winner," *Journal of Organizational Excellence* (Winter 2000), pp. 55–68; Sonia Alleyne and Nicole Marie Richardson, "The 40 Best Companies for Diversity," *Black Enterprise* (July 2006), p. 100ff; and "Denny's Diversity Facts," accessed at http://www.dennys.com.

Chapter 12

Your Leadership Challenge

After reading this chapter, you should be able to:

- Use power and politics to help accomplish important organizational goals.

- Practice aspects of charismatic leadership by pursuing a vision or idea that you care deeply about and want to share with others

- Apply the concepts that distinguish transformational from transactional leadership

- Identify types and sources of power in organizations and know how to increase power through political activity.

- Use the influence tactics of rational persuasion, friendliness, reciprocity, developing allies, direct appeal, and scarcity.

Chapter Outline

Leadership Power and Influence

To the crash of applause, Bill Strickland strides to the podium. Then he says softly, "Over the next few minutes, I'm going to show you some pictures of what I do for a living." The attention of every person in the audience is focused on this big, graceful black man and what he has to say. The excitement of the crowd might lead you to think Strickland is a football hero or a music star. Instead, he's a man who used the force of his personality to build a center of hope in a crumbling Pittsburgh area neighborhood and is now spreading his vision across the country.

Strickland was a rootless teenager about to flunk out of high school when he met a special teacher, Frank Ross, who changed his life by turning him on to the power of art and music. When Ross took the 16-year-old to see Fallingwater, the famous Frank Lloyd Wright-designed house that has a creek running through the middle of it, Strickland's life changed forever. "It was a very interesting way of looking at water," Strickland tells people in the audience, "and a very interesting way of looking at light." His husky voice a mixture of salesman, CEO, and preacher, Strickland draws out the last word, making the audience feel its—and his—power. "I said to myself, if I could ever bring that light to my neighborhood. . . ."

Thus were planted the seeds of a vision that turned into Manchester Bidwell, a nonprofit corporation that provides after-school and summer programs for at-risk middle and high-school students, along with job training for low-income adults. The way Strickland built Manchester-Bidwell's state-of-the-art greenhouse for the center's horticultural training program is a lesson in the power of vision. Rep. Melissa Hart, a U.S. congresswoman from Pennsylvania, recalls: "Ten years ago, he and I stood together in this bombed-out industrial area, and Bill was saying, 'This is where we're going to have the irrigation system, and this is going to be the computerized control room, and we're going to sell our orchids to [supermarket chain] Giant Eagle.' I said, 'Sure, uh-huh, Bill.' But he actually saw that greenhouse standing in that bombed-out field. He was absolutely convinced it was a done deal." Today, Manchester-Bidwell students grow and sell top-grade orchids as they learn new skills.

Strickland has now helped establish smaller Manchester Bidwell centers in San Francisco, Cincinnati, and Grand Rapids, Michigan. His long-term goal is to open 25 more centers in inner-city neighborhoods around the country. Strickland isn't shy about admitting that he's out to save the world. Practically every member of the audience hears the passion in his voice and wants to help him do it.[1]

When you think of powerful people, you may think of politicians, top business leaders, or highly paid sports and entertainment figures. Bill Strickland reminds us of a different kind of power, the power that comes from being deeply passionate about an idea or vision and believing it can become a reality. An associate of Strickland says his power is that he doesn't just overcome obstacles, he refuses to even recognize them. Leaders such as Bill Strickland see beyond current realities and problems and help followers believe in a brighter future. Not everyone has the personal charisma of Bill Strickland, but all leaders use personal power and influence to have an impact on their world.

This chapter explores the topic of leadership power and influence in detail. The chapter opens with a consideration of charismatic and transformational leadership, two leadership styles that rely strongly on a leader's personal characteristics as a source of power. We next examine what we mean by the terms *power* and *influence*, look at some sources and types of power, and outline ways leaders exercise power and influence through political activity. Finally, we briefly consider some ethical aspects of using power and influence.

Transformational and Charismatic Leadership

Charismatic and transformational leadership have been of great interest to researchers. One of the key characteristics of both charismatic and transformational leadership is that they are based largely on the strength of the leader's personal power rather than on a position of authority granted by an organization.

Transformational versus Transactional Leadership

Transformational leadership typically has a substantial impact on followers and can potentially renew an entire organization. One way to understand transformational leadership is to compare it to transactional leadership.[2] The basis of **transactional leadership** is a transaction or exchange process between leaders and followers. The transactional leader recognizes followers' needs and desires and then clarifies how those needs and desires will be satisfied in exchange for meeting specified objectives or performing certain duties. Thus, followers receive rewards for job performance, whereas leaders benefit from the completion of tasks.

> **Transactional leadership**
> a transaction or exchange process between leaders and followers

Transactional leaders focus on the present and excel at keeping the organization running smoothly and efficiently. They are good at traditional management functions such as planning and budgeting and generally focus on the impersonal aspects of job performance. Transactional leadership can be quite effective. By clarifying expectations, leaders help build followers' confidence. In addition, satisfying the needs of subordinates may improve productivity and morale. However, because transactional leadership involves a commitment to "follow the rules," transactional leaders maintain stability within the organization rather than promoting change. Transactional skills are important for all leaders. However, in today's world, in which organizational success often depends on continuous change, effective leaders also use a different approach.

> **Transformational leadership**
> leadership characterized by the ability to bring about significant change in followers and the organization

Transformational leadership is characterized by the ability to bring about significant change in both followers and the organization.[3] Transformational leaders have the ability to lead changes in an organization's vision, strategy, and culture as well as promote innovation in products and technologies. Rather than analyzing and controlling specific transactions with followers using rules, directions, and incentives, transformational leadership focuses on intangible qualities such as vision, shared values, and ideas in order to build relationships, give larger meaning to separate activities, and provide common ground to enlist followers in the change process. Transformational leadership is based on the personal values, beliefs, and qualities of the leader rather than on an exchange process between leaders and followers.

> **Action Memo**
> As a leader, you can act like a transformational leader by rallying people around an inspiring vision, expressing optimism about the future, helping followers' develop their potential, and empowering people to make change happen.

Recent studies support the idea that transformational leadership has a positive impact on follower development and follower performance. Moreover, transformational leadership skills can be learned and are not ingrained personality characteristics.[4] However, some personality traits may make it easier for a leader to display transformational leadership behaviors. For example, studies of transformational leaders have found that the trait of agreeableness, as described in Chapter 4 of this text, is positively associated with transformational leadership.[5] In addition, transformational leaders are typically emotionally stable and positively engaged with the world around them, and they have a strong ability to recognize and understand others' emotions (emotional intelligence).[6] This is not surprising considering that these leaders accomplish change by building networks of positive relationships.

Transformational leadership differs from transactional leadership in four significant areas.[7]

1. *Transformational leadership develops followers into leaders.* Followers are given greater freedom to control their own behavior. Transformational leadership rallies people around a mission and vision and defines the boundaries within which followers can operate in relative freedom to accomplish organizational goals. The transformational leader arouses in followers an awareness of problems and issues and helps people look at things in new ways so that productive change can happen.

2. *Transformational leadership elevates the concerns of followers from lower-level physical needs (such as for safety and security) to higher-level psychological needs (such as for self-esteem and self-actualization).* It is important that lower-level needs are met through adequate wages, safe working conditions, and other considerations. However, the transformational leader also pays attention to each individual's need for growth and development. Therefore, the leader sets examples and assigns tasks not only to meet immediate needs but also to elevate followers' needs and abilities to a higher level and link them to the organization's mission. Transformational leaders change followers so that they are empowered to change the organization.

3. *Transformational leadership inspires followers to go beyond their own self-interests for the good of the group.* Transformational leaders motivate people to do more than originally expected. They make followers aware of the importance of change goals and outcomes and, in turn, enable them to transcend their own immediate interests for the sake of the organizational mission. Followers admire these leaders, want to identify with them, and have a high degree of trust in them. However, transformational leadership motivates people not just to follow the leader personally, but to believe in the need for change and be willing to make personal sacrifices for the greater purpose.

4. *Transformational leadership paints a vision of a desired future state and communicates it in a way that makes the pain of change worth the effort.*[8] The most significant role of the transformational leader may be to find a vision for the organization that is significantly better than the old one and to enlist others in sharing the dream. It is the vision that launches people into action and provides the basis for the other aspects of transformational leadership we have just discussed. Change can occur only when people have a sense of purpose as well as a desirable picture of where the organization is going. Without vision, there can be no transformation.

Action Memo
Complete the questions in Leader's Self-Insight 12.1 on page 358 to learn how a supervisor of yours rates on transformational leadership. Then, answer the questions for how you would behave in a leadership situation.

Whereas transactional leaders promote stability, transformational leaders create significant change in followers as well as in organizations. Leaders can learn to be transformational as well as transactional. Effective leaders exhibit

Think of a situation where someone (boss, coach, teacher, group leader) was in a leadership position over you. Indicate whether each item below is Mostly False or Mostly True for you.

In general, the leader over me:

	Mostly False	Mostly True
1. Listened carefully to my concerns	_____	_____
2. Showed conviction in his/her values	_____	_____
3. Helped me focus on developing my strengths	_____	_____
4. Was enthusiastic about our mission	_____	_____
5. Provided coaching advice for my development	_____	_____
6. Talked optimistically about the future	_____	_____
7. Encouraged my self development	_____	_____
8. Fostered a clear understanding of important values and beliefs	_____	_____
9. Provided feedback on how I was doing	_____	_____
10. Inspired us with his/her plans for the future	_____	_____
11. Taught me how to develop my abilities	_____	_____
12. Gained others' commitment to his/her dream	_____	_____

Scoring and Interpretation

These questions represent two dimensions of transformational leadership. For the dimension of *develops followers into leaders,* sum your Mostly True responses to questions 1, 3, 5, 7, 9, and 11. For the dimension of *inspires followers to go beyond their own self-interest,* sum your Mostly True responses for questions 2, 4, 6, 8, 10, and 12. The scores for my leader are:

Develops followers into leaders _____
Inspires followers to go beyond their own self-interest _____

These two scores represent how you saw your leader on two important aspects of transformational leadership. A score of 5 or above on either dimensions is considered high because many leaders do not practice transformational skills in their leadership or group work. A score of 2 or below would be below average. Compare your scores with other students to understand your leader's practice of transformational leadership. How do you explain your leader's score?

Remember, the important learning from this exercise is about yourself, not your leader. Analyzing your leader is simply a way to understand the transformational leadership concepts. How would you rate on the dimensions of *developing followers into leaders* or *inspiring followers to go beyond their own self-interest?* These are difficult skills to master. Answer the 12 questions for yourself as a leader. Analyze your pattern of transformational leadership as revealed in your 12 answers.

Source: These questions are based on B. Bass and B. Avolio, *Multifactor Leadership Questionnaire,* 2nd ed. (Mind Garden, Inc); and P. M. Podsakoff, S. B. MacKenzie, R. H. Moorman, and R. Fetter, "Transformational Leader Behaviors and Their Effects on Followers' Trust in Leader, Satisfaction, and Organizational Citizenship Behaviors," *Leadership Quarterly* 1, no. 2 (1990), pp. 107–142.

both transactional and transformational leadership patterns. They accentuate not only their abilities to build a vision and empower and energize others, but also the transactional skills of designing structures, control systems, and reward systems that can help people achieve the vision.[9] One leader who reflects a balance of transactional and transformational leadership is Mike Eskew of UPS.

Michael L. Eskew, UPS

IN THE LEAD

Mike Eskew has spent his entire career at UPS, beginning in 1972 as an engineer and moving through the ranks until he became chairman and CEO in 2002. As CEO, Eskew has helped transform UPS from a company that just delivers packages into a company that "enables global commerce." Since he took over the top job, the giant company's international profits have soared and its revenue from "supply chain solutions"—running other companies' operations for them—has more than doubled. Today, UPS employees repair Toshiba laptops, manage warehouses full of spare parts for Bentley automobiles, pick and pack Nike athletic shoes, and ship Birkenstock sandals from German factories directly to U.S. retail stores. Over the past several years, UPS has acquired six logistics companies, e-brokerage firm, small companies that specialize in so-called less-than-truckload shipments, freight forwarders, an airline, and even a small bank.

No one would doubt Eskew's careful attention to the structures, systems, and processes that have kept UPS humming. His first job at UPS in 1972 was redesigning a parking lot so that it could accommodate more trucks, and Eskew still pays close attention to the details that help employees accomplish their jobs smoothly and efficiently. Yet he sees his most important role as helping people understand the vision and how they fit—that is, where the company wants to go and how each person can help it get there. Eskew doesn't like the attention that comes with being CEO; he prefers that the focus be on the people who do the day-to-day work of the company. When he visits facilities, he tells employees: "What you do is noble. . . . You make business better. You make communities better. You bring order to chaos."[10]

Transformational leaders like Mike Eskew give people a chance to make significant contributions as well as recognition for their accomplishments. "People want to accomplish great things," says Eskew. "They want to make a difference."[11]

Charismatic Leadership

Many transformational leaders have *charisma*, a seemingly-innate ability to inspire enthusiasm, interest, and affection from followers. However, charismatic leadership typically instills both awe and submission in followers, whereas transformational leadership seeks to increase the engagement of followers.[12]

Charisma has been called "a fire that ignites followers' energy and commitment, producing results above and beyond the call of duty."[13] **Charismatic leaders** have the ability to inspire and motivate people to do more than they would normally do, despite obstacles and personal sacrifice. In describing the charismatic leader, one business writer says, "He persuades people—subordinates, peers, customers, even the S.O.B. you both work for—to do things they'd rather not. People charge over the hill for him. Run through fire. Walk barefoot on broken glass. He doesn't demand attention, he commands it."[14]

Charismatic leaders have an emotional impact on people because they appeal to both the heart and the mind. They may speak emotionally about putting themselves on the line for the sake of a mission and they are perceived as people who persist in spite of great odds against them. Charismatic leaders often emerge in troubled times, whether in society or in organizations, because a strong, inspiring personality can help to reduce stress and anxiety among followers. For example, Amr Khaled emerged as a young, charismatic Muslim religious leader in Egypt during the Mideast crisis of the early twenty-first century. Khaled's sermons, delivered in an emotional, impassioned manner, touched people who were searching for a moderate approach to living as a good Muslim. An organizational example is Lloyd Ward, who was brought in as chief executive of the United States Olympic Committee (USOC) at a time when the organization was torn by internal strife and suffering a loss of public trust. The USOC believed Ward, known as a master motivator with the ability to unite and inspire people with a vision, could use his charisma to heal the fractures in the organization and restore the U.S. Olympics to glory.[15]

Charismatic leaders
leaders who have the ability to inspire and motivate people to do more than they would normally do, despite obstacles and personal sacrifice

Used wisely and ethically, charisma can lift the entire organization's level of performance. Charismatic leaders can raise people's consciousness about new possibilities and motivate them to transcend their own interests for the sake of the team, department, or organization.

Although charisma itself cannot be learned, there are aspects of charismatic leadership that anyone can use. For one thing, charisma comes from pursuing activities that you have a true passion for, such as Bill Strickland in the opening example. Charismatic leaders are engaging their emotions in everyday work life, which makes them energetic, enthusiastic, and attractive to others. Their passion galvanizes people to action. Consider Major Tony Burgess, the U.S. Army tactical officer attached on a full-time basis to Company C-2 at West Point. Burgess planned to get out of the Army after five years and become a millionaire businessman. "Then, somewhere along the way," he says, "I fell in love with leading." To Burgess, there's no better job in the world than commanding an Army company. He is so passionate about his work that he started his own Web site, CompanyCommand.com, a resource for company commanders, and has written a book on the topic.[16]

Action Memo

As a leader, you can use aspects of charismatic leadership by articulating a vision, making personal sacrifices to help achieve it, and appealing to people's emotions more than to their minds. Expand your charismatic potential by pursuing activities that you genuinely love.

What Makes a Charismatic Leader?

Understanding charismatic leadership qualities and behavior can help anyone become a stronger leader. A number of studies have identified the unique qualities of charismatic leaders, documented the impact they have on followers, and described the behaviors that help them achieve remarkable results.[17] Exhibit 12.1 compares distinguishing characteristics of charismatic and non-charismatic leaders.[18]

Exhibit 12.1 Distinguishing Characteristics of Charismatic and Non-Charismatic Leaders

	Non-Charismatic Leaders	Charismatic Leaders
Likableness:	Shared perspective makes leader likable	Shared perspective and idealized vision make leader likable and an honorable hero worthy of identification and imitation
Trustworthiness:	Disinterested advocacy in persuasion attempts	Passionate advocacy by incurring great personal risk and cost
Relation to status quo:	Tries to maintain status quo	Creates atmosphere of change
Future goals:	Limited goals not too discrepant from status quo	Idealized vision that is highly discrepant from status quo
Articulation:	Weak articulation of goals and motivation to lead	Strong and inspirational articulation of vision and motivation to lead
Competence:	Uses available means to achieve goals within framework of the existing order	Uses unconventional means to transcend the existing order
Behavior:	Conventional, conforms to norms	Unconventional, counter-normative
Influence:	Primarily authority of position and rewards	Transcends position; personal power based on expertise and respect and admiration for the leader

Source: Jay A. Conger and Rabindra N. Kanungo and Associates, *Charismatic Leadership: The Elusive Factor in Organizational Effectiveness* (San Francisco: Jossey-Bass, 1988), 91.

Charismatic leaders create an atmosphere of change and articulate an idealized vision of a future that is significantly better than what now exists. They have an ability to communicate complex ideas and goals in clear, compelling ways, so that everyone from the vice president to the janitor can understand and identify with their message. Charismatic leaders inspire followers with an abiding faith, even if the faith can't be stated in specific goals that are easily attained. The faith itself becomes a "reward" to followers.[19] Charismatic leaders also act in unconventional ways and use unconventional means to transcend the status quo and create change. Charismatic leaders may sometimes seem like oddballs, but this image only enhances their appeal.

Charismatic leaders earn followers' trust by being willing to incur great personal risk. Putting themselves on the line affirms charismatic leaders as passionate advocates for the vision. According to a personal friend of the King family, Martin Luther King received death threats against himself and his family almost every day during the civil rights movement.[20] By taking risks, leaders enhance their emotional appeal to followers.

The final characteristic of charismatic leaders is that their source of influence comes from personal characteristics rather than a formal position of authority. People admire, respect, and identify with the leader and want to be like him or her. Although charismatic leaders may be in formal positions of authority, charismatic leadership transcends formal organizational position because the leader's influence is based on personal qualities rather than the power and authority granted by the organization.

Action Memo
Take the short quiz in Leader's Self-Insight 12.2 on page 362 to help you determine whether you have the potential to be a charismatic leader.

The Black Hat of Charisma

One characteristic of charisma noted by most researchers is that it can be a curse as well as a blessing. Leaders such as Winston Churchill, John F. Kennedy, and Mohandas Gandhi had tremendous charisma. So did leaders such as Adolf Hitler, Charles Manson, and Idi Amin. Charisma isn't always used to benefit the group, organization, or society. It can also be used for self-serving purposes, which leads to deception, manipulation, and exploitation of others. Because the basis of charisma is emotional rather than logical or rational, it is risky and potentially dangerous.[21]

One explanation for the distinction between charisma that results in positive outcomes and that which results in negative outcomes relates to the difference between *personalized* leaders and *socialized* leaders.[22] Leaders who react to organizational problems in terms of their own needs rather than the needs of the whole often act in ways that can have disastrous consequences for others. Personalized charismatic leaders are characterized as self-aggrandizing, non-egalitarian, and exploitative, whereas socialized charismatic leaders are empowering, egalitarian, and supportive. Personalized behavior is based on caring about self; socialized behavior is based on valuing others. Studies have shown that personalized charismatic leaders can have a significant detrimental impact on long-term organizational performance. Leaders who have been consistently successful in improving organizational performance show a pattern of socialized behavior.[23]

Power, Influence, and Leadership

Power and influence are highly important concepts in the study of leadership; indeed, leadership relies on the use of power to get things done. However, getting a grasp on the meaning of the terms power and influence can be difficult.[24]

This short quiz will help you determine whether you have characteristics that are associated with charismatic leaders. Circle the answer that best describes you.

1. I am most comfortable thinking in
   a. Generalities
   b. Specifics
2. I worry most about
   a. Current competitive issues
   b. Future competitive issues
3. I tend to focus on
   a. The opportunities I've missed
   b. The opportunities I've seized
4. I prefer to
   a. Promote traditions and procedures that have led to success in the past
   b. Suggest new and unique ways of doing things
5. I tend to ask
   a. How can we do this better?
   b. Why are we doing this?
6. I believe
   a. There's always a way to minimize risk
   b. Some risks are too high
7. I tend to persuade people by using
   a. Emotion
   b. Logic

8. I prefer to
   a. Honor traditional values and ways of thinking
   b. Promote unconventional beliefs and values
9. I would prefer to communicate via
   a. A written report
   b. A one-page chart
10. I think this quiz is
    a. Ridiculous
    b. Fascinating

Scoring and Interpretation

The following answers are associated with charismatic leadership:

   1. a; 2. b; 3. a; 4. b; 5. b; 6. a; 7. a; 8. b; 9. b; 10. b

   If you responded in this way to seven or more questions, you have a high charisma quotient and may have the potential to be a charismatic leader. If you answered this way to four or fewer questions, your charisma level is considered low. Do you believe a person can develop charisma?

Source: Based on "Have You Got It?" a quiz that appeared in Patricia Sellers, "What Exactly Is Charisma?" *Fortune* (January 15, 1996), pp. 68–75. The original quiz was devised with the assistance of leadership expert Jay Conger.

Power is an intangible force in organizations. It cannot be seen, but its effect can be felt. Power is often defined as the potential ability of one person (or department) to influence other persons (or departments) to carry out orders[25] or to do something they otherwise would not have done.[26] Other definitions stress that power is the ability to achieve goals or outcomes that power holders desire.[27] The achievement of desired outcomes is the basis of the definition used here. **Power** is the ability of one person or department in an organization to influence other people to bring about desired outcomes. It is the potential to influence others within the organization with the goal of attaining desired outcomes for power holders. Potential power is realized through the processes of politics and influence.[28] Sometimes, the terms power and influence are used synonymously, but there are distinctions between the two. Basically, **influence** is the effect a person's actions have on the attitudes, values, beliefs, or actions of others. Whereas power is the capacity to cause a change in a person, influence may be thought of as the degree of actual change. For example, as a child you may have had the experience of playing a game you didn't really want to play because one person in the group influenced others to do what he or she wanted. Or you may have changed your college major because of the influence of someone important in your life, or shifted your beliefs about some social issue based on the influence of political or religious leaders.

Although we usually think of power and influence as belonging to the leader, in reality they result from the interaction of leaders and followers in specific

Power
the ability of one person or department in an organization to influence other people to bring about desired outcomes

Influence
the effect a person's actions have on the attitudes, values, beliefs, or actions of others

situations. As we learned in Chapter 7 on followership, followers may also influence a leader's behavior in any number of ways, for better or worse. Later in this chapter, we will examine some specific *influence tactics* that may be used to change another's attitudes or behavior. Leaders can improve their effectiveness by understanding the various types and sources of power as well as the influence tactics they or their followers may use.

Five Types of Leader Power

Power is often described as a personal characteristic, but as described above, organizational position also influences a leader's power. Most discussions of power include five types that are available to leaders.[29]

The five types of leader power are illustrated in Exhibit 12.2. The first three—legitimate, reward, and coercive power—may all be considered types of *position power* that are defined largely by the organization's policies and procedures. A person's position in the organization determines what amount of power he or she has, particularly in regard to the ability to reward or punish subordinates to influence their behavior. However, it is important to remember that position power and leadership are not the same thing. As we discussed in Chapter 1, a person might hold a formal position of authority and yet not be a leader. Effective leaders don't rely solely on formal position to influence others to accomplish goals. Two sources of *personal power,* called expert power and referent power, are based on the leader's special knowledge or personal characteristics.

> **Action Memo**
> As a leader, you can expand your personal power by developing good relationships and acquiring advanced knowledge and experience. You can use power to gain the commitment of others to achieve the vision. Use position power when appropriate, but don't overdo it.

Legitimate Power Legitimate power is the authority granted from a formal position in an organization. For example, once a person has been selected as a supervisor, most workers understand that they are obligated to follow his or her direction with respect to work activities. Subordinates accept this source of power as legitimate, which is why they comply. Certain rights, responsibilities, and prerogatives accrue to anyone holding a formal leadership position. Followers accept the legitimate rights of formal leaders to set goals, make decisions, and direct activities. Most North Americans accept the legitimate right of appointed leaders to direct an organization.

Legitimate power
authority granted from a formal position

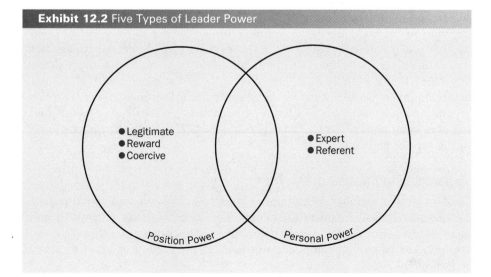

Exhibit 12.2 Five Types of Leader Power

- Legitimate
- Reward
- Coercive

- Expert
- Referent

Position Power

Personal Power

Reward Power This kind of power stems from the authority to bestow rewards on other people. For example, appointed leaders may have access to formal rewards, such as pay increases or promotions. Moreover, organizations allocate huge amounts of resources downward from top leaders. Leaders control resources and their distribution. Lower-level followers depend on leaders for the financial and physical resources to perform their tasks. Leaders with **reward power** can use rewards to influence subordinates' behavior.

Reward power
authority to bestow rewards on other people

Coercive Power The opposite of reward power is **coercive power**. It refers to the power to punish or recommend punishment. Supervisors have coercive power when they have the right to fire or demote subordinates, criticize, or withdraw pay increases. For example, if a salesman does not perform as well as expected, the sales manager has the coercive power to criticize him, reprimand him, put a negative letter in his file, and hurt his chance for a raise. Coercive power is the negative side of legitimate and reward power.

Coercive power
authority to punish or recommend punishment

Expert Power Power resulting from a leader's special knowledge or skill regarding tasks performed by followers is referred to as **expert power**. When a leader is a true expert, subordinates go along with recommendations because of his or her superior knowledge. Leaders at supervisory levels often have experience in the production process that gains them promotion. At top management levels, however, leaders may lack expert power because subordinates know more about technical details than they do. An exception is Mike Eskew of UPS, described earlier. Eskew has worked at UPS for so long and understands so much about all aspects of the business that employees accept that he knows what he's doing when he peers into delivery vehicles, inspects warehouses, or walks along conveyor belts. People throughout the organization with expertise and knowledge can use it to influence or place limits on decisions made by people above them in the organization.[30] Furthermore, specialized information may be withheld or divulged in ways designed to achieve particular outcomes desired by the leaders.[31]

Expert power
authority resulting from a leader's special knowledge or skill

Referent Power This kind of power comes from leader personality characteristics that command followers' identification, respect, and admiration so they want to emulate the leader. When workers admire a supervisor because of the way he or she deals with them, the influence is based on referent power. **Referent power** depends on the leader's personal characteristics rather than on a formal title or position and is especially visible in the area of charismatic leadership. Charismatic leadership is intensely based on the relationship between leader and followers and relies almost entirely on either referent or expert power. With charismatic leadership, there is often a strong identification of followers with the leader and an unquestioning acceptance of his or her ideas and plans. All good leaders make use of referent power. The *Consider This* box talks about the far-reaching impact of this type of power.

Referent power
authority based on personality characteristics that command followers' attention, respect, and admiration so that they want to emulate the leader

Responses to the Use of Power

Leaders use the various types of power to influence others to do what is necessary to accomplish organizational goals. The success of any attempt to influence is a matter of degree, but there are three distinct outcomes that may result from the use of power: compliance, resistance, and commitment, as illustrated in Exhibit 12.3.[32]

Consider This!

The Ripple Effect

Do you want to be a positive influence in the world? First, get your own life in order. Ground yourself in this single principle so that your behavior is wholesome and effective. If you do that, you will earn respect and be a powerful influence.

Your behavior influences others through a ripple effect. A ripple effect works because everyone influences everyone else. Powerful people are powerful influences.

If your life works, you influence your family.

If your family works, your family influences the community.

If your community works, your community influences the nation.

If your nation works, your nation influences the world.

If your world works, the ripple effect spreads throughout the cosmos.

Source: John Heider, *The Tao of Leadership: Leadership Strategies for a New Age* (New York: Bantam Books, 1985), p. 107. Copyright 1985 Humanic Ltd., Atlanta, GA. Used with permission.

When people successfully use position power (legitimate, reward, coercive), the response is compliance. **Compliance** means that people follow the directions of the person with power, whether or not they agree with those directions. They will obey orders and carry out instructions even though they may not like it. The problem is that in many cases, followers do just enough work as is necessary to satisfy the leader and may not contribute their full potential. In addition, if the use of position power, especially the use of coercion, exceeds a level people consider legitimate, people may resist the attempt to influence. **Resistance** means that employees will deliberately try to avoid carrying out instructions or they will attempt to disobey orders. Thus, the effectiveness of leaders who rely solely on position power is limited.

The follower response most often generated by personal power (expert, referent) is commitment. **Commitment** means that followers adopt the leader's viewpoint and enthusiastically carry out instructions. Leader Anu Shukla, who currently heads the startup RubiconSoft, learned that she was much more effective in gaining the commitment of employees when she stopped relying on position power alone to influence subordinates.

Compliance
following the directions of the person with power, regardless of how much agreement there is with that person's directions

Resistance
the act of disobeying orders or deliberately avoiding carrying out instructions

Commitment
adopting the leader's viewpoint and enthusiastically carrying out instructions

Exhibit 12.3 Responses to the Use of Power

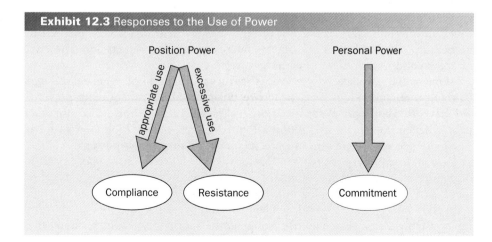

IN THE LEAD

Anu Shukla, RubiconSoft

When she began her leadership career in the technology industry as vice-president of marketing and product development at Compuware, Anu Shukla says she thought leaders got results by giving orders. "I thought I would force my will on people and make them follow me whether they wanted to or not," Shukla says. "I didn't understand that my employees were the prize stallions and my job was to unblock things for them and help them succeed."

As she moved through jobs at different companies, Shukla gradually learned a different way of leading, finding that she got far better results when she stopped barking orders and instead got her employees to understand and embrace her ideas. She began listening to employees' ideas and contributions as well, which increased her referent power. When she started her own company Rubric, an Internet software firm, Shukla found that acknowledging her dependence on her employees was the key to retaining her most talented workers. It was the height of the dot-com boom, and the competition for talent was fierce. Shukla believes if she had relied on formal authority alone, she would have lost many of her most valued employees to other startups.

After Shukla sold Rubric, many of her colleagues followed her to her new venture, RubiconSoft. Both Rubric's former CFO and its former vice president of marketing, who had also worked with Shukla at three other companies, even invested in the new company. Ted Mihara, Rubric's former western regional sales manager, also joined RubiconSoft as vice president of sales. He explains why: "I want a leader who makes my own efforts easier, and Anu's intellect, competitiveness, and great customer skills are very compelling."[33]

Rather than relying on her position of authority in the organization, Anu Shukla now leads primarily with referent and expert power, gaining strong commitment from employees. Needless to say, commitment is preferred to compliance or resistance. Although compliance alone may be enough for routine matters, commitment is particularly important when the leader is promoting change. Change carries risk or uncertainty, and follower commitment helps to overcome fear and resistance associated with change efforts. Successful leaders exercise both personal and position power to influence others.

The Role of Dependency

You probably know from personal experience that when a person has control over something that others want and need, he or she gains power. A simple example is a star high school quarterback graduating at a time when there are few excellent quarterbacks coming out of high schools. The star will be courted by numerous colleges who will vie for his interest and make increasingly attractive offers to entice him to sign on with their team.

One of the key aspects of power is that it is a function of dependence—that is, the greater Individual B's dependence on Individual A, the greater power A will have over B. People in organizations, as elsewhere, have power because other people depend on them—for information, resources, cooperation, and so forth. The more people depend on someone, the greater that person's power.[34]

The nature of dependency relationships between leaders and subordinates in organizations fluctuates depending on economic circumstances. When unemployment is low and jobs are plentiful, people feel less dependent on their supervisors, and managers are more dependent on employees because they are hard to replace. Only a few years ago, for example, the shortage of engineers and other high-tech talent was so severe that many employees could shop around, gather several offers, and then demand more money and benefits from their employers. With a struggling economy and massive downsizing, however, such as occurred in the early 2000s, the situation reversed. Once again, managers gained more clout over workers because people would have a hard time finding comparable jobs and salaries elsewhere.[35] When jobs are hard to come by and unemployment is high, organizational leaders have greater power over employees because most people are dependent on the organization for their livelihood.

This type of dependency primarily affects a leader's position power, which is based on formal authority and the ability to bestow rewards and punishments. When supervisors are dependent on employees, such as in a tight labor market, leaders must gain and exercise personal power to a greater extent, because people will often stay in a job where they admire and respect the leader, even if other opportunities are plentiful. When jobs are scarce, it is easier for leaders to get by relying on position power, but they won't get the full benefit of employees' enthusiasm and commitment.

Control over Resources

Dependency within organizations is related to a person's control over resources. Resources include such things as jobs, rewards, financial support, expertise, knowledge, materials, information, and time. As illustrated in Exhibit 12.4, people are more dependent—therefore leaders and organizations have more control and power—when resources are high on three characteristics—importance, scarcity, and nonsubstitutability.[36] People in the organization must perceive the resource to be *important*—that is, if nobody wants what you've got, it's not going to create dependency. Resources can be important for a variety of reasons. For example, they may be essential elements of a key product, they may directly generate sales, or they may be critical to reducing or avoiding uncertainty for the organization's top decision makers. Chief information officers have gained a tremendous amount of power in many organizations because of the critical role of information technology for both business and non-profit organizations. Similarly, ethics and compliance officers are highly powerful today because they help reduce uncertainty for top leaders concerning ethical lapses and financial malfeasance.

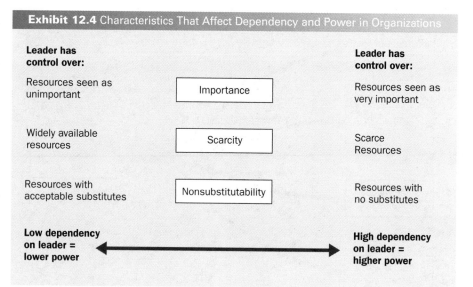

Exhibit 12.4 Characteristics That Affect Dependency and Power in Organizations

Scarcity refers to whether the resource is easy or difficult to obtain. A resource that is difficult or expensive to acquire is more valuable and creates more dependency than one that is widely available. In Ireland, for example, an influx of information technology and finance companies over the past 15 years has left top managers scrambling to find employees with skills and experience in these fields. Irish engineers who once had to come to the United States to get jobs now find themselves highly valued in their own country, and U.S. technology and finance professionals are learning that companies in Ireland will gladly help them with the necessary work permits, visas, information on taxes and real estate, and moving expenses to get them to sign on.[37] Leaders and employees with specialized knowledge in U.S. firms also serve to illustrate this aspect of dependency. In companies moving toward e-business, some young Internet-literate managers have gained power over senior leaders who have no computer expertise.

The third characteristic, *nonsubstitutability,* means that leaders or employees with control over resources with no viable substitute will have more power. These resources may include knowledge and expertise as well as access to people with high power. For example, an executive secretary that has daily access to the CEO might have more power than middle managers, who must compete for a few minutes of the top leader's time.

Sources of Leader Power in Organizations

An understanding of dependency and control over resources provides the foundation for examining several sources of leader power in organizations. The five types of power we discussed earlier are derived from either formal position or the leader's personal qualities. These sources provide a basis for much of a leader's influence. In organizations, however, additional sources of power and influence have been identified. The strategic contingencies theory identifies power sources not linked to the specific person or position, but to the role the leader plays in the overall functioning of the organization.[38] Sources of power in this regard are interdepartmental dependency, control over information, centrality, and coping with uncertainty, as illustrated in Exhibit 12.5.

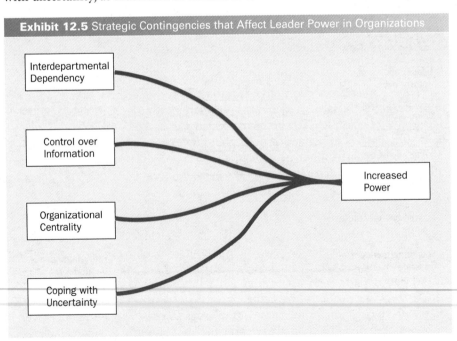

Exhibit 12.5 Strategic Contingencies that Affect Leader Power in Organizations

Interdepartmental Dependency

One key source of leader power in many organizations is interdepartmental dependency. Materials, resources, and information may flow between departments in one direction. In such cases, leaders in the department receiving resources will have less power than those in the department that provides them. For example, consider the case of leaders at a cigarette factory.[39] One might expect that the production department would be more powerful than the maintenance department, but this was not the case in a cigarette plant near Paris. The production of cigarettes was a routine process. The machinery was automated. On the other hand, maintenance department workers and their leaders were responsible for repair of the automated machinery, which was a complex task, and they had many years of experience. Because the maintenance department had the ability to fix unpredictable assembly-line breakdowns, production managers became dependent on maintenance, and maintenance leaders called the shots about machine repair and assembly line maintenance.

Control over Information

Despite the trend toward empowerment and broader information-sharing, the fact remains that some people will almost always have access to more information than others. Control over information—which involves both access to information and control over how and to whom it is distributed—is an important source of power for leaders. Consider the example of Jay S. Sidhu, an émigré from India who has served as chief executive of Sovereign Bancorp for more than 15 years. Sidhu has negotiated more than 27 acquisitions that both transformed the troubled savings and loan into a major regional bank as well as increased his own power over shareholders and board members. In the most recent acquisition, Sidhu structured the deal in such a way that it diluted the power of investors who have been critical of the top leader and want more control. Insiders say Sidhu often withholds information from the board or waits until the last minute to brief them in order to accomplish his objectives.[40]

Most leaders recognize that information is a primary business resource and that by controlling what information is collected, how it is interpreted, and how it is shared, they can influence how decisions are made.[41] To some extent, access to information is determined by a person's position in the organization. Top leaders typically have access to more information than do lower-level supervisors or other employees. They can release information selectively to influence others and shape actions and decisions. However, control over information can also be a source of power for lower-level leaders and employees. Employees who have exclusive access to information needed by leaders to make decisions gain power as a result. For example, top executives may be dependent on the production manager for analyzing and interpreting complex operations data.

> **Action Memo**
> As a leader, you can gain power by helping the organization deal with strategic contingencies. You can use information to shape decisions and actions, strive to become involved in the central activities of the organization, and stay alert to ways you can help the organization cope with critical uncertainties.

Organizational Centrality

Centrality reflects a leader's or a department's role in the primary activity of an organization.[42] One measure of centrality is the extent to which the work of the leader's department affects the final output of the organization. At a company such as Intel, which is heavily technology-oriented, engineers have a high degree of power because the organization depends on them to maintain the technical superiority of its products. In contrast, engineers at a company such as Procter & Gamble or Kimberly-Clark, where marketing is the name of the game, have a lower degree of power. In these organizations, marketers are typically the most powerful group of employees.[43]

Centrality
a leader's or a department's role in the primary activity of an organization

Centrality is associated with more power because it reflects the contribution made to the organization. At the University of Illinois, for example, important resources come from research grants and the quality of students and faculty. Departments that provide the most resources to the university are rated as having the most power. Also, departments that generate large research grants are more powerful because the grants contain a sizable overhead payment to university administration.[44]

Coping with Uncertainty

The environment can change swiftly and create uncertainty and complexity for leaders. In the face of uncertainty, little information is available to leaders on appropriate courses of action. Leaders in departments that cope well with this uncertainty will increase their power.[45] When market research personnel accurately predict changes in demand for new products, for example, they gain power and prestige because they have reduced a critical uncertainty. Leaders in industrial relations departments may gain power by helping the organization deal with uncertainties created by labor unions. Consider the following example of coping with uncertainty in the health care industry.

HCA and Aetna, Inc.

Once upon a time, insurers called all the shots, forcing hospitals to take lower reimbursements, forego price increases, and discharge patients more quickly. HCA, based in Nashville, Tennessee, says it routinely signed contracts that barely covered its costs. But HCA is now the largest hospital owner in the United States, and it owns a huge percentage of the hospital market in major metropolitan areas such as Denver, Las Vegas, and Houston. Thus, HCA now has enough power to push around large insurance companies.

HCA's legal department has been instrumental in absorbing critical uncertainties for the organization. Beginning in 1996, when a Medicare scandal surfaced, the legal department swung into action to help the organization weather the storm and develop clear guidelines and compliance programs to make sure similar legal problems didn't happen again. The department again played a critical role in negotiating a series of mergers and acquisitions that enabled HCA to grow in size and power and turn the tables on big insurers such as Aetna, Inc. In Houston, for example, HCA now operates 10 hospitals, a 22 percent share of the market. In that city, HCA officials began warning doctors that it will terminate its contract with Aetna, the country's largest health insurer, unless the company meets its demands for price increases.

At the same time, hospitals are facing another critical uncertainty concerning billing practices that sometimes require uninsured patients to pay excessively high rates. A congressional committee has been investigating billing practices at HCA and other large hospitals, again requiring shrewd attention from the legal department. So long as legal issues represent a critical strategic contingency for HCA, the legal department will remain a powerful force in the organization.[46]

Because hospitals have to deal with so many complex legal and regulatory matters, it is likely that leaders in the legal department at systems such as HCA are typically in a high power position. Yet power relationships in organizations change as strategic contingencies change. In a hospital dealing with a major health crisis, leaders in the public relations department might gain power, for example, by soothing public fears and keeping people informed about the hospital's efforts to control the spread of disease.

Strategic issues and uncertainties are continually changing for organizations, which leads to shifting power relationships. Departments that help organizations cope with new uncertainties will increase their power.

Increasing Power Through Political Activity

Action Memo
To learn about your own political orientation, go to Leader's Self-Insight 12.3 on page 372 and complete the questions.

Another aspect of power is that it isn't enough to be performing central activities or coping with organizational uncertainties—one's efforts must also be recognized as important by others.[47] People who want to increase their power make sure their activities are visible and appreciated by others. Acquiring and using power is largely a political process.

Politics involves activities to acquire, develop, and use power and other resources to obtain desired future outcomes when there is uncertainty or disagreement about choices.[48] Politically skillful leaders strive to understand others' viewpoints, needs, desires, and goals, and use their understanding to influence people to act in ways that help the leader accomplish his or her goals for the team or organization.[49] Russell Chew, who runs the nation's air traffic control system for the Federal Aviation Administration (FAA), has been criticized for his lack of political savvy. Although Chew has had some notable successes since he took the job as the first leader of the newly created semiautonomous Air Traffic Organization, many of his efforts to cut bureaucracy and trim costs have been frustrated by the resistance of Congressional leaders. Cost-saving proposals that involve closing facilities, for example, frequently are stalled because lawmakers fight the loss of jobs in their districts. Although Chew insists he won't let up on his cost-cutting drive as he serves out his term, some observers think he will continue to run up against roadblocks because he "doesn't get the politics."[50] Leaders at most organizations engage in some degree of political activity aimed at influencing government policies, because government choices represent a critical source of uncertainty for businesses as well as non-profit organizations.[51] Consider such U.S. government decisions as the activation of a national "do not call" registry, which dramatically changes the rules of the game for telemarketers, a Supreme Court ruling that endorsed the continuation of affirmation action guidelines for hiring and college admissions, or changes in Medicare and Medicaid that enable states to wring discounts from health care providers. Organizations use political activity to try to influence decisions that will be to their benefit.

Individuals and departments within organizations also engage in political activity. Political behavior can be either a positive or negative force. Uncertainty and conflict are natural in organizations, and politics is the mechanism for accomplishing things that can't be handled purely through formal policies or position power. The appropriate use of power and politics to get things done is an important aspect of leadership, as further discussed in this chapter's Leader's Bookshelf.

Leaders also use politics to increase their personal power. One way leaders increase their power is by seeking greater responsibility, such as serving on committees or volunteering for difficult projects. This often enables them to make connections with powerful people in the organization and build their reputation among those people. When lower-level leaders are perceived as having "friends in higher places," their own power is increased.

Another political approach is called *impression management*, which means people seek to control how others perceive them, often creating an impression of greater power as well as helping them gain more power. A whole new industry has

Politics
activities to acquire, develop, and use power and other resources to obtain desired future outcomes when there is uncertainty or disagreement about choices

This questionnaire asks you to describe yourself as a leader. For each item below, give the number "4" to the phrase that best describes you, "3" to the item that is next best, and on down to "1" for the item that is least like you.

1. My strongest skills are:
   _____ a. Analytical skills
   _____ b. Interpersonal skills
   _____ c. Political skills
   _____ d. Flair for drama

2. The best way to describe me is:
   _____ a. Technical expert
   _____ b. Good listener
   _____ c. Skilled negotiator
   _____ d. Inspirational leader

3. What has helped me the most to be successful is my ability to:
   _____ a. Make good decisions
   _____ b. Coach and develop people
   _____ c. Build strong alliances and a power base
   _____ d. Inspire and excite others

4. What people are most likely to notice about me is my:
   _____ a. Attention to detail
   _____ b. Concern for people
   _____ c. Ability to succeed in the face of conflict and opposition
   _____ d. Charisma

5. My most important leadership trait is:
   _____ a. Clear, logical thinking
   _____ b. Caring and support for others
   _____ c. Toughness and aggressiveness
   _____ d. Imagination and creativity

6. I am best described as:
   _____ a. An analyst
   _____ b. A humanist
   _____ c. A politician
   _____ d. A visionary

Scoring and Interpretation

Compute your scores as follows:

Structural = 1a + 2a + 3a + 4a + 5a + 6a = _____

Human Resource = 1b + 2b + 3b + 4b + 5b + 6b = _____

Political = 1c + 2c + 3c + 4c + 5c + 6c = _____

Symbolic = 1d + 2d + 3d + 4d + 5d + 6d = _____

Your answers reveal your preference for four distinct leader orientations. The higher your score, the greater your preference for that orientation. A low score may mean a blind spot. "Structural" means to view the organization as a machine that operates with efficiency to be successful. "Human Resource" means to view the organization primarily as people and to treat the family well to succeed. "Political" means to view the organizations as a competition for resources and the need to build alliances to succeed. "Symbolic" means to view the organization as a system of shared meaning and values and to succeed by shaping the culture.

Do you view politics in a positive or negative light? Most new leaders succeed first by using either or both of the structural or people orientations. New leaders often have a blind spot about politics. As managers move up the hierarchy, they learn to be more political or they miss out on key decisions. The symbolic view usually comes last in a leader's development. Compare your scores to other students and see which orientations are more widely held.

Source: © 1988, Leadership Frameworks, 440 Boylston Street, Brookline, Massachusetts 02146. All rights reserved. Used with permission.

emerged aimed at helping leaders hone their impression management skills. For example, consultant Debra Benton helps executives at companies such as Mattel, Hewlett-Packard, and PepsiCo develop what she calls *executive presence*—"the impact you have when you walk into a room, a collection of subtle . . . visual cues, including everything from how your clothes fit to how you walk."[52] Impression management may include a wide variety of tactics. Subtle name-dropping can give the impression that a leader associates with high-status people. Likewise, flattery is a form of impression management that can help a person appear to be perceptive

Leader's Bookshelf

Leadership on the Line: Staying Alive Through the Dangers of Leading

Getty Images

by Ronald A. Heifetz and Marty Linsky

In *Leadership on the Line,* Ronald Heifetz and Marty Linsky start with the premise that leadership is hard and lonely work. Each of us has opportunities to lead every day, but many avoid the challenge. And with good reason, say the authors: "To lead is to live dangerously because when leadership counts, when you lead people through difficult change, you challenge what people hold dear—their daily habits, tools, loyalties, and ways of thinking—with nothing more to offer perhaps than a possibility." Heifetz and Linsky, who teach at Harvard University's Kennedy School of Government, wrote *Leadership on the Line* as a guide for "surviving and thriving amidst the dangers of leadership."

STRATEGIES FOR THRIVING AS A LEADER

Here are a few of the strategies Heifetz and Linsky offer for how leaders can accomplish change and avoid being put down or pushed aside.

- *Think politically.* A key step is acknowledging the political nature of leadership. Leaders cannot get anything done unless they create and nurture networks of people they can call on and work with to accomplish goals. At the start of any change campaign, good leaders line up their supporters, start working closely with their opponents, and develop tactics for influencing the uncommitted.
- *Manage conflict.* Any tough issue is bound to be accompanied by conflict. While the natural tendency for most of us is to limit conflict, Heifetz and Linsky point out that people learn and grow only when they encounter ideas that challenge their own experience

and assumptions. The job for leaders is to work with differing ideas, opinions, emotions, and attitudes in a way that harnesses the energy of conflict but minimizes its destructive potential.

- *Keep your hungers in check.* Everyone has *hungers,* expressions of our normal human needs, but leaders are careful not to let their hungers disrupt their capacity for acting with wisdom and purpose. For example, a lust for power becomes an end in itself, distracting a eader's attention from organizational needs and goals. Inappropriate personal behavior damages trust, creates confusion, and destroys relationships. An inflated sense of self-importance limits the capacity for self-understanding and meaningful, caring relationships with others. Good leaders understand where their vulnerabilities are and work to keep them from taking charge of their lives.

EMOTIONAL AND PRACTICAL SUPPORT

Leadership on the Line can help people from all walks of life accept the challenge of leadership and "survive to delight in the fruits of your labor." Taking the opportunity to lead—to make a difference in the lives of people around you—is not always easy, but it is worth the costs. With the tips, strategies, and guidelines in *Leadership on the Line,* Heifetz and Linsky lend emotional and practical support for those who rise to the challenge.

Leadership on the Line: Staying Alive Through the Dangers of Leading, by Ronald A. Heifetz and Marty Linsky, is published by Harvard Business School Press.

and pleasant. These political tactics can be helpful when they enable others to perceive a leader's value to the organization. However, they can also backfire if leaders are perceived as being insincere, dishonest, or arrogant.

One example of the effective use of impression management is Steve Harrison, who at the age of 50 was afraid younger superiors as well as subordinates might perceive him as behind the times. Not only does Harrison make sure others know that he keeps up with current business issues, but he also peppers his informal conversations with references to his "youthful" hobbies of running and collecting electric guitars.[53] Followers use impression management too, as we discussed in our section on *strategies for managing up* in Chapter 7. For example, followers may seek feedback from their leaders as a way to create a favorable impression and increase their power, or, conversely, try to evade feedback in an attempt to avoid creating a negative impression.[54]

Tactics for Asserting Leader Influence

The next issue is how leaders use their power to implement decisions, facilitate change, and pursue organizational goals. That is, leaders use power to influence others, which requires both skill and willingness. Much influence is interpersonal and one-on-one. This is social influence, which involves coalitions, rewards, and inspiration. Other influence has broader appeal, such as to influence the organization as a whole, or to influence those outside the organization. However, not all attempts to use power result in actual influence. Some power moves are rejected by followers, particularly if they are seen to be self-serving. Leaders have to determine the best approach for using their power—that is, the approach that is most likely to influence others—by considering the individuals, groups, and situations involved.[55] In addition, they understand the basic principles that can cause people to change their behavior or attitudes.

Leaders frequently use a combination of influence strategies, and people who use a wider variety of tactics are typically perceived as having greater power and influence. One survey of a few hundred leaders identified more than 4,000 different techniques by which these people were able to influence others to do what the leader wanted.[56] However, the myriad successful influence tactics used by leaders fall into basic categories of influence actions. Exhibit 12.6 lists seven principles for asserting leader influence. Notice that most of these involve the use of personal power, rather than relying solely on position power or the use of rewards and punishments.

1. *Use rational persuasion.* Perhaps the most frequently used influence tactic is rational persuasion, which means using facts, data, and logical arguments to persuade others that a proposed idea or request is the best way to complete a task or accomplish a desired goal. It can be effective whether the influence attempt is directed upward toward superiors, downward toward subordinates, or horizontally, because most people have faith in facts and analysis.[57] Rational persuasion is most effective when a leader has technical knowledge and expertise related to the issue (expert power), although referent power is also used. Frequently, some parts of a rational argument cannot be backed up with facts and figures, so people have to believe in the leader's credibility to accept his or her argument.

2. *Make people like you.* We all know it's easier to say yes to someone we like than to someone we don't like.[58] One author of a book on influence tells a story about an American working in Saudi Arabia, who learned that getting information or action from government offices was easy when he'd drop by, drink tea, and chat for a while.[59] Cultural values in Saudi Arabia

---

Exhibit 12.6 Seven Principles for Asserting Leader Influence

1. Use rational persuasion.
2. Make people like you.
3. Rely on the rule of reciprocity.
4. Develop allies.
5. Ask for what you want.
6. Remember the principle of scarcity.
7. Extend formal authority with expertise and credibility.

put great emphasis on personal relationships, but people in all cultures respond to friendliness and consideration. When a leader shows concern for others, demonstrates trust and respect, and treats people fairly, people are more likely to want to help and support the leader by doing what he or she asks. In addition, most people will like a leader who makes them feel good about themselves. Leaders never underestimate the importance of praise.

3. *Rely on the rule of reciprocity.* Recall the discussion of dependency, and how leaders gain power by having something that others value. A primary way to turn that power into influence is to share what you have—whether it be time, resources, services, or emotional support. There's a near universal feeling among people that others should be paid back for what they do in one form or another. This "unwritten law of reciprocity" means that leaders who do favors for others can expect others to do favors for them in return. Leaders also elicit the cooperative and sharing behavior they want from others by first demonstrating it with their own actions.[60] Some researchers argue that the concept of exchange—trading something of value for what you want—is the basis of all other influence tactics. For example, rational persuasion works because the other person sees a benefit from going along with the plan, and making people like you is successful because the other person receives liking and attention in return.[61]

4. *Develop allies.* Reciprocity also plays an important role in developing networks of allies, people who can help the leader accomplish his or her goals. Leaders can influence others by taking the time to talk with followers and other leaders outside of formal meetings to understand their needs and concerns, as well as to explain problems and describe the leader's point of view.[62] Leaders consult with one another and reach a meeting of minds about a proposed decision, change, or strategy.[63] A recent study found that political skill, particularly network-building, has a positive impact on both followers' perceptions of a leader's abilities and performance as well as on the actual, objective performance of the work unit.[64]

A leader can expand his or her network of allies by reaching out to establish contact with additional people. Some leaders expand their networks through the hiring, transfer, and promotion process. Identifying and placing in key positions people who are sympathetic to the desired outcomes of the leader can help achieve the leader's goals. However, if power building is perceived as self serving, key people may become alienated, as Philip Purcell learned at Morgan Stanley.

Philip Purcell and John Mack, Morgan Stanley

During negotiations for the 1997 merger of Morgan Stanley and Dean Witter, Dean Witter's long-time head, Philip Purcell, argued that since his firm was technically the acquirer in the deal, it was only right that the first CEO come from Dean Witter. Morgan's heir apparent, John Mack, who was generally respected and admired by his employees, agreed to the terms, saying the merger was too important to make an issue over the top job. The arrangement was that Purcell would serve for 5 years and then be succeeded by Mack, from the Morgan Stanley side of the merger.

But the Morgan managers soon learned that Purcell was out to gain total control for himself. He quickly installed trusted Dean Witter veterans in key positions and often supported them over higher-level Morgan managers. Executives loyal to Purcell successfully resisted any efforts Mack made for change in the business.

Purcell gradually shifted more and more aspects of the business away from Mack and to his trusted aides. Frustrated, Mack launched a campaign to have himself named co-CEO, but the balance of power had already swung too far toward Purcell. As terms of directors expired, Purcell was able to stack the board with new directors who were loyal to him and would support his proposals for management changes over those of Mack.[65] When the dust settled at Morgan Stanley, Phillip Purcell had gained complete control of the firm, with all core operations reporting directly to him. John Mack was effectively forced out.

But by 2005, Purcell's aggressive power moves had led to serious strife within Morgan Stanley. As previous Morgan Stanley managers saw their responsibilities taken away and perceived that Purcell's favored executives were given special privileges, they began leaving the firm in droves. A management shake-up in early 2005 led to the departure of three more high-level Morgan Stanley executives and prompted public calls by shareholders and former executives for Purcell's ouster. The open antagonism combined with weak financial performance and a sagging stock price caused the board and Purcell to reconsider. They made a joint decision that Purcell would resign from the firm. John Mack was later brought back as chairman and CEO.[66]

One problem for Philip Purcell was that he failed to build support among shareholders, clients, and lower level employees. He was considered a remote manager who interacted primarily with his top trusted executives and board members and failed to include outsiders in his network. Some major clients said they were never visited or even phoned by Purcell. When the tide began to turn, Purcell was unable to deflect the open antagonism from former executives and chagrined shareholders. Directors, managers, employees, and shareholders hope Mack's more inclusive style of leadership will resolve the discord and set Morgan Stanley on a smoother course.

Many top executives strive to build a cadre of loyal and supportive managers to help them achieve their goals for the organization. For example, former New York Stock Exchange Chairman Dick Grasso placed his friends and allies in critical positions and pushed favored candidates for board posts. As another example, the U.S. government hand-picked the advisers and committee members who would influence decisions made by the interim Iraqi government.[67]

Action Memo

As a leader, you can influence others by using rational persuasion, developing allies, and expanding your expertise and credibility. Remember that people respond to friendliness and consideration, and they typically feel obligated to return favors.

5. *Ask for what you want.* Another way to have influence is to make a direct appeal by being clear about what you want and asking for it. If leaders do not ask, they seldom receive. Political activity is effective only when the leader's vision, goals, and desired changes are made explicit so the organization can respond. Leaders can use their courage to be assertive, saying what they believe to persuade others. An explicit proposal may be accepted simply because other people have no better alternatives. Also, an explicit proposal for change or for a specific decision alternative will often receive favorable treatment when other options are less well defined. Effective political behavior requires sufficient forcefulness and risk-taking to at least try to achieve desired outcomes.[68]

6. *Remember the principle of scarcity.* This principle means that people usually want more of what they can't have. When things are less available, they become more desirable. An interesting dissertation study on the purchase decisions of wholesale beef buyers found that buyers more than doubled their orders when they were told that because of weather conditions there was likely to be a scarcity of foreign beef in

the near future. Interestingly, though, their orders increased 600 percent when they were informed that no one else had that information yet.[69] Retailers often use this principle by sending advance notice of sales to credit card holders, making them feel they're getting information that the general shopping public doesn't have. Leaders can learn to frame their requests or offers in such a way as to highlight the unique benefits and exclusive information being provided. One approach is to selectively release information that is not broadly available and that supports the leaders' ideas or proposals. Letting people know they're getting a sneak peak at information captures their interest and makes them more likely to support the leader's position.

7. *Extend formal authority with expertise and credibility*. The final principle for asserting influence is the leader's legitimate authority in the organization. Legitimate authorities are in a position to be particularly influential. However, research has found that the key to successful use of formal authority is to be knowledgeable, credible, and trustworthy. Managers who become known for their expertise, who are honest and straightforward with others, and who inspire trust can exert greater influence than those who simply try to issue orders.[70] In addition, effective leaders keep the six previous influence principles in mind, realizing that influence depends primarily on personal rather than position power. By understanding the importance of rational persuasion, liking and friendship, reciprocity, networks of alliances, direct appeal, and scarcity, leaders can extend the power of their formal position and strengthen their influence over others.

Ethical Considerations in Using Power and Politics

Harry Truman once said that leadership is the ability to get people to do what they don't want to do and like it.[71] His statement raises an important issue: Leadership is an opportunity to use power and influence to accomplish important organizational goals, but power can also be abused. Consider the behavior of a colleague of Scott Rosen, an assistant manager at a financial services company: Rosen says his colleague would routinely go to their boss's office and lead him to believe that Rosen was mishandling his job. The rival also undermined Rosen with his staff. "Whatever I did," Rosen says, "I lost." Eventually, Rosen was demoted, while his colleague received a promotion.[72] Unfortunately, like Rosen's associate, there are frequently people in organizations who use power and politics primarily to serve their own interests, at the expense of others and the organization.

Recall our earlier discussion of *personalized* versus *socialized* leaders. This distinction refers primarily to their approach to the use of power.[73] Personalized leaders are typically selfish, impulsive, and exercise power for their own self-centered needs and interests rather than for the good of the organization. Socialized leaders exercise power in the service of higher goals that will benefit others and the organization as a whole.

One specific area in which the unethical use of power is of increasing concern for organizations is sexual harassment. People in organizations depend on one another—and especially on leaders—for many resources, including information, cooperation, and even their jobs. When access to resources seems to depend on granting sexual favors or putting up with sexually intimidating or threatening comments, the person in a dependent position is being personally violated,

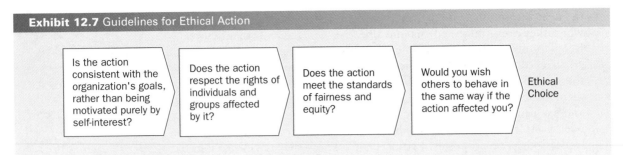

Exhibit 12.7 Guidelines for Ethical Action

Is the action consistent with the organization's goals, rather than being motivated purely by self-interest? → Does the action respect the rights of individuals and groups affected by it? → Does the action meet the standards of fairness and equity? → Would you wish others to behave in the same way if the action affected you? → Ethical Choice

Sources: Based on G. F. Cavanaugh, D. J. Mobert, and M. Valasques, "The Ethics of Organizational Politics, "*Academy of Management Journal,* (June 1981), pp. 363–374; and Stephen P. Robbins, *Organizational Behavior,* 8th ed. (Upper Saddle River, NJ: Prentice Hall, 1998), p. 422.

whether or not the leader actually withholds the resources. Partly in response to pressures from the courts, many organizations are developing policies and procedures that protect individuals from sexual harassment on the job and offer mechanisms for reporting complaints. Sexual harassment is not just unethical, it is illegal, and it is a clear abuse of power.

However, there are many other situations in organizations that are not so clear-cut, and leaders may sometimes have difficulty differentiating ethical from unethical uses of power and politics. Exhibit 12.7 summarizes some criteria that can guide ethical actions. First and foremost is the question of whether the action is motivated by self-interest or whether it is consistent with the organization's goals. One Internet company has a rule that any employee can be terminated for a political act that is in the individual's own self-interest rather than in the interest of the company, or that harms another person in the organization.[74] Once a leader answers this primary question, there are several other questions that can help determine whether a potential influence action is ethical, including whether it respects the rights of individuals and groups affected by it, whether it meets the standards of fairness, and whether the leader would want others to behave in the same way. If a leader answers these questions honestly, they can serve as a guide to whether an intended act is ethical.

In the complex world of organizations, there will always be situations that are difficult to interpret. The most important point is for leaders to be aware of the ethical responsibilities of having power and take care to use their power to help rather than harm others. Leaders should think not in terms of getting their own way, but rather in terms of building long-term productive relationships that can achieve goals and benefit the entire organization.

> **Action Memo**
>
> As a leader, you can be ethical in your use of power and politics. You can build long-term productive relationships to achieve important goals and benefit the entire team or organization.

Summary and Interpretation

This chapter looked at how leaders use power and political processes to get things done. Power and politics are an important, though often hidden, part of all organizations. Two leadership styles that rely strongly on a leader's personal characteristics as a source of power are transformational and charismatic leadership. Charismatic leaders have an emotional impact on people by appealing to both the heart and mind. They create an atmosphere of change, articulate an idealized vision of the future, inspire faith and hope, and frequently incur personal risks to influence followers. Charisma can be used to benefit organizations and society, but it can also be dangerous. Transformational leaders also create an atmosphere of change, and they inspire followers not just to follow them personally but to believe in the vision of organizational transformation. Transformational leaders inspire followers to go beyond their own self-interest for the good of the whole.

All leaders use power and politics to influence people and accomplish goals. Power is the ability to influence others to reach desired outcomes. The best known types of power are legitimate, reward, expert, referent, and coercive, which are associated with a leader's position and personal qualities. Three distinct outcomes may result from the use of power: compliance, resistance, and commitment. The effective use of position power generally leads to follower compliance, whereas the excessive use of position power—particularly coercive power—may result in resistance. The follower response most often generated by personal power is commitment.

A key aspect of power is that it is a function of dependency, which is related to a person's control over resources. Dependency is greatest for resources that are highly important, scarce, and have no readily available substitutes. Leaders may gain power by contributing to the organization's purpose via interdepartmental dependencies, centrality, control over information, and coping with uncertainty.

Power is acquired, developed, and exercised through political activities. Leaders use a wide variety of influence tactics, but they fall within some broad categories based on general principles for asserting influence. Seven principles for asserting leader influence are rational persuasion, liking and friendliness, reciprocity, developing allies, direct appeal, scarcity, and formal authority. One important consideration for leaders is how to use power and politics ethically and responsibly. Ethical leaders use power to serve the organization's goals, respect the rights of individuals and groups, and strive to be fair in their dealings with others.

Discussion Questions

1. What do you consider the most important difference between transformational leadership and transactional leadership? Between transformational and charismatic leadership? How is transformational leadership similar to charismatic leadership? Discuss.

2. Why is charismatic leadership considered to have potentially negative consequences? Think of two or three current social, political, or business leaders that you would consider to be charismatic. To what extent do they display characteristics of socialized or personalized charisma?

3. Do you agree that politics is a natural and healthy part of organizational life? Discuss.

4. What types and sources of power would be available to a leader of a student government organization? To a head nurse in a small hospital?

5. Do you think impression management is an appropriate political approach for a business leader? Discuss. Can you name some ways in which you have personally used this tactic?

6. How does control over information give power to a person? Have you ever used control over information to influence a decision with friends or co-workers? Explain.

7. Describe ways in which you might increase your personal power.

8. Which of the seven influence tactics would you be most comfortable with as leader of a study group? Of a work team? Discuss.

9. Lord Acton, a British historian of the late 19th century, said that "power tends to corrupt; absolute power corrupts absolutely," suggesting that a person's sense of morality lessens as his or her power increases. Do you agree? Considering this idea, is it ethical for leaders to try to increase their power? Discuss.

Leadership at Work

Circle of Influence

How do you personally try to influence others? Think carefully about how you get others to agree with you or do something you want. Watch the way you influence others in a team, at home, or during your work. Make a list below of your influence tactics:

1. _____   4. _____
2. _____   5. _____
3. _____   6. _____

Of the influence and political tactics discussed in the chapter, which ones do you typically not use?

_____

_____

_____

During the next two days, your assignment is to (1) monitor the influence tactics you typically use, and (2) try one new tactic that you don't normally use. The new influence tactic you will try is: _____

_____

Another important concept is called the *circle of influence*. Think carefully about the people who have influence *over you*. These people are your circle of influence. You may have one circle of influence at work, another at home, and others for your social life or career. Write down the people who would have some influence over you at work or school:

_____

_____

This is your circle of influence.

A person's circle of influence can be important when you really want to influence that person. If the person doesn't respond to your normal influence attempts, think about identifying their circle of influence—the people who have influence over them. You can then influence people in the "circle" as an indirect way to influence the person you want to change.

Pick a person at work or school, or even your instructor, and plot out their circle of influence. List the key people you believe are in their circle of influence:

_____

_____

_____

How would you get more information on the person's true circle of influence?

_____

_____

_____

How can you use your knowledge of the person's circle to have influence over him/her? What are possible disadvantages of using this approach to influence someone?

_____

_____

_____

In Class: The instructor can ask students to sit in small groups of three to five people and share the circles of influence they identified for themselves. After listing the circle of influence at work or school, students can also talk about the circles of people who might influence them in their professional, social, or family activities. Key questions for this discussion are: What are the common themes in the students' circles of influence? When and how could the circle idea be applied to influence someone? How might it be misapplied and backfire on your effort to influence another?

Leadership Development: Cases for Analysis

The Unhealthy Hospital

When Bruce Reid was hired as Blake Memorial Hospital's new CEO, the mandate had been clear: Improve the quality of care, and set the financial house in order.

As Reid struggled to finalize his budget for approval at next week's board meeting, his attention kept returning to one issue—the future of six off-site clinics. The clinics had been set up six years earlier to provide primary health care to the community's poorer neighborhoods. Although they provided a valuable service, they also diverted funds away from Blake's in-house services, many of which were underfunded. Cutting hospital personnel and freezing salaries could affect Blake's quality of care, which was already slipping. Eliminating the clinics, on the other hand, would save $256,000 without compromising Blake's internal operations.

However, there would be political consequences. Clara Bryant, the recently appointed commissioner of health services, repeatedly insisted that the clinics were an essential service for the poor. Closing the clinics could also jeopardize Blake's access to city funds. Dr. Winston Lee, chief of surgery, argued forcefully for closing the off-site clinics and having shuttle buses bring patients to the hospital weekly. Dr. Susan Russell, the hospital's director of clinics, was equally vocal about Blake's responsibility to the community, and suggested an entirely new way of delivering health care: "A hospital is not a building," she said, "it's a service. And wherever the service is needed, that is where the hospital should be." In Blake's case, that meant funding *more* clinics. Russell wanted to create a network of neighborhood-based centers for all the surrounding neighborhoods, poor and middle income. Besides improving health care, the network would act as an inpatient referral system for hospital services. Reid considered the proposal: If a clinic network could tap the paying public and generate more inpatient business, it might be worth looking into. Blake's rival hospital, located on the affluent side of town, certainly wasn't doing anything that creative. Reid was concerned, however, that whichever way he decided, he was going to make enemies.

Source: Based on Anthony R. Kovner, "The Case of the Unhealthy Hospital," *Harvard Business Review* (September– October 1991), pp. 12–25.

QUESTIONS

1. What sources of power does Reid have in this situation? Do you believe using legitimate power to implement a decision would have a positive effect at Blake Memorial? Discuss.

2. What influence tactics might you use if you were in Reid's position?

3. Do you see ways in which Reid might use the ideas of transformational leadership to help resolve this dilemma?

Waite Pharmaceuticals

Amelia Lassiter is chief information officer at Waite Pharmaceuticals, a large California-based company. In an industry where it generally takes $500 million and 10 to 12 years to bring a new drug to market, companies such as Waite are always looking for ways to increase productivity and speed things up. After about eight months on the job, Lassiter suggested to company president James Hsu that Waite implement a new global knowledge-sharing application that promises to cut development time and costs in half. She has done extensive research on knowledge-sharing systems, and has talked closely with an IT director at global powerhouse Novartis, a company on the cutting edge in pharmaceuticals and animal health care, as well as other diverse products. The Novartis director believes the knowledge-sharing system plays an important role in that company's competitiveness.

Hsu presented the idea to the board of directors, and everyone agreed to pursue the project. He has asked Lassiter to investigate firms that could assist Waite's IT department in developing and implementing a global knowledge-sharing application that would be compatible with Waite's existing systems. Hsu explained that he wants to present the information to the board of directors for a decision next month.

Lassiter identified three major firms that she believed could handle the work and took a summary of her findings to Hsu's office, where she was greeted by Lucy Lee, a young, petite, attractive woman who served as a sort of executive assistant to Hsu. Word was that the relationship between Lee and Hsu was totally proper, but besides the value of her good looks, no one in the company could understand why she was working there. Her lack of talent and experience made her a liability more than a help. She was very deferential to Hsu, but condescending to everyone else. Lee was a constant source of irritation and ill will among managers throughout the company, but there was no doubt that the only way to get to Hsu was through Lucy Lee. Lee took the information from Lassiter and promised the president would review it within two days.

The next afternoon, Hsu called Lassiter to his office and asked why Standard Systems, a small local consulting firm, was not being considered as a potential provider. Lassiter was surprised—Standard was known primarily for helping small companies computerize their accounting systems. She was not aware that they had done any work related to knowledge-sharing applications, particularly on a global basis. Upon further investigation into the company, she learned that Standard was owned by an uncle of Lucy Lee's, and things began to fall into place. Fortunately, she also learned that the firm did have some limited experience in more complex applications. She tried to talk privately with Hsu about his reasons for wanting to consider Standard, but Hsu insisted that Lee participate in all his internal meetings. At their most recent meeting, Hsu insisted that Standard be included for possible consideration by the board.

During the next two weeks, representatives from each company met with Hsu, his two top executives, and the IT staff to explain their services and give demonstrations. Lassiter had suggested that the board of directors attend these presentations, but Hsu said they wouldn't have the time and he would need to evaluate everything and make a recommendation to the board. At the end of these meetings, Lassiter prepared a final report evaluating the pros and cons of going with each firm and making her first and second-choice recommendations. Standard was dead last on her list. Although the firm had some excellent people and a good reputation, it was simply not capable of handling such a large and complex project.

Lassiter offered to present her findings to the board, but again, Hsu declined her offer in the interest of time. "It's best if I present them with a final recommendation; that way, we can move on to other matters without getting bogged down with a lot of questions and discussion. These are busy people." The board meeting was held the following week. Lassiter was shocked when the president returned from the meeting and informed her that the board had decided to go with Standard Systems as the consulting firm for the knowledge-sharing application.

Sources: Based on "Restview Hospital," in Gary Yukl, *Leadership,* 4th ed. (Upper Saddle River, NJ: Prentice Hall, 1998), pp. 203–204; "Did Somebody Say Infrastructure?" in Polly Schneider, "Another Trip to Hell," *CIO,* (February 15, 2000), pp. 71–78; and Joe Kay, "Digital Diary," Part I, http://*www.forbes.com/asap/2000/*, accessed on November 19, 2000.

QUESTIONS

1. How would you explain the board's selection of Standard Systems?

2. Discuss the types, sources, and relative amount of power for the three main characters in this story.

3. How might Lassiter have increased her power and influence over this decision? If you were in her position, what would you do now?

References

1 John Brant, "What One Man Can Do," *Inc.* (September 2005), pp. 145–153.

2 The terms transactional and transformational leadership are from James MacGregor Burns, *Leadership* (New York: Harper & Row, 1978), and Bernard M. Bass, "Leadership: Good, Better, Best," *Organizational Dynamics* 13 (Winter 1985), pp. 26–40.

3 Bernard M. Bass, "Theory of Transformational Leadership Redux," *Leadership Quarterly* 6, no. 4 (1995), pp. 463–478; Noel M. Tichy and Mary Anne Devanna, *The Transformational Leader* (New York: John Wiley & Sons, 1986); and Badrinarayan Shankar Pawar and Kenneth K. Eastman, "The Nature and Implications of Contextual Influences on Transformational Leadership: A Conceptual Examination," *Academy of Management Review* 22, no. 1 (1997), pp. 80–109.

4 Taly Dvir, Dov Eden, Bruce J. Avolio, and Boas Shamir, "Impact of Transformational Leadership on Follower Development and Performance: A Field Experiment," *Academy of Management Journal* 45, no. 4 (2002), pp. 735–744.

5 Robert S. Rubin, David C. Munz, and William H. Bommer, "Leading From Within: The Effects of Emotion Recognition and Personality on Transformational Leadership Behavior," *Academy of Management Journal* 48, no 5 (2005), pp. 845–858; and Timothy A. Judge and Joyce E. Bono, "Five-Factor Model of Personality and Transformational Leadership," *Journal of Applied Psychology* 85, no. 5 (October 2000), p. 751ff.

6 Rubin et al., "Leading From Within."

7 Based on Bernard M. Bass, "Theory of Transformational Leadership Redux," *Leadership Quarterly* 6, no. 4 (Winter 1995), pp. 463–478, and "From Transactional to Transformational Leadership: Learning to Share the Vision," *Organizational Dynamics* 18, no. 3 (Winter 1990), pp. 19–31; Francis J. Yammarino, William D. Spangler, and Bernard M. Bass, "Transformational Leadership and Performance: A Longitudinal Investigation," *Leadership Quarterly* 4, no. 1 (Spring 1993), pp. 81–102; and B. M. Bass, "Current Developments in Transformational Leadership," *The Psychologist-Manager Journal* 3, no. 1 (1999), pp. 5–21.

8 Noel M. Tichy and Mary Anne Devanna, *The Transformational Leader* (New York: John Wiley & Sons, 1986), pp. 265–266.

9 Manfred F. R. Kets De Vries, "Charisma in Action: The Transformational Abilities of Virgin's Richard Branson and ABB's Percy Barnevik," *Organizational Dynamics,* (Winter 1998), pp. 7–21.

10 Daniel J. Lynch, "Thanks to Its CEO, UPS Doesn't Just Deliver; Up-Through-the-Ranks Eskew Oversees New Directions," *USA Today* (July 24, 2006), p. B1; Paul B. Brown, "What I Know Now," *Fast Company* (November 2005), p. 108; and John Murawski, "UPS Working as One," *News & Observer* (September 25, 2005), p. E1.

11 Brown, "What I Know Now."

12 Rakesh Khurana, "The Curse of the Superstar CEO," *Harvard Business Review* (September 2002), pp. 60–66.

13 Katherine J. Klein and Robert J. House, "On Fire: Charismatic Leadership and Levels of Analysis," *Leadership Quarterly* 6, no. 2 (1995), pp. 183–198.

14 Patricia Sellers, "What Exactly is Charisma?" *Fortune* (January 15, 1996), pp. 68–75.

15 Gretel C. Kovach, "Moderate Muslim Voice Falls Silent: Charismatic Young Leader Leaves Egypt As His Popular Sermons Come Under Government Scrutiny," *The Christian Science Monitor* (November 26, 2002), p. 6; Selena Roberts, "U.S.O.C. Elects Former Maytag Chairman as Chief," *The New York Times* (October 21, 2001), p. D7.

16 Keith H. Hammonds, "You Can't Lead Without Making Sacrifices," *Fast Company,* (June 2001), pp. 106–116.

17 Jay A. Conger, Rabindra N. Kanungo and Associates, *Charismatic Leadership: The Elusive Factor in Organizational Effectiveness* (San Francisco: Jossey-Bass, 1988); Robert J. House and Jane M. Howell, "Personality and Charismatic Leadership," *Leadership Quarterly* 3, no. 2 (1992), pp. 81–108; Klein and House, "On Fire: Charismatic Leadership and Levels of Analysis"; and Harold B. Jones, "Magic, Meaning, and Leadership: Weber's Model and the Empirical Literature," *Human Relations* 54, no. 6 (June 2001), pp. 753–771.

18 The following discussion is based primarily on Conger et al., *Charismatic Leadership*.

19 Boas Shamir, Michael B. Arthur, and Robert J. House, "The Rhetoric of Charismatic Leadership: A Theoretical Extension, A Case Study, and Implications for Future Research," *Leadership Quarterly* 5, no. 1 (1994), pp. 25–42.

20 Richard L. Daft and Robert H. Lengel, *Fusion Leadership: Unlocking the Subtle Forces that Change People and Organizations* (San Francisco: Berrett-Koehler, 1998), p. 169.

21 Rakesh Khurana, "The Curse of the Superstar CEO," *Harvard Business Review,* (September 2002), pp. 60–66; Joseph A. Raelin, "The Myth of Charismatic Leaders," *Training & Development* 57, no. 3 (March 2003), p. 46; and Janice M. Beyer, "Taming and Promoting Charisma to Change Organizations," *Leadership Quarterly* 10, no. 2 (1999), pp. 307–330.

22 Robert J. House and Jane M. Howell, "Personality and Charismatic Leadership," *Leadership Quarterly* 3, no. 2 (1992), pp. 81–108; and Jennifer O'Connor, Michael D. Mumford, Timothy C. Clifton, Theodore L. Gessner, and Mary Shane Connelly, "Charismatic Leaders and Destructiveness: An Historiometric Study," *Leadership Quarterly* 6, no. 4 (1995), pp. 529–555.

23 O'Connor et. al. "Charismatic Leaders and Destructiveness."

24 James MacGregor Burns, *Leadership* (New York: Harper & Row, 1978); and Earle Hitchner, "The Power to Get Things Done," *National Productivity Review* 12 (Winter 1992/93), pp. 117–122.

25 Robert A. Dahl, "The Concept of Power," *Behavioral Science* 2 (1957), pp. 201–215.

26 W. Graham Astley and Paramijit S. Pachdeva, "Structural Sources of Intraorganizational Power: A Theoretical Synthesis," *Academy of Management Review* 9 (1984), pp. 104–113; and Abraham Kaplan, "Power in Perspective," in Robert L. Kahn and Elise Boulding, eds., *Power and Conflict in Organizations* (London: Tavistock, 1964), pp. 11–32.

27 Gerald R. Salancik and Jeffrey Pfeffer, "The Bases and Use of Power in Organizational Decision Making: The Case of the University," *Administrative Science Quarterly* 19 (1974), pp. 453–473.

28 Earle Hitchner, "The Power to Get Things Done."

29 John R. P. French, Jr. and Bertram Raven, "The Bases of Social Power," in *Group Dynamics,* D. Cartwright and A. F. Zander, eds. (Evanston, IL: Row Peterson, 1960), pp. 607–623.

30 Jeffrey Pfeffer, *Power in Organizations* (Marshfield, MA: Pitman Publishing, 1981).

31 Erik W. Larson and Jonathan B. King, "The Systemic Distortion of Information: An Ongoing Challenge to Management," *Organizational Dynamics,* 24, no. 3 (Winter 1996), pp. 49–61; Thomas H. Davenport, Robert G. Eccles, and Lawrence Prusak, "Information Politics," *Sloan Management Review* (Fall 1992), pp. 53–65.

32 Gary A. Yukl and T. Taber, "The Effective Use of Managerial Power," *Personnel* (March–April 1983), pp. 37–44.

33 Carol Hymowitz, "The Best Leaders Have Employees Who Would Follow Them Anywhere," (In the Lead column), *The Wall Street Journal* (February 10, 2004), p. B1.

34 R. E. Emerson, "Power-Dependence Relations," *American Sociological Review* 27 (1962), pp. 31–41.

35 Carol Hymowitz, "Managers Are Starting to Gain More Clout Over Their Employees," (In the Lead column), *The Wall Street Journal* (January 30, 2001), p. B1.

36 Henry Mintzberg, *Power In and Around Organizations* (Englewood Cliffs, NJ: Prentice-Hall, 1963).

37 Lauren Tara LaCapra, "Ireland Taps U.S. to Fill Need for Skilled Workers," *The Wall Street Journal* (October 31, 2006), p. B4.

38 Jeffrey Pfeffer, *Managing with Power: Politics and Influence in Organizations* (Boston: Harvard University Press, 1992); Gerald R. Salancik and Jeffrey Pfeffer, "Who Gets Power—and How They Hold onto It: A Strategic Contingency Model of Power," *Organizational Dynamics* (Winter 1977), pp. 3–21; Pfeffer, *Power in Organizations;* Carol Stoak Saunders, "The Strategic Contingencies Theory of Power: Multiple Perspectives," *Journal of Management Studies* 27 (1990), pp. 1–18.

39 Michel Crozier, *The Bureaucratic Phenomenon* (Chicago: University of Chicago Press, 1964).

40 Carrick Mollenkamp, Jesse Eisinger, and Clint Riley, "Boardroom Survivor; Behind Sovereign's Growth: A Chief Who Plays Hardball," *The Wall Street Journal* (November 25, 2005), pp. A1, A6.

41 Larson and King, "The Systemic Distortion of Information;" and Davenport, Eccles, and Prusak, "Information Politics."

42 D. J. Hickson, C. R. Hinings, C. A. Lee, R. C. Schneck, and J. M. Pennings, "A Strategic Contingencies Theory of Intraorganizational Power," *Administrative Science Quarterly* 16 (1971): pp. 216–229.

43 Stephen P. Robbins, *Organizational Behavior,* 8th ed. (Upper Saddle River, NJ: Prentice Hall, 1998), p. 401.

44 Jeffrey Pfeffer and Gerald Salancik, "Organizational Decision Making as a Political Process: The Case of a University Budget," *Administrative Science Quarterly* (1974), pp. 135–151.

45 Hickson, et al., "Strategic Contingencies Theory."

46 Barbara Martinez, "Strong Medicine; With New Muscle, Hospitals Sqeeze Insurers on Rates," *The Wall Street Journal* (April 12, 2002), p. A1; James V. DeLong, "Rule of Law: Just What Crime Did Columbia/HCA Commit?" *The Wall Street Journal* (August 20, 1997), A15; and Lucette Lagnado, "House Panel Begins Inquiry Into Hospital Billing Practices," *The Wall Street Journal* (July 17, 2003), p. B1.

47 Allan R. Cohen, Stephen L. Fink, Herman Gadon, and Robin D. Willits, *Effective Behavior in Organizations,* 7th ed. (New York: McGraw-Hill Irwin, 2001), p. 264; Rosabeth Moss Kanter, *Men and Women of the Corporation* (New York: Basic Books, 1977).

48 Pfeffer, *Power in Organizations,* p. 70.

49 Gerald R. Ferris, Darren C. Treadway, Robert W. Kolodinsky, Wayne A. Hochwarter, Charles J. Kacmar, Ceasar Douglas, and Dwight D. Frink, "Development and Validation of the Political Skill Inventory," *Journal of Management* 31, no. 1 (February 2005), pp. 126–152.

50 Laura Meckler, "Flight Plan; Amid Turbulence, FAA's Mr. Chew Fights Bureaucracy," *The Wall Street Journal* (January 30, 2006), pp. A1, A16.

51 See Amy J. Hillman and Michael A. Hitt, "Corporate Political Strategy Formulation: A Model of Approach, Participation, and Strategy Decisions," *Academy of Management Review* 24, no. 4 (1999), pp. 825–842, for a recent examination of organizational approaches to political action.

52 Anne Fisher, "Ask Annie: Studying in Charm School, and Meeting Laggards," *Fortune* (June 7, 1999), p. 226.

53 Hal Lancaster, "For Some Managers, Hitting Middle Age Brings Uncertainties," *The Wall Street Journal* (April 20, 1999), p. B1.

54 Sherry E. Moss, Enzo R. Valenzi, and William Taggart, "Are You Hiding From Your Boss? The Development of a Taxonoomy and Instrument to Assess the Feedback Management Behaviors of Good and Bad Performers," *Journal of Management* 29, no. 4 (2003), pp. 487–510.

55 John R. Carlson, Dawn S. Carlson, and Lori L. Wadsworth, "The Relationship Between Individual Power Moves and Group Agreement Type: An Examination and Model," *SAM Advanced Management Journal* (Autumn 2000), pp. 44–51.

56 D. Kipnis, S. M. Schmidt, C. Swaffin-Smith, and I. Wilkinson, "Patterns of Managerial Influence: Shotgun Managers, Tacticians, and Bystanders," *Organizational Dynamics* (Winter 1984), pp. 58–67.

57 Ibid., and Pfeffer, *Managing with Power,* Chapter 13.

58 This discussion is based partly on Robert B. Cialdini, "Harnessing the Science of Persuasion," *Harvard Business Review* (October 2001), pp. 72–79.

59 Judith Tingley, *The Power of Indirect Influence* (New York: AMACOM, 2001), as reported by Martha Craumer, "When the Direct Approach Backfires, Try Indirect Influence," *Harvard Management Communication Letter* (June 2001), pp. 3–4.

60 Cialdini, "Harnessing the Science of Persuasion."

61 Allan R. Cohen and David L. Bradford, "The Influence Model: Using Reciprocity and Exchange to Get What You Need," *Journal of Organizational Excellence* (Winter 2005), pp. 57–80.

62 Pfeffer, *Power in Organizations,* p. 70.

63 V. Dallas Merrell, *Huddling: The Informal Way to Management Success* (New York: AMACON, 1979).

64 Ceasar Douglas and Anthony P. Ammeter, "An Examination of Leader Political Skill and Its Effect on Ratings of Leader Effectiveness," *Leadership Quarterly* 15 (2004), pp. 537–550.

65 Charles Gasparino and Anita Raghavan, "Survivor: How Dean Witter Boss Got the Upper Hand in Merger with Morgan," *The Wall Street Journal* (March 22, 2001), pp. A1, A6.

66 Bethany McLean and Andy Serwer, "Brahmins at the Gate," *Fortune* (May 2, 2005), pp. 59–68; Ann Davis, "Closing Bell; How Tide Turned Against Purcell In Struggle at Morgan Stanley," *The Wall Street Journal* (June 14, 2005), pp. A1, A11; and Randall Smith and Ann Davis, "Purcell Deputy Backed Effort to Make Peace," *The Wall Street Journal* (April 19, 2005), p. C1.

67 Greg Ip, Kate Kelly, Susanne Craig, and Ianthe Jeanne Dugan, "A Bull's Market; Dick Grasso's NYSE Legacy: Buffed Image, Shaky Foundation," *The Wall Street Journal* (December 30, 2003), pp. A1, A6; Yochi J. Dreazen and Christopher Cooper, "Lingering Presence; Behind the Scenes, U.S. Tightens Grip on Iraq's Future," *The Wall Street Journal* (May 13, 2004), A1.

68 Richard L. Daft, *Organization Theory and Design,* 6th ed. (Cincinnati, OH: South-Western, 1998), Chapter 12.

69 Cialdini, "Harnessing the Science of Persuasion."

70 Robert B. Cialdini, *Influence: Science and Practice,* 4th ed. (Boston: Pearson Allyn & Bacon, 2000).

71 Quoted in Cohen, Fink, Gadon, and Willits, *Effective Behavior in Organizations,* p. 254.

72 Jared Sandberg, "Sabotage 101: The Sinister Art of Back-Stabbing," *The Wall Street Journal* (February 11, 2004), p. B1.

73 For a discussion of personalized and socialized power, see David C. McClelland, *Power: The Inner Experience* (New York: Irvington, 1975).

74 "Stop the Politics," *Forbes ASAP* (April 3, 2000), p. 126.

PART 5
The Leader as Social Architect

Getty Images

Chapter 13

Your Leadership Challenge

After reading this chapter, you should be able to:

- Explain the relationship among vision, mission, strategy, and implementation mechanisms.

- Create your personal leadership vision.

- Use the common themes of powerful visions in your life and work.

- Describe four basic approaches for framing a noble purpose that followers can believe in.

- Understand how leaders formulate and implement strategy.

- Apply the elements of effective strategy.

Chapter Outline

Creating Vision and Strategic Direction

Burt Rutan was a teenager when President John F. Kennedy set for NASA a clear and visionary goal of putting a man on the moon by the end of the decade. In July of 1969, he watched along with millions around the world as that vision became a reality. Nearly 40 years later, Rutan has his own ambitious vision: to make human space flight as routine as airplane travel. Rutan has pulled off extraordinary accomplishments by bucking conventional wisdom about aerodynamics and inspiring people to do things differently. In the 1980s, his company, Scaled Composites, gained international acclaim for Voyager, a twin-engine propeller plane that completed his vision for the first nonstop flight around the world without refueling. But when Rutan first announced to his 125 or so employees his vision of building a space craft, chief engineer Michael Gionta recalls that it was overwhelming. "We had done low-speed subsonic flight for 17 years. What did we know about going to space?" But the vision was so powerful and energizing that every single employee at Scaled Composites wanted a chance to contribute to the space project.

In October of 2004, SpaceShipOne landed in the Mojave Desert after having carried humans to space twice within a week, earning its owners the $10 million Ansari-X prize, which was set up to encourage non–government-funded development of manned space travel. It marked the first time a private business successfully launched humans into space. Space fanatic Paul Allen backed the original spacecraft, setting up a separate company called Mojave Aerospace Ventures, which owns the technology. Virgin Atlantic's Richard Branson has since contracted with the company to move to the next step of producing a space airliner, called Virgin Galactic, for which tickets have already gone on sale.

SpaceShipOne is a small step, and there are significant hurdles to overcome before routine space travel becomes a reality. But Rutan's passion for the vision is infectious, and the excitement generated by the Ansari-X prize may open the door to an entire space tourism industry and change the way we think about the universe.[1]

One of the most important functions of a leader is to articulate and communicate a compelling vision that will motivate and energize people toward the future. The vision of routine space travel is out of the ordinary, but so was Kennedy's idea of putting a man on the moon in 1961. Both illustrate how inspiring and energizing an idealistic vision can be. Good leaders are always looking forward, setting a course for the future and getting everyone moving in the same direction. Lorraine Monroe, former principal of the renowned Frederick Douglass Academy in Harlem and founder of the Lorraine Monroe Leadership Institute, refers to a leader as "the drum major, the person who keeps a vision in front of people and reminds them of what they're about." People naturally "gravitate toward leaders who have a vision," Monroe says. "When people see that you love your work, they want to catch your energy."[2]

Follower motivation and energy are crucial to the success of any endeavor; the role of leadership is to focus everyone's energy on the same path. At City Bank, the predecessor of Citigroup, leaders energized employees with a vision of becoming "the most powerful, the most serviceable, the most far-reaching world financial institution that has ever been." That vision, first articulated in 1915 by a small regional bank, motivated and inspired generations of employees until it was eventually achieved.[3]

In this chapter, we first provide an overview of the leader's role in creating the organization's future. Then, we examine what vision is, the underlying themes that are common to effective visions, and how vision works on multiple levels. The distinction between vision and the organization's mission is also explained. We then discuss how leaders formulate vision and strategy and the leader's contribution to achieving the vision. The last section discusses the impact this leadership has on organizations.

Strategic Leadership

Superior organizational performance is not a matter of luck. It is determined largely by the choices leaders make. Top leaders are responsible for knowing the organization's environment, considering what it might be like in 5 or 10 years, and setting a direction for the future that everyone can believe in. Strategic leadership is one of the most critical issues facing organizations.[4] **Strategic leadership** means the ability to anticipate and envision the future, maintain flexibility, think strategically, and work with others to initiate changes that will create a competitive advantage for the organization in the future.[5] In a fast-changing world, leaders are faced with a bewildering array of complex and ambiguous information, and no two leaders will see things the same way or make the same choices.

Strategic leadership
the ability to anticipate and envision the future, maintain flexibility, think strategically, and initiate changes that will create a competitive advantage for the organization in the future

The complexity of the environment and the uncertainty of the future can overwhelm a leader. Thus, many are inclined to focus on internal organizational issues rather than strategic activities. It is easier and more comforting for leaders to deal with routine, operational issues where they can see instant results and feel a sense of control. In addition, many leaders today are inundated with information and overwhelmed by minutiae. They may have difficulty finding the quiet time needed for "big-picture thinking." One study looked at the time executives in various departments spend on long-term, strategic activities and found discouraging results. In the companies studied, 84 percent of finance executives' time, 70 percent of information technology executives' time, and 76 percent of operational managers' time is focused on routine, day-to-day activities.[6] Another study found that, on average, senior executives spend less than 3 percent of their energy on building a corporate perspective for the future, and in some companies, the average is less than 1 percent.[7] Yet no organization can thrive for the long term without a clear viewpoint and framework for the future.

> **Action Memo**
> As a leader, you can learn to think strategically. You can anticipate and envision the future, and initiate changes that can help the group or organization thrive over the long term.

Exhibit 13.1 illustrates the levels that make up the domain of strategic leadership. Strategic leadership is responsible for the relationship of the external environment to choices about vision, mission, strategy, and their implementation.[8] At the top of Exhibit 13.1 is a clear, compelling vision of where the organization wants to be in 5 to 10 years. The vision reflects the environment and works in concert with the company's mission—its core values, purpose, and reason for existence. Strategy provides direction for translating the vision into action and is the basis for the development of specific mechanisms to help the organization achieve goals. Strategies are intentions, whereas implementation is through the basic organization architecture (structure, incentives) that makes things happen. Each level of the hierarchy in Exhibit 13.1 supports the level above it. Each part of this framework will be discussed in the remainder of this chapter.

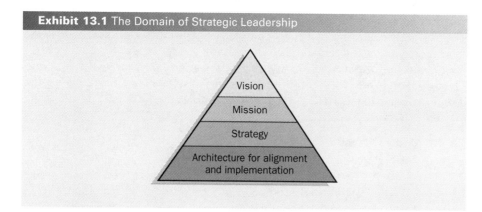

Exhibit 13.1 The Domain of Strategic Leadership

Leadership Vision

A vision can be thought of as a dream for the future. Stanford R. Ovshinsky spent 40 years pursuing his dream of making giant sheets of thin photovoltaic material that can convert sunlight to electricity, and making them cheaply enough that solar can compete with fossil fuels. "I said we were going to make it by the mile," the 84-year-old Ovshinsky says. "Nobody believed me [at first], not even in my own company." Today, Energy Conversion Devices uses a mammoth machine the size of a football field to spool out long thin sheets of solar material that is used on the roofs of homes and businesses. Even running at full capacity, the factory can't keep up with the orders.[9]

A vision is also more than a dream—it is an ambitious view of the future that everyone involved can believe in, one that can realistically be achieved, yet one that offers a future that is better in important ways than what now exists. For organizations, a **vision** is an attractive, ideal future that is credible yet not readily attainable. In the 1950s, Sony Corporation wanted to "[b]ecome the company most known for changing the worldwide poor-quality image of Japanese products."[10] Since that time, Japanese companies have become known for quality, but in the 1950s this was a highly ambitious goal that fired people's imaginations and sense of national pride. Sometimes, visions are brief, compelling, and slogan-like, easily communicated to and understood by everyone in the organization. For example, Coca-Cola's "A Coke within arm's reach of everyone on the planet" and Komatsu's "Encircle Caterpillar" serve to motivate all employees. William Wrigley Jr., the fourth-generation leader of Wm. R. Wrigley, Jr. Company, crafted the slogan, "Wrigley brands woven into the fabric of everyday life around the world," to capture the company's vision of moving beyond chewing gum such as Juicy Fruit to become a broader food and confectionery company competitive with Europe's Cadbury Schweppes.[11]

Exhibit 13.2 lists a few more brief vision statements that let people know where the organization wants to go in the future. Not all successful organizations have such short, easily communicated slogans, but their visions are powerful because leaders paint a compelling picture of where the organization wants to go. The vision expressed by civil rights leader Martin Luther King Jr. in his "I Have a Dream" speech is a good example of how leaders paint a vision in words. King articulated a vision of racial harmony, where discrimination was nonexistent, and he conveyed the confidence and conviction that his vision would someday be achieved.

Action Memo
Go to Leader's Self-Insight 13.1 on page 390 and answer the questions to learn where you stand with respect to a personal vision.

Vision
an attractive, ideal future that is credible yet not readily attainable

How much do you think about the positive outcomes you want in your future? Do you have a personal vision for your life? Indicate whether each item below is Mostly False or Mostly True for you.

	Mostly False	Mostly True
1. I can describe a compelling image of my future.	_____	_____
2. Life to me seems more exciting than routine.	_____	_____
3. I have created very clear life goals and aims.	_____	_____
4. I feel that my personal existence is very meaningful.	_____	_____
5. In my life, I see a reason for being here.	_____	_____
6. I have discovered a satisfying "calling" in life.	_____	_____
7. I feel that I have a unique life purpose to fulfill.	_____	_____
8. I will know when I will have achieved my purpose.	_____	_____
9. I talk to people about my personal vision.	_____	_____
10. I know how to harness my creativity and use my talents.	_____	_____

Scoring and Interpretation

Add the number of Mostly True answers above for your score: _____. A score of 7 or above indicates that you are in great shape with respect to a personal vision. A score of 3 or below would suggest that you have not given much thought to a vision for your life. A score of 4–8 would be about average.

Creating a personal vision is difficult work for most people. It doesn't happen easily or naturally. A personal vision is just like an organizational vision in that it requires focused thought and effort. Spend some time thinking about a vision for yourself and write it down.

Source: The ideas for this questionnaire were drawn primarily from Chris Rogers, "Are You Deciding on Purpose?" *Fast Company* (February/March 1998), pp. 114–117; and J. Crumbaugh, Cross-Validation of a Purpose-in-Life Test Based on Frankl's Concepts. *Journal of Individual Psychology*, 24 (1968), pp. 74–81.

Exhibit 13.2 Examples of Brief Vision Statements

Motorola: Become the premier company in the world.

Ritz-Carlton (Amelia Island) engineering department: To boldly go where no hotel has gone before—free of all defects.

Johnson Controls Inc.: Continually exceed our customers' increasing expectations.

New York City Transit: No graffiti.

Texas Commerce Bank: Eliminate what annoys our bankers and our customers.

BP: Beyond Petroleum.

Egon Zehnder: Be the worldwide leader in executive search.

Sources: Examples from Jon R. Katzenbach and the RCL Team, *Real Change Leaders: How You Can Create Growth and High Performance in Your Company* (New York: Times Business, 1995), pp. 68–70; Andrew Campbell and Sally Yeung, "Creating a Sense of Mission," *Long Range Planning*, (August, 1991), pp. 10–20; Alan Farnham, "State Your Values, Hold the Hot Air," *Fortune* (April 19, 1993), pp. 117–124; and Christopher K. Bart, "Sex, Lies, and Mission Statements," *Business Horizons* (November–December 1997), pp. 23–28.

Strong, inspiring visions have been associated with higher organizational performance.[12] When people are encouraged by a picture of what the organization can be in the future, they can help take it there. Recall from the previous chapter that vision is an important aspect of transformational leadership. Transformational leaders typically articulate visions that present a highly optimistic view of the future and express high confidence that the better future can be realized.[13] Leaders at the Greater Chicago Food Depository have a vision of transforming the nonprofit agency from an organization that just feeds the hungry to one that helps end hunger.

Michael P. Mulqueen and Kate Maehr, Greater Chicago Food Depository

It has been referred to as "culinary boot camp," an intense 12-week program aimed at teaching low-income, low-skilled workers the basics of cooking, along with life skills such as punctuality, teamwork, commitment, and personal responsibility, with the goal of landing each person a good job.

The Community Kitchens chef-training program was begun in 1998 by Michael Mulqueen, who was then executive director of the Greater Chicago Food Depository, based on a concept originated at a Washington, D.C. soup kitchen. Mulqueen, a former Brigadier General in the U.S. Marine Corps, set the agency toward a vision of solving the problem of hunger by moving people out of poverty, not just giving hungry people a meal.

While in the training program, participants prepare about 1,500 meals a day that are served in after-school programs around the city that give low-income children an alternative to gangs and drugs. Executive Chef Instructor Lisa Gershenson, who acts as a counselor and cheerleader as well as a teacher for Community Kitchens, had grown bored and cynical in her previous job as owner of a company that catered to the well-to-do. She calls the Community Kitchens job the "perfect antidote" to her cynicism of being a chef.

Under Mulqueen's leadership, the Greater Chicago Food Depository graduated around 300 people from Community Kitchens, with almost all of them finding jobs soon after leaving. Some 63 percent stayed in their positions for at least a year, a high number in a typically high-turnover industry. "For those who succeed," says current executive director Kate Maehr, "this is the beginning of the end of the cycle of poverty."[14]

Poverty is a big problem, and its causes are many and complex. Yet one thing is clear: As Mike Mulqueen points out, people can't begin to move out of poverty unless they can get good jobs. The vision of helping people change their lives has energized employees at the Greater Chicago Food Depository in a way that simply providing food to low-income clients never did.

Vision is just as important for nonprofit agencies like the Greater Chicago Food Depository, the United Way and the Salvation Army as it is for businesses such as Coca-Cola, Google, or General Electric. Indeed, some have argued that nonprofits need vision even more than do businesses, since they operate without the regular feedback provided by profit and loss.[15]

In Exhibit 13.3, vision is shown as a guiding star, drawing everyone along the same path toward the future. Vision is based in the current reality but is concerned with a future that is substantially different from the status quo.[16] Taking the group or organization along this path requires leadership. Compare this to rational management (as described in Chapter 1), which leads to the status quo.

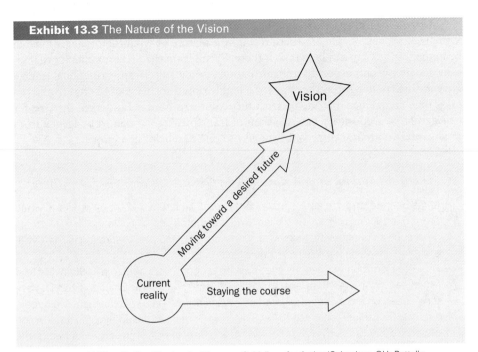

Exhibit 13.3 The Nature of the Vision

Source: Based on William D. Hitt, *The Leader-Manager: Guidelines for Action* (Columbus, OH: Battelle Press, 1988).

What Vision Does

Vision works in a number of important ways. An effective vision provides a link between today and tomorrow, serves to energize and motivate employees toward the future, provides meaning for people's work, and sets a standard of excellence and integrity in the organization.[17]

Vision Links the Present to the Future Vision connects what is going on right now with what the organization aspires to. A vision is always about the future, but it begins with the here and now. Consider the Microsoft advertising slogan, "Your potential inspires us to create products that help you reach it." Microsoft employees create software products that help meet current needs, but they also strive to envision and create products that might encourage other, broader applications for the future. Similarly, at the Wm. R. Wrigley, Jr. Company, described earlier, leaders aren't abandoning the company's leading global position in chewing gum, which still accounts for 90 percent of sales. However, to achieve the broader vision, they are pushing people to take risks and think about such questions as "What else is out there?" "Who are we competing with?" and "Why can't we do some of that too?"

In organizations, the pressures to meet deadlines, make the big sale, solve immediate problems, and complete specific projects are very real. Some have suggested that today's leaders need "bifocal vision," the ability to take care of the needs of today and meet current obligations while also aiming toward dreams for the future.[18] The ability to operate on both levels can be seen in

Visionary Leadership

Getty Images

Think about a situation in which you either assumed or were given a leadership role in a group. Imagine your own behavior as a leader. To what extent do the following statements characterize your leadership? Indicate whether each item below is Mostly False or Mostly True for you.

	Mostly False	Mostly True
1. I have a clear understanding of where we are going.	_____	_____
2. I work to get others committed to our desired future.	_____	_____
3. I initiate discussion with others about the kind of future I would like us to create together.	_____	_____
4. I show others how their interests can be realized by working toward a common vision.	_____	_____
5. I look ahead and forecast what I expect in the future.	_____	_____
6. I make certain that the activities I manage are broken down into manageable chunks.	_____	_____
7. I seek future challenges for the group.	_____	_____
8. I spend time and effort making certain that people adhere to the values and outcomes that have been agreed on.	_____	_____
9. I inspire others with my ideas for the future.	_____	_____
10. I give special recognition when others' work is consistent with the vision.	_____	_____

Scoring and Interpretation

The odd-numbered questions pertain to creating a vision for the group. The even-numbered questions pertain to implementing the vision. Calculate your score for each set of questions. Which score is higher? Compare your scores with other students.

This questionnaire pertains to two dimensions of visionary leadership. Creating the vision has to do with whether you think about the future, whether you are excited about the future, and whether you engage others in the future. Implementing the vision is about the extent to which you communicate, allocate the work, and provide rewards for activities that achieve the vision. Which of the two dimensions is easier for you? Are your scores consistent with your understanding of your own strengths and weaknesses? What might you do to improve your scores?

a number of successful companies, such as DuPont. Top executives routinely review short-term operational goals with managers throughout the company, reflecting a focus on the present. However, DuPont has succeeded over the long haul because of its leaders' ability to look to the future and shift gears quickly to take advantage of new opportunities. Since its beginning, DuPont's business portfolio has shifted from gunpowder to specialty chemicals, and today, the company is moving into biotechnology and life sciences.[19]

Vision Energizes People and Garners Commitment People want to feel enthusiastic about their work. Many people commit their time and energy voluntarily to causes they believe in—a political campaign, community events, or environmental causes, for example. These same people often leave their energy and enthusiasm at home when they go to work, because they don't have anything to inspire them. People are not generally willing to make emotional commitments just for the sake of increasing profits and enhancing shareholder wealth. Vision needs to transcend the bottom line because people are willing, and even eager, to commit to something truly worthwhile, something that makes life better for others or improves their communities.[20] Consider Henry Ford's original vision for Ford Motor Company:

I will build a motor car for the great multitude. . . . It will be so low in price that no man making a good salary will be unable to own one and enjoy with his family the blessings of hours of pleasure in God's open spaces. . . . When I'm through, everybody will be able to afford one, and everyone will have one. The horse will have disappeared from our highways, the automobile will be taken for granted [and we will give many people] employment at good wages.[21]

Action Memo

As a leader, you can frame a vision that sets a standard of excellence and integrity, connects to core values, and helps people find meaning in their work.

Employees were motivated by Ford's vision because they saw an opportunity to make life better for themselves and others.

Vision Gives Meaning to Work People also need to find dignity and meaning in their work. Recall how the chef at the Community Kitchens program described earlier had grown pessimistic about her work as a chef to the affluent. "It's taken me by surprise to see how meaningful this job is to me," she says of her work at the food bank. Even people performing routine tasks can find pride in their work when they have a larger purpose for what they do. For example, a clerk who thinks of his job as "processing insurance claims" will feel very differently than one who thinks of her job as helping victims of fire or burglary put their lives back in order.[22] As another example, one housekeeper at ServiceMaster Co. explained that she is enthusiastic about her work at a community hospital because leaders help her see the job as more than just cleaning floors. The housekeeper considers herself an important member of a team that is dedicated to helping sick people get well. Without quality cleaning, she points out, the hospital could not serve its patients well and would soon be out of business.[23]

People are drawn to companies that offer them a chance to do something meaningful. Today, prospective employees often ask about a company's vision when interviewing for a job because they want to know what the organization aims for and how, or whether, they will fit in.

Vision Establishes a Standard of Excellence and Integrity A powerful vision frees people from the mundane by providing them with a challenge that requires them to give their best. In addition, vision provides a measure by which employees can gauge their contributions to the organization. Most workers welcome the chance to see how their work fits into the whole. Think of how frustrating it is to watch a movie when the projector is out of focus. Today's complex, fast-changing business environment often seems just like that—out of focus.[24] A vision is the focus button. It clarifies an image of the future and lets people see how they can contribute. A vision presents a challenge, asks people to go where they haven't gone before. Thus, it encourages workers to take risks and find new ways of doing things. This chapter's *Consider This* box discusses three qualities a powerful vision can inspire.

Vision clarifies and connects to the core values and ideals of the organization and thus sets a standard of integrity for employees. A good vision brings out the best in people by illuminating important values, speaking to people's

Consider This!

Vision's Offspring

A compelling vision inspires and nurtures three qualities, here personified as individuals. Do you think followers would benefit from contact with the following "people" in an organization?

CLARITY

My visits to Clarity are soothing now. He never tells me what to think or feel or do but shows me how to find out what I need to know. . . . he presented me with a sketchbook and told me to draw the same thing every day until the drawing started to speak to me.

COMMITMENT

Commitment has kind eyes. He wears sturdy shoes. . . . You can taste in [his] vegetables that the soil has been cared for. . . . He is a simple man, and yet he is mysterious. He is more generous than most people. His heart is open. He is not afraid of life.

IMAGINATION

Some people accuse Imagination of being a liar. They don't understand that she has her own ways of uncovering the truth. . . . Imagination has been working as a fortune-teller in the circus. She has a way of telling your fortune so clearly that you believe her, and then your wishes start to come true. . . . Her vision is more complex, and very simple. Even with the old stories, she wants us to see what has never been seen before.

Source: J. Ruth Gendler, *The Book of Qualities* (New York: Harper & Row, 1988). Used with permission.

hearts, and letting them be part of something bigger than themselves. Consider how Walt Disney painted a picture of Disneyland that unified and energized employees.

Walt Disney

Walt Disney created a clear picture of what he wanted Disneyland to be. His vision translated hopes and dreams into words and allowed employees to help create the future. Notice how the vision says nothing about making money—the emphasis is on a greater purpose that all employees could believe in.

> "The idea of Disneyland is a simple one. It will be a place for people to find happiness and knowledge. It will be a place for parents and children to spend pleasant times in one another's company, a place for teachers and pupils to discover greater ways of understanding and education. Here the older generation can recapture the nostalgia of days gone by, and the younger generation can savor the challenge of the future. Here will be the wonders of Nature and Man for all to see and understand. Disneyland will be based on and dedicated to the ideals, the dreams, and hard facts that have created America. And it will be uniquely equipped to dramatize these dreams and facts and send them forth as a source of courage and inspiration for all the world. Disneyland will be something of a fair, an exhibition, a playground,

a community center, a museum of living facts, and a showplace of beauty and magic. It will be filled with the accomplishments, the joys and hopes of the world we live in. And it will remind us and show us how to make these wonders part of our lives." [25]

A clear, inspiring picture such as that painted by Walt Disney can have a powerful impact on people. His vision gave meaning and value to workers' activities. Painting a clear picture of the future is a significant responsibility of leaders, yet it cannot always be the leader's alone. To make a difference, a vision can be widely shared and is often created with the participation of others. Every good organizational vision is a shared vision.

Common Themes of Vision

Five themes are common to powerful, effective visions: they have broad, widely shared appeal; they help organizations deal with change; they encourage faith and hope for the future; they reflect high ideals; and they define both the organization's destination and the basic rules to get there.

Vision Has Broad Appeal Although it may be obvious that a vision can be achieved only through people, many visions fail to adequately involve employees. Isolated top leaders may come up with a grand idea that other employees find ridiculous, or they might forget that achieving the vision requires understanding and commitment throughout the organization. For example, most people originally thought Stanford Ovshinsky's idea of inexpensive films for solar power was ridiculous. If he had not been able to involve investors, managers, engineers, and other employees in the vision, it would never have become a reality. The vision cannot be the property of the leader alone.[26] The ideal vision is identified with the organization as a whole, not with a single leader or even a top leadership team. It "grabs people in the gut" and motivates them to work toward a common end.[27] It allows each individual to act independently but in the same direction.

Vision Deals with Change Visions that work help the organization achieve bold change. Vision is about action and challenges people to make important changes toward a better future. Change can be frightening, but a clear sense of direction helps people face the difficulties and uncertainties involved in the change process. When employees have a guiding vision, everyday decisions and actions throughout the organization respond to current problems and challenges in ways that move the organization toward the future rather than maintain the status quo.

Vision Encourages Faith and Hope Vision exists only in the imagination—it is a picture of a world that cannot be observed or verified in advance. The future is shaped by people who believe in it, and a powerful vision helps people believe that they can be effective, that there is a better future they can move to through their own commitment and actions. Vision is an emotional appeal to our fundamental human needs and desires—to feel important and useful, to believe we can make a real difference in the world.[28] A powerful, clearly articulated vision helps people believe in a future they cannot see.[29]

Vision Reflects High Ideals Good visions are idealistic. Visions that portray an uplifting future have the power to inspire and energize people. Referring back to our opening example, when Kennedy announced the "man on the moon" vision, NASA had only a small amount of the knowledge it would need to accomplish the feat. William F. Powers, who worked at NASA during the 1960s, later helped Ford Motor Company develop an idealistic vision for the world's first high-volume, aerodynamically styled car that featured fuel economy (the 1980s Taurus). It was a big risk for Ford at a time when the company was down and out. But leaders portrayed this as a chance not only to save the company but to establish a whole new path in automotive engineering, which tapped into employees' imaginations and idealism.[30]

Vision Defines the Destination and the Journey A good vision for the future includes specific outcomes that the organization wants to achieve. It also incorporates the underlying values that will help the organization get there. For example, a private business school might specify certain outcomes such as a top 20 ranking, placing 90 percent of students in summer internships, and getting 80 percent of students into jobs by June of their graduating year. Yet in the process of reaching those specific outcomes, the school wants to increase students' knowledge of business, values, and teamwork, as well as prepare them for lifelong learning. Additionally, the vision may espouse underlying values such as no separation between fields of study or between professors and students, a genuine concern for students' welfare, and adding to the body of business knowledge. A good vision includes both the desired future outcomes and the underlying values that set the rules for achieving them.[31]

> **Action Memo**
> As a leader, you can create a shared vision so that every individual, team, and department is moving in the same direction. You can help people see the values, activities, and objectives that will attain the vision.

A Vision Works at Multiple Levels

Most of the visions we have talked about so far are for the company as a whole. However, divisions, departments, and individuals also have visions, which are just as important and powerful. Successful individuals usually have a clear mental picture of their vision and how to achieve it. People who do not have this clear vision of the future have less chance of success. Three young Pepperdine University graduates started an organization to help other young people find and pursue their personal vision.

Roadtrip Productions

Several years ago, Mike Marriner, Nathan Gebhard, and Brian McAllister set out in a 1985 neon-green Fleetwood RV on an epic pilgrimage to find out what they wanted to do with their lives. One thing they knew: They weren't ready and willing to play it safe and follow the expected paths of medicine, consulting, and the family landfill business (respectively).

Armed with a video camera, the three interviewed successful leaders in a wide variety of professions, asking questions such as: "When you were our age, what were you thinking?" and "How did you get to where you are?" The answers all boiled down to this simple message, says McAllister: "Block out the noise and really pave your own road guided by what lights you up." Following their three-month, 17,342-mile journey across the country, the three founded Roadtrip Productions to help other young people experience their own journeys and find their own visions. Roadtrip produces a television series for PBS, has published three books, and is launching an XM radio program. It has formed partnerships with career centers at some 100 American and 22 British colleges.

Many young people today, the three founders of Roadtrip believe, are desperately searching for meaning in their work, but don't know how to find it or lack the confidence to pursue it. Marriner suggests that most people know deep down what they're passionate about, but they lack the confidence or courage to pursue that vision. They have been conditioned to look for the safe paths and to pick jobs, careers, or other pursuits where they can be successful. Yet, as Howard Schultz, chairman and former CEO of Starbucks, told the team during his interview, success shouldn't be the target. Instead, success comes from pursuing your vision. Roadtrip's favorite advice to anyone who is hesitant to follow their vision comes from Michael Jager, the founder of a design firm: "When you really magnify what it is you believe in and follow it, the world conspires for you."[32]

Roadtrip also reminds people that making an initial career choice is just one aspect of a personal vision that will grow and change over time. Some successful organizations ask employees to write a personal vision statement because leaders know that people who have a vision of where they want their life to go are more effective. In addition, this enables leaders to see how an employee's personal vision and the team or organizational vision can contribute to one another.

Organizational visions grow and change as well. Within organizations, top leaders develop a vision for the organization as a whole, and at the same time a project team leader five levels beneath the CEO can develop a vision with team members for a new product they are working on. Leaders of functional departments, divisions, and teams can use vision with the same positive results as do top leaders. The vision becomes the common thread connecting people, involving them personally and emotionally in the organization.[33]

Consider the facility manager for a large corporation. His department received requests to fix toilets and air conditioners. Rather than just seeing this as menial work, the manager framed it for employees in a way that inspired them. He told them people's feelings about their work environment were important to them personally and to the organization, and employees in his department had the chance to "use physical space to make people feel good." Department employees started planting flowers outside office windows and created an environment that lifted people's spirits.[34] In innovative companies, every group or department creates its own vision, as long as the vision is in line with the overall company's direction.

When every person understands and embraces a vision, the organization becomes self-adapting. Although each individual acts independently, everyone is working in the same direction. In the new sciences, this is called the principle of self-reference. **Self-reference** means that each element in a system will serve the goals of the whole system when the elements are imprinted with an understanding of the whole. Thus, the vision serves to direct and control people for the good of themselves and the organization.

To develop a shared vision, leaders share their personal visions with others and encourage others to express their dreams for the future. This requires openness, good listening skills, and the courage to connect with people on an emotional level. A leader's ultimate responsibility is to be in touch with the hopes and dreams that drive employees and find the common ground that binds

Self-reference

a principle stating that each element in a system will serve the goals of the whole system when the elements are imprinted with an understanding of the whole personal dreams into a shared vision for the organization. As one successful top leader put it, "My job, fundamentally, is listening to what the organization is trying to say, and then making sure it is forcefully articulated."[35] Another successful leader refers to leadership as "discovering the company's destiny and having the courage to follow it."[36]

Mission

Mission is not the same thing as a company's vision, although the two work together. The **mission** is the organization's core broad purpose and reason for existence. It defines the company's core values and reason for being, and it provides a basis for creating the vision. Whereas vision is an ambitious desire for the future, mission is what the organization "stands for" in a larger sense. James Collins compares Zenith and Motorola to illustrate the importance of a solid organizational mission. Both Zenith and Motorola were once successful makers of televisions. Yet while Zenith stayed there, Motorola continued to move forward—to making microprocessors, integrated circuits, cellular phones, modems, and other products—and became one of the most highly regarded companies in the country. The difference is that Motorola defined its mission as "applying technology to benefit the public," not as "making television sets."[37]

Mission
the organization's core broad purpose and reason for existence

What Mission Does

Whereas visions continue to grow and change, the mission persists in the face of changing technologies, economic conditions, or other environmental shifts. It serves as the glue that holds the organization together in times of change and guides strategic choices and decisions about the future. The mission defines the enduring character—the spiritual DNA—of the organization and can be used as a leadership tool to help employees find meaning in their work.[38]

Recall the discussion of intrinsic rewards from Chapter 8. When people connect their jobs to a higher purpose, the work itself becomes a great motivator. The Gallup organization's Q12 study, also discussed in Chapter 8, has found that when employees believe the company's mission makes their job important, they are typically more engaged with their work, feel a greater sense of pride and loyalty, and are more productive. Exhibit 13.4 compares the Gallup results for those who agree that the mission makes their job important to those who do not feel that the mission of the company makes their job important. The differences are quite striking. For example, 60 percent of respondents who agreed that the mission makes their job important reported feeling engaged with their work, whereas none of the respondents who disagreed felt engaged with their work. Sixty-six percent would recommend their company's products or services, compared to only 20 percent of those who did not believe the mission made their job important.[39]

Typically, the mission is made up of two critical parts: the core values and the core purpose. The *core values* guide the organization "no matter what." As Ralph Larsen, former CEO of Johnson & Johnson, explained it, "The core values embodied in our credo might be a competitive advantage, but that is not *why* we have them. We have them because they define for us what we stand for, and we would hold them even if they became a competitive *dis*advantage in certain situations."[40] Johnson & Johnson's core values led the company, for

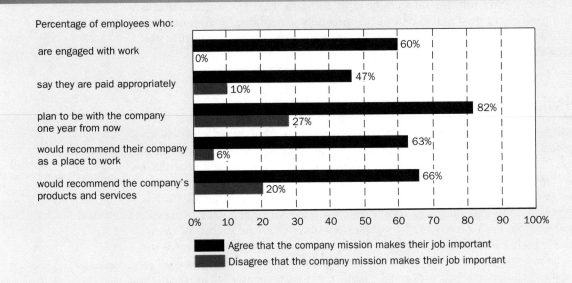

Exhibit 13.4 The Power of a Strong Mission

Percentage of employees who:

- are engaged with work — 60% / 0%
- say they are paid appropriately — 47% / 10%
- plan to be with the company one year from now — 82% / 27%
- would recommend their company as a place to work — 63% / 6%
- would recommend the company's products and services — 66% / 20%

■ Agree that the company mission makes their job important
■ Disagree that the company mission makes their job important

Source: Susan Ellingwood, "On a Mission," *Gallup Management Journal* (Winter 2001), pp. 6–7.

Action Memo
As a leader, you can keep in mind what the organization stands for in a broader sense—its core purpose and values—and create the vision around that central mission.

example, to voluntarily remove Tylenol from the market after the cyanide poisoning of some Tylenol capsule users, even though this act cost the company more than $100 million.

The mission also includes the company's *core purpose*. The core values and core purpose are frequently expressed in a *mission statement*. Exhibit 13.5 shows the vision, mission, and core values of DuPont Canada. Consider how DuPont's specific vision grows out of the company's mission and works with it.

A Framework for Noble Purpose

An effective mission statement doesn't just describe products or services; it captures people's idealistic motivations for why the organization exists. Most successful companies have missions that proclaim a noble purpose of some type, such as Motorola's "applying technology to benefit the public," Mary Kay's "to enrich the lives of women," or Wal-Mart Stores' "to give ordinary folk the chance to buy the same things as rich people."[41]

Leaders are responsible for framing a noble purpose that inspires and leads followers to high performance and helps the organization maintain a competitive advantage. People like to have a sense that what they are doing matters and makes a positive difference in the world. Consider the purpose that inspires employees at Genentech, which topped *Fortune* magazine's list of the 100 Best Companies to Work For in 2006.

IN THE LEAD

Genentech

Genentech was the world's first biotechnology company, and after 29 years it is the brightest star in the burgeoning industry. The company's core purpose, which imbues employees with idealism, has a lot to do with its success. Genentech's motto, *In Business For Life,* captures its mission to use human genetic information to develop medicines for serious and life-threatening diseases.

Exhibit 13.5 Mission, Vision, and Values of DuPont Canada

DuPont Mission, Vision, and Values

Our Mission

Sustainable Growth: Increasing shareholder and societal value while reducing our environmental footprint.

Our Vision

Our vision is to be the world's most dynamic science company, creating sustainable solutions essential to a better, safer, healthier life for people everywhere.

We will be a pacesetter in improving every aspect of our operations with a total commitment to meeting the needs of our customers in Canada and abroad with continuosly improving, high-value offerings.

Our Core Values

Safety, concern and care for people, protection of the environment, and personal and corporate integrity are this company's highest values, and we will not compromise them.

Life. Improved by DuPont Science

Source: "DuPont Mission, Vision, and Values," DuPont Canada Website, "Our Company; Company at a Glance: Our Mission, Vision, Values," accessed on April 10, 2007 at http://www2.dupont.com/Our_Company/en_CA/glance/vision/

Employees say they work at the company because it gives them a chance to make a difference. Scientists and researchers have the time, freedom, and support at Genentech to answer big research questions that could have a big impact on curing diseases such as cancer. Genentech puts great effort into attracting people with a passion for science and a commitment to improving human life. It can take several visits and as many as 20 interviews to land a job. Part of the process is designed to screen out those who are preoccupied with salary, title, and personal advancement. CEO Art Levinson emphasizes that people who need to feel special with assigned parking spaces and executive dining rooms won't fit in at Genentech.

Genentech managers by no means consider the company a philanthropy. They are focused on growth and profits as much as any other business. However, as Levinson puts it: "At the end of the day, we want to make drugs that really matter. That's the transcendent issue."[42]

Exhibit 13.6 A Leader's Framework for Noble Purpose

Purpose	Description	Basis for Action	Examples
Discovery	Finding the new	Pioneer, entrepreneur	IBM, 3M, Virgin
Excellence	Being the best	Fulfillment	Berkshire Hathaway, Apple, BMW
Altruism	Providing service	Happiness	ServiceMaster, Wal-Mart
Heroism	Being effective	Achievement	Microsoft, Dell, ExxonMobil

Source: Nikos Mourkogiannis, *Purpose: The Starting Point of Great Companies* (New York: Palgrave Macmillan, 2006); and Nikos Mourkogiannis, "The Realist's Guide to Moral Purpose," *Strategy + Business* Issue 41 (Winter 2005), pp. 42–53.

It is easy to understand how employees at Genentech can feel that they are serving a noble purpose. But what about a mutual fund company, a fashion retailer, or a soft drink manufacturer? Leaders in any type of organization can tap into people's desire to contribute and make a difference.[43] Exhibit 13.6 describes four basic approaches leaders take in framing an organizational purpose that helps people feel that their work is worthwhile. Each of these approaches is described in more detail below.

Discovery Many people are inspired by the opportunity to find or create something new. Discovery for its own sake can serve as a noble purpose, as it does for employees at 3M, where researchers are given time to explore ideas and work on their own projects. Another example is Google, where people are energized by the psychic rewards they get from working on intellectually stimulating and challenging technical problems.[44] Leaders at Samsung Electronics have reenergized the company by focusing employees on discovery rather than imitation, aiming to transform Samsung into a world-class innovator rather than a manufacturer known for cheap, low-quality knockoffs. This shift in purpose has led to amazing results.[45] Samsung's record of innovation will be discussed in more detail in Chapter 15. This type of purpose inspires people to see the adventure in their work and experience the joy of a pioneering or entrepreneurial spirit.

Excellence With this approach, leaders focus people on being the best, both on an individual and an organizational level. Excellence is defined by the work itself rather than by customers. Indeed, organizations that pursue excellence would rather turn customers away than compromise their quality. Apple, for instance, has always built high-quality, cleverly designed computers, yet it holds less than 5 percent of the personal computer market. Leaders would like to increase their share of the market, but they aren't willing to sacrifice their commitment to high quality and what they consider superior technology.[46] In companies with excellence as a guiding purpose, managers and employees are treated as valuable resources and provided with support to perform at their peak. People are motivated by the opportunity to experience intrinsic rewards and personal fulfillment.

Altruism Many nonprofit organizations are based on a noble purpose of altruism, but businesses can use this approach as well. Recall the examples of employees at

ServiceMaster from Chapter 6 and from earlier in this chapter. One of ServiceMaster's core values is to treat employees with respect and help low-skilled manual workers see the worth and dignity of their service to society. Similarly, leaders at Dollar General emphasize the purpose of giving low-income people a good deal, not just making sales and profits. Any company that puts a high premium on customer service can be considered to fall in this category as well. Marriott encapsulates its purpose in the slogan, "The Spirit to Serve."[47] The basis of action for this type of purpose is to increase personal happiness. Most people feel good when they are doing something to help others or make their communities or the world a better place.

Heroism The final category, heroism, means the company's purpose is based on being strong, aggressive, and effective. Companies with this basis of noble purpose often reflect almost an obsession with winning. Bill Gates imbued Microsoft with a goal of putting the Windows operating system into every personal computer, for example.[48] At General Electric, former CEO Jack Welch wanted the company to strive to be number one or number two in each industry in which it did business. As another example, Southwest Airlines was founded with a heroic goal of winning against much larger competitors such as American and Delta. With this approach, the basis of action is people's desire to achieve and to experience *self-efficacy,* as described in Chapter 8. People want to feel capable of being effective and producing results.

Companies that remain successful over the long term have top executives who lead with a noble purpose. A well-chosen noble purpose taps into the emotions and instincts of employees and customers and can contribute to better morale, greater innovativeness, and higher employee and organizational performance.

Strategy in Action

Strong missions that reflect a noble purpose and guiding visions are both important, but they are not enough alone to make strong, powerful organizations. For organizations to succeed, they need ways to translate vision, values, and purpose into action, which is the role of strategy. Formulating strategy is the hard, serious work of taking a specific step toward the future. **Strategic management** is the set of decisions and actions used to formulate and implement specific strategies that will achieve a competitively superior fit between the organization and its environment so as to achieve organizational goals.[49] It is the leader's job to find this fit and translate it into action.

Strategic management
the set of decisions and actions used to formulate and implement specific strategies that will achieve a competitively superior fit between the organization and its environment so as to achieve organizational goals

Deciding Where to Go

Strategy can be defined as the general plan of action that describes resource allocation and other activities for dealing with the environment and helping the organization attain its goals. In formulating strategy, leaders ask questions such as "Where is the organization now? Where does the organization want to be? What changes and trends are occurring in the competitive environment? What courses of action can help us achieve our vision?"

Developing effective strategy requires actively listening to people both inside and outside the organization, as well as examining trends and discontinuities in the environment that can be used to gain an edge. Rather than reacting to

Strategy
the general plan of action that describes resource allocation and other activities for dealing with the environment and helping the organization attain its goals

environmental changes, strategic leaders study the events that have already taken place and act based on their anticipation of what the future might be like.[50] An example is Progressive Insurance, which was the first to offer rate quotes online. Other companies had the same information about the growth of personal computers and the Internet, but they didn't interpret it in the same way or formulate the same strategy for taking advantage of the new technology. Good leaders anticipate, look ahead, and prepare for the future based on trends they see in the environment today, which often requires radical thinking. The Leader's Bookshelf describes a successful application of radical thinking in the Oakland A's baseball team.

Innovative thinking carries a lot of risk. Sometimes leaders have to shift their strategy several times before they get it right.[51] In addition, strategy necessarily changes over time to fit shifting environmental conditions. To improve the chances for success, leaders develop strategies that focus on three qualities: core competence, developing synergy, and creating value for customers.

An organization's **core competence** is something the organization does extremely well in comparison to competitors. Leaders try to identify the organization's unique strengths—what makes their organization different from others in the industry. L.L. Bean succeeds with a core competence of excellent customer service and a quality guarantee. A customer can return a purchase at any time and get a refund or exchange, no questions asked. One story told about the company is that a manager approached a young boy with his mother and commented that his L.L. Bean jacket was frayed at the sleeves and collar. The mother commented that it was no wonder considering how much he had worn it, but the manager said, "That shouldn't happen; we need to replace that for you."[52]

Synergy occurs when organizational parts interact to produce a joint effect that is greater than the sum of the parts acting alone. As a result the organization may attain a special advantage with respect to cost, market power, technology, or employee skills. One way companies gain synergy is through alliances and partnerships. North General Hospital, a small community hospital in Harlem that caters mostly to the poor and elderly, had lost money every year since it was founded in 1979—until 2005, when leaders focused on a new strategy that included an alliance with Mount Sinai Medical Center, one of New York City's most prominent teaching hospitals. In return for an annual fee, North General uses Mount Sinai physicians and surgeons who perform highly specialized procedures and treat specific diseases that affect African Americans in high rates. The deal boosts revenue for Mount Sinai, as well, and brings in more patients because North General acts as a referral service for patients with complex medical issues.[53]

Focusing on core competencies and attaining synergy helps companies create value for their customers. **Value** can be defined as the combination of benefits received and costs paid by the customer.[54] Delivering value to the customer is at the heart of strategy. At Pottery Barn, for example, president Laura Alber points to a thick, $24 bath towel as an icon of what Pottery Barn aspires to: "For us this represents a combination of design, quality, and price," Alber says. "If this were $60, you'd still like it. But at $24, you go, 'This is incredible.'"[55]

Strategy formulation integrates knowledge of the environment, vision, and mission with the company's core competence in such a way as to achieve synergy and create value for customers. When these elements are brought together, the company has

Core competence
something the organization does extremely well in comparison to competitors

Synergy
the interaction of organizational parts to produce a joint effect that is greater than the sum of the parts

Action Memo
As a leader, you can prepare for the future based on trends in the environment today. Don't be afraid to think radically. You can shift your strategies to fit changing conditions.

Value
the combination of benefits received and costs paid by the customer

Strategy formulation
integrating knowledge of the environment, vision, and mission with the core competence in such a way as to achieve synergy and create customer value

Moneyball: The Art of Winning an Unfair Game

by Michael Lewis

How do you turn a bunch of undervalued baseball players, many of them deemed unfit for the big leagues, into one of the Major League's most successful franchises? The Oakland A's general manager Billy Beane did it by having a different vision than the rest of the pack. Beane's unique vision and strategy built one of Major League Baseball's winningest teams with one of its smallest budgets. Unlike successful teams such as the New York Yankees, which can afford to lavish millions on high-profile free-agents, Beane looks for the hidden talents among unwanted or undiscovered players.

FINDING A DIAMOND IN THE ROUGH

Beane's skill at finding baseball's hidden gems comes partly from his own rocky experiences as a big-league outfielder, where he learned that there's more to being a good ball player than raw talent. The other part is his unique vision and strategy for fielding a ball team. Here are some of Beane's guiding principles:

- *Buy low and sell high.* Beane and his managers look for players at all levels—from high school and college to the minor and major leagues—who are undervalued by others, whether because of a quirk in their playing style or other managers' narrow mindsets. When other managers don't see a player's potential, Beane can swoop in and get him for a bargain. Then, he has the discipline and sense of timing to trade a player once he's turned him into a star who is highly desired by other teams. Beane picks up several new, low-cost players with combined talents that roughly equal that of the player traded.

- *Forget the traditional measures.* In choosing players, Beane makes much greater use of sophisticated statistical analysis than other general managers, and he looks at different measures. For example, he favors stats such as on-base percentage over batting average. Beane believes the ability to get on base—even with a walk—is a valuable long-term asset, whereas traditional measures such as batting average or base steals may mean nothing over the long haul.

- *The stats always rule.* Scouting is de-emphasized in Oakland. Other managers sometimes reject a player because he doesn't "look" like a major leaguer, but not Beane. If the statistics say an overweight college catcher that nobody else wants should be a number one draft pick, Beane goes for it. One player was signed on without anyone from the A's ever seeing him.

THINKING RADICALLY

The new statistical models and sophisticated tools Beane is using to spot high-potential players have been around for years, but they were used mostly by amateur baseball enthusiasts: software engineers, statisticians, Wall Street analysts, lawyers, physics professors, and just run-of-the-mill geeks. Billy Beane looked at the cache of numbers compiled over the years and saw a new vision: the traditional yardsticks of success for baseball players are fatally flawed. By thinking differently and paying attention to obscure numbers, Beane has built a highly successful organization—and perhaps revolutionized baseball management.

Moneyball: The Art of Winning an Unfair Game, by Michael Lewis, is published by W. W. Norton & Company.

---

an excellent chance to succeed in a competitive environment. But to do so, leaders have to ensure that strategies are implemented—that actual behavior within the organization reflects the desired direction.

Deciding How to Get There

Strategy is implemented through specific mechanisms, techniques, or tools for directing organizational resources to accomplish strategic goals. This is the basic architecture for how things get done in the organization. **Strategy implementation** is the most important as well as the most difficult part of strategic management, and leaders must carefully and consistently manage the implementation process to achieve results.[56] One recent survey found that only 57 percent of responding firms reported that managers successfully implemented the new strategies they had devised over the past three years.[57] Other research has estimated that

Strategy implementation
putting strategy into action by adjusting various parts of the organization and directing resources to accomplish strategic goals

as much as 70 percent of all business strategies never get implemented, reflecting the complexity of strategy implementation.[58]

Strategy implementation involves using several tools or parts of the organization that can be adjusted to put strategy into action. Strong leadership is one of the most important tools for strategy implementation. Follower support for the strategic plan is essential for successful implementation, and leaders create the environment that determines whether people understand and feel committed to the company's strategic direction. People who feel trust in their leaders and commitment to the organization are typically more supportive of strategy and put forth more effort to implement strategic decisions.[59]

As an example of using leadership in strategy implementation, the manager of a department store might implement a strategy of better customer service by pumping up morale, encouraging greater interaction with customers, being physically present on the sales floor, and speaking enthusiastically with employees about providing quality service. Strategy is also implemented through organizational elements such as structural design, pay or reward systems, budget allocations, and organizational rules, policies, or procedures. Leaders are responsible for making decisions about changes in structure, systems, policies, and so forth, to support the company's strategic direction. When she was general manager of the Applebee's Neighborhood Grill & Bar in Mankato, Minnesota, Lisa Hofferbert implemented a strategy of increased sales by budgeting for newspaper and radio ads asking customers to help the store break a sales record, designing daily incentive-based contests for employees, redesigning employee parking policies to give greater access for customers to park near the store, and making the sales target a mandatory topic on the agenda for every staff meeting. These changes, combined with Hofferbert's inspirational leadership and commitment to taking care of her employees, helped the store meet her ambitious goal of $3 million in sales for the year.[60]

Leaders make decisions every day—some large and some small—that support company strategy. Exhibit 13.7 provides a simplified model for how leaders make strategic decisions. The two dimensions considered are whether a particular choice will have a high or low strategic impact on the business

Exhibit 13.7 Making Strategic Decisions

	Ease of Implementation	
	Hard	Easy
Strategic Impact — High	**High Impact, Hard to Implement.** Major changes, but with potential for high payoff	**High Impact, Easy to Implement.** Simple changes that have high strategic impact—take action here first
Strategic Impact — Low	**Low Impact, Hard to Implement.** Difficult changes with little or no potential for payoff—avoid this category	**Low Impact, Easy to Implement.** Incremental improvements, "small wins;" pursue for symbolic value of success

Source: Adapted from Amir Hartman and John Sifonis, wtih John Kador, *Net Ready: Strategies for the New E-conomy* (McGraw-Hill, 2000), p. 95.

and whether implementation of the decision will be easy or difficult. A change that both produces a high strategic impact and is easy to implement would be a leader's first choice for putting strategy into action. For example, leaders at Payless ShoeSource have shifted the company's strategy to try to appeal to young, fashion-conscious women with trendier shoes at reasonable prices, or as CEO Matt Rubel puts it, to "democratize fashion." One of the first steps leaders took was to give the stores a new look. The tall, crowded wire racks have been replaced with low countertops and displays arranged by fashion rather than by size. The walls are curved to give a feeling of movement and energy. Even the lighting is strategic. Modern white ceiling lamps brighten the whole store and accent lamps highlight the higher-fashion items. "It makes a $12 shoe look like a $20 shoe," says Rubel. It's too early to tell if Payless's move into fashion is a success, but the redesign of stores is already having a big strategic impact. As one fashion-conscious shopper said, "Everything looks so much nicer. Is this Payless?"[61]

Some strategic decisions, however, are much more difficult to implement. For example, pursuing growth through mergers and acquisitions can present difficulties of blending production processes, accounting procedures, corporate cultures, and other aspects of the organizations into an effectively functioning whole. Structural reorganizations, such as a shift to horizontal teams or breaking a corporation into separate divisions, is another example of a high-risk decision. Leaders frequently initiate major changes despite the risks and difficulties because the potential strategic payoff is very high.

Leaders also sometimes pursue activities that have a low strategic impact but which are relatively easy to implement. Incremental improvements in products, work processes, or techniques are examples. Over time, incremental improvements can have an important effect on the organization. In addition, small changes can sometimes be needed to symbolize improvement and success to people within the organization. It may be important for leaders to produce quick, highly visible improvements to boost morale, keep people committed to larger changes, or keep followers focused on the vision. For example, the manager of a purchasing department wanted to re-engineer the purchasing process to increase efficiency and improve relationships with suppliers. He wanted requisitions and invoices to be processed within days rather than the several weeks it had been taking. Employees were skeptical that the department could ever meet the new standards and pointed out that some invoices currently awaiting processing were almost two months old. The manager decided to make some simple revisions in the flow of paperwork and employee duties, which enabled the department to process all the old invoices so that no remaining invoice was more than a week old. This "small win" energized employees and helped keep them focused on the larger goal.[62] The positive attitude made implementation of the larger change much smoother.

The final category shown in Exhibit 13.7 relates to changes that are both difficult to implement and have low strategic impact. An illustration of a decision in this category was the attempt by new management at a highly successful mail-order clothing company to implement teams. In this case, the decision was not made to support a new strategic direction but simply to try out a new management trend—and it was a miserable failure that cost the organization much time, money, and employee goodwill before the teams were finally disbanded.[63] Effective leaders try to avoid making decisions that fall within this category.

The Leader's Contribution

Although good leadership calls for actively involving everyone, leaders are still ultimately responsible for establishing direction through vision and strategy. When leadership fails to provide direction, organizations flounder. Consider the example of Eastern Mountain Sports (EMS), which was founded as a sporting goods store selling serious gear for serious outdoor enthusiasts. In recent years, leaders decided to spur growth by appealing to a broader array of customers, selling fleece jackets, khaki slacks, and cotton sweaters to soccer moms and dads. In the process, EMS lost most of its core customers and became nothing more than a fuzzy also-ran in the outdoor retail industry. Since Will Manzer came in as CEO, he has been striving to provide EMS with a more coherent and focused strategic direction. "EMS wasn't safe," Manzer says. "It wasn't clear and it wasn't differentiated. If we're not precise in our answer to the outdoor athlete, then we mean nothing to anybody."[64]

> **Action Memo**
>
> Strategic management is one of the most critical jobs of a leader, but leaders may exhibit different strategy styles that can be effective. Leader's Self-Insight 13.3 lets you determine your strengths based on two important ways leaders can bring creativity to strategic management.

Stimulating Vision and Action

In the waiting lounge of a fine lakeside restaurant a sign reads, "Where there is no hope in the future, there is no power in the present." The owner explains its presence there by telling the story of how his small, picturesque village with its homes and businesses was sacrificed to make way for a flood-control project. After losing their fight to reverse the decision, most business leaders simply let their businesses decline and die. Soon, the only people who came to the village did so to eat at the cheery little diner, whose owner became the butt of jokes because he continued to work so hard. Everyone laughed when he chose to open a larger and fancier restaurant on the hill behind the village. Yet, when the flood-control project was finally completed, he had the only attractive restaurant on the edge of a beautiful, newly constructed lake that drew many tourists. Anyone could have found out, as he did, where the edge of the lake would be, yet most of the business owners had no vision for the future. The restaurant owner had a vision and he took action on it.

Hopes and dreams for the future are what keep people moving forward. However, for leaders to make a real difference, they have to link those dreams with strategic actions. Vision has to be translated into specific goals, objectives, and plans so that employees know how to move toward the desired future. An old English churchyard saying applies to organizations as it does to life:

Life without vision is drudgery.

Vision without action is but an empty dream.

Action guided by vision is joy and the hope of the earth.[65]

Exhibit 13.8 illustrates four possibilities of leadership in providing direction. Four types of leaders are described based on their attention to vision and attention to action. The person who is low both on providing vision and stimulating action is *uninvolved*, not really a leader at all. The leader who is all action and little vision is a *doer*. He or she may be a hard worker and dedicated to the job and the organization, but the doer is working blind. Without a sense of purpose and direction, activities have no real meaning and do not truly serve the organization, the employees, or the community. The *dreamer*, on the other hand, is good at providing a big idea with meaning for self and others. This leader may

Leader's Self-Insight 13.3

Your Strategy Style

Think about *how you handle challenges and issues* in your current or a recent job. Then circle a or b for each item below depending on which is generally more descriptive of your behavior. There are no right or wrong answers. Respond to each item as it best describes how you respond to work situations.

1. When keeping records, I tend to
   a. be very careful about documentation.
   b. be more haphazard about documentation.

2. If I run a group or a project, I
   a. have the general idea and let others figure out how to do the tasks.
   b. try to figure out specific goals, time lines, and expected outcomes.

3. My thinking style could be more accurately described as
   a. linear thinker, going from A to B to C.
   b. thinking like a grasshopper, hopping from one idea to another.

4. In my office or home, things are
   a. here and there in various piles.
   b. laid out neatly or at least in reasonable order.

5. I take pride in developing
   a. ways to overcome a barrier to a solution.
   b. new hypotheses about the underlying cause of a problem.

6. I can best help strategy by making sure there is
   a. openness to a wide range of assumptions and ideas.
   b. thoroughness when implementing new ideas.

7. One of my strengths is
   a. commitment to making things work.
   b. commitment to a dream for the future.

8. For me to work at my best, it is more important to have
   a. autonomy.
   b. certainty.

9. I work best when
   a. I plan my work ahead of time.
   b. I am free to respond to unplanned situations.

10. I am most effective when I emphasize
    a. inventing original solutions.
    b. making practical improvements.

Scoring and Interpretation

For Strategic Innovator style, score one point for each "a" answer circled for questions 2, 4, 6, 8, and 10 and for each "b" answer circled for questions 1, 3, 5, 7, and 9. For Strategic Adaptor style, score one point for each "b" answer circled for questions 2, 4, 6, 8, and 10, and for each "a" answer circled for questions 1, 3, 5, 7, and 9. Which of your two scores is higher and by how much? The higher score indicates your Strategy Style.

Strategic Innovator and Strategic Adaptor are two important ways leaders bring creativity to strategic management. Leaders with an adaptor style tend to work within the situation as it is given and improve it by making it more efficient and reliable. They succeed by building on what they know is true and proven. Leaders with the innovator style push toward a new paradigm and want to find a new way to do something. Innovators like to explore uncharted territory, seek dramatic break-throughs, and may have difficulty accepting an ongoing strategy. Both innovator and adaptor styles are essential to strategic management, but with different approaches. The strategic adaptor asks, "How can I make this better?" The strategic innovator asks, "How can I make this different?" Strategic innovators often use their skills in the formulation of whole new strategies, and strategic adaptors are often associated with strategic improvements and strategy implementation.

If the difference between the two scores is two or less, you have a mid-adaptor/innovator style, and work well in both arenas. If the difference is 4–6, you have a moderately strong style and probably work best in the area of your strength. And if the difference is 8–10, you have a strong style and almost certainly would want to work in the area of your strength rather than in the opposite domain.

Sources: Adapted from Dorothy Marcic and Joe Seltzer, *Organizational Behavior: Experiences and Cases* (Cincinnati: South-Western, 1998), pp. 284–287; and William Miller, *Innovation Styles* (Global Creativity Corporation, 1997). The adaptor-innovator concepts are from Michael J. Kirton, "Adaptors and Innovators: A Description and Measure," *Journal of Applied Psychology* 61, no. 5 (1976), p. 623.

effectively inspire others with a vision, yet he or she is weak on implementing strategic action. The vision in this case is only a dream, a fantasy, because it has little chance of ever becoming reality. To be an *effective leader,* one both dreams big *and* transforms those dreams into significant strategic action, either through his or her own activities or by hiring other leaders who can effectively

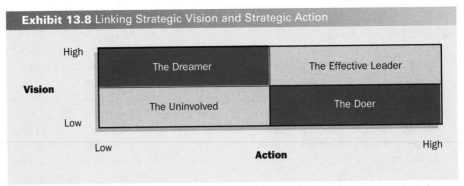

Exhibit 13.8 Linking Strategic Vision and Strategic Action

Source: Based on William D. Hitt, *The Leader–Manager: Guidelines for Action* (Columbus, OH: Battelle Press, 1988), p. 7.

implement the vision and strategy. For example, Steve Jobs of Apple has been hailed as a visionary leader whose dream of merging the worlds of technology and creative design keep Apple on the cutting edge. Yet Jobs also understand the importance of implementation.

Steve Jobs, Apple

Steve Jobs transformed Apple from a personal computer manufacturer into a dominant force in the digital entertainment business with the creation of the sleek, stylish iPod and the iTunes music store, changing the rules of the game in consumer electronics, entertainment, and software. But now Apple faces growing competition from Microsoft, Cingular, and other companies that are coming out with digital players and launching online music services. Jobs wants to make sure the iPod stays a step ahead, and he wants to increase sales of Macintosh computers in direct competition with Windows-based systems.

Jobs made a strategic decision in 2001 to get into the retail business in order to increase visibility and sales. He hired Ron Johnson, a fast-track Target executive, to help create a store experience that would be a physical embodiment of the Apple brand. The showcase store in Manhattan, which customers enter through a huge glass cube with a suspended Apple logo inside, reflects the company's reputation for clever design and is open 24 hours a day, seven days a week.

Jobs's vision broke all the standard rules about computer retailing. For example, conventional wisdom says stores selling expensive products like computers that are purchased infrequently should be located on inexpensive sites. But Jobs wanted to sell *digital experiences,* not just products. So, rather than building stand-alone stores on cheap land, he decided to locate in expensive sites like shopping malls and bustling downtown areas. Most employees are not there to sell but rather to provide free help on how to use Macintosh computers, iPods, Apple software, and accessories like digital cameras. Staff members are paid on salary rather than commission, unlike employees in most other computer retailers, so they don't feel pressure to push products. Apple stores "can be seen as solution boutiques," says Ted Schadler, an analyst at Forrester Research.

Getting into retailing was risky, but it has paid off. The Apple chain has become a retailing phenomenon. Revenue for each square foot at Apple stores last year was $2,489, compared to $971 at Best Buy, the huge computer and electronics chain. Stores are buzzing with people checking e-mail, browsing the Web, or listening to music. Think Starbucks without the lattes. Steve Jobs hopes the "Apple experience" can grow as large and powerful as the Starbucks one has.[66]

Steve Jobs "felt with every bone in his body that Apple had to do retailing" in order to meet it's strategic goals, says Ron Johnson, the former Target executive who is now senior vice president for retail operations at Apple.[67] Observers credit Jobs with the vision—and with the smarts to hire a talented retailer like Johnson to help him achieve it.

How Leaders Decide

To determine strategic direction for the future, leaders look inward, outward, and forward. Leaders scan both the internal and external organizational environment to identify trends, threats, and opportunities for the organization.

Organizations need both a broad and inspiring vision and an underlying plan for how to achieve it. To decide and map a strategic direction, leaders strive to develop industry foresight based on trends in technology, demographics, government regulation, values and lifestyles that will help them identify new competitive advantages. One approach leaders take in setting a course for the future is through hard analysis. Situation analysis, for example, includes a search for SWOT—strengths, weaknesses, opportunities, and threats that affect organizational performance. Leaders using situation analysis obtain external information from a variety of sources, such as customers, government reports, suppliers, consultants, or association meetings. They gather information about internal strengths and weaknesses from sources such as budgets, financial ratios, profit and loss statements, and employee surveys. Another formula often used by leaders is a five-force analysis developed by Michael Porter, who studied a number of businesses and proposed that strategy is often the result of five competitive forces: potential new entrants into an industry; the bargaining power of buyers; the bargaining power of suppliers; the threat of substitute products; and rivalry among competitors. By carefully examining these five forces, leaders can develop effective strategies to remain competitive.

Vision and strategy have to be based on a solid factual foundation, but too much rationality can get in the way of creating a compelling vision. Leaders do conduct rational analysis, but successful visions also reflect their personal experiences and understandings.[68] When leaders rely solely on formal strategic planning, competitor analysis, or market research, they miss new opportunities. Consider that when Ted Turner first talked about launching a 24-hour news and information channel in the 1970s, many dismissed him as delusional. Every source of conventional wisdom, from market research to broadcast professionals, said the vision was crazy and bound to fail. Yet Turner looked at emerging social and demographic trends, listened to his intuition, and launched a global network that generates 35 percent gross margins.[69]

To formulate a vision, leaders also look inward to their hopes and dreams, and they listen to the hopes and dreams of followers. Foresight and the ability to see future possibilities emerge not just from traditional strategic planning tools and formulas, but from curiosity, instinct and intuition, emotions, deep thinking, personal experience, and hope. To connect with people's deeper yearning for something great, vision can transcend the rational. Although it is based on reality, it comes from the heart rather than the head.

The Leader's Impact

When leaders link vision and strategy, they can make a real difference for their organization's future. A leader's greatest discretion is often over strategic vision and strategic action. Research has shown that strategic thinking and planning for the future can positively affect a company's performance and financial success.[70] Another study has shown that as much as 44 percent of the variance in profitability of major firms may be attributed to strategic leadership.[71]

One way leader impact has been evaluated is to examine whether top executive turnover makes a difference. Several studies of chief executive turnover have been conducted, including a sample of 167 corporations studied over a 20-year period, 193 manufacturing companies, a large sample of Methodist churches, and retail firms in the United Kingdom.[72] These studies found that leader succession was associated with improved profits and stock prices and, in the case of churches, with improved attendance, membership, and donations. Although good economic conditions and industry circumstances play a part in improved performance for any organization, the top leader had impact beyond these factors. Overall, when research has been carefully done, top leader succession typically explains from 20 percent to 45 percent of the variance in organizational outcomes.[73]

More recent research has explored the notion of top leadership teams, as opposed to an individual executive. The makeup of the top leadership group is believed to affect whether an organization develops organizational capability and the ability to exploit strategic opportunities. A team provides diverse aptitudes and skills to deal with complex organizational situations. Many researchers believe the configuration of the top leadership team to be more important for organizational success than the characteristics of a single CEO. For example, the size, diversity, attitudes, and skills of the team affect patterns of communication and collaboration, which, in turn, affect company performance.[74]

The emerging focus on teams is more realistic in some ways than focusing on individual leadership. In a complex environment, a single leader cannot do all things. An effective team may have a better chance of identifying and implementing a successful strategy, of discerning an accurate interpretation of the environment, and of developing internal capability based on empowered employees and a shared vision. Without a capable and effectively interacting top leadership team, a company may not adapt readily in a shifting environment. Although research in the area of leader impact is still relatively limited, it does seem to affirm the belief that the choices leaders make have significant impact on an organization's performance.

Summary and Interpretation

Leaders establish organizational direction through vision and strategy. They are responsible for studying the organization's environment, considering how it may be different in the future, and setting a direction everyone can believe in. The shared vision is an attractive, ideal future for the organization that is credible yet not readily attainable. A clear, powerful vision links the present and the future by showing how present actions and decisions can move the organization toward its long-range goals. Vision energizes employees and gives them an inspiring picture of the future to which they are eager to commit themselves. The vision can also give meaning to work and establish a standard of excellence by presenting a challenge that asks all workers to give their best.

The mission includes the company's core values and its core purpose or reason for existence. Visions for the future change, whereas the mission should persist, as a reflection of the enduring character of the organization. Effective leaders frame a noble purpose that inspires followers and helps the organization maintain a competitive advantage. To frame an organizational purpose that helps people find their work meaningful, leaders can choose among four basic concepts as the basis of purpose: discovery, excellence, altruism, and heroism.

Strategy is the serious work of figuring out how to translate vision and mission into action. Strategy is a general plan of action that describes resource allocation and other activities for dealing with the environment and helping the organization reach its goals. Like vision, strategy changes, but successful companies develop strategies that focus on core competence, develop synergy, and create value for customers. Strategy is implemented through the systems and structures that are the basic architecture for how things get done in the organization.

Leaders decide on direction through rational analysis as well as intuition, personal experience, and hopes and dreams. Leaders make a real difference for their organization only when they link vision to strategic action, so that vision is more than just a dream. Superior organizational performance is not a matter of luck. It is determined by the decisions leaders make.

Discussion Questions

1. A management consultant said that strategic leaders are concerned with vision and mission, while strategic managers are concerned with strategy. Do you agree? Discuss.

2. A vision can apply to an individual, a family, a college course, a career, or decorating an apartment. Think of something you care about for which you want the future to be different from the present and write a vision statement for it.

3. If you worked for a company like Apple or Google that has a strong vision for the future, how would that affect you compared to working for a company that did not have a vision?

4. Do you agree with the principle of self-reference? In other words, do you believe if people know where the organization is trying to go, they will make decisions that support the desired organizational outcome?

5. What does it mean to say that the vision can include a description of both the journey and the destination?

6. Many visions are written and hung on a wall. Do you think this type of vision has value? What would be required to imprint the vision within each person?

7. What is the difference between mission and vision? Can you give an example of each?

8. Do you think every organization needs a noble purpose in order to be successful over the long term? Discuss. Name one company that seems to reflect each category of noble purpose as defined in the chapter.

9. Strategic vision and strategic action are both needed for a leader to be effective. Which do you think you are better at doing? Why?

10. If a new top leader is hired for a corporation, and performance improves, to what extent do you think the new top leader was responsible compared to other factors? To what extent do you think a new coach is responsible if her basketball team did better after she took over?

Leadership at Work

Future Thinking

Think of some problem you have in your life right now. It could be any problem you are having at school, home, or work that you would like to solve. Write a few words that summarize the problem:

_____

_____

_____

Now write brief answers to the following questions for that specific problem. (Do not look ahead to the next set of four questions below. This exercise is more effective if the questions are seen in sequence.)

1. Why do I have this problem?

_____

_____

_____

2. Who/what caused this problem?

_____

_____

_____

3. What stands in the way of a solution?

_____

_____

_____

4. How likely is it that I'll solve this problem?

_____

_____

_____

After you have answered these four questions, write down what are you feeling about the problem.

_____

_____

_____

Now, for the same problem, write brief answers to the four questions below.

1. What do I really want instead of this problem? (Your answer equals your desired future outcome.)

_____

_____

_____

2. How will I know I've achieved this future outcome? (What will I see, hear, and feel?)

_____

_____

_____

3. What resources do I need to pursue this future outcome?

_____

_____

_____

4. What is the first step I can take to achieve this outcome?

_____

_____

_____

After you have answered these four questions, what are you feeling about the problem?

_____

_____

_____

The human mind is effective at focusing on problems to diagnose what is wrong and who to blame. The first four questions reflect that approach, which is called problem-focused thinking.

The second set of four questions reflects a different approach, called outcome-directed thinking. It focuses the mind on future outcomes and possibilities rather than on the causes of the problem. Most people feel more positive emotion, more creative ideas, and more optimism about solving the problem after answering the second four questions compared to the first four questions. Shifting the mind to the future harnesses the same power that a vision has to awaken creativity and inspire people to move forward. Future thinking is using the idea of future vision on a small, day-to-day scale.

In Class: This exercise is very effective when each student selects a problem, and then students interview each other about their problems. Students should work in pairs—one acting the role of leader and the other acting as a subordinate. The subordinate describes his or her problem (one minute), and then the leader simply asks the first four questions above (_changing each "I" to "you"_) and listens to the answers (four minutes). Then the two students can switch leader/subordinate roles and repeat the process for the same four questions. The instructor can then gather students' observations about what they felt when answering the four questions.

Then, students can be instructed to find a new partner, and the pairs can again adopt the role of leader and subordinate. The subordinate will relate the same problem as before to the leader, but this time the leader will ask the second four questions (outcome-directed thinking, _again changing each "I" to "you"_). After the subordinate answers the four questions, the pair switches leader/subordinate roles and repeats the process. Then the instructor can ask for student observations about how they felt answering these four questions compared to the first four questions. Generally the reaction is quite positive. The key questions for students to consider are: How did the questions about future outcomes affect your creative thoughts for solving the problem compared to the first four questions that were problem-oriented? As a leader, can you use future-oriented questions in your daily life to shape your thinking and the thinking of others toward more creative problem solving? Future-oriented thinking is a powerful leadership tool.

Sources: This approach to problem solving was developed by Robert P. Bostrom and Victoria K. Clawson of Bostrom and Associates, Columbia Missouri, and is based on a write-up appearing in "Inside USAA," (September 11, 1996), pp. 8–10; and Victoria K. Clawson and Robert P. Bostrom, "Research-Driven Facilitation Training for Computer-Supported Environments," _Group Decision and Negotiation_ 5 (1996), pp. 7–29.

Leadership Development: Cases for Analysis

Metropolis Police Department

You are in a hotel room watching the evening news as a local reporter interviews people who complain about abuse and mistreatment by police officers. These reports have been occurring in the news media with increasing frequency over the last three years. Some observers believe the problem is the police department's authoritarian style. Police managers encourage paramilitary values and a "them-against-us" attitude. The police orientation has been toward a spit-and-polish force that is efficient and tolerates no foolishness. The city believes that a highly professional, aloof police force is the best way to keep the city under control. Training emphasizes police techniques, the appropriate use of guns, and new technology, but there is no training on dealing with people. Several citizens have won large lawsuits against the police force, and many suits originated with minority groups. Critics believe the police chief is a major part of the problem. He has defended the rough actions of police officers, giving little public credence to complaints of abuse. He resists the community-oriented, people-friendly attitudes of other city departments. The chief has been considered insensitive toward minorities and has been heard to make disparaging public comments about African-Americans, women, and Hispanics.

One vocal critic alleges that police brutality depends on the vision and moral leadership set by the chief of police and lays responsibility for incidents of abuse on the current chief. Another critic believes there is a relationship between his intemperate remarks and the actions of police officers.

The reason you are in Metropolis, watching the news in a hotel room, is that you have been invited to interview for the job of police chief. The mayor and selected council members are preparing to fire the chief and name a replacement. You are thinking about what you would do if you took the job.

QUESTIONS

1. Identify themes that you would like to make a part of your vision for the police department.

2. If you get the job, how will you gain acceptance for your vision? How will you implement changes that will support the new vision and values?

3. Would you relish the challenge of becoming police chief of Metropolis? Why or why not?

The Visionary Leader

When Frank Coleman first began his job as president of Hi-Tech Aerostructures, most managers and employees felt a surge of hope and excitement. Hi-Tech Aerostructures is a 50-year-old family-owned manufacturing company that produces parts for the aircraft industry. The founder and owner had served as president until his health began to decline, and he felt the need to bring in someone from outside the company to get a fresh perspective. It was certainly needed. Over the past several years, Hi-Tech had just been stumbling along.

Coleman came to the company from a smaller business, but one with excellent credentials as a leader in advanced aircraft technology. He had a vision for transforming Hi-Tech into a world-class manufacturing facility. In addition to implementing cutting-edge technology, the vision included transforming the sleepy, paternalistic culture to a more dynamic, adaptive one and empowering employees to take a more active, responsible role in the organization. After years of just doing the same old thing day after day, vice president David Deacon was delighted with the new president and thrilled when Coleman asked him to head up the transformation project.

Deacon and his colleagues spent hours talking with Coleman, listening to him weave his ideas about the kind of company Hi-Tech could become. He assured the team that the transformation was his highest priority, and inspired them with stories about the significant impact they were going to have on the company as well as the entire aircraft industry. Together, the group crafted a vision statement that was distributed to all employees and posted all over the building. At lunchtime, the company cafeteria was abuzz with talk about the new vision. And when the young, nattily dressed president himself appeared in the cafeteria, as he did once every few weeks, it was almost as if a rock star had walked in.

At the team's first meeting with Coleman, Deacon presented several different ideas and concepts they had come up with, explaining the advantages of each for ripping Hi-Tech out of the past and slamming it jubilantly into the twenty-first century. Nothing, however, seemed to live up to Coleman's ambitions for the project—he thought all the suggestions were either too conventional or too confusing. After three hours the team left Coleman's office and went back to the drawing board. Everyone was even more fired up after Coleman's closing remarks about the potential to remake the industry and maybe even change the world.

Early the next day, Coleman called Deacon to his office and laid out his own broad ideas for how the project should proceed. "Not bad," thought Deacon, as he took the notes and drawings back to the team. "We can take this broad concept and really put some plans for action into place." The team's work over the next few months was for the most part lively and encouraging. Whenever Coleman would attend the meetings, he would suggest changes in many of their specific plans and goals, but miraculously, the transformation plan began to take shape. The team sent out a final draft to colleagues and outside consultants and the feedback was almost entirely positive.

The plan was delivered to Coleman on a Wednesday morning. When Deacon had still not heard anything by Friday afternoon, he began to worry. He knew Coleman had been busy with a major customer, but the president had indicated his intention to review the plan immediately. Finally, at 6 P.M., Coleman called Deacon to his office. "I'm afraid we just can't run with this," he said, tossing the team's months of hard work on the desk. "It's just . . . well, just not right for this company."

Deacon was stunned. And so was the rest of the team when he reported Coleman's reaction. In addition, word was beginning to get out around the company that all was not smooth with the transformation project. The cafeteria conversations were now more likely to be gripes that nothing was being done to help the company improve. Coleman assured the team, however, that his commitment was still strong; they just needed to take a different approach. Deacon asked that Coleman attend as many meetings as he could to help keep the team on the right track. Nearly a year later, the team waited in anticipation for Coleman's response to the revised proposal.

Coleman called Deacon at home on Friday night. "Let's meet on this project first thing Monday morning," he began. "I think we need to make a few adjustments. Looks like we're more or less headed in the right direction, though." Deacon felt like crying as he hung up the phone. All that time and work. He knew what he could expect on Monday morning. Coleman would lay out his vision and ask the team to start over.

Sources: Based on "The Vision Failed," Case 8.1 in Peter G. Northouse, *Leadership—Theory and Practice,* 2nd ed. (Thousand Oaks, CA: Sage, 2001), pp. 150–151; and Joe Kay, "My Year at a Big High Tech Company," *Forbes ASAP* (May 29, 2000), pp. 195–198; "Digital Diary (My Year at a Big High Tech Company)," *http://www.forbes. com/asap/2000/* accessed on November 19, 2000; and "Digital Diary, Part Two: The Miracle," *Forbes ASAP* (August 21, 2000), pp. 187–190.

QUESTIONS

1. How effective would you rate Coleman as a visionary leader? Discuss.

2. Where would you place Coleman on the chart of types of leaders in Exhibit 13.8? Where would you place Deacon?

3. If you were Deacon, what would you do?

References

1   David H. Freedman, "Burt Rutan: Entrepreneur of the Year," *Inc.* (January 2005), pp. 59–66; and Andy Pasztor, "In Race to Take Tourists Into Orbit, Partners Split, Spar," *The Wall Street Journal* (February 13, 2007), pp. A1, A22.

2   Keith H. Hammonds, "The Monroe Doctrine," *Fast Company* (October 1999), pp. 230–236.

3   James C. Collins and Jerry I. Porras, "Building Your Company's Vision," *Harvard Business Review* (September–October 1996), pp. 65–77.

4   R. Duane Ireland and Michael A. Hitt, "Achieving and Maintaining Strategic Competitiveness in the 21st Century: the Role of Strategic Leadership," *Academy of Management Executive* 13, no. 1 (1999), pp. 43–57; M. Davids, "Where Style Meets Substance", *Journal of Business Strategy* 16, no. 1 (1995), pp. 48–60; and R. P. White, P. Hodgson, and S. Crainer, *The Future of Leadership* (London: Pitman Publishing, 1997).

5   Ireland and Hitt, "Achieving and Maintaining Strategic Competitiveness."

6   Louisa Wah, "The Dear Cost of 'Scut Work,'" *Management Review* (June 1999), pp. 27–31.

7   Gary Hamel and C. K. Prahalad, "Seeing the Future First," *Fortune* (September 5, 1994), pp. 64–70.

8   Ray Maghroori and Eric Rolland, "Strategic Leadership: The Art of Balancing Organizational Mission with Policy, Procedures, and External Environment," *The Journal of Leadership Studies* no. 2 (1997), pp. 62–81.

9   John J. Fialka, "Power Surge; After Decades, A Solar Pioneer Sees a Spark in Sales," *The Wall Street Journal* (November 27, 2006), pp. A1, A11.

10 Collins and Porras, "Building Your Company's Vision."

11 Janet Adamy, "Father, Son, and Gum," *The Wall Street Journal* (March 11–12, 2006), pp. A1, A10; and Jeremy W. Peters, "New Chief at Wrigley is Outsider," *The New York Times* (October 24, 2006), p. C1.

12 R. J. Baum, E. A. Locke, and S. Kirkpatrick, "A Longitudinal Study of the Relations of Vision and Vision Communication to Venture Growth in Entrepreneurial Firms," *Journal of Applied Psychology* 83 (1998), pp. 43–54.

13 Yair Berson, Boas Shamir, Bruce J. Avolio, and Micha Popper, "The Relationship Between Vision Strength, Leadership Style, and Context," *The Leadership Quarterly* 12 (2001), pp. 53–73.

14 Roger Thurow, "Different Recipe; To Tackle Hunger, A Food Bank Tries Training Chefs," *The Wall Street Journal* (November 28, 2006), pp. A1, A13; and "Joseph Weber, "Waging War on Hunger," *BusinessWeek* (May 16, 2005), pp. 94, 96.

15 Andrea Kilpatrick and Les Silverman, "The Power of Vision," *Strategy & Leadership* 33, no. 2 (2005), pp. 24–26.

16 Andrew Douglas, John O. Burtis, and L. Kristine Pond-Burtis, "Myth and Leadership Vision: Rhetorical Manifestation of Cultural Force," *The Journal of Leadership Studies* 7, no. 4 (2001), pp. 55–69.

17 This section is based on Burt Nanus, *Visionary Leadership* (San Francisco: Jossey-Bass, 1992), pp. 16–18; and Richard L. Daft and Robert H. Lengel, *Fusion Leadership: Unlocking the Subtle Forces that Change People and Organizations* (San Francisco: Berrett-Koehler, 1998).

18 Oren Harari, "Looking Beyond the Vision Thing," *Management Review* (June 1997), pp. 26–29; and William D. Hitt, *The Leader-Manager: Guidelines for Action* (Columbus, OH: Battelle Press, 1988), p. 54.

19 Nancy Chambers, "The Really Long View," *Management Review* (January 1998), pp. 11–15, and Arie de Geus, "The Living Company," *Harvard Business Review* (March–April 1997), pp. 51–59.

20 Nanus, *Visionary Leadership,* p. 16.

21 Collins and Porras, "Building Your Company's Vision," p. 74.

22 Roger E. Herman and Joyce L. Gioia, "Making Work Meaningful: Secrets of the Future-Focused Corporation," *The Futurist* (December 1998), pp. 24–26.

23 Stephen J. Garone, "Motivation: What Makes People Work?" *Across the Board* (May–June 2001), pp. 79–80.

24 James M. Kouzes and Barry Z. Posner, *The Leadership Challenge: How to Get Extraordinary Things Done in Organizations* (San Francisco: Jossey-Bass, 1988), p. 98.

25 B. Thomas, *Walt Disney: An American Tradition* (New York: Simon & Schuster, 1976), pp. 246–247.

26 Marshall Sashkin, "The Visionary Leader," in Jay Conger and Rabindra N. Kanungo, eds., *Charismatic Leadership: The Elusive Factor in Organizational Effectiveness* (San Francisco: Jossey-Bass, 1988), pp. 122–160.

27 James C. Collins and Jerry I. Porras, "Organizational Vision and Visionary Organizations," *California Management Review* (Fall 1991), pp. 30–52.

28 Nanus, *Visionary Leadership,* 26; John W. Gardner, "Leadership and the Future," *The Futurist* (May–June 1990), pp. 9–12; and Warren Bennis and Burt Nanus, *Leaders: The Strategies for Taking Charge* (New York: Harper & Row, 1985), p. 93.

29 Gardner, "Leadership and the Future."

30 William F. Powers, segment in Polly LaBarre, ed., "What's New, What's Not," (Unit of One), *Fast Company* (January 1999), p. 73.

31 Daft and Lengel, *Fusion Leadership.*

32 Danielle Sacks, "Inspiration Junkies," *Fast Company* (November 2005), p. 95ff.

33 Peter M. Senge, *The Fifth Discipline: The Art and Practice of the Learning Organization* (New York: Doubleday/Currency, 1990), pp. 205–225.

34 Kouzes and Posner, *The Leadership Challenge,* p. 82.

35 Quoted in Senge, *The Fifth Discipline,* p. 218.

36 Joe Jaworski, quoted in Alan M. Webber, "Destiny and the Job of the Leader," *Fast Company* (June–July 1996), pp. 40, 42.

37 James Collins, "It's Not What You Make, It's What You Stand For," *Inc.* (October 1997), pp. 42–45.

38 Susan Ellingwood, "On a Mission," *Gallup Management Journal* (Winter 2001), pp. 6–7.

39 Ibid.

40 Collins and Porras, "Building Your Company's Vision."

41 Art Kleiner, George Roth, and Nina Kruschwitz, "Should a Company Have a Noble Purpose?" *The Conference Board Review* (January–February 2001).

42 Betsy Morris, "The Best Place to Work Now," *Fortune* (January 23, 2006), pp. 78–86.

43 This discussion is based on Nikos Mourkogiannis, "The Realist's Guide to Moral Purpose," *Strategy + Business* Issue 41 (Winter 2005), pp. 42–53.

44 Alan Deutschman, "Can Google Stay Google?" *Fast Company* (August 2005), pp. 62–68.

45 Bill Breen, "The Seoul of Design," *Fast Company* (December 2005), pp. 90–99; Peter Lewis, "A Perpetual Crisis Machine," *Fortune* (September 19, 2005), pp. 58–76; Steve Hamm with Ian Rowley, "Speed Demons," *BusinessWeek* (March 27, 2006), pp. 68–76; and Martin Fackler, "Electronics Company Aims to Create Break-Out Product," *The New York Times* (April 25, 2006), p. C1.

46 Steve Lohr, "Apple, a Success at Stores, Bets Big on Fifth Avenue," *The New York Times* (May 19, 2006), p. C1.

47 Mourkogiannis, "The Realist's Guide to Moral Purpose."

48 Ibid.

49 John E. Prescott, "Environments as Moderators of the Relationship between Strategy and Performance," *Academy of Management Journal* 29 (1986), p. 329–346.

50 Ireland and Hitt, "Achieving and Maintaining Strategic Competitiveness."

51 Christopher Hoenig, "True Grit," *CIO* (May 1, 2002), pp. 50–52.

52 Personal story heard at Farmer's Restaurant in Tenants Harbor, Maine.

53 Rafael Gerena-Morales, "How a Harlem Hospital Healed Itself," *The Wall Street Journal* (June 22, 2006), pp. B1, B5.

54 Gregory M. Bounds, Gregory H. Dobbins, and Oscar S. Fowler, *Management: A Total Quality Perspective* (Cincinnati, OH: South-Western, 1995), p. 244, and Michael Treacy, "You Need a Value Discipline—But Which One?" *Fortune* (April 17, 1995), p. 195.

55 Linda Tischler, "How Pottery Barn Wins With Style," *Fast Company* (June 2003), p. 106.

56 L. J. Bourgeois III and David R. Brodwin, "Strategic Implementation: Five Approaches to an Elusive Phenomenon," *Strategic Management Journal* 5 (1984), pp. 241–264; Anil K. Gupta and V. Govindarajan, "Business Unit Strategy, Managerial Characteristics, and Business Unit Effectiveness at Strategy Implementation," *Academy of Management Journal* (1984), pp. 25–41; and Michael K. Allio, "A Short Practical Guide to Implementing Strategy," *Journal of Business Strategy* 26, no. 4 (2005), pp. 12–21.

57 2004 *Economist* survey, reported in Allio, "A Short, Practical Guide to Implementing Strategy."

58 M. Corboy and D. O'Corrbui, "The Seven Deadly Sins of Strategy," *Management Accounting* 77, no. 10 (1999), pp. 29–33.

59 W. Robert Guffey and Brian J. Nienhaus, "Determinants of Employee Support for the Strategic Plan," *SAM Advanced Management Journal* (Spring 2002), pp. 23–30.

60 James Peters, "Applebee's Neighborhood Grill & Bar: Lisa Hofferbert," *Nation's Restaurant News* (January 26, 2004), p. 16.

61 Bruce Horovitz, "Payless Is Determined to Put a Fashionably Shod Foot Forward," *USA Today* (July 28, 2006), p. B1.

62 Thanks to Russell Guinn for the story on which this example is based.

63 Based on Gregory A. Patterson, "Land's End Kicks Out Modern New Managers, Rejecting a Makeover," *The Wall Street Journal* (April 3, 1995), pp. A1, A6.

64 Lucas Conley, "Back Up the Mountain," *Fast Company* (April 2005), pp. 85–86.

65 Quoted in Pat McHenry Sullivan, "Finding Visions for Work and Life," *Spirit at Work* (April 1997), p. 3.

66 Brent Schlender, "How Big Can Apple Get?" *Fortune* (February 21, 2005), pp. 66–76; and Steve Lohr, "Apple, a Success at Stores, Bets Big on Fifth Avenue," *The New York Times* (May 19, 2006), p. C1.

67 Lohr, "Apple, a Success at Stores."

68 Jill M. Strange and Michael D. Mumford, "The Origins of Vision: Effects of Reflection, Models, and Analysis," *The Leadership Quarterly* 16 (2005), pp. 121–148.

69 Oren Harari, "Catapult Your Strategy Over Conventional Wisdom," *Management Review* (October 1997), pp. 21–24.

70 C. Chet Miller and Laura B. Cardinal, "Strategic Planning and Firm Performance: A Synthesis of More than Two Decades of Research," *Academy of Management Journal* 37, no. 6 (1994), pp. 1649–1665.

71 Sydney Finkelstein and Donald C. Hambrick, *Strategic Leadership: Top Executives and Their Effect on Organizations* (St. Paul, MN: West Publishing, 1996), p. 23.

72 Stanley Lieberson and James F. O'Connor, "Leadership and Organizational Performance: A Study of Large Corporations," *American Sociological Review* 37 (1972), p. 119; Nan Weiner and Thomas A. Mahoney, "A Model of Corporate Performance as a Function of Environmental, Organizational, and Leadership Influences," *Academy of Management Journal* 24 (1981), pp. 453–470; Ralph A. Alexander, "Leadership: It Can Make a Difference," *Academy of Management Journal* 27 (1984), pp. 765–776; and Alan Berkeley Thomas, "Does Leadership Make a Difference to Organizational Performance?" *Administrative Science Quarterly* 33 (1988), pp. 388–400.

73 David G. Day and Robert G. Lord, "Executive Leadership and Organizational Performance: Suggestions for a New Theory and Methodology," *Journal of Management* 14 (1988), pp. 453–464.

74 Ken G. Smith, Ken A. Smith, Judy D. Olian, Henry P. Sims, Jr., Douglas P. O'Bannon, and Judith A. Scully, "Top Management Team Demography and Process: The Role of Social Integration and Communication," *Administrative Science Quarterly* 39 (1994), pp. 412–438.

Chapter 14

Your Leadership Challenge

After reading this chapter, you should be able to:

- Understand why shaping culture is a critical function of leadership.

- Recognize the characteristics of an adaptive, as opposed to an unadaptive, culture.

- Understand and apply how leaders shape culture and values through ceremonies, stories, symbols, language, selection and socialization, and daily actions.

- Identify the cultural values associated with adaptability, achievement, clan, and bureaucratic cultures and the environmental conditions associated with each.

- Act as an ethical leader and instill ethical values in the organizational culture.

- Apply the principles of spiritual leadership to help people find deeper life meaning and a sense of membership through work.

Chapter Outline

Shaping Culture and Values

Commerce Bank is one of the fastest growing banks in the United States—but it's also one of the goofiest places of business you're likely to find. Commerce's two costumed mascots regularly visit branches and mingle with customers at special events. Mr. C, a jolly, oversized, red letter, serves as the bank's walking logo. On "Red Fridays," Mr. C joins the "Wow Patrol" visiting branches and taking photos of staffers and customers. The second mascot, Buzz, an exuberant giant bee, also gets in on the act, making sure employees are creating buzz within the branches. "It sounds juvenile, but people love getting their picture taken with Mr. C," says John Manning, vice president of the Wow Department.

The *What* Department? "*Wow* is more than a word around here," Manning emphasizes. "It's a feeling that you give and get." That's right—all this silliness has a very serious purpose. Leaders rely on this playful culture to create and maintain Commerce Bank's obsession with customer service. In Commerce lingo, that means its focus on "wowing" customers. Through the company's *Kill a Stupid Rule* program, any employee who identifies a rule that prevents Commerce from wowing customers wins $50. Each week, Dr. Wow (no one knows his or her real identity) reviews hundreds of letters and e-mails from employees and customers. Branches compete to out-wow one another and take home the coveted Hill Cup (named for president and CEO Vernon Hill).

Whereas most banks try to steer customers from branches to ATMs and online banking, Commerce looks for ways to lure more customers in. Buildings are designed to attract visitors, with floor-to-ceiling windows and historic murals on the walls. Most are open from 7:30 A.M. to 8:00 P.M. seven days a week—and the company's 10-minute rule means that if you arrive at 7:20 A.M. or 8:10 P.M. you can still get service.

Commerce Bank's approach is working. Customers who are tired of being treated shabbily by other banks are enamored of Commerce's service and convenience orientation. "There's a different attitude around here, like we're all in this together," said one customer. As the organization grows, what tools does Commerce plan to use to keep its focus on superior service? President and CEO Vernon Hill gives one answer: "Culture, culture, culture." Without the wow, he says, Commerce would be just another bank.[1]

Commerce Bank has definite cultural values that make it unique in the banking industry. New managers and employees who attend sessions at Commerce University, the bank's training department inspired by McDonald's Hamburger University, learn that they've joined a service cult. A one-day course called Traditions—part game show, part training session, and part culture festival—begins socializing people into Commerce's unique way of doing things. Weekly activities such as Red Fridays and the care and attention of Dr. Wow help to keep the culture strong.

In the previous chapter, we talked about creating a vision that inspires and motivates people and defining the strategies to help achieve it. Successful leaders recognize that culture is a core element in helping the organization meet strategic goals and attain the vision. Leaders align people with the vision by influencing organizational culture and shaping the environment that determines morale and performance. The nature of the culture is highly important because it impacts a company for better or worse. Thriving companies such as Southwest Airlines and Starbucks have often attributed their success to the cultures their leaders helped create. Leaders at other companies, including Ford Motor Company, Boeing Corporation, and J. C. Penney, are trying to shift their cultural values to remain competitive in today's environment. Many leaders recognize that organizational culture is an important mechanism for attracting, motivating, and retaining talented employees, a capability that may be the single best predictor of overall organizational excellence.[2] One long-term study discovered that organizations with strong cultures outperform organizations with weak cultures two-to-one on several primary measures of financial performance.[3]

This chapter explores ideas about organizational culture and values, and the role of leaders in shaping them. The first section describes the nature of corporate culture and its importance to organizations. Then we turn to a consideration of how shared organizational values can help the organization stay competitive and how leaders influence cultural values for high performance. Leaders emphasize specific cultural values depending on the organization's situation. The final section of the chapter briefly discusses ethical and spiritual values and how values-based leadership shapes an organization's cultural atmosphere.

Action Memo
Complete Leader's Self-Insight 14.1, "How Spiritual are You," before reading the rest of this chapter.

Organizational Culture

As uncertainty and global competition has grown, the concept of culture has become increasingly important to organizational leaders because the new environment often calls for new values and ways of doing things. Most leaders now understand that when a company's culture fits the needs of its external environment and company strategy, employees can create an organization that is tough to beat.[4]

What Is Culture?

Some people think of culture as the character or personality of an organization. How an organization looks and "feels" when you enter it is a manifestation of the organizational culture. For example, you might visit one company where you get a sense of formality the minute you walk in the door. Desks are neat and orderly, employees wear professional business attire, and there are few personal items such as family photos or other decorations on walls and desks. At another company, employees may be wearing jeans and sweaters, have empty pizza boxes and cola cans on their desks, and bring their dogs to work with them. Both companies may be highly successful, but the underlying cultures are very different.

Culture
the set of key values, assumptions, understandings, and norms that is shared by members of an organization and taught to new members as correct

Culture can be defined as the set of key values, assumptions, understandings, and norms that is shared by members of an organization and taught to new members as correct.[5] *Norms* are shared standards that define what behaviors are acceptable and desirable within a group of people. At its most basic, culture is a pattern of shared assumptions about how things are done in an organization. As organizational members cope with internal and external problems, they develop shared assumptions and norms of behavior that are taught to new members as the correct way to think, feel, and act in relation to those problems.[6]

Culture can be thought of as consisting of three levels, as illustrated in Exhibit 14.1, with each level becoming less obvious.[7] At the surface level are visible artifacts, such as manner of dress, patterns of behavior, physical symbols,

Getty Images

How Spiritual Are You?

Think about your current life. Indicate whether each item below is Mostly False or Mostly True for you.

	Mostly False	Mostly True
1. I often reflect on the meaning of life.	_____	_____
2. I want to find a community where I can grow spiritually.	_____	_____
3. I have made real personal sacrifices in order to make the world a better place.	_____	_____
4. Sometimes when I look at an ordinary thing I feel that I am seeing it fresh for the first time.	_____	_____
5. I sometimes have unexpected flashes of insight or understanding while relaxing.	_____	_____
6. It is important to me to find meaning and mission in the world.	_____	_____
7. I often feel a strong sense of unity or connection with all the people around me.	_____	_____
8. I have had experiences that made my role in life clear to me.	_____	_____
9. After reflecting on something for a long time, I have learned to trust my feelings rather than logical reasons.	_____	_____
10. I am often transfixed by loveliness in nature.	_____	_____

Scoring and Interpretation

Spiritual leadership engages people in higher values and mission, and tries to create a corporate culture based on love and community rather than fear and separation. Spiritual leadership is not for everyone, but when spiritual ideals guide a leader's behavior, an excellent culture can be created. Values-based and spiritual leadership are discussed later in the chapter.

Add the number of Mostly True answers above for your score: _____. A score of 7 or above indicates that you are highly spiritual and will likely become a values-based or spiritual leader. A score of 4–6 would suggest that you are spiritually average. A score of 0–3 means that you may be skeptical about developing spiritual awareness.

Source: Kirsi Tirri, Petri Nokelainen, and Martin Ubani, "Conceptual Definition and Empirical Validation of the Spiritual Sensitivity Scale," *Journal of Empicial Theology* 19, no. 1 (2006), pp. 37–62; and Jeffrey Kluger, "Is God in Our Genes?" *Time* (October 25, 2004), pp. 62–72.

Exhibit 14.1 Levels of Corporate Culture

Culture that can be seen at the surface level

Visible
1. Artifacts, such as dress, office layout, symbols, slogans, ceremonies

Invisible
2. Expressed values, such as "The Penney Idea," "The HP Way"
3. Underlying assumptions and deep beliefs, such as "people here care about one another like a family"

Deeper values and shared understandings held by organization members organizational ceremonies, and office layout—all the things one can see, hear, and observe by watching members of the organization. Consider some visible artifacts of culture at John Lewis, one of Britain's most successful retailers. People working in John Lewis stores are typically older than staff members at other retailers and are called partners, not employees. Everyone shares in company profits and has a say in how the business is run. The entrance to leaders' offices is small and functional rather than ostentatious, and stores exude an air of simplicity, calmness, and order.[8] At a deeper level of culture are the expressed values and beliefs, which are not observable but can be discerned from how people explain and justify what they do. These are values that members of the organization hold at a conscious level. For example, John Lewis partners consciously know that dependability, service, and quality are highly valued and rewarded in the company culture.

Some values become so deeply embedded in a culture that organizational members may not be consciously aware of them. These basic, underlying assumptions are the deepest essence of the culture. At John Lewis, these assumptions might include (1) that the company cares about its employees as much as it expects them to care about customers, (2) that individual employees should think for themselves and do what they believe is right to provide exceptional customer service, and (3) that trust and honesty are an essential part of successful business relationships. Assumptions generally start out as expressed values, but over time they become more deeply embedded and less open to question— organization members take them for granted and often are not even aware of the assumptions that guide their behavior, language, and patterns of social interaction.

Importance of Culture

When people are successful at what they undertake, the ideas and values that led to that success become institutionalized as part of the organization's culture.[9] Culture gives employees a sense of organizational identity and generates a commitment to particular values and ways of doing things. Culture serves two important functions in organizations: (1) it integrates members so that they know how to relate to one another, and (2) it helps the organization adapt to the external environment.

Internal Integration Culture helps members develop a collective identity and know how to work together effectively. It is culture that guides day-to-day working relationships and determines how people communicate in the organization, what behavior is acceptable or not acceptable, and how power and status are allocated. Culture can imprint a set of unwritten rules inside employees' minds, which can be very powerful in determining behavior, thus affecting organizational performance.[10]

Many organizations are putting increased emphasis on developing strong cultures that encourage teamwork, collaboration, and mutual trust.[11] In an environment of trust, people are more likely to share ideas, be creative, and be generous with their knowledge and talents. At the Container Store, a chain of retail stores that sells boxes, garbage cans, shelving, and just about anything else you might need to organize your home, office, or car, the culture encourages employees to do whatever needs to be done. Simple maxims like "treat people the way you want to be treated" and "be helpful to others" are granted policy status at the Container Store. Cultural values that promote open communication, cooperation, and equality have helped the company consistently win top spots on *Fortune* magazine's list of the best companies to work for in America.[12]

External Adaptation Culture also determines how the organization meets goals and deals with outsiders. The right cultural values can help the organization respond rapidly to customer needs or the moves of a competitor. Culture can encourage employee commitment to the core purpose of the organization, its specific goals, and the basic means used to accomplish goals.

The culture should embody the values and assumptions needed by the organization to succeed in its environment. If the competitive environment requires speed and flexibility, for example, the culture should embody values that support adaptability, collaboration across departments, and a fast response to customer needs or environmental changes. Consider how the cultural values at FedEx meet the needs of its competitive environment.

Nicky Cava, FedEx

Ever wonder how FedEx consistently manages to get things delivered right on time? It's partly because the company lets its drivers decide the best way to get packages where they need to be. Daniel Roth, a writer at *Fortune* magazine, rode with FedEx driver Nicky Cava to get a glimpse of how FedEx operates.

One of the first things Roth noticed was that Cava proudly pointed out "his truck." Drivers feel like owners of their delivery vehicles because once they leave the station, they're their own boss. FedEx believes in efficiency, but there are no monitoring systems tracking where drivers go or how long it takes them to get there. All the company cares about is that drivers stay safe and make their deliveries fast to the right people. What seemed to Roth, for example, to be unnecessary circling of the same blocks was actually Cava's way of calculating in his head the best routes to take to make sure he got the priority packages delivered on time and still had plenty of time to deliver all his standard packages by the end of the day.

FedEx thrives on a culture of innovation and adaptability, and the hands-off approach with drivers is an illustration of how leaders encourage and support that culture. Decision making is decentralized so that people throughout the company can do what is needed to make sure customers are satisfied. Promotion from within is gospel; every person is valued and seen as a leader with potential to rise through the ranks. In addition, managers emphasize listening, so that employees feel free to share their ideas for how to do things better or faster. Cross-functional teams support collaboration across departments and help to ensure that creative ideas get implemented.

FedEx leaders often attribute their company's success to front-line employees who go above and beyond the call of duty. They instill and support cultural values of trust, innovation, risk-taking, and flexibility, which gives people freedom to explore and create. As FedEx driver Cava puts it, "the only way you lose your job at FedEx is if you make yourself lose your job."[13]

At FedEx, a strong culture helps bind people together, making the organization a community rather than just a collection of individuals. However the culture also encourages adaptation to the environment in order to keep the organization healthy and profitable. This chapter's *Consider This* highlights the importance of individual learning and adaptability. Just like people, organizational cultures have to grow and change to meet new challenges.

Culture Strength, Adaptation, and Performance

Culture strength
the degree of agreement among employees about the importance of specific values and ways of doing things

Culture strength refers to the degree of agreement among employees about the importance of specific values and ways of doing things. If widespread consensus exists, the culture is strong and cohesive; if little agreement exists, the culture is weak.[14] The effect of a strong culture is not always a positive one. Sometimes a strong culture can encourage the wrong values and cause harm to the organization and its members. Think of Enron Corp., which failed largely because of a strong culture that supported pushing everything to the limits: business practices, rules, personal behavior, and laws. Executives drove expensive cars, challenged employees to participate in dangerous competitive behavior, and often celebrated big deals by heading off to a bar or club for a night of carousing.[15]

Thus, a strong culture increases employee cohesion and commitment to the values, goals, and strategies of the organization, but companies can sometimes have unethical values or values that are unhealthy for the organization because they don't fit the needs of the environment. Research at Harvard into some 200 corporate cultures found that a strong culture does not ensure success unless it also encourages a healthy adaptation to the external environment.[16] A strong culture that does not encourage adaptation can be more damaging to an organization than a weak culture. For example, J. C. Penney Company has a deeply-entrenched corporate culture rooted in the company's 1902 founding as "The Golden Rule Store." Penney's founder emphasized values such as agreeableness, thriftiness, discipline, and dignity. Over time, these values led to a degree of formality and a paternalistic attitude among many managers that prevented employees from proposing changes and participating fully in the organization. Only senior managers, for example, were eligible for awards and ceremonies honoring employees for a commitment to service and cooperation. New CEO Mike Ullman is trying to shift Penney's to a more democratic and egalitarian culture, emphasizing the use of first names among colleagues and their superiors, selling off the company's art collection and replacing it with photos of rank-and-file employees, and giving everyone access to all parts of headquarters, including the executive suite. Ullman has adapted the company's core values for modern times in a statement called *Winning Together Principles*. "If I had a choice to honor the past and lose, or move forward and win, I pick winning," Ullman says.[17]

Adaptive Cultures

As illustrated in Exhibit 14.2, adaptive corporate cultures have different values and behavior from unadaptive cultures. In adaptive cultures, leaders are concerned with customers and those internal people, processes, and procedures that bring about useful change. In unadaptive cultures, leaders are concerned with themselves or their own special projects, and their values tend to discourage risk-taking and change. Thus, a strong culture is not enough,

Action Memo

To improve your understanding of adaptive versus unadaptive cultures, go to Leader's Self-Insight 14.2 on page 428 and assess the cultural values of a place you have worked.

	Exhibit 14.2 Adaptive Versus Unadaptive Cultures	
	Adaptive Organizational Culture	**Unadaptive Organizational Culture**
Visible Behavior	Leaders pay close attention to all their constituencies, especially customers, and initiate change when needed to serve their legitimate interests, even if it entails taking some risks.	Managers tend to behave somewhat insularly, politically, and bureaucratically. As a result, they do not change their strategies quickly to adjust to or take advantage of changes in their business environments.
Expressed Values	Leaders care deeply about customers, stockholders, and employees. They also strongly value people and processes that can create useful change (e.g., leadership initiatives up and down the management hierarchy).	Managers care mainly about themselves, their immediate work group, or some product (or technology) associated with that work group. They value the orderly and risk-reducing management process much more highly than leadership initiatives.
Underlying Assumption	Serve whole organization, trust others.	Meet own needs, distrust others.

Source: Reprinted with the permission of The Free Press, a Division of Simon & Schuster Adult Publishing Group, from *Corporate Culture and Performance* by John P. Kotter and James L. Heskett. Copyright © 1992 by Kotter Associates, Inc. and James L. Heskett. All rights reserved.

Think of a specific full-time job you have held. Indicate whether each item below is Mostly False or Mostly True according to your perception of the *managers above you* when you held that job.

	Mostly False	Mostly True
1. Good ideas got serious consideration from management above me.	_____	_____
2. Management above me was interested in ideas and suggestions from people at my level in the organization.	_____	_____
3. When suggestions were made to management above me, they received fair evaluation.	_____	_____
4. Management did not expect me to challenge or change the status quo.	_____	_____
5. Management specifically encouraged me to bring about improvements in my workplace.	_____	_____
6. Management above me took action on recommendations made from people at my level.	_____	_____
7. Management rewarded me for correcting problems.	_____	_____
8. Management clearly expected me to improve work unit procedures and practices.	_____	_____
9. I felt free to make recommendations to management above me to change existing practices.	_____	_____
10. Good ideas did not get communicated upward because management above me was not very approachable.	_____	_____

Scoring and Interpretation

To compute your score: Give yourself one point for each Mostly True answer to questions 1, 2, 3, 5, 6, 7, 8, and 9 and for each Mostly False answer to questions 4 and 10. Total points _____.

An adaptive culture is shaped by the values and actions of top and middle managers. When managers actively encourage and welcome change initiatives from below, the organization will be infused with values for change. These 10 questions measure your management's openness to change. A typical average score for management's openness to change is about 4. If your average score was 5 or higher, you worked in an organization that expressed cultural values of adaptation. If your average score was 3 or below, the culture was probably unadaptive.

Thinking back to your job, was the level of management openness to change correct for that organization? Why? Compare your score to that of another student, and take turns describing what it was like working for the managers above you. Do you sense that there is a relationship between job satisfaction and management's openness to change? What specific manager characteristics and corporate values accounted for the openness (or lack of) in the two jobs?

Sources: S. J. Ashford, N. P. Rothbard, S. K. Piderit, and J. E. Dutton, "Out on a Limb: The Role of Context and Impression Management in Issue Selling," *Administrative Science Quarterly* 43 (1998), pp. 23–57; and E. W. Morrison and C. C. Phelps, "Taking Charge at Work: Extrarole Efforts to Initiate Workplace Change," *Academy of Management Journal* 42, (1999), pp. 403–419.

because an unhealthy culture may encourage the organization to march resolutely in the wrong direction. Healthy cultures help companies adapt to the external environment.

An organization's culture may not always be in alignment with the needs of the external environment. The values and ways of doing things may reflect what worked in the past, as they did at J. C. Penney. The difference between desired and actual values and behaviors is called the **culture gap**.[18] Many organizations have some degree of culture gap, though leaders often fail to realize it. An important step toward shifting the culture toward more adaptive values is to recognize when people are adhering to the wrong values or when important values are not held strongly enough.[19]

Culture gap
the difference between desired and actual values and behaviors

Culture gaps can be immense, particularly in the case of mergers. Consider what happened after Chicago's Tribune Co. (*Chicago Tribune*) acquired Times Mirror Co. (*Los Angeles Times*). People at the *Times* consider the *Chicago Tribune* a provincial newspaper and see their new owners as bean-counters in business suits who care little about journalistic excellence. Many people at the *Tribune*, on the other hand, think the *Los Angeles Times* is arrogant and spoiled. The two sides have battled in particular over whether to focus on local news, which the *Tribune* does, at the expense of national and international coverage, which the *Times* considers essential. Trying to merge the two widely different philosophies and cultures has exacerbated the troubles both companies were having prior to the acquisition. "It's a tragic, bad marriage," said *Times* former editor Dean Baquet.[20]

Despite the popularity of mergers and acquisitions as a corporate strategy, many fail. Almost one-half of all acquired companies are sold within five years, and some experts claim that 90 percent of mergers never live up to expectations.[21] One reason for this is the difficulty of integrating cultures. Organizational leaders should remember that the human systems—in particular, the norms and values of corporate culture—are what make or break any change initiative. The problem of integrating cultures increases in scope and complexity with global companies and cross-cultural mergers or acquisitions.

The High-Performance Culture

Culture plays an important role in creating an organizational climate that enables learning and innovative response to challenges, competitive threats, or new opportunities. A strong culture that encourages adaptation and change enhances organizational performance by energizing and motivating employees, unifying people around shared goals and a higher mission, and shaping and guiding employee behavior so that everyone's actions are aligned with strategic priorities. Thus, creating and influencing an adaptive culture is one of the most important jobs for organizational leaders. The right culture can drive high performance.[22]

A number of studies have found a positive relationship between culture and performance.[23] In *Corporate Culture and Performance*, Kotter and Heskett provided evidence that companies that intentionally managed cultural values outperformed similar companies that did not.[24] Some companies have developed systematic ways to measure and manage the impact of culture on organizational performance. At Caterpillar Inc., leaders used a tool called the Cultural Assessment Process (CAP), to give top executives hard data documenting millions of dollars in savings they could attribute directly to cultural factors.[25] Even the U.S. government is recognizing the link between culture and effectiveness. The U.S. Office of Personnel Management created its Organizational Assessment Survey as a way for federal agencies to measure culture factors and shift values toward high performance.[26]

Strong adaptive cultures that facilitate high performance often incorporate the following values:

1. *The whole is more important than the parts and boundaries between parts are minimized.* People are aware of the whole system, how everything fits together, and the relationships among various organizational parts. All members consider how their actions affect other parts and the total organization. This emphasis on the whole reduces boundaries both within the organization and with other companies. Although subcultures may form, everyone's primary attitudes and behaviors reflect the organization's dominant culture. The free flow of people, ideas, and information allows coordinated action and continuous learning.

2. *Equality and trust are primary values.* The culture creates a sense of community and caring for one another. The organization is a place for creating a web of relationships that allows people to take risks and develop to their full potential. The emphasis on treating everyone with care and respect creates a climate of safety and trust that allows experimentation, frequent mistakes, and learning. Managers emphasize honest and open communications as a way to build trust.

3. *The culture encourages risk taking, change, and improvement.* A basic value is to question the status quo. Constant questioning of assumptions opens the gates to creativity and improvement. The culture rewards and celebrates the creators of new ideas, products, and work processes. To symbolize the importance of taking risks, an adaptive culture may also reward those who fail in order to learn and grow.

In addition, high-performance cultures emphasize both values and solid business performance as the drivers of organizational success. Leaders align values with the company's day-to-day operations—hiring practices, performance management, budgeting, criteria for promotions and rewards, and so forth. A 2004 study of corporate values by Booz Allen Hamilton and the Aspen Institute found that managers in companies that report superior financial results typically put a high emphasis on values and link them directly to the way they run the organization.[27] A good example is Commerce Bank, which was described in the chapter opening example, where recruitment, training, incentives, and other practices are tied directly to the cultural values leaders want to encourage.

Cultural Leadership

An organization exists only because of the people who are a part of it, and those people both shape and interpret the character and culture of the organization. That is, an organization is not a slice of objective reality; different people may perceive the organization in different ways and relate to it in different ways. Leaders in particular formulate a viewpoint about the organization and the values that can help people achieve the organization's mission, vision, and strategic goals. Therefore, leaders enact a viewpoint and a set of values that they think are best for helping the organization succeed. A primary way in which leaders influence norms and values to build a high-performance culture is through *cultural leadership*.

Cultural leader
A leader who actively uses signals and symbols to influence corporate culture

A **cultural leader** defines and uses signals and symbols to influence corporate culture. Cultural leaders influence culture in two key areas:

1. *The cultural leader articulates a vision for the organizational culture that employees can believe in.* This means the leader defines and communicates central values that employees believe in and will rally around. Values are tied to a clear and compelling mission, or core purpose.

2. *The cultural leader heeds the day-to-day activities that reinforce the cultural vision.* The leader makes sure that work procedures and reward systems match and reinforce the values. Actions speak louder than words, so cultural leaders "walk their talk."[28]

For values to guide the organization, leaders model them every day. Canada's WestJet Airlines, which ranked in a survey as having Canada's most admired corporate culture, provides an illustration. Employees (called simply "people" at WestJet) regularly see CEO Clive Beddoe and other top leaders putting the values of equality, teamwork, participation, and customer service into action. At the end of a flight, for example, everyone on hand pitches in to pick up garbage—even the CEO. Top executives spend much of their time chatting informally with employees and customers, and they regularly send notes of thanks to people who have gone above and beyond the call of duty. Top executives have been known to visit the call center on Christmas Day to pitch in and to thank people for working the holiday. Leaders don't receive perks over and above anyone else. There are no assigned parking spaces and no club memberships. Every person at WestJet is treated like first-class, exactly the way leaders want employees to treat every passenger on a WestJet flight.[29]

Creating and maintaining a high-performance culture is not easy in today's turbulent environment and changing workplace, but through their words—and particularly their actions—cultural leaders let everyone in the organization know what really counts. Some of the mechanisms leaders use to enact cultural values are organizational rites and ceremonies, stories, symbols, and specialized language. In addition, they emphasize careful selection and socialization of new employees to keep cultures strong. Perhaps most importantly, leaders signal the cultural values they want to instill in the organization through their day-to-day behavior.

Action Memo

As a leader, you can build a high-performance culture that is strong and adaptive by showing concern for customers and other stakeholders in the external environment and by supporting people and projects that bring about useful change. You can be alert to culture gaps and influence values to close them.

Ceremonies

A **ceremony** is a planned activity that makes up a special event and is generally conducted for the benefit of an audience. Leaders can schedule ceremonies to provide dramatic examples of what the company values. Ceremonies reinforce specific values, create a bond among employees by allowing them to share an important event, and anoint and celebrate employees who symbolize important achievements.[30]

A ceremony often includes the presentation of an award. At Mary Kay Cosmetics, one of the most effective companies in the world at using ceremonies, leaders hold elaborate award ceremonies at an annual event called "Seminar," presenting jewelry, furs, and luxury cars to high-achieving sales consultants. The most successful consultants are introduced by film clips like the ones used to present award nominees in the entertainment industry.[31] These ceremonies recognize and celebrate high-performing employees and help bind sales consultants together. Even when they know they will not personally be receiving awards, consultants look forward to Seminar all year because of the emotional bond it creates with others.

Ceremony
a planned activity that makes up a special event and is generally conducted for the benefit of an audience

Stories

A **story** is a narrative based on true events that is repeated frequently and shared among employees. Stories are told to new employees to illustrate the company's primary values. As we discussed in Chapter 9, storytelling is a powerful way to connect with others on an emotional level, and leaders can use stories to transmit and reinforce important values and provide a shared meaning for organization members. Employees at IBM tell a story about a female security supervisor who challenged IBM's chairman because he didn't have the proper clearance identification to enter a security area. Rather than chastising the officer, the chairman thanked her for doing her job.[32] One FedEx story concerns the driver who had lost the key to a drop box. Not wanting to risk the packages being delivered late, he unbolted the box, loaded it in his truck, and hauled it back to the station where it could be opened. As the story goes, FedEx rewarded the driver's initiative. By telling this story, workers communicate that

Story
a narrative based on true events that is repeated frequently and shared among employees

the company stands behind its commitment to values of worker autonomy and customer service.

In some cases, stories may not be supported by facts, but they are consistent with the values and beliefs of the organization. At Nordstrom, for example, leaders do not deny the story about a customer who got his money back on a defective tire, even though Nordstrom does not sell tires. The story reinforces the company's no-questions-asked return policy.[33]

Symbols

Another tool for conveying cultural values is the **symbol**. A symbol is an object, act, or event that conveys meaning to others. In a sense, stories and ceremonies are symbols, but leaders can also use physical artifacts to symbolize important values. Recall the earlier example from J. C. Penney, where Mike Ullman is selling the company's expensive art collection and instead putting up photos of employees. Ullman wants to symbolize a new cultural value that recognizes the worth of front-line employees and considers their efforts and contributions to be the lifeblood of the company.

Specialized Language

Language can shape and influence organizational values and beliefs. Leaders sometimes use slogans or sayings to express key corporate values. Slogans can easily be picked up and repeated by employees. For example, at Averitt Express, the slogan "Our driving force is people," applies to customers and employees alike. The culture emphasizes that drivers and customers, not top executives, are the power that fuels the company's success.

Leaders also express and reinforce cultural values through written public statements, such as corporate mission statements or other formal statements that express the core values of the organization. Leaders at Eli Lilly and Company developed a formal statement of corporate values, including respect for all people, honesty and integrity, and striving for continuous improvement.[34] Eaton Corporation's philosophy statement, called "Excellence Through People," includes values such as encouraging employee involvement in all decisions, regular face-to-face communication between executives and employees, emphasizing promotion from within, and always focusing on the positive behavior of workers.[35]

Selection and Socialization

To maintain cultural values over time, leaders emphasize careful selection and socialization of new employees. Companies with strong, healthy cultures, such as Genentech, described in the previous chapter, Nordstrom, Southwest Airlines, and PSS World Medical, often have rigorous hiring practices. PSS, for example, doesn't call candidates back for follow-up interviews. Requiring the candidate to take the initiative through every step of the recruiting and hiring process, which takes six to eight weeks, ensures that PSS hires people with the right values and attitudes to fit its achievement-oriented culture.[36]

Once the right people are hired, the next step is socializing them into the culture. **Socialization** is the process by which a person learns the values, norms, perspectives, and expected behaviors that enable him or her to successfully participate in the group or organization.[37] When people are effectively socialized, they "fit in," because they understand and adopt the norms and values of the group. Socialization is a key leadership tool for transmitting the culture and enabling it to survive over time. Leaders act as role models for the values they want new employees

Action Memo
As a leader, you can shape cultural values through rites and ceremonies, stories, symbols, and language. You can keep the culture strong by carefully selecting and socializing people, and by making sure your actions match the espoused values.

to adopt, as well as implement formal training programs, which may include pairing the newcomer with a key employee who embodies the desired values.

Newcomers learn about values by watching other employees, as well as paying attention to what gets noticed and rewarded by leaders. But good leaders don't leave socialization to chance. At The Walt Disney Company, for example, all new employees attend training sessions to learn about Disney's unique culture, where employees are referred to as "cast members," work either "on stage" or "backstage," and wear "costumes" rather than uniforms. After their initial training, each new hire is paired with a role model to continue the socialization process.[38] Starbucks Coffee also emphasizes socialization to maintain its strong culture. CEO Howard Schultz compares an employee's first days with the company to the early years of childhood, when you want to instill good values, high self-esteem, and the confidence to begin taking risks and making decisions. Schultz himself welcomes each new employee by video, tells about the company's history and culture, and shares some of his own personal experiences at Starbucks. All employees receive 24 hours of training, during which they talk about the Starbucks mission and values and the qualities that make Starbucks a unique company.[39] Even though Schultz believes an employee's first two weeks may be the most important, socialization also continues throughout an employee's tenure with the organization.

Formal socialization programs can be highly effective. One study of recruits into the British Army surveyed newcomers on their first day and then again eight weeks later. Researchers compared the findings to a sample of experienced "insider" soldiers and found that after eight weeks of training, the new recruits' norms and values had generally shifted toward those of the insiders.[40] Another field study of around 300 people from a variety of organizations found that formal socialization was associated with less stress for newcomers, less ambiguity about expected roles and behaviors, and greater job satisfaction, commitment, and identification with the organization.[41]

Daily Actions

One of the most important ways leaders build and maintain the cultures they want is by signaling and supporting important cultural values through their daily actions. Employees learn what is valued most in a company by watching what attitudes and behaviors leaders pay attention to and reward, how leaders react to organizational crises, and whether the leader's own behavior matches the espoused values.[42] Steel company Nucor's CEO Daniel DiMicco supports the egalitarian cultural values by doing without perks such as an executive jet or assigned parking space; and when he takes the last cup of coffee in the break room, DiMicco is always careful to brew another pot.[43] Good leaders understand how carefully they are watched by employees.

Leaders can also change unadaptive cultures by their actions. For example, at Marriott, as at many hotels, the pursuit of superior round-the-clock performance led to a deeply ingrained culture of *face time*—the more hours a manager put in, the better. By the late 1990s, though, this philosophy was making it tough for Marriott to find and keep talented people. When leaders wanted to instill values that encouraged work–life balance and an emphasis on results rather than hours worked, one of their most important steps was to make a point of leaving work early whenever possible. Encouraging lower-level managers to take more time off did no good until top leaders demonstrated the new value with their own behavior.[44]

Through ceremonies, stories, symbols, language, selection and socialization practices, and their own behavior, leaders influence culture. When culture change is needed to adapt to the environment or bring about smoother internal integration, leaders are responsible for instilling new values.

The Competing Values Approach to Shaping Culture

Organizational values are the enduring beliefs that have worth, merit, and importance for the organization. The crisis in corporate ethics and the crash of once-promising companies such as WorldCom, Qwest, Enron, and Arthur Andersen have brought values to the forefront. One review of recent company failures revealed that unhealthy cultural values played a crucial role in many of the mistakes these companies made.[45] Ethical values will be discussed later in the chapter. Changes in the nature of work, increasing diversity in the workforce, and other shifts in the larger society have also made the topic of values one of considerable concern to leaders. They are faced with such questions as, "How can I determine what cultural values are important? Are some values 'better' than others? How can the organization's culture help us be more competitive?"

In considering what values are important for the organization, leaders consider the external environment and the company's vision and strategy. Cultures can vary widely across organizations; however, organizations within the same industry often reveal similar values because they are operating in similar environments.[46] Key values should embody what the organization needs to be effective. Rather than looking at values as either "good" or "bad," leaders look for the right combination. The correct relationship among cultural values, organizational strategy, and the external environment can enhance organizational performance.

Organizational cultures can be assessed along many dimensions, such as the extent of collaboration versus isolation among people and departments, the importance of control and where control is concentrated, or whether the organization's time orientation is short-range or long-range.[47] Here, we will focus on two specific dimensions: (1) the extent to which the competitive environment requires flexibility or stability; and (2) the extent to which the organization's strategic focus and strength is internal or external. Four categories of culture associated with these differences, as illustrated in Exhibit 14.3, are adaptability, achievement, clan, and bureaucratic.[48] These four categories relate to the fit among cultural values, strategy, structure, and the environment, with each emphasizing specific values, as shown in the exhibit.

An organization may have cultural values that fall into more than one category, or even into all categories. However, successful organizations with strong cultures will lean more toward one particular culture category.

Adaptability Culture

The **adaptability culture** is characterized by strategic leaders encouraging values that support the organization's ability to interpret and translate signals from the environment into new behavior responses. Employees have autonomy to make decisions and act freely to meet new needs, and responsiveness to customers is highly valued. Leaders also actively create change by encouraging and rewarding creativity, experimentation, and risk-taking. A good example of an adaptability culture is 3M Corp., where leaders encourage experimentation and taking risks as an everyday way of life. All employees attend a class on risk-taking where they are encouraged to defy their supervisors if necessary to pursue a promising idea. Researchers are allowed to use 15 percent of their time to explore ideas outside their assigned projects. This encouragement of *experimental doodling*, as an early 3M manager called it, has led to the creation of hundreds of innovative projects and entrenched 3M as a leader in some of today's most dynamic global markets.[49] Many technology and Internet companies also use this type of culture because they must move quickly to satisfy customers.

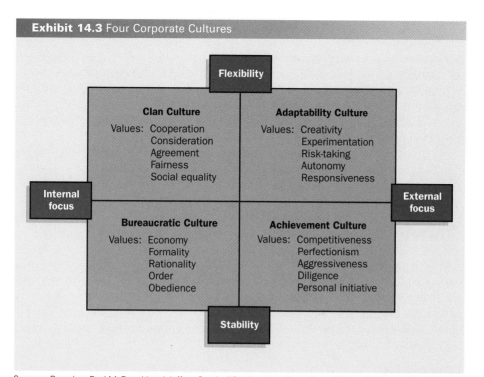

Exhibit 14.3 Four Corporate Cultures

Sources: Based on Paul McDonald and Jeffrey Gandz, "Getting Value from Shared Values," *Organizational Dynamics* 21, no. 3 (Winter 1992), pp. 64–76; Deanne N. Den Hartog, Jaap J. VanMuijen, and Paul L. Koopman, "Linking Transformational Leadership and Organizational Culture," *The Journal of Leadership Studies* 3, no. 4 (1996), pp. 68–83; Daniel R. Denison and Aneil K. Mishra, "Toward a Theory of Organizational Culture and Effectiveness," *Organizational Studies* 6, no. 2 (March–April 1995), pp. 204–223; Robert Hooijberg and Frank Petrock, "On Cultural Change: Using the Competing Values Framework to Help Leaders Execute a Transformational Strategy," *Human Resource Management* 32, no. 1 (1993), pp. 29–50; and R.E. Quinn, *Beyond Rational Management: Mastering the Paradoxes and Competing Demands of High Performance* (San Francisco: Jossey-Bass, 1998).

Achievement Culture

The **achievement culture** is characterized by a clear vision of the organization's goals, and leaders focus on the achievement of specific targets such as sales growth, profitability, or market share. An organization concerned with serving specific customers in the external environment but without the need for flexibility and rapid change is suited to the achievement culture. This is a results-oriented culture that values competitiveness, aggressiveness, personal initiative, and the willingness to work long and hard to achieve results. An emphasis on winning is the glue that holds the organization together.[50]

One good example of an achievement culture is Synapse, where leaders have built what they call a "culture for winners."

Achievement culture
culture characterized by a clear vision of the organization's goals and leaders' focus on the achievement of specific targets

Michael Loeb, Synapse

IN THE LEAD

Michael Loeb started the marketing firm Synapse in 1991 with a clear vision of *becoming the largest distributor of magazine subscriptions on the planet.* "We did not pretend to have a grand, greater good in mind and never masked our singular purpose," company leaders stated in a recent article. Synapse provides services to help publishers gain new subscriptions through various marketing partnerships and loyalty programs, then handles automatic renewals, which doubles the rate at which people renew their subscriptions.

An emphasis on winning defines the corporate culture. Synapse hires people who have an innate achievement drive and a positive attitude. People who succeed at

Synapse are typically assertive, self-confident, and take pride in doing a superior job. The company's commitment to quality means "setting high standards and aspiring to perfection in everything we do." Those who perform well and meet, aggressive goals are handsomely rewarded. Those who don't are fired. Synapse doesn't tolerate underperformers because leaders believe winners want to be with winners. And although leaders encourage risk-taking and accept that failure is sometimes a necessary collateral of progress, they refuse to forgive failure that is a result of carelessness or sloppy thinking.

The culture of winning at Synapse helped the company achieve its vision of becoming the largest distributor of magazine subscriptions before its tenth birthday. After becoming a subsidiary of Time Inc. in 2001, leaders set a new vision to become a billion-dollar global business. With the aggressive goals set by top leaders and employees who thrive on the intense, competitive culture, it's likely Synapse will achieve that vision in record time as well.[51]

The emphasis on competitiveness and achieving results should not be taken to mean that leaders at Synapse don't care about their employees. They strive to create an environment that is inspiring and fun in order to both motivate and reward people. Yet the primary culture values are aggressiveness, achievement, personal initiative, and striving for perfection. People who don't want to work hard and reach high standards don't last long at Synapse.

Clan Culture

Clan culture
culture with an internal focus on the involvement and participation of employees to meet changing expectations from the external environment

The **clan culture** has an internal focus on the involvement and participation of employees to meet changing expectations from the external environment. More than any other, this culture places value on meeting the needs of organization members. Companies with clan cultures are generally friendly places to work, and employees may seem almost like a family. Leaders emphasize cooperation, consideration of both employees and customers, and avoiding status differences. Leaders put a premium on fairness and reaching agreement with others.

One company that achieves success with a clan culture is Sargento Foods Inc., which processes and markets cheese. Sargento's commitment to employees started with its founder, Leonard Gentine, Sr., whose philosophy was "hire good people and treat them like family." At Sargento, one of the most important values is taking care of employees and making sure they have whatever they need to be satisfied and productive. Even in difficult times, Sargento maintains a commitment to comprehensive employee benefits and rewards such as profit sharing. The company's lifelong learning program offers 100 percent tuition reimbursement for full-time employees to take classes from the associate to the doctoral level, even if the classes aren't related to their work at Sargento. Sargento also offers flexible hours, and leaders encourage people to live a balanced life rather than work long hours and express a hard-charging, competitive spirit. Other key values include trust, fairness, and cooperation. At Sargento, employees care about each other and the company, a focus that helps the company do more with fewer resources and remain competitive against larger rivals such as Kraft and Borden.[52]

Action Memo
As a leader, you can align the organization's culture to its strategy and the needs of the external environment. You can choose to implement the appropriate culture (adaptability, achievement, clan, or bureaucratic) depending on environmental requirements and the organization's strategic focus.

Bureaucratic Culture

Bureaucratic culture
culture with an internal focus and consistency orientation for a stable environment

The **bureaucratic culture** has an internal focus and consistency orientation for a stable environment. The culture supports a methodical, rational, orderly way of doing business. Following the rules and being thrifty are valued. The organization succeeds by being highly integrated and efficient.

Safeco Insurance has functioned well with a bureaucratic culture. Employees take their coffee breaks at an assigned time, and a dress code specifies white shirts and suits for men and no beards. However, employees like this culture—reliability is highly valued and extra work isn't required. The bureaucratic culture works for the insurance company, and Safeco succeeds because it can be trusted to deliver on insurance policies as agreed.[53] In today's fast-changing world, very few organizations operate in a stable environment, and most leaders are shifting away from bureaucratic cultures because of a need for greater flexibility.

Each of the four cultures can be successful. The relative emphasis on various cultural values depends on the organization's strategic focus and the needs of the external environment. Leaders might have preferences for the values associated with one type of culture, but they learn to adjust the values they emulate and encourage, depending on the needs of the organization. It is the responsibility of leaders to ensure that organizations don't get "stuck" in cultural values that worked in the past but are no longer successful. As environmental conditions and strategy change, leaders work to instill new cultural values to help the organization meet new needs.

> **Action Memo**
> Determine your own cultural preferences by completing the exercise in Leader's Self-Insight 14.3 on page 438.

For example, leaders at Ford Motor Company are trying to instill new values to get the struggling automaker back on track. The culture, which past and present employees have described with words like "cautious," "cliquish," and "hierarchical," reflects values that fall primarily in the bureaucratic category. As the new head of Ford's North and South American auto operations, Mark Fields is trying to instill a sense of urgency for change and shift the culture toward values that encourage adaptability rather than predictability. In his "Way Forward" conference room, where teams of workers from all parts of the company meet to plot a new course for the future, team members wear wristbands that say "Red, White, and Bold" and talk about phrases such as "Culture eats strategy for breakfast."[54]

Ethical Values in Organizations

Of the values that make up an organization's culture, ethical values are considered highly important for leaders and have gained renewed emphasis in today's era of financial scandals and moral lapses. Most organizations that remain successful over the long term have leaders who include ethics as part of the formal policies and informal cultures of their companies. Some companies place significant emphasis on ethics in their business conduct. For example, leaders at Baxter International Inc. quickly yanked a product from the market when a number of people died after undergoing dialysis using a Baxter blood filter. It's a CEO's nightmare, but top leaders at Baxter did the right thing by investigating the problem, admitting their role in the deadly mistake, and providing financial compensation to families of the victims. Moreover, in atonement for the error, CEO Harry M. Jansen Kraemer, Jr. slashed his annual bonus by 40 percent and the bonuses of other top executives by 20 percent.[55]

Ethics is difficult to define in a precise way. In general, **ethics** is the code of moral principles and values that governs the behavior of a person or group with respect to what is right or wrong. Ethics sets standards as to what is good or bad in conduct and decision making.[56] Many people believe that if you are not breaking the law, then you are behaving in an ethical manner, but ethics often goes far beyond the law.[57] The law arises from a set of codified principles and regulations

Ethics
the code of moral principles and values that governs the behavior of a person or group with respect to what is right and wrong

The inventory below consists of 14 sets of four responses that relate to typical values or situations facing leaders in organizations. Although each response to a question may appear equally desirable or undesirable, your assignment is to rank the four responses in each row according to your preference. Think of yourself as being in charge of a major department or division in an organization. Rank the responses in each row according to how much you would like each one to be a part of your department. There are no correct or incorrect answers; the scores simply reflect your preferences for different responses.

Rank each of the four in each row using the following scale. You must use all four numbers for each set of four responses.

1. Would not prefer at all
2. Would prefer on occasion
4. Would prefer often
8. Would prefer most of all

	I	II	III	IV
1.	___Aggressiveness	___Cost efficiency	___Experimentation	___Fairness
2.	___Perfection	___Obedience	___Risk-taking	___Agreement
3.	___Pursue goals	___Solve problems	___Be flexible	___Develop people's careers
4.	___Apply careful analysis	___Rely on proven approaches	___Look for creative approaches	___Build consensus
5.	___Initiative	___Rationality	___Responsiveness	___Collaboration
6.	___Highly capable	___Productive and accurate	___Receptive to brainstorming	___Committed to the team
7.	___Be the best in our field	___Have secure jobs	___Recognition for innovations	___Equal status
8.	___Decide and act quickly	___Follow plans and priorities	___Refuse to be pressured	___Provide guidance and support
9.	___Realistic	___Systematic	___Broad and flexible	___Sensitive to the needs of others
10.	___Energetic and ambitious	___Polite and formal	___Open-minded	___Agreeable and self-confident
11.	___Use key facts	___Use accurate and complete data	___Use broad coverage of many options	___Use limited data and personal opinion
12.	___Competitive	___Disciplined	___Imaginative	___Supportive
13.	___Challenging assignments	___Influence over others	___Achieving creativity	___Acceptance by the group
14.	___Best solution	___Good working environment	___New approaches or ideas	___Personal fulfillment

Scoring and Interpretation

Add the points in each of the four columns—I, II, III, IV. The sum of the point columns should be 210 points. If your sum does not equal 210 points, check your answers and your addition.

The scores represent your preference for I, achievement culture; II, bureaucratic culture; III, adaptability culture; and IV, clan culture. Your personal values are consistent with the culture for which you achieved the highest score, although all four sets of values exist within you just as they exist within an organization. The specific values you exert as a leader may depend on the group situation, particularly the needs of the external environment. Compare your scores with other students and discuss their meaning. Are you pleased with your preferences? Do you think your scores accurately describe your values?

Source: Adapted from Alan J. Rowe and Richard O. Mason, *Managing with Style: A Guide to Understanding, Assessing, and Improving Decision Making* (San Francisco: Jossey-Bass, 1987).

that are generally accepted in society and are enforceable in the courts. Ethical standards for the most part apply to behavior not covered by law. Although current laws often reflect minimum moral standards, not all moral standards are codified into law. The morality of aiding a drowning person, for example, is not specified by law.

The standards for ethical conduct are embodied within each employee as well as within the organization itself. In a survey about unethical conduct in the workplace, more than half of the respondents cited poor leadership as a factor.[58] Leaders can create and sustain a climate that emphasizes ethical behavior for all employees.

Values-Based Leadership

Ethical values in organizations are developed and strengthened primarily through **values-based leadership**, a relationship between leaders and followers that is based on shared, strongly internalized values that are advocated and acted upon by the leader.[59] Leaders influence ethical values through their personal ethics and spiritual leadership. These leaders give meaning to followers by connecting their deeply held values to organizational goals.

Values-based leadership
a relationship between leaders and followers that is based on shared, strongly internalized values that are advocated and acted upon by the leader

Personal Ethics

Employees learn about values from watching leaders. Values-based leaders generate a high level of trust and respect from employees, based not just on stated values, but on the courage, determination, and self-sacrifice they demonstrate in upholding those values. When leaders are willing to make personal sacrifices for the sake of values, employees become more willing to do so. John Mackey, CEO of Whole Foods Markets, recently slashed his salary to $1 a year. Mackey has never believed top executives should take huge salaries while employees are paid a paltry wage, and he advocates finding meaning in one's work and making a contribution to society. When asked about his decision to take the salary cut, Mackey said he just felt like it was the right thing to do because he had enough money and wanted his motivation to come primarily from serving others.[60]

Action Memo
Answering the questions in Leader's Self-Insight 14.4 on the following page will give you an idea of how you feel about some ethical issues that students typically face.

For organizations to be ethical, leaders need to be openly and strongly committed to ethical conduct. In addition, ethical leaders uphold their commitment to values during difficult times or crises, as illustrated by the example of Bill Greehey at Valero.

Bill Greehey, Valero

When Hurricane Katrina hit New Orleans in late August of 2005, companies throughout the region set their disaster plans into action. But few matched the heroic efforts put forth by employees at Valero's St. Charles oil refinery. Just eight days after the storm, the St. Charles facility was up and running, whereas a competitor's plant across the road was weeks away from getting back online. During the same time period, St. Charles's disaster crew managed to locate every one of the plant's 570 employees.

Part of the credit goes to Valero's culture, which includes ethical values of caring, honesty, trust, and doing the right thing. Valero's culture has given the company a distinctive edge during an era of cutthroat global competition in the oil industry. As CEO Bill Greehey transformed Valero, once primarily a natural-gas-pipeline company,

Cheating is a common problem on college campuses today; 67 percent of students confess that they have cheated at least once. Many pressures cause students to engage in unethical behavior, and these are similar to pressures they will later face in the workplace. Answer the following questions to see how you think and feel about certain student behaviors that could be considered unethical. Circle a number on the scale from 1–5 based on the extent to which you approve of the behavior described, with 5 = Strongly approve and 1 = Strongly disapprove. *Please answer based on whether you approve or disapprove of the behavior, not whether you have ever acted in such a way.*

	Strongly disapprove				Strongly approve
1. Receiving a higher grade through the influence of a family or personal connection	1	2	3	4	5
2. Communicating answers to a friend during a test	1	2	3	4	5
3. Using a faked illness as an excuse for missing a test	1	2	3	4	5
4. Visiting a professor's office frequently to seek help in a course	1	2	3	4	5
5. "Hacking" into the university's computer system to change your grade	1	2	3	4	5
6. Getting extra credit because the professor likes you	1	2	3	4	5
7. Using formulas programmed into your pocket calculator during an exam	1	2	3	4	5
8. Attending commercial test preparatory courses such as those offered by Kaplan	1	2	3	4	5
9. Asking a friend to sign you in as attending when you are absent from a large class	1	2	3	4	5
10. Peeking at your neighbor's exam during a test	1	2	3	4	5
11. Brown-nosing your professor	1	2	3	4	5

	Strongly disapprove				Strongly approve
12. Overhearing the answers to exam questions when your neighbor whispers to another student	1	2	3	4	5
13. Using a term paper that you purchased or borrowed from someone else	1	2	3	4	5
14. Contributing little to group work and projects but receiving the same credit and grade as other members	1	2	3	4	5
15. Hiring someone or having a friend take a test for you in a very large class	1	2	3	4	5
16. Comparing work on assignments with classmates before turning the work in to the instructor	1	2	3	4	5
17. Receiving favoritism because you are a student athlete or member of a campus organization	1	2	3	4	5
18. Using unauthorized "crib notes" during an exam	1	2	3	4	5
19. Taking advantage of answers you inadvertently saw on another student's exam	1	2	3	4	5
20. Having access to old exams in a particular course that other students do not have access to	1	2	3	4	5
21. Receiving information about an exam from someone in an earlier section of the course who has already taken the test	1	2	3	4	5
22. Being allowed to do extra work, which is not assigned to all class members, to improve your grade	1	2	3	4	5

Continued

Scoring and Interpretation

There are five subscale scores that reflect your attitudes and beliefs about different categories of behavior.

For the category of *actively benefiting from unethical action,* sum your scores for questions 2, 5, 10, 13, 15, and 18 and divide by 6 _____.

For the category of *passively benefiting from questionable action,* sum your scores for questions 1, 6, 11, 14, 17, 20, and 22 and divide by 7_____.

For the category of *actively benefiting from questionable action,* sum your scores for questions 3, 7, 9, and 21 and divide by 4 _____.

For the category of *acting on an opportunistic situation,* sum your scores for questions 12 and 19 and divide by 2 _____.

For the category of *no harm/no foul* (actions perceived to cause no harm to anyone are considered okay) sum your scores for questions 4, 8, and 16 and divide by 3 _____.

The higher the score, the more you find that category of behaviors acceptable. When the scale was administered to 291 students in marketing and finance classes at a medium-sized university, the mean scores were as follows: *actively benefiting from unethical behavior*: 1.50; *passively benefiting from questionable action*: 2.31; *actively benefiting from questionable action*: 2.46; *acting on an opportunistic situation*: 2.55; and *no harm/no foul*: 4.42. How do your scores compare to these averages? The students in this sample had high approval for the *no harm/no foul* category. Do you agree that these behaviors are acceptable? Why might some people consider them unethical? If you feel comfortable doing so, compare your scores to another student's and discuss your beliefs about categories that you strongly disapprove or strongly approve of.

Source: Mohammed Y. A. Rawwas and Hans R. Isakson, "Ethics of Tomorrow's Business Managers: The Influence of Personal Beliefs and Values, Individual Characteristics, and Situational Factors," *Journal of Education for Business* (July 2000), p. 321. Reprinted with permission of the Helen Dwight Reid Educational Foundation. Published by Heldref Publications, 1319 Eighteenth St., NW, Washington, DC 20036-1802. Copyright © 2000.

IN THE LEAD

into the nation's largest oil refinery business, he also instilled a culture where people care about one another and the company. Many of the refineries Valero bought were old and run-down. After buying a refinery, Greehey's first steps would be to assure people their jobs were secure, bring in new safety equipment, and promise employees that if they worked hard he would put them first, before shareholders and customers. Employees held up their end of the bargain, and so did Greehey.

Greehey maintains a strict no-layoff policy, believing people need to feel secure in their jobs to perform at their best. "I see this cycle with companies where they fire and they hire and they fire and they hire," he says. "Fear does not motivate people." Of course, Greehey occasionally has to do some firing of his own—specifically, he'll fire any executive who is condescending or uses profanity when addressing subordinates. "Right now morale is so high in this refinery you can't get at it with a space shuttle," an electrical superintendent at St. Charles said in the aftermath of Hurricane Katrina. "Valero has been giving away gas, chain saws, putting up trailers for the employees. They've kept every employee paid. Other refineries shut down and stopped paying. What else can you ask?"[61]

When leaders like Bill Greehey maintain their commitment to ethical values through hard times, they help the organization weather a crisis and come out stronger on the other side. Several factors contribute to an individual leader's ethical stance. Every individual brings a set of personal beliefs, values, personality characteristics, and behavior traits to the job. The family backgrounds and spiritual beliefs of leaders often provide principles by which they conduct business. Personality characteristics such as ego strength, self-confidence, and a strong sense of independence may enable leaders to make ethical decisions even if those decisions might be unpopular.

One important personal factor is the leader's stage of moral development, as described in Chapter 6, which affects an individual's ability to translate values into behavior.[62] For example, some people make decisions and act only to obtain rewards and avoid punishment for themselves. Others learn to conform to expectations of good behavior as defined by society. This means willingly upholding the law and responding to the expectations of others. At the highest level of moral development are people guided by high internal standards. These are self-chosen ethical principles that don't change with reward or punishment. Leaders can strive to develop higher moral principles so that their daily actions reflect important ethical values.

Leaders have to discover their own personal ethical values and actively communicate values to others through both words and actions.[63] When faced with difficult decisions, values-based leaders know what they stand for, and they have the courage to act on their principles. In addition, by clearly communicating the ethical standards they expect others to live by, leaders can empower people throughout the organization to make decisions within that framework. This chapter's Leader's Bookshelf describes a unique, 450-year old organization that has succeeded by emphasizing personal values as the basis of leadership.

Spiritual Values

Managers who include spiritual values in addition to the traditional mental and behavioral aspects of leadership tend to be successful as leaders. Values and practices considered as spiritual ideals include integrity, humility, respect, appreciation for the contributions of others, fair treatment, and personal reflection.[64] This approach to leadership can be effective because many people are struggling with how to combine their spiritual journey and their work life. Many employees want to express their individuality in their work, and when they can do so work is more satisfying. Polls have reported that American managers as well as workers would like deeper fulfillment on the job, and evidence suggests that workplace spirituality programs provide increased productivity along with reduced absenteeism and turnover.[65]

Spiritual leadership is the display of values, attitudes, and behaviors necessary to intrinsically motivate one's self and others toward a sense of spiritual expression through calling and membership.[66] As illustrated in Exhibit 14.4, spiritual leaders can start by creating a vision through which organization participants experience a sense of calling that gives meaning to their work. An appropriate vision would have broad appeal, reflect high ideals, and establish a standard of excellence. Second, spiritual leaders establish a corporate culture based on altruistic love. Altruistic love includes forgiveness, genuine caring, compassion, kindness, honesty, patience, courage, and appreciation, which enables people to experience a sense of membership and feel understood. Spiritual leaders also engage hope/faith to help the organization achieve desired outcomes. Faith is demonstrated through action. Faith means believing in the ability to excel, exercising self-control, and striving for excellence to achieve a personal best. A leader's hope/faith includes perseverance, endurance, stretch goals, and a clear expectation of victory through effort.[67] As illustrated in Exhibit 14.4, spiritual leadership behaviors enable employees to have a sense of calling that provides deeper life meaning through work. Spiritual leadership also provides a sense of membership through a work community in which one is understood and appreciated. The outcome for the organization is improved commitment and productivity.

Leader's Bookshelf

Heroic Leadership: Best Practices From a 450-Year Old Company That Changed the World

Getty Images

by Chris Lowney

Many of today's organizations struggle to find leadership. Top executives hire talented, ambitious young people only to find that they crumble under pressure, can't inspire and motivate their teams, or lack the courage to innovate and take risks. Chris Lowney, author of *Heroic Leadership,* believes these companies can look to a sixteenth-century priest for guidance. In 1540, St. Ignatius Loyola founded the 10-man Jesuits with no capital and molded it into the most successful "company" of its time. Now the world's largest religious order, the Jesuits have operated a highly efficient international network of trade, education, military work, and scholarship for almost five centuries.

PILLARS OF LEADERSHIP SUCCESS

With fascinating historical examples and anecdotes, Lowney explores how the Jesuits have grappled with many of the same problems that face today's organizations—"forging seamless multinational teams, motivating inspired performance, remaining change ready and strategically adaptable." He believes the Jesuits' enduring success comes from molding leaders at all levels based on four core leadership pillars:

- *Self-Awareness*. To be a leader, one must understand his or her strengths, weaknesses, values, and beliefs. The Jesuits are trained to reflect on their goals, values, and performance throughout each day. Once a year, each sits down with a superior for an "account of conscience" to reinforce an understanding of common goals and success.
- *Ingenuity*. Innovating and adapting to a changing world is one of the things the Jesuits have done best. St. Ignatius Loyola described the ideal Jesuit as "living with one foot raised," always ready to respond to opportunities. Although education was not one of the Jesuit's initial goals, for example, they spotted a need and began plowing money into building a college. Within a decade, they had opened more than 30 colleges all over the world.
- *Love*. Loyola believed people perform best in environments that are supportive, caring, and charged with positive emotion. He counseled leaders to create a climate filled with "greater love than fear," and be passionately committed to unlocking the potential in themselves and others.
- *Heroism*. "Heroes extract gold from the opportunities around them rather than waiting for golden opportunities to be handed to them." Leaders aim high and energize others with their ambitions for something *more,* something greater than what is. This Jesuit idea contributed to the first European forays into Tibet, for example, and created the world's highest-quality secondary education available.

LIVING LEADERSHIP

The Jesuit approach focuses not on what leaders do, but on who they are. The principles aim to make each individual a better person, which in turn makes a stronger organization. Leadership cannot be separated from everyday life. The four pillars of leadership form a foundation for a way of living that is based on strong values and allows any individual to respond positively to the leadership opportunities all around us every day.

Heroic Leadership, by Chris Lowney, is published by Loyola Press.

One example of a spiritual leader is Tom Chappell, owner of Tom's of Maine, a health care products company. Chappell was financially successful but he reached a point where he decided something was missing. He enrolled in divinity school and subsequently applied his theological training to Tom's of Maine, creating a successful example of a values-led business. Another example is the CEO of BioGenex, Kris Kalra. He realized he was a workaholic living entirely for material success. His higher purpose was lost. Kalra focused on spiritual studies for three months, and he returned to work with a new attitude and respect for others' ideas. The outcome was 12 new company patents and a sharp increase in sales. His spiritual leadership likely saved a business that was stumbling.[68]

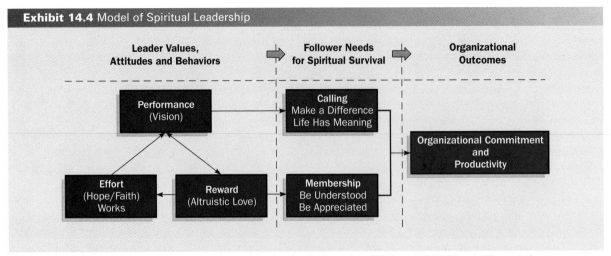

Exhibit 14.4 Model of Spiritual Leadership

Source: L. W. Fry, "Toward a Theory of Spiritual Leadership," *The Leadership Quarterly* 14 (2003), pp. 693–727. Used with permission.

Spiritual leadership is related to ideas discussed in Chapter 8 on motivation and Chapter 6 on moral leadership. The spiritual leader addresses followers' higher order needs for membership and self-actualization. This is intrinsic motivation at its best because work provides interest and enjoyment for its own sake. People are actively engaged in tasks they find interesting and fun. Intrinsic motivation is typically associated with better learning, higher performance, and enhanced well being. Spiritual leadership provides substantial autonomy and self-management, for example, through participation in empowered teams that direct activities and do work that is significant and meaningful. An employee's task involvement is under the control of the individual or team, thereby providing feedback and satisfaction through achievement, performance, and problem solving. Servant leadership, discussed in Chapter 6, holds that business organizations can create a positive impact on employees and the community. The spiritual leader, like the servant leader, engages people in work that provides both service and meaning.

Another impact of spiritual leadership is the dramatic reduction of negative feelings, emotions, and conflicts that are typically present in organizations. The four main types of destructive emotions are (1) fear, including anxiety and worry; (2) anger, including hostility, resentment, and jealousy; (3) sense of failure, including discouragement and depressed mood; and (4) pride, including prejudice, selfishness, and conceit. These destructive emotions arise from fear of losing something important or not getting something one desires. A more loving atmosphere based on care and concern can remove fear and worry, anger and jealousy, and provide a stronger foundation for personal well-being.[69]

Summary and Interpretation

Leaders influence organizational culture and ethical values. Culture is the set of key values, norms, and assumptions that is shared by members of an organization and taught to new members as correct. Culture serves two critically important functions—to integrate organizational members so they know how to relate to one another and to help the organization adapt to the environment.

Strong, adaptive cultures have a positive impact on organizational outcomes. Creating and influencing an adaptive culture is important because the right culture can drive high performance. Leaders build high performance cultures by emphasizing both values and solid business operations as the drivers of organizational success.

A culture gap exists when an organization's culture is not in alignment with the needs of the external environment or company strategy. Leaders use ceremonies, stories, symbols, specialized language, selection, and socialization to influence cultural values. In addition, leaders shape cultural values most strongly through their daily actions.

Leaders consider the external environment and the company's vision and strategy in determining which values are important for the organization. Four types of culture may exist in organizations: adaptability, achievement, clan, and bureaucratic. Each type emphasizes different values, although organizations may have values that fall into more than one category.

Of the values that make up an organization's culture, ethical values are among the most important. Ethics is the code of moral principles and values that governs the behavior of a person or group with respect to what is right or wrong. Leaders shape ethical values through values-based leadership. Leaders' personal beliefs and level of moral development influence their personal ethics. For organizations to be ethical, leaders have to be openly and strongly committed to ethical conduct in their daily actions. Many good leaders practice spiritual leadership, which means displaying values, attitudes, and behaviors that motivate people toward a sense of spiritual expression through calling and membership. The principles of spiritual leadership can improve both organizational performance and employee well-being.

Discussion Questions

1. Describe the culture for an organization you are familiar with. Identify the physical artifacts and discuss what underlying values and assumptions these suggest. What did you learn?

2. Name one or two companies in the news that seem to have strong corporate cultures, and describe whether the results have been positive or negative. Discuss how a strong culture could have either positive or negative consequences for an organization.

3. What is a culture gap? What are some techniques leaders might use to influence and change cultural values when necessary?

4. Compare and contrast the achievement culture with the clan culture. What are some possible *disadvantages* of having a strong clan culture? A strong achievement culture?

5. In which of the four types of culture (adaptability, achievement, clan, bureaucratic) might you expect to find the greatest emphasis on ethical issues? Why?

6. Discuss the meaning of *calling* and *membership*, as related to spiritual leadership. Identify an organization or leader that uses these concepts. To what extent were these concepts present where you have worked?

7. If a leader directs her health care company to reward hospital managers strictly on hospital profits, is the leader being ethically responsible? Discuss.

8. What is meant by the idea that culture helps a group or organization solve the problem of internal integration?

9. Some people believe that all good leadership is spiritual in nature. Others think spiritual values have no place at work. Discuss these two opposing viewpoints.

Leadership at Work

Walk the Talk

Often in an organization the culture is characterized both by what people say (talk) and by what people actually do (walk). When this happens there is a gap between organizational leaders' espoused values and the values in action within the company. One example would be an espoused value of "a balanced life for employees," whereas managers and employees are actually expected to work nights and weekends to meet demanding performance goals. This is the difference between the "walk" and the "talk" in an organization.

Your assignment for this exercise is to think of one example in your own student or work experience where the walk and talk in a corporate culture did not align. Why do you think the gap occurred? Then interview four other people for examples of when an organization's espoused values did not align with the values in action. Also ask them why they think the walk and talk differed. Summarize the findings from your interviews below:

My example (and why):

_____

_____

_____

_____

_____

Second person's examples (and why):

_____

_____

_____

_____

_____

Third person's examples (and why):

_____

_____

_____

_____

_____

Fourth person's examples (and why):

_____

_____

_____

_____

_____

_____

Fifth person's examples (and why):

_____

_____

_____

What patterns and themes do you see in the responses? Is there a common type of walk/talk gap? What is the most common reason why these gaps occur? Which is the real culture—the leader's espoused values or the values in action?

In Class: Students can be organized into small groups in class and do the above exercise all at once. Each person in the circle can give examples of an organization's walk not fitting its talk from their work and student experiences, and explain why they think the gaps occurred. Then students can identify the common themes from their discussion. The instructor can help students probe into this issue by writing good examples from students on the board and asking students to help identify key themes. Students can be engaged to discuss the walk versus talk phenomenon via key questions, such as: What does it mean to you when you discover a walk/talk gap in your organization? Are espoused values or values-in-action more indicative of a company's culture (or are both the culture)? Are walk/talk gaps likely to be associated with an adaptive culture? A strong culture? Do symbols, stories, ceremonies, and other signals of corporate culture mean what they imply?

Leadership Development: Cases for Analysis

Lisa Benavides, Forest International

Lisa Benavides has just been hired as the vice president of human resources for Forest International. Previously, the company had only a personnel officer and a benefits specialist, who spent most of their time processing applications and benefit forms and tracking vacation and sick days. However, a new CEO came to Forest believing that HR could play a key strategic role in the organization, and he recruited Benavides from a well-known HR consulting firm soon after he took over the top job. The new CEO has lots of ideas about empowerment, shared leadership, and teamwork that he hopes to eventually implement at the company.

Forest International operates in one of the most dangerous industries around. Paper mills, sawmills, and plywood factories are filled with constant noise, giant razor-toothed saw blades, caustic chemicals, and chutes loaded with tons of lumber. Even in this notoriously hazardous industry, Forest's safety record stinks. Within a four-year period, 29 workers were killed on the job. There are an average of 9 serious injuries per 100 employees each year. In addition, productivity has been declining in recent years, and Forest's competitors are gaining market share. As one of her first major projects, the CEO has asked Benavides for her advice on how to improve the company's safety record and increase productivity.

The company, based outside Atlanta, Georgia, has around $11 billion in annual revenues and employs 45,000 people. Many employees' parents and grandparents also worked in Forest's mills and factories. Among many of the workers, missing a finger or two is considered a badge of honor. Taking chances is a way of proving that you're a true *Forest-man* (the term persists even though the company now has a good percentage of female workers). During lunch or break, groups of workers routinely brag about their "close calls" and share stories about parents or grandparents' dangerous encounters with saw blades or lumber chutes.

It is clear to Benavides that worker attitudes are part of the problem, but she suspects that management attitudes may play a role as well. Production managers emphasize the importance of keeping the line moving, getting the product out no matter what. Rather than finding a supervisor and asking that the production line be shut down, most line employees take chances on sticking their hands into moving equipment whenever there is a minor problem. As Benavides talks with workers, she learns that most of them believe managers care more about productivity and profits than they do about the well-being of people in the plant. In fact, most Forest employees don't feel that they're valued at all by the company. One saw operator told Benavides that he has made several suggestions for improving productivity and safety on his line, but has been routinely ignored by management. "They never listen to us; they just expect us to do what we're told," he said. This same employee was one of the most vocal in opposing some recent safety-oriented changes requiring that all workers wear safety gear anytime they're on the production floor, not just when they are on the line. "They don't really care about our safety," he boomed. "They just want another way to push us around." Many of the other workers also oppose the new rules, saying that "managers walk around the production floor all the time without goggles and ear plugs, so why shouldn't we?"

Sources: Based in part on information in Anne Fisher, "Danger Zone," *Fortune* (September 8, 1997), pp. 165–167; and Robert Galford, "Why Doesn't This HR Department Get Any Respect?" *Harvard Business Review* (March–April 1998), pp. 24–26.

QUESTIONS

1. How would you describe the culture of Forest International as it relates to internal integration and external adaptation?
2. Would you expect that changing the culture at Forest would be easily accomplished now that a new CEO is committed to change? Why or why not?
3. If you were Lisa Benavides, what suggestions would you make to Forest's new CEO?

Acme and Omega

Acme Electronics and Omega Electronics both manufacture integrated circuits and other electronic parts as subcontractors for large manufacturers. Both Acme and Omega are located in Ohio and often bid on contracts as competitors. As subcontractors, both firms benefited from the electronics boom of the 1980s, and both looked forward to growth and expansion. Acme has annual sales of about $100 million and employs 950 people. Omega has annual sales of $80 million and employs about 800 people. Acme typically reports greater net profits than Omega.

The president of Acme, John Tyler, believed that Acme was the far superior company. Tyler credited his firm's greater effectiveness to his managers' ability to run a "tight ship." Acme had detailed organization charts and job descriptions. Tyler believed that everyone should have clear responsibilities and narrowly defined jobs, which generates efficient performance and high company profits. Employees were generally satisfied with their jobs at Acme, although some managers wished for more empowerment opportunities.

Omega's president, Jim Rawls, did not believe in organization charts. He believed organization charts just put artificial barriers between specialists who should be working together. He encouraged people to communicate face-to-face rather than with written memos. The head of mechanical engineering said, "Jim spends too much time making sure everyone understands what we're doing and listening to suggestions." Rawls was concerned with employee satisfaction and wanted everyone to feel part of the organization. Employees were often rotated among departments so they would be familiar with activities throughout the organization. Although Omega wasn't as profitable as Acme, they were able to bring new products on line more quickly, work bugs out of new designs more accurately, and achieve higher quality because of superb employee commitment and collaboration.

It is the end of May, and John Tyler, president of Acme, has just announced the acquisition of Omega Electronics. Both management teams are proud of their cultures and have unflattering opinions of the other's. Each company's customers are rather loyal, and their technologies are compatible, so Tyler believes a combined company will be even more effective, particularly in a time of rapid change in both technology and products.

The Omega managers resisted the idea of an acquisition, but the Acme president is determined to unify the two companies quickly, increase the new firm's marketing position, and revitalize product lines—all by year end.

Sources: Adapted from John F. Veiga, "The Paradoxical Twins: Acme and Omega Electronics," in John F. Veiga and John N. Yanouzas, *The Dynamics of Organization Theory* (St. Paul: West Publishing, 1984), pp. 132–138; and "Alpha and Omega," Harvard Business School Case 9-488-003, published by the President and Fellows of Harvard College, 1988.

QUESTIONS

1. Using the competing values model in Exhibit 14.3, what type of culture (adaptability, achievement, clan, bureaucratic) would you say is dominant at Acme? At Omega? What is your evidence?

2. Is there a culture gap? Which type of culture do you think is most appropriate for the newly merged company? Why?

3. If you were John Tyler, what techniques would you use to integrate and shape the culture to overcome the culture gap?

References

1 Chuck Salter, "The Problem with Most Banks Is That They Abuse Their Customers Every Day. We Want to Wow Ours," *Fast Company* (May 2002), pp. 80–91.

2 Jeremy Kahn, "What Makes a Company Great?" *Fortune* (October 26, 1998), p. 218; James C. Collins and Jerry I. Porras, *Built to Last: Successful Habits of Visionary Companies* (New York: HarperBusiness, 1994); and James C. Collins, "Change is Good—But First Know What Should Never Change," *Fortune* (May 29, 1995), p. 141.

3 T. E. Deal and A. A. Kennedy, *The New Corporate Cultures: Revitalizing the Workforce after Downsizing, Mergers, and Reengineering* (Perseus Books, 1999).

4 Yoash Wiener, "Forms of Value Systems: A Focus on Organizational Effectiveness and Culture Change and Maintenance," *Academy of Management Review* 13 (1988), pp. 534–545; V. Lynne Meek, "Organizational Culture: Origins and Weaknesses," Organization Studies 9 (1988), pp. 453–473; and John J. Sherwood, "Creating Work Cultures with Competitive Advantage," *Organizational Dynamics* (Winter 1988), pp. 5–27.

5 W. Jack Duncan, "Organizational Culture: Getting a 'Fix' on an Elusive Concept," *Academy of Management Executive* 3 (1989), pp. 229–236; Linda Smircich, "Concepts of Culture and Organizational Analysis," *Administrative Science Quarterly* 28 (1983), pp. 339–358; and Andrew D. Brown and Ken Starkey, "The Effect of Organizational Culture on Communication and Information," *Journal of Management Studies* 31, no. 6 (November 1994), pp. 807–828.

6 Edgar H. Schein, "Organizational Culture," *American Psychologist* 45, no. 2 (February 1990), pp. 109–119.

7 This discussion of the levels of culture is based on Edgar H. Schein, *Organizational Culture and Leadership*, 2nd ed. (San Francisco: Jossey-Bass, 1992), pp. 3–27.

8 Chris Blackhurst, "Sir Stuart Hampson," *Management Today* (July 2005), pp. 48–53.

9 John P. Kotter and James L. Heskett, *Corporate Culture and Performance* (New York: The Free Press, 1992), p. 6.

10 Peter B. Scott-Morgan, "Barriers to a High-Performance Business," *Management Review* (July 1993), pp. 37–41.

11 Arthur Ciancutti and Thomas Steding, "Trust Fund," *Business 2.0* (June 13, 2000), pp. 105–117.

12 Robert Levering and Milton Moskowitz, "And the Winners Are," *Fortune* (January 23, 2006), pp. 89–108; Daniel Roth, "My Job at the Container Store," *Fortune* (January 10, 2000), pp. 74–78; and Robert Levering and Milton Moskowitz, "The 100 Best Companies to Work For," *Fortune* (January 20, 2003), pp. 127–152.

13 Daniel Roth, "Trading Places," *Fortune* (January 23, 2006), pp. 120–128; and David Flaum, "The Innovation Man—Former FedEx Facilitator Praises Company's Culture," *The Commercial Appeal* (July 23, 2005), p. C1.

14 Bernard Arogyaswamy and Charles M. Byles, "Organizational Culture: Internal and External Fits," *Journal of Management* 13 (1987), pp. 647–659.

15 Anita Raghavan, Kathryn Kranhold, and Alexei Barrionuevo, "Full Speed Ahead: How Enron Bosses Created a Culture of Pushing Limits," *The Wall Street Journal*, (August 26, 2002), pp. A1, A7.

16 Kotter and Heskett, *Corporate Culture and Performance*.

17 Ellen Byron, "'Call Me Mike!' To Attract and Keep Talent, J. C. Penney CEO Loosens Up Once-Formal Workplace," *The Wall Street Journal* (March 27, 2006), p. B1.

18 Ralph H. Kilmann, Mary J. Saxton, Roy Serpa, and Associates, *Gaining Control of the Corporate Culture* (San Francisco: Jossey-Bass, 1985).

19 Larry Mallak, "Understanding and Changing Your Organization's Culture," *Industrial Management* (March–April 2001), pp. 18–24.

20 Sarah Ellison, "Bulldog Edition; Clash of Cultures Exacerbates Woes for Tribune Co.," *The Wall Street Journal* (November 10, 2006), pp. A1, A12.

21 Oren Harari, "Curing the M&A Madness," *Management Review* (July/August 1997): 53–56; Morty Lefkoe, "Why So Many Mergers Fail," *Fortune* (June 20, 1987), pp. 113–114.

22 Jennifer A. Chatman and Sandra Eunyoung Cha, "Leading by Leveraging Culture," *California Management Review* 45, no. 4 (Summer 2003), pp. 20–34; and Jeff Rosenthal and Mary Ann Masarech, "High-Performance Cultures: How Values Can Drive Business Results," *Journal of Organizational Excellence* (Spring 2003), pp. 3–18.

23 Abby Ghobadian and Nicholas O'Regan, "The Link Between Culture, Strategy and Performance in Manufacturing SMEs," *Journal of General Management* 28, no. 1 (Autumn, 2002), pp. 16–34; G. G. Gordon and N. DiTomaso, "Predicting Corporate Performance from Organisational Culture," *Journal of Management Studies* 29, no. 6 (1992), pp. 783–798; G. A. Marcoulides and R. H. Heck, "Organizational Culture and Performance: Proposing and Testing a Model," *Organization Science* 4 (1993), pp. 209–225.

24 John P. Kotter and John Heskett, *Corporate Culture and Performance* (New York: Free Press, 1992).

25 Micah R. Kee, "Corporate Culture Makes a Fiscal Difference," *Industrial Management* (November–December 2003), pp. 16–20.

26 Tressie Wright Muldrow, Timothy Buckley, and Brigitte W. Schay, "Creating High-Performance Organizations in the Public Sector," *Human Resource Management* 41, no. 3 (Fall 2002), pp. 341–354.

27 Reggie Van Lee, Lisa Fabish, and Nancy McGaw, "The Value of Corporate Values: A Booz Allen Hamilton/Aspen Institute Survey," *Strategy + Business*, Issue 39 (Summer 2005), pp. 52–65.

28 Rosenthal and Masarech, "High-Performance Cultures;" Patrick M. Lencioni, "Make Your Values Mean Something," *Harvard Business Review* (July 2002), pp. 113–117; and Thomas J. Peters and Robert H. Waterman, Jr., *In Search of Excellence* (New York: Warner, 1988).

29 Andrew Wahl, "Culture Shock," *Canadian Business* (October 10–23, 2005), pp. 115–116; and Calvin Leung, Michelle Magnan, and Andrew Wahl, "People Power," *Canadian Business* (October 10–23, 2005), pp. 125–126.

30 Harrison M. Trice and Janice M. Beyer, "Studying Organizational Culture Through Rites and Ceremonials," *Academy of Management Review* 9 (1984), pp. 653–669.

31 Alan Farnham, "Mary Kay's Lessons in Leadership," *Fortune* (September 20, 1993), pp. 68–77.

32 Joanne Martin, *Organizational Culture: Mapping the Terrain* (Thousand Oaks, CA: Sage Publications, 2001), pp. 71–72.

33 Joan O'C. Hamilton, "Why Rivals Are Quaking As Nordstrom Heads East," *BusinessWeek* (June 15, 1987), pp. 99–100.

34 "About Lilly: Overview: Our Values." Accessed August 9, 2000, from http://www.lilly.com/about/overview/values.html.

35 Gerald E. Ledford, Jr., Jon R. Wendenhof, and James T. Strahley, "Realizing a Corporate Philosophy," *Organizational Dynamics* 23, no. 3, (Winter 1995), pp. 5–19.

36 Charles A. O'Reilly III and Jeffrey Pfeffer, "PSS World Medical: Opening the Books Boosts Commitment and Peformance," *Journal of Organizational Excellence* (Spring 2001), pp. 65–80.

37 D. C. Feldman, "The Multiple Socialization of Organization Members," *Academy of Management Review* 6 (1981), 309–318; J. Van Maanen, "Breaking In: Socialization to Work," in *Handbook*

of Work, Organization, and Society, R. Dubin, ed. (Chicago: Rand-McNally, 1976), p. 67; and Blake E. Ashford and Alan M. Saks, "Socialization Tactics: Longitudinal Effects on Newcomer Adjustment," *Academy of Management Journal* 39, no. 1 (February 1996), p. 149ff.

38 Debra L. Nelson and James Campbell Quick, *Organizational Behavior,* 5th ed. (Cincinnati, OH: South-Western, 2006), p. 544.

39 Stephanie Gruner, "Lasting Impressions," *Inc.* (July 1998), p. 126.

40 Helena D. C. Thomas and Neil Anderson, "Changes in Newcomers' Psychological Contracts During Organizational Socialization: A Study of Recruits Entering the British Army," *Journal of Organizational Behavior* 19, no. S1 (1998), pp. 745–767.

41 Ashford and Saks, "Socialization Tactics."

42 Deanne N. Den Hartog, Jaap J. Van Muijen, and Paul L. Koopman, "Linking Transformational Leadership and Organizational Culture," *The Journal of Leadership Studies* 3, no. 4 (1996), pp. 68–83; and Schein, "Organizational Culture."

43 Nanette Byrnes, "The Art of Motivation," *BusinessWeek* (May 1, 2006), pp. 57–62.

44 Bill Munck, "Changing a Culture of Face Time," *Harvard Business Review* (November 2001), pp. 125–131.

45 Ram Charan and Jerry Useem, "Why Companies Fail," *Fortune* (May 27, 2002), pp. 50–62.

46 Jennifer A. Chatman and Karen A. Jehn, "Assessing the Relationship Between Industry Characteristics and Organizational Culture: How Different Can You Be?" *Academy of Management Journal* 37, no. 3 (1994), pp. 522–553.

47 James R. Detert, Roger G. Schroeder, and John J. Mauriel, "A Framework for Linking Culture and Improvement Initiatives in Organizations," *Academy of Management Review* 25, no. 4 (2000), pp. 850–863.

48 Paul McDonald and Jeffrey Gandz, "Getting Value from Shared Values," *Organizational Dynamics* 21, no. 3 (Winter 1992), pp. 64–76; and Daniel R. Denison and Aneil K. Mishra, "Toward a Theory of Organizational Culture and Effectiveness," *Organization Science* 6, no. 2 (March–April 1995), pp. 204–223.

49 Joel Hoekstra, "3M's Global Grip," *WorldTraveler* (May 2000), pp. 31–34; and Thomas A. Stewart, "3M Fights Back," *Fortune* (February 5, 1996), pp. 94–99.

50 Robert Hooijberg and Frank Petrock, "On Cultural Change: Using the Competing Values Framework to Help Leaders Execute a Transformational Strategy," *Human Resource Management* 32, no. 1 (1993), pp. 29–50.

51 Dorothy Brill and Kristin Kish, "Success at Synapse: Investing in People Reaps Big Dividends for a Small Company," *Journal of Organizational Excellence* (Spring 2005), pp. 65–73.

52 Barbara Gannon and John Sterling, "Company Culture Provides Competitive Edge for Sargento Foods," *Strategy & Leadership* 32, no. 3 (2004), pp. 31–35.

53 Carey Quan Jelernter, "Safeco: Success Depends Partly on Fitting the Mold," *Seattle Times* (June 5, 1986), p. D8.

54 Jeffrey McCracken, "'Way Forward' Requires Culture Shift at Ford," *The Wall Street Journal* (January 23, 2006), p. B1.

55 Michael Arndt, "How Does Harry Do It?" *BusinessWeek* (July 22, 2002), pp. 66-67.

56 Gordon F. Shea, *Practical Ethics* (New York: American Management Association, 1988); and Linda Klebe Treviño, "Ethical Decision Making in Organizations: A Person-Situation Interactionist Model," *Academy of Management Review* 11 (1986), pp. 601–617.

57 Dawn-Marie Driscoll, "Don't Confuse Legal and Ethical Standards," *Business Ethics* (July/August 1996), p. 44.

58 Alison Boyd, "Employee Traps—Corruption in the Workplace," *Management Review* (September 1997), p. 9.

59 Robert J. House, Andre Delbecq, and Toon W. Taris, "Values-Based Leadership: An Integrated Theory and an Empirical Test" (Working Paper).

60 Steven Gray, "Natural Competitor," *The Wall Street Journal* (December 4, 2006), pp. B1, B3.

61 Janet Guyon, "The Soul of a Moneymaking Machine," *Fortune* (October 3, 2005), pp. 113–120.

62 Lawrence Kohlberg, "Moral Stages and Moralization: The Cognitive-Developmental Approach," in *Moral Development and Behavior: Theory, Research, and Social Issues,* T. Likona, ed. (New York: Holt, Rinehart & Winston, 1976), pp. 31–53; and Jill W. Graham, "Leadership, Moral Development, and Citizenship Behavior," *Business Ethics Quarterly 5*, no. 1, (January 1995), pp. 43–54.

63 Kathy Whitmire, "Leading Through Shared Values," *Leader to Leader* (Summer 2005), pp. 48–54.

64 Laura Reave, "Spiritual Values and Practices Related to Leadership Effectiveness," *The Leadership Quarterly* 16 (2005), pp. 655–687.

65 R. A. Giacalone and C. L. Jurkiewicz, "Toward a Science of Workplace Spirituality," in R. A. Giacalone and C. L. Jurkiewicz, eds., *Handbook of Workplace Spirituality and Organizational Performance* (New York: M. E. Sharp, 2003), pp. 3–28; Louis W. Fry, "Toward a Theory of Ethical and Spiritual Well-Being, and Corporate Social Responsibility Through Spiritual Leadership." In R. A. Giacalone, ed., *Positive Psychology in Business Ethics and Corporate Responsibility,* (Greenwich, CT: Information Age Publishing, 2005), pp. 47–83; and I. I. Mitroff and E. A. Denton, *A Spiritual Audit of Corporate America* (San Francisco: Jossey Bass, 1999).

66 Louis W. Fry, "Toward a Theory of Spiritual Leadership," *The Leadership Quarterly* 14 (2003), pp. 693–727.

67 Ibid.

68 Reave, "Spiritual Values and Practices."

69 Fry, "Toward a Theory of Spiritual Leadership."

Chapter 15

Your Leadership Challenge

After reading this chapter, you should be able to:

- Recognize social and economic pressures for change in today's organizations.

- Implement the eight-stage model of planned major change and use everyday strategies for gradual change.

- Expand your own and others' creativity and facilitate organizational innovation.

- Use techniques of communication, training, and participation to overcome resistance to change.

- Effectively and humanely address the negative impact of change.

Leading Change

You've seen them on store shelves. Maybe you even use some in your home, office, or dorm room. We're talking about those squiggly bulbs that cost four or five dollars but promise to last five times as long as bulbs that cost less than a buck—and help save the environment in the process.

Compact fluorescent bulbs that fit in standard light fixtures have been around for more than 20 years. Yet two-thirds of the lighting technology used in homes and offices today dates to before 1960, practically the dark ages as far as leaders at Philips Electronics NV, the world's largest lighting manufacturer, are concerned. Philips invented the compact fluorescent bulb in the early 1980s and has been trying ever since to get people to use it. The company has spent millions on research and development and millions more on marketing, yet most consumers still reach for the familiar bell-shaped incandescent bulb. The higher up-front cost has been a major turn-off for many consumers, as well as for builders, organizations, and city governments. Yet equally significant is that the bulbs just don't look right. Recent versions of compact fluorescents look more like an old-fashioned light bulb, but they still conjure up in people's minds the idea that the light they produce won't be as desirable. When the bulbs first came out, they indeed emitted light that was not as warm and inviting as that of incandescent bulbs. Years of research have solved that problem, but many people still associate fluorescent lighting with harsh office settings and don't want to use the bulbs in their homes.

Philips, as well as rival lighting makers General Electric (GE) and Siemens, have embarked on a massive campaign to make the compact fluorescent bulb—which uses 75 percent to 80 percent less electricity to produce the same amount of light as an incandescent bulb—the first choice for lighting homes, offices, public buildings, and street lamps around the world. GE, for example, teamed up with Wal-Mart for displays that educate consumers about compact fluorescents. Philips is sending marketers to talk to city governments around the globe. All three companies are offering rebates and special offers. How many marketing campaigns does it take to get people to change a light bulb? The answer remains to be discovered.[1]

Companies produce new products and services every day, and many have been huge successes. Yet the story of compact fluorescent light bulbs illustrates that getting people to change long-entrenched habits—whether it be changing their style of light bulb or changing the way they work together in an organization—is not easy. The hard fact is that most people don't like change. By some estimates, two-thirds of all organizational change efforts fail.[2] Scientific studies suggest that people tend to resist change even when their lives depend on it. Ninety percent of patients who have had coronary artery bypass surgery, for example, don't change their lifestyle habits, even for seemingly simple changes.[3]

Within organizations, leaders almost always encounter some degree of resistance when they attempt to implement changes. However, change is necessary if organizations are to survive and thrive. Leaders in many organizations, from small companies such as Gemmy Industries, which invented inflatable holiday yard figures, to major corporations such as Boeing and large government agencies such as the Federal Emergency Management Agency (FEMA), have had to reconceptualize almost every aspect of how they do business to meet the changing needs of customers or clients, keep employees motivated and satisfied, and remain effective and competitive in a complex, global environment. Even the United States Army is finding it needs to undergo massive changes to fight a new kind of war. Rather than launching an all-out assault, the Army is struggling to learn that "the more force you use when battling insurgents, the less effective you are," as stated in the organization's new counterinsurgency doctrine.[4] The pressing need for change management is reflected in the fact that many companies are hiring "transformation officers" who are charged with radically rethinking and remaking either the entire organization or major parts of it.[5]

Recall from our definition used throughout this book that leadership is about change rather than stability. In recent years, though, the pace of change has increased dramatically, presenting significant challenges for leaders. Many leaders today feel as if they are "flying the airplane at the same time they are building it."[6] The patterns of behavior and attitudes that were once successful no longer work, but new patterns are just emerging—and there are no guarantees that the new ways will succeed. Leaders are responsible for guiding people through the discomfort and dislocation brought about by major change.

This chapter explores how leaders facilitate creativity, innovation, and change. We first look briefly at the need for change in today's organizations and examine a step-by-step model for leading major change. We also explore everyday change strategies and examine how leaders facilitate innovation by fostering creative people and organizations. The final sections of the chapter consider why people resist change and how leaders can overcome resistance and help people cope with the potentially negative consequences of change.

Change or Perish

"When the rate of change outside exceeds the rate of change inside, the end is in sight."[7] That's how Jack Welch, the former long-time chairman and CEO of General Electric, emphasized the fact that internal organizational changes must keep pace with what is happening in the external environment. What a challenge that is today. The rapidity of social, economic, and technological change means that organizations have to be perpetually changing and adapting to keep pace. As illustrated in Exhibit 15.1, environmental forces such as rapid technological changes, a globalized economy, shifting geopolitical forces, changing markets, the growth of e-business, and the swift spread of information via the Internet are creating more threats as well as more opportunities for organizational leaders.

A big problem for today's organizations is the failure to adapt to all these changes in the environment. Although there are many reasons for the failure to change and adapt, a primary solution to the problem is better change leadership. Leaders serve as the main role models for change and provide the motivation and communication to keep change efforts moving forward. Strong, committed leadership is crucial to successful change, and research has identified some key characteristics of leaders who can accomplish successful change projects:[8]

- They define themselves as change leaders rather than people who want to maintain the status quo.
- They demonstrate courage.
- They believe in employees' capacity to assume responsibility.
- They are able to assimilate and articulate values that promote adaptability.
- They recognize and learn from their own mistakes.

How Innovative Are You?

Think about your current life. Indicate whether each item below is Mostly False or Mostly True for you.

	Mostly False	Mostly True
1. I am always seeking out new ways to do things.	_____	_____
2. I consider myself creative and original in my thinking and behavior.	_____	_____
3. I prefer to be slow to accept a new idea.	_____	_____
4. I rarely trust new gadgets until I see whether they work for people around me.	_____	_____
5. I am usually one of the last people among my peers to adopt something new.	_____	_____
6. I like to feel that the old way of doing things is the best way.	_____	_____
7. In a group or at work I am often skeptical of new ideas.	_____	_____
8. I typically buy new foods, gear, and other innovations before other people.	_____	_____
9. My behavior influences others to try new things.	_____	_____
10. I like to spend time trying out new things.	_____	_____

Scoring and Interpretation

Innovativeness reflects an awareness of the need to innovate and a positive attitude toward change. Innovativeness is also thought of as the degree to which a person adopts innovations earlier than other people in the peer group. Innovativeness is a positive thing for leaders today because individuals and organizations are faced with a constant need to change.

Add the number of Mostly True answers to items 1, 2, 8, 9, and 10 above and the Mostly False answers to items 3, 4, 5, 6, and 7 for your score: _____. A score of 8 or above indicates that you are very innovative and likely are one of the first people to adopt changes. A score of 4–7 would suggest that you are average or slightly above average in innovativeness compared to others. A score of 0–3 means that you may prefer the tried and true and hence be slow and skeptical about adopting new ideas or innovations.

Source: Based on H. Thomas Hurt, Katherine Joseph, and Chester D. Cook, "Scales for the Measurement of Innovativeness," *Human Communication Research* 4, no. 1 (1977), pp. 58–65.

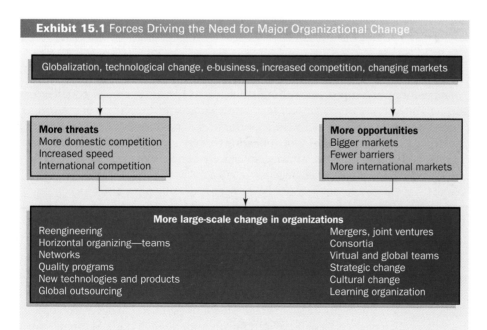

Exhibit 15.1 Forces Driving the Need for Major Organizational Change

Globalization, technological change, e-business, increased competition, changing markets

More threats
More domestic competition
Increased speed
International competition

More opportunities
Bigger markets
Fewer barriers
More international markets

More large-scale change in organizations

Reengineering
Horizontal organizing—teams
Networks
Quality programs
New technologies and products
Global outsourcing

Mergers, joint ventures
Consortia
Virtual and global teams
Strategic change
Cultural change
Learning organization

Source: Adapted with permission of The Free Press, a division of Simon & Schuster Adult Publishing Group, from *The New Rules: How to Succeed in Today's Post-Corporate World* by John P. Kotter. Copyright © 1995 by John P. Kotter. All rights reserved.

- They are capable of managing complexity, uncertainty, and ambiguity.
- They have vision and can describe their vision for the future in vivid terms.

One leader who illustrates many of the characteristics of change leadership is Barbara Waugh of Hewlett-Packard.

Barbara Waugh, Hewlett-Packard

Barbara Waugh began her career at Hewlett-Packard Company in a mid-level personnel position at HP Labs—not the place one would think of for instituting massive change. Yet Waugh always identified herself as an agent for change and looked for opportunities to make things better. She had a vision that the organization could be the "world's best industrial research lab" and she activated dozens of people to talk about what that would mean and how it could be accomplished. She also had the courage to question and challenge senior executives, serving as a reality check for leaders who had gotten too far away from the day-to-day work of the organization. Waugh believes to be a change leader, "You have to always be willing to lose your job."

Waugh quickly developed a reputation for getting things done, and many people from various parts of the organization would come to her with problems. Rather than solving the problems herself, Waugh helped each individual assume responsibility and take steps toward accomplishing their own change goals. For example, Tan Ha, a former Vietnamese refugee working at HP Labs, regularly sent money to a Buddhist orphanage in Bangladesh, only to have the money disappear en route. When he learned about a new HP project developing low-cost telecommunications and computing services for developing countries, he contacted Waugh and asked her to do something about his money transit problems. Waugh told Ha that she couldn't solve the problem for him, but that she would help him take the steps needed to become personally involved in the project and make sure his concerns were addressed.

During her time in personnel, Waugh contributed directly or indirectly to numerous change projects, including new products, new mentoring relationships among engineers, and a 20 percent reduction in R & D development life cycles. Her passion and ability as a change leader eventually led her to a position as worldwide change manager at HP Labs.[9]

Change does not happen easily, but as illustrated by this example, good leaders throughout the organization can facilitate change and help their organizations adapt to external threats and new opportunities. One does not need to be a top leader to be a change leader. In the following section, we examine a model for leading major changes, and later in the chapter we will give some tips for how leaders can overcome resistance to change.

Leading a Major Change

When leading a major change project, it is important for leaders to recognize that the change process goes through stages, each stage is important, and each may require a significant amount of time. Leaders are responsible for guiding employees and the organization through the change process.

Exhibit 15.2 presents an eight-stage model of planned change.[10] To successfully implement change, leaders pay careful attention to each stage. Skipping stages or making critical mistakes at any stage can cause the change process to fail.

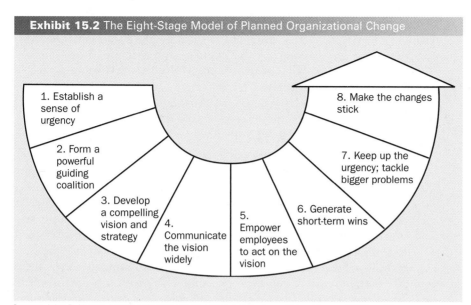

Exhibit 15.2 The Eight-Stage Model of Planned Organizational Change

1. Establish a sense of urgency

2. Form a powerful guiding coalition

3. Develop a compelling vision and strategy

4. Communicate the vision widely

5. Empower employees to act on the vision

6. Generate short-term wins

7. Keep up the urgency; tackle bigger problems

8. Make the changes stick

Source: John P. Kotter, *Leading Change* (Boston: Harvard Business School Press, 1996), p. 21.

1. At stage 1, leaders *establish a sense of urgency* that change is really needed. Crises or threats will thaw resistance to change. Consider the situation at Volkswagen, Europe's largest automaker. Already stumbling as a result of weak sales, high costs, and an overcapacity of more than a million cars a year, Volkswagen spiraled into crisis after accusations that executives solicited bribes, siphoned money into fake companies, and arranged visits to prostitutes using company funds. Wolfgang Bernhard, who was brought in to lead a transformation, is getting support for many of his efforts because employees know the organization has serious problems and might not survive without change.[11] In many cases, though, there is no obvious crisis and leaders have to make others aware of the need for change. Leaders carefully scan the external and internal environment—looking at competitive conditions; market position; social, technological, and demographic trends; profit and loss; operations; and other factors. After identifying potential crises or problems, they find ways to communicate the information broadly and dramatically.

2. Stage 2 involves *establishing a coalition* with enough power to guide the change process and then developing a sense of teamwork among the group. For the change process to succeed, there must be a shared commitment to the need and possibilities for organizational transformation. Middle management change will seek top leader support in the coalition. It is also essential that lower-level executives become involved. Mechanisms such as off-site retreats can get people together and help them develop a shared assessment of problems and how to approach them. At MasterBrand Industries, transformation began with an off-site meeting of some 75 key managers who examined the need for change and discussed ways to remake MasterBrand into a team-based organization.[12]

3. Stage 3 requires *developing a vision and strategy*. Leaders are responsible for formulating and articulating a compelling vision that will guide the change effort, then developing the strategies for achieving that vision. A "picture"

of a highly desirable future motivates people to change. A new CEO at Yellow Freight System had a vision of transforming the traditional trucking company into a service company that could quickly respond to customers' changing needs. Bill Zollars' vision involved using a sophisticated, integrated information system and redesigning jobs so that employees had more autonomy, enabling Yellow Freight to offer one-stop shopping for a range of services and allowing customers get deliveries exactly when they wanted them.[13]

4. In stage 4, leaders use every means possible to widely *communicate the vision and strategy*. At this stage, the coalition of change agents should set an example by modeling the new behaviors needed from employees. They must communicate about the change at least 10 times more than they think necessary. Transformation is impossible unless a majority of people in the organization are involved and willing to help, often to the point of making personal sacrifices. At Yellow Freight, Bill Zollars regularly visited terminals across the country to communicate the new direction. "Repetition is important, especially when you're trying to change the way a company thinks about itself," Zollars advises. "You're trying to create new behaviors."[14]

5. Stage 5 involves *empowering employees throughout the organization to act on the vision*. This means getting rid of obstacles to change, which may require revising systems, structures, or procedures that hinder or undermine the change effort. People are empowered with knowledge, resources, and discretion to make things happen. A primary purpose of investing in information technology at Yellow Freight was to give employees on the front lines the information they needed to solve customer problems quickly. The management system was also changed to give people freedom to make many decisions themselves without waiting for a supervisor to review the problem.

6. At stage 6, leaders *generate short-term wins*. Leaders plan for visible performance improvements, enable them to happen, and celebrate employees who were involved in the improvements. Major change takes time, and a transformation effort loses momentum if there are no short-term accomplishments that employees can recognize and celebrate. For example, Philip Diehl of the U.S. Mint wanted to transform the clumsy, slow-moving government bureaucracy into a fast, energetic organization that was passionate about serving customers, particularly coin collectors. Diehl publicly set an early goal of processing 95 percent of orders within six weeks. Even though that sounds agonizingly slow in today's fast-paced business world, it was a tremendous improvement for the Mint. Achieving the goal energized employees and kept the transformation efforts moving.[15] A highly visible and successful short-term accomplishment boosts the credibility of the change process and renews the commitment and enthusiasm of employees.[16]

7. Stage 7 *keeps up the urgency*, building on the credibility and momentum achieved by short-term wins to *tackle bigger problems*. Successful change leaders don't simply declare victory after small wins and become complacent. They use courage and perseverance to give people the energy and power to take on more difficult issues. This often involves changing systems, structures, and policies; hiring and promoting people who can implement the vision; and making sure employees have the time, resources,

and authority they need to pursue the vision. Leaders at one company striving to improve collaboration, for example, found employees' energy flagging after they had achieved a short-term win that improved on-time and complete shipments from 50 percent to 99 percent. They decided to invest significant time and money in reconfiguring the plant to increase interaction of production and office personnel, thereby creating a feeling of community that reinforced and continued the change effort in a highly visible way.[17]

8. Stage 8 is where leaders *make the changes stick*.[18] The transformation isn't over until the changes have well-established roots. Leaders instill new values, attitudes, and behaviors so that employees view the changes not as something new but as a normal and integral part of how the organization operates. They use many of the ideas we discussed in Chapter 14 for changing organizational culture, such as tapping into people's emotions, telling vivid stories about the new organization and why it is successful, selecting and socializing employees to fit the desired culture, and acting on the espoused values so that people know what leaders care about and reward. Leaders celebrate and promote people who act according to the new values. This stage also requires developing a means to ensure leadership development and succession so that the new values and behaviors are carried forward to the next generation of leadership.

Stages in the change process generally overlap, but each is important for successful change to occur. When dealing with a major change effort, leaders can use the eight-stage change process to provide a strong foundation for success.

Action Memo
Answer the questions in Leader's Self-Insight 15.2 on page 460 to see if you have what it takes to initiate changes and follow the 8-stage model of change.

Leading Everyday Change

Sometimes leaders see that significant changes need to be made but they are constrained by various circumstances from initiating bold changes or they recognize that aggressive moves would provoke strong resistance. In addition, the nature of leadership means influencing others in many small ways on a regular basis. Good leaders work daily to gradually shift attitudes, assumptions, and behaviors toward a desired future. When individual leaders throughout the organization are involved in daily change efforts, they have a powerful cumulative effect.[19]

Leaders can learn strategies for everyday change that will have significant constructive impact as everyday conversations and small actions spread to others throughout the organization. Exhibit 15.3 illustrates a range of incremental change strategies that leaders can use. The strategies range from the individual leader working alone to effect gradual change to working directly with others in a more directed and extensive change effort.[20] Each of the strategies is described below:

- *Creative self-expression.* This is the least conspicuous way to promote change and involves a single leader acting in a way that others will notice and that reflects the values or behaviors he or she wishes to instill in followers. Creative self-expression quietly unsettles others' expectations and routines, whether it be a leader who wears casual pants and sweaters in an organization where most people wear suits, or a leader who shifts working hours to balance work and family life. One manager, for example, shifted his work hours so he could always be home by 6:00 P.M. and

Think specifically of your current or a recent full-time job. Please answer the 10 questions below according to *your perspective and behaviors in that job.* Indicate whether each item below is Mostly False or Mostly True for you.

	Mostly False	Mostly True
1. I often tried to adopt improved procedures for doing my job.	_____	_____
2. I often tried to change how my job was executed in order to be more effective.	_____	_____
3. I often tried to bring about improved procedures for the work unit or department.	_____	_____
4. I often tried to institute new work methods that were more effective for the company	_____	_____
5. I often tried to change organizational rules or policies that were nonproductive or counterproductive.	_____	_____
6. I often made constructive suggestions for improving how things operate within the organization.	_____	_____
7. I often tried to correct a faulty procedure or practice.	_____	_____
8. I often tried to eliminate redundant or unnecessary procedures.	_____	_____
9. I often tried to implement solutions to pressing organizational problems.	_____	_____
10. I often tried to introduce new structures, technologies, or approaches to improve efficiency.	_____	_____

Scoring and Interpretation

Please add the number of items for which you marked Mostly True, which is your score: _____. This instrument measures the extent to which people take charge of change in the workplace. Change leaders are seen as change initiators. A score of 7 or above indicates a strong take-charge attitude toward change. A score of 3 or below indicates an attitude of letting someone else worry about change.

Before change leaders can champion large planned change projects via the model in Exhibit 15.2, they often begin by taking charge of change in their workplace area of responsibility. To what extent do you take charge of change in your work or personal life? Compare your score with other students' scores. How do you compare? Do you see yourself being a change leader?

Source: *Academy of Management Journal* by E. W. Morrison and C. C. Phelps. Copyright 1999 by Academy of Management. Reproduced with permission of Academy of Management in the format Textbook via Copyright Clearance Center.

Exhibit 15.3 A Range of Everyday Change Strategies

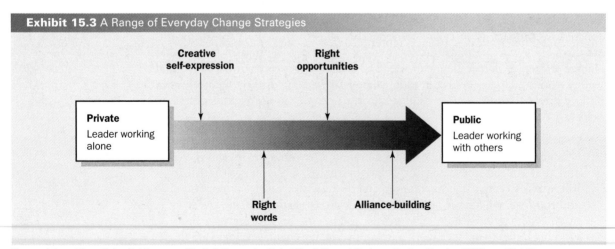

Source: Adapted from Debra E. Meyerson, "Radical Change the Quiet Way," *Harvard Business Review* (October 2001), pp. 92–100.

refused to take calls during the evening between 6:30 and 9:00. In the hard-charging, fast-paced organization, his behavior raised eyebrows, but gradually, as colleagues saw that he actually became more rather than less productive, they also began leading more balanced lives.

- *Right words.* With this strategy, a leader turns an opponent's negative attitudes, comments, or behaviors into opportunities for change that others will notice. One good example relates to diversity and the challenges that minorities face in organizations, as described in Chapter 11. A sales executive was disturbed by the fact that the few minority managers in his organization had a hard time getting noticed and listened to. At a staff meeting, Carol, a new female marketing director, raised several concerns and questions, but was routinely ignored. Later in the meeting, a white male manager raised similar concerns, and everyone directed their attention toward him. The sales executive quickly jumped in, saying, "That's a really important point and I'm glad you picked up on Carol's comments. Carol, did he correctly capture your thinking on this issue?" By casually calling attention to the fact that Carol had been ignored and her ideas co-opted, the executive made an important point without accusing or embarrassing anyone. In addition, he raised Carol's visibility and drew her directly into the discussion.

- *Right opportunities.* A more public approach is for leaders to look for, create, and capitalize on opportunities for motivating others to change. One woman who was hired as a division president at a technology company was opposed to the company's prevailing command-and-control leadership style but knew she would make enemies by attacking it directly. She focused on leading her own division in a participative way and sharing as much power and authority with followers as she could. Moreover, when she was asked to make presentations to the company's executive staff, she passed the opportunity to those who had worked directly on the project. The employees gained greater skills and experience and other executives were able to see and recognize their abilities and contributions.

> **Action Memo**
> As a leader, you can model the behaviors and values you want others to follow. You can use your opponents' negative comments, attitudes, or behaviors as opportunities to illustrate the value of a different approach. You can make allies and work with them to move important change issues to the forefront.

- *Alliance building.* With strategic alliance building, the leader works closely with others to move issues to the forefront more quickly and directly than would be possible working alone. This is the most public and most political approach to everyday change. Recall the discussion of coalitions and allies from Chapter 12. The leader enlists the support and assistance of people who agree with his or her ideas for change. In addition, smart leaders look at everyone, even those who may be opposed to their ideas or projects, as a potential ally, as illustrated by the following example.

Paul Wielgus, Allied Domecq

Paul Wielgus doesn't consider himself a revolutionary, but he sparked a transformation at the global company Allied Domecq, whose brands include Courvoisier and Beefeater, by effectively persuading people who were originally opposed to his plans. Wielgus headed a new learning and training department designed to help people throughout the company break out of outdated thinking and be more creative and adaptable. The problem was, even though the department had the support of top management, many executives thought it was a waste of time and money.

One senior executive from Allied Domecq's internal audit department took aim at the learning and training unit when he was asked to identify areas of unnecessary expense. He soundly berated Wielgus and criticized the department's activities. However, rather than becoming defensive and treating the audit executive as an enemy, Wielgus used the meeting as an opportunity to sell him on the benefits of the program. His strategy was to treat the opposition as a friend and potential ally. Wielgus began excitedly telling him about how the workshops functioned and the dramatic changes he had seen in people who'd been through the training program. He enthusiastically explained how people left the workshops feeling more excited about their work and with a renewed commitment to the organization and its goals.

Before long, the senior executive was scheduling training for the internal audit department itself, and he became one of Wielgus's most enthusiastic supporters. The image of the Audit Services Department gradually changed from that of a policing unit to that of a partner helping people do their jobs better.[21]

Paul Wielgus understood the importance of building strategic alliances by reaching out to the opposition as well as to those who already agreed with and supported his ideas.

Leaders use a variety of everyday change strategies depending on the organization, the circumstances, and their own personalities. There are many ways to bring about change, and one of the most important ways is through individual leaders working every day—quietly and alone or publicly in connection with others—to effect small changes that ultimately have a powerful impact on the organization and its members.

Leading for Innovation

In response to the question, "What must one do to survive in the twenty-first century?" the top answer among 500 CEOs surveyed by the American Management Association was "practice creativity and innovation." However, only 6 percent of the respondents felt that their companies were successfully accomplishing this goal.[22] Similarly, another survey by *Business Week* and the Boston Consulting Group found that 72 percent of top executives said innovation is a top priority in their companies, yet almost half said they are dissatisfied with their results in that area.[23]

Many organizational leaders in the United States, Europe, and Japan are recognizing a need for greater innovation to keep pace with technological and societal advances and compete with the growing power of companies in China and other developing countries. Rather than focusing on ways to improve efficiency and cut costs, today's leaders are rewiring their organizations for creativity and innovation. Some observers of business trends suggest that the *knowledge economy* of the late 1990s and early 2000s is rapidly being transformed into the *creativity economy*. As more high-level knowledge work is outsourced to less-developed countries, companies in the United States, Europe, and Japan are evolving to the next level—generating economic value from creativity, imagination, and innovation.[24]

Today's leaders are adopting structures and systems that promote rather than squelch the creation and implementation of new ideas. Effective leaders find ways to promote creativity in the departments where it is most needed. For example, some organizations, such as hospitals, government agencies, and non-profit organizations, may need frequent changes in policies and procedures, and leaders can promote creativity among administrative workers. For companies that rely on new products, leaders need to promote the generation and sharing of ideas across departments. In most successful companies, leaders want everyone to come up with new ideas for solving problems and meeting customer needs.

One of the best ways for leaders to facilitate continuous change is to create an environment that nourishes creativity. **Creativity** is the generation of ideas that are both novel and useful for improving efficiency and/or effectiveness of an organization.[25] Creative people come up with ideas that may meet perceived needs, solve problems, or respond to opportunities and are therefore adopted by the organization. However, creativity itself is a process rather than an outcome, a journey rather than a destination. One of the most important tasks of leaders today is to harness the creative energy of all employees to spur innovation and further the interests of the organization.

Creativity
the generation of ideas that are both novel and useful for improving efficiency and effectiveness of the organization

The Creative Organization

Leaders can build an environment that encourages creativity and helps the organization be more innovative. Five elements of innovative organizations are listed in the left column of Exhibit 15.4, and each is described below.[26] These elements correspond to the characteristics of creative individuals, listed in the right column of the exhibit.

Alignment For creative acts that benefit the organization to occur consistently, the interests and actions of everyone should be aligned with the organization's purpose, vision, and goals. Leaders make clear what the company stands for, consistently promote the vision, and clarify specific goals. In addition, they make a commitment of time, energy, and resources to activities that focus people on innovation. Many organizations set up separate creative departments or venture teams. One increasingly popular approach is the **idea incubator,** which is being used at companies such as Boeing, Ziff-Davis, and UPS. An idea incubator provides a safe harbor where ideas from people throughout the organization can be developed without interference from company bureaucracy or politics.[27]

Idea incubator
a safe harbor where ideas from employees throughout the organization can be developed without interference from company bureaucracy or politics

Exhibit 15.4 Characteristics of Innovative Organizations and Creative People

The Innovative Organization	The Creative Individual
Alignment	Commitment
	Focused approach
Creative Values	Interdependence
	Persistence
	Energy
Unofficial activity	Self-confidence
	Nonconformity
	Curiosity
Diverse stimuli	Open-mindedness
	Conceptual fluency
	Enjoys variety
Within-company communication	Social competence
	Emotionally expressive
	Loves people

Source: Based on Alan G. Robinson and Sam Stern, *Corporate Creativity: How Innovation and Improvement Actually Happen* (San Francisco: Berrett-Koehler, 1997); Rosabeth Moss Kanter, "The Middle Manager as Innovator," *Harvard Business Review,* (July–August 1982), pp. 104–105; and James Brian Quinn, "Managing Innovation: Controlled Chaos," *Harvard Business Review,* (May–June 1985), pp. 73–84.

Creative Values Most people have a natural desire to explore and create, which leads them to want to initiate creative activity on their own. Unfortunately, this desire is sometimes squelched early in life by classroom teachers who insist on strict adherence to the rules. Leaders can unleash deep-seated employee motivation for creativity and innovation. Leaders encourage an entrepreneurial spirit by instilling values of risk-taking and exploration and providing the structures and systems that encourage people to explore new ideas. This **corporate entrepreneurship** can produce a higher-than-average number of innovations. One important outcome is to facilitate idea champions. **Idea champions** are people who passionately believe in an idea and fight to overcome natural resistance and convince others of its value. Change does not happen by itself. Personal energy and effort are needed to successfully promote a new idea. Champions make sure valuable ideas get accepted and carried forward for implementation.

Corporate entrepreneurship
internal entrepreneurial spirit that includes values of exploration, experimentation, and risk taking

Idea champions
people who passionately believe in a new idea and actively work to overcome obstacles and resistance

Unofficial Activity Employees need to be able to experiment and dream outside of their regular job description. Leaders can give people free time for activities that are not officially sanctioned. One study of creativity found that in almost every case the essence of the creative act came during the "unofficial" time period.[28] Dream time is what makes it possible for companies to go where they never expected to. The best-known example is 3M's Post-it Notes, one of the five most popular 3M products and one that resulted from an engineer's free-time experiments with another worker's "failure"—a not-very-sticky glue. 3M lets employees spend 15 percent of their time on any project of their own choosing, without management approval.[29] Managers at Google also keep creativity alive by letting people spend 20 percent of their time—one day each week—working on any project they choose, even if the project doesn't tie in with the company's central mission.[30]

Diverse Stimuli It is impossible to know in advance what stimulus will lead any particular person to come up with a creative idea. The seeds of the idea for Post-it Notes were planted when an engineer's bookmarks kept falling out of his church hymnal. Leaders can help provide the sparks that set off creative ideas. Companies such as Hallmark, Nortel Networks' Broad Band, and Bell Laboratories/ Lucent Technologies bring in outside speakers on diverse topics to open people up to different ideas. Advertising agency Leo Burnett holds a regular "Inspire Me" day, when one team takes the rest of the department out to do something totally unrelated to advertising. One team took the group to a Mexican wrestling match, where team members showed up in costumes and masks like some of the more ardent wrestling fans. One idea that grew out of the experience was a new slogan for The Score, a sports network: "The Score: Home for the Hardcore."[31]

Leaders can also provide employees with diverse stimuli by rotating people into different jobs, allowing them time off to participate in volunteer activities, and giving them opportunities to mix with people different from themselves. Organizations can give people opportunities to work with customers, suppliers, and others outside the industry.

Internal Communication Creativity flourishes when there is frequent contact with interdisciplinary networks of people at all levels of the organization.[32] Without adequate internal communication and coordination, ideas from creative departments or idea champions can't be implemented. Leaders foster an environment that encourages people to communicate across boundaries. For example, at appliance maker Electrolux, CEO Hans Straberg introduced a new approach to product development that has designers, engineers, marketers, and production people working side-by-side to come up with hot new products such as the Pronto cordless stick vacuum, which gained a 50 percent market share in Europe within two years. "We never used to create new products together," says engineer Giuseppe Frucco. "The designers would come up with something and then tell us to build it." The new cooperative approach enhances creativity and saves both time and money at Electrolux by avoiding the technical glitches that crop up as a new design moves through the development process.[33]

Leaders can use the characteristics of innovative organizations to ignite creativity in specific departments or the entire organization. Consider how leaders at Samsung Electronics have applied these ideas to encourage creativity and get designers and engineers to come up with innovative products rather than crank out cheap imitations.

> **Action Memo**
> As a leader, you can help the organization be more innovative. You can encourage curiosity, playfulness, and exploration and provide people with diverse stimuli to open their minds to new ideas. You can also build in mechanisms for cross-functional collaboration and information sharing.

Kun-Hee Lee, Samsung Electronics

IN THE LEAD

When Kun-Hee Lee, chairman of Samsung Electronics, realized that consumers had come to regard Samsung products as cheap, low-quality knockoffs suitable only for the bargain bin, he vowed that the company would become a world-class innovator. "We must change no matter what," the chairman proclaimed.

One step executives took to create a new mindset that values creativity, cooperation, and innovation was to set up the Innovative Design Lab (IDS), where designers, engineers, marketers, and managers from various disciplines took a year-long series of courses aimed at fostering a creative, collaborative environment. The courses gave people the skills and confidence to risk thinking differently. Ongoing programs at the IDS help designers learn how to better champion their ideas, and cross-discipline teams study consumers and create what-if scenarios about the world's future buying patterns. Samsung further stimulates creativity with the Global Design Workshop, which sends employees to the world's great art and design centers. Designers get Wednesday afternoons off to explore for ideas outside the office. To put cutting edge ideas into action, people from different functional areas work side-by-side in the Value Innovation Program (VIP) Center. At the VIP, there are no interrupting phone calls, no annoying administrative tasks or other day-to-day matters to distract people from the project.

Today, Samsung is the global leader in 8 consumer electronics categories, and the consulting firm Interbrand calculates it is the world's most valuable electronics brand, outstripping previous leader Sony. Between the years of 2000 and 2005, the company won more awards from the Industrial Design Society of America than any other firm on the planet.[34]

By encouraging entrepreneurship, allowing for unofficial activity, providing employees with diverse stimuli, and encouraging internal communication and collaboration, leaders have transformed Samsung Electronics into a hotbed of creativity and innovation.

Many organizations that want to encourage innovation also strive to hire people who display the characteristics of creative individuals, as listed in the right hand column of Exhibit 15.4. Creative people are often known for open-mindedness, curiosity, independence, self-confidence, persistence, and a focused approach to problem-solving. Clearly, these characteristics are stronger in some people than in others. However, recent research on creativity suggests that everyone has roughly equal creative potential. The problem is that many people don't use that potential. Leaders can help both individuals and organizations be more creative.

> **Action Memo**
> Complete the exercise in Leader's Self-Insight 15.3 on page 466 to see if you have a creative personality.

Leader's Self-Insight 15.3

Do You Have a Creative Personality?

In the list below, check each adjective that you believe accurately describes your personality. Be very honest. Check all the words that fit your personality.

1. affected ___
2. capable ___
3. cautious ___
4. clever ___
5. commonplace ___
6. confident ___
7. conservative ___
8. conventional ___
9. egotistical ___
10. dissatisfied ___
11. honest ___
12. humorous ___
13. individualistic ___
14. informal ___
15. insightful ___
16. intelligent ___
17. narrow interests ___
18. wide interests ___
19. inventive ___
20. mannerly ___
21. original ___
22. reflective ___
23. resourceful ___
24. self-confident ___
25. sexy ___
26. snobbish ___
27. sincere ___
28. submissive ___
29. suspicious ___
30. unconventional ___

Scoring and Interpretation

Add one point for checking each of the following words: 2, 4, 6, 9, 12, 13, 14, 15, 16, 18, 19, 21, 22, 23, 24, 25, 26, and 30. Subtract one point for checking each of the following words: 1, 3, 5, 7, 8, 10, 11, 17, 20, 27, 28, and 29. The highest possible score is +18 and the lowest possible score is −12.

The average score for a set of 256 assessed males on this creativity scale was 3.57, and for 126 females was 4.4. A group of 45 male research scientists and a group of 530 male psychology graduate students both had average scores of 6.0, and 124 male architects received an average score of 5.3. A group of 335 female psychology students had an average score of 3.34. If you received a score above 6.0, your personality would be considered above average in creativity.

The adjective checklist above was validated by comparing the respondents' scores to scores on other creativity tests and to creativity assessments of respondents provided by expert judges of creativity. This scale does not provide perfect prediction of creativity, but it is reliable and has moderate validity. Your score probably indicates something about your creative personality compared to other people.

To what extent do you think your score reflects your true creativity? Compare your score to others in your class. What is the range of scores among other students? Which adjectives were most important for your score compared to other students? Can you think of types of creativity this test might not measure? How about situations where the creativity reflected on this test might not be very important?

Source: Harrison G. Gough, "A Creative Personality Scale for the Adjective Check List," *Journal of Personality and Social Psychology* 37, no. 8 (1979), pp. 1398–1405.

Leading Creative People

Leaders of today's organizations have powerful reasons to encourage creativity. As we discussed in Chapter 1, many organizations are undergoing fundamental transformations to respond to new challenges. They need employees to contribute new ideas. In addition, people can be more creative when they are helped to be open-minded, curious, and willing to take risks. Leaders can increase individual creativity by facilitating brainstorming, lateral thinking, and creative intuition.

Brainstorming One good way leaders encourage creativity is to set up brainstorming sessions. Assume your organization faces a problem such as how to reduce losses from shoplifting, speed up checkout, reduce food waste, or lessen noise from a machine room. **Brainstorming** uses a face-to-face interactive group to spontaneously suggest a wide range of creative ideas to solve the problem. The keys to effective brainstorming are:

Brainstorming
a technique that uses a face-to-face group to spontaneously suggest a broad range of ideas to solve a problem

1. *No Criticism.* Group members should not criticize or evaluate ideas in any way during the spontaneous generation of ideas. All ideas are considered valuable.

2. *Freewheeling is welcome.* People should express any idea that comes to mind no matter how weird or fanciful. Brainstormers should not be timid about expressing creative thinking. As a full-time developer of ideas at Intuit said, "It's more important to get the stupidest idea out there and build on it than not to have it in the first place."[35]

3. *Quantity desired.* The goal is to generate as many ideas as possible. The more ideas the better. A large quantity of ideas increases the likelihood of finding excellent solutions. Combining ideas is also encouraged. All ideas belong to the group and members should modify and extend ideas whenever possible.[36]

Brainstorming has been found to be highly effective for quickly generating a wide range of creative alternatives. After all the ideas are expressed and recorded, the group can have another session to discuss and evaluate which ideas or combination will best solve the problem. Marissa Mayer, Director of Consumer Web Products at Google, has eight hour-long brainstorming sessions each year. At each session, six concepts are pitched to 100 engineers and discussed for 10 minutes each. The goal is to build on and modify each concept.[37]

Recent improvements in the brainstorming process are to have people write down their ideas before coming to the brainstorming session, and to go back and write down ideas immediately after the session. Taking advantage of each person's before and after thinking will increase creative output.[38] Another recent approach, called **electronic brainstorming**, or *brainwriting*, brings people together in an interactive group over a computer network.[39] One member writes an idea, another reads it and adds other ideas, and so on. Studies show that electronic brainstorming generates about 40 percent more ideas than individuals brainstorming alone, and 25 percent to 200 percent more ideas than regular brainstorming groups, depending on group size.[40] Why? Because each person is anonymous, and the sky's the limit in terms of what people feel free to say. Creativity also increases because people can write down their ideas immediately, avoiding the possibility that a good idea might slip away while the person is waiting for a chance to speak in a face-to-face group. Social inhibitions and concerns are avoided, which typically allows for a broader range of participation. Another advantage is that electronic brainstorming can potentially be done with groups made up of employees from around the world, further increasing the diversity of ideas.

Electronic brainstorming
bringing people together in an interactive group over a computer network sometimes called *brainwriting*

Action Memo
As a leader, you can expand the creative potential of yourself and others by using the techniques of brainstorming, lateral thinking, and creative intuition.

Lateral Thinking Most of a person's thinking follows a regular groove and somewhat linear pattern from one thought to the next. But linear thinking does not often provide a creative breakthrough. Linear thinking is when people take a problem or idea and then build sequentially from that point. A more creative approach is to use lateral thinking. **Lateral thinking** can be defined as a set of systematic techniques used for changing mental concepts and perceptions and generating new ones.[41] With lateral thinking, people move "sideways" to try different perceptions, different concepts, and different points of entry to gain a novel solution. Lateral thinking appears to solve a problem by an unorthodox or apparently illogical method. Lateral thinking makes an unusual mental connection that is concerned with possibilities and "what might be."

Lateral thinking
a set of systematic techniques for changing mental concepts and generating new ones

To stimulate lateral thinking, leaders provide people with opportunities to use different parts of their brain and thus to make novel, creative connections. When people take time off from working on a problem and change what they are doing, it is possible to activate different areas of the brain. If the answer isn't in the part of the brain being used, it might be in another that can be stimulated by a new experience. For example, a NASA scientist was taking a shower in a German hotel while pondering how to fix the distorted lenses in the Hubble telescope in 1990. Nobody could figure out how to fit a corrective mirror into the hard-to-reach space inside the orbiting telescope. The engineer noticed the European-style showerhead mounted on adjustable rods. This perception connected with the Hubble problem as he realized that corrective mirrors could be extended into the telescope on similar folding arms. Lateral thinking came to the rescue.[42]

To facilitate the creative flash from people, some managers reorganize frequently to mix people into different jobs and responsibilities, or they hire people with diverse experiences. Frequent change can be traumatic but it keeps people's minds fresh and innovative. Having someone with a real estate background run a bank branch brings a fresh perspective to problems. People with diverse skills challenge the status quo when developing strategies or responses to customers.[43]

Personal approaches to stretch your mind when solving problems could include behaviors such as changing your sleeping hours, taking a different route to work, reading a different newspaper or listening to a different radio station, meeting new people, trying new recipes, or changing your restaurant, recreation or reading habits, all of which might stimulate a new part of the brain and trigger a lateral response. Unilever Best Foods asks 1500 managers to leave their offices, laboratories, or factories for three days, twice a year, to visit customers and learn more about them. Card designers at American Greetings are free to change their work location, enjoy a library of hundreds of magazines and thousands of books, and confer with counterparts in other industries, such as automotive and appliance manufactures. Nike designers got the idea for the high gloss finish on the Air Jordan XIX at the Detroit auto show.[44]

Alex Osborn, the originator of brainstorming, developed many creative techniques. One effective technique that is widely used to stimulate lateral thinking is the checklist in Exhibit 15.5. The checklist seems to work best when there is a current product or service for sale that needs to be improved. If the problem is to modify a cell phone design to increase its sales, for example, the checklist verbs in

Exhibit 15.5 Lateral Thinking Checklist	
Verb	**Description**
Put to other uses?	New ways to use as is? Other uses if modified?
Adapt?	What else is like this? What other idea does this suggest?
Modify?	Change meaning, color, motion, sound, odor, form, shape? Other changes?
Magnify?	What to add: Greater frequency? Stronger? Larger? Plus ingredient? Exaggerate?
Minify?	What to subtract: Eliminate? Smaller? Slower? Lower? Shorter? Lighter? Split up? Less frequent?
Substitute?	Who else instead? What else instead? Other place? Other time?
Rearrange?	Other layout? Other sequence? Change pace?
Reverse?	Transpose positive and negative? How about opposites? Turn it backward? Turn it upside down? Reverse role?
Combine?	How about a blend, an alloy, an assortment, an ensemble? Combine units? Combine purposes? Combine appeals? Combine ideas?

Source: Alex Osborn, *Applied Imagination*, New York: Charles Scribner's Sons, 1963.

Exhibit 15.5 can stimulate an array of different perceptions about the item being analyzed.

An exercise of *considering opposites* will also stretch the mind in a lateral direction. Physical opposites include back/front, big/small, hard/soft, and slow/fast. Biological opposites include young/old, sick/healthy, male/female, and tortoise/hare. Management opposites would be bureaucratic/entrepreneurial, or top-down/bottom-up. Business opposites are buy/sell, profit/loss, and hire/fire.[45]

Action Memo

Right now, see if you can think of three additional opposites in each of the categories of physical, biological, management, and business. Look at opposites to stretch your thinking for a problem you face.

Creative Intuition The creative flash of insight leaders want to awaken is actually the second stage of creativity. The first stage is data gathering. The mind is gathering data constantly, especially when you are studying background material on a problem to be solved. Then the creative insight bubbles up as an intuition from the deeper subconscious. It may be hard to trust that intuitive process because it seems "soft" to many business executives. The subconscious mind remembers all experiences that the conscious mind has forgotten. Intuition has a broader reach than any analytical process focused solely on the problem at hand.

Where or when do you get your best ideas? The most popular response is "in the shower." One man got good ideas so consistently in the shower that he regularly experienced a 20-minute mental core dump of ideas. He purchased a piece of clear plastic and a grease pencil to write down the creative ideas while in his "think tank." Creativity often occurs during a mental pause, a period of mixed tension and relaxation. In the shower, or while exercising, driving, walking, or meditating, the mind reverts to a neutral, somewhat unfocused state in which it is receptive to issues or themes that have not been resolved. A temporary activity that is relatively simple and mindless can provide the moment for a creative flash from deep in the subconscious. If the analytical part of the mind is too focused and active, it shuts down the spontaneous part. Thus, the semi-relaxed mental "pause" is like putting the analytical left brain on hold and giving room for the intuitive right brain to find the solution in the subconscious mind.[46] C. S. Lewis, author of *The Chronicles of Narnia,* was fond of long, contemplative walks to facilitate his creative juices. Novelist Stephen King runs several miles most mornings. One study suggested that a single aerobic workout is enough to kick the brains of college students into high gear for a couple of hours. Thus, physical exercise may be as effective as the shower for triggering the appropriate relaxed state that enables creative intuition to break through.[47]

To understand your own creative intuition, consider the problems below. Each set of three words has something in common.[48] Do not over-analyze. Instead just relax and see if the common element pops up from your intuition.

1. April   locker room   bride-to-be
2. curtain   fisherman   nuclear reactor
3. catcher   dinner table   armadillo
4. watermelon   tennis tournament   idea
5. bowling alley   tailor   wrestling match

Don't rush to find the answers. Give your intuitive subconscious time to work. After it's finished working on these problems, consider the following question you might be asked if you interview for a job at Microsoft: *How would you weigh a large jet aircraft without a scale?* This question combines logical thinking and intuition. Before reading on, how might you compute the airplane's weight doing something that is technologically feasible even if not realistic?[49]

The next challenge may appear to have no solution until your intuition shows you the obvious answer. In the illustration below, remove three matches to leave four.[50]

Here is another problem that may force your mind to respond from a different place to get the answer. The matches are an equation of Roman numerals made from ten matches. The equation is incorrect. Can you correct the equation without touching the matches, adding new matches, or taking away any matches?

Have you given adequate time to your creative intuition? The answers to these creative challenges follow:

For the word sets, the correct answers are: (1) shower, (2) rods, (3) plates, (4) seeds, and (5) pins.

One answer to weighing the jet aircraft would be to taxi the jet onto a ship big enough to hold it. You could put a mark on the hull at the water line and then remove the jet and reload the ship with items of known weight until it sinks to the same mark on the hull. The weight of the items will equal the weight of the jet.

The answer to the first match puzzle depends on how you interpret the word "four." Rather than counting four matches, remove the matches at the top, bottom, and right and the answer is obvious—the Roman numeral IV. For the second match puzzle, you can solve this problem by looking at it from a different perspective—turn the page upside down. Did your creative intuition come up with good answers?

Implementing Change

Leaders frequently see innovation, change, and creativity as a way to strengthen the organization, but many people view change only as painful and disruptive. A critical aspect of leading people through change is understanding that resistance to change is natural—and that there are often legitimate reasons for it. This chapter's *Consider This* box takes a lighthearted look at why employees may resist changes in some overly bureaucratic organizations.

The underlying reason why employees resist change is that it violates the **personal compact** between workers and the organization.[51] Personal compacts are the reciprocal obligations and commitments that define the relationship between employees and organizations. They include such things as job tasks, performance requirements, evaluation procedures, and compensation packages. These aspects of the compact are generally clearly defined and may be in written form. Other aspects are less clear-cut. The personal compact incorporates elements such as mutual trust and dependence, as well as shared values. When employees perceive that change violates the personal compact, they are likely to resist. For example, a new general manager at the Dallas-Fort Worth Marriott wanted to change the incentive system to offer bonuses tied to the hotel's financial performance, but employees balked. "They were thinking, 'Here comes the Wicked Witch of the West taking my stuff away,'"

Personal compact
the reciprocal obligations and commitments that define the relationship between employees and the organization

Consider This!

Dealing with a Dead Horse

Ancient wisdom says that when you discover you are astride a dead horse, the best strategy is to dismount. In government and other overly bureaucratic organizations, many different approaches are tried. Here are some of our favorite strategies for dealing with the "dead horse" scenario:

1. Change the rider.
2. Buy a stronger whip.
3. Beat the horse harder.
4. Shout at and threaten the horse.
5. Appoint a committee to study the horse.
6. Arrange a visit to other sites to see how they ride dead horses.
7. Increase the standards for riding dead horses.
8. Appoint a committee to revive the dead horse.
9. Create a training session to improve riding skills.
10. Explore the state of dead horses in today's environment.
11. Change the requirements so that the horse no longer meets the standards of death.
12. Hire an external consultant to show how a dead horse can be ridden.
13. Harness several dead horses together to increase speed.
14. Increase funding to improve the horse's performance.
15. Declare that no horse is too dead to ride.
16. Fund a study to determine if outsourcing will reduce the cost of riding a dead horse.
17. Buy a computer program to enhance the dead horse's performance.
18. Declare a dead horse less costly to maintain than a live one.
19. Form a work group to find uses for dead horses.
    And . . . if all else fails . . .
20. Promote the dead horse to a supervisory position. Or, in a large corporation, make it a Vice President.

Source: Author unknown. Another version of this story may be found at http://www.abcsmallbiz.com/funny/deadhorse.html

the manager said. There are management tools available to help implement innovation and change.

Tools for Implementation

Leaders can improve the chances for a successful outcome by following the eight-stage model discussed earlier in this chapter and using the strategies we discussed for incremental everyday change. In addition, leaders mobilize people for change by engaging their hearts as well as their minds. Effective leaders use elements such as storytelling, metaphor, humor, symbolism, and a personal touch to reach people on an emotional level and sell them on proposed changes.[52] As discussed in Chapter 9, emotional elements are essential for persuading and influencing others; thus, leaders should not overlook the importance of emotional elements to overcome resistance to change.[53] The Leader's Bookshelf further describes how leaders can use emotion

Action Memo
As a leader, you can understand the reasons for resistance to change and use tools such as communication, training, and follower participation to overcome resistance. Use coercion only as a last resort and when the change is urgent.

The Heart of Change: Real-Life Stories of How People Change Their Organizations

by John P. Kotter and Dan S. Cohen

In his 1996 book, *Leading Change*, John Kotter, professor emeritus at Harvard Business School, outlined an eight-stage process that leaders should follow in leading major change. With this book, *The Heart of Change*, Kotter teamed up with consultant Dan Cohen to look at the typical problems leaders face at each of the eight stages. The authors' main finding is that the biggest barriers to change involve people's attitudes and behaviors.

HOW PEOPLE CHANGE

Change comes easier, the authors argue, when people see potent reasons for change that touch their emotions rather than being presented with rational analysis that attempts to change their thinking. Consider these examples connected to three of the eight change stages:

- *Stage 1: Establish a sense of urgency.* One leader at a company struggling to cut costs was curious about what his company was spending on gloves in its manufacturing plants. His summer intern found that the plants purchased 424 different types of gloves that were roughly equal in quality but varied widely in cost. The two gathered a sample of each type of glove, tagged it with a price on it, and made a pile in the executive boardroom. When division managers saw the display, they were astounded. The gloves became a traveling road show that managers used to show people how bad things had gotten.

- *Stage 4: Widely communicate the vision and strategy.* At a company in the United Kingdom, leaders personally communicated a new vision with people all around the company, but they wanted to keep the vision fresh in everyone's mind. One morning, when employees turned on their computers, the first thing they saw was a multicolored map of the United

Kingdom surrounded by a bright blue circle. As the image moved around the screen, the words "We will be #1 in the UK market by 2001" appeared. The screen saver technique took everyone by surprise and got people talking about the vision.

- *Stage 5: Empowering employees.* One manufacturing plant's early efforts at empowerment were total chaos. Employee involvement meetings deteriorated into gripe sessions, and morale declined rather than improved. Leaders decided to try a different approach. With the approval of some of their best teams, they began videotaping what they did on the factory floor—everything from grabbing the raw material off the shelf to taking the finished product off the line. When people later viewed the tape, ideas for improvement started flowing immediately—such as reorganizing the machines to cut down on how far people had to walk or setting up a rack with all the tools needed for a process right at hand. Teams now have "before and after" tapes and feel a sense of pride as they show the quality, safety, and cost improvements they have made.

REAL-LIFE STORIES; PRACTICAL GUIDELINES

The Heart of Change is based on interviews with about 400 leaders at 130 organizations in the midst of major changes. The numerous personal anecdotes include both successes and fumbles, and each chapter ends with a "What Works/What Does Not Work" guide for each of the eight change stages. With *The Heart of Change*, Kotter and Cohen have combined a lively, highly readable story with a practical, no-nonsense guide to leading successful change.

Source: *The Heart of Change*, by John P. Kotter and Dan S. Cohen, is published by Harvard Business School Press.

in following the eight-stage change process discussed earlier. Leaders also use a number of specific implementation techniques to smooth the change process.

- *Communication and training.* Open and honest communication is perhaps the single most effective way to overcome resistance to change because it reduces uncertainty, gives people a sense of control, clarifies the benefits of the change, and builds trust. In one study of change efforts, the most commonly cited reason for failure was that employees learned of the change from outsiders.[54] Top leaders concentrated on communicating with the public and shareholders, but failed to communicate with the people who would be most intimately affected by the changes—their own employees. It is important that leaders communicate with people face-to-face rather than relying solely on newsletters, memos, or electronic communication. For example, the CEO of one information technology company embarking on a major restructuring held a meeting with all employees to explain the changes, answer questions, and reassure people that the changes were not going to result in job losses.[55]

Employees frequently also need training to acquire skills for their role in the change process or their new responsibilities. Good change leaders make sure people get the training they need to feel comfortable with new tasks, such as when Canadian Airlines International spent a year and a half training employees in new procedures before changing its entire reservations, airport, cargo, and financial systems.[56]

- *Participation and involvement.* Participation involves followers in helping to design the change. Although this approach is time-consuming, it pays off by giving people a sense of control over the change activity. They come to understand the change better and become committed to its successful implementation. A study of the implementation and adoption of new computer technology at two companies, for example, showed a much smoother implementation process at the company that introduced the change using a participatory approach.[57]

- *Coercion.* As a last resort, leaders overcome resistance by threatening employees with the loss of jobs or promotions or by firing or transferring them. Coercion may be necessary in crisis situations when a rapid response is needed. For example, a number of top managers at Coca-Cola had to be reassigned or let go after they refused to go along with a new CEO's changes for revitalizing the sluggish corporation.[58] Coercion may also be needed for administrative changes that flow from the top down, such as downsizing the workforce. However, as a general rule, this approach to change is not advisable because it leaves people angry at leaders, and the change may be sabotaged. Leaders at Raytheon Missile Systems faced an urgent need for change, but they wisely realized that participation and involvement, communication, and training would lead to far better results than trying to force the changes on employees.

Raytheon Missile Systems

In the early 2000s, leaders at Raytheon Missile Systems (RMS) were reeling from the challenges brought about by the merger of four different companies into one. Employees were from different geographical areas; used different processes, methods, and tools; held different corporate cultural values and norms; and even used different words for the same products or technologies.

Top leaders put together a core change team to write a clear vision for change that would align the entire organization into one smoothly functioning manufacturing operation. The team also created a powerful tool that provided bite-sized action steps the factories could take to achieve manufacturing improvement goals. However, leaders realized that imposing these changes from above might provoke strong resistance. Instead, they set up three off-site workshops that involved people from all parts of the organization and assigned subgroups to tackle the issue of describing steps needed to achieve manufacturing excellence. With facilitation from core team members, the employee groups developed descriptions that were parallel to those originally developed by the change team but which were also richer and more detailed.

Next, leaders actively involved factory managers in the changes by assigning them to assess one another's operations. Careful thought went into the assignments so that managers who were particularly good in one area were assigned to factories that were weak in that area, which led to learning and cross-pollination of ideas. In short order, factory mangers were helping one another implement the best manufacturing methods of the entire organization across boundaries.

Leaders set broad improvement goals for each factory, but allowed the factory manager to determine the specific elements to improve during each year of the five-year improvement plan. They reasoned that, even if some managers chose only easy improvements, at least everyone's efforts were focused in the same direction. Training was provided to help managers and improvement teams accomplish results faster.[59]

The change journey at Raytheon Missile Systems was not without challenges, but by communicating with employees, allowing people to participate in the change, actively involving factory managers, and providing training, leaders overcame most of the resistance and facilitated a smoother implementation. After two years, they decided to apply for the Shingo Prize for Excellence in Manufacturing as a way to gauge the organization's progress. Surprisingly, RMS won the award on its first attempt, which served both as a reminder of how far the organization had come and a way to celebrate and reward factory managers for all their hard work.

The Two Faces of Change

Effectively and humanely leading change is one of the greatest challenges for leaders. The nature and pace of change in today's environment can be exhilarating and even fun. But it can also be inconvenient, painful, and downright scary. Even when a change appears to be good for individual employees as well as the organization, it can lead to decreased morale, lower commitment, and diminished trust if not handled carefully.

In addition, some changes that may be necessary for the good of the organization can cause real, negative consequences for individual employees, who may experience high levels of stress, be compelled to quickly learn entirely new tasks and ways of working, or possibly lose their jobs. Consider what's happening at Hewlett-Packard Co., where new CIO Randy Mott is leading a $1 billion makeover of HP's internal IT systems, which will cut the company's IT costs in half and increase sales by enabling managers to analyze buying trends and other data. The transformation calls for slashing thousands of small IT projects and replacing 85 loosely-connected data centers with six cutting edge facilities. Tearing up the entire IT infrastructure is causing tremendous stress for many employees. In addition, the new centralized approach means some people have had their projects terminated, and thousands of employees may lose their jobs. Referring to the stress level at HP, one veteran manager said, "At some point, you hit a breaking point."[60]

Some of the most difficult changes are those related to structure, such as redefining positions and responsibilities, re-engineering the company, redesigning jobs, departments, or divisions, or downsizing the organization. In many cases, these types of changes mean that some people will be seriously hurt because they will lose their jobs. Downsizing is one of the most difficult situations leaders face; they have to handle the layoffs in a way that eases the pain and tension for departing employees and maintains the trust, morale, and performance of employees who remain with the organization.

Leadership and Downsizing

Downsizing
intentionally reducing the size of a company's workforce

Downsizing refers to intentionally reducing the size of a company's workforce. During the boom years of the 1990s, few leaders had to be concerned with the need for laying off employees, but the economic downturn of the early 2000s made massive downsizing a common practice in American corporations. In addition, downsizing is a part of many change initiatives in today's organizations.[61] Re-engineering projects, mergers and acquisitions, global competition, the trend toward outsourcing, and the transition from an industrial to an information economy have all led to job reductions.[62]

Some researchers have found that massive downsizing has often not achieved the intended benefits, and in some cases has significantly harmed the organization.[63] Nevertheless, there are times when downsizing is a necessary part of a thoughtful restructuring of assets or other important change initiatives.

When job cuts are necessary, leaders should be prepared for increased conflict and stress, even greater resistance to change, and a decrease in morale, trust, and employee commitment.[64] A number of techniques can help leaders smooth the downsizing process and ease tensions for employees who leave as well as those who remain.[65] Some leaders seem to think that the less said about a pending layoff, the better. Not so. Leaders should provide advance notice with as much information as possible. Even when they're not certain about exactly what is going to happen, leaders should be as open and honest with employees as possible. Leaders can also involve employees in shaping the criteria for which jobs will be cut or which employees will leave the company. Another option is to offer incentive packages for employees to leave voluntarily and offer alternative work arrangements such as job-sharing and part-time work.

> **Action Memo**
> As a leader, you can be compassionate when making changes such as downsizing that will hurt some people in the organization. You can provide assistance to displaced workers, and remember to address the emotional needs of remaining employees to help them stay motivated and productive.

Providing assistance to displaced workers, such as through training programs, severance packages, extended benefits, outplacement assistance, and counseling services for both employees and their families can ease the trauma associated with a job loss. In addition, this shows remaining workers that leaders care about people, which can help to ease their own feelings of confusion, guilt, anger, and sadness over the loss of colleagues. Many companies provide counseling to help remaining employees handle the emotional difficulties associated with the downsizing, as well.

Even the best-led organizations may sometimes need to lay off employees in a turbulent environment. Leaders can attain positive results if they handle downsizing in a way that enables remaining organization members to be motivated, productive, and committed to a better future.

Summary and Interpretation

The important point of this chapter is that tools and approaches are available to help leaders facilitate creativity and innovation and manage change. Change is inevitable, and the increased pace of change in today's global environment has led to even greater problems for leaders struggling to help their organizations adapt. A major factor in the failure of organizations to adapt to changes in the global environment is the lack of effective change leadership. Leaders who can successfully accomplish change typically define themselves as change leaders, describe a vision for the future in vivid terms, and articulate values that promote change and adaptability. Change leaders are courageous, are capable of managing complexity and uncertainty, believe in followers' capacity to assume responsibility for change, and learn from their own mistakes.

Major changes can be particularly difficult to implement, but leaders can help to ensure a successful change effort by following the eight-stage model of planned change—establish a sense of urgency; create a powerful coalition; develop a compelling vision and strategy; communicate the vision; empower employees to act; generate short-term wins; keep up the energy and commitment to tackle bigger problems; and institutionalize the change in the organizational culture. Leaders also facilitate change on a daily basis by using several everyday change strategies, including creative self-expression, right words, right opportunities, and alliance building.

Leading for innovation is a significant challenge for today's leaders. One way is by creating an environment that nourishes creativity in particular departments or the entire organization. Five elements of innovative organizations are alignment, creative values, unofficial activity, diverse stimuli, and within-company communication. These correspond to characteristics of creative individuals. Creative people are less resistant to change. Although some people demonstrate more creativity than others, research suggests that everyone has roughly equal creative potential. Leaders can increase individual creativity by facilitating brainstorming, lateral thinking, and creative intuition.

Implementation is a critical aspect of any change initiative. Leaders can understand why people resist change and how to overcome resistance. Leaders use communication and training, participation and involvement, and—as a last resort—coercion to overcome resistance. Leaders should recognize that change can have negative as well as positive consequences. One of the most difficult situations leaders may face is downsizing. They can use techniques to help ease the stress and hardship for employees who leave as well as maintain the morale and trust of those who remain.

Discussion Questions

1. Of the eight stages of planned change, which one do you think leaders are most likely to skip? Why?

2. Which of the everyday change strategies (Exhibit 15.3) would you be most comfortable using and why? What are some situations when a passive, private strategy such as creative self-expression might be more effective than an active, public strategy such as alliance building?

3. Do you think creative individuals and creative organizations have characteristics in common? Discuss.

4. How could you increase the number of novel and useful solutions you can come up with to solve a problem?

5. What advice would you give a leader who wants to increase innovation in her department?

6. What are some ways leaders can overcome resistance to change?

7. Why are idea champions considered to be essential to innovation? Do you think these people would be more important in a large organization or a small one? Discuss.

8. Planned change is often considered ideal. Do you think unplanned change could be effective? Discuss. Can you think of an example?

9. Is the world really changing faster today, or do people just assume so?

Leadership at Work

Organizational Change Role Play

You are the new director of the Harpeth Gardens not-for-profit nursing home. Harpeth Gardens is one of 20 elder care centers managed by Franklin Resident Care Centers. Harpeth Gardens has 56 patients and is completely responsible for their proper hygiene, nutrition, and daily recreation. Many of the patients can move about by themselves, but several require physical assistance for eating, dressing, and moving about the nursing home. During daytime hours, the head of nursing is in charge of the four certified nursing assistants (CNAs) who work on the floors. During the night shift, a registered nurse is on duty, along with three CNAs. The same number of CNAs are on duty over the weekend, and either the head of nursing or the registered nurse is on call.

Several other staff also report to you, including the heads of maintenance, bookkeeping/MIS, and the cafeteria. The on-call physician stops by Harpeth Gardens once a week to check on the residents. You have 26 full- and part-time employees who cover the different tasks and shifts.

During your interviews for the director's job, you became aware that the previous director ran a very tight ship, insisting that the best way to care for nursing home patients was though strict rules and procedures. He personally approved almost every decision, including decisions for patient care, despite not having a medical degree. Turnover has been rather high and several beds are empty because of the time required to hire and train new staff. Other elder care facilities in the area have a waiting list of people wanting to be admitted.

At Harpeth Gardens, the non-nursing offices have little interaction with nurses or each other. Back office staff people seem to do their work and go home. Overall, Harpeth Gardens seems to you like a dreary place to work. People seem to have forgotten the compassion that is essential for patients and each other working in a health care environment. You believe that a new strategy and culture are needed to give more responsibility to employees, improve morale, reduce turnover, and fill the empty beds. You have read about the concept of a learning organization (Chapter 15), and would like to implement some of those ideas at Harpeth Gardens. You decide to start with the ideas of increasing empowered roles and personal networks and see how it goes. If those two ideas work, then you will implement other changes.

During your first week as the director, you have met all the employees, and you have confirmed your understanding of the previous director's rigid approach. You call a meeting of all employees for next Friday afternoon.

Your assignment for this exercise is to decide how you will implement the desired changes and what you will tell employees at the employee meeting. Start by deciding how you will accomplish each of the first three steps in the model in Exhibit 15.2. Write your answers to these three questions:

1. How will you get employees to feel a sense of urgency?

2. How will you form a guiding coalition, and who will be in it?

3. What is your compelling vision?

_____

_____

_____

Your next task is to prepare a *vision speech* to employees for the changes you are about to implement. In this speech, explain your dream for Harpeth Gardens and the urgency of this change. Explain exactly what you believe the changes will involve and why the employees should agree to the changes and help implement them. Sketch out the points you will include in your speech:

_____

_____

_____

In Class: The instructor can divide the class into small groups to discuss the answers to questions 1 to 3 above and to brainstorm the key points to cover in the vision speech to employees. After student groups have decided what the director will say, the instructor can ask for volunteers from a few groups to actually give the speech to employees that will start the Harpeth Gardens transition toward a learning organization. The key questions are: Did the speech touch on the key points that inspire employees to help implement changes? Did the speech convey a high purpose and a sense of urgency? Did the speech connect with employees in a personal way, and did it lay out the reality facing Harpeth Gardens?

Leadership Development: Cases for Analysis

Southern Discomfort

Jim Malesckowski remembers the call of two weeks ago as if he just put down the telephone receiver: "I just read your analysis and I want you to get down to Mexico right away," Jack Ripon, his boss and chief executive officer, had blurted in his ear. "You know we can't make the plant in Oconomo work any more—the costs are just too high. So go down there, check out what our operational costs would be if we move, and report back to me in a week."

At that moment, Jim felt as if a shiv had been stuck in his side, just below the rib cage. As president of the Wisconsin Specialty Products Division of Lamprey, Inc., he knew quite well the challenge of dealing with high-cost labor in a third-generation, unionized U.S. manufacturing plant. And although he had done the analysis that led to his boss's knee-jerk response, the call still stunned him. There were 520 people who made a living at Lamprey's Oconomo facility, and if it closed, most of them wouldn't have a journeyman's prayer of finding another job in the town of 9,900 people.

Instead of the $16-per-hour average wage paid at the Oconomo plant, the wages paid to the Mexican workers—who lived in a town without sanitation and with an unbelievably toxic effluent from industrial pollution—would amount to about $1.60 an hour on average. That's a savings of nearly $15 million a year for Lamprey, to be offset in part by increased costs for training, transportation, and other matters.

After two days of talking with Mexican government representatives and managers of other companies in the town, Jim had enough information to develop a set of comparative figures of production and shipping costs. On the way home, he started to outline the report, knowing full well that unless some miracle occurred, he would be ushering in a blizzard of pink slips for people he had come to appreciate.

The plant in Oconomo had been in operation since 1921, making special apparel for persons suffering injuries and other medical conditions. Jim had often talked with employees who would recount stories about their fathers or grandfathers working in the same Lamprey company plant—the last of the original manufacturing operations in town.

But friendship aside, competitors had already edged past Lamprey in terms of price and were dangerously close to overtaking it in product quality. Although both Jim and the plant manager had tried to convince the union to accept lower wages, union leaders resisted. In fact, on one occasion when Jim and the plant manager tried to discuss a cell manufacturing approach, which would cross-train employees to perform up to three different jobs, local union leaders could barely restrain their anger. Yet probing beyond the fray, Jim sensed the fear that lurked under the union reps' gruff exterior. He sensed their vulnerability, but could not break through the reactionary bark that protected it.

A week has passed and Jim just submitted his report to his boss. Although he didn't specifically bring up the point, it was apparent that Lamprey could put its investment dollars in a bank and receive a better return than what its Oconomo operation is currently producing.

Tomorrow, he'll discuss the report with the CEO. Jim doesn't want to be responsible for the plant's dismantling, an act he personally believes would be wrong as long as there's a chance its costs can be lowered. "But Ripon's right," he says to himself. "The costs are too high, the union's unwilling to cooperate, and the company needs to make a better return on its investment if it's to continue at all. It sounds right but feels wrong. What should I do?"

Source: Doug Wallace, "What Would You Do?" *Business Ethics* (March/April 1996), pp. 52–53. Reprinted with permission from *Business Ethics*, P.O. Box 8439, Minneapolis, MN 55408. 612/879-0695.

QUESTIONS

1. If you were Jim Malesckowski, would you fight to save the plant? Why?

2. Assume you want to lead the change to save the plant. Describe how you would enact the eight stages outlined in Exhibit 15.2.

3. How would you overcome union leader resistance?

MediScribe Corporation

MediScribe provides medical transcription, insurance claims, and billing and collection services for doctors, clinics, and hospitals in south Florida. As a production supervisor, Ramona Fossett is responsible for the work of approximately 40 employees, 25 of whom are classified as data entry clerks. Fossett recently agreed to allow a team of outside consultants to come to her production area and make time and systems-analysis studies in an effort to improve efficiency and output. She had little choice but to do so—the president of the company had personally issued instructions that supervisors should cooperate with the consultants.

The consultants spent three days studying job descriptions, observing employees' daily tasks, and recording each detail of the work of the data entry clerks. After this period of observation, they told Fossett that they would begin more detailed studies and interviews on the following day.

The next morning, four data entry clerks were absent. On the following day, 10 failed to show up for work. The leader of the systems analysis team explained to Fossett that, if there were as many absences the next day, his team would have to drop the study and move on to another department, as a valid analysis would be impossible with 10 out of 25 workers absent.

Fossett, who had only recently been promoted to the supervisor's position, knew that she'd be held responsible for the failure of the systems analysis. Concerned both for her employees and her own job, she telephoned several of the absent workers to find out what was going on. Each told approximately the same story, saying they were stressed out and exhausted after being treated like "guinea pigs" for three days.

One employee said she was planning to ask for a leave of absence if working conditions didn't improve.

At the end of the day, Fossett sat at her desk considering what could be done to provide the necessary conditions for completion of the study. In addition, she was greatly concerned about implementing the changes that she knew would be mandated after the consultants finished their work and presented their findings to the president. Considering how her employees had reacted to the study, Fossett doubted they would instantly comply with orders issued from the top as a result of the findings—and, again, she would be held responsible for the failure.

Source: Adapted from "Resistance to Change" in John M. Champion and John H. James, *Critical Incidents in Management: Decision and Policy Issues,* 6th ed. (Homewood, IL: Irwin, 1989), pp. 230–231.

QUESTIONS

1. Why do you think employees are reacting in this way to the study?
2. How could leaders have handled this situation to get greater cooperation from employees?
3. If you were Ramona Fossett, what would you do now? What would you do to implement any changes recommended by the study?

References

1 Leila Abboud, "Philips Pushes Energy-Saving Bulbs: Why This Bright Idea is a Hard Sell," *The Wall Street Journal* (December 5, 2006), pp. B1, B4.

2 M. Beer and N. Nohria, "Cracking the Code of Change," *Harvard Business Review* 78 (May–June 2000), pp. 133–141.

3 Studies reported in Alan Deutschman, "Change or Die," *Fast Company* (May 2005), p. 53ff.

4 Greg Jaffe, "Next Chapter; As Iraq War Rages, Army Re-Examines Lessons of Vietnam," *The Wall Street Journal* (March 20, 2006), p. A1.

5 Marlene Piturro, "The Transformation Officer," *Management Review* (February 2000), pp. 21–25.

6 Nicholas Imparato and Oren Harari, "When New Worlds Stir," *Management Review* (October 1994), pp. 22–28.

7 Jack Welch, quoted in *Inc.* (March 1995), p. 13.

8 Alain Vas, "Top Management Skills In a Context of Endemic Organizational Change: The Case of Belgacom," *Journal of General Management* 27, no. 1 (Autumn 2001), pp. 71–89.

9 Art Kleiner, "Diary of a Change Agent," *Strategy + Business,* Issue 28 (Third Quarter 2002), pp. 18–21

10 The following discussion is based heavily on John P. Kotter, *Leading Change* (Boston: Harvard Business School Press, 1996), pp. 20–25; and "Leading Change: Why Transformation Efforts Fail," *Harvard Business Review* (March–April 1995), pp. 59–67.

11 Mark Landler, "From a Scandal Springs a Chance For an Overhaul at Volkswagen," *The New York Times* (July 14, 2005), p. C1.

12 Patrick Flanagan, "The ABCs of Changing Corporate Culture," *Management Review* (July 1995), pp. 57–61.

13 Chuck Salter, "On the Road Again," *Fast Company* (January 2002), pp. 50–58.

14 Ibid.

15 Anna Muoio, "Mint Condition," *Fast Company* (December 1999), pp. 330–348.

16 Kotter, "Leading Change: Why Transformation Efforts Fail," p. 65.

17 John P. Kotter, *The Heart of Change: Real-Life Stories of How People Change Their Organizations* (Boston, MA: Harvard Business School Press, 2002), pp. 143–159.

18 Ibid.

19 Debra Meyerson, *Tempered Radicals: How People Use Difference to Inspire Change at Work* (Boston: Harvard Business School Press, 2001).

20 These strategies and examples are from Debra E. Meyerson, "Radical Change the Quiet Way," *Harvard Business Review* (October 2001), pp. 92–100.

21 Meyerson, "Radical Change the Quiet Way."

22 Stanley S. Gryskiewicz, "Cashing In On Creativity at Work," *Psychology Today* (September–October 2000), pp. 63–66.

23 Jena McGregor, Michael Arndt, Robert Berner, Ian Rowley, Kenji Hall, Gail Edmondson, Steve Hamm, Moon Ihlwan, and Andy Reinhardt, "The World's Most Innovative Companies," *BusinessWeek* (April 24, 2006), p. 62ff.

24 Bruce Nussbaum, with Robert Berner and Diane Brady, "Get Creative," *BusinessWeek* (August 1, 2005), pp. 60–68; McGregor et al., "The World's Most Innovative Companies."

25 Dorothy A. Leonard and Walter C. Swap, *When Sparks Fly: Igniting Creativity in Groups* (Boston: Harvard Business School Press, 1999), pp. 6–8.

26 The elements of creative organizations come from Alan G. Robinson and Sam Stern, *Corporate Creativity: How Innovation and Improvement Actually Happen* (San Francisco: Berrett-Koehler, 1997).

27 Sherry Eng, "Hatching Schemes," *The Industry Standard* (November 27–December 4, 2000), pp. 174–175.

28 Robinson and Stern, *Corporate Creativity,* p. 14.

29 Gail Dutton, "Enhancing Creativity," *Management Review* (November 1996), pp. 44–46.

30 Joann S. Lublin, "Nurturing Innovation," *The Wall Street Journal* (March 20, 2006), p. B1; and Ben Elgin, "Managing Google's Idea Factory," *BusinessWeek* (October 3, 2005), pp. 88–90.

31 "Fast Talk: Creative to the Core," Interviews by Micheal A. Prospero, *Fast Company* (December 2005), pp. 25–32.

32 Cameron M. Ford, "Creativity Is a Mystery: Clues from the Investigators' Notebooks," in Cameron M. Ford and Dennis A. Gioia, eds., *Creative Action in Organizations: Ivory Tower Visions & Real World Voices* (Thousand Oaks, CA: Sage Publications, 1995), pp. 12–49.

33 Ariane Sains and Stanley Reed, with Michael Arndt, "Electrolux Cleans Up," *BusinessWeek* (February 27, 2006), pp. 42–43.

34 Bill Breen, "The Seoul of Design," *Fast Company* (December 2005), pp. 90–99; Peter Lewis, "A Perpetual Crisis Machine," *Fortune* (September 19, 2005), pp. 58–76; Steve Hamm with Ian Rowley, "Speed Demons," *BusinessWeek* (March 27, 2006), pp. 68–76; and Martin Fackler, "Electronics Company Aims to Create Break-Out Products," *The New York Times* (April 25, 2006), p. C1.

35 David Kirkpatrick, "Throw It at the Wall and See if it Sticks," *Fortune* (December 12, 2005), pp. 142–150.

36 Leigh Thompson, "Improving the Creativity of Organizational Work Groups," *Academy of Management Executive* 17 (2003), pp. 96–109; and Bruce Nussbaum, "The Power of Design," *BusinessWeek* (May 17, 2004), pp. 86–94.

37 Ben Elgin, "Managing Google's Idea Factory," *BusinessWeek* (October 3, 2005), pp. 88–90.

38 Jared Sandberg, "Brainstorming Works Best if People Scramble for Ideas on Their Own," *The Wall Street Journal* (January 13, 2006), p. B1.

39 R. B. Gallupe, W. H. Cooper, M. L. Grise, and L. M. Bastianutti, "Blocking Electronic Brainstorms," *Journal of Applied Psychology* 79 (1994), pp. 77–86; R. B. Gallupe and W. H. Cooper, "Brainstorming Electronically," *Sloan Management Review* (Fall 1993), pp. 27–36; and Alison Stein Wellner, "A Perfect Brainstorm," *Inc.* (October 2003), pp. 31–35.

40 Wellner, "A Perfect Brainstorm"; Gallupe and Cooker, "Brainstorming Electronically."

41 Edward D. Bono, *Serious Creativity: Using the Power of Lateral Thinking to Create New Ideas* (New York: HarperBusiness, 1992).

42 Francine Russo, "The Hidden Secrets of the Creative Mind," *Time* (January 16, 2006), pp. 89–90.

43 Ronald T. Kadish, "Mix People Up," *Harvard Business Review* (August 2002), pp. 39–49.

44 Carol Glover and Steve Smethurst, "Creative License" *People Management* (March 20, 2003), pp. 31–34; Michael Michalko, *Thinkertoys*, 2nd ed, (Berkeley, CA: Ten Speed Press, 2006); Joseph Weber, "Keeping the Whimsy Coming," *BusinessWeek* (December 5, 2005), pp. 54–55.

45 Derm Barrett, *The Paradox Process: Creative Business Solutions . . . Where You Least Expect to Find Them* (New York: American Management Association, 1997).

46 R. Donald Gamache and Robert Lawrence Kuhn, *The Creativity Infusion: How Managers Can Start and Sustain Creativity and Innovation* (New York: Harper & Row, 1989); Alison Stein Wellner, "Cleaning Up," *Inc.* (October 2003), p. 35; Roger von Oech, *A Kick in the Seat of the Pants* (New York, Harper & Row, 1986).

47 Richard A. Lovett, "Jog Your Brain," *Psychology Today* (May/June 2006), pp. 55–56; Mary Carmichael, "Stronger, Faster, Smarter," *Newsweek* (March 26, 2007), pp. 38–46.

48 This word challenge (and the answers given for it later in the chapter) is from Will Shortz, "Rdchallenge," *Readers Digest* (March 2004), p. 204.

49 This question and the answer given later is from Tahl Raz, "How Would You Design Bill Gates' Bathroom?" *Inc.* (May, 2003), p. 35.

50 These match puzzles are from Michael Michalko, *Thinkertoys*, 2nd ed. (Berkeley, CA: Ten Speed Press, 2006).

51 Based on Paul Stebel, "Why Do Employees Resist Change?" *Harvard Business Review* (May–June 1996), pp. 86–92.

52 Michael A. Roberto and Lynne C. Levesque, "The Art of Making Changes Stick," *MIT Sloan Management Review* (Summer 2005), pp. 53–60.

53 Shaul Fox and Yair Amichai-Hamburger, "The Power of Emotional Appeals in Promoting Organizational Change Programs," *Academy of Management Executive* 15, no. 4 (2001), pp. 84–95.

54 Peter Richardson and D. Keith Denton, "Communicating Change," *Human Resource Management* 35, no. 2 (Summer 1996), pp. 203–216.

55 Dan S. Cohen, "Why Change Is an Affair of the Heart," *CIO* (December 1, 2005), pp. 48–52.

56 T. J. Larkin and Sandar Larkin, "Reaching and Changing Frontline Employees," *Harvard Business Review* (May–June 1996), pp. 95–104; and Rob Muller, "Training for Change," *Canadian Business Review* (Spring 1995), pp. 16–19.

57 Phillip H. Mirvis, Amy L. Sales, and Edward J. Hackett, "The Implementation and Adoption of New Technology in Organizations: The Impact of Work, People, and Culture," *Human Resource Management* 30 (Spring 1991), pp. 113–139.

58 Dean Foust with Gerry Khermouch, "Repairing the Coke Machine," *BusinessWeek* (March 19, 2001), pp. 86–88.

59 Mark Jepperson, "Focused Journey of Change," *Industrial Management* (July–August 2005), pp. 8–13.

60 Peter Burrows, "Stopping the Sprawl at HP" *BusinessWeek* (May 29, 2006), pp. 54–56.

61 William McKinley, Carol M. Sanchez, and Allen G. Schick, "Organizational Downsizing: Constraining, Cloning, Learning," *Academy of Management Executive* 9, no. 3 (1995), pp. 32–42.

62 Gregory B. Northcraft and Margaret A. Neale, *Organizational Behavior: A Management Challenge*, 2nd ed. (Fort Worth: The Dryden Press, 1994), p. 626. "Executive Commentary" on McKinley, Sanchez, and Schick, "Organizational Downsizing: Constraining, Cloning, Learning," *Academy of Management Executive* 9, no. 3 (1995), pp. 43–44.

63 James R. Morris, Wayne F. Cascio, and Clifford E. Young, "Downsizing After All These Years: Questions and Answers About Who Did It, How Many Did It, and Who Benefited from It," *Organizational Dynamics* (Winter 1999), pp. 78–86; McKinley, Sanchez, and Schick, "Organizational Downsizing," Stephen Doerflein and James Atsaides, "Corporate Psychology: Making Downsizing Work," *Electrical World* (September–October 1999), pp. 41–43; and Brett C. Luthans and Steven M. Sommer, "The Impact of Downsizing on Workplace Attitudes," *Group and Organization Management* 2, no. 1 (1999), pp. 46–70.

64 K. S. Cameron, S. J. Freeman, and A. K. Mishra, "Downsizing and Redesigning Organizations," in G. P. Huber and W. H. Glick, eds., *Organizational Change and Redesign* (New York: Oxford University Press, 1993), pp. 19–63.

65 This section is based on Bob Nelson, "The Care of the Un-downsized," *Training and Development* (April 1997), pp. 40–43; Shari Caudron, "Teach Downsizing Survivors How to Thrive," *Personnel Journal,* (January 1996), p. 38ff; Joel Brockner, "Managing the Effects of Layoffs on Survivors," *California Management Review* (Winter 1992), pp. 9–28; Kim S. Cameron, "Strategies for Successful Organizational Downsizing," *Human Resource Management* 33, no. 2 (Summer 1994), pp. 189–211; and Matt Murray, "Stress Mounts as More Firms Announce Large Layoffs, But Don't Say Who or When" (Your Career Matters column), *The Wall Street Journal* (March 13, 2001), pp. B1, B12.

index

Name Index

Index of Organization

Subject Index